BRAIN & BEHAVIOR

AN INTRODUCTION TO PHYSIOLOGICAL PSYCHOLOGY

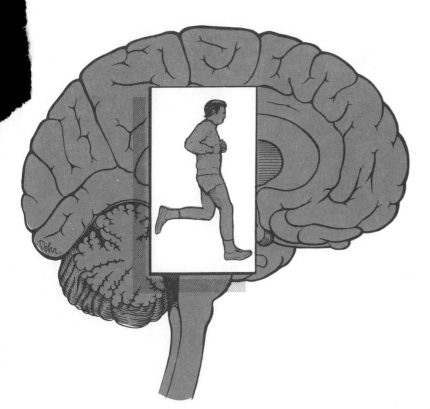

ROD PLOTNIK
SAN DIEGO STATE UNIVERSITY

SANDRA MOLLENAUER
SAN DIEGO STATE UNIVERSITY

Canfield Press c͞p San Francisco
A Department of Harper & Row, Publishers, Inc.
New York   Hagerstown   London

Sponsoring Editor Theodore C. Ricks
Production Editor Pearl C. Vapnek
Production Manager Laura Argento
Interior and Cover Designer Bill Yenne
Medical Illustrators Nelva B. Richardson and Marsha J. Dohrmann
Photo Researchers Kay Y. James and Myra Schachne
Compositor Chapman's Phototypesetting
Printer and Binder Kingsport Press

**BRAIN & BEHAVIOR An Introduction to Physiological
Psychology**
Copyright © 1978 by Rod Plotnik and Sandra Mollenauer

Library of Congress Cataloging in Publication Data

Plotnik, Rod
  Brain behavior.

  Includes bibliographical references and index.
  1. Psychology, Physiological. 2. Brain. 3. Human
behavior. I. Mollenauer, Sandra, joint author.
II. Title.
QP360.P58   152   78-507

78 79 80 81 10 9 8 7 6 5 4 3 2 1

Contents

1

DEVELOPMENT

How Cells Become a Brain   1

2

NEURON

It's All Done with Chemicals   17

3

ANATOMY

How the Brain Controls the Body   37

4

STRESS, BIOFEEDBACK, AND AUTONOMIC NERVOUS SYSTEM

How Your Heart Knows What Your Head Is Thinking   55

5

SEEING AND HEARING

Why Your Eye Does Not Hear and Your Ear Does Not See

6

SMELLING, TASTING, AND TOUCHING

How Your Nose, Tongue, and Skin Make Sense

7

SEXUAL BEHAVIOR

How Your Head Knows about Your Sex 107

8

EMOTIONS

Loving, Hating, Crying, and Laughing 125

9

HUNGER, OBESITY, AND THIRST

Does Your Mouth Have a Mind of Its Own?   143

10

SLEEP AND WAKEFULNESS

Why You Spend One-Third of Your Life Asleep   163

11

LEARNING AND MEMORY

How Neurons Learn to Remember 179

12

HUMAN BRAIN
AND HIGHER FUNCTIONS

One Brain Is Actually Two 197

13

BEHAVIOR DISORDERS AND DRUGS

Can Pills Change Your Mind? 219

SELECTED READINGS 242

To the Instructor

After teaching physiological psychology for many semesters, we thought the subject could be much more interesting than most texts made it. Starting with this idea, we tried to write a text that includes all of the basic core material but presents it in a more functional way; that includes all of the usual animal research but stresses data from human studies; that includes all of the traditional areas but also has chapters on stress, human sexual behavior, brain damage, and drugs.

This book is specifically written for psychology students with little or no background in the sciences, for nonpsychology majors, and for students in the health sciences. To arouse the student's interest, some of the chapters begin with real-life examples, such as taking a "lie-detector" test, experiencing 264 hours of sleep deprivation, having misassigned sex gender, coping after split-brain surgery, suffering amnesia, or having schizophrenic episodes. Other chapters begin with hypothetical situations, such as a three-neuron creature, brain transplants from different organisms, or assembling a human nervous system. By the use of these lead-ins, the core material is presented in a functional context. For example, in the chapter on anatomy (Chapter 3), students see a body develop more and more complex responses as the nervous system is assembled piece by piece. In the chapter on sexual behavior (Chapter 7), which is usually given very little coverage, emphasis is on human sexual behavior with a discussion of hormones affecting preference, motivation, and interest. In the chapter on higher functions (Chapter 12), there is a discussion of the left and right brain functions and there are examples of many behavioral deficits following stroke damage: problems in speaking, naming, writing, reading, and comprehending. From these few examples, we hope that you can see how this book is different in its functional approach and in its use of human data and examples.

Designed for a one-semester course, this text can be used either with the more traditional lecture format or with the personalized system of instruction known as PSI. Whichever format is used—and each of us uses a different one—we have found that the Self-Test at the end of each chapter helps the student focus on what should be restudied and eliminates questions like, "Is it enough to read the material twice?"

In teaching this course, we found that students often wanted information and had questions on related areas. For example, in discussing amnesia, they wanted to know about electroconvulsive shock; in discussing hunger, they wanted to know about diets and fasting; in discussing sex, they wanted more information on therapies. Since there is never enough class time, we have tried to provide this information by including a series of Selected Readings. These articles not only provide additional information on related topics, but also spark discussion and give students an appreciation of how scientists go about answering questions.

We have also tried to show how scientists' work is applied to real-world situations by inserting throughout the text brief articles from newspapers and magazines. This feature, titled "The Headliner," covers such topics as why it is so difficult to find a sweet-tasting substitute; whether knowledge about autonomic responses can be useful in measuring truthfulness in presidential debates; whether implanted electrodes can help deaf persons hear; why people go into shock after experiencing a highly emotional event. These headliners can be used to spark discussion of the problems and applications of scientific data.

The Instructor's Manual has a number of special features that make it suitable for either a PSI or a lecture approach. For each chapter there are two sets of multiple-choice items, think-type questions (together with answers) that can be used in either a verbal or written format, more traditional essay questions, and projects that the student may complete for additional credit or experience.

We have used earlier versions of the text and the instructor's manual in our classes and have tried to eliminate the rough spots, rewrite difficult sections, and add examples that help the students understand. With all the work that went into this book, there is still undoubtedly room for improvement. We would like to invite instructors to send us their reactions and suggestions to help us in formulating plans for subsequent editions.

We would like to express our appreciation to the following individuals for reviewing preliminary drafts of the manuscript and for providing us with valuable suggestions: Jane Dallinger, Contra Costa Community College; Donald M. Johnson, West Valley College; Marie S. Marshall, El Camino College; and Parks Whitmer, American River College.

For reviewing the final manuscript to ensure factual accuracy, we extend our gratitude to Jerry W. Koppman, San Diego State University.

Rod Plotnik
Sandra Mollenauer
Department of Psychology
San Diego State University
San Diego, CA 92182

To the Student

Lie-detection, sexual behavior, epilepsy, strokes, marihuana, nerve cells, and schizophrenia—these are only a few of the interesting topics covered in the text. Physiological psychology is ten times more stimulating than the title suggests. The text is essentially about how it is possible for you to dream, think, walk, remember, cry, and laugh.

The brain has hundreds of parts, and each of these parts is printed in boldface type (for example, **hippocampus**) to indicate that it should probably be remembered. Other important terms are also printed in boldface type on first occurrence, where they are defined. If you forget the definition of a term, there is a Glossary in the back of the book to refresh your memory.

How often have you said, ''I read that chapter twice and think I know it''? To find out if you do know it, each chapter is followed by a Self-Test. If you can answer 90 percent of these items correctly, you know most of the material. If you cannot, you will know which material should be restudied.

Throughout the text there are newspaper and magazine articles describing how knowledge about the nervous system is applied to everyday problems—why people sleep, how one detects lies, how drugs cure behavioral disorders, and why people become fat. These articles, titled ''The Headliner,'' show you how scientific data can be used to explain real-life situations.

Each chapter is introduced either with a real-life situation, such as the boy who went without sleep for 264 hours (Chapter 10), or with a hypothetical one, such as a brain transplant operation (Chapter 1). Each of these situations raises questions about the material: What happens to you after being sleepless for 264 hours? Why can't brain transplants be done today? The chapter then tries to answer these questions.

When you finish a chapter, see if you can answer these questions and that will tell you how well you understand the material.

The first time you see the term **extrapyramidal,** you will notice that is is printed in boldface type. This means that it is an important term and that a pronunciation guide follows. This guide is based on the way you pronounce everyday sounds. For example, the guide looks like this

extra-per-RAM-id-all

and should be pronounced as follows: ''extra'' is like the work *extra*; ''per'' is like the first part of *person*; RAM is like the animal and because the syllable is capitalized, it means that is where the accent goes; ''id'' is like the Freudian term *id*; and ''all'' is pronounced like the word *all*.

As you finish each chapter, you will probably have many related questions; some of these are answered in the Selected Readings section of the book. For example, after studying about emotions, you may wonder if brain stimulation can change emotional behavior; after studying sleep, you may wonder about the meaning of dreams; after studying about drugs, you may wonder why the brain has its own morphine-like chemical. These are the kinds of interesting topics covered in the Selected Readings that relate to each chapter.

If you have particular difficulty in remembering terms or want more practice in testing yourself, there is a Study Guide that includes multiple-choice questions to test your memory, essay questions and analogies to test your thinking, and projects to give you a chance to gain practical experience.

The only question that is not answered in the book is why you cannot tickle yourself. We're working on that one. We really do hope you will find the text more enjoyable and readable than most.

Development 1

How Cells Become a Brain

Brain Library

Although somewhat worried, you enter the library and walk quickly to the brain-trust section. Picking up a loan card, you think a moment and then begin filling in the necessary information: 1.8 m (6 ft), 81 k (180 lb), excellent kidneys, blood type AB, normal skull, brain weight 1,398 g, two-day loan. Your first choice is "romantic" and your second choice is "humorous."

The loan card is processed and your first choice is available. You are led into a sterile room and are given an instruction card. "If you decide to continue, please place your head in the skull holder, relax your muscles, and place the mask over your face." A red light comes on, followed by the smell of anesthetic vapors.

The neurosurgeon enters the room and carefully sets the container labeled "romantic" next to the skull holder. She removes your wig and loosens the titanium skull fasteners. The top of your skull comes off easily. Your brain has a healthy pinkish color and there should be no problem.

The neurosurgeon starts the timer and begins the first of 12 steps that must be finished in 85 seconds. A miniature valve is turned, blood supply is interrupted, spinal cord detached, brain removed, and brain placed in life support storage. Forty-two seconds have passed and the most difficult steps begin. New brain delicately removed from container labeled "romantic," brain inserted in skull, padding added, spinal cord reattached, valve opened, and blood supply returned.

Within seconds, the new brain has a healthy color and normal brain waves. The neurosurgeon replaces your skull and tightens the fasteners. Pleased with her efficiency, she goes on to the next brain transplant. You awake an hour later and are told your name, where you live, and your

class schedule. The last instruction is: "Return in two days."

Obstacles in Transplanting Brains

Imagine the excitement at having a different brain put into your head. Not just any brain, but one that could turn you into a romantic or a wit or allow you to understand a math book as though it were a comic book or write a brilliant 20-page English paper or compose a hit song. And all you would have to do is check out your choice at the library.

At present, part of the brain transplant procedure is possible. The brain from a monkey or human can be removed from the skull and, with life support systems, can be kept alive for days (1–1). But transplanting a brain into a new skull is, at present, impossible. It is impossible because the body forms antibodies that destroy foreign substances such as a new brain or heart. However, even if the problem of the body rejecting a transplanted brain is solved, there is a second hurdle. It would be exceedingly difficult to pair up correctly the thousands and thousands of severed connections or nerve tracts. There is no known method for connecting a transplanted brain to the existing spinal cord.

Peripheral and Central Nervous Systems

If your arm were cut off in an accident, a surgeon could sew it back on. There is a good possibility that your arm would live and that the feelings and movements would return. When an arm or finger is sewn back on, the severed nerves will grow back into the arm or finger. Nerves in your limbs and trunk, outside the brain and spinal cord, are called peripheral nerves. They make up your **peripheral nervous system** and have the capacity to regrow or regenerate. If your toe were cut off and resewn, during the following months most of the movement and feeling would return. That is because the nerves in your toe are peripheral nerves which have the capacity to regenerate.

If your spinal cord were severed in an accident, the nerve tracts in the spinal cord would not regrow; you would be paralyzed and have no sensations from that part of your body below the cut. If you were shot in the head, the bullet would damage cells in the brain, called **neurons**, and these neurons would not regrow. The surviving neurons might fill in for some of the destroyed neurons in a process called sprouting, but the damaged neurons would never regrow. The neurons and nerve tracts in your brain and spinal cord make up the **central nervous system**. These neurons and tracts do not have the capacity to regrow or regenerate if damaged. This means that there would be two problems in transplanting a brain: the first would be correctly pairing up the thousands of nerve tracts, and the second would be

getting the nerve tracts to reconnect since they usually die after damage. Individuals confined to wheel chairs because of damaged spinal cords or stroke victims paralyzed because of damaged brains hope for a breakthrough in the ability to regenerate neurons and tracts in the central nervous system. In spite of sustained research, this hope has not been realized.

Experiencing a Different Brain

Jellyfish: No Brain at All

You may wonder what it would be like to have the brain of another person or perhaps even that of another animal. Suppose you decided to have your brain removed and replaced with a jellyfish's. The nervous system of a jellyfish is very primitive and existed millions of years before man's. After this transplant, you would be incapable of having many sensations or movements. The problem is that a jellyfish really does not have a structure that could be called a brain. Instead, scattered around the jellyfish's body are

Figure 1–1 Both of these patients had their arms severed in separate motor accidents. Barry's arm, although still in a cast, began functioning 17 days after it was sewn back on. The return of feeling and movement to his hand demonstrates the capacity for regrowth of nerves in the peripheral nervous system. The other patient had her arm sewn back on in a 14-hour operation, and the doctors are optimistic about its recovery. (United Press International Photo.)

Development

the specialized cells called neurons. These neurons are interconnected but are not organized under any central control. With a jellyfish's nervous system, you could not maintain your basic bodily functions, such as breathing, blood pressure, or temperature. You would have to be kept alive by life support machines. You would have no sensations, could not stand or open your eyes or say the word ''help.'' If jellyfish neurons were connected to the nerves that control your fingers, you would be unable to coordinate their movements. Part of one finger might be bending while another was straightening. No amount of effort would enable you to move two fingers to make the victory sign. This is because the jellyfish does not have a group of neurons that controls and organizes other neurons which in turn control the muscles and glands throughout the body. Without a central control, which is the function of a brain, it would be impossible to control all finger muscles involved in making the victory sign.

Cells and Neurons

The neurons in the jellyfish's body are not unlike the neurons in your brain. Compared with other cells, such as fat or muscle cells, neurons are different in that they are specialized for **communication**. But all cells—whether fat, muscle, gland, or neuron—share similar characteristics. All cells have mechanisms for protecting themselves, for converting food into energy and for manufacturing various chemicals necessary to function.

The cell is enclosed in a baglike structure called a membrane. The **cell membrane** not only separates and protects one cell from another, but is active in regulating which substances enter and leave the cell. There are certain chemical substances necessary for the cell to carry out its functions. The genetic instructions for the manufacture of these chemicals are contained in another baglike structure inside the cell body called the **nucleus**. As explained later, the cell has a method of transporting these genetic instructions out of the nucleus into the cell body where the chemical substances are manufactured. The cell receives much of its energy from breaking down blood sugar or glucose; this process occurs in the **mitochondria**. If the cell secretes a hormone such as insulin or other chemicals, this occurs in the **ribosomes**, which are in the **endoplasmic reticulum**, shown in Figure 1–3. After a hormone or other chemical is manufactured by the ribosomes, the substance is wrapped or contained by a membrane produced by the **Golgi complex**. The substance, in its wrapper, moves toward the cell membrane. When it reaches the cell membrane, the wrapper breaks and the substance is released into the fluid or blood surrounding the cell. Most of the cell interior is filled with a jellylike substance in which the chemical reactions occur; it is called the **cytoplasm**.

The neuron, like any other cell, has all the above components with one addition. It has several extensions that allow it to reach and communicate with other neurons. Some of these extensions come together to form nerves or nerve tracts. How neurons communicate is explained in Chapter 2. This basic cell, the neuron, multiplied billions of times, makes up most of your brain.

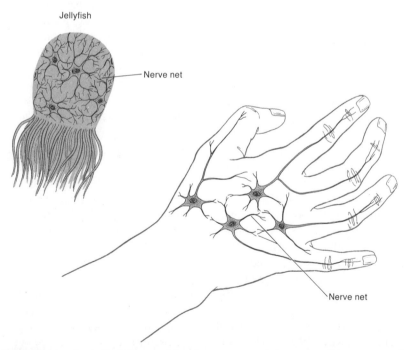

Jellyfish

Nerve net

Nerve net

Figure 1–2 The nervous system of a jellyfish consists of a nerve net. Suppose this nerve net could be connected to the nerves in your fingers. Individual fingers might be able to move, but the movement would not be coordinated. This is because the nerve net does not have a group of controlling cells.

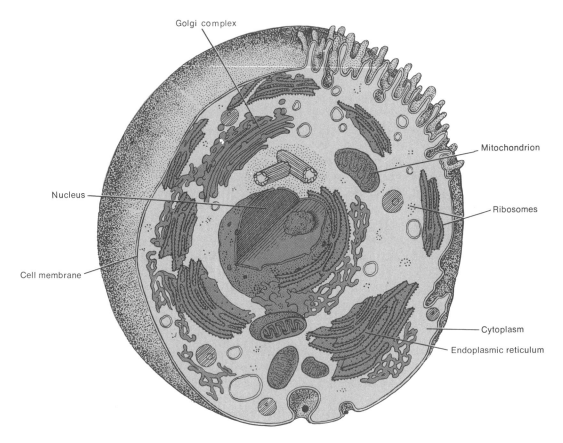

Golgi complex

Mitochondrion

Nucleus

Ribosomes

Cell membrane

Cytoplasm

Endoplasmic reticulum

Figure 1–3 Your brain and your body are composed of billions of cells, all of which share the same basic components illustrated here: cell membrane, nucleus, cytoplasm, and mitochondrion.

Flatworm: The Beginnings

Your next transplant is from an animal that is a considerable step forward in the evolutionary development of the nervous system. Only 2 or 3 cm long, the flatworm was the first beast to evolve an organized nervous system. It has a primitive forerunner of a brain called a **ganglion** that is located at the top of a **nerve network** resembling a primitive spinal cord. This ganglion, a cluster of neurons analogous to our brain, organizes and controls the flatworm body through the nerve network.

The flatworm has the distinction of being one of the first creatures to have a nervous system whose basic structure is somewhat similar to ours. However, if you had a flatworm brain, you would still have to be kept alive by machines. You might respond differently to darkness and light, but that would be about the limit of your sensory world. The flatworm ganglion is not developed enough to allow you to get off the table and walk. Rising and walking are very complicated motor tasks, requiring the integration of many sensations and muscle movements. If the flatworm ganglion were connected to the nerves controlling your fingers, you might be able to move two fingers together and make the victory sign. This is because the ganglion and nerve network enable the flatworm to make coordinated movements. It can swim in one direction and it is a champion at curling up.

The tendency for a group of neurons to develop at the head end of the nerve network is called **encephalization**. The jellyfish brain has no encephalization. Thus, the jellyfish has less control over its tentacles and has less ability to learn new responses. In contrast, the flatworm has the forerunner of a brain and can organize primitive movements and learn simple responses. The advantage, then, of encephalization is greater control. But even with a flatworm nervous system in your skull, your chances of going out the door, much less going on a date, are nil.

Crocodile: A Basic Brain

The neurosurgeon takes out the flatworm brain and replaces it with one that is another big advance in the evolution of the nervous system. This brain will allow you to get off the table and walk out of the library. The brain is that of a crocodile, a creature that evolved millions of years before humans.

The crocodile has a spinal cord similar to ours and a brain that has the three basic divisions of the human brain: **hindbrain**, **midbrain**, and **forebrain**. The crocodile brain would maintain your vital bodily functions (breathing and blood pressure) because a structure in the hindbrain, the **medulla** (mah-DULL-ah), controls respiration and blood pressure. The crocodile brain would also let you make movements that were well coordinated because another structure in the

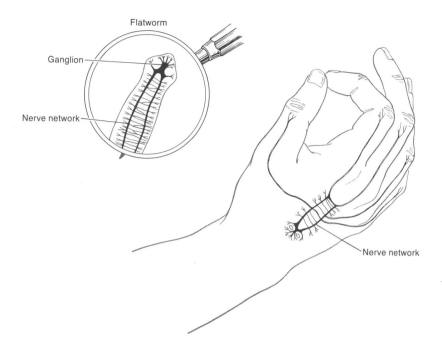

Figure 1-4 The nervous system of a flatworm has a nerve network at whose top is a group of neurons called a ganglion. Suppose the flatworm nervous system could be connected to the nerves in your fingers. With this nervous system, the movement of the fingers could be coordinated because the ganglion provides central control over the nerve network.

hindbrain, the **cerebellum** (ser-ah-BELL-ahm), regulates coordination. The crocodile brain would let you distinguish between the surgeon and the table according to smell because sensations are received and analyzed by structures in the midbrain and forebrain. The crocodile brain would also let you get off the table and organize a biting attack on the surgeon because the initiation of complex movements is made possible by structures in the forebrain. The coordination for these movements comes from the cerebellum in the hindbrain. So the crocodile brain would allow you to walk around campus and attack people. If you wanted to do some serious thinking about why you were attacking people, you would need a more evolved brain.

In any case, the crocodile nervous system is hundreds of times more developed than the jellyfish's. The jellyfish only had interconnected neurons and permitted you to make only very simple, uncoordinated movements. The flatworm had nerves arranged in a ladderlike structure with a group of controlling neurons at the top—an example of encephalization. The flatworm brain permitted coordinated, though still simple, movements and primitive sensations such as distinguishing between light and dark. The crocodile brain, having all three basic divisions of the human brain, would let you regulate your bodily functions, get off the table, experience basic sensations, and make complex motor responses like attacking. But the crocodile brain does not have sufficient development to think about whether it is better to attack or not to attack, or whether it is or is not

an example of encephalization—it is. For serious thinking, you need a new brain, specifically one that has more forebrain.

Chimpanzee: An Advanced Brain

The neurosurgeon takes out the crocodile's brain and replaces it with a chimpanzee's brain. Yes, after waking up, you would like bananas. Compared to the brain of crocodiles and other animals, the chimp brain has a very well-developed forebrain and, at 500 g, is about one-third as large as a human brain.

The chimp brain evolved long after the crocodile brain, retaining many of the same structures found in the reptilian brain. However, the forebrain, which is very tiny in the crocodile, became the largest part of the chimp brain and proportionally a still larger part of the human brain. It is the forebrain that allows you to understand this sentence.

Even though the chimp brain and human brain have some of the same structures found in the crocodile brain, these structures may have one function in the crocodile and another in chimps and humans. For example, a large part of the crocodile brain, called the **limbic area**, helps the crocodile identify and locate prey through smell. The human brain also contains a limbic area, but instead of helping us locate prey through smell, it is involved in our memory and emotions. On the other hand, when a crocodile swims in

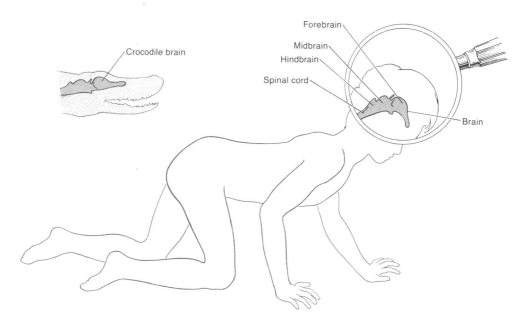

Figure 1–5 The nervous system of a crocodile consists of a spinal cord and a brain with the three major divisions found in the more developed human brain. Imagine that a crocodile brain could be placed in the human skull and connected to the spinal cord. This brain could maintain vital bodily functions, allow fairly complex movements, and experience basic sensations.

the water or a chimp swings through the trees or a tennis player makes a sizzling shot, the same brain structure, the cerebellum, is coordinating these movements. Thus, in the evolution of the human brain, some of the structures found in primitive brains (cerebellum) have retained approximately the same function; other structures found in primitive brains (limbic area) have evolved different functions in the human brain.

When you awakened with a chimp's brain in your head, you would be able to get off the table, figure out how to open the door, use the elevator, and get a banana or apple from the vending machine. If you saw yourself in a mirror, you would probably know that you did not look like a chimp. It seems that chimps, like humans, develop a self concept and know what they look like or who they are (1–3, 1–4). If your chimp brain had been taught a sign language, you could use the sign language to ask for a glass of water or a hug or a banana. Chimpanzees have been taught to use sign language similar to that used by people who are mute (1–2, 1–5). Your chimp brain could do these complex tasks, even use sign language, because of the well-developed forebrain. But if you wanted to read a book or do library research and write a paper on intelligence in chimps, you would find that your chimp brain was not well enough developed for these more complex tasks. If you went on a date with a chimp's brain in your skull, you could engage in simple conversation using sign language and would probably spend the evening in the fruit section of the supermarket.

PKU Brain

The neurosurgeon removes the chimp brain from your skull and replaces it with a human brain. The average human brain weighs about 1,350 g (3 lb) and contains about 10 billion nerve cells or neurons. But human brains are not all alike. Suppose the surgeon put in a human brain that was labeled **PKU**, for phenylketonuria. PKU is a metabolic disorder that prevents normal development of the brain. After you woke up, you could do everything you had done with a chimp brain but probably not much more.

A human brain may fail to develop properly because of some problem with the **chromosomes**, or **genes**, material located in every cell of your body. Each cell nucleus contains chromosomes which in turn contain genes. At conception, an ovum (egg), which contains 23 chromosomes, is penetrated by a sperm, which contains 23 chromosomes, resulting in one cell that has two sets of paired chromosomes, for a total of 46. The chromosomes are very tiny structures that look like X's and Y's, and there are 46 found in every cell of your body. It is the genes in each chromosome that contain the instructions for how your brain and body will develop. The genes are like a set of instructions for putting a bicycle together. If the instructions are written correctly, listing each step in order, your bike should work properly. On the other hand, if the steps in the instructions are mixed up, your bike might end up with some serious defects. Likewise, if a gene is in the wrong place on a chromosome, the result can be a child who has serious defects,

Development

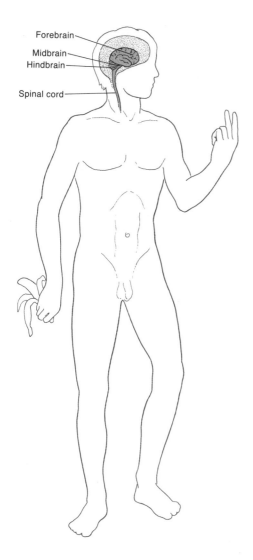

Figure 1-6 The nervous system of a chimpanzee consists of a spinal cord and a brain with a well-developed forebrain. Suppose the chimp's brain could be placed in a human skull and connected to the spinal cord. This brain would make it possible for the human to perform very complex and coordinated movements, to receive and analyze complicated stimuli, and to learn and use sign language.

such as a smaller than normal head and a lower than normal IQ score. The disorder PKU is caused by a misplaced gene on a chromosome, which in turn prevents the body from converting one chemical (phenylalanine) into another (tyrosine). When this conversion does not take place, phenylpyruvic acid accumulates and causes the formation of other acids that are toxic to the nervous system (1–9).

If PKU is not diagnosed early and treated, severe brain damage will occur in the first three to six months of life. Since this disorder can be diagnosed at birth, PKU infants can be fed a special diet low in phenylalanine that prevents brain damage and serious mental retardation. Without nor-

mal brain development, PKU children are poor in reading, writing, and thinking, as reflected in low scores on intelligence tests. Intelligence here means actual performance on tasks involving reasoning, identifying objects, and solving various kinds of puzzles. The score received for completing these tasks is called an **IQ score** and does not indicate your potential or native intelligence. It indicates, rather, how well you perform certain tasks that are thought to relate to intelligence.

The average IQ score is 100, while many PKU children have IQ scores in the 30's. The misplaced gene in PKU does not directly cause the mental retardation but rather starts a chain of events: the gene causes a metabolic disorder, which in turn interferes with brain development, which finally results in mental retardation. Thus, genes can indirectly affect very complex behaviors such as reading, writing, and thinking.

DNA and RNA

As stated earlier, the genes are chains of chemicals that carry the instructions for the development of that original single cell formed by an ovum and sperm into a human body. Instructions contained in the genes determine that your finger is to be a finger and not a kidney. In fact, instructions in the genes determine how each cell in the body is to develop and how these cells are to be combined into organs. Because the genes come from your parents, the genes carry instructions for cells to develop characteristics similar to those of your parents: eye color, bone structure, hair texture, color blindness, and hundreds of other traits. Genes can also carry instructions for characteristics that were not evident in your parents but were carried in their genes from their parents.

How do the genes carry all these instructions? The gene is composed of a chemical called **DNA** (deoxyribonucleic acid). Each DNA molecule looks like a ladder that was held at the top and bottom and twisted a number of times. The rungs of this ladder are made up of four different chemicals with two of the four chemicals combining to form each rung. These four chemicals combine in certain ways to form a sequence of rungs on the ladder, and it is this sequence of rungs that contains the genetic instructions.

The instructions for the development of a toe are arranged in a different sequence of rungs on the ladder than are the instructions for the development of a nose. Thus, the DNA molecule structure of a ladder with rungs arranged in certain sequences contains the coded instructions for all cell development.

There is still the question of how the instructions contained in DNA become known to the cell. DNA is involved in the production of chemicals that regulate the development of the cell. These chemicals are called **enzymes**. The reason the cells that make up a toe do not instead become

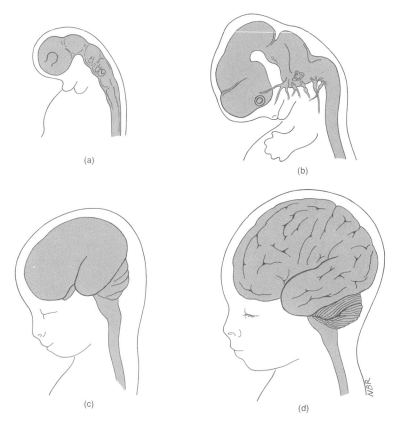

Figure 1–7 As the cells in the developing brain multiply, the human brain takes shape from (a) the 3-week embryo, (b) the 7-week embryo, (c) the 4-month fetus, (d) to the newborn infant. At birth the infant's brain weighs about 350 g. At puberty, when it is completely developed, it weighs between 1,300 and 1,500 g.

a nose is that different enzymes are involved in the development of a toe than those in a nose. The development of each cell of the body into a particular structure, toe versus nose, is determined by the kind of enzyme produced by DNA. Thus, the genetic instructions contained in the DNA molecule are put into operation through the production of enzymes which in turn tell cells whether to become neurons, eyes, or fingers.

There is a series of steps in the production of enzymes by DNA. The DNA is contained in the cell nucleus while the enzymes are manufactured in the cell body, in the jellylike cytoplasm. Thus, it is necessary for DNA to transfer its instructions from the nucleus to the cytoplasm. This transfer is accomplished by a chemical called messenger **RNA** (ribonucleic acid), which carries the instructions from the DNA in the nucleus to the cytoplasm. When the instructions carried by messenger RNA reach the cytoplasm, enzymes are formed which in turn control the cell's development into a toe or kidney or nose.

If the structure of the DNA molecule—that is, the ladder and its rungs—is damaged by x rays or drugs or other causes, the instructions contained in the DNA structure are changed. If the genetic instructions are changed, the proper enzymes are not formed and the cell does not develop appropriately. The development of the single-celled zygote

(egg and sperm) into a human body is accomplished through the genetic instructions contained in the DNA molecule. Discovery of the structure of this molecule, called a **double helix**, was accomplished by James Watson and Francis Crick. It was one of the most important scientific breakthroughs of our time.

Brain Aging

Just as the structure of the body changes with age, so does the structure of the brain. The following Headliner describes interesting research that shows exactly how the brain changes with age.

Down's Syndrome

People with **Down's syndrome** have abnormal physical features such as slanting eyes and a large, protruding tongue. Their brains are maldeveloped; they can learn to dress and feed themselves and engage in simple conversation, but on IQ tests their scores usually range between 20 and 60.

In the case of Down's syndrome, the cause for maldeveloped brain is not a misplaced gene, as with PKU, but rather a misplaced chromosome. Since chromosomes carry

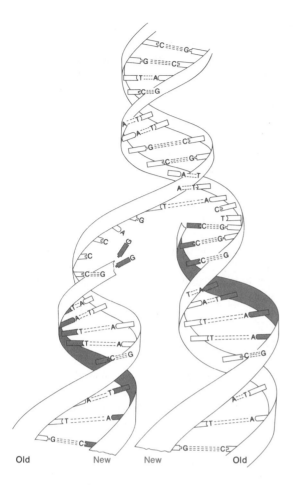

Figure 1–8 The structure of the DNA molecule, called a double helix, resembles a ladder twisted around a number of times. When the DNA molecule divides, the ladder unwinds and splits down its length. Two new sides are formed and attached to the original ladder sides, resulting in two DNA molecules.

genes, the change in a chromosome's placement results in defective genetic instructions. Abnormal brain and body development occur as Down's syndrome when an extra chromosome has joined a pair of chromosomes or a chromosome from one pair has been exchanged with that of another pair (1–9). The PKU infant can be treated with proper diet to prevent retardation but there is as yet no cure for Down's syndrome.

Protein-Deficient Brain

If the brain is severely deprived of nourishment, especially protein, during prenatal development or the first three years of life, the brain will not develop fully. Generalizing from animal brains deprived of protein, scientists think that human brains deprived of protein may lack many of the connections between neurons that normal brains have (1–8, 1–11). Thus, the brain cells are not able to communicate as they normally should. A person with a brain that has been severely deprived of protein has a lower IQ score, has trouble in school with reading, writing, and thinking, and has difficulty being admitted to college. It appears that the brain damage from protein deficiency is irreversible if it occurs in the uterus or during the child's first three years.

In the case of the protein-deficient brain, the genes and chromosomes are perfectly normal. But for the genetic instructions to be carried out, there must be the right environment—in this example, a sufficient amount of protein in the diet. Thus, the way your brain develops is partly determined by *environmental* factors, for example, what your mother eats or drinks or the kinds of pills she takes while you are a fetus, and the kind of food you eat or do not eat once you are born. The development of your brain depends both on genetic instructions and on environmental factors.

Genius' Brain

No one knows exactly what makes a brain a genius. It is not the size or weight, since brains of geniuses like Einstein were about the same size and weight as the brains of normal college sophomores. You may hear people say that the brain of a genius is more efficient or better organized than normal. If this is true, you might expect some physical or chemical differences that allow the genius brain to be more efficient. To find possible physical differences, the scientist would have to explore the actual brain: dissecting neurons, counting the number of neurons, weighing the neurons, counting the connections between neurons, analyzing the chemicals in the neurons. However, with present techniques, analyzing a living brain would result in damage or destruction of neurons. Since neurons in the brain do not regenerate when damaged or destroyed, most geniuses would not be very enthusiastic about having their brains damaged. Thus, it is difficult to determine any physical differences between the brain of a genius and the brain of a person who only wishes to be one.

Parent's Brain

Suppose your parents were geniuses or dullards, cowards or murderers. Would you inherit these traits from your mother and father? There is no question that you do inherit physical traits from your parents, such as eye color, bone structure, skin coloring, and hair texture. But whether you inherit psychological or behavioral traits is much more difficult to determine. You have heard the saying, ''She takes after her mother.'' This saying could mean that the child *inherited* the behavior from her parents or that the child *learned* the behavior from her parents or that she experienced some combination of inheriting and learning. If the child inherited the behavior, it means that somehow the genes carried instructions for a certain kind of brain development. One way scientists attempt to determine which behaviors are inherited is by studying twins.

Genetic Factor

Twins come in two kinds: **identical** twins, which have the same genetic makeup and thus look identical; and **fraternal** twins, which have different genetic makeups and thus look different. If a certain behavior like "genius" were inherited, you would expect the identical twins with identical genetic makeups to have about the same degree of genius and the fraternal twins with different genetic makeups to have different degrees of genius. Although no one knows if you inherit "genius," there is evidence that performance on intelligence tests is affected by inherited factors. If performance on intelligence tests is affected by inherited factors, then identical twins should have more similar IQ scores than do fraternal twins. In fact, identical twins, whether raised together or apart, *do* have more similar IQ scores than do fraternal twins. Thus, performance on IQ tests is partly determined by genetic factors. But this is only part of the story.

Environmental Factor

Even though you may be born to parents who have very low IQ scores, this does not mean that you will automatically have a low IQ score. Although it is true that some aspect of how you perform on IQ tests is inherited, twin studies have shown that your performance on IQ tests also depends on the kind of environment in which you were raised. If you inherited genes that somehow resulted in poor performance on IQ tests but you were raised in an exciting, stimulating environment, then you might do very well on IQ tests. If you inherited genes that somehow resulted in poor performance on IQ tests and you were raised in a dull, boring environment, you might in fact do poorly on IQ tests. Genes alone do not determine your IQ score. Your home, parents, friends, schools—your environment—interact with your genetic makeup. Exactly how your genetic makeup will be expressed in your behavior is greatly influenced by your environment.

Interaction of Heredity and Environment

When captured, he was approximately 12 years old. He could not speak and was interested only in eating, sleeping, and trying to escape. From an early age, he had lived in the woods, adopting the ways of an animal, not knowing human contact. Upon his capture, he was judged more animal than human and, for a while, was kept on a leash. During the next six years, a doctor patiently tried to teach this wild boy how to eat, dress, speak, and behave like other humans. The doctor had some success in teaching him to develop human behaviors although the boy never learned to speak (1-7). This case illustrates how an individual, presumably with normal genes for human development, became more animal than human because of his deprived environment. The presence of normal genes does not guarantee that an individual will develop human behaviors.

Mother monkeys guard, protect, and defend their infants, never letting them out of sight, never failing to respond to their cries. Thus, the scientist Harry Harlow thought it very strange to observe several mothers showing little interest in their infants, dropping or stepping on them and not responding to their cries. The abnormal mothers had *not* been raised by monkeys themselves, but by dummy-mothers. The scientist had thought a dummy-mother might be ideal: never punishing, always being available, and providing plenty of milk. However, monkeys raised by dummy-mothers became adults with abnormal sexual and maternal behaviors (1-6). This is another instance of how the environment interacts with the genetic makeup to determine behavior patterns.

The isolated human boy and the monkeys raised by dummy-mothers probably had brains that were physically different from individuals raised normally. Even if there are no dietary problems during brain development, lack of sensory stimulation can result in brains with areas that actually weigh less and have less chemical activity than normal (1-10). These data come from studies on rats raised in isolated or deprived environments. The studies indicate how the physical structure of the brain can be modified by sensory stimulation. Too little sensory stimulation can produce a brain that is less developed than a brain from an environment full of sensory input. If you ever do have the opportunity to borrow a brain, it would be as important to know the kind of environment in which it has lived as it would be to know the brain's genetic background.

The Mind: Is It the Brain?

If your brain were removed and another put into your skull, who would you be? Your friends would recognize your face but you would not recognize your friends or know their names. You would not know where you lived or who your parents were. You would not joke like or think like or dream like the original you. You would be a different you since the original you was stored in the brain that was removed. With a new brain, you would have a different mind and personality even though your original body remained. Thus, if you changed your brain, you also would be literally changing your mind. The courts and insurance companies would have to figure out whether your body or your brain was the real you.

With a new brain, you would have new thoughts, dreams, and fantasies, and this is to say that you would have a new mind. Scientists have never been comfortable with the word *mind* because it is not easy to bring a "mind" into the lab-

SCIENTISTS DESCRIBE HOW BRAIN CHANGES WITH AGE

In the beginning, neurons in the developing brain stand like young saplings, sinewy looking and strong but almost bare of spreading branches.

Soon, tiny hair-like structures appear on the sides of the nerve shaft and spread horizontally to form connections with tissues spreading from other neurons. By the time of maturity—say, 20 to 30 years of age—an amazing intergrowth of connections has developed between millions of nerve cells.

Then, as the years go by, the neurons change shape, the tiny hairs swell and become lumpy, and finally, toward the end, the branches fall off, leaving a nerve shaft that is drooping and almost bare.

This is the picture of infancy, maturity and senility in the brain.

The tiny hairs are dendritic spines.

The horizontal mesh they form is called dendritic branches. The trillions of interconnections between these spines provide the matrix within which information ultimately is received, processed and acted upon by neurons within the brain. They [dendritic branches] are, therefore, extremely important objects for study.

The correlation between the number of dendritic branches and aging—increasing numbers until maturity, then decreasing numbers—has been found by a husband and wife team at UCLA's Brain Research Institute, Drs. Mila and Arnold Scheibel.

Their discovery provides scientists with a kind of anatomical standard which can be used to evaluate those influences on humans which may affect the normal balances.

What effects do drugs and diet have on the presence of dendritic spines? Can the spines be made more profuse or, at least, their ultimate demise delayed? Because the brain is the control center of all the organs in the body, can the physical effects of aging, as well as the intellectual, be delayed by prolonging healthy dendritic profusion?

The answers to those questions are unknown. The Scheibels stress that their work has no practical application at the moment.

Recently the Scheibels, Dr. Jesu Machada-Sala, Dr. Robert D. Lindsay and Dr. Uwamie Tomiyasu, a neuropathologist at Wadsworth Veterans Administration Hospital, studied brain tissue from 10 recently deceased patients who were between 58 and 96 years old.

Six of the patients had been senile from one to four years before dying. The other four had not been considered to have lost significant intellectual or emotional capabilities.

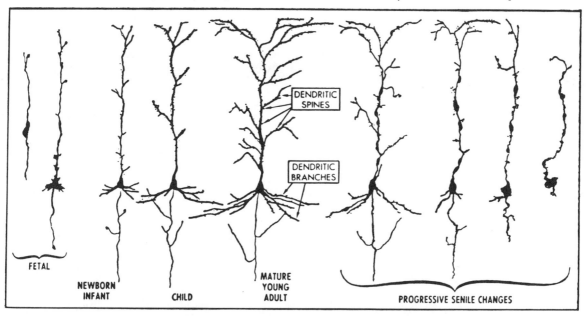

Changes in the neuron's structure from infancy through senility. Notice how the newborn infant's neuron has few dendritic branches, while in the mature adult the branching is profuse. In senility the dendritic branches disappear. This means that there would be less communication between neurons and thus loss of behavioral functions. (Los Angeles Times Photo.)

11

Using a special method of staining called the Golgi technique, the researchers were able to study microscopic changes in the neurons which are not obvious when other techniques are used.

By combining the observations made from these senile and nonsenile patients with their previous findings using animals of different ages, the researchers have been able to map the cyclic patterns of spines and dendritic branch growth. They noted that the degree of change seemed more related to degree of senility than to calendar age.

Researchers have long suspected that large numbers of neurons are being lost continuously as a result of the aging process. One estimate is that 30% of the 8 to 10 billion nerve cells in the brain are lost between the ages of 20 and 90.

But the structures being studied by the Scheibels are not so much the neurons alone as they are the densely massed and interwoven spines and dendrite branches which, they believe, may be "program libraries" responsible for a significant amount of brain function.

The effects on the individual of gradually losing parts of this system would at first be subtle because of the enormous amount of tissue involved.

However, the Scheibels say, eventually the total amount of deficit would begin to show up as decreasing motor strength, lack of dexterity and agility and problems with memory and making associations.

The severity of these symptoms of early senility, they believe, is related not only to the total number of lost cells, but—perhaps more importantly—to the number of cells which have become more isolated due to loss of the mesh formed by the dendrite branches.

The Scheibels' work is one of a number of basic research projects with potential clinical applications under way at the Brain Research Institute.

"We are preparing for the era of explosive advances in the field of neuroscience in the decade ahead," says Dr. John D. French, a neurosurgeon and physiologist who has been BRI director since its opening in 1959.

SOURCE: Harry Nelson, Times Medical Writer, *Los Angeles Times*, May 14, 1976. Copyright © 1976 by Los Angeles Times.

oratory for investigation. You have often heard the statements, "My mind is a blank," or "She has a brilliant mind," or "He lost his mind." This sounds as though your mind is separate from your brain. But since it is true that without a brain you could not think or reason or dream, and with a new brain you would have different thoughts and reasons and dreams, your mind and brain must be closely connected. In fact, scientists often define the *mind* as those things—thinking, reasoning, dreaming—that the brain does. Instead of saying your mind is a blank, the scientist might say your brain is a blank.

Comment

You have seen how the nervous system and brain have developed over millions of years of evolution, from a few scattered neurons into a highly developed, complex nervous system. You have seen how genetic factors are transmitted and how they can affect the way your brain develops. Finally, you have seen that the environment can affect the physical structure of the brain and your actual behavior patterns. If brain transplants did become possible, what kind of brain would you choose?

SELF-TEST 1

1 If your finger were cut off, it could be sewn back on and would regain feelings because the nerves involved are part of the _____ system.

peripheral nervous

2 If your spinal cord were severed, the neurons involved would not regrow because they are part of the _____ system.

central nervous

3 The central nervous system is made up of neurons and nerve tracts in the _____ and neurons in the _____ . None of these neurons have the capacity to _____ if they are destroyed.

spinal cord / brain / regenerate or regrow

4 In the evolution of the nervous system, one of the very early systems is that of the jellyfish. It has specialized cells called _____ , but does not have anything that could be called a _____

neurons / brain or ganglion

5 A cell is surrounded by a _____ , and the genetic instructions for the development of the cell are contained in the _____ . Energy is supplied to the cell by the _____ . The manufacture of hormones occurs on the _____ , and these hormones are wrapped in a membrane by the _____ .

membrane
nucleus / mitochondria
ribosomes
Golgi complex

6 A big leap forward in the evolution of the nervous system is found in the flatworm. It has a system of nerves arranged in a manner resembling a primitive _____ , at the top of which is a group of neurons called a _____ which is the forerunner of your _____ , but much, much simpler.

spinal cord
ganglion / brain

7 The advantage of having a controlling group of neurons such as the ganglion is that the flatworm could do many more _____ tasks than could the jellyfish.

complex or difficult or complicated

8 The tendency for a group of neurons to develop at the head end of a nerve network is an example of _____ .

encephalization

9 A nervous system much more developed than that of the flatworm is the crocodile's. The crocodile has a spinal cord similar to yours and a brain with the three basic divisions of the human brain: _____, _____ , and _____ .

hindbrain / midbrain / forebrain

10 The structure in the crocodile's hindbrain that controls respiration and _____ is called the _____ .

blood pressure
medulla

11 The crocodile can distinguish between a body and a log by smell sensations that are received and processed by structures in the _____ and _____ .

midbrain / forebrain

12 The division of your brain that allows you to think about being eaten by a crocodile is your _____ .

forebrain

13 In the evolutionarily old brain of the crocodile, the limbic area was involved mainly with _____ while in the newer human brain it is involved with _____ .

smell
emotions and memory

14 The cerebellum is present in the evolutionarily old brain of the crocodile, as well as in the later-evolved brain of humans. In both crocodiles and human brains, the cerebellum is involved with _____ .

coordination

15 A chimpanzee can be taught complicated tasks such as the use of sign language because of the well-developed division of the brain called the _____ .

forebrain

16 The instructions for how your brain develops are contained in the _____ , which are carried in the chromosomes.

genes

17 A misplaced gene can prevent the body from converting one chemical, phenylalanine, into another, and this disorder is called _____ .

PKU or phenylketonuria

18 If the metabolic disorder produced in PKU is not treated, the results will be brain damage and the child will be _____ .

mentally retarded

19 There are 23 pairs of chromosomes, and if one pair is exchanged or another chromosome is added a disorder can result called _____ .

Down's syndrome

20 The gene is composed of a chemical called _____ . The structure of this chemical resembles a _____ with sides and rungs made of other _____ .

DNA
ladder / chemicals

21 The chemicals that make up the rungs of the DNA ladder combine in certain ways to form a _____ of rungs that carry the genetic _____ .

sequence / instructions

22 DNA is involved in the production of chemicals called _____ that control the development of each cell. The reason your heart is not an elbow is that there are different _____ controlling the development of the heart from those of the elbow.

enzymes
enzymes

23 The genetic instructions contained in DNA, which is located in the _____ of the cell, are transferred to the _____ of the cell by messenger _____ .

nucleus
cytoplasm / RNA

24 If there is damage to the DNA molecule by drugs or x rays or other causes, the result is a change in genetic instructions and the cell does not develop correctly. This is because the proper _____ are lacking.

enzymes

25 PKU and Down's syndrome are examples of genetic and chromosomal defects that directly affect _____ development and indirectly affect very complex behaviors such as _____ .

brain / thinking or reading or writing

26 Even though the genes and chromosomes may be normal, the brain may not develop properly if there is a severe _____ deficiency in the womb or during the first three years of life.

protein

27 The PKU brain illustrates the importance of _____ factors in brain development, while the protein-deficient brain illustrates the importance of _____ factors.

genetic
environmental

28 It is not known how the brain of a genius differs *physically* from your own brain. To measure any physical differences, scientists would damage some of the _____ , and once damaged these would not _____ .

neurons or brain cells
regrow

29 Identical twins have an identical _____ makeup while fraternal twins have a dissimilar _____ makeup.

genetic
genetic

30 There is evidence from studies of identical twins that performance on IQ tests can be influenced by _____ makeup.

genetic

31 If you have inherited genes that will lead to a high IQ score, you will probably show a high IQ score only if you have been raised in a stimulating _____ .

environment

32 If you have inherited genes that will lead to a low IQ score, you may still show a high performance on IQ tests if you were raised in a _____ environment.

stimulating or exciting

33 If you have inherited some behavior through your genes, this behavior might occur, might be modified, or might not occur depending on the kind of _____ in which you were raised.

environment

34 The brain and the mind are closely connected; if it were possible to change your brain, you would also be changing your mind. One definition of mind is those things (thinking, dreaming, fantasizing, reasoning) that the _____ does.

brain

REFERENCES

1–1   Fallaci, O. The dead body and the living brain. *Look* November 28, 1967.

1–2   Fleming, J. D. The Lucy and Roger talk show. *Psychology Today* January 1974.

1–3   Gallup, G. G., Jr. Chimpanzees: self-recognition. *Science* 1970, 167: 86–87.

1–4   Gallup, G. G., Jr. Chimps and self-concept. *Psychology Today* March 1971.

1–5   Gardner, R. A. and Gardner, B. T. Teaching sign language to a chimpanzee. *Science* 1969, 196: 664–672.

1–6   Harlow, H. F. Heterosexual affectional systems in monkeys. *American Psychologist* 1962, 17: 1–9.

1–7   Lane, H. *The wild boy of Aveyron*. Cambridge, MA: Harvard University, 1976.

1–8   Lewin, R. Starved brains. *Psychology Today* September 1975.

1–9   McClearn, G. E. and DeFries, J. C. *Introduction to behavioral genetics*. San Francisco: W. H. Freeman, 1973.

1–10   Rosenzweig, M. R., Bennett, E. L., and Diamond, M. C. brain changes in response to experience. *Scientific American* 1972, 226: 2–29.

1–11   Sheour, E. A. *The malnourished mind*. Garden City, NY: Anchor, 1975.

Neuron

2

It's All Done with Chemicals

Neuron Visitor

It was a Friday afternoon when the Director of Neuro-physiology found the visitor on his laboratory table. No one could tell him where it had come from or what kind of organism it might be. Soon a group of scientists were gathered around, peering, probing, and talking about the creature. Each one had a different opinion, but all agreed on one point; the visitor was quite unlike any living organism they had ever seen. It had—or rather was—a medium-sized head, and it was transparent! You could look inside and see that it was mostly empty, except for fluid and three peculiar structures that seemed to glow and flash. After a great deal of excited discussion, the scientists agreed that they were looking at the creature's "brain" and that the three structures were actually enormous nerve cells. They gave the visitor the name X Neuron because nerve cells are called neurons.

On the front of its head (or it may have been the back) was what looked like an ear with a neuron attached. On top of its head (or possibly the bottom) was what looked like a mouth with a second neuron attached. Between the neurons of the ear and the mouth was a middle one. The glowing and flashing of the neurons resembled a miniature fireworks display.

When X Neuron heard a laugh, the ear neuron flashed, then the middle one flashed, and lastly the mouth neuron flashed. When all three had flashed, there would be a splendiforous smile. When X Neuron was neither hearing nor smiling, the neurons could be seen glowing softly. X Neuron seemed not the least disturbed that everyone could read its mind by watching its neurons. It got on quite well with three neurons and was content to spend its day smiling or glowing.

Neuron

Being a creature of fiction, X Neuron could smile using only three neurons. If X Neuron had been human, its brain would have had approximately 10 billion neurons. Neurons in the human brain are incredibly small and can be seen only with powerful microscopes. Each **neuron** has the very special property of being able to store information and to *communicate* with other neurons or glands or muscles. Other cells in the body, such as muscle cells, can receive information, but only neurons can transmit information. If there were only fat and muscle cells in your brain, you could not think or move or smile. When someone laughs, X Neuron's ear receives this information and the ear neuron passes this information on to the next neuron. If there is enough laughter, the middle neuron is activated and it causes the last neuron to flash and produce the smile. When you multiply by millions this simple chain of three neural events, you have some notion of what happens when you smile. You are able to hear, think, smile, and do the millions of things that you do because cells called neurons have been specialized to store, receive, and transmit information.

The neurons in the human nervous system come in an almost endless variety of sizes and shapes. Some are shaped like simple spheres, others like pyramids or beautifully branched trees; still others resemble tadpoles or starfish. The shape of the neuron reflects its function. The shapes of X Neuron's three neurons are good examples of some of the neurons found in the human nervous system.

Afferent Neuron

The neuron that is attached to X Neuron's "ear" has a shape similar to the neurons that transmit information from your skin to your spinal cord. This neuron has two long tubes that attach to a protuberance that is the cell body. One of these tubes begins in the skin and carries information toward the cell body. The other tube begins at the cell body and carries information into the spinal cord. The neuron shape is called **unipolar** and is shown in Figure 2–1. If your skin were pinched, this information would be received and transmitted by **sensory** or **afferent** neurons, one of which has a unipolar shape.

The end of the sensory neuron that begins in the skin is called the **dendrite**. It has many branches which receive information from the skin or other neurons. The dendrite includes the branches and that part of the tube that extends to the cell body. Without dendrites, you would not be able to receive information from the world around you. The tip of the dendrite, located in your skin, is specialized to react to environmental information and is called a **receptor**. In order to register pressure or pain or cold, the receptor part of the dendrite reacts by changing these stimuli into electrical or neural information. All dendrites can receive information, but only dendrites with specialized receptors at their tips can react to stimulation from the environment, changing *environmental* information into neural information.

The dendrite extends to the round protuberance that is called the **cell body** or **soma**. The cell body functions to provide nourishment for the rest of the neuron. If the cell body were snipped off or damaged, the rest of the neuron would die. The dendrites transmit their information to the cell body. Extending from the cell body is a long tube called the **axon** that carries information away from the cell body. At the very end of the axon are many hairlike extensions called **telodendria** (tel-oh-DEN-dree-ah). The telodendria are specialized for transmitting information by secreting chemicals that affect neighboring neurons. The telodendria secrete their chemicals into a tiny space between neurons called a **synapse** (SIN-aps). It is at the synapse that the information from one neuron is chemically transmitted to the next neuron.

The unipolar afferent neuron, consisting of a dendrite, cell body, and axon, carries information from areas on your skin into your spinal cord or brain. If you are very tall, some of your unipolar neurons may be more than 1 m (over 3 ft) long.

The unipolar neuron does not actually transmit a sensation of pressure or pain or cold. It transmits a combination of electrical and chemical changes that is called **neural information** or **nerve impulses**. You experience a sensation of cold or pain only after neural information from the receptors has been transmitted across many synapses and finally activates neurons in certain parts of your brain. Some unipolar neurons carry information that eventually results in sensations of pain or cold. Others carry information that does not result in sensations. For example, some unipolar neurons carry information for reflexes such as the knee jerk

response, that occurs when the doctor taps your knee with a rubber hammer. Since some unipolar neurons carry information that does not cause sensations, it is better to refer to them as afferent rather than sensory. An **afferent neuron** is one that carries information toward the central nervous system.

Interneuron

Between X Neuron's ear and mouth is a middle neuron or **interneuron**. The interneuron forms a link between the afferent neuron that receives information and the motor neuron that moves its mouth. While X Neuron has only one interneuron, there are literally billions of these neurons in your central nervous system. They are found in the spinal cord and also in the brain. The term *interneuron* is *not* applied to all neurons of the brain. It is used to refer to neurons whose primary function is linking neurons from different areas of the nervous system.

X Neuron's interneuron looks something like a tadpole and is specialized for receiving information from only one neuron. In your nervous system, interneurons differ in appearance depending on whether they are specialized to receive information from one or many neurons. Most interneurons have numerous dendrites whose function is to receive information from other neurons. Thus, they are called **multipolar**. Most of the neurons in your brain are multipolar in shape.

When X Neuron's ear hears laughter, the attached afferent neuron is activated. This neural information is transmitted from the telodendria of the afferent neuron to the dendrites of the interneuron. If enough information is transmitted by the telodendria, that is, enough chemicals are secreted, the interneuron will be activated and neural information or a nerve impulse will be transmitted down its axon to its telodendria. The interneuron's telodendria will transmit the neural information to the dendrites of the motor neuron that will cause X Neuron to smile. The interneuron functions to modulate the neural information transmitted by afferent neurons. In the case of X Neuron, if only a little laughter is heard, the afferent neuron may be activated, but it may not be activated frequently enough to trigger the interneuron. Thus, X Neuron would have no sensation of hearing the laugh and there would be no smile. In your case, if you touched a hot surface, afferent nerves might be activated but we would not see a reflex unless the afferent neurons were able to trigger the interneurons, which in turn trigger motor neurons. In addition to reflexes, interneurons are involved in all the activities you do, from sleeping to thinking, moving, and reading. Some of the sensory information that is transmitted on afferent neurons never results in any conscious sensations or behaviors because the interneurons are not activated. On the other hand, some information carried in afferent neurons does result in sensations or behavior because interneurons have gathered information from many afferent neurons. By the time you have experienced the sensation of your knee moving or have thought about why your knee moves, literally millions of interneurons in both your spinal cord and brain have been activated.

Motor Neuron

When X Neuron smiles, a motor neuron has caused a muscle to move. When you move reflexively or drive to work or fight a bear, you are depending on the action of motor neurons on muscles. Motor neurons in your spinal cord, called **alpha motor neurons**, have dendrites, cell bodies, and axons similar to other neurons. However, the axons of most motor neurons are quite long since they must travel from the spinal cord to the muscles of your toes, fingers, and other parts of your body. Most motor neurons, like that shown in Figure 2–2, have axons that are wrapped with a fatty material called the **myelin sheath** (MY-lin). This sheath varies in thickness and in some places along the axon is very thin. These thin places or interruptions in the myelin sheath are called **nodes of Ranvier** (ron-vee-AYE). The myelin sheath stops just before and does not cover the telodendria. Nor does it cover the cell body or dendrites. As we will explain later, the myelin is thought to help the axon conduct neural impulses at higher rates of speed. Most large axons, motor as well as nonmotor, are myelinated; smaller axons have some myelination or may share myelin with other axons.

To produce a smile, only one interneuron activates X Neuron's motor neuron. In contrast, your motor neurons receive information from thousands of other neurons. The telodendria of these other neurons, mostly interneurons, synapse with the motor neuron's cell body and dendrites. Figure 2–3 shows, greatly magnified, thousands of telodendria making contact or synapsing on the cell body of a motor neuron. For one motor neuron to be activated, there has been an extraordinary amount of neural input from other neurons. An individual motor neuron may activate one muscle fiber or it may branch and activate as many as 100 fibers. To contract an entire muscle, which is composed of many muscle fibers, interneurons activate hundreds of motor neurons at approximately the same time. The motor neurons, in turn, excite the muscle fibers with which they connect. Thus, running or jumping rope may appear to be simple movements, but each of these activities depends upon the activation of millions of neurons.

How Neurons Function

If neurons in your brain were visible, you would not see them glow or flash when you were thinking or smiling. But they would be the site of considerable chemical activity. There are chemical particles in and around your neurons that actually carry electrical charges and generate electrical forces. Whether you are awake or asleep, moving or still, this **electrochemical activity** is occurring in each of the billions of neurons in your nervous system. The electrochemical activity results from two things: the presence of small chemical particles called ions, and the properties of the outside covering of the neuron, or cell **membrane**.

Ions

Each time you put salt on your food, you are actually adding two chemical particles called sodium and chloride. Sodium is represented by the symbol Na, and chloride by Cl. Thus, table salt is NaCl. When salt or NaCl is dissolved in water, the chemical particles separate or **dissociate** into Na and Cl. Each of these particles has an important property: it carries an electrical charge. A chemical particle that carries an electrical charge is called an **ion**. Ions have either **positive** (plus) charges or **negative** (minus) charges. You can understand how these electrical charges on ions work if you think about a magnet. A magnet will attract metal objects, that are oppositely charged from itself and will repel another magnet that has a like charge. Similarly, an ion will attract other particles that have a different or opposite charge and will repel other particles that have the same charge. In other words, ions with positive charges are attracted to ions with negative charges and vice versa. Ions with positive charges are repelled by ions with positive charges, and ions with negative charges are repelled by those with negative charges. It is important to remember that oppositely charged ions ($+-$ or $-+$) are attracted or move toward each other; similarly charged ($++$ or $--$) are repulsed or move away from each other.

There are fluids in and around the neuron and there are ions in this fluid. The fluid inside the neuron is called **intracellular** fluid (*intra* meaning "inside"), and the fluid outside the neuron is called **extracellular** fluid (*extra* meaning "outside"). Chemicals dissolved in the intra- and extracellular fluids form ions. These fluids contain varying concentrations of sodium ions (Na^+), chloride ions (Cl^-), potassium ions (K^+), and other ions. As you will see, all of your thinking, planning, smiling, and moving can be traced to the activity of these small ions.

Semipermeable Membrane

You can think of the outside covering or membrane of the neuron as having holes or pores. These pores are large enough for the small ions, such as potassium (K^+), to pass through. However, inside the neuron are ions composed of proteins that are too large to leave and are trapped in the intracellular fluid. Because some ions can pass through the membrane while others cannot, the membrane is said to be **semipermeable**. As illustrated in Figure 2–4, these large protein ions have negative charges, which means they will

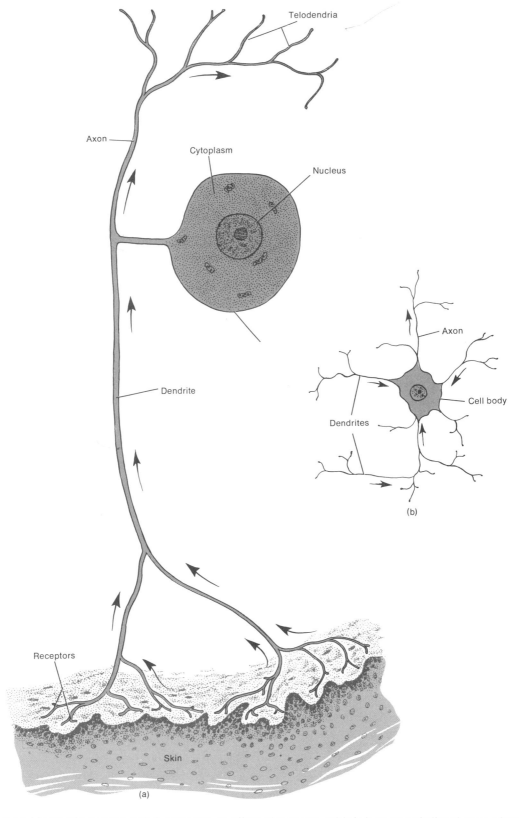

Telodendria

Axon

Cytoplasm

Nucleus

Axon

Cell body

Dendrites

Dendrite

(b)

Receptors

Skin

(a)

Figure 2-1 Two kinds of neurons. (a) A sensory or afferent neuron, which has specialized receptors to receive information from stimulation of the skin. (b) An interneuron, which transmits information between neurons.

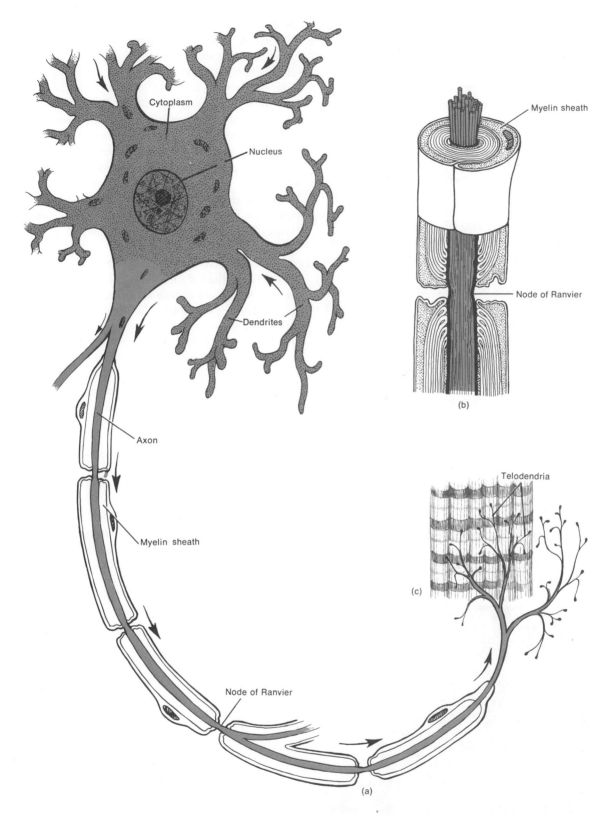

Cytoplasm

Nucleus

Dendrites

Axon

Myelin sheath

Myelin sheath

Node of Ranvier

Telodendria

Node of Ranvier

(a)

(b)

(c)

Figure 2–2 Motor neuron. (a) Notice the long axon whose telodendria make contact with muscles or glands. (b) Enlargement of the myelin sheath and break in the myelin, called node of Ranvier. (c) Enlargement of muscle fibers with which neuron makes contact.

attract ions with positive charges. In fact, it takes several of the smaller positive ions to balance the negative charges of the large protein ions. Clustered around the negative protein ions are positive K^+ ions, but only a few positive Na^+ ions. The fact that there are *not* more Na^+ ions inside the neuron is explained by another property of the neuron's membrane, the sodium pump.

Sodium-Potassium Pump

Normally, Na^+ ions would move through the membrane pores, attracted to the negative protein ions inside the neuron. However, the membrane resists the entry of Na^+ ions or acts as a sodium **barrier**. The Na^+ ions that do manage to enter the neuron are expelled by something called the **sodium-potassium pump**. The pump is not something you can see, like a tiny mechanical pump. Rather, it is a function of the membrane. The sodium-potassium pump means that the membrane actively pumps Na^+ ions out of the neuron and actively pumps K^+ ions into the neuron. In other words, Na^+ ions are actively pumped to the extracellular fluid, and most are prevented from reentering by the sodium barrier. On the other hand, K^+ ions are actively pumped to the intracellular fluid, but are also able to pass relatively freely through the membranes pores. It is not known exactly how the sodium-potassium pump and sodium barrier function, but we do know that they function because there are more Na^+ ions in the extracellular fluid than in the intracellular fluid. If they were not functioning, Na^+ ions would flow into the neuron until there would be about an equal number in the fluids inside and outside the neuron.

Resting Membrane Potential

Even when X Neuron's three neurons are not flashing to produce a smile, they continue to glow and show electrical produce a smile, they continue to glow and show electrical activity. Although your neurons would not be glowing if you could see them, they, too, show a great amount of electrochemical activity in between nerve impulses. When your neurons are not conducting nerve impulses, they are said to be in a **resting state**. During the resting state, there is a constant movement of ions. K^+ ions are continuously passing into and out of the membrane, and both Na^+ and K^+ ions are continuously being transported by the sodium-potassium pump. In spite of these movements, the relative distribution of ions inside and outside the neuron remains about the same. Thus, during the resting state, there is a miniature turbulence of ion activity at the neuron's membrane, but the overall distribution of ions remains fairly stable.

Although there is a high concentration of K^+ ions in the intracellular fluid during the resting state, there are not enough K^+ ions to completely balance the negative charges of the large protein ions. This means there are more negative charges inside the membrane than outside. If it were not for the sodium barrier, the positive Na^+ ions would flow through the membrane into the neuron to balance these negative charges. Since the actual movement of Na^+ ions into the cell is prevented by the sodium pump, there is only a potential for ion movement at the membrane. This potential for movement during the resting state is called the **resting membrane potential**.

During the resting membrane potential, the difference in the amount of negative charge between inside and outside is actually very tiny. In the giant squid axon, where it has been studied most extensively, the average difference or average potential amounts to $-70mV$ or $-70/1000$ of a volt. In other words, the intracellular fluid is $-70mV$ more negative than the extracellular fluid. **Voltage** is a measurement that describes the potential for ionic movement. This small voltage difference across the membrane is the value

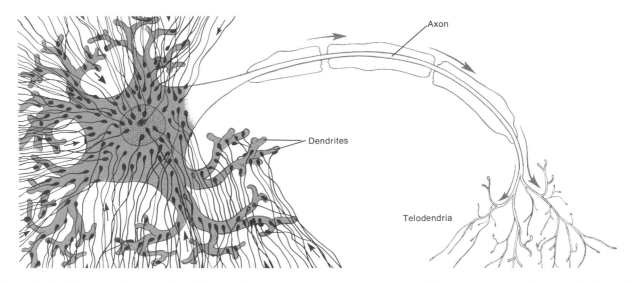

Figure 2–3 The dendrites and cell body of a motor neuron are covered with thousands of telodendria bringing neural information from other neurons.

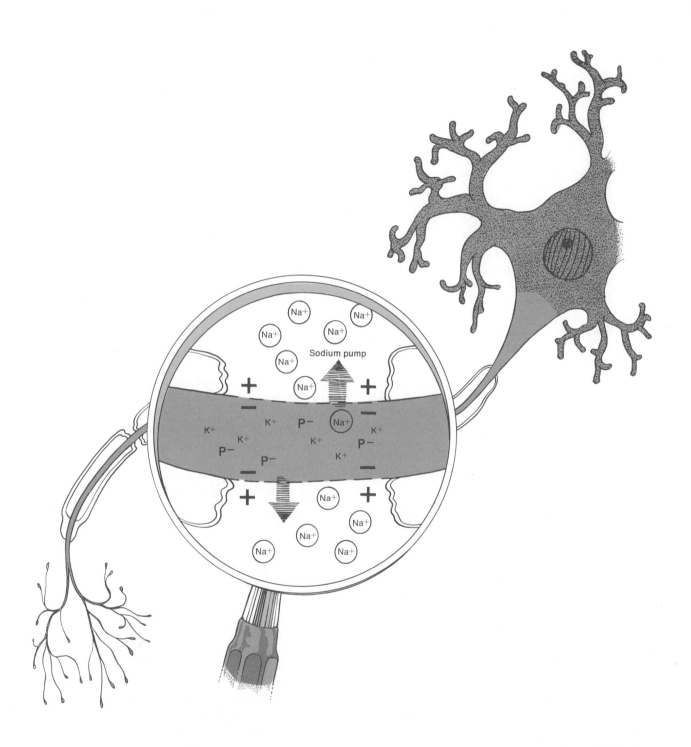

Figure 2–4 An axon in the resting state. Sodium (Na⁺) ions are kept outside the membrane by the sodium pump. Potassium (K⁺) ions are more concentrated inside the membrane. There are also large protein (P⁺) ions that carry negative charges. The resulting membrane potential results because there are more negative charges inside the membrane than outside.

Resting Membrane Potential

of the resting membrane potential. The voltage difference remains fairly constant during the resting state, even though individual ions such as K^+ and Cl^- are continuously passing through the pores of the membrane. When X Neuron's neurons were said to be glowing, it meant they were in the resting state. Except for the instant of the impulse, neurons remain continuously in the resting state. During the resting state, a neuron is neither transmitting nor receiving information. It is in a state of relatively low-level, consistent electrical activity. It is prepared for the next impulse.

Threshold of Neuron

When the neuron connected to X Neuron's ear is in the resting state, the sound of laughter causes the neuron's specialized receptors to have a change in the permeability of their membrane. The membrane's permeability changes so that more Na^+ ions enter the neuron. The influx of Na^+ ions causes an electrochemical change that upsets the resting membrane potential. A small amount of laughter will cause a small electrochemical change while a large amount of laughter will cause a larger change. The dendrites and the cell body respond to a weak stimulus with a small electrochemical change and to a strong stimulus with a larger change. This change in electrochemical activity spreads over the cell body and dendrites, but not necessarily the axon. The axon will only respond or have a change in its membrane's permeability to Na^+ when the electrochemical charge generated by the cell body reaches a certain level. This certain level is called the **threshold**. If the cell body generates an electrochemical charge that is below the axon's threshold, the axon will not become active. Axons have fixed thresholds while dendrites and cell bodies will respond to small or large stimuli, with the size of their responses depending upon the intensity of the stimulation. Reaching the axon's threshold involves an incredible amount of electrochemical activity in a very short period of time.

Nerve Impulse or Action Potential

Initiation of Action Potential

On the axons of motor neurons, there is an area near the cell body where the threshold is lower than in the rest of the axon. This area is called the **axon hillock**. It is at this point that the axon's membrane first becomes permeable to Na^+ ions and a special electrochemical change begins. The change is called the **nerve impulse** or **action potential**. During the resting state, the axon hillock has a resting membrane potential of about $-70mV$. An electrical change generated in the cell body results in sodium ions leaking into the axon hillock. This leak causes the resting potential in the axon hillock to become less negative, going from $-70mV$ to $-68mV$ to $-65mV$, thus weakening the sodium barrier. The effect is the same as a small leak in a weakened dam. As Na^+ ions flow into the intracellular fluid, the resting potential is reduced more, causing further weakening in the sodium barrier. When the resting membrane potential lowers to the threshold of the axon, approximately $-60mV$, the sodium barrier at the axon hillock suddenly collapses and Na^+ ions gush in. This sudden influx of Na^+ ions into the axon is the action potential or nerve impulse. Figure 2–5 shows the distribution of ions during the action potential.

Electrochemical Events during Action Potential

Once the action potential or impulse begins, it travels down the length of the axon much like a flame traveling down a fuse. The impulse represents a torrent of electrochemical activity that lasts about a millisecond, or a thousandth of a second. This electrochemical activity, the impulse, happens at a single point on the axon and is then repeated over and over down its length to the end feet.

The change in the electrochemical activity from the resting membrane potential to the action potential and back to resting potential happens in a few milliseconds. Figure 2–6 shows the sequence of changes in the membrane potential. During the resting state, before the action potential, the membrane is said to be **polarized**, meaning that there is a difference in electrical charge between the inside and outside ($-70mV$). During the action potential, there is a brief fraction of a millisecond during which the inrushing Na^+ ions have balanced all the negative charges inside the axon and there is no charge across the membrane. When the difference in charge is eliminated, the membrane is said to be **depolarized**. In Figure 2–6, depolarization is the point at which the value of the potential reaches zero.

After the membrane is depolarized, Na^+ ions continue to flow into the neuron, and for a brief period there are more positive charges inside than negative ones. When there are more positive than negative charges inside, the intracellular fluid actually becomes positively charged for a fraction of a millisecond. In Figure 2–6, this fraction of a millisecond is the point at which the action potential reaches its peak or spike.

Immediately following the peak of the action potential, two things happen. First, the K^+ ions follow the law that like ions are repelled and they are driven outside the axon by the positive charges. Second, the sodium barrier is reactivated more strongly than ever; thus, the Na^+ ions that flooded the intracellular fluid during the action potential are driven out, and very few Na^+ ions remain inside the axon. With both Na^+ and K^+ ions reduced in concentration inside the axon, the negative protein ions are less balanced than usual and the potential across the axon's membrane becomes even more negative than during the resting state. When the membrane becomes more negative, it is said to be **hyperpolarized**. In Figure 2–6, hyperpolarization is the point at which the potential drops below the original resting potential. Whether the membrane is polarized (resting potential), depolarized (no potential), or hyperpolarized (more negative than the resting potential) is important in determining whether the axon can conduct another impulse.

Refractory Periods

After the action potential, there is a brief period when the membrane is hyperpolarized and the sodium barrier is said to be virtually absolute, meaning that Na$^+$ ions cannot enter the axon. During this time, the axon cannot conduct another impulse because the impulse can only occur when Na$^+$ ions enter the axon. This period, during which the neuron cannot be fired or conduct an impulse, is called the **absolute refractory period**. Next follows a period of several milliseconds during which K$^+$ ions begin to return to the intracell-

ular fluid, but do not yet reach their resting level of concentration. During this time, the membrane is still hyperpolarized, or more negative than during the resting state. The axon can conduct an impulse at this stage, but its threshold is higher than during the resting state. In other words, it would take a larger electrical charge to reach the axon's threshold and cause an impulse. This period is termed the **relative refractory period**. Sensory neurons in the relative refractory period require a *more intense* environmental stimulus—more sound, more pressure, more cold—to create an impulse. Other neurons, such as interneurons, in this period require greater than normal stimulation from other neurons to cause an impulse. Because of these refractory periods, neurons cannot be fired continuously. However, the refractory periods are so brief that neurons can be fired or have impulses as frequently as a thousand times per second.

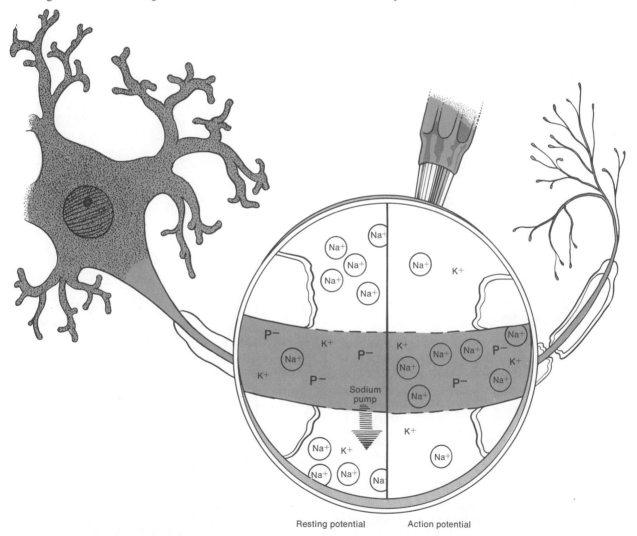

Resting potential   Action potential

Figure 2–5 A comparison of the difference in location of ions during the resting and action potentials. An action potential occurs because there is a breakdown in the sodium barrier, which allows an enormous influx of Na$^+$ ions. During the action potential, the inside of the membrane is positive and the outside is negative — exactly the opposite of the resting state.

Nerve Impulse or Action Potential

Traveling Action Potential

The impulse traveling down the axon cannot reverse and travel backward over the area it has just covered. This is because the sodium barrier is absolute in the period following the impulse. Since no Na⁺ can enter the axon where an impulse has just occurred, the impulse cannot be repeated at that point. Instead the impulse moves forward, down the length of the axon.

The impulse moves forward because of something that happens during the action potential. At the point where the action potential is taking place, there is a flow of electrical current. The flow of current changes the permeability of the membrane at the next point down the axon and initiates the sodium leakage into the axon. The sodium leakage finally causes the collapse of the sodium barrier that results in an action potential at this point. In this way, the action potential repeats itself, or is **propagated** down the length of the axon. Since the sodium cannot enter the membrane behind the impulse, the impulse continues forward down the axon. If an axon were artificially stimulated in the middle, an impulse would travel outward in both directions from the point of stimulation. Normally, impulses travel down the axon from the cell body toward the telodendria of the axon.

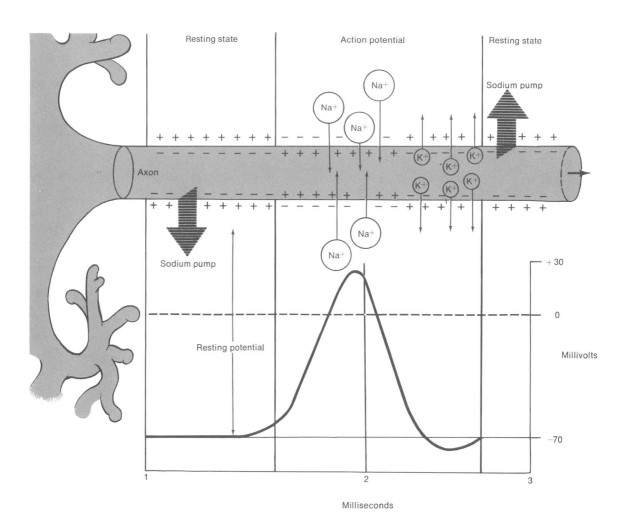

Figure 2–6 Changes in electrical membrane potential related to ion movements. During the resting state there are more negative ions inside the membrane, and the membrane potential is −70mV. During the action potential, Na⁺ ions rush into the cell, and for a brief period there are more positive charges inside. The membrane potential is then positive, about +30mV. Immediately after the action potential, both Na⁺ and K⁺ leave the inside, and for a brief period the membrane potential becomes even more negative than during the normal resting state. Finally the membrane returns to the resting potential of −70mV. Thus the changes in membrane potential shown in the curve are caused by different concentrations of ions inside and outside the membrane.

Squid Axon

The squid is a sea creature whose survival depends upon shooting rapidly away from predators. It does this by sucking in water and then expelling it suddenly with great force. The muscles that activate the expulsion of water are activated by motor neurons. Although the squid is an ugly creature, it is the darling of the neurophysiologists. These scientists can easily study the functions of the squid's axon because of its great size, 1 mm in diameter, and its length, almost one-third of a meter long.

In the 1930's, two independent teams of scientists, Hodgkin and Huxley (2–7) in England and Cole and Curtis (2–2) in the United States, used the squid axon to study the electrochemical events underlying the resting and action potentials. Because of the size of the axon, they were able to insert extremely fine wires, called microelectrodes, into the axon's intracellular fluid and record the electrical events taking place. The drawing in Figure 2–6 is hypothetical, but with slight changes in values could represent the electrical changes recorded from microelectrodes placed in the squid axon.

It was also through studies of the squid axon that the roles of various chemical particles were determined. By changing the concentration of various chemicals in and around the axons, scientists calculated the value of the resting potential from the concentration of potassium in the intracellular and extracellular fluids. It was determined that the action potential was characterized by a sudden inrush of sodium ions (2–6, 2–8). In other experiments, the axon was depleted of energy, which caused a breakdown in the sodium barrier or pump, indicating that the sodium barrier was an active, energy-dependent process (2–1). These findings represent only a few of the important experiments on the squid axon. Virtually everything you have learned in this chapter about the neuron's resting and action potentials have resulted from these early studies on the squid axon.

All-or-None Law

For the dendrites and cell bodies, a weak stimulus causes a small reaction or electrochemical change while a stronger stimulus causes a larger reaction. This is not true for the axon. If a stimulus reaches the threshold of the axon, the action potential will occur. There is no such thing as a partial action potential or impulse. Because the impulse either does or does not occur, the axon is said to follow the **all-or-none law**. According to the law, if the threshold of the axon hillock is reached, there will be an impulse. If the threshold is not reached, there will not be an impulse.

The strength or amplitude of the action potential (Figure 2–6) remains the same as it is propagated down the length of the axon. As there is no loss in the amplitude of the potential, the axon is said to conduct **without decrement**. This is not true for dendrites or cell bodies. As a potential travels across the dendrites or cell bodies, it loses strength. Thus dendrites and cell bodies are said to conduct **with decrement**.

Speed of Action Potential

If you could see impulses traveling down the axons, some would appear as quick flashes, while others would be slower. Quick impulses can travel as fast as 120 m per second (268 mph), which is similar to the speeds at the Indy 500. Slower impulses travel at approximately 1 m per second (2.5 mph), which is similar to the speed of jogging. You can probably remember experiences that reflect these different rates of neural conduction. When you hurt yourself, at first you sometimes feel a sharp pain, and then a fraction of a second later, a dull aching pain. The reason is that sharp pain is carried in fast-conducting axons and dull pain is carried in slow-conducting axons. When you trip and almost fall, you may recover your balance and move on before you feel responses such as rapid heartbeat or sweating. This is because the axons that control these responses are slow conducting.

The speed of the action potential in a given axon seems to depend on the diameter of the axon. The larger the diameter of the axon, the more rapidly the impulse is conducted. Most of the large-diameter axons are myelinated, and this covering permits the axons to conduct at a faster rate of speed. In Figure 2–2 you can see the interruptions in the myelin sheath called nodes of Ranvier. Actually the myelin sheath itself seems to insulate the axon, so that the ion flow cannot take place except at the nodes. Thus, instead of the impulse creeping down the axon, it jumps from node to node and the result is faster conduction. The impulse jumping from node to node is called **saltatory conduction**.

Synapse

If we were to build a giant model of two neurons coming together, you would see that there is actually a small space between one neuron and the next. Neurons do not make physical contact with each other; instead, there is a small space called the **synaptic cleft** between them. The area where neurons come together, that includes the synaptic cleft and a small area of the membrane of each cell, is called the **synapse**. This space at the synapse is so small that it is difficult to imagine; it is only 200 millionths of a millimeter (1 mm = 4/100 inch), written as 200 angstroms. Despite the small size of the space, the nerve impulse cannot leap across it by itself. Instead, when the nerve impulse reaches the telodendria of the first neuron, it causes chemicals to be secreted. These chemicals move across the synaptic cleft and act on the neighboring dendrites and cell body. The neuron on the transmitting side of the synaptic cleft is called the **presynaptic** neuron, and the neuron on the receiving side is called the **postsynaptic** neuron. The presynaptic neuron transmits its information across a synapse it forms with the postsynaptic neuron.

The telodendria of a presynaptic neuron have small spherical packets called **synaptic vesicles** (VES-icles) that contain chemicals. When a nerve impulse reaches the telodendria of a presynaptic neuron, the chemicals, called **neurotransmitters** or **transmitter substances**, are released. The transmitter substances travel across the synaptic cleft to act upon the postsynaptic neuron's dendrite, cell body, or, on rare occasions, the axon. Some transmitters tend to excite the postsynaptic neuron or form excitatory synapses. Others tend to inhibit the postsynaptic neuron or form inhibitory synapses. As Figure 2–3 shows, a single postsynaptic neuron, such as a motor neuron, may be bombarded by chemical secretions from thousands of presynaptic neurons. Some of these are excitatory and some are inhibitory. Whether the postsynaptic neuron is excited or inhibited depends on whether there are more excitatory or inhibitory transmitters. Among the many scientists who

have contributed to our knowledge of the synapse, two in particular have made enormous contributions and have received Nobel prizes for their work: John Eccles (2–5) and Bernard Katz (2–9).

Postsynaptic Potentials

When a neurotransmitter reaches the dendrites or cell body of a neighboring neuron, it changes the cell membrane's permeability and thus changes the resting potential of the cell. Because the dendrites and cell body are continuously bombarded by transmitters, the resting potential varies slightly from moment to moment. Sometimes it will be slightly more positive than −70mV and other times slightly more negative. The neuron becomes excited when the resting potential of the cell body and dendrites becomes *more positive*. For example, if the resting potential changes from −70mV to −65mV, it has moved in the positive direction and the neuron tends to be excited, or more likely to begin an action potential. Eccles has termed this event an **exci-**

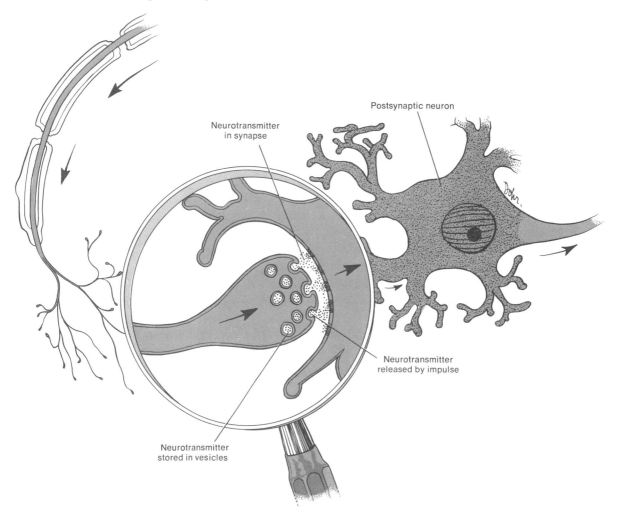

Neurotransmitter in synapse

Postsynaptic neuron

Neurotransmitter released by impulse

Neurotransmitter stored in vesicles

Figure 2–7 The telodendria of a presynaptic neuron contain neurotransmitters that are secreted upon arrival of the impulse. The neurotransmitters move across the synapse and act on the postsynaptic membrane.

tatory postsynaptic potential or EPSP. When the post-synaptic potential becomes positive enough to exceed the threshold of the neuron, the action potential occurs. On the other hand, the neuron tends to be inhibited when the resting potential of the cell body and dendrite becomes *more negative*. For example, if the resting potential changes from -70mV to -75mV, it has moved in a negative direction and the neuron tends to be inhibited, or less likely to initiate an action potential. This occurrence is termed an **inhibitory postsynaptic potential** or **IPSP**. Thus, when transmitters cause the resting potential of the cell body and dendrites to become more positive, they cause an EPSP that excites the neuron and may trigger an action potential. When they cause that potential to become more negative, they cause an IPSP that inhibits the neuron, making an action potential less likely to occur.

Transmitter substances cause the resting potential of the cell body and dendrites to become more positive or more negative by changing the balances of ions at the cell membrane. **Excitatory transmitters** are thought to make the membrane more permeable to positive ions, including Na^+. These positive ions reduce the negative charge of the intracellular fluid and cause the resting potential to become more positive (2–4). When a membrane potential becomes more positive, it is said to be depolarized. This is another way of saying that an excitatory postsynaptic potential or EPSP has developed.

Graded Potential

Some neurons have thousands of telodendria secreting transmitters on their dendrites and cell bodies. Some of these transmitters are excitatory and some are inhibitory, so the resting potential of the dendrites and cell body is continually changing between more negative and more positive. Thus, the dendrites and cell body have a resting potential that shows degrees or grades of change and is, therefore, called a **graded potential**.

At any given moment, the postsynaptic potential of a neuron represents the average of all the excitatory and inhibitory transmitters acting on the cell membrane. If the excitatory and inhibitory transmitters average out to be excitatory, an EPSP will develop and continue for a brief period of time, a hundredth to a tenth of a second. If there are no further excitatory effects, the EPSP will die out and the membrane will return to its resting level. Because the EPSP dies out or decreases over time, it is said to be **decremental**. When the resting potential moves in a positive direction, from -70mV to -65mV, an EPSP develops. Following ten or so milliseconds, the potential returns to the resting value of about -70mV.

If other excitatory influences occur, that is, if more end feet secrete excitatory transmitters before the first EPSP has decreased, these influences will add to the first EPSP and cause the resting potential to move still further in the pos-

itive direction. In other words, two EPSP's that occur close together in time can add together to produce one large EPSP, and this is called **summation**. If one EPSP is too weak to make the resting potential positive enough to exceed threshold and to activate the neuron, this weak EPSP may summate with another weak EPSP and together they may fire the neuron. For example, the first EPSP may change the resting potential from -70mV to -68mV. This change alone is not enough to fire the neuron. However, the second EPSP changes the potential further, from -68mV to -65mV, and this *is* enough to fire the neuron. Either of these EPSP's alone could only have changed the potential to -68 or -67mV, but together they can change it to -65mV, the threshold of the neuron. Summation can happen when the second EPSP arrives a few milliseconds after the first, in a process called **temporal summation**. Or summation can happen when the two EPSP's begin at different points on the dendrites or cell body; this is called **spatial summation**.

Like EPSP's, IPSP's decay over time, or are decremental, and also show summation. However, when two IPSP's summate, the effect is to make the potential still more negative (-70mV to -75mV) than either IPSP alone could have done. If an IPSP and EPSP happen at the membrane at approximately the same time, the resulting change in the membrane's potential is the approximate average of their effects. In fact, the postsynaptic potential may represent hundreds of thousands of EPSP's and IPSP's. Thus, the membrane of the dendrites and cell body acts like a miniature computer, processing and averaging the effects of transmitters.

Importance of Graded Potential

Only the membrane of the dendrites and cell body has the capacity to average the transmitters and become more or less negative, that is, show a graded potential. In the case of X Neuron, laughter activates the neuron attached to its ear and causes an impulse to travel down its axon. When this impulse reaches the end feet, a transmitter substance is released, crosses the synaptic cleft, and acts on the dendrites and cell body of the interneuron. This transmitter, which happens to be excitatory, changes the balance of ions at the cell membrane and causes the potential of the cell body and dendrites to become more positive; thus, a small EPSP develops. This EPSP is not strong enough to activate the interneuron. Fortunately, the EPSP continues in effect for a few milliseconds. As X Neuron hears another laugh, the neuron attached to its ear carries another impulse. This impulse causes additional transmitter substances to be secreted in the interneuron and causes a second EPSP to develop. The first and second EPSP's summate (temporal summation) and push the membrane potential far enough in a positive direction so that the interneuron is activated. As a result, an impulse travels down the axon of the interneuron. When the impulse reaches the interneuron's telodendria, a transmitter is secreted onto the motor neuron causing an EPSP to develop in that neuron. If the EPSP in the dendrite and cell body of the motor neuron is large enough, an action potential will travel down the axon to the telodendria, neurotransmitters will be released to stimulate the muscle fibers, and the result will be a smile.

Without the ability of EPSP's to show spatial or temporal summation, we might never see X Neuron smile. Summation of EPSP's and IPSP's happens in your own nervous system, but on a much grander scale. When one of the neurons in your brain fires, this action may represent the combined input from thousands of other neurons. Similarly, when one of the neurons in your brain is inhibited, this occurrence may represent inhibitory influences from thousands of other neurons coming from many different areas of your brain. There are probably days when you wish you had only three neurons and could spend your time simply smiling or glowing.

A Nerve

It may be surprising to learn that X Neuron does not have any nerves. This is because X Neuron does not have a peripheral nervous system. You, on the other hand, do have a peripheral nervous system. This means that you have hundreds of feet of nerves that carry information from your body to your central nervous system (brain and spinal cord) and from your central nervous system to your body. **Nerves** are simply groups of axons that carry information to and from your central nervous system. The nerves resemble lengths of white cord or thread because many of the longer axons are myelinated, and myelin is white in appearance. The term **nerve** is applied only to groups of axons outside the central nervous system.

Gray Matter and White Matter

If you could peer inside a human skull and see the brain, you would see a cortex with a gray-pinkish color. This is because the cortex is composed mainly of cell bodies and dendrites, which tend to be gray in color. A slice through the brain would show areas of gray-pink containing cell bodies, alternating with areas of white containing myelinated axons. When a slice of brain is immersed in certain chemicals, the cell bodies are stained a different color than the axons; in this way the various pathways in the brain and spinal cord can be studied. Some of these stained brain slices resemble an incredibly detailed psychedelic painting.

Frequency Code

You can easily tell the difference between a light touch and a hard squeeze, between soft music and loud rock, between a pinprick and a deep cut. X Neuron smiles more frequently to loud laughter and less frequently to soft laughter. When X Neuron hears soft laughter, the three neurons fire and X Neuron smiles. After a smile, the axons pass through the absolute refractory period, the relative refractory period, and the resting state. More soft laughter cannot trigger these neurons again until they have returned to the resting state. Loud laughter, on the other hand, can trigger the neurons while they are still in the relative refractory period. In other words, a strong stimulus can fire the axon during the relative refractory period while a weak stimulus can fire it only during the resting state. Thus, a strong stimulus, such as a loud laugh, makes X Neuron smile more frequently because the axons can fire sooner, during the relative refractory period. A weak stimulus, such as a soft laugh, makes X Neuron smile less frequently because the axons must pass through the absolute and relative refractory periods into the resting state before being activated. You can tell the difference between weak and strong stimuli, such as soft and loud music, because soft music fires the neuron less frequently. Soft music cannot fire the neuron until the axon has returned to the resting state. Loud music fires the neuron more frequently because it can fire the neuron as soon as the axon enters the relative refractory period. The fact that a stronger stimulus can fire the neuron more frequently is referred to as the **frequency code**. The frequency code is one of the ways your nervous system makes life interesting.

In addition to the frequency code, there is another way your nervous system tells you that one stimulus is more intense than another. A stimulus, such as salt on the tongue, usually excites many receptors, which excite many neurons, which have many axons that come together to form a nerve. Each axon in a nerve may have a slightly different threshold. Lightly salted food fires axons only during the resting state and fires only those axons with lower thresholds. Heavily salted food fires axons during the relative refractory periods (thus more frequently) and, in addition, fires those axons with higher thresholds. Weak stimuli fire only the low-threshold axons; strong stimuli fire these axons plus those with higher thresholds. The firing of more axons results in your feeling something as stronger or louder or more salty. Although this does not have an official name, you could think of it as the number code, because a larger number of axons is fired. The frequency and number codes are the cues your brain uses to tell the difference between a pinprick and a deep cut, between a weak and strong stimulus.

Studying the Neuron

The squid axon described earlier has a diameter of about 1 mm (1/25 inch) (width of pencil line) and a length of approximately 30 cm (1 ft). It can be removed from the squid for study and seen with the naked eye. The neurons in your own nervous system are much smaller and can be seen only with a microscope. Although the length of some

FRONTIER IN NERVE CELL RESEARCH

Not long ago scientists would have scoffed at the notion that regeneration of nerve cells in the brain and spinal cord is possible in humans.

Today many leading neuroscientists are convinced that they are well on the way to doing it.

While it will probably be decades before such knowledge can be applied to help paraplegics, stroke victims and similar sufferers of central nervous system (brain and spinal cord) damage, there is a growing excitement among scientists who see new vistas opening.

Two weeks ago about 50 neuroscientists met in Florida to discuss the latest findings on this frontier of biological research.

By far the most dramatic report was from a Russian who showed motion pictures of rats that had regained a remarkable degree of locomotion after having suffered completely severed spinal cords.

Speaking through an interpreter, Dr. Levon A. Matinian of the Orbeli Institute of Physiology in Armenia reported a 33% recovery rate for young rats treated with combinations of enzymes injected into the area of spinal cord damage.

At the beginning of the film the rats dragged their legs behind them as they walked. They were given daily injections of the enzymes for three months.

Within 22 to 27 days, Matinian reported he could record nerve impulses passing through the severed parts of the spinal cord, although the animals' hind legs were still totally paralyzed and they displayed other signs of internal impairment.

It was not clear from Matinian's films at what point the rats achieved maximum use of their rear legs. But a summary of his work in English indicated that recovery—in those rats that did recover—took somewhere between two and eight months.

The animals were shown scampering on all four legs after food pellets were tossed across their paths. Their coordination appeared good although the summary said the rate of conduction of nerve impulses was still 2½ to three times slower than normal.

Many of the American scientists were privately critical of the Russian's scientific methods. But they were impressed by the dramatic filmed evidence that certain combinations of enzymes injected immediately following the injury can result in spinal cord regeneration in an impressive percentage of cases.

The meaning the Russian work has for human spinal cord injury victims may be another matter, however.

The Russians have used the enzyme treatment on human patients and reported "a positive effect." But they have been unwilling to disclose details or rates of success.

Word that there exists in Russia a treatment said to be better than what is available in this country has been circulating among American paraplegics for more than a year.

Matinian was in this country as part of a delegation of Russian spinal cord specialists headed by Dr. V. M. Ueryumov, director of the Polenov Neurological Research Institute near Leningrad.

Several weeks ago, Ugryumov, Matinian and Dr. E. I. Babychenko, a neurosurgeon at the Saratov Medical Institution, examined four paraplegic Americans in Washington, D.C. The Americans' hopes were high but the Soviet doctors told them there was nothing they could do beyond what had already been done.

According to a report in the Washington Post, Matinian told the parents of one quadruplegic, a 15-year-old boy injured in a football accident, that the enzymes are most successful when given immediately after an accident and that they don't work at all when the spinal cord damage is as severe as it was in his case.

The goal of enzyme therapy, according to the Russians, is to create conditions favorable to the growth of nerve fiber. They find that two enzymes used in combination, trypsin and hyaluronidase, give the best results.

★ ★ ★

Perhaps the chief reason for the lack of interest in central nervous system regeneration research in this country until recently has been the widespread conviction that neurons in the brain and spinal cord simply do not regrow in higher animals like mammals.

There are sound reasons for this deep-seated belief. One is the simple observation that once an individual becomes paralyzed due to a break or severe bruise of the spinal cord, he never overcomes the paralysis.

Another reason—the one on which most scientists have based their conviction—is a finding made 60 years ago by Dr. Santiago Ramon y Cajal, perhaps the most famous neuroscientist of all time.

Cajal observed that nerve fibers in the spinal cord of a mammal do begin to regenerate but that the process stops after several weeks and no return of function occurs.

The idea was thus firmly implanted in the minds of most scientists that effective regeneration does not occur in mammals.

It has been commonly accepted that the structure of the central nervous system could degenerate—for example, following a stroke or polio or spinal cord injury—but never regenerate.

According to Dr. Carmine Clemente, the new director of UCLA's Brain Research Institute, there are several reasons why this view has slowly begun to change. (Clemente was a student at Windle's in the 1950s and based his doctoral thesis on regeneration research.)

One has to do with the closing of the gap between "mind" and "brain." Another is that neuroscientists have become more mechanistic in their thinking, Clemente says.

They now commonly make references to the brain as a computer and use terms like "systems approach to understanding the nervous system."

At the same time, much has been learned in the past 25 years about the neurological mechanisms of such abstractions of the mind as emotions, learning, memory, sleep, consciousness, dreams, pleasure and pain.

Although people had considered the so-called structure of the mind as being nonrigid, or plastic, the structure of the brain was considered to be very rigid and nonplastic except in the early months of life.

But, Clemente said, it finally became apparent that since the brain is the organ of the mind, the plasticity formerly ascribed only to the mind had to be the result of things occuring in the central nervous system. Therefore the ground was laid for accepting the concept of plasticity, or nonrigidity, in the central nervous system.

By plasticity, neuroscientists mean the ability of central nervous neurons to grow beyond their normal development period or to reestablish old or develop new connections or to regenerate after injury.

The tendency to be more accepting of the notion or plasticity was enhanced by the results of work like Windle's in 1950 and that of C. N. Liu in 1958.

Liu showed for the first time that it is possible for uninjured neurons in the spinal cord to send out shoots or sprouts when stimulated to do so.

The ability of uninjured neurons to sprout is distinctly different from the sprouting of new fibers by a neuron which has been cut.

This finding drastically altered how scientists viewed the organization of the central nervous system because it revealed for the first time an anatomical plasticity in the spinal cord which nobody has suspected.

More recently, several scientists have shown that intact neurons in the brain also have the capability of sending out collateral sprouts under certain circumstances. Dr. Carl W. Cotman of the department of psychobiology at UC Irvine is one of the leaders in this field.

Using rats as experimental animals, Cotman cut out some of the neurons that feed impulses into a part of the brain called the hippocampus.

Within six or seven days, he reported at the Florida meeting, unharmed neurons adjacent to those which were removed sent out collateral sprouts. After nine to 14 days, the sprouts formed connections (synapses) with the stumps of the severed nerves.

Cotman is uncertain whether the new connections successfully restored function that was lost following removal of the original neurons. But he suspects that they did.

He and others believe that collateral sprouting may occur naturally following a stroke which has killed off an area of the brain. This could account for the recovery from paralysis some stroke victims experience.

Similarly, Carmine Clemente at UCLA speculates that paralyzed polio patients who regained some functions after undergoing physical manipulation and reeducation of paralyzed muscles may have been beneficiaries of collateral sprouting.

Elizabeth Kenny, an Australian nurse, was a controversial figure during the 1930s and '40s because she insisted that her physical manipulations had an effect on damaged neurons. Doctors who believed in the rigidity of the central nervous system were among her loudest critics.

Clemente says the barrage of nerve impulses initiated by Sister Kenny's procedure in fact may have caused neurons in the spinal cord to bypass injured areas and make new connections.

"Had that statement been made by a neuroanatomist in 1945, he would have been derided even more than the Australian nurse," Clemente adds.

Scientists would like to be able to control the sprouting—to make it happen when and where they would like—so that it could be used therapeutically not only in the case of strokes but also other kinds of degeneration due to aging or disease.

But that is a long way off yet, and before it can happen a great deal more must be learned about the physiology and biochemistry of neurons and the nonneuron cells of the central nervous system.

★ ★ ★

SOURCE: Excerpt from a longer article by Harry Nelson, Times Medical Writer, *Los Angeles Times*, June 17, 1976. Copyright © 1976 by Los Angeles Times.

of your axons may reach 1 m (over 3 ft), their diameter is only about 20 thousandths of a millimeter or 20 microns (1/1250 inch); the diameter of the cell bodies is about 50 microns (1/500 inch). Although most of your neurons are too small to observe directly, scientists have been able to observe their function. When the neuron is in the resting state or is fired, there are electrical potentials generated and these can be accurately measured. It has been possible to insert wires with tips so thin they cannot be seen by the naked eye into the cell bodies of large spinal motor neurons of experimental animals. These wires are called **microelectrodes** and can record the graded potentials of cell bodies. Microelectrodes have also been inserted into the brains of experimental animals to record resting and action potentials of axons. When these electrical events are magnified and written out on paper, they produce a pattern that looks very much like that in Figure 2–7.

The electrical activity from groups of neurons can also be recorded with **electrodes**, thin wires inserted into the brain or disks fixed to the scalp, to produce brain recordings or brain waves. There are no pain receptors in the brain, so the introduction of a microelectrode or the larger electrode causes no pain to the experimental animal or to a human undergoing brain surgery.

Comment

It would be a very simple world if you had only three neurons like X Neuron. But whether you have three or three billion, the neuron's function is the same. It's all done with chemicals. Your ability to read this sentence or to think about a neuron derives from the movement of certain ions in and out of the neuron's membrane. This movement depends on the action of various chemicals. Since a neuron's proper functioning involves chemicals, you have some idea of why drugs can affect your behavior. If the chemicals involved in neural functioning are somehow changed by drugs, the neurons will either fire more or less, and the result may be anything from your going to sleep to going berserk. As far as the neuron is concerned, the way you are may be affected by what you eat, drink, or sniff.

SELF-TEST 2

1 There are approximately 10 billion neurons in the human brain, each of them specialized for _____ .
storing and communicating or transmitting and receiving information

2 If a neuron has a two long tubes attached to either side of its cell body, it is called a _____ neuron.
unipolar

3 Some unipolar neurons have a section at the tip of the dendrite that is called the _____ and is specialized for converting environmental stimulation to _____ .
receptor / neural information or impulse

4 One type of neuron has many _____ but only one _____ and is an example of an _____ .
dendrites/axon interneuron (also motor neuron)

5 Afferent neurons are specialized to receive information from the _____ and to transmit this information to other _____ .
environment neurons

6 Motor neurons are specialized to receive information from _____ and to transmit this information to _____ .
neurons muscle fibers

7 The interneuron, like most of the neurons in your brain, is specialized to receive information from other _____ and to transmit this information to other _____ .
neurons / neurons

8 When you move reflexively or when you play volleyball, the muscles for the movements are controlled by _____ .
alpha motor neurons

9 Throughout every moment of life, _____ activity continues in your neurons.
electrochemical

10 This activity results from the presence of electrically charged chemical particles called _____ .
ions

11 Ions having plus charges tend to _____ ions having plus charges and tend to _____ ions having minus charges.
repel / attract

12 The membrane of the neuron allows passage of some ions but not others; thus, it is said to be _____ .
semipermeable

13 The fluid inside the cell membrane is known as _____ fluid and that outside is known as _____ fluid.
intracellular extracellular

14 During the resting state the negative charges of the large _____ ions in the intracellular fluid are not balanced by positive charges.
protein

15 Sodium ions cannot balance the negative intracellular fluid because the _____ actively _____ any Na^+ ions that manage to pass the _____ .
sodium-potassium pump rejects or expels / sodium barrier

16 The fact that there are more negative charges in the intracellular fluid than in the extracellular fluid results in the _____ .
resting membrane potential

17 During the resting state _____ are concentrated in the extracellular fluid, and _____ and _____ are concentrated in the intracellular fluid.
sodium ions or Na^+ / potassium ions or K^+ negative protein ions

18 During the resting state the overall distribution of ions remains about the same, while individual ions are continuously _____ the membrane.
passing through or moving in and out of

19 In the squid axon, the value of the resting membrane potential or voltage difference is approximately _____ .
−70mV

20 The nerve impulse or _____ occurs when the change in the resting potential exceeds the _____ of the neuron.
action potential threshold

21 The nerve impulse usually occurs when the resting potential has moved in a _____ direction. The value of the threshold is approximately _____ .
positive −60mV

22 In neurons such as the motor neuron the action potential begins at the _____ .
axon hillock

23 During the action potential, _____ flood into the intracellular fluid because there is a break-down in the _____ .

sodium ions or Na+
sodium barrier

24 At the peak of the action potential, the intracellular fluid becomes _____ charged for a fraction of a millisecond.

positively

25 After the action potential, there is a brief period when the sodium barrier is _____ . During this time, which is called the _____ period, a strong stimulus _____ fire the neuron.

absolute/absolute
refractory / cannot

26 For several more milliseconds after the action potential there is a period when the intracellular fluid is more _____ charged than usual.

negatively

27 During this period, called the _____ period, the neuron can only be fired by a _____ stimulus.

relative refractory
more intense

28 The impulse is propagated down the axon because the flow of _____ at the point of the action potential weakens the _____ at the next point on the membrane.

current
sodium barrier

29 The all-or-none law applies to the _____ but not to the _____ .

axon / cell body and
dendrites

30 Because it follows the all-or-none law, the axon's resting potential remains _____ until an action potential occurs.

constant or about the
same

31 The axon conducts _____ decrement, and the cell body and dendrites conduct _____ decrement.

without / with

32 The speed of the impulse in the axon depends upon the _____ of the axon; the larger it is, the _____ the impulse.

diameter
faster

33 In myelinated fibers, the impulse jumps from one node of Ranvier to the next. This is called _____ conduction; it greatly increases the _____ of the impulse.

saltatory / speed

34 At the synapse, the telodendria of the _____ neuron secretes _____ .

presynaptic / transmitter
chemical

35 If the transmitter is excitatory, it causes the postsynaptic potential to be more _____ and to show an _____ .

positive
excitatory postsynaptic
potential or EPSP

36 If the transmitter is inhibitory, it causes the postsynaptic potential to be more _____ and to show an _____ .

negative
inhibitory postsynaptic
potential or IPSP

37 The most important thing about the postsynaptic potential of dendrites and cell body is that it is _____ , meaning that it varies depending on the amount of _____ .

graded / transmitters

38 If two excitatory synapses occur on the same cell body at the same time, they cause _____ and result in a _____ EPSP.

spatial summation
larger or more positive

39 If two excitatory synapses occur at slightly different points in time, they cause _____ and result in a _____ EPSP.

temporal summation
larger or more positive

REFERENCES

2–1 Caldwell, P. C. and Keynes, R. D. The utilization of phosphate bond energy for sodium extrusion from giant axons. *Journal of Physiology* 1957, 137: 12–13.

2–2 Cole, K. S. and Curtis, H. J. Electric impedance of squid giant axon during activity. *Journal of General Physiology* 1939, 22: 649–670.

2–3 Coombs, J. S., Curtis, D. R., and Eccles, J. C. The generation of impulses in motoneurons. *Journal of Physiology* 1957, 139:232–249.

2–4 Eccles, J. C. *The Physiology of Nerve Cells.* Baltimore: Johns Hopkins Press, 1957.

2–5 Eccles, J. C. *The Physiology of Synapses.* New York: Academic Press, 1964.

2–6 Hodgkin, A. L. Ionic movements and electrical activity in giant nerve fibers. *Proceedings of the Royal Society, Series B* 1958, 148: 1–37.

2–7 Hodgkin, A. L. and Huxley, A. F. Action potentials recorded from inside nerve fiber. *Nature* 1939, 144: 710–711.

2–8 Hodgkin, A. L. and Katz, B. The effect of sodium ions on the electrical activity of the giant axon of the squid. *Journal of Physiology* 1949, 108: 37–77

2–9 Katz, B. *Nerve, Muscle and Synapse.* New York: McGraw-Hill, 1966.

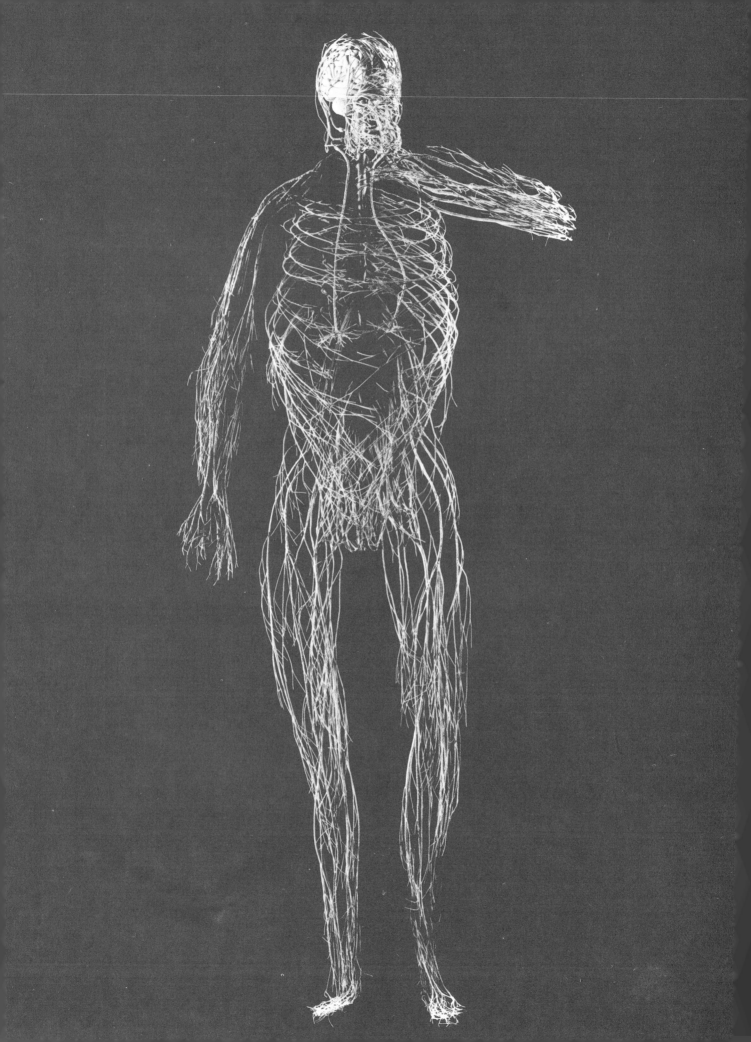

Anatomy

3

How the Brain Controls the Body

Assembling a Person

It is sometime in the future. The young couple are looking forward to the arrival of their first son. He is not going to be an ordinary son, since the mother is not pregnant and the father is not the father. Rarely is anyone born in the usual sense these days. Instead, everyone is recycled.

The couple look through the person catalogue that lists thousands of bodies and brain pieces. They try to be diligent in selecting pieces that will result in the best combination of looks, intelligence, and personality. Of course, once all the pieces are connected, no one knows for certain exactly which traits the new person will have. Try to imagine what an individual would be like if pieces of brain were combined from a hockey player, a poet, and a banker. Yet everyone, including this couple, thinks they know how to combine different parts from different brains to create the best personality.

After they select the body and thousands of brain pieces from the catalogue, the couple will have the exacting task of assembling them. If any of the pieces or nerves are damaged or misconnected, the new person might be abnormal. There have been cases of misassembled individuals who thought that up was down, who could not understand what they said, who could read but not write, and who could see with their fingers. Needless to say, these persons had to be disassembled and begun again.

As the couple picks out the various pieces of brain, they wonder how one puts a human nervous system together. How many pieces of brain must be connected before an individual can breathe, walk, speak, or think? This couple selects the body of a young adult male and thousands of brain pieces that they hope will result in a bright, humorous, and warm personality. In four weeks, the body and brain pieces will arrive and assembly will begin.

The Nervous System

Spinal Cord

The body and brain pieces come packed in a sealed liquid nitrogen container. After breaking the seal, the couple remove the body and place it on a sterile sheet. Next they cautiously remove the thousands of nerves and brain pieces and arrange them in order of assembly.

Impatient to see his son the father does not read the instructions and begins by inserting a brain piece called the *pons.* He waits for the body to react, but nothing happens. The instructions read, ''The spinal cord must be inserted before the body can execute any movements.'' Grudgingly, the father inserts the **spinal cord** into a tubelike structure comprised of a series of connected bones called **vertebrae.** The cord looks like a long, white, smooth rope that reaches from the body's neck to the small of the back. With the spinal cord in place, the father waits for something to happen. The body does nothing.

Spinal Nerves

The instructions continue, ''After spinal cord is inserted, connect spinal cord to **spinal nerves**.'' The spinal nerves had been preconnected to the various muscles and organs of the body, so it remained only for the couple to attach them to the spinal cord. There are thirty-one pairs of spinal nerves, with one nerve of each pair connected to the right side of the spinal cord and the other in each pair to the left side. Depending on their location, spinal nerves have different names. Spinal nerves in the neck area are called **cervical** (SIR-vee-cul); those in the upper back area, **thoracic** (thor-ASS-ic); those in the lower back area, **lumbar** (LUM-bar); and those at the very bottom of the back, **sacral** (SAY-crull).

The mother carefully places each of the spinal nerves near the appropriate area of the spinal cord. The instructions read, "Danger: it is very easy to commit an error at this step. Each spinal nerve is composed of two kinds of cells called neurons. Sensory or afferent neurons, attached to sensors in the skin, muscles, and joints, carry information into the spinal cord. Motor neurons, attached to muscles, carry information out of the spinal cord. Afferent and motor neurons must be attached at different points on the spinal cord."

The mother notices that a spinal nerve looks like a piece of white string that has been split in two parts just before it reaches the spinal cord. The afferent part has a lump, called a *ganglion*, that is a cluster of cell bodies; the motor part of the spinal nerve has no lump. The afferent neurons are attached to the back of the spinal cord in a branch called the **dorsal root**. The motor neurons are attached to the front or stomach side in a branch called the **ventral root**. Hours later, the couple has all 31 pairs of spinal nerves in place.

Reflex

With the spinal nerves attached to the spinal cord, the father tells the body to walk. Nothing. He reads on, "To make sure the spinal cord is functioning, complete the following test. Stick a pin into the thumb. The hand should withdraw." He sticks a pin into the thumb and the hand withdraws. The hand withdrawal is an example of a **reflex**. Reflex behavior is automatic, requires no thinking, and occurs in response to certain kinds of stimuli.

Next he taps below the knee cap and the leg jerks. Another reflex: quick, automatic, no thinking involved. When the knee is tapped, sensors in the knee send this information through afferent neurons in the spinal nerve, through the dorsal root, and into the spinal cord. Once in the spinal cord, the afferent neuron connects with a motor neuron. The motor neuron carries the message through the ventral root and the spinal nerve to the muscles that make the knee jerk. Different parts of the spinal cord control different reflexes: knee jerk is controlled by the lower spinal cord, while hand withdrawal is controlled by the upper spinal cord. Without any control from the brain, the knee is able to jerk and the hand to withdraw. No matter how much the father shouts "walk," a body with just a spinal cord cannot walk, but it can have reflexes. Reflexes are important in protecting your body from many harmful stimuli: removing your hand from a hot stove or blinking your eye at dust or lifting your foot from a sharp stone. These are simple reflexes and do not require any control by the brain. More complex reflexes, such as breathing, require some control by the brain. In addition to controlling some of our reflexes, the spinal cord also carries information to and from the brain, but this function will have to wait until the brain is assembled.

Medulla

Checking the diagram, the father finds the first brain piece that fits on top of the spinal cord, the medulla. It is bigger around than the spinal cord and approximately 8 cm (3–4 inches) in length. Once the medulla is connected to the spinal cord, dramatic changes occur. With the medulla in place, breathing and heart rate are regulated, blood pressure in partly regulated, and intestines may start to contract. The medulla controls many of the more complex reflexes that are vital to staying alive. There is wisdom in the old saying, "Without a medulla you are as good as dead."

Pons

With the spinal cord and medulla in place, the body is capable of many different reflexes, but still no voluntary movements. Back to the instructions. "To the top of the medulla, attach the structure that is approximately 5 cm (2 inches) long, bigger around than the medulla, and called the **pons**." With the pons in place, the body still does nothing. The pons is involved in the regulation of sleep, but unless more of the brain is assembled it is difficult to tell if the body is asleep or awake. As the brain is assembled, many other brain structures will be connected to the pons. Without the pons, the new son would have trouble getting a good night's sleep and would be missing important connections to the rest of his brain.

Reticular Formation

The father and mother name the body "Jack." With each new brain piece added, the father checks to see if Jack will respond to his name or a command, but Jack does not move. Actually, the brain part that allows Jack to wake up is already in place. About as big around as your middle finger, it is a structure that lies in the center of the medulla and pons and is called the **reticular formation** (rah-TICK-you-ler). When more brain is assembled, the reticular formation will help wake Jack up.

When your alarm goes off in the morning, the reticular formation alerts other parts of the brain. Here's how you wake up. As the information from the senses (sound of alarm) is transmitted to the brain, some of this information branches off and goes to the reticular formation. After receiving this information, the reticular formation excites or alerts a certain part of the brain that some message is coming. Once alerted, the brain is ready to process the sensory information. The reticular formation arouses that part of the brain that will be assembled last, the outside layer of the brain called the *cortex*.

If Jack's reticular formation were severely damaged, his cortex could not be aroused and could not process sensory information. If he had no reticular formation, we could not wake him up. He would be in a coma.

The reticular formation has two parts. The part that alerts and arouses the brain and helps to keep Jack in an awake state is called the **reticular activating system** or **RAS**. The other part is involved with muscle movement. With just the spinal cord assembled, it was possible to tap Jack's knee and get a knee-jerk reflex. With the addition of the reticular formation, the movement of the knee jerk can be made larger or smaller. The reticular formation does not cause muscle movements, but it does influence how much tension the muscle has. Whether the muscle is tense or relaxed influences how much the muscle will move. The part of the reticular formation involved in regulation of muscle tension is called the **descending reticular formation** . This area does not initiate movement but rather modifies the movement once it has begun.

Cerebellum

With the pieces of the brain assembled so far—medulla, pons, and reticular formation—Jack is capable of showing only reflexive movements. When his knee is tapped, the

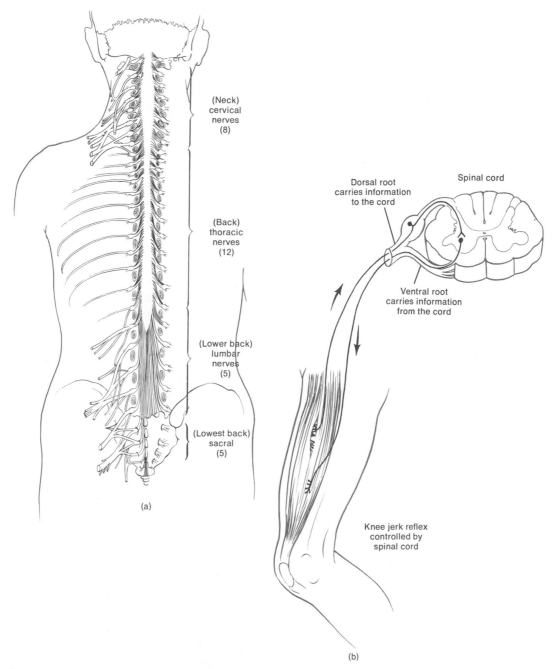

(Neck)
cervical
nerves
(8)

(Back)
thoracic
nerves
(12)

(Lower back)
lumbar
nerves
(5)

(Lowest back)
sacral
(5)

(a)

Dorsal root
carries information
to the cord

Spinal cord

Ventral root
carries information
from the cord

Knee jerk reflex
controlled by
spinal cord

(b)

Figure 3–1 How information is carried back and forth to the spinal cord. (a) The spinal nerves receive information from different parts of the body and also send information back to the muscles and glands. (b) An enlargement of one spinal nerve shows that it branches into a dorsal root, which carries information into the spinal cord, and a ventral root, which carries information out to the body.

The Nervous System

movement is very sluggish. At first, the couple thinks something is wrong with Jack's spinal cord, since it controls this reflex. But the instructions read, "Muscles will be very weak or lack muscle tone until the **cerebellum** is attached." The cerebellum, about the size of a baseball, is attached right in back of the pons and has many connections with the pons. With the cerebellum in place, Jack's hand withdrawal is a smooth, coordinated movement. The cerebellum provides the muscle tone that is necessary for smooth, coordinated reflexes and for voluntary movements—which Jack cannot yet make. The cerebellum will also help Jack maintain his balance by making adjustments in posture. Without a cerebullum, Jack would have jerky movements and a very uncoordinated walk similar to a drunkard's. If he were to reach for a glass of water without benefit of cerebellum, his hand would shoot past the glass or crash into it, knocking it over. Certain disorders of the cerebellum do cause a drunkard's walk or lack of hand control in reaching for an object.

Hindbrain

The parents are completely baffled by reference to something called the **hindbrain**. They cannot remember assembling it. The instructions read, "Hindbrain check: the hindbrain consists of the medulla, which controls vital reflexes; the pons, which is involved in sleep and makes connections with other parts of the brain, especially the cerebellum; and the cerebellum, which is involved in the coordination of movements." The couple know that the medulla and pons also contain the reticular formation, which is involved in alerting the brain, in maintaining wakefulness, and in controlling muscle tension. The father is pleased that he has single-handedly assembled the hindbrain. Jack is neither pleased nor displeased. Much more brain needs to be assembled before Jack even knows he has a hindbrain.

Midbrain

The instructions read, "It is important to assemble the brain piece by piece. Careless assemblage may lead to the creation of a monster. The next piece of brain, the **midbrain**, is connected to the top of the pons." The mother attaches the midbrain to the top of the pons. There are a series of tests to determine if the midbrain is working. "Stand out of sight and drop a large book on the floor. The head should turn reflexively toward the loud noise. Again, stand out of sight. Take the same large book and throw it close to, but do not hit, the head. The eyes should reflexively detect and blink as the book goes hurling by. Repeat, do not hit the head with the book." The father drops the book and nothing happens. He jumps on top of the book and makes a tremendous racket. Nothing. He reads on, "If the test is a failure, you have omitted a step. Go back and complete the previous step."

Cranial Nerves

Before Jack can turn his head toward a loud noise or blink his eyes or stick out his tongue or smile or taste food, 12 different nerves must be assembled. Ten of these 12 nerves, called **cranial nerves**, are attached at various places along the medulla, pons, and midbrain; two cranial nerves are connected to pieces of the brain not yet assembled. At their other end, the cranial nerves are connected to various sensors, glands, and muscles in the face, head, and neck; and also to the heart and visceral organs, such as intestines. The cranial nerves and their major functions are listed in Table 3–1. It is your cranial nerves that allow you to make faces at the idea of memorizing the names of these 12 nerves.

With the cranial nerves in place, Jack's midbrain functions correctly. The area in the midbrain involved in the reflex of turning toward a noise is called the **inferior colliculus** (ko-LICK-u-lus). The area involved in the reflex of detecting moving objects and blinking is called the superior colliculus.

If the mother had damaged the midbrain in assembly, Jack might not have the above reflexes. Jack might also have muscle weakness, a shuffling walk, a very inexpressive face, and shakes or tremors. Together, these symptoms are called **Parkinson's disease** and can be caused by damage to the midbrain.

The midbrain also contains the top part of the reticular formation that stretches across the medulla and pons into the midbrain. Together the medulla, pons, and midbrain are called the **brainstem**. It would be most correct to say that the reticular formation is located in the brainstem, meaning the medulla, pons, and midbrain. Although Jack now has a large part of the central nervous system assembled—spinal nerves, spinal cord, medulla, pons, cerebellum, midbrain, and cranial nerves—the only responses he can make are reflexes.

Forebrain

The instructions read, "If you have completed the brainstem, you are now ready to assemble the forebrain." All of the structures that will be added above the midbrain are part of the **forebrain**. You will remember from Chapter 1 that the forebrain is the most forward part of the brain and is greatly expanded in humans. The forebrain actually consists of two large **hemispheres** (meaning "half-spheres") and is symmetrical in the same way that your body is symmetrical. In other words, each brain structure found in the left hemisphere is also found in the right. For example, the first forebrain area we will be adding is the hypothalamus (hype-po-THAL-mus). There is actually a hypothalamus in the left hemisphere and one in the right hemisphere, but these are usually referred to in the singular. Thus, you would discuss the hypothalamus, but it would be understood that you meant the hypothalamus in both hemispheres.

Hypothalamus

The instructions read, "This structure is critical to a well-functioning body. Attach the **hypothalamus** above and in front of the midbrain." Jack needs a hypothalamus to regulate his eating, drinking, temperature, secretion of hormones, emotional responses, and possibly sexual behavior. Not only is the hypothalamus involved in all of these func-

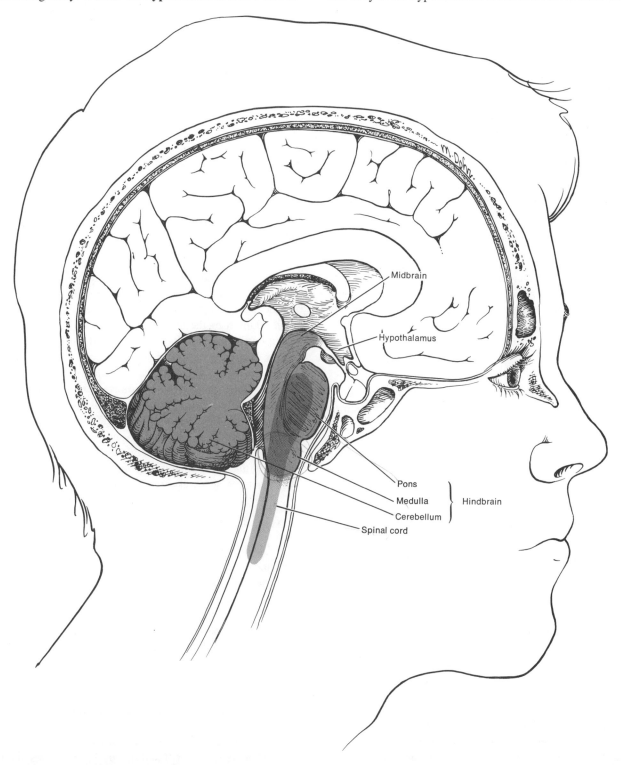

Figure 3–2 A middle view of the brain showing the location of the hindbrain, including medulla, pons, and cerebellum; the midbrain; and the hypothalamus. The reticular formation lies in the medulla and pons, extending slightly into the midbrain.

TABLE 3–1 The Cranial Nerves

Designated by Number	Name	Functions	Point Where Nerve Begins or Ends in Brain
I	Olfactory	Smell	Under front part of brain
II	Optic	Vision	Thalamus
III	Oculomotor	Eye movement	Midbrain
IV	Trochlear	Eye movement	Midbrain
V	Trigeminal	Eating movements and sensations from face	Midbrain and pons
VI	Abducens	Eye movement	Medulla
VII	Facial	Face movements and taste	Medulla
VIII	Auditory	Hearing and balance	Medulla
IX	Glossopharyngeal	Taste and pharynx movements	Medulla
X	Vagus	Heart, blood vessels, and viscera	Medulla
XI	Spinal accessory	Neck muscles and viscera	Medulla
XII	Hypoglossal	Tongue muscles	Medulla

These are the 12 cranial nerves; they are referred to either by name or by number. Some of these nerves carry sensory information, some carry motor information, and still others carry both sensory and motor information.

tions, but it is connected to many other brain areas with even more functions. Without a hypothalamus, Jack would starve, not drink, be unable to retain water, be generally miserable, and die.

Thalamus

The next instruction reads, "Right above the hypothalamus, insert a structure about the size of a walnut, the **thalamus** (THAL-mus). If you damage the thalamus in assembly, the body will be blind, deaf, and unable to feel any sensations when touched." But even with the thalamus in place, Jack still cannot see or hear. For Jack to hear, understand, and respond to his name, he will need both the thalamus and the piece of brain that comes last, the cortex. The thalamus is involved in the relay of information coming from the senses to the cortex. Sensors in the body send information into the spinal nerves and up to the spinal cord. Sensors in the face and head send information into the cranial nerves. Much of the sensory information carried by the spinal cord and cranial nerves goes to the thalamus. The thalamus has been called a great relay center because it relays the sensory information about vision goes to the **lateral geniculate** (jen-ICK-you-lit) nuclei, and information about hearing goes ral of *nucleus*. A nucleus is a group of cell bodies of neurons that are gathered together in one place in the central nervous system.)

Sensory information about touch, temperature, and pain goes to the **ventrobasal** (ven-tro-BASE-all) nuclei of the thalamus. If Jack's ventrobasal nuclei were damaged, he would not know if he were being touched because this information could not be transmitted to the cortex. Sensory information about vision goes to the **lateral geniculate** (jen-ICK-you-lit) nuclei, and information about hearing goes

to the **medial geniculate** nuclei. If the lateral and medial geniculate nuclei were damaged, Jack would be just as blind and deaf as if his eyes and ears had been destroyed.

In addition to the above nuclei, the thalamus has many others. Some are involved in sleep and waking and others gather information from many different areas and send it to the cortex. The thalamus is called the relay station because most of the sensory information that goes to the cortex must pass through the thalamus; however the thalamus is more that a relay station. The thalamus changes or modulates sensory information and also integrates information from many different brain areas. With his thalamus in place, Jack still cannot hear his name but he has one of the structures necessary for hearing.

Basal Ganglia

The father is confident that the next brain structure will get Jack moving. The label reads, "Brain part #14, **basal ganglia**, part of motor system." The instructions state, "Place the next three parts above and to the side of the thalamus. All three parts must be assembled together, or severe problems in movement will develop." Slightly larger than the thalamus, these three areas together are the basal ganglia. If Jack is ever to play tennis, he must have his basal ganglia. Earlier it was said that Parkinson's disease was caused by damage to an area of the midbrain. More often, in Parkinson's disease there is damage to both the midbrain and the basal ganglia.

If Jack develops Parkinson's disease his muscles will become increasingly stiff and he will have tremors and difficulty in starting movements. For example, he will have trouble starting a swing with his racket and, once he has started, he will have trouble stopping. Both the midbrain and

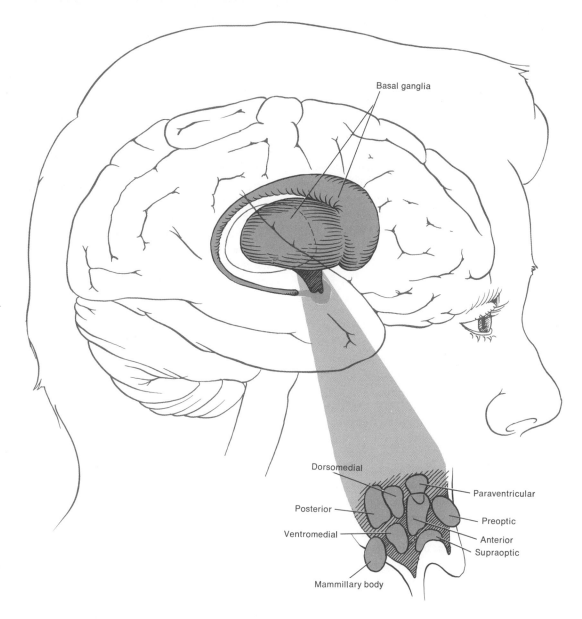

Basal ganglia

Dorsomedial
Paraventricular
Posterior
Preoptic
Ventromedial
Anterior
Supraoptic
Mammillary body

Figure 3–3 The location of the basal ganglia, above and to the side of the hypothalamus. The enlargement of the hypothalamus shows its many separate nuclei.

the basal ganglia are involved in the control of muscles for walking, swinging the arms, and starting and stopping.

These areas, midbrain and basal ganglia, together with the cerebellum, make up the **extrapyramidal motor system** (extra-per-RAM-id-all). The extrapyramidal system, alone, does not make voluntary movement possible, but it is very important for the regulation of muscle tone and movements. If your extrapyramidal motor system is damaged, you should consider selling your tennis racket.

Hippocampus and Amygdala

Jack would need only one novel for the rest of his life if he had no **hippocampus.** He could read the same story over

and over, thinking he was reading it for the first time. The hippocampus is involved in memory. It is approximately the size of the bent hotdog and is located below and to the side of the basal ganglia.

A structure that looks like an olive is placed right in front of the hippocampus; it has an equally strange name. This is the **amygdala** (a-MIG-da-la) and it is involved in emotional behavior. If Jack had no amygdala, he might show very little emotion or enthusiasm. He would not care whether he won or lost at tennis and he would never get mad at a bad shot. The amygdala and hippocampus are connected to many other brain structures and, because of these connections, are involved in other behaviors.

Cortex

Only two pieces of brain remain to be assembled. Either Jack will soon move and respond to his name or the entire brain will have to be reassembled. The mother picks up a structure that is about as thick as a piece of cardboard and very wrinkled, and places it on top of all other structures in the forebrain. This is the cortex. If you wanted to put a large piece of paper in a very small box, you might wrinkle up the paper. That is essentially what happened to the cortex. The skull, like a small box, did not provide enough space; by evolving in a wrinkled fashion, the cortex was able to have more area that if it were smooth. The top of a wrinkle is called a **gyrus** (JI-russ) and the bottom of a wrinkle is called a **fissure** or **sulcus** (SUL-kus). (Use your hippocampus to remember that).

Jack is capable of acting like a human because of the cortex. It contains approximately 10 billion neurons that allow you to think, dream, reason, talk, walk, see, hear, and learn. Beginning with the day you were born, and even in the womb, you were constantly experiencing, integrating, and responding to the world around you. The cortex is involved to a large extent in processing these millions of experiences and learning or not learning from them. In the year 2880, these millions of experiences are programmed into Jack's cortex by computer.

The cortex has a number of curious features. For example, the *left* side of the cortex receives information from the right side of the body and controls the movements of the right side. The *right* side of the cortex receives information from the left side of the body and controls movements on the left side. Exactly how this arrangement came about probably is to be found in your evolutionary past.

Auditory Area

The father begins assembling the cortex. When it is assembled, the wrinkled cortex will look the same throughout. However, different areas of the cortex have different functions. The instructions say there are four lobes and that the first one to look for is the **temporal lobe**. He finds this lobe and discovers that it actually has two parts that are positioned at either side of the brain.

At the moment when the father places the right temporal cortex alongside and near the bottom of the forebrain, Jack can hear. The medial geniculate nucleus of the thalamus relays information from the ears to this area in the temporal lobe. The boundary of the temporal lobe is a fissure running laterally up the brain and called the **lateral fissure**.

When Jack's left temporal cortex is in place, he will also have the part of the brain needed for speaking. For most people, speech is controlled in the left temporal lobe, but much more that that is needed for speech.

Motor Area

Another piece of cortex is placed over the front part of the brain. At this moment, Jack can reach for his tennis racket.

He now has a **frontal lobe**, which, among other functions, controls voluntary movements. The system that controls voluntary movements is called the **pyramidal system**. It is named for the pyramidal shape of the neurons in the motor area. When Jack reaches for his tennis racket, messages to move his arm start in the motor area of the frontal lobe and travel down his spinal cord. There, they activate other neurons that travel to the muscles in his arm. At the same time, the extrapyramidal motor system (basal ganglia and cerebellum) are involved in regulating and coordinating the arm's movements. But, without the portion of the frontal lobe called the **motor area**, Jack could not make any voluntary movements. The rear boundary of the frontal lobe is the **central sulcus**, which runs down the side of the brain. The motor area is immediately in front of the central sulcus.

When Jack picks up the racket with his right hand, it is the motor area in the cortex of the left hemisphere that controls the movement. If there were damage to Jack's motor area on the right side, the left side of his body would be paralyzed. As the neurons leave the right motor area, they travel through other areas of the brain, cross over to the left side in the brainstem, and travel down the left side of the spinal cord to control the left side of the body. If only a tiny spot in the motor area were damaged, only an arm might be paralyzed, and the other parts of the body spared. This is because all of the different areas of the body are represented at different locations in the motor area. As you see in Figure 3–5, the control of mouth movements is on the side of the motor area, while the control of knee movements is on the very top.

A curious feature of the motor area is that it has a large area for mouth and face movements and a very small area for chest movements. The rule is: the more complex the movement, the larger the area on the motor cortex. A large area of the motor cortex is devoted to finger movements, because it requires millions of neurons to control all the complex movements the fingers can make. A smaller area of the motor cortex is devoted to back movements, because it requires fewer neurons to control the general movements of the back.

Somatosensory Area

Jack can hear and can reach for the tennis racket, but he cannot yet feel the racket. Behind the frontal lobe and therefore behind the central sulcus, goes a piece of cortex forming the **parietal lobe** (pear-ee-EYE-tall). An area in the parietal lobe called the **somatosensory area** enables Jack to experience touch and temperature. Jack can feel that the racket handle is smooth and cold because of this **somesthetic cortex**. The ventrobasal nucleus of the thalamus relays information from the sensors in the body to the somesthetic area in the parietal lobe. If Jack grabs the racket with his right hand, the sensory information goes to the left somesthetic cortex. As in the motor area, different parts of the body are represented at different locations in the somesthetic area.

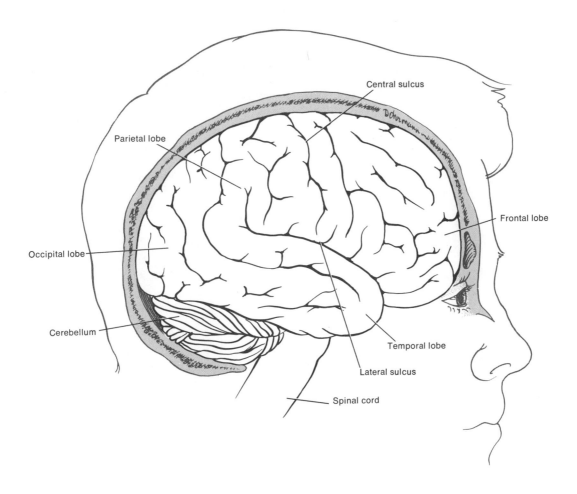

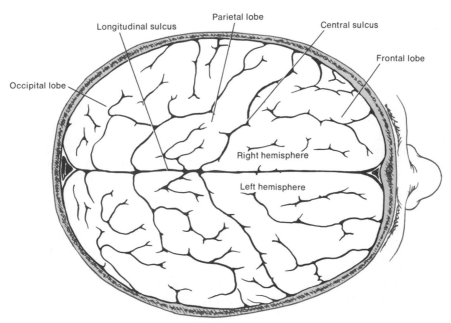

Figure 3–4 The side view of the brain shows the four lobes: frontal, parietal, temporal, and occipital. The top view shows how the brain is divided down the middle by the longitudinal sulcus into a right and left hemisphere. The central sulcus lies between the frontal and parietal lobes, and the lateral sulcus separates the temporal lobe. There is no sulcus defining the occipital lobe.

The Nervous System

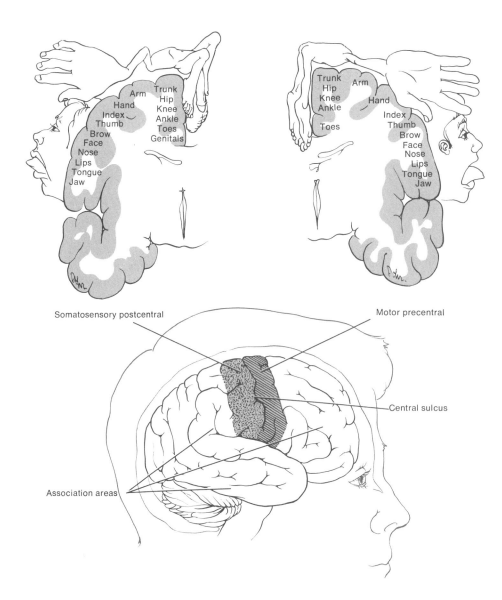

Figure 3–5 This side view of the brain shows how the central sulcus separates the motor area (precentral) in the frontal lobe from the somatosensory area (postcentral) in the parietal lobe. The figures above are schematic representations of cortical functions. Different parts of the body have larger or smaller areas on the motor cortex depending upon the complexity of movement. For example, fingers have greater complexity of movement and therefore have a larger area on the cortex than toes have. Similarly, different parts of the body have larger or smaller areas on the somatosensory cortex depending upon the sensitivity. For example, the tongue is very sensitive and therefore has a larger area than a knee has.

Visual Area

Finally, the mother places the last piece of cortex on the very back of the brain. At that moment, Jack can see. This fourth lobe, called the **occipital lobe** (awk-SIP-ah-tall), is the area involved in vision. The lateral geniculate nucleus of the thalamus relays information from the eyes to an area in the occipital lobe. There is no noticeable sulcus separating the parietal and occipital lobes.

Association Areas

Perhaps Jack is thinking about playing tennis, or is fantasizing about winning, or is figuring out how to serve better.

There is no one area of the cortex responsible for these complex responses of thinking, reasoning, and fantasizing. Areas involved in thinking and reasoning and associating are called **association areas**. Association areas are scattered throughout the four lobes and comprise a large part of the cortex.

Cortex Alerted

Only when the cortex was assembled, could Jack hear and understand his name or think about playing tennis. For the cortex to process sensory information from the ears or other senses, the cortex must be alerted or aroused. When the father shouts "Jack," sensory information from the ears enters the brain and does two things. Some of the information goes into the reticular formation, which immediately sends messages to alert the cortex that some information is coming. Additionally, sensory information from the ears goes to the thalamus (medial geniculate nuclei), which relays the information to the cortex in the temporal lobe. With the cortex alerted, these sensory messages are processed and understood.

Corpus Callosum

One last piece must be added to make the brain complete. The brain is separated into a right and left hemisphere by a wide sulcus called the **longitudinal sulcus**. With the brain in two halves, there must be some way for the right hemisphere to know what the left hemisphere is doing. The final instructions read, "To connect the two hemispheres, place a structure called the **corpus callosum** between the two halves." The corpus callosum is about 1 cm (½ inch) thick and is a bundle of nerve fibers that connects the two hemispheres. If Jack did not have a corpus callosum, his left hemisphere would not always know what his right hemisphere was doing, which could be embarrassing. Without a corpus callosum, he might be swinging his racket at the ball with one hand and trying to catch the ball with the other.

A Functioning Body

With Jack's brain assembled and working, it is time for the couple to determine whether his body is functioning normally. There are a number of glands which secrete chemicals necessary for his well being. If one of these glands had malfunctioned, Jack might have been very short like a dwarf, or very tall like a giant, or have diabetes or muscle spasms. Jack's body came with these glands preassembled, so the couple must check to see that they are in working order.

The various glands that secrete hormones operate automatically and are not under conscious control. Glands that secrete their hormones directly into the blood stream are called **endocrine glands**. Once released into the blood stream, the hormones act on target organs or glands in various parts of the body. The level of hormones in the body is regulated through a feedback system. Normally, your hormones are regulated without problem. If this regulation should break down, there can be physiological problems or psychological problems.

Thyroid: Metabolism Control

Jack's body has two **thyroid glands**, one on each side of his neck just below the voice box. The thyroid secretes a hormone called **thyroxin**. If too little thyroxin is secreted when a child is growing and replacement hormones are not administered, the child will be short for his age, have a pot belly and a protruding tongue, and be mentally retarded. A child with this thyroxin deficiency is called a *cretin*. The secretion of thyroxin causes the cells of the body to increase their activity or metabolic rate. An abnormally low metabolic rate would mean slower growth, resulting in an inability to reach full potential, as seen in the cretin.

If you had normal secretion of thyroxin as a child but too little as as adult, you would be sluggish, have reduced muscle tone, and experience lowered motivation and alertness. These symptoms can be cleared up with the administration of thyroxin. If an adult has too much thyroxin, which is less common than too little, the result is nervousness, irritability, and a high metabolism rate. As a result of the higher metabolic rate, this individual eats large amounts of food but does not gain weight. Treatment for too much secretion entails removal of part of the thyroid gland.

Pituitary: Master Gland

In a bony cavity at the base of the brain, hanging directly below the hypothalamus, is the **pituitary** gland. This gland controls many other glands throughout the body. The pituitary is divided into two parts: the **anterior pituitary**, which is controlled by hormones released from the hypothalamus; and the **posterior pituitary**, which is controlled by nerve impulses from the hypothalamus. The hypothalamus, then, controls the pituitary, which in turn controls other glands, such as the thyroid.

It is thought that the hypothalamus releases a hormone called **thyroid releasing factor**, or **T-RF**, that triggers the anterior pituitary to release a thyroid stimulating hormone, **thyrotropin**, or **TSH**. TSH triggers the thyroid gland to produce thyroxin. If secretion of thyroxin were to continue unchecked, the rate of metabolism would be too high and we would see the symptoms of an overactive thyroid. There is a mechanism to turn off secretion of thyroxin. When thyroxin builds up in the blood, it suppressess T-RF from the hypothalamus. Without this releasing factor, the production of thyrotropin stops and the thyroid is no longer stimulated to release thyroxin. Thus, the level of the hormone in the blood effects the hypothalamus, causing it either to start or stop secreting the releasing factor. This interaction between hormone level in the blood and secretion of releasing factors by the hypothalamus is called a **feedback system** and is characteristic of how normal levels of hormones are maintained in the body.

Parathyroid: Calcium Control

Following early attempts to remove thyroid glands from patients with too much thyroxin secretion, it was discovered that these patients sometimes developed uncontrollable muscle contractions, called **tetany**. The amount of calcium in these patients' blood was lower than normal, and it was the reduced calcium that caused the tetany. In removing the thyroid glands, the surgeon had accidentally removed four tiny glands, two on each side of the thyroid. These glands, called the **parathyroid glands**, regulate the amount of calcium in the blood. Low levels of calcium cause the nerves to fire spontaneously, and because nerves innervate muscles, the result is tetany. Removal of the parathyroid glands

can also cause mental problems, since nerves firing spontaneously in the brain disrupt normal mental functioning. These symptoms are relieved when the calcium level is restored to normal.

In the normal person, there is a feedback system that regulates the level of calcium. A low level of calcium in the blood causes the parathyroid glands to secrete more hormone to raise the level. If Jack's body had arrived without parathyroid glands, he would have had an abnormally low

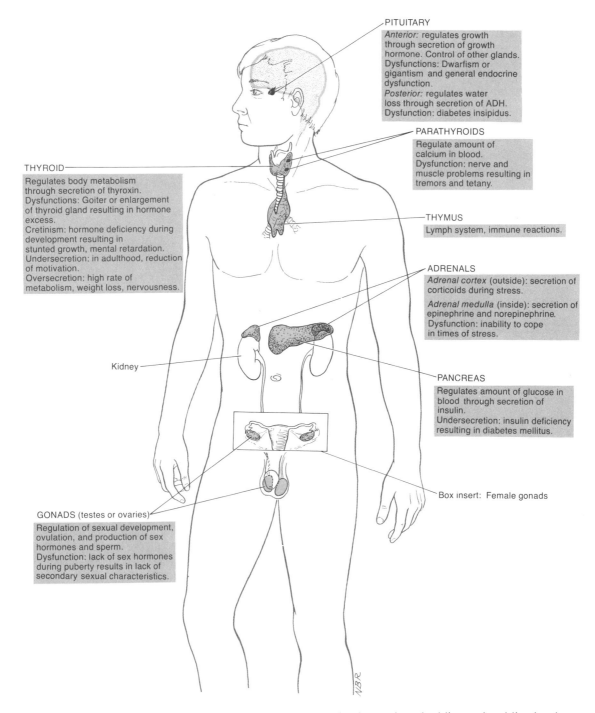

PITUITARY
Anterior: regulates growth through secretion of growth hormone. Control of other glands. Dysfunctions: Dwarfism or gigantism and general endocrine dysfunction.
Posterior: regulates water loss through secretion of ADH. Dysfunction: diabetes insipidus.

PARATHYROIDS
Regulate amount of calcium in blood. Dysfunction: nerve and muscle problems resulting in tremors and tetany.

THYROID
Regulates body metabolism through secretion of thyroxin. Dysfunctions: Goiter or enlargement of thyroid gland resulting in hormone excess. Cretinism: hormone deficiency during development resulting in stunted growth, mental retardation. Undersecretion: in adulthood, reduction of motivation. Oversecretion: high rate of metabolism, weight loss, nervousness.

THYMUS
Lymph system, immune reactions.

ADRENALS
Adrenal cortex (outside): secretion of corticoids during stress.
Adrenal medulla (inside): secretion of epinephrine and norepinephrine. Dysfunction: inability to cope in times of stress.

Kidney

PANCREAS
Regulates amount of glucose in blood through secretion of insulin. Undersecretion: insulin deficiency resulting in diabetes mellitus.

Box insert: Female gonads

GONADS (testes or ovaries)
Regulation of sexual development, ovulation, and production of sex hormones and sperm. Dysfunction: lack of sex hormones during puberty results in lack of secondary sexual characteristics.

Figure 3-6 Glands that secrete various hormones and chemicals are located throughout the body.

FETAL TRANSPLANTS MAY HELP DIABETICS

Researchers at UCLA medical school believe it may be possible to salvage insulin-producing organs from aborted fetuses and transplant them into patients with diabetes.

While the researchers say the first human case is three to five years into the future, recent experiments with animals suggest the idea has possibilities.

An improved method of freezing organs is one recent development that makes such transplants feasible. Another is a trick learned in the animal experiments that enables the tiny fetal pancreas to maximize its insulin production in animal experiments.

The UCLA researchers, headed by Dr. Josiah Brown, an endocrinologist, have succeeded in reversing diabetes in fully grown rats by supplying them with insulin from a transplanted rat fetus pancreas.

Although the pancreas of a rat fetus is only about 1/16th of an inch long, it is the largest organ to function successfully after being frozen and then thawed, according to Brown. The freezing technique was developed at Oak Ridge National Laboratories.

The problem with freezing organs is that the ice crystals that form inside cells cause lethal damage. The Oak Ridge scientists found a way to freeze organs up to the size of a rat fetal pancreas without forming ice crystals. Success depends on selecting the proper freezing rate and warming rate and the use of a special additive.

When the tiny fetal pancreas was placed inside the rat with diabetes, it grew to one-half inch within six weeks. In fact, Brown said in an interview, the organ had formed new blood vessels attaching the pancreas to the adult rat within 24 hours.

The pancreas from a 12- to 18-week human fetus is larger than the rat fetus organ and therefore more difficult to freeze and thaw and still function. Solving that problem—perhaps by cutting it into sections before freezing—is one reason why it will be three to five years before a human case is attempted.

One problem is that methods must be worked out to tissue-type fetal tissue. While scientists know a lot about tissue-typing adult tissues—kidneys, for example—nobody has done it for fetal organs, Brown said. Tissue-typing is necessary in order to make the organ as compatible as possible with the recipient's tissues, thereby lessening the chances of rejection.

Still another obstacle is that no one is sure at what stage of development the fetal pancreas will work best. It is believed to be between 12 and 13 weeks.

Other members of the UCLA team are Drs. Yoko S. Mullen, William R. Clark and I. Gabriella Molnar.

SOURCE: Harry Nelson, Times Medical Writer, *Los Angeles Times,* May 16,1977. Copyright © 1977 by Los Angeles Times.

---

level of calcium. Thus, he would have had an abnormally functioning brain and his body would have had tetany.

Growth Hormone

There are people called **pituitary giants** who are 2.5 m (8 ft) tall but have normal intelligence. Their problem occurs during their growth period, from birth to adolescence. In these early years, the hypothalamus secretes **growth releasing hormone**, **GH-RF**, that triggers the anterior pituitary to release **growth hormone**. Growth hormone does not act on other glands, but acts directly on the body's cells to stimulate growth by making proteins available. If there is too much secretion of growth hormone during the period from birth to adolescence, the result can be a pituitary giant. If there is too little secretion of growth hormone during this period, the result can be a **pituitary dwarf** who has normal body proportions and normal intelligence but is only 1 m (3 to 4 ft) tall as an adult. If this hormonal malfunction is discovered early, it is possible to prevent the person from becoming a pituitary dwarf by administering growth hormone.

Hormones and Stress

If Jack were pursued by a rabid dog, he would be stressed. As discussed in greater detail in Chapter 4, stressors trigger the hypothalamus to secrete a releasing factor, **ACTH-RF**, that triggers the anterior pituitary to release **ACTH** (adrenocorticotrophic hormone). The ACTH acts on the two glands sitting above the kidneys, the **adrenal glands**.

Each adrenal gland has an outside layer called the **adrenal cortex** and an inside layer called the **adrenal medulla**. The adrenal cortex and medulla are activated by different mechanisms and secrete different hormones, but both layers are active in times of stress. The release of ACTH from the pituitary causes the adrenal cortex to secrete hormones called **corticoids** that help the body cope with stress. The stress of being chased by a rabid dog would also cause the hypothalamus, acting through the nervous system, to stimulate the adrenal medulla to secrete two hormones, **epinephrine** (ap-ah-NEF-ah-rin) and **norepinephrine** (nor-ap-ah-NEF-ah-rin). Those two hormones cause many physiological reactions that prepare the body for stress.

Anterior Pituitary

To avoid being a dwarf or giant or cretin and to function in times of stress, you need a normally functioning anterior pituitary. The chain of command begins with the releasing factors secreted by the hypothalamus that act on the anterior pituitary to control secretion of growth hormone, ACTH, and thyroxin. When you reach puberty, the anterior pituitary also secretes two sex hormones, **FSH** and **LH**, that are involved in sexual development.

Posterior Pituitary

If Jack had **diabetes insipidus**, which is different from the diabetes you normally think of, he would drink large quantities of water and urinate frequently and in large amounts. This condition occurs if the posterior pituitary does not secrete enough **antidiuretic hormone**, or **ADH**, which normally causes the kidneys to reabsorb water. When this system is functioning properly, cells in the hypothalamus react to the level of water in the blood. When the cells in the hypothalamus sense that there is not enough water in the blood, the hypothalamus sends a neural message to the posterior pituitary to release more ADH, which causes more water to be reabsorbed by the kidneys. In the absence of ADH, the kidneys fail to reabsorb. Thus water is lost in the urine and the individual must replace it by drinking large quantities.

One other hormone is secreted by the posterior pituitary and it is called **oxytocin** (ox-ee-TOX-in). In the female, oxytocin causes contractions of the uterus during birth and

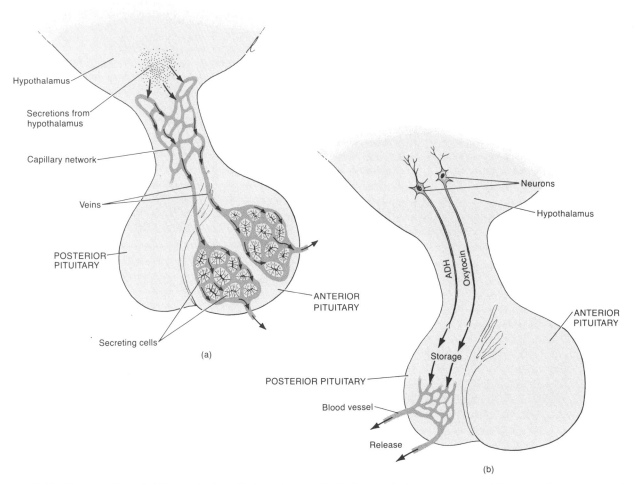

Figure 3–7 The pituitary. (a) The anterior pituitary has cells that secrete hormones, and these cells are regulated by releasing factors coming from the blood supply of the hypothalamus. (b) The posterior pituitary has cells that store and release ADH and oxytocin, which are manufactured in the hypothalamus. These cells are regulated by nerve impulses from the hypothalamus.

release of milk from the breast during nursing. It is not known what function oxytocin has in males, but it is present in their blood streams.

As explained earlier, the anterior pituitary, and posterior pituitary secrete different hormones and are under different kinds of control by the hypothalamus. The anterior pituitary is activated by releasing hormones secreted by the hypothalamus. In contrast, axons from hypothalamic neurons actually extend down into the posterior pituitary and control the gland's release of hormones.

Diabetes Mellitus

There are thousands of people who must regularly give themselves insulin. Without insulin, diabetics go into a coma and die. In the normal person, the ability of the cells to use glucose from the blood is regulated by the secretion of insulin from the **pancreas**, an organ located between the stomach and the small intestine. After you've eaten a candy bar or a meal, the level of glucose in your blood rises. Cells in the pancreas are sensitive to the level of glucose in the blood. When your glucose level rises, these cells begin secreting insulin. Insulin lowers the glucose level in the blood by increasing glucose usage and storage in your body tissues and muscles. When the glucose level drops, the secretion of insulin drops.

When a diabetic person eats a candy bar or a meal, the level of glucose in the blood rises but the pancreas does not secrete enough insulin to cause glucose to be used by the cells. Thus the level of glucose in the blood remains high and the cells starve from lack of glucose. In addition, the body tries to rid itself of the excess glucose by excreting it in the urine. The kidneys excrete more water in the attempt to expel glucose in urine, and the diabetic may be-

come dehydrated because of the water loss. This condition is called **diabetes mellitus**. Thus, there are two kinds of diabetes: one is caused by loss of water due to excretion of glucose and is called *diabetes mellitus*; the other is caused by loss of water due to lack of ADH and is called *diabetes insipidus*. In the old days, laboratory technicians had to taste the urine to see which kind of diabetes the person had. If it tasted sweet, it was mellitus, which means "sweet"; if it was bitter, it was insipidus, which means "insipid" or "bitter." Today, these technicians have been replaced with machines that have no complaints.

Comment

You have seen how Jack developed from a nameless body with reflexes into a human being with the ability to think, reason, and fantasize. It was not until a final piece of brain, the cortex, was added that Jack took on those complex behaviors that distinguish a human from other animals.

As the pieces of the brain were assembled, each piece was connected to the preceding piece, resulting in thousands and thousands of interconnections. Because of these many interconnections, it is difficult to determine the exact function of a certain brain area. You have been told that the hippocampus is involved in memory. That is true. But the hippocampus has thousands of connections with other parts of the brain. Thus, the hippocampus also influences these other areas and is involved in many other functions.

Many parts of the brain are called into play for a relatively simple response like breathing. A complex response like thinking requires thousands of parts.

SELF-TEST 3

1 The spinal cord is connected to the body by spinal nerves. A spinal nerve is composed of _____ neurons and _____ neurons.

afferent
motor

2 Messages from sensors in the body are carried by afferent neurons and enter the spinal cord through the _____ root.

dorsal

3 Information leaving the spinal cord is carried by motor neurons that leave the spinal cord through the _____ root.

ventral

4 If stuck with a pin, your hand would withdraw. This movement is controlled by the _____ and is called a _____ .

spinal cord
reflex

5 Connected to the top of the spinal cord is a piece of brain called the _____ that controls vital reflexes that are involved in regulating _____ , _____ , _____ , and intestinal movement.

medulla
breathing / heart rate
blood pressure

6 Connected to the top of the medulla is a part of the brain called the _____ that is involved in the regulation of _____ and has many connections with the rest of the brain, especially the _____ .

pons
sleep
cerebellum

7 In the middle of the medulla and pons lies a structure that alerts the brain and helps to keep you awake. It is called the _____ system.

reticular activation

8 The part of the reticular formation that influences how much tension the muscles have is called the _____ formation.

descending reticular

9 If most of the reticular formation were damaged, you would be in a _____ because the brain could not be _____ .

coma
aroused or alerted

10 If your cerebellum were damaged, your reflexive movements would be _____ ; your walk would be _____ ; and you would have trouble _____ for a glass of water.

weak or sluggish
uncoordinated / reaching

11 When referring to these three structures, medulla, pons, and cerebellum, you can use the term _____ .

hindbrain

12 The brain structure that is attached to the top of the pons is called the _____ .

midbrain

13 The area in the midbrain involved in the reflex of turning your head toward a noise is called the _____ .

inferior colliculus

14 The area in the midbrain involved in the reflex of detecting moving objects and blinking is called the _____ .

superior colliculus

15 There are 12 nerves attached to various places in the medulla, pons, and midbrain. These nerves are called _____ nerves.

cranial

16 Among their various functions, the cranial nerves are involved in controlling your heart and intestines and in allowing you to feel sensations from and move the muscles in your _____ , _____ , and _____ .

head / neck
face

17 An area in the forebrain that is involved in the regulation of eating, drinking, temperature, and secretion of hormones is called the _____ .

hypothalamus

18 The thalamus has a number of nuclei; the one involved with touch, temperature, and pain is called the _____ nucleus; with vision, the _____ nucleus; with audition, the _____ nucleus.

ventrobasal
lateral geniculate
medial geniculate

19 In addition to relaying sensory information to the cortex, the thalamus is also involved in _____ sensory informatin before it is relayed to the cortex.

changing or modulating

20 One of the systems that controls motor movements, the extrapyramidal system, is composed of the _____ , _____ , and _____ .

basal ganglia
midbrain
cerebellum

21 The basal ganglia regulate muscle movements used in complex activities such as _____ or _____ . (Give any two.)

walking / swinging arms
starting or stopping
movement

22 Damage to the basal ganglia and midbrain can result in the disorder known as _____ .

Parkinson's disease

23 The hippocampus is involved in many functions, and one of these is _____ .

memory

24 Right in front of the hippocampus is a structure called the _____ , which is involved in emotional behavior.

amygdala

25 The outermost layer of the brain, called the cortex, is divided into four lobes: _____ , _____ , _____ , and _____ .

frontal / parietal
temporal / occipital

26 The motor system that controls voluntary movements, is called the _____ system. This system originates in the _____ lobe.

pyramidal motor
frontal

27 The thalamus relays sensory information from the ear to the _____ lobe; sensory information from the eye to the _____ lobe; and sensory information about touch and temperature to the _____ lobe.

temporal
occipital
parietal

28 A curious feature of the brain is that the right side of the brain controls the _____ side of the body; the left side of the brain controls the _____ side of the body.

left
right

29 In the motor cortex, each part of the body is represented in a different _____ .

place or area

30 Muscles that are involved in very precise and complex movements have a _____ area in the motor cortex than muscles used in gross movements.

larger

31 There are many areas of the cortex that are involved in the complicated activities of thinking, reasoning, and figuring. The general name for these areas is _____ areas.

association

32 The two hemispheres are connected by the _____ .

corpus callosum

33 The hypothalamus controls the _____ pituitary through releasing factors and controls the _____ pituitary through neural impulses.

anterior
posterior

34 In order for thyroxin to be produced, the hypothalamus must secrete _____ , that acts on the anterior pituitary to produce _____ , that triggers the thyroid to secrete _____ .

thyroid releasing factor
or T-RF / TSH or
thyrotropin / thyroxin

35 If a child were a cretin, that would mean that he had not had enough _____ secreted by the _____ gland.

thyroxin
thyroid

36 If a surgeon carelessly removed your thyroid gland, he might also remove your _____ glands, and this would cause a lower level of _____ in the blood resulting in _____ .

parathyroid
calcium / tetany

37 If you saw a pituitary giant or dwarf, you would know that the problem was too much or too little secretion of _____ hormone from the _____ .

growth / anterior
pituitary

38 If you were run over by a car, your hypothalamus would activate your nervous system, which would send neural impulses to trigger your _____ to secrete _____ and _____ to help you cope with the stress.

adrenal medulla
epinephrine
norepinephrine

39 At the same time, your hypothalamus would, through secretion of a releasing factor, _____ , trigger the anterior pituitary to secrete _____ , that would act on the adrenal _____ to trigger the secretion of corticoids.

ACTH-RF

ACTH / cortex

40 If your posterior pituitary were removed, you would develop _____ because there would be no secretion of _____ , that causes the kidneys to reabsorb water normally lost through urination.

diabetes insipidus

ADH

41 After you eat a sundae, the level of glucose in the blood rises, and this rise triggers cells in the _____ to secrete _____ that lowers the level of glucose.

pancreas / insulin

42 If there were no secretion of insulin after a rise in blood glucose level, the body would try to rid itself of the excess glucose through excretion in the urine. This condition is known as _____ .

diabetes mellitus

43 The glands that secrete hormones into the blood stream are called _____ glands. Normal levels of hormones in the body are maintained through _____ systems.

endocrine

feedback

Stress, Biofeedback, and Autonomic Nervous System

How Your Heart Knows What Your Head Is Thinking

Lie Detector

When Harold saw a wart, he worried about cancer; when he noticed a bald spot, he worried about losing his hair; and when he tripped, he worried about having muscular dystrophy. Harold was a worrier, and at the moment he had one of his biggest worries: before getting his new job, he had to take a lie detector test. As he waited for the test, he thought about all the past lies he had told, how he was beginning to perspire, and how he wanted to run. Just then his name was called.

He was led into a small room. The examiner told him to relax and be seated. He tried to relax, but his palms became sweaty and his mouth felt like dry sand. The examiner attached two metal disks to his fingers, put a cuff around his arm, and tied a flexible rubber belt around his chest. All of these sensors were attached to a small gray machine with many lights and indicators that seemed in constant motion. Harold was bewildered and felt his heart pounding like a drum. The examiner said the test was painless and warned Harold to tell the truth on each question. If he lied, she would be able to tell and, of course, Harold would not get the job. He worried about the job, passing out, or laughing uncontrollably. The questions began.

"Is your name Harold?" He said yes.

"Are you a student?" He said yes.

"Have you ever lied when applying for a job?" He swallowed and said no. It was a lie. Harold knew it. He thought he had been very calm when he had said no. He wondered what the machine had recorded.

The questions continued. Harold kept his face very straight and his eyes fixed and did not move a muscle. In answering the next nine questions, he told two more lies. What worried

him was the examiner writing down something after one of his answers. Was she trying to scare him or had she detected his lies? The questions continued.

A Lie or the Truth?

The sensors that had been attached to Harold's body were connected to a machine sometimes called a **lie detector** or, more accurately, a **polygraph**. The sensors recorded Harold's bodily activities—respiration, blood pressure, and skin changes—which were then fed into and magnified by the polygraph. The polygraph had four pens that moved back and forth across a sheet of paper depending upon how much bodily activity the sensors were recording. Before and after Harold said yes to who he was and what he was, there was little change in the pens' movements. But when Harold said no to the question about never lying in a job interview, the pens' movements increased. There were several more questions about his habits and family that produced little change in the pens' activity. Harold was asked, "Have you ever stolen money from a cash register?" The mere thought made Harold tremble. He said no. It was the truth, but the pens showed increased movements. More questions. Harold was asked if he had ever helped a friend steal from a store. He thought for a while. Before he had even spoken the word ʾno, which was the truth, the pens showed increased activity.

The polygraph was measuring physiological responses going on in the body before Harold actually said yes or no. Some bodily responses change when you lie, but they can also change when you are telling the truth about an event that is emotionally disturbing. The polygraph only records bodily responses. The polygraph cannot tell the examiner

55

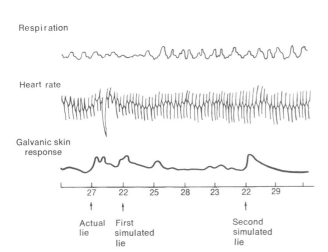

Respiration

Heart rate

Galvanic skin
response

27 22 25 28 23 22 29

Actual   First   Second
lie   simulated   simulated
         lie   lie

Figure 4-1 As part of an experiment, a subject tells a lie and then simulates lying. His physiological responses (respiration, heart rate, and galvanic skin response) are measured. Since these responses are controlled by the ANS, they occur automatically when he is aroused or stressed. Telling an actual lie or even a simulated lie caused him to be stressed, which triggered involuntary ANS responses. (Courtesy of Merit Protective Service, Inc., photo by Audrey Ross, Berkeley.)

if the changed responses occurred from telling a lie or from telling an emotionally disturbing answer that is true. It is the trained examiner who decides whether or not a person has lied. The examiner uses carefully chosen questions that are designed to reduce general nervousness and increase the likelihood that the person will show physiological arousal only to the critical questions. Although the polygraph is commonly called a lie detector, it does not detect lies. It only detects the bodily responses occurring during emotions or stress.

Autonomic Nervous System

Involuntary Responses

The small metal disks that were attached to Harold's fingers are called **electrodes**. When Harold responded to the ques-

tion about his name, there was some movement in the pens connected to these sensors or electrodes. Even when he was sitting quietly, there was some pen movement. When Harold said "No," he had never stolen from a store, there was more than the usual pen movement. The skin on his fingers indicated that Harold felt differently about answering this question.

The skin of his fingers, as well as other parts of the body, contains tiny **sweat glands** that secrete fluids. As the glands secrete more or less fluid, the ability of the skin to pass an electrical current changes. The electrodes on Harold's fingers were measuring the activity of these glands by measuring how easily the current passed through his skin. The comparative ease with which current passes through the skin was previously known as the **galavinic skin response** or **GSR** or the **electrodermal response** or **EDR**, but is now called the **skin resistance response** or **SRR**. When you are nervous or emotional the SRR will be different than when you are calm or relaxed.

The finger electrodes detected a change in Harold's SRR when he answered certain questions. Although his face looked calm when he responded with a lie, he felt guilty and was afraid of being found out. His emotions caused activation of his sweat glands, along with a number of other involuntary **physiological responses**. These involuntary responses were controlled by the involuntary or **autonomic nervous system**, or **ANS**.

A cuff tied around Harold's arm had sensors that recorded blood pressure and heart rate. When Harold answered routine questions, the pens recorded steady, rhythmical heart rate and blood pressure. When he was asked, "Did you ever help a friend steal from a store?" there was a greater change in heart rate and blood pressure. Changes in heart rate and blood pressure are two other involuntary responses that occur during stress and emotional states, and they are controlled by the autonomic nervous system.

At this very moment, you probably could not cause your heart to beat slower. Without prolonged training, people have very little voluntary control over the responses of the autonomic nervous system. Harold could lie with a straight face because many facial muscles are under voluntary control by way of the motor cortex. But involuntarily he sent out signals to the polygraph via his autonomic nervous system. Whether you are worried, elated, fearful, or relaxed, the ANS continues to function automatically, and often unnoticed.

Sympathetic Arousal

Not only did Harold's fingers sweat, his heart pound, and his blood race when he became anxious, but a number of other physiological responses occurred. His digestion was inhibited, glucose (a kind of sugar) was released from his liver into his blood stream, and blood was diverted from his intestines and stomach to his brain and limb muscles. All of these responses occurred involuntarily and made Harold's body ready for running or fighting or engaging in some other action. The physiological responses involved in preparing the body for action are controlled by a part of the ANS called the **sympathetic division**. It is thought that the hypothalamus is involved in activating the sympathetic division. Whenever you are stressed or feeling an emotion, your sympathetic division prepares the body for action. You may run or fight or just stare fiercely, but you are ready.

The question "Did you ever lie during an interview?" caused Harold to feel as though he had just received an injection of adrenalin, and he had. Above each kidney is a gland, called the adrenal gland, which secretes hormones. The inside of the gland is called the adrenal medulla, and the outside is called the adrenal cortex. In times of stress or emotion, such as telling a serious lie, the sympathetic division causes the adrenal medula to secrete two different hormones: **adrenalin** (ah-DREN-ah-lin), usually called **ep-**

inephrine, and **noradrenalin** (NOR-ah-dren-ah-lin), usually called **norepinephrine**. These two hormones enter the blood stream and affect other organs. For example, they make the heart beat faster and cause the liver to release glucose. Glucose is an important source of energy for muscles and cells and is especially needed during stress or emotions.

Hypothalamus and ANS

The question, "Did you steal from a store?" triggers a **chain of events**: Harold feels guilty; he experiences fear and nervousness; his hypothalamus becomes involved; the hypothalamus and perhaps other brain areas activate the sympathetic division; the sympathetic division causes increased heart rate, blood pressure, sweating, diversion of blood, release of glucose, and release of epinephrine and norepinephrine from the adrenal medulla; epinephrine and norepinephrine cause additional increases in heart rate and release of glucose.

The polygraph measures Harold's physiological responses that are primarily under the control of the sympathetic division. It does not matter whether Harold actually says or just thinks the answer. Thinking about the question arouses some emotional feelings that cause the hypothalamus to trigger the sympathetic division. Since the sympathetic division can be activated by many kinds of emotions, how can the "lie detector" know whether Harold is really lying or just anxious?

At the age of 15, Harold watched a policeman arrest one of his friends for shoplifting. He never forgot how terrified he was. When the examiner asked Harold, "Have you ever helped a friend steal from a store?" he remembered his friend's arrest. This memory caused him to be anxious. The feeling of anxiety activated the sympathetic division of the ANS and the polygraph recorded this increased activity. Harold was not lying, he was only very anxious. But the polygraph could not tell the difference. The polygraph is not a detector of lies but rather a device to measure the body's arousal level (4–16). The examiner administering the polygraph test has to decide whether Harold was lying or anxious about a past emotional event. The examiner uses a series of questions to help decide which it is.

Sympathetic Division

Suppose you took a drug which deactivated the sympathetic division. Could you then fool the polygraph? Without the sympathetic division, there would be few physiological signs of bodily arousal during emotional or stressful states. The sympathetic division has cell bodies that originate in the spinal cord. These cell bodies send axons out of the spinal cord to a group of neurons paralleling the spinal cord. Starting at the top of the back and extending down to the lower back, groups of cell bodies that resemble beads

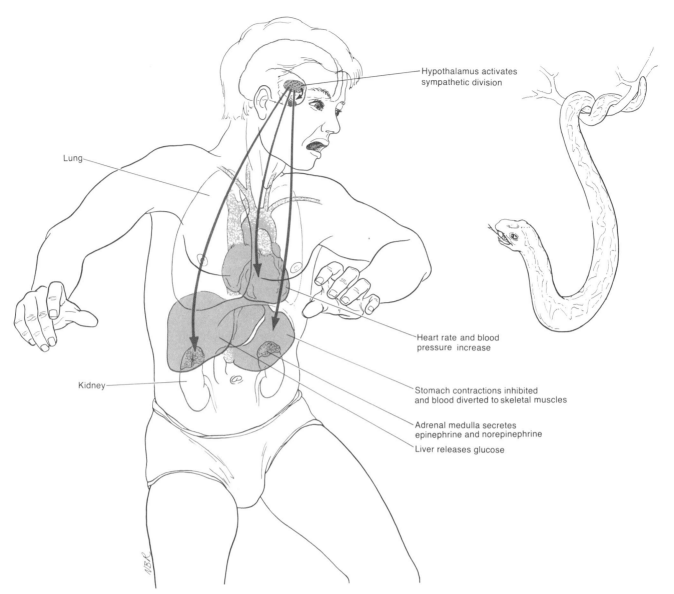

Figure 4-2 If you were frightened by a snake, the physiological responses controlled by the sympathetic division would prepare your body for action by increasing your heart rate, inhibiting digestion, releasing sugar, and increasing blood flow to the muscles of your limbs.

Hypothalamus activates sympathetic division

Lung

Heart rate and blood pressure increase

Kidney

Stomach contractions inhibited and blood diverted to skeletal muscles

Adrenal medulla secretes epinephrine and norepinephrine

Liver releases glucose

on a string run alongside the spinal cord. Shown in Figure 4–3, these clusters of cell bodies, or ganglia, are called the **sympathetic ganglia**. Axons going from the spinal cord to these ganglia are called **preganglionic**. All preganglionic fibers of the sympathetic division originate in the thoracic (chest) and lumbar (upper back) sections of the spinal cord, which are shortened to **thoracicolumbar**. From the thoracicolumbar area of the spinal cord, axons leave and synapse with cells in the sympathetic ganglia.

A drug could destroy or block the transmitter chemical secreted by the telodendria of preganglionic axons as they synapse in the sympathetic ganglia. Without this transmitter, the sympathetic impulses would stop at the ganglia and never reach or be able to control the body's organs. The transmitter substance secreted by preganglionic sympathetic axons is called **acetylcholine** (ah-seat-tul-KO-lean), usually abbreviated **ACh**. If a drug destroyed or blocked the action

of ACh, the preganglionic transmitter, the sympathetic division would be deactivated. There would also be many other effects, since ACh is the transmitter for the other division of the ANS and also for voluntary muscles.

Cell bodies in the sympathetic ganglia send out axons that make contact with or synapse on the stomach, heart, adrenal medulla, and other glands and muscles throughout the body. Axons that leave the sympathetic ganglia and synapse on the organs and muscles of the body are called **postganglionic**. Impulses in the postganglionic axons cause the telodendria to secrete the transmitter substance norepinephrine. Norepinephrine, the postganglionic transmitter, acts on the organs, glands, and muscles to increase heart rate and blood pressure; release glucose from the liver; release additional epinephrine and norepinephrine from the adrenal medulla; and cause other responses that prepare the body for action. Theoretically, you could deactivate the

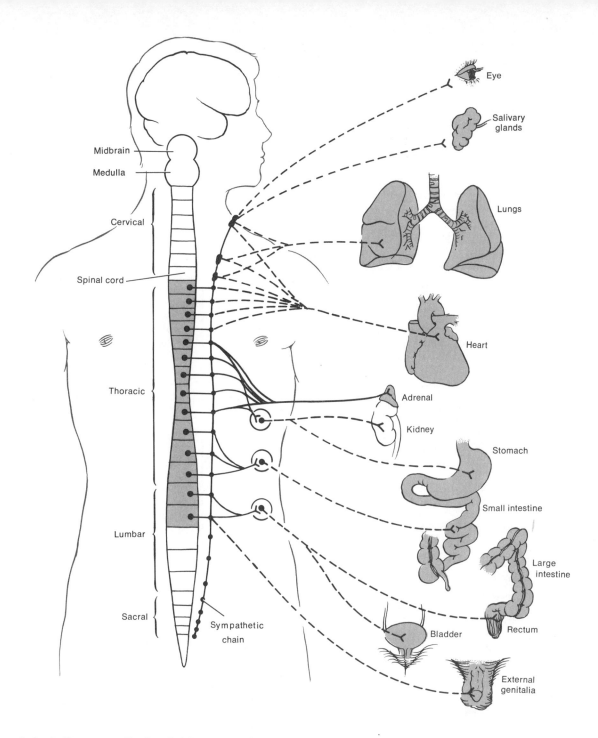

Figure 4–3 In the sympathetic division, nerve impulses leave the spinal cord from the thoracicolumbar region. These impulses travel in short preganglionic fibers (solid lines) to the sympathetic ganglia that lie parallel to the spinal cord. Long postganglionic fibers (broken lines) then travel to muscles and glands to prepare the body for action.

sympathetic division by destroying or blocking either the preganglionic transmitter ACh (although this would have many other effects) or the postganglionic transmitter norepinephrine.

If the sympathetic division were deactivated, you would have difficulty responding to stress or emotions, since there would be no increase in blood pressure, heart rate, or release of epinephrine. Without these physiological changes that enable the body to respond to stress, you might faint or go into shock. If you told a lie with your sympathetic division deactivated, you would still feel some guilt or nervousness, but the guilt you felt could not cause physiological arousal if the sympathetic division were deactivated. If no physiological arousal accompanied a lie, the polygraph would record no change in heart rate, blood pressure, or breathing. Thus, the answer to the question, could a drug that deactivates the sympathetic division make it possible to fool a lie detector, is "Possibly, yes." However, the

Sympathetic Division

"VOICE STRESS ANALYZER" USED TO TEST TRUTHFULNESS IN PRESIDENTIAL DEBATES

The Ford campaign used a controversial machine called a "voice stress analyzer" to try to audit Jimmy Carter's truthfulness in the first two presidential debates, a Republican National Committee official said Saturday.

In the process, the machine's manufacturer told a reporter, he found that President Ford's voice registered "heavy stress" each time he mentioned the word "Congress."

For undisclosed reasons, the President Ford Committee chose not to publicize the result of the Carter or Ford analyses.

"Obviously, whatever they found in those recordings was not used," Peter B. Teeley, a committee spokesman, said.

Eddie Mahe, Jr., executive director of the Republican National Committee, said he and Stuart Spencer, the deputy campaign director, had been reluctant to publicize the Carter results because "this was the kind of thing that can whip around on you and blow up on you 14 ways from Sunday."

The maker of the device, Rick Bennett of the Seattle suburb of Issaquah, said he had hoped to have the Carter results publicized before the election, contending that it would have changed the outcome.

Bennett refused to detail his findings Saturday, saying that in the post election period 51% of the voters —those who voted for the President-elect—had a "vested interest" in Carter and that disclosure might destroy his fledgling manufacturing enterprise.

When asked why Ford had shown heavy stress whenever he mentioned the word "Congress" during the Sept. 23 and Oct. 6 debates, Bennett said he believed the President's tension reflected difficulty of dealing with a House and Senate dominated by Democrats. For that reason, he said, he urged publicizing the finding.

However, Spencer feared that voters would view Ford's stress as meaning that if elected he could not work with a Congress certain to be Democratic and for that reason preferred silence, Bennett said in a phone interview.

If the Ford campaign had contended that the machine impugned Carter's truthfulness or verified Ford's, questions about the voice analysis technique might have been raised.

Voice analyzers are supposed to measure giveaway modulations in the human voice when a lie is told. By 1974 more than 500 of the machines were being used by police agencies and private organizations here and abroad. The principal producer was Dektor Counterintelligence and Security, Inc., of Springfield, Va.

The Army, which owned three of the devices, had a study made by a Fordham University psychologist. In a report in February, 1974, the Army said the study indicated a "clear inferiority of voice analysis . . . not only to the polygraph, but also to judgments made on the basis of simply observing subjects' behavior."

Last year, New York writer George O'Toole, who used electronic equipment to make analyses for the CIA for three years, contended that his tests with a voice stress analyzer had shown that Lee Harvey Oswald told the truth when he said he had not killed President John F. Kennedy.

Bennett said the devices were "very reliable." One "proof," he said, was that in his six months in business he had sold more than 50 of them with an unconditional guarantee of a refund of the $1,500 purchase price and no one had asked for a refund.

The Washington connection began last month when Roger McLoughlin of Denver, a vice president of Bennett's firm, told a former Ford aide that Bennett had monitored Carter's voice and had obtained "damning information."

As Mahe tells it, McLoughlin contacted him to offer to do an analysis, free of charge, of stress registered in tapes of Carter's voice in the first two debates. "McLoughlin was particularly aggressive, wanting to get exposure and to get to the press," Mahe said.

Mahe recalled being skeptical, saying it would not surprise him if stress showed in men whose "goals, ambitions, dreams" rode on their performance in the debates.

But it "sure as hell wasn't my business to make the decision," he said, and so he put the matter before Spencer.

The upshot was that on Oct. 20, McLoughlin and Bennet demonstrated the machine in Spencer's office, then at the Republican National Committee. They spent about 12 hours reviewing debate tapes. They underlined sections of the transcripts where the needle on the machine swung, purportedly showing Carter to be under stress.

The next day—the eve of the final debate on Oct. 22—Mahe sent the underlined transcript to Spencer. The response of the Ford campaign official was silence.

SOURCE: Morton Mintz, *Washington Post*, November 7, 1976. Copyright © 1976 by The Washington Post.

effects of such a drug would be devastating, because it would render you incapable of responding appropriately to stress.

Parasympathetic Division

Taking a lie detector test would probably cause you to feel anxious. After you completed the test, it would take some time before the anxious feeling left and your heart rate, blood pressure, and other responses returned to a normal or relaxed state. To help your heart rate and blood pressure return to a relaxed state, there is a division of the autonomic nervous system (ANS) called the **parasympathetic division**. Thus, the ANS has two divisions: the sympathetic division, that prepares the body for action in times of stress or emotions, and the parasympathetic division, that helps the body return to a relaxed state and conserve energy.

During feelings of anxiety or stress, your heart rate is increased by the sympathetic division. As you return to a relaxed state, your heart rate is slowed by the action of the parasympathetic division. The parasympathetic impulses to the heart and other organs are carried by axons that leave either the brain stem, or cranial area, or the very bottom, or sacral area, of the spinal cord. Thus, the parasympathetic division is called **craniosacral** while the sympathetic division is called **thoracicolumbar**.

To slow down the heart, an impulse travels along axons that leave the cranial area and go to a ganglion near the heart. Axons that travel to the parasympathetic ganglia are called **preganglionic**. Impulses in these preganglionic axons cause the telodendria to secrete the transmitter, ACh on neurons in the parasympathetic ganglia. From the ganglia, axons travel to and make contact with the heart muscle. These axons are called **postganglionic**, and impulses in them cause the telodendria to secrete ACh on the heart muscle. In the parasympathetic division, the chemical transmitter for both pre- and postganglionic axons is the same: ACh. In addition to controlling the heart, the parasympathetic division controls many other organs and muscles, as shown in Figure 4–4. For each of these organs or muscles there are preganglionic axons that leave the craniosacral area of the spinal cord and travel to the parasympathetic ganglia near the target organ. Postganglionic axons leave the parasympathetic ganglia to make contact with and control the target organ.

Following periods of stress or emotion, the parasympathetic division is activated to slow the heart, lower blood pressure, and return the body to a relaxed state. When you are eating, it is the parasympathetic division that stimulates the stomach to digest the food. When you urinate or defecate, parasympathetic neurons are involved in emptying the bladder or bowel. Automatically, without your conscious control, the parasympathetic and sympathetic divisions control various organs and muscles throughout the body.

Homeostasis

Your heart rate and blood pressure are increased by the sympathetic and decreased by the parasympathetic division. Digestion is stimulated by the parasympathetic and inhibited by the sympathetic division. Many glands, organs, and muscles throughout your body are controlled by both divisions of the ANS. These two divisions work together to maintain your blood pressure, heart rate, digestion, temperature, and bodily fluids in proper balance for optimum functioning. Maintaining your body's internal environment in a state of optimal functioning is called **homeostasis**. The internal environment can be upset by a virus, infection, cold, or flu or by psychological stressors such as anger, rage, or anxiety. The autonomic nervous system responds to these stressors by trying to maintain homeostasis. Responses of the ANS may include shivering to warm the body when you are cold; perspiring to cool the body when you are hot; secreting hormones to regulate metabolism; and raising the heart rate and blood pressure and releasing adrenalin when you are angry. When the body can no longer maintain homeostasis, tissue damage may occur—for example, frost bite, heat stroke, ulcers, or various vascular problems, such as high blood pressure.

Muscle Control

Under a microscope the muscular lining of your stomach looks very different from the muscle of your leg. The muscle of your legs or arms looks striped and is called **striated muscle**. You can control striated muscles. You can quickly and voluntarily move your fingers, legs, lips, and tongue because these are striated muscles controlled by neurons in the motor cortex.

The muscles lining your stomach as well as those controlling urination and defecation have no stripes and are called **smooth muscle**. Neither smooth nor striated, the muscle that comprises your heart is simply called **heart muscle**. The muscular lining of the stomach, the heart muscle, and the muscles involved in urination and defecation; and various glands (sweat, tear, salivary) are not controlled by neurons in the motor cortex and so are not under voluntary control. Instead, the heart muscle and smooth muscles are under reflexive control by the two divisions of the ANS. You may think that the belly dancer has learned to control her smooth stomach muscle voluntarily. What she is actually doing is controlling the abdominal muscles, which are striated. However, with training, it may be possible to gain some degree of voluntary control over some smooth muscles.

Voluntary Control and Yogis

You probably have very little voluntary control over the muscles and glands controlled by the ANS. There are some

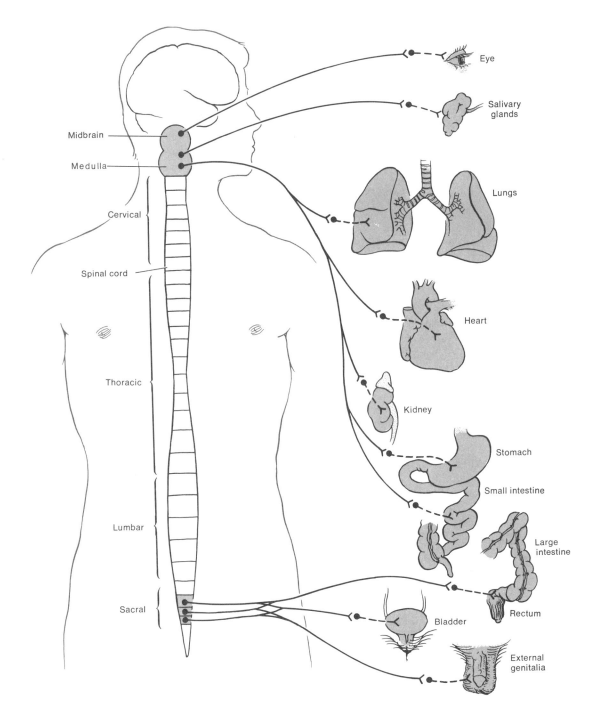

Figure 4–4 In the parasympathetic division, nerve impulses leave the central nervous system from the cranio-sacral region. These impulses travel in long preganglionic fibers (solid lines) to ganglia located on or near the organ to be controlled. Short postganglionic fibers (broken lines) make contact with muscles and glands that help the body conserve energy.

people who seem to have more. It is reported that some yogis can voluntarily increase their heart rate from a normal 75 beats a minute to 300 or voluntarily slow it to 50 per minute; can cause one side of the hand to warm and one side to cool; can hold one hand in very cold water without any physiological signs of being uncomfortable; and can lower the body metabolism to well below normal levels (4–2, 4–8). Apparently some yogis have learned to control parts of their autonomic nervous system voluntarily.

Few scientists believed that yogis could directly control their ANS responses until Neal Miller and his associates reported that rats could learn to control directly their heart rate and blood pressure (4–7). However, these data from rats have been questioned. Other scientists have not been able to train rats to exert voluntary control over their heart rate, blood pressure, or other ANS responses. At present it appears that yogis can but rats probably cannot control their ANS. Miller's research did raise the possibility that

Stress, Biofeedback, and Autonomic Nervous System

people might learn more control over their ANS. Being able to control the ANS would be extremely beneficial to those with medical problems such as hypertension (high blood pressure) or irregular heart rates. These patients might learn to lower their blood pressure or control irregular heart beat voluntarily, reducing or eliminating the need for medications.

Biofeedback

During Harold's physical for his new job, it was discovered that he had hypertension or high blood pressure. One probable cause is the constant stress from his continual worrying. A possible treatment for him would be to learn to control his ANS.

Harold sits quietly in a chair with a cuff around his arm to measure blood pressure. The cuff is attached to a machine that will signal when his blood pressure goes down. Normally there is some fluctuation in blood pressure, and whenever his blood pressure drops a little, a light comes on. His task is to make some response to keep the light on as much as possible. The machine is used to magnify and display the blood pressure changes for Harold because these changes otherwise may be too small for him to notice. Being made aware of the physiological changes occurring

in your body is called **biofeedback**. Clammy hands, pounding heart, or dry mouth are examples of bodily functions you probably do notice, and your awareness of them is an example of biofeedback that does not require instrumentation. Achieving awareness, often with help from instruments, is the first phase of the biofeedback procedure.

The second phase is learning to control these responses. With continued practice, Harold gradually learns to make a response to keep the light on. Studies show that although he is learning to lower his blood pressure, he may not be able to explain exactly what response he is making (4–2). Each time he makes some response to lower his blood pressure as indicated by the light, he has a feeling of success. The light and the feeling of success are called **reinforcements**. This sequence of making some response (lowering blood pressure) to receive a reinforcement (light on and feeling of success) is called **operant conditioning**. Operant conditioning involves learning to make a certain response more and more frequently to obtain some reinforcement. After a number of operant conditioning sessions, Harold will learn to keep the light on for longer and longer periods, which means that he will be learning to lower his blood pressure. Studies on patients with hypertension and with normal blood pressure have reported that both groups can learn to lower their blood pressure 5–15% in 10–20 one-hour sessions (4–2).

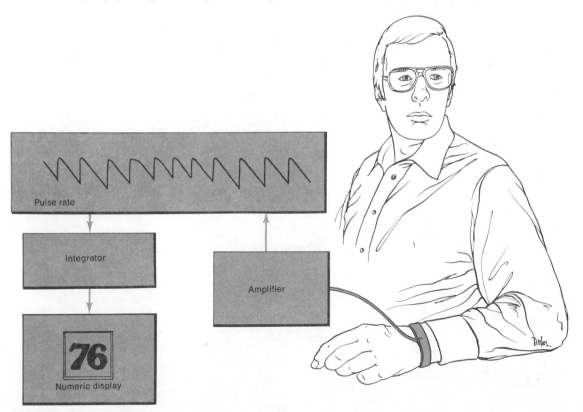

Figure 4–5 In biofeedback training, an involuntary response such as pulse rate, which is controlled by the autonomic nervous system (ANS), is recorded, amplified, and shown to the subject. He then tries to think or imagine something in order to increase or decrease the pulse rate, depending upon which result is desired.

Meditation

Using biofeedback and operant conditioning, Harold can try to control his blood pressure independently of other bodily responses. Or, instead of trying to control a specific bodily function, such as blood pressure, he can try to relax his entire body. Relaxation of his whole body would lead to a lowering of his blood pressure. There is evidence that learning relaxation, yoga, or meditation does enable you to relax and lower such responses as blood pressure and heart rate (4–2).

During relaxation or meditation exercises, you are generally trying to slow the sympathetic division and activate the parasympathetic division of the ANS. When Harold was learning to lower his blood pressure through biofeedback, perhaps he was not affecting just blood pressure. Perhaps he was depressing activity in the whole sympathetic division and increasing activity in the parasympathetic. If this were true, then a decrease in blood pressure during biofeedback would always be accompanied by a decrease in heart rate. But in fact, there is evidence that Harold would be able to learn to raise his blood pressure without affecting heart rate or to raise and lower heart rate without affecting blood pressure (4–12). This evidence suggests that you can learn control over one specific organ without having to change the entire sympathetic or parasympathetic division. If you had an irregular heart rate you would want to eliminate this symptom without affecting other functions, such as blood pressure.

Treatment without Drugs

There have been reports of success—varying from little to considerable—for patients using biofeedback and operant conditioning to lower blood pressure, eliminate irregular heart rate, lower heart rate, reduce occurrence of migraine headaches, and reduce asthma attacks. There also have been reports of patients succeeding in doing the above using relaxation exercises or meditation. While meditation, relaxation, or biofeedback can help you learn to control ANS responses, one of these procedures may help you more than another (4–2). Studies show that one problem with using these techniques is that certain people are better at learning

Figure 4–6 In meditation the individual tries to calm and relax the body, which is another way of saying that the person is trying to deactivate the sympathetic division and activate the parasympathetic division.(©Suzanne Arms / Jeroboam, Inc.)

Stress, Biofeedback, and Autonomic Nervous System

to control their ANS responses than others, and no one yet knows what accounts for the difference (4–19). To use any of the techniques for ANS control you must be very motivated, because these techniques take much time and require more effort than taking a pill (4–12). Even so, it is not known whether high levels of motivation can overcome the fact that some people seem better than others at learning control over ANS responses. Another problem is that, after learning to lower blood pressure with biofeedback, relaxation, or meditation, it is difficult for some patients to transfer this learning to stressful job or home situations (4–12). Despite these difficulties, biofeedback techniques are being used with some success to treat a range of medical problems, from migraine headaches, to irregular heart rate, to high blood pressure, to tension and coping with stress (4–5).

Stress Response

In his new job, Harold is constantly worrying about accepting a bad check, giving the wrong change, or overcharging a customer. Each of these worries causes him to feel stressed and in turn causes his body to initiate a stress response. His body's response to stress always is basically the same, whether it results from his being accused of stealing or his being promoted to store manager. Both situations, pleasant and unpleasant, are stressors because they demand that he make some adjustment to a new situation. If accused of stealing, he must defend himself; if promoted, he must assume new responsibilities. Even though he may feel fear when accused of stealing and feel joy when told of his promotion, these opposite emotional experiences may cause the same kind of stress response (4–14). Each stressor, whether pleasant or unpleasant, causes the following series of reactions known as the **stress response**.

1 The accusation of stealing or news of promotion are interpreted by Harold's brain as being *stressful* because either situation places new demands on him.

2 Many areas of Harold's brain are involved in interpreting the situation as stressful. One of these areas, the hypothalamus, is thought to activate the sympathetic division of the ANS.

3 Once activated, the sympathetic division automatically initiates a series of responses that prepare the body to deal with stress.

4 The sympathetic division, by way of the preganglionic axons, sympathetic ganglia, and postganglionic axons, increases the heart rate and blood pressure and causes the adrenal medulla to release epinephrine and norepinephrine. These hormones travel through the blood stream causing the heart to beat faster, blood pressure to rise, and glucose to be released from the liver. Glucose is used by muscles during exertion and is a source of energy for neurons in the brain.

5 In addition to activating the sympathetic division, the hypothalamus also stimulates the anterior pituitary, that is located immediately below the hypothalamus. In response to stress, the hypothalamus sends releasing factors through blood vessels to the anterior pituitary, which causes the release of other hormones.

6 When activated by releasing factors from the hypothalamus, the anterior pituitary releases adrenocorticotropic hormone, or ACTH. ACTH travels through the blood stream to the adrenal cortex, the outside part of the adrenal gland.

7 ACTH causes the adrenal cortex to release a number of hormones called **corticoids**: **glucocorticoids** and **mineralcorticoids.**

8 Among their other effects, the glucocorticoids raise the level of glucose in the blood and the mineralcorticoids help regulate the level of sodium and potassium in the body. These corticoids are so critical that if the adrenal cortex were not functioning, a person would die if severely stressed.

Each time Harold is stressed, these eight steps occur, often without his awareness. These eight steps involve two different mechanisms: one is the activation of the sympathetic division, which prepares the body for action; the second is the hypothalamus stimulating the anterior pituitary to release ACTH, which prepares the body to deal with the stress. Because Harold is a worrier and interprets many situations as stressful, the eight-step response occurs many times throughout his day.

Stressors

If the sound in a record shop were increased until it was painful, everyone in the store would be stressed by the noise and the eight-step response would occur. There are some stressors that would probably cause the eight-step stress response to occur in everyone: extremely loud noise, intense cold, falling from a cliff, profuse bleeding, or being run over by a car. Whether an upcoming test or a long-sought-after date or getting stopped by a police car are stressful and cause the stress response depend upon how you evaluate the situation (4–6). An upcoming test might produce little stress for a graduating senior and produce extreme stress for a sophomore on academic probation.

Experiences as different as extreme heat and the news that a good friend has been killed would probably produce the eight-step stress response. Because very different kinds of events can initiate the same eight-step response, it is called a **nonspecific response** to stress. People also have specific responses to stress. At the news of a friend's death, one person may break out in a rash while another may get headaches. The same stressor may result in different *specific responses* (rash, headaches) in different individuals. The kind of specific response you develop to stress depends upon your genetic background, conditioning, diet, sex, and age (4–15). When you respond to extreme stress, there will

Figure 4–7 The girl on the left has just won a Miss Teenage America contest, while the one on the right has just lost. Although the winning girl is extremely happy and the losing girl is very sad, many of their internal responses, which are under control of the ANS, are approximately the same. Winning and losing are both stressful situations, causing the body's stress responses to be activated. (Wide World Photos.)

be a nonspecific response (eight-step stress response) and a specific response (rash, headaches) that depends upon your individual makeup.

Stages of Stress

Alarm

Thinking about starting a new job or taking a final examination is stressful. During the initial response to stress, the body is said to be in the **alarm stage**. During the alarm stage, the eight-step response prepares the body to deal with stress. If you adjust to your new job or do well on the final exam, the stress decreases and the alarm stage ends.

Resistance

If you have trouble on your new job or fail the final exam, the stress may persist and cause the body to enter the **re-**

sistance stage of the stress reaction. During the resistance stage, the adrenal cortex and medulla lower their hormonal output ·and the body appears to be handling the prolonged stress. But all is not well. With these hormone levels suppressed during prolonged stress, you may become more susceptible to colds, flu, or other infectious diseases. Also, if stress persists during the resistance stage, various organs in the body may be damaged. The diseases that one gets during prolonged stress are said to be **psychosomatic**. For Harold, the psychosomatic ailment was hypertension. It could have been ulcers, migraine headaches, colitis, or allergies.

Psychosomatic Disease

It would have been difficult to predict beforehand that Harold would develop hypertension rather than ulcers or migraines in response to prolonged stress. There is evidence that it is not the kind of stress that determines which organ will be attacked. Rather, it is the vulnerability of the organ

Stress, Biofeedback, and Autonomic Nervous System

NO *DEUS EX MACHINA*

Bio-feedback was once hailed as "the single greatest development in the history of psychology." The development of new machines in the '60s offered the possibility of monitoring one's own brain waves, heartbeat, blood pressure, body temperature and other involuntary body functions. The theory: the buzzes, lights or other indicators of biofeedback machines instantly report the body's reaction to thoughts or feelings. Once a patient discovers, for example, which feelings or tensions are associated with a warning buzz or light in the machine, he can learn by trial and error to shift his thoughts or relax his tensions and thereby avoid the warning.

Suddenly, all things seemed possible. Joe Kamiya, a pioneer of biofeedback training, thought "people will soon control phobias and anxieties." Psychopharmacologist Barbara Brown (*New Mind, New Body*) predicted a drastic drop in the use of medication and the number of hospitals within a decade. Among other heady predictions bio-feedback would eliminate the need for psychotherapy, provide a foolproof birth control method (by teaching males to lower their scrotal temperatures), produce superathletes, prove the reality of ESP and enable mankind to solve problems during sleep by "programming dreams."

Mixed Results. With that kind of buildup, a letdown was almost inevitable. "Impossible expectations have been raised." Physiological Psychologist Neal Miller of Rockefeller University, a leader in feedback research, told a New York symposium last week. Indeed, actual gains have been modest. Researchers have helped some incontinent patients to gain control of their urination and defecation through biofeedback. Among other researchers, Dr. John Basmaijian, a professor of anatomy and rehabilitation medicine at Emory University, reports success in eliminating foot drop—difficulty in raising the foot while walking—though efforts to extend the technique to cerebral palsy victims have failed.

The most common experiments—to lower blood pressure and end migraine headaches—have had mixed results. Bio-feedback clearly can affect blood pressure. In one experiment, baboons were trained to maintain a large increase in pressure for 40 days. However, attempts to lower human blood pressure have generally not been significant or lasting outside the laboratory. Despite claims of 80% success, migraine research has been a headache for some bio-feedback experimenters because of the placebo effect—a certain number of ailments vanish, not as a result of bio-feedback but simply because the patient has faith in the method. Says Miller: "Many of these headaches would have disappeared if the patients were treated with extract of watermelon."

The inflated hopes for bio-feedback may have been related to the growth of interest in Eastern mysticism. Glowingly described by fans as "electronic yoga," bio-feedback seemed to offer inner exploration without drugs, religion or psychotherapy. The revelation that biofeedback machines could monitor the brain's alpha waves—associated with relaxation and meditation—led to the proliferation of "alpha" institutes and training centers, many of them now defunct. "Getting high on alpha" peaked in 1973, when some colleges offered credit for alpha experience.

Limited Acceptance. One problem was that "electronic yoga" was upstaged by other marketable versions of yoga—Transcendental Meditation, for example—that do not require relatively expensive machines. Another has been the sheer quackery of some promoters who were quick to jump on the bio-feedback bandwagon, and the limitations of the equipment for home use. According to Brain Researcher Robert Ornstein, "Commercial machines are not good enough to get alpha feedback, and certainly wouldn't help a person much. They might be fun."

With the faddish phase of biofeedback over, serious researchers are continuing to inch ahead, recording small but solid gains and winning limited acceptance from the medical establishment. In Ornstein's words, bio-feedback still "needs a lot of work." Says Thomas Mulholland, former president of the Bio-Feedback Research Society and head of the Psychophysiology Laboratory at the Bedford, Mass., Veterans Administration Hospital: "It is one technique, and not the kind that will lead to a great theoretical breakthrough. I would say bio-feedback will have arrived when it is unobtrusive again and taken for granted as one method in the stream."

itself that results in its eventual damage from prolonged stress (4–6). Possibly Harold was born with a circulatory system that was disposed toward hypertension. Or his circulatory system may have developed some problem while he was growing up. Or he may have learned to raise his blood pressure through operant conditioning, without his even being aware of what he was doing. Neal Miller suggests that this psychosomatic disease, hypertension, might develop in the following way.

As a child, Harold was afraid to go to school. His fear activated the sympathetic division of the ANS, which, among other responses, constricted peripheral blood vessels and caused his face to turn white from fear. His mother noticed the paleness and, sympathizing with Harold, let him stay home. Harold began to turn pale every time he was afraid or angry, and each time his mother responded to his paleness by giving him his way (reinforcement). Harold made a response (paleness) and got a reinforcement (his way), which is an example of operant conditioning. Harold learned through operant conditioning to control his ANS, specifically his circulatory system, without having any awareness that he was doing so. Having learned this response, he continued through the years to become pale and to control his circulatory system in response to many different fearful situations. He still was unaware that he was controlling his circulatory response. Finally, the response became so frequent that he developed hypertension. Now when Harold worries about all the psychosomatic diseases he may yet develop, he turns very pale and his hypertension becomes worse.

Your Own Response

Other than hypertension, there are a number of diseases that can be caused or made worse by prolonged stress: allergies, asthma attacks, ulcers, heart diseases, and intestinal colitis (4–1). If you are the type of person who is very aggressive, competitive, and ambitious and who desires to have everything in a very short time, your chances of developing a coronary heart attack are twice as great as someone who feels no pressing urgency and is willing to wait for what he wants. The first type of personality has been called **Type A** and the second, **Type B** (4–11). Compared with a Type B, the person with a Type A personality has double the chance for coronary heart disease, apparently because of the constant stress from this way of life.

If a job is stressing and also calls for great responsibility, the result can be higher risk and earlier onset of hypertension and high incidence of ulcers, as found in air traffic controllers (4–3, 4–4). There is some evidence that major changes in your life, such as marriage, divorce, death of a spouse, or change in job—which are all stressors—can increase your chance of developing a disease (4–9). Just how stressful a situation will be, to a large extent depends upon how stressful you think it is. Others may or may not perceive your situation as stressful, but what determines your physiological response is whether you perceive it as

threatening, harmful, or anxiety-producing (4–6). If you perceive the situation as stressful and continue to perceive it as stressful over a long period of time, the result can be a breakdown in a particular organ.

Exhaustion

If Harold continued year after year to interpret his job as being very stressful, his hypertension might lead to heart disease serious enough to cause his death. The final stage of stress is called **exhaustion**. The physiological state in the exhaustion stage is similar to what it was in the alarm stage in that the eight-step response occurs again. However, in the exhaustion stage the body's defenses cannot cope with the continued stress, and death follows. Physiological stressors do not often lead to the exhaustion stage because the stressed person feels pain or distress during the resistance stage and seeks help. However, exhaustion and death can occur from prolonged physiological stressors such as being stranded in the desert or adrift in the ocean without any provisions. If you died from exposure in the desert, and an autopsy were conducted, the coroner would find certain evidence of stress: an adrenal gland that was enlarged because it had produced so much hormone; shrunken thymus, spleen, and lymph glands that had been involved in producing antibodies to ward off infection; and some breakdown in body organs, perhaps ulcers. These last three symptoms are characteristic of what happens to the body during the exhaustion stage.

General Adaptation Syndrome

The three stages of stress—alarm, resistance, and exhaustion—were identified and named the **general adaptation syndrome (GAS)** by Hans Selye (4–13, 4–14). Most stressors do not last long enough to go beyond the alarm stage. If the stressor does persist, the body enters the resistance stage, when psychosomatic disease may appear. If the stressor persists even longer, exhaustion and death may follow. The stages of the GAS were first identified in animals, but it is thought that the process is similar in humans.

Coping with Stress

There are some stressors—intense cold, extremely loud noises, prolonged diarrhea, jumping out of a burning building—that are stressful to almost everyone. **Physical** stressors such as these are usually difficult to cope with. There are other kinds of stressors—exams, jobs, personal problems—that are **psychological** stressors, and you can learn to cope with them if you can identify them. That is, by studying very hard for an exam, taking some action to make the job better, or reinterpreting your personal problems as less serious, you can make the situation less stressful. There is evidence that if you interpret or think of the event as

Stress, Biofeedback, and Autonomic Nervous System

being less stressful, your body's physiological stress responses will be lessened. For example, in cases where parents denied the seriousness of their children's having leukemia, the parents showed evidence of less stress than parents who did not deny the seriousness of their children's disease. More specifically, the parents who coped with this stress (leukemia) by denying its seriousness showed less evidence of ACTH secretion than parents who did not cope by denying (4–17).

There is debate over which methods to use in coping with stress. The stress of a final exam could be lessened by studying very hard and enabling yourself to say, "I have nothing to worry about." Thus, coping with stress can be a combination of taking action (studying) and reevaluating the stressor (I'm not worried). But what relieves stress in one person (studying) may cause more stress in another (the more I study, the more I worry). Exactly which coping or defensive methods will be effective against stress depends upon the individual's personality. Harold is now worried about whether he has adopted the best possible defensive or coping behaviors. Harold has missed the point.

Comment

Whether you are relaxed or stressed, your autonomic nervous system is functioning automatically. Usually without your awareness, the ANS regulates many physiological responses to prepare your body for action, or calm it down. The action of the ANS helps maintain the body in homeostasis. Stressing events set off a series of eight physiological steps that prepare the body to deal with the stress. If the stressful situation persists, the stress response itself can cause damage to organs throughout the body. Biofeedback, meditation, and relaxation procedures are being used to help people deal with problems that are caused by stress. When your head thinks "stress," the physiological responses that follow tell your heart and other body organs what your head is thinking.

SELF-TEST 4

1   There are many brain areas activated by feelings of anxiety or guilt, and one of these areas is thought to be the _____ .

hypothalamus

2   After telling a lie, you might feel guilt, which could affect the hypothalamus, which in turn is thought to activate or trigger the _____ division of the ANS.

sympathetic

3   When the sympathetic division is activated during worry, emotions, or stress, it prepares the body for action by causing _____ heart rate and blood pressure; release of _____ ; diversion of blood from intestines to _____ muscle; and activation of the adrenal _____ and _____ glands.

increased / glucose
striated / medulla
sweat

4   The sympathetic division causes the adrenal medulla to secrete two hormones called _____ and _____ , which intensify the sympathetic responses.

epinephrine
norepinephrine

5   If you were accused of cheating on a test, the sympathetic division would activate many physiological responses. These responses would occur _____ and probably without your notice, because normally you do not have much _____ over responses of the ANS.

automatically or
reflexively or immediately
control

6   The theory behind the lie detector test is, that after telling a lie, you feel some emotion like guilt that activates the sympathetic division, that produces _____ responses you cannot control.

physiological

7   When asked a loaded question, you may feel guilty, anxious, nervous, or embarrassed, even though you answer with the truth. Therefore, there is no machine that can detect lies, as such. Rather, the polygraph detects physiological responses primarily regulated by the _____ division.

sympathetic

8   One of the measures of how nervous or aroused you are involves measuring how easily a tiny electrical current passes through the skin. This response is now called the _____ , abbreviated _____ .

skin resistance response
SRR

9   If you wanted to deactivate the sympathetic division for research purposes, you could destroy the spinal cord in the _____ area, from which the sympathetic axons originate.

thoracicolumbar

10 A few inches from the spinal cord, a chain composed of ganglia runs parallel to the spinal cord. The ganglia on this chain are called the _____ ganglia.

sympathetic

11 Sympathetic axons that leave the spinal cord and synapse with the sympathetic ganglia are called _____ axons. They secrete _____ as a transmitter.

preganglionic /
acetylcholine or ACh

12 Sympathetic axons that leave the ganglia and go to synapse with the organs and glands in the body are called _____ axons and secrete _____ as a transmitter.

postganglionic /
norepinephrine

13 The parasympathetic division is called the _____ division because it originates in the brainstem (cranium) and in the sacral region of the spinal cord.

craniosacral

14 Parasympathetic axons leave the spinal cord and go to synapse with ganglia located near the organs and glands in the body. These axons are called _____ and secrete _____ as a transmitter.

preganglionic /
acetycholine or ACh

15 Axons that leave the parasympathetic ganglia and synapse with the actual organs and glands in the body are called _____ axons and secrete _____ as a transmitter.

postganglionic/
acetylcholine or ACh

16 After an emotional upset, the parasympathetic division would help you calm down and relax by slowing _____ rate and lowering _____ pressure. In addition, this division is also involved in stimulating _____ , urination, and _____ , and other _____ processes important in maintaining the body's resources.

heart / blood / digestion
defecation / metabolic

17 Many of the glands and organs in the body are regulated by both the sympathetic and parasympathetic divisions. These two divisions help maintain your body in an optimum state called _____ .

homeostasis

18 Normally, you cannot directly control your stomach, which is composed of _____ muscle, or your heart, which is composed of _____ muscle, but you can voluntarily control your limbs, which are composed of _____ muscle.

smooth
heart
striated

19 Although it was once thought uncontrollable, there is evidence you can learn to control some responses regulated by the _____ system.

autonomic nervous

20 If you had an irregular heart rate, you could possibly learn to correct this symptom through the use of _____ and _____ conditioning.

biofeedback / operant

21 You might also learn to correct your irregular heart rate by learning to relax your entire body through practicing _____ .

relaxation or yoga or meditation

22 There is evidence that you can learn to lower your blood pressure using operant conditioning and biofeedback without affecting heart rate. This indicates that you have learned to control a _____ response rather than depress the entire _____ division.

specific or particular
sympathetic

23 There are some stimuli that only you respond to as stressful (a blind date), and there are other stimuli that are stressful for everyone (being hit by a bus). If a stimulus is stressful, your body will react with the _____ response.

eight-step

24 One part of the eight-step stress response involves the hypothalamus triggering the sympathetic division to prepare the body for action by _____ , _____ , _____ , and _____ . (Give four responses.)

increasing heart rate and blood pressure / releasing glucose / diverting blood / causing adrenal medulla to secrete hormones

25 Another part of the eight-step response involves the hypothalamus sending releasing factors via the blood supply to the _____ .

anterior pituitary

26 Releasing factors from the hypothalamus cause the anterior pituitary to secrete _____ , that travels through the blood stream to act on the _____ .

adrenocorticotropic hormone or ACTH
adrenal cortex

27 In response to ACTH, the adrenal cortex secretes hormones called corticoids that include _____ and _____ .

glucocorticoid
mineralcorticoid

28 If the adrenal cortex were damaged or removed, you might die if exposed to a _____ situation.

stressful

29 Stressors come and go throughout the day. The initial stage of stress is called the _____ phase and is characterized by the eight-step response.

alarm

30 If the stressor persists past the alarm stage the body is said to be in the _____ phase of the stress response.

resistance

31 If the stress persists during the resistance phase, there may be damage to a bodily organ, and this type of illness is called _____ disease.

psychosomatic

32 If you were trapped on a barren island with no provisions, the stress of exposure to the elements would lead to the last stage of stress, called _____ , which is followed by death.

exhaustion

33 The three stages of the stress reaction—alarm, resistance, and exhaustion—are called the _____

general adaptation syndrome

REFERENCES

4–1 Backus, F. I. and Dudley, D. L. Observations of psychosocial factors and their relationship to organic diseases. *International Journal of Psychiatry in Medicine* 1974, 5: 499–515.

4–2 Blanchard, E. B. and Young, L. D. Self-control of cardiac functioning: a promise as yet unfulfilled. *Psychological Bulletin* 1973, 79: 145–163.

4–3 Cobb, S. and Rose, R. Hypertension, peptic ulcer and diabetes in air traffic controllers. *Journal of the American Medical Association* 1973, 224: 489–492.

4–4 Grayson, R. R. Air controllers syndrome: peptic ulcer in air traffic controllers. *Illinois Medical Journal* 1972, 142: 111–115.

4–5 Katz, R. C. and Zlutnick, S. *Behavior therapy and health care: principles and applications*. New York: Pergamon, 1975.

4–6 Lazarus, R. S. Psychological stress and coping in adaptation and illness. *International Journal of Psychiatry in Medicine* 1974, 5: 321–333.

4–7 Miller, N. E. Learning of visceral and glandular responses. *Science* 1969, 163: 434–445.

4–8 Pines, M. *The brain changers*. New York: Harcourt, 1973.

4–9 Rabkin, J. G. and Struening. Life events, stress and illness. *Science* 1976, 194: 1013–1020.

4–10 Ray, W. J. The relationship of locus of control, self-report measures and feedback to the voluntary control of heart rate. *Psychophysiology* 1974, 11: 527–534.

4–11 Roseman, R. H. and Friedman, M. Neurogenic factors in pathogenesis of coronary heart disease. *Medical Clinics of North America* 1974, 58: 269–279.

4–12 Schwartz, G. E. Biofeedback as therapy. *American Psychologist* August 1973, 666–673.

4–13 Selye, H. Stress: it's a G.A.S. *Psychology Today* September 1969.

4–14 Selye, H. *Stress without distress*. New York: The New American Library, 1975.

4–15 Selye, H. *Stress in health and disease*. Boston: Butterworths, 1976.

4–16 Smith, B. M. The polygraph. *Scientific American* 1967, 216: 25–31.

4–17 Wolff, C. T., Friedman, S. B., Hofer, M. A., and Mason, J. W. Relationship between psychological defenses and mean urinary 17-hydroxycorticosteriod excretion rates: I and II. *Psychosomatic Medicine* 1964, 26, 576–609.

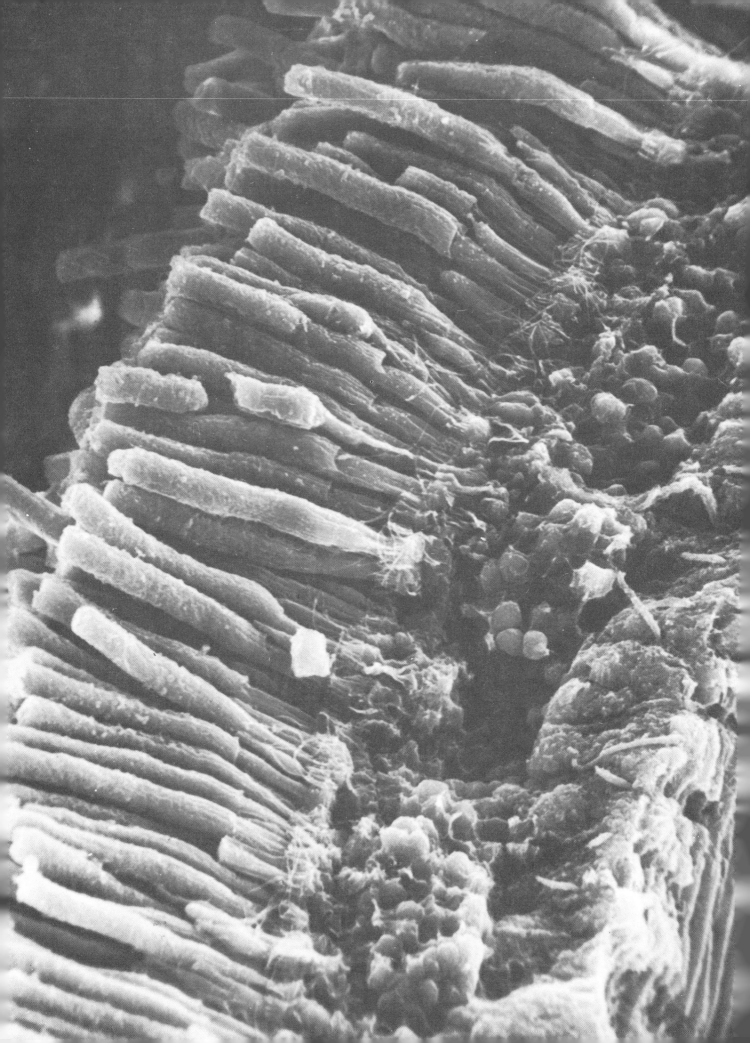

Seeing and Hearing 5

Why Your Eye Does Not Hear and Your Ear Does Not See

One Way of Sensing

It was a picture of three Roman gladiators. They were standing in an empty arena. Their faces showed no fear. Joan was staring at the picture as she had a hundred times before. One of the gladiators began to move. His head turned in her direction and he stared at her. The second gladiator walked out of the picture and stood at the far end of the room. The third began to swing his sword over his head. She knew she could reach out and touch them. She was terrified to move. The first gladiator spoke to her. Joan saw his mouth move. She saw him gesture in her direction. She replied that she could not hear him. She thought to ask them their names. She could hear herself asking them over and over to speak louder. She could hear them talking among themselves. There was a noise. They stopped talking. They stopped moving. She was looking at a picture of three gladiators, nothing more. She could not tell whether she had looked at the picture for minutes or hours.

There was that sound again. She felt it come into her ears. It was a lion's roar. It was a mountain of falling water. It was a friend calling her name, slowly and quietly. The sound filled her head. It was overpowering. Someone was calling her name in Spanish. She could not answer. Now it was peaceful. She saw nothing, heard nothing. She waited for sleep.

Some hours later the hallucinogenic drug wore off. When Joan woke up, she looked around the room. There was the picture of the gladiators. There was the sound of her cat meowing for its food. It all seemed so ordinary. She remembered seeing the gladiators and hearing her cat's meows sound like her name. It was too vivid to deny. Joan had seen what was not there and had heard what was not spoken.

Sensation and Perception

There are many ways to experience seeing and hearing. You can see something that is not actually there, such as a person walking out of a picture. This is called an **hallucination** or **delusion**. You can see a bird and think it is a plane or misread a traffic sign while looking right at it. This is called a **misperception**. You can find yourself seeing only food ads in a magazine when you are hungry or failing to see a friend walk by when thinking about a final exam. On the other hand, you may hear someone call your name even though you are at a noisy football game. These are all examples of **selective perception** or attention. Seeing or not seeing a friend or a food ad or a traffic sign or the thousands of other stimuli is influenced by your mood, mental state, motivation, and past learning experiences. When you look at a person's face, what you see is influenced by whether you love, hate, or like the person, by how the person has treated you in the past, by whether you are in a good, terrible, or depressed mood, by what happened the last time you saw the person, and hundreds of other things.

It may never be possible to experience stimuli, that is to see or hear or touch or smell, without bringing in your past and present learning and feelings. Stimuli that are colored by your mood, motivation, and past and present learning experiences are called **perceptions**. Either consciously or unconsciously, you are constantly coloring, filtering, and selecting stimuli from the world around you. You may have heard someone say he had a sensation of "floating space," or "absolute darkness," or "not being able to breathe," or "seeing someone for the first time." Since each of these experiences was probably colored by past and present learning—fear of darkness or not breathing or pleasure at seeing someone in a different way—they should actually be considered perceptions rather than sensations. A sensory experience would be considered a **sensation** if it were not colored by your past or present learning or feelings. However, it is likely that any sensory impulses that enter your brain automatically set off associations with previous learning and feelings. Therefore, it may be that no stimulus is ever experienced as a pure sensation. Certainly, in your day-to-day life, very few if any of your sensory experiences can be considered sensations in the technical sense. In some cases, such as experiencing a drug, a person's perceptions can be so distorted that she experiences an event as though it is actually happening, even though it is not and cannot happen. Hallucinations are probably the ultimate example of how your brain can use past and present learning to change ordinary stimuli. It will be easier to explain hallucinations if we first explain how Joan can look at a picture and identify three Roman gladiators in all their detail and color.

Vision

Light

As Joan looked at the picture, light waves that were reflected from it entered her eye. Light is a form of energy conceptualized by physicists as waves or as movement of particles, called **photons**. Photons are generated by a light source, such as the sun or a light bulb. Waves used in radio broadcast are approximately 550 m (one-third mi) long, while those used in x rays are only 118 nm (5 ten-millionths of an inch) long. You cannot see radio waves or x rays because these waves are either too long or too short to activate receptors in the eye. Waves you can see are called **light waves**. Usually, the length of light waves is expressed in **nanometers** (**nm**); one nm is one billionth of a meter. Light waves are from 380 to 760 nm (16–32 millionths of an inch) long.

The different pigments in the gladiator picture absorb some wave lengths and reflect others. The length of light wave reflected determines the color you see. The shortest visible light waves cause the color violet, and the longest visible light waves cause the color red. If the gladiators in the picture were wearing robes that reflected light waves 400 nm long, the color would be violet. If the reflected light waves were 600 to 700 nm, the color would be red. So it is the length and other properties of light waves that the visual system translates into three gladiators wearing red robes and standing in an empty arena.

There are three steps in turning light waves into gladiators:

1 Light waves must be converted into nerve impulses.

2 Nerve impulses must be sent to a certain area of the brain called the **visual cortex** or **Area 17**.

3 The visual cortex and other brain areas known as **association areas** organize and recognize the pattern of neural impulses as three gladiators.

Eye Structure

You have never seen an animal with square eyeballs, and for good reason. Light rays from a picture or from any other source tend to spread out in space before reaching the eye. As shown in Figure 5–1, the front of the eye is curved, and this curvature helps to gather and bend the scattered light waves into a concentrated beam. If the waves that reached the receptors in the back of your eye were scattered, the result would be a blurred image. As light waves enter the eye, the first structure they pass through is a curved transparent covering called the **cornea**. As light waves pass through the cornea, they are gathered together. The light waves gathered together by the cornea next pass through the pupil. The **pupil** is a hole in the center of a colored muscular disk known as the **iris**. The color of your eye comes from the color of the iris. By varying its shape, the iris controls the amount of light entering through the pupil. If Joan looks at the picture under bright lights, her pupil constricts to let in less light. If she looks at the picture in dim light, her pupil opens or **dilates** to let in more light.

Lens

At this point in the process, the light waves passing through the pupil have not yet been sufficiently focused to provide a clear image. Looking at Figure 5–1, you can see that these light waves next pass through the **lens**. If you have ever operated a slide projector or focused a camera, you know that you must adjust the lens to see the picture clearly. As a projector or camera lens is adjusted, it bends or gathers light waves to focus them on a screen. Similarly, the lens in your eye is adjusted to focus light waves on the receptors at the back of your eye. Adjustments in the shape of your lens are controlled by tiny muscles called **ciliary** (SILL-ee-airy) muscles. When you look at something up close, these muscles cause the lens to become thick in shape and to focus the light waves very sharply. When you look at something in the distance, they make the lens flat, and it focuses the light waves less sharply. In this way, light waves are focused on the area at the back of your eye called the **retina**. The retina contains the receptors that change light waves into nerve impulses.

If the light waves that strike the retina are not focused into a concentrated beam, the result is blurred vision that must be corrected with glasses. As shown in Figure 5–2, people who are nearsighted have unusually long eyeballs, which means that the light waves are focused just in front of the retina. People who are farsighted have unusually short eyeballs, so that the point of focus is behind the retina. Glasses and contact lenses are artificial lenses that help the lenses in people's eyes to focus light waves directly on the retina. As people grow old, the lenses in their eyes become less elastic and cannot thicken enough to focus light waves from near objects on their retinas. Many older people are farsighted, but this condition can be corrected with glasses. If the lens becomes cloudy through disease or injury, the

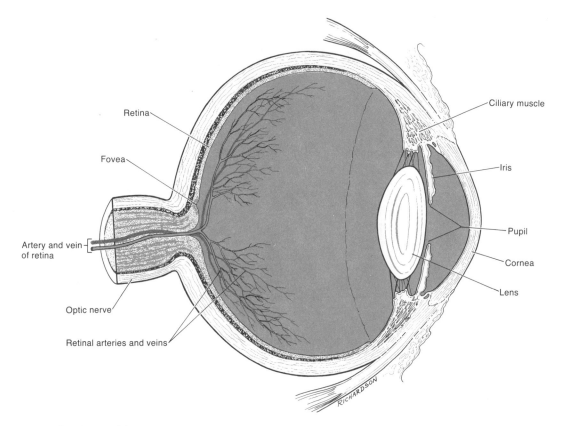

Figure 5-1 The structure of the eye.

result is blurred vision and a condition known as **cataracts**, which cannot be corrected with glasses. For vision to occur, light waves must pass through the lens and be clearly focused on the retina.

Retina

As Joan looks at the picture, the light waves entering her eye are focused on the retina. As you can see in Figure 5–3, there are three layers of cells in the retina, and the receptors are at the back. This means that the light waves actually pass through the fibers that will become the optic nerve and the other layers of cells before reaching the receptors. If you look at the receptors, you can see that there are two types. According to their shapes, these receptors are called **rods** and **cones**. We will see that the rods and cones have different roles. The second layer of cells in the retina is composed of **bipolar** cells. As you can see from Figure 5–3, the bipolar cells are also named for their shape. They have a single dendrite and single axon, extending from opposite sides of the cell body. You'll notice that some of the bipolar cells in layer two are connected to several different receptors. It is the function of the bipolar cells to pass along information from the receptors to the third layer of cells in the retina, the ganglion cells. You can see that the ganglion cells have huge cell bodies, and it is their axons that form the optic nerve and leave the retina. Often, many receptors and bipolar cells must be activated before

there is enough stimulation to activate one of these large ganglion cells. Only when the ganglion cell is activated are impulses sent along the optic nerve into the brain. This description of the retina is greatly simplified. As we discuss its function, you will see there are other cells in the retina that make connections between adjacent receptors. It is enough for now to remember there are three layers in the retina: the receptors, the bipolar cells, and the ganglion cells, whose axons make up the optic nerve.

Transduction

When light waves strike the retina, they set off the events that will ultimately cause you to see. Since awareness of seeing occurs in your brain rather than in your eye, the light waves must first be converted into neural impulses that can travel to your brain. When a physical stimulus, such as light, is converted into a nerve impulse, the process is called **transduction**. In the visual system transduction results from chemical changes that are triggered by light. Rods and cones are neurons that are specialized to be reactive to light; they are the only cells in the body capable of changing light into nerve impulses. When light waves strike the rods or cones there is a breakdown in the chemicals contained in these cells. As described in Chapter 2, chemical changes are the basis for almost all neural activity. When light causes a change in the cell's chemistry, it causes a change

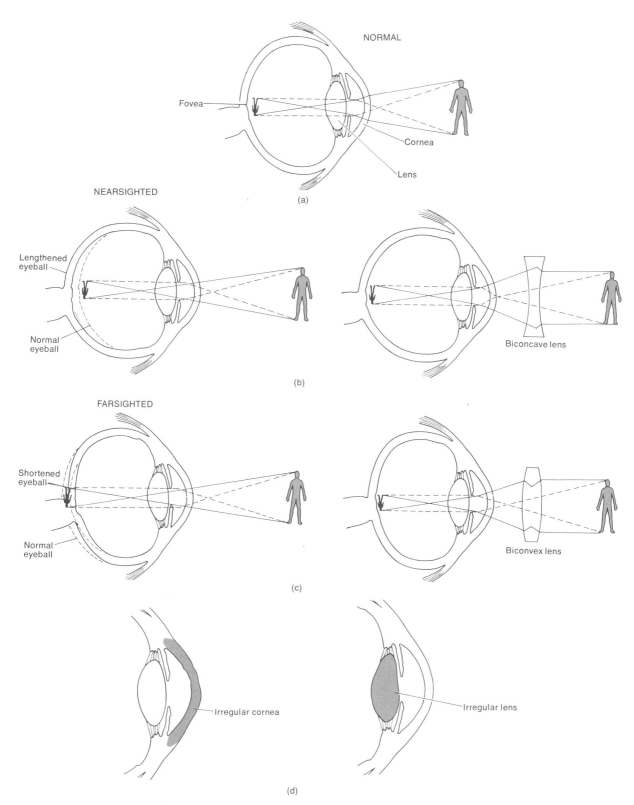

Figure 5–2 Focusing an image on the retina. (a) If you have a normal-shaped eye, the lens focuses the image directly on the retina. (b) If you are nearsighted, you have a lengthened eyeball so that the image is focused in front of the retina. (c) If you are farsighted, you have a shortened eyeball so that the image is focused in back of the retina. (d) If you have an irregularly shaped cornea or lens, the image is not focused properly on the retina. This condition is called astigmatism.

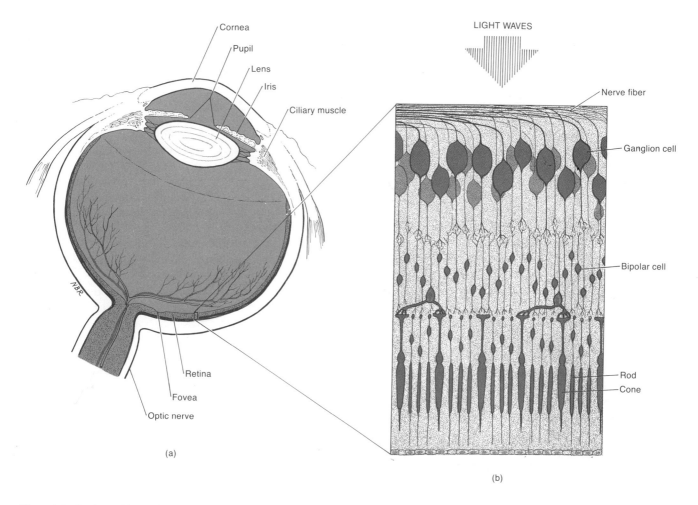

Figure 5-3 Location of the receptors in the eye. (a) The retina, in the back of the eye, contains the receptors, which are the rods and cones. (b) An enlargement of part of the retina shows how light waves must pass through several layers of cells before reaching the rods and cones.

in its electrical potential, and this change is called a **generator potential**. When the change or generator potential becomes great enough, it stimulates the bipolar cells, and these cause impulses to be formed in the ganglion cells. In this way light waves are transformed into nerve impulses that begin the journey to your brain.

Receptors

If Joan looks at the painting at night or in very dim light, she is dependent upon her rod receptors. Rods contain the chemical **rhodopsin** (row-DOP-sin), which is extremely sensitive to light. In response to even the smallest beam of light, rhodopsin breaks down into **opsin**, which is a protein, and into a chemical very similar to vitamin A. When rhodopsin breaks down into these two chemicals, it causes the rod to develop a generator potential, the first step in seeing.

Because rhodopsin is composed partly of vitamin A, night vision is especially dependent upon this vitamin. If you were deprived of vitamin A for two weeks or more, you would have great difficulty seeing at night or in dim light.

When you walk from bright sunlight into a darkened movie theater, you may be temporarily blinded. It takes several minutes for your eyes to adapt to the dark, so that you can see which seats are empty. The temporary blindness results from the fact that there is very little rhodopsin present in your rods. When you were in bright sunlight, the rhodopsin was broken down into its two components. The time that it takes your eyes to adjust to darkness, called **dark adaptation**, is the time that is required for these chemicals to recombine into rhodopsin. Once rhodopsin has been restored, your rods are capable of forming generator potentials, and you can see in dim light.

Although you can see in very dim light because of your rods, you cannot distinguish colors. This is because rods contain only one chemical, rhodopsin, and it cannot respond differently to different wave lengths of light. If you look around in the darkened movie theater, you will not be able to distinguish the colors of people's clothes. At night, when we are dependent upon the rods and rhodopsin, we can see only black and white and shades of gray.

If you came out of the theater into bright sunlight, you would not be dependent upon the rods. Instead, both rods and cones would be activated. With the cones activated, you would be able to distinguish the colors of people's clothes. This is because there are three different kinds of cones in the human retina, containing three different color-sensitive chemicals called **iodopsins** (eye-oh-DOP-sins). The iodopsins are similar to rhodopsin in that they break down into a chemical that resembles vitamin A and into an opsin or protein. In the case of the cones, however, there are three different opsins, making three different iodopsins. Some cones tend to absorb wave lengths of the color red, and they contain an iodopsin that breaks down in response to these red waves. Other cones tend to absorb wave lengths of the color green, and they contain an iodopsin that breaks down to these waves. A third type of cone tends to absorb wave lengths of the color blue and it contains an iodopsin that breaks down to these waves. These three colors—red, green, and blue—are called **primary colors** because all others can be derived from them. As cones pass on their information, other neurons respond in an **opponent** fashion. That is, a single neuron will be excited by one color (for example, red) and inhibited by a different color (for example, blue). This means that neurons stationed later on in the visual system receive information from more than one cone. These later neurons are excited by the information from some cones and inhibited by the information from others. However, all of the information seems to originate from three different cones, having three different types of iodopsin. You cannot see colors in dim light because the iodopsins, which are about ten times less sensitive than rhodopsin, do not break down in dim light.

Although the retina itself is no larger than a postage stamp, it contains approximately 125 million rods and 6 million cones. The different locations of these rods and cones explain one of the strange things about night vision. At night or in dim light, your peripheral vision is superior. In other words, at night you can actually see things better when they occur in the periphery of your visual field than when they occur in the center. This is because an area in the center of your retina called the **fovea** (FOH-vee-ah) contains only cones, which are not activated by dim light. In the area surrounding the fovea, cones and rods are intermixed, with the number of cones decreasing and the number of rods increasing toward the edge of the retina. Around the periphery of the retina is an area that contains only rods, which are sensitive in dim light. These rods in the periphery of your retina are activated by stimuli that occur in the periphery of your visual field.

Seeing Details

The gladiators are wearing bronze medallions around their necks. On the medallions are tiny figures of pagan gods. If Joan looks at the painting in dim light, with only her rods activated, she cannot distinguish these details. However, if she looks at the painting in bright light, so that her cones are also activated, she can distinguish the details easily. Joan has much better **acuity** (ah-CUE-it-tee), or vision for detail, with her cones than with her rods. When details on the medallion reflect light waves to the eye, different rods are activated by light waves from different details. However, the detail is lost because hundreds of rods connect with the same optic nerve fiber. This process, illustrated in Figure 5–4, is called **convergence**. Information from many rods converges or comes together on a single cell. Although there are more than 100 million rods in the retina, there are only 1 million optic nerve fibers. Thus, a great deal of convergence is taking place.

When light waves from details on the medallion activate cones, the information from only a few cones is transmitted to a single nerve fiber. Thus there is much less convergence and much less loss of detail. In fact, in the fovea, which contains only cones, each individual cone sends its information to a single optic nerve fiber. This means that detail is almost perfectly preserved. The fovea, which receives most of its information from the center of the visual field, is the area of greatest acuity.

Seeing Boundaries

There are three gladiators, each distinct from the other. Joan can distinguish the three separate figures because each has its own outline or boundary. You can see outlines or boundaries, also called **contours**, partly because of what happens even before the information leaves the retina. When light waves from a figure activate cells in the retina, those cells not only pass along information to the optic nerve, they also inhibit or decrease the activity in nearby cells (5–8). In other words, when you see a figure in your visual field, that figure is reproduced in miniature on your retina, and the cells surrounding the figure are inhibited. This effect, called **contour sharpening**, causes the boundary of the figure to stand out more clearly against its background.

Seeing Changes

If the figures move or the light in the room becomes brighter or dimmer, Joan can detect these changes partly because of events that take place in the retina. From research on the eye of a frog (5–2, 5–3), it was learned that some ganglion cells change their rate of firing as the level of illumination changes. As the light becomes dimmer, the cells fire less frequently, and as it becomes brighter, they fire more frequently.

Other ganglion cells respond to the onset or offset of light: some fire when light is turned on, and are called **on cells**; some fire when light is turned off, and are called **off cells**; and still others fire at both the onset and offset of

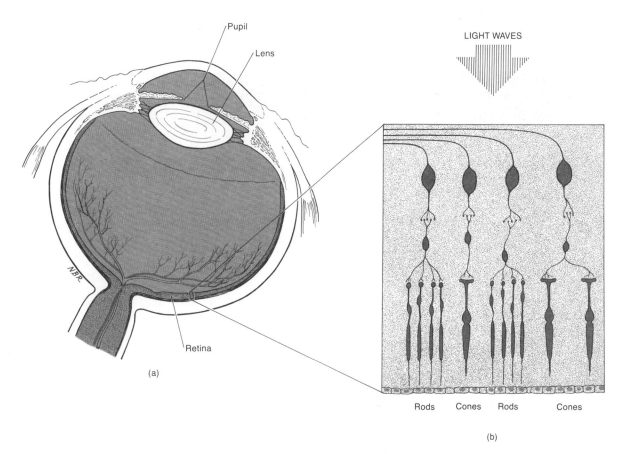

Figure 5–4 How convergence differs for rods and cones. (a) The location of the receptors in the retina. (b) An enlarged and simplified diagram of the receptors. Notice that many rods meet or converge on a single bipolar cell, while only one or two cones converge on a single cell. The less the convergence, the less information is lost and the better the acuity or ability to see details. Because the cones have less convergence than the rods, visual acuity is better for cones than for rods.

light, and are called **on-off cells**. When a stimulus moves across your visual field, it turns on some cells and turns off others, providing the basis for the sensation of movement.

In the frog retina are still more complex ganglion cells that have been dubbed **bug detectors** (5–6). These cells fire only when a small stimulus moves across the visual field. You may wonder how this can happen, but if you look back at Figure 5–4, you will see that a single ganglion cell can receive input from many receptors. In the case of the bug detectors, the ganglion cell is fired only when several of these receptors are activated sequentially. Joan has no bug detectors in her retina, but we will see later that there are cells in her cortex that operate in a similar fashion.

Optic Pathway

With all of the processing that takes place in the retina— color coding, contour sharpening, on-off discriminating—

you can see why the retina is frequently referred to as a miniature brain. In a sense, the **optic nerve** carries information from the small brain in your retina to the larger brain where you will experience seeing.

When a ganglion cell is activated, it may represent the occurrence or nonoccurrence of light, it may represent converging information from hundreds of receptors, or it may represent the output of a single cone in the fovea. In any case, when the ganglion cell is fired, an impulse is formed and travels down the cell's long axon into the brain. The axons of the ganglion cells gather together to form the optic nerve. The point at which the optic nerve leaves the back of the eyeball is your **blind spot**, since there are no rods or cones located there, and you are blind to light striking this area.

The path followed by the optic nerves to the brain is shown in Figure 5–5. A short distance after the optic nerves leave the eyeballs, they come together at a point known as the **optic chiasma** (ky-AZ-muh). If you were a frog, all the fibers from your left eye would cross over and go to your right brain, and vice versa for the other eye. In your human visual pathway, only about half the fibers cross over to the opposite side of the brain. The remaining fibers continue on to the same side of the brain. As you can see from the figure, the fibers from the inner or nasal side of the retina cross over, and those from the outer or temporal side continue to the same side of the brain (Area 17). It may sound a little complicated in words. However, it is very easy to see in the figure that information from the left half of your visual field goes to the right side of your brain, and infor-

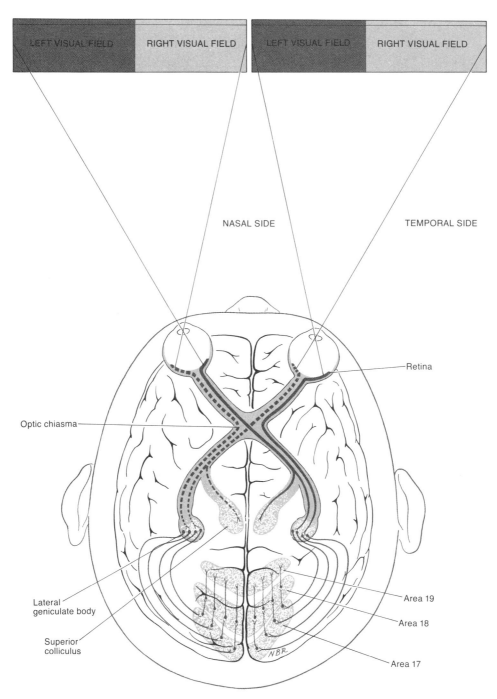

LEFT VISUAL FIELD   RIGHT VISUAL FIELD

LEFT VISUAL FIELD   RIGHT VISUAL FIELD

NASAL SIDE

TEMPORAL SIDE

Retina

Optic chiasma

Lateral
geniculate body

Superior
colliculus

Area 19

Area 18

Area 17

Figure 5–5 Tracing the visual pathways from the retina to the cortical areas in the brain. The right eye sends half of its fibers to the right hemisphere and half to the left. The same is true for the left eye. The result is that the right hemisphere receives information from the left visual field from both right and left eyes; the opposite is true for the left hemisphere. The primary cortical area for vision is Area 17. Areas 18 and 19 are visual association areas.

mation from the right half of your visual field goes to the left side of the brain. Information coming from the very center of your visual field is sent to both sides of your brain.

Thalamus

Of the million axons traveling in the optic tract, only a small proportion have to do with reflexes. The great majority carry the neural information you will eventually experience as a painting. As you can see in Figure 5–5, these axons travel to the thalamus and synapse on cells in the **lateral geniculate nucleus**, or **LGN**. We can make a very good guess about how the LGN cells function in Joan's thalamus because microelectrodes have been inserted into the brains of monkeys and used to study the activity of LGN cells (5–10). From these studies we know that each LGN cell has a specific visual field. In other words, each LGN cell receives information that has come from a small group of receptors in the retina. The LGN cell acts as a tiny processor or integrator of this information from the retina.

Opponent Process Cells

One of the most important functions of the lateral geniculate cells is the coding of color. They do this by responding differently to information coming from the various cones in their receptor fields. For example, some LGN cells are turned on (increase their rate of firing) by the color red and

are turned off by the color green. Others are turned on by green and off by blue, and so on. Because the LGN cells tend to increase firing to one wave length and decrease it to another, they have been called **opponent process cells**. There are other opponent process cells in the LGN that receive information from rods and respond in an opponent fashion to light and dark.

Although the coding that is necessary for color vision takes place in the thalamus, Joan does not see the colors of the painting until the information reaches her cortex. In fact, it is unlikely that she will see anything until impulses reach the cortex. Another important function of the LGN cells is to send information to the cortex.

Visual Cortex

After processing information from the retina, the lateral geniculate cells send impulses to the **primary projection** area for vision, Area 17, located in the occipital lobe of the cortex (see Figure 5–6). At the instant impulses reach this area, Joan might have the experience of seeing something, but it would not be a picture of three gladiators. This is because a neuron in Area 17 responds to individual elements of its visual field. For example, some neurons in Area 17 respond only to vertical lines, and others respond only to horizontal lines (5–4). If Area 17 were stimulated electrically, you would report seeing stars or flashes of light

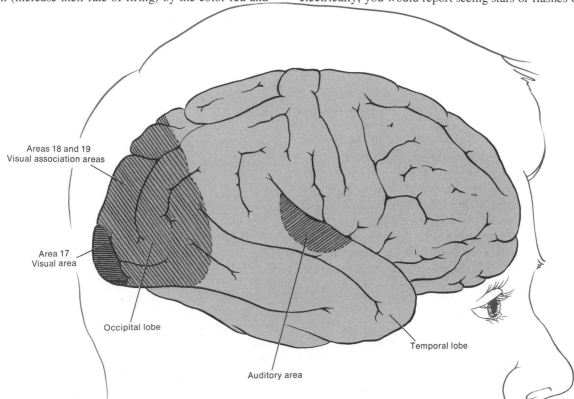

Figure 5–6 Location of the cortical areas for vision in the occipital lobe. Area 17 is the primary area, and Areas 18 and 19 are the association areas. The primary cortical area for audition is located in the temporal lobe.

Vision

but no complex forms, such as gladiators, kangaroos, or rocks. Although activation of Area 17 alone cannot cause you to see a painting, the area is vitally important to your vision. If Area 17 were destroyed on both sides of your brain, your vision would be severely impaired. One of the important functions of Area 17 is to send information to association areas of the cortex.

Association Areas

Surrounding Area 17 are the association areas, 18 and 19 (see Figure 5–6). A fraction of a second after Area 17 is activated, impulses arrive in these association areas, which contain cells that respond to complex stimuli. For example, some cells may respond to lines of particular length or angle and others to lines that are moving across the visual field (5–5). In the cells of the association areas, the neural information is finally integrated into a coherent pattern. For the pattern to become three gladiators, cells in many areas of association cortex are activated. Some of these cells may even be in the parietal or temporal lobes. When an association area in the temporal lobe is electrically stimulated, patients report seeing billboards or having visual memories or flashbacks (5–7). As Joan looks at the painting, cells in her retina, thalamus, and visual cortex respond differently to colors, outlines, movements, and so forth. However, she does not actually see the picture until this information is analyzed by cells in the association cortex. Thus, it is in her association cortex that she sees the picture.

What Joan sees when she looks at the painting depends on information stored in her association areas. If she were an historian, she might see the gladiators not only as figures, but as symbols of their time. On the other hand, if Joan as a child was frightened by a movie with gladiators, she might see them as threatening. You very rarely, or possibly never, see something such as a face without supplying some meaning—enemy, friend, lover. This is the same as saying we usually experience perception, rarely sensation. For the many stimuli you experience throughout the day, the association areas of the brain automatically add meaning, very often without your awareness. The kind of meaning that is added to the stimuli you see, hear, or smell depends upon your past experience as well as your present state. Since each of us has different experiences, we tend to perceive stimuli in our own individual ways. This is why two people ''seeing'' the same person may have two very different impressions.

Hallucinations and Dreams

Now that you know how we see, you can probably explain how Joan saw the gladiators walk out of the picture after she took an hallucinogenic drug. We see things in our association cortex, not our eyes. When a certain pattern of cells in your association cortex is activated, you will have a visual experience, regardless of how those cells are activated. In Joan's case the cells were activated partly by information coming from her receptors and partly by the drug acting on neurons somewhere along the visual pathway or in the association cortex itself. The same kind of thing happens when we dream. Cells in the association cortex are activated while we sleep and tell us we are seeing something even though our receptors have not been activated. Hallucinations and dreams are extreme examples of the way in which perceptions can be distorted. When your brain is functioning in its normal awake state, your perceptions are far less distorted and bear a closer relationship to events in your visual field.

One Sense at a Time

All the time Joan was looking at the picture, her cat was meowing in the background. While she was absorbed in looking at the picture, she did not hear the cat. As you read this sentence, you are not aware of your watch band or ring until it is brought to your attention. If your radio is on, you may not hear it if you are watching an elephant walk by your window. These are examples of how you selectively attend to one sense or another. At one time it was believed that when you attended to one stimulus, the brain somehow turned off sensory impulses coming in through other sensory nerves. For example, if you looked at the elephant, the auditory nerve would be turned off so that you could not hear the radio. Since it was believed that sensory impulses were actually prevented from entering the brain, the process was referred to as **sensory gating**. It may well be that some sensory gating takes place, because in most sensory systems it has been shown that there are neurons that carry impulses *from the brain to the sensory receptor area*. These neurons may inhibit the activity of the sensory cells. Still, it now seems that selective attention occurs primarily in the cortex. When you are watching the elephant, sensory impulses from the sounds of the radio do reach the cortex and can be recorded there as brain waves called **evoked potentials**. However, something often happens in the cortex to prevent you from registering or noticing these stimuli. Exactly how this happens is not yet understood.

Audition

What you know as sound begins with vibrations. A radio's speaker or your vocal apparatus is designed to produce vibrations. These vibrations cause molecules in the air to move back and forth, creating sound waves. If you banged a bass drum, the vibrations produced by the drum would have a slow frequency. Let's say you were moving or vibrating a paddle in water. If you moved the paddle slowly, a wave would travel out a long distance before another wave occurred. If you moved the paddle rapidly, waves would occur in shorter bursts. Slow frequency vibrations, such as the beat of the bass drum, create longer sound waves that are heard as lower tones. In contrast, a cat's meow produces vibrations with a faster frequency, causing shorter sound waves heard as higher tones. Thus, a drum or a cat's vocal apparatus causes vibrations of different frequencies that in turn cause molecules to move back and forth at different speeds, creating sound waves of different lengths and the experience of hearing high and low tones.

The length of the sound wave is measured in terms of how many waves or cycles occur per second. The human ear can hear sound waves beginning at approximately 16 cycles per second (cps)—very long sound waves—and will continue to hear through approximately 20,000 cps—very short sound waves. The unit cps is now called a Hertz (Hz) after one of the early scientists in acoustics. Stereo equipment is designed to produce sounds in the range of 16 to 20,000 Hz, since that is the range for human hearing. Some animals, such as bats and porpoises, can hear sound waves up to 100,000 Hz, extremely short sound waves.

Outer Ear

The shape of your ears helps them gather in sound waves. The shape of rabbits' ears helps even more. Rabbits' large movable ears collect sound waves efficiently and make it easier for them to avoid predators. This part of the ear you can see is called the **pinna**. If you looked into the pinna, you would see a small tunnel approximately 2.5 cm (1 inch) long, the **ear canal**. It directs sound into the ear. If wax builds up in your ear canal, it impedes the entry of sound waves and decreases your hearing, or **audition**.

At the end of the ear canal is the **tympanic membrane**, more commonly known as the **eardrum**. The eardrum is elastic, and when it is struck by sound waves, it vibrates. If your eardrum were badly punctured, sound waves would pass through the hole without causing the eardrum to vibrate. If the eardrum did not vibrate, you would hear very little, if anything. The pinna, ear canal, and eardrum comprise the **outer ear**.

Middle Ear

The sound waves produced by a cat's meow enter the outer ear, travel down the ear canal and strike the eardrum, causing it to vibrate. Attached to the eardrum is a tiny bone called the **malleus** that is attached to a second tiny bone

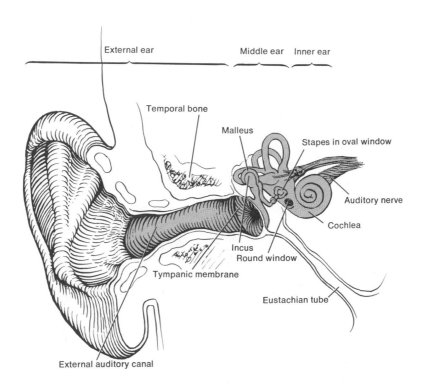

Figure 5-7 The structure of the external, middle, and inner ear.

called the **incus** that is attached to a third bone called the **stapes** that is finally attached to a membrane called the **oval window**. The three bones, together called **ossicles** (as in popsicles) make up the **middle ear**. When the eardrum vibrates, it causes these three bones to vibrate, which in turn causes the oval window to vibrate. The ossicles not only transmit vibrations from the eardrum to the oval window, but they are so designed that they increase the force of the vibrations.

During landing or takeoff in an airplane, you may notice pressure in your ears. The middle ear is a cavity filled with air, and you need to maintain a balance in pressure between air outside and inside the ear. Air pressure changes quickly when you go up in an airplane, and sometimes you must help your middle ear adjust to the rapid change. There is a tube connecting the middle ear to the back of the mouth.

If you yawn or swallow, air passes through the tube and balances the pressure inside the middle ear with that outside, relieving the uncomfortable feeling in your ear.

Sometimes calcium deposits or growths develop on the ossicles. When this happens the ossicles do not vibrate strongly enough, and the person develops a general hearing loss. This loss can be minimized with a hearing aid, which essentially replaces the ossicles and helps transmit the vibrations to the oval window. The oval window is the beginning of the inner ear.

Inner Ear

The inner ear, called the **cochlea** (COKE-lee-ah), resembles a coiled snake. If the cochlea were partially uncoiled, as in Figure 5–8, it would look like a straight tube divided

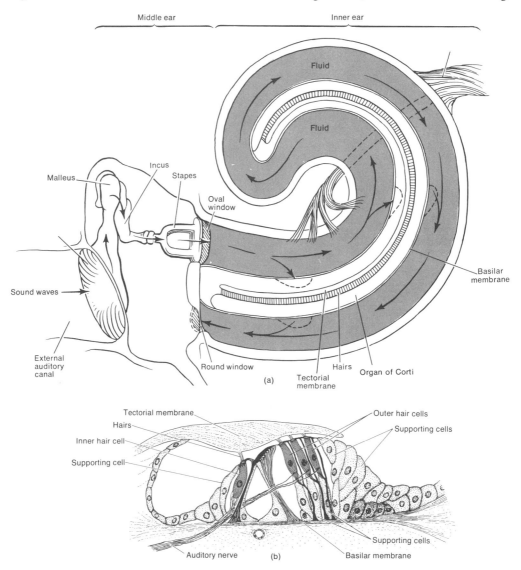

Figure 5–8 Receptors in the ear. (a) In the inner ear, the hair cells on the basilar membrane are the receptors for audition and, together with other membranes, are called the organ of Corti. The movement of fluid bends the membranes supporting the hair cells, and this bending causes generator potentials. (b) An enlargement of the organ of Corti showing the hair cells located between the tectorial and basilar membranes.

down the middle into three compartments filled with fluid. The fluid is held in the tube by the oval window, which is attached to the ossicles. When the ossicles vibrate, they cause the oval window to vibrate, and the vibrations of the oval window cause the fluid in the tube to vibrate.

The membrane that divides the tube down the middle is called the **basilar** (BAZ-ah-ler) membrane. The receptors for hearing, that change vibrations into impulses, are located in a structure called the **organ of Corti** (CORE-tee), found on the basilar membrane. When the oval window vibrates, the fluid in the tube vibrates, causing the basilar membrane to vibrate. Since the organ of Corti is on the basilar membrane, it is affected by the vibrations. In the organ of Corti are tiny **hair cells**, so named because they look like hairs. The vibrations of the basilar membrane cause the hair cells to bend. When the hair cells bend, they produce electrical changes or generator potentials. When the generator potential in a hair cell becomes large enough, it triggers a nerve impulse. Thus, the auditory receptors are located in the structure with the strange name, organ of Corti, and it is here that vibrations are changed into impulses.

Pitch

You can easily tell the difference between the high-pitched whine of a police siren and the low-pitched throb of a bass drum. Your ear, or more specifically your basilar membrane, functions in two different ways to tell you whether a sound has the high pitch of a siren or the low pitch of a drum (5–1). When a drum is struck, it produces vibrations that cause molecules in the air to move back and forth producing sound waves. Vibrations produced by a drum have a slow frequency and produce longer sound waves. The middle ear changes these long sound waves into slow vibrations. The inner ear changes these slow vibrations into impulses. If the sound is very low, 16 to 1,000 Hz, the long sound waves will cause impulses to fire at approximately the same rate as sound waves. For example, the lowest note on a piano generates long sound waves, 28 Hz, that are changed by the inner ear into impulses firing 28 times per second. Thus, sound waves that are long, which means they have a frequency of from 16 to 1,000 Hz, are translated into nerve impulses that match their frequency and fire from 16 to 1,000 times per second.

Sound waves generated during human conversation are in a somewhat higher range, from approximately 1,000 to 4,000 Hz. This is the range to which the human ear is most sensitive. But because of the physiological limitations of the neuron, it cannot fire more than 1,000 times per second. In order for tones in this range to be heard, one group of neurons may fire at their maximum rate of 1,000 times per second, and then a different group of neurons also fires at 1,000 times per second. The two groups of neurons fire two separate volleys of impulses at 1,000 times per second. The brain adds these two separate volleys of impulses and reads

them as 2,000 times per second. This type of coding follows the **volley theory**: there are volleys or discharges of impulses that follow the frequency of the tone.

For the lower end of the range, from 16 to 1,000 Hz, volleys of impulses from *one* group of neurons are fired at the same rate as the sound waves. For tones from 1,000 to 4,000 Hz, different groups of neurons send volleys of impulses that the brain adds together and reads as one group of impulses. Thus, the volley principle explains how you discriminate tones from 16 to 4,000 Hz. For tones from 16 to 1,000 Hz, the volley comes from a single set of neurons; for tones from 1,000 to 4,000 Hz, volleys from several sets of neurons are added.

You can also hear sounds above 4,000 Hz, which is approximately the sound of the highest note on a piano. For tones in the range 4,000 to 20,000 Hz, the basilar membrane functions in a slightly different way. Our understanding of basilar-membrane function comes in large part from the work of Georg von Bekesy (5–1), who was awarded the Nobel prize for his research on auditory coding. For a very high-pitched sound, one near 16,000 Hz, the area of the basilar membrane closest to the oval window vibrates more than any other part of the membrane. Sounds between 4,000 and 20,000 Hz cause different areas on the basilar membrane to vibrate more than other areas depending on the number of Hz's. This is called the **place theory**: you can discriminate among tones from 4,000 to 20,000 Hz on the basis of which place on the basilar membrane vibrates the most. Since different hair cells are located at different places on the basilar membrane, the place theory means that different tones activate different receptors. Thus, a tone of 4,000 Hz will cause maximal firing in one set of auditory nerve fibers, and a tone of 10,000 Hz will cause maximal firing in another set. The information carried in these auditory fibers eventually reaches different areas of the auditory cortex and is perceived as differences in pitch.

Loudness

Movements of the basilar membrane also explain how you distinguish between a whisper and a shout, or in other words, how you code loudness. Compared to a whisper, a shout or any loud noise causes a larger section of the basilar membrane to vibrate, and it causes the membrane to vibrate with more force. When a larger section of the membrane vibrates, more hair cells are bent, and therefore more nerve impulses are generated. When the basilar membrane vibrates with greater force, hair cells are bent to a greater degree. When more hair cells are bent more strongly, generator potentials are sufficient to cause nerve impulses in neurons with higher thresholds and in neurons that are in the relative refractory period. Because impulses can be generated during the relative refractory period, they are generated more frequently. Thus, the perception of loudness depends on how large an area of the basilar membrane is vibrated and how forceful the vibrations are. Greater activation of the membrane in these two ways results in more nerve impulses, which the brain interprets as increased loudness.

Pathways to Brain

Although sound waves are transformed into nerve impulses in the inner ear or cochlea, these impulses must travel to the brain before you can hear. The hair cells in the cochlea synapse with other neurons whose long axons form the **auditory nerve**. On their way to the cortex, some fibers from the left auditory nerve stay on the same side and reach the left brain, while others cross over and reach the right brain. So each side of the brain receives impulses from both ears. This is similar to the visual system, in which each side of the brain receives impulses from both eyes. As the auditory fibers ascend toward the cortex, they synapse at several different nuclei, one of which is the **inferior colliculus**. If you heard a loud noise off to the right, the inferior colliculus would automatically or reflexively help to orient your head toward the noise. Other auditory fibers synapse in the thalamus, specifically the **medial geniculate nucleus**. The thalamus is the great relay and analyzing center in the brain through which all senses, except smell, are processed. The medial geniculate nucleus of the thalamus begins the task of sorting and combining information that has arrived from the receptors in the organ of Corti. The activation of one cell in the medial geniculate probably represents input from many hair cells in the organ of Corti. One of the important functions of the medial geniculate cells is to send impulses to the cortex, where sensations of hearing will occur.

Auditory Cortex

After leaving the thalamus, impulses proceed along nerve fibers that terminate in the auditory cortex or **primary projection area** for hearing. This cortical area is located in the temporal lobe (see Figure 5–6). Each neuron in the cortex receives input from many thalamic neurons, and thalamic neurons send impulses to many different cortical neurons. From studies on the dog's auditory cortex, it is thought that different tones or frequencies terminate in different parts of the cortex (5–9). This means that the part of the basilar membrane that responds to high tones is sending impulses to a different part of the cortex than the part of the basilar membrane that responds to low tones. At the instant that impulses reach the auditory cortex in the temporal lobe, you might experience some sound, but it would not be recognizable. If the auditory cortex were stimulated electrically, you might report hearing tones or noise, but nothing as complex as your name or your cat's meow. (When your brain is functioning normally, the auditory cortex is probably never activated by itself.) One function of the auditory cortex is to activate association areas of cortex.

Understanding What You Hear

When someone says your name, a pattern of impulses reaches your auditory cortex. These impulses are the same as those produced by any other receptors, such as the rods and cones in your eye. If the impulses are all the same, why then do you hear a sound and not see it? One reason is that the receptors in your ear are specialized for, or have a low threshold to, the kind of energy or stimulation produced by sound waves. Suppose the receptors in your ear were sensitive to both light waves and sound waves. Would your ear both hear and see? The answer is still no. Unless your brain had also been rewired, the impulses from your ear would still be sent to the auditory cortex, which is involved in hearing. Just as you see with your visual cortex rather than your eyes, you hear with your auditory cortex rather than your ears. The area of the cortex where the impulses terminate is an important determinant of which kind of perceptions you will have. When your auditory association areas are stimulated, you will hear something, regardless of how the stimulation occurs.

In order for Joan to recognize that pattern of impulses as a cat's meow or her name, impulses from the primary projection area are sent to other association areas in the cortex. These association areas somehow recognize the impulse patterns as a ''cat's meow'' or ''my name'' or other complex sounds. In addition to recognition of sounds, the association areas also add other kinds of meanings, such as the feeling that a sound is pleasant, eerie, or disturbing, or that it has something to do with feeding the cat. You probably never hear a sound (your name) without your brain automatically adding some meaning to the sound (said by a friend, stranger, someone wanting a favor). The world you know through your senses is a world different from the world someone else knows through her senses. Each of us has different experience and different learning, and so our brains add different kinds of meaning to stimuli affecting our senses. To a cat lover, a cat's meow is a nice sound, while to a cat hater, a cat's meow is a terrible sound—even though the cat's meow is physically the same in both situations.

Sound Localization

If your ears were located close together on the same side of your head, you would have trouble telling where sounds come from. When a car backfires, you automatically turn toward the direction of the noise and are able to say where the noise originated. This reflexive turning is controlled by the inferior colliculus. The reason you know that the sound is coming from the right or left is that your ears are separated by your head. Sound waves from a sound on your right side reach your right ear first and, depending on how thick your head is, reach your left ear a short time later. If the sound waves arrive at the right ear before the left, that is your cue for localizing the sound on the right. Sometimes

GREATER USE OF IMPLANTED HEARING DEVICE URGED

A Los Angeles surgeon who is a pioneer in the experimental technique of implanting an electronic hearing device in the inner ear of totally deaf persons says the time has come for more widespread use of the device.

Many of his colleagues disagree. They say that more animal experimentation is needed before the device is implanted in large numbers of deaf persons.

But Dr. William F. House is quite insistent: "I personally think the results we are getting justify more widespread clinical work. I feel it should be done by centers around the world."

An estimated 300,000 Americans have so-called nerve-type deafness. According to House, about 200,000 could benefit from a "cochlear" implant, so-called because it replaces some of the function of damaged cells inside that inner ear structure.

House, vice president and director of research of the Los Angeles-based Ear Research Institute, has implanted 22 artificial cochleas, more than any other American surgeon. He did his first in 1961, but the majority were performed during the last three years.

★ ★ ★

The cochlea is a tiny snail-shaped structure in the ear whose job is to translate mechanical sound forces into electrical impulses which can be carried along the hearing nerve to the brain.

In most persons with nerve-type deafness the hearing nerve is intact but they are deaf because the tiny hair cells which act as sensors for the nerve inside the cochlea are either missing or damaged.

The cochlear implant is intended to replace the lost function of these hair cells. However, the artificial cochleas that are now available fall far short of providing anywhere near the normal ability to discriminate between different sounds.

For example, it is not now possible for a deaf person with an implant to understand speech. All they hear is a sound. They must rely on lip reading to understand what is being said to them.

★ ★ ★

In the safety studies, one of the interests is in learning what ill effect, if any, the continual electrical stimulation by the device may have on the hearing nerve. It is conceivable—although there is no strong evidence yet—that the stimulation may destroy the nerve.

★ ★ ★

But House does not agree that more animal studies are necessary. He said that followup studies of human cases for as long as six years have produced no evidence that the device has caused any harm.

★ ★ ★

SOURCE: Excerpt from a longer article by Harry Nelson, Times Medical Writer, *Los Angeles Times*, April 25, 1977. Copyright © 1977 by Los Angeles Times.

---

you cannot easily tell where a sound is coming from. When this happens, it means that the sound waves are reaching both ears simultaneously. For example, if the sound is coming from directly in front or behind you, the sound waves reach both ears simultaneously. You then have to turn your head back and forth so that sound waves reach one ear before the other. For a sound to be localized, the sound waves must reach one ear before the other.

Deafness

If both your primary projection areas for hearing were destroyed, your hearing would be severely impaired, because it is in your cortex that you hear. If your auditory nerve were damaged, you would also have a hearing loss (nerve deafness), since impulses could not reach the brain. If a part of your basilar membrane were damaged by extremely loud sounds, such as those from a jet plane or jackhammer or rock concert, you would have a hearing loss. This is because the organ of Corti, the receptor for hearing, is on the basilar membrane. Depending upon how much of the basilar membrane was damaged, your hearing loss might be extensive or just for certain tones. Damage to any of the above areas cannot be completely corrected by a hearing aid.

Comment

It seems a simple thing to see a flower or hear a song. Yet because of the way your brain adds meaning to incoming stimuli, you and I probably never see a flower or hear a song in the same way. The world perceived through your senses is most likely different from the world perceived through my senses. You can now understand why philosophers have argued about how you perceive the world around you. You can understand why two eye witnesses to a crime can rarely agree about what they saw. You can understand why rock music sounds like noise to some and like great music to others. And you can understand how a drug that affects the brain could make Joan see her picture come alive and her cat sound like a lion.

1 When you look at a dog, besides seeing a small, hairy creature with four legs, you also see an animal that you like or dislike or think is cute or ugly. Awareness of a stimulus, such as a dog, that is colored by past and present learning and feelings is called _____ .   *perception*

2 Radio waves are too long and xrays are too short to be seen. The waves you can see are 16–32 millionths of an inch long, which is usually expressed as _____ nm long.   *380–760*

3 The curved shape of the cornea helps to _____ the light waves, which tend to scatter before they reach the eye.   *bend or gather*

4 If you have blue eyes, it means that a muscular disk called the _____ is blue.   *iris*

5 If a bright light were shined into your eye, your iris would _____ . In a dim light, the iris would _____ to let in more light.   *constrict* *dilate*

6 After passing through the pupil, light waves next pass through the _____ , which helps to further bend or focus the _____ into a single beam.   *lens* *light waves*

7 When you look at your watch, the shape of your lens is _____ . When you look at a sign in a distance, the shape of your lens is _____ .   *thick* *thin*

8 If you had blurred vision because of a cloudy lens, you would have a condition known as _____ .   *cataract*

9 The function of the lens is to further bend the light waves and focus them into a single beam on the receptors located in the _____ .   *retina*

10 The retina has three layers of cells. Those cells in the layer farthest back in the eye are receptors for vision and are called _____ and _____ .   *rods / cones*

11 Along the outside or periphery of the retina are located mostly _____ , while in the center of the retina, especially in the fovea, are located mostly _____ .   *rods* *cones*

12 The cones contain three types of a chemical called _____ , which breaks down only in _____ light.   *iodopsin* *bright*

13 The rods contain one chemical, _____ , and allow you to see in dim light and to see _____ , but not color.   *rhodopsin* *black, white, or shades of gray*

14 The cones contain iodopsin, which is activated by bright light. There are three kinds of iodopsin, which are sensitive to the wave lengths of the three primary colors _____ , _____ , and _____ .   *red / green* *blue*

15 The breakdown of chemicals in the receptors causes _____ , which, if large enough, will cause an _____ to occur in a ganglion cell.   *generator potentials* *impulse*

16 As you read this sentence, you can see the fine details of the letters because of the way your _____ are connected to adjoining cells.   *cones*

17 The reason you cannot see fine details with your rods is that many rods connect with one neuron, showing _____ . Thus, the fine details are lost.   *convergence*

18 You can distinguish the outline or boundaries of a person walking on the sidewalk because some cells in the retina cause other cells to fire more _____ .   *slowly*

19 In order for you to see details, outlines, movements, and changes in illumination, ganglion cells in the _____ must fire and either _____ or _____ their rate of firing.   *retina / increase* *decrease*

20 The ganglion cells in the retina have long axons which come together to form the _____ .   *optic nerve*

21 A short distance after leaving the back of each eye, the optic nerves join together at the optic _____ . At this point, half of the nerves from each eye cross over and join together to form the _____ .   *chiasma* *optic tracts*

22 Some fibers from the optic tracts terminate in a structure involved in controlling reflexive blinking and eye movements. This structure is called the _____ .   *superior colliculus*

23 Most of the fibers in the optic tracts go to the _____ of the thalamus. One of the important functions of this nucleus is _____ coding.   *lateral geniculate nucleus* *color*

24 When cells in the lateral geniculate nucleus are activated, impulses travel to the cortex in Area _____ , which is the primary projection area for _____ .   *17 / vision*

25 Theoretically, when impulses reach Area 17, you might see a _____ but not a _____ .   *simple stimulus or flash of light / complex stimulus*

26 In order for you to identify an object as an elephant, impulses would have to reach other areas of your brain known in general as _____ areas.   *association*

27 The association areas somehow recognize the pattern of impulses as an elephant. They also add other kinds of _____ .   *meaning*

28 When you speak, your vocal apparatus produces vibrations that cause molecules in the air to move back and forth, creating _____ .   *sound waves*

29 Sound waves have different lengths, and it is the length of the sound wave that determines the sound's
_____ .   *pitch*

30 Sound waves are measured according to how many waves or cycles occur per second. The range of human hearing is from _____ to _____ Hz.   *16 / 20,000*

31 The purpose of the outer ear is to gather sound waves which then travel down the ear canal and strike the _____ .   *eardrum*

32 Sound waves cause the eardrum to vibrate, which in turn causes three tiny bones, the _____ , to vibrate.   *ossicles*

33 The ossicles transmit the vibrations to the _____ , which is the start of the inner ear.   *oval window*

34 The inner ear, called the _____ , looks like a coiled snake. If it were uncoiled, it would look like a straight tube filled with _____ and divided down the middle by the _____ membrane.   *cochlea* / *fluid / basilar*

35 Located on the basilar membrane is the _____ , that contains the receptors for hearing known as _____ cells.   *organ of Corti* / *hair*

36 When the oval window vibrates, it causes the fluid in the cochlea to vibrate, which causes the _____ to vibrate, which causes the hair cells to _____ .   *basilar membrane / bend*

37 If you wanted to explain how you hear low sounds, from 16 to 4,000 Hz, you would discuss the _____ theory or principle.   *volley*

38 The volley principle states that for low tones from _____ to _____ Hz, the neurons fire or send a volley of impulses that match the vibrations of these tones. And for low tones from _____ to _____ Hz, different groups of neurons must send separate volleys of impulses because the neurons cannot fire more than 1,000 times per second.   *16 / 1,000* / *1,000 / 4,000*

39 If you were to explain how we hear tones from 4,000 to 20,000 cps, you would discuss the _____ theory.   *place*

40 The place theory states that for high tones it is the place on the _____ where the maximum vibrations occur that determines the tone or pitch   *basilar membrane*

41 You can tell the difference between someone shouting and speaking normally because a shout causes a larger part of the _____ to vibrate, and it vibrates with more _____ .   *basilar membrane / force*

42 After leaving the ear, auditory nerves synapse in several structures, one of which helps to orient the head in the direction of a noise. This structure is called the _____ .   *inferior colliculus*

43 Auditory fibers also synapse in a structure that analyzes and integrates the information coming from the receptors. This structure is the _____ of the thalamus.   *medial geniculate nucleus*

44 After leaving the thalamus, auditory fibers terminate in the primary projection area for hearing, located in the _____ .   *temporal lobe*

45 When impulses reach the primary projection area for hearing, you might experience hearing _____ .   *noise or tone or simple stimulus*

46 In order for you to recognize a pattern of impulses as being a song, impulses would have to reach your _____ areas.   *association*

47 You know a car is coming from your right side because the sound waves from the car will reach your _____ ear before your _____ ear.   *right / left*

REFERENCES

5-1 Bekesy, G. von. *Experiments in hearing*. New York: McGraw-Hill, 1960.

5-2 Hartline, H. K. The effects of spatial summation in the retina on the excitation of the fibers of the optic nerve. *American Journal of Physiology* 1940, 130: 700–711.

5-3 Hartline, H. K. Receptive field of the optic nerve fibers. *American Journal of Physiology* 1940, 130: 690–699.

5-4 Hubel, D. H. The visual cortex of the brain. *Scientific American* 1963, 209: 54–62.

5-5 Hubel, D. H. and Wiesel, T. N. Receptive field and functional architecture in two nonstriate visual areas (18 and 19) of the cat. *Journal of Neurophysiology* 1965, 28: 229–289.

5-6 Lettvin, J. Y., Maturana, H. R., McCulloch, W. S., and Pitts, W. H. What the frog's eye tells the frog's brain. *Proceedings of the Institute of Radio Engineering* 1959, 47: 1940–1951.

5-7 Penfield, W. Functional localization in temporal and deep sylvian areas. *Academy for Research in Nervous and Mental Disease* 1958, 36: 210–226.

5-8 Ratliff, F. and Hartline, H. K. The response of limulus optic nerve fibers to patterns of illumination on the receptor mosaic. *Journal of General Physiology* 1959, 42: 1242–1255.

5-9 Tunturi, A. R. A difference in the representation of auditory signals for the left and right ears in the iso-frequency contours of the right middle ectosylvian cortex of the dog. *American Journal of Physiology* 1952, 168:712–727.

5-10 Wiesel, T. N. and Hubel, D. H. Spatial and chromatic interactions in the lateral geniculate body of the Rhesus monkey. *Journal of Neurophysiology* 1966, 29: 1115–1116.

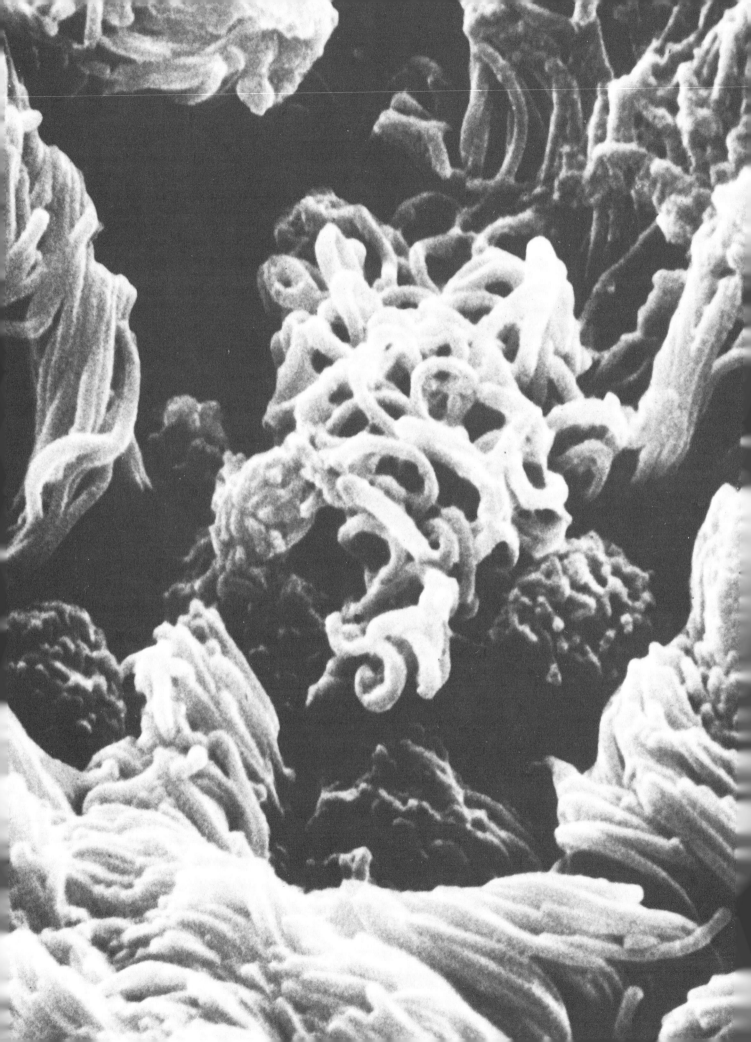

Smelling, Tasting, and Touching 6

How Your Nose, Tongue, and Skin Make Sense

A Sure Thing

Charlie liked to bet on sure things. It did not matter that most of his sure winners turned out to be losers. Each time, Charlie thought he had a sure bet. The first sure thing was the perfume bet. The dog trainer told Charlie he could use any kind of perfume he wanted, any container he wanted, and any hiding place he wanted, and the dog would find it in less than two minutes. Charlie considered this an excellent bet. He used a very weak perfume and placed the tiniest amount on a wad of cotton. When he held the cotton two feet from his nose, he could smell nothing. Next he placed the cotton in a plastic container, and although he sniffed and sniffed, he could smell nothing. The dog found the container in 64 seconds.

The second sure thing was the soft drink bet. He wagered that, while blindfolded and holding his nose, he could taste the difference and correctly distinguish between a glass of Coca-Cola and a glass of Seven-Up. He took a long taste of the first glass and a long taste of the second. Then he tried the first again and then the second. The more he drank, the less he could taste. In the end he guessed wrong and lost.

The third thing was the cigarette bet. A puny-looking man boasted to Charlie that he could stand a lot of pain. The man wagered that he could hold a burning cigarette against his hand for 15 seconds without withdrawing his hand. The only condition was that the man would decide where to place the cigarette. The man lit a cigarette and smoked it until there was a red glowing end. He gave it to Charlie and told him to place it against the heel of his hand. When the burning cigarette touched his hand, the man did not even flinch. For 15 seconds he talked about being a handball player. Then he collected his money.

The fourth sure thing was the magic fingers bet. A woman stated that she could distinguish colors on a page by using only her fingers. She said over the years she had trained herself to have such sensitive fingers that she could feel light waves. The ends of her fingers seemed to be very smooth and to have no ridges. Charlie wagered that she could not distinguish the colors on the page of a magazine. After she was blindfolded, Charlie gave her the page. It took some time and apparently much effort, but the woman correctly identified each color on the page.

If Charlie had known more about the function of the senses, he might not have made some of these bets.

Smelling

Dogs have been trained to sniff out hidden marijuana, cocaine, and various explosives. Bloodhounds can track lost persons through all kinds of terrain. Although your sense of smell is not as sensitive as that of a dog, some individuals, such as perfume testers and wine testers, do have excellent noses. These professionals have developed their sense of smell so highly that they can detect minute differences in perfumes or wines. Apparently you can train yourself to increase your smell sensitivity, but you probably would never be as good at sniffing as a dog.

Nose

One reason a dog can find a hidden cache of perfume is simply the size of the animal's nose. The larger the nose, the more the receptors for smelling. In the upper part of your nose is a tissue known as the **olfactory membrane**. This membrane contains literally millions of **olfactory cells**, the receptors for smell. In your small nose, the olfactory membrane is approximately the size of a postage stamp. In the large nose of a German shepherd, the olfactory membrane is approximately the size of a handkerchief. The olfactory membrane in both dogs and humans is covered by a viscous substance called **mucus**. Since the mucus covers the olfactory membrane, it also covers the olfactory cells. In order for you to smell an onion, the onion must give off something that can be dissolved in the mucus that covers the olfactory cells.

Smell

When a dog tries to locate hidden explosives, it sniffs constantly. When you smell a flower or a new perfume, you usually take a large sniff. Sniffing helps to increase the air flow through the nose and brings the odor in contact with the olfactory cells. The reason a flower or an onion has an odor is that the flower and onion release molecules into the air. Your sniffing draws these airborne molecules into your nose. Once in your nose, the molecules dissolve in the mucus and affect the olfactory cells. A substance such as glass does not give off molecules and thus has no odor. Flowers and onions are said to be **volatile** substances since they can release molecules into the air. Glass is not a volatile substance.

If Charlie had known about volatile substances and the

size of the dog's olfactory membrane, he probably would not have made his wager. Some molecules from the perfume probably escaped through the plastic container. The dog was able to notice the weak odor because its nose, with millions and millions of olfactory cells, can detect a lower concentration of perfume molecules than your nose can. Some animals, such as dolphins, have little or no sense of smell. A better bet for Charlie might be to wager that a dolphin cannot smell a few drops of perfume in the water.

Smell Variation
You can certainly smell the difference between brownies and gasoline. Scientists have been trying to determine why a brownie smells different from gasoline, or how the olfactory cells code the hundreds of different odors. It is known that brownies release molecules into the air and that these molecules are dissolved in the olfactory mucus and affect the olfactory cells. The stimulus for the olfactory cells is a series of molecules, or a chemical. For that reason, the sense of smell, or **olfaction**, is called a **chemical sense**. One researcher has proposed that differences in odor are caused by differences in the size and shape of the molecular structure of the chemicals and the receptors (6–3). As illustrated in Figure 6–1, you can imagine different odors as being the result of different shapes or "keys" (volatile chemicals) being fitted into certain "locks" (olfactory receptors). Only the chemical having the appropriate molecular size and shape can fit into a receptor having a particular

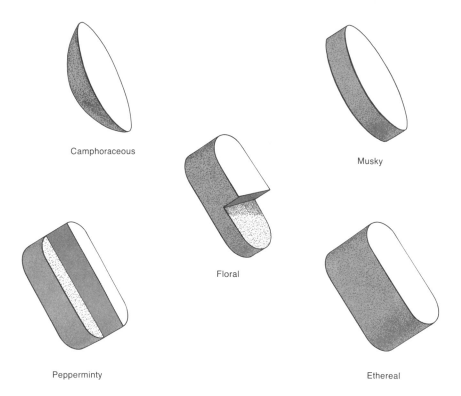

Camphoraceous

Musky

Floral

Pepperminty

Ethereal

Figure 6–1 Substances that smell musky may be shaped like the "musky" molecule shown here. How something smells may be coded by the shape of the molecule that fits into a certain olfactory receptor — similar to a lock-and-key arrangement. Shown here are some molecular shapes for a number of smells.

Smelling, Tasting, and Touching

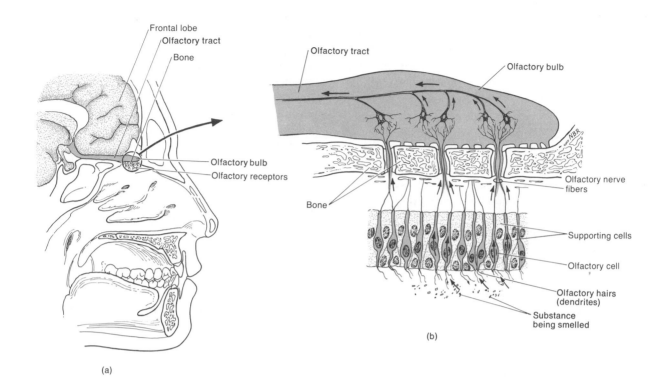

(a)

(b)

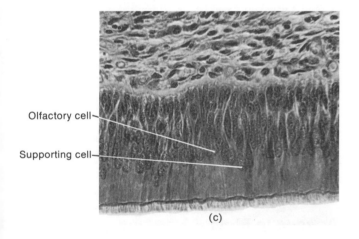

Olfactory cell
Supporting cell

(c)

Figure 6-2 The olfactory or smell sense. (a) The location of the olfactory receptors in the roof of the nose. (b) An enlargement of the receptors showing the olfactory nerve passing into the olfactory bulb, which is part of the brain. (c) Photomicrograph of the olfactory mucosa at a magnification of 400×. (Courtesy of Donald I. Patt, from *Comparative Vertebrate Histology*, by Donald I. Patt and Gail R. Patt, Harper & Row, Publishers, Inc., New York, 1969.)

size and shape. The idea that odors are coded by the shape of chemical keys fitting appropriate olfactory receptors is the **stereochemical theory**. Following this theory, another researcher went on to classify seven primary odors based on the shape of the molecular structure (6–1). There is evidence for both the stereochemical theory and for seven primary odors, but, because of conflicting data, neither of these ideas has been completely validated.

Nose to Brain

As you sniff a rose, molecules released into the air by the rose are drawn into your nose and dissolved in the mucus covering the olfactory membrane. Once the molecules are

dissolved in the mucus, these chemicals affect the olfactory cells, perhaps according to the stereochemical theory. The dissolved chemicals cause the olfactory cells to produce electrical changes, or generator potentials. When a receptor produces a sufficient generator potential to reach the threshold of a neuron, a nerve impulse is triggered. The nerve impulse travels in the **olfactory nerve** to the brain.

Unlike the other senses, the sense of smell does not synapse within the thalamus. Figure 6–2 shows you how the olfactory receptors in your nose send information to your brain. As you can see in the figure, the brain structure known as the **olfactory bulb** lies just a few millimeters, or a fraction of an inch, above your nasal passage. The olfactory nerve fibers, which are very short, travel straight up through a spongy, perforated section of the skull and synapse in the olfactory bulb. Cells in the olfactory bulb then send impulses to other areas at the base of the brain, such as the **olfactory tubercle** (TWO-burr-cle) and **prepyriform** (pre-PEER-ah-form) **cortex**, which is in the temporal lobe. You probably first have a sensation of smell when impulses reach the olfactory area in the temporal lobe.

Adaptation

When you apply your deodorant, you can smell its odor. After some time, you are no longer aware of any odor. In the same way, you initially may be aware of your own bad breath or body odor, but after some time you no longer smell yourself. The explanation for this process is unclear, but the name for it is **adaptation**. Adaptation is a decrease in your ability to detect an odor (your deodorant) that occurs when your receptors stop responding after continuous exposure to the same odor. Another process also causes a decrease in your sense of smell. After a while, neurons in the central nervous system stop responding to input from the receptors. This is called **habituation**. It is very fortunate that you have the processes of adaptation and habituation, since without them you would be smelling the same smells for hours on end.

Tasting

Charlie was not able to taste the difference between Coca-Cola and Seven-Up with his nasal passages blocked. What you consider to be taste actually involves your nose as well as your tongue. Foods or liquids on the way to your mouth release molecules into the air. These molecules reach the olfactory receptors in your nose. When you taste food, which is called **gustation**, you also smell it, which is olfaction. A good example of how much olfaction affects your sense of taste is the lack of taste you experience during a cold. Usually a cold causes excess mucus in the nasal passages, and this overabundant mucus prevents the airborne molecules from reaching the olfactory cells. During a cold, you are deprived of olfaction and must rely solely on the sense of taste. Taste, like smell, is a chemical sense because the stimulus for taste is a chemical in solid (food) or liquid (beverage) form. Charlie had to learn the hard way that taste and smell are both chemical senses and that smell helps determine the way things taste.

Tongue

There are approximately 10,000 taste buds. They are located mostly on your tongue, but some are found in your throat. Each taste bud contains many **taste cells**, the receptors for taste. As Charlie drank some Seven-Up, the chemicals in the liquid affected his taste cells, causing them to produce generator potentials. When the generator potential in a taste cell becomes great enough, a neuron's threshold is reached and a nerve impulse is triggered.

After drinking very hot coffee and burning your tongue, you may have noticed a temporary decrease in your taste sensitivity. This is because the heat actually destroyed some of your taste cells. You probably also noticed that your taste sensitivity returned shortly. This is because taste cells are continuously being replaced. Any given cell is replaced about every seven days. As you get older and reach the late 40's, taste buds begin to degenerate and taste sensitivity decreases.

Four Kinds of Taste

When you drink a Coca-Cola, it tastes sweet because the receptors on the tip of the tongue are activated more than any of the other cells (Figure 6–3). When you eat salted nuts, they taste salty because the cells most stimulated are those on the edges near the front of the tongue. Lemonade tastes sour because the taste cells most affected are those on the edges of the tongue near the back. If you have ever tasted quinine, you know it tastes bitter, and this is because the cells most affected are those on the middle of the tongue near the back. It is thought that these four basic tastes—**sweet**, **salty**, **sour**, and **bitter**—form the basis for all other tastes. Each of these four tastes is produced by a different group of chemicals. Some chemicals affect only one set of receptors, such as sweet taste cells. Other chemicals affect several sets of receptors at once, producing tastes that are in between sweet and sour or salty and bitter. If you burned your tongue, the receptors on the tip, the sweet cells, would probably be affected most. But the taste for sweetness would not be lost completely, because the other receptors on the tongue can also respond to sweetness. Your taste sensitivity may change from day to day, and taste sensitivity certainly varies among people.

Tongue to Brain

The sensations you know as sweet or salty begin when different chemicals activate taste cells. The taste cells produce generator potentials that eventually trigger nerve impulses. Impulses leave the tongue on nerves that synapse with several nuclei before reaching the thalamus. Which nucleus of the thalamus receives taste has not been established. The thalamus integrates the information and sends it on to the **primary projection area** for taste. This area is located on the side and near the bottom of the parietal lobe, in the part of the cortex that receives information from most of the body's senses, the somatosensory cortex. Impulses coming from the four different types of receptors terminate in slightly different areas of the somatosensory cortex. When impulses reach the taste area in the somatosensory cortex, you might have very simple taste sensations, such as sweet,

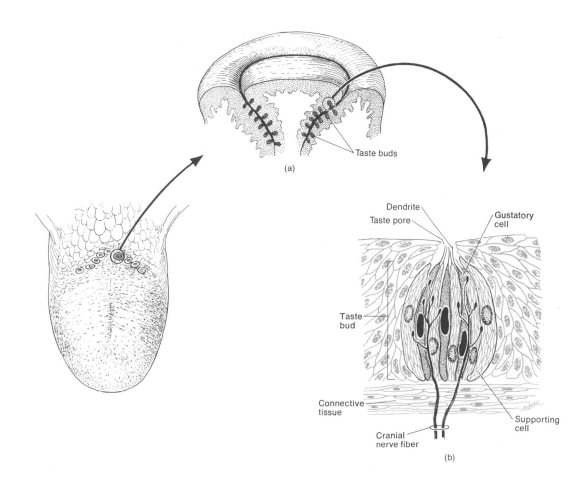

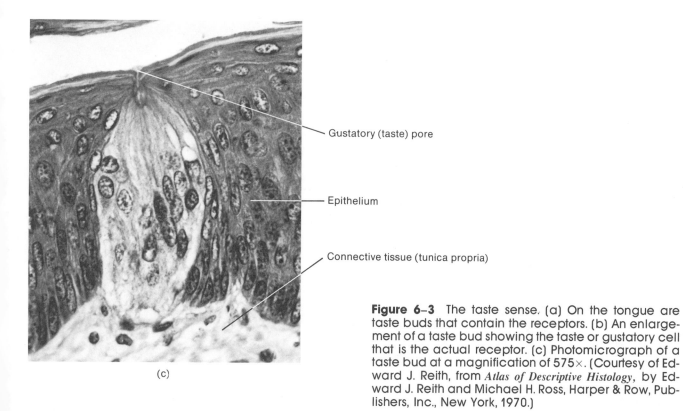

Gustatory (taste) pore

Epithelium

Connective tissue (tunica propria)

Figure 6-3 The taste sense. (a) On the tongue are taste buds that contain the receptors. (b) An enlargement of a taste bud showing the taste or gustatory cell that is the actual receptor. (c) Photomicrograph of a taste bud at a magnification of 575×. (Courtesy of Edward J. Reith, from *Atlas of Descriptive Histology*, by Edward J. Reith and Michael H. Ross, Harper & Row, Publishers, Inc., New York, 1970.)

sour, bitter, or salty. However, you do not know what the taste is (hamburger) or how much you like it until impulses reach the association areas of the cortex. In the normally functioning brain, the primary projection area for taste is probably never activated by itself. Milliseconds after an impulse reaches the primary projection area, other impulses reach the association areas and tell you that the stimulus is a hamburger and that it tastes good.

First Bite versus Last Bite

Your first bite into a brownie may taste fantastic, while your last bite may not taste nearly as good. The brownie has not lost its flavor, your taste receptors have become less sensitive. As the receptors, in this case mostly sweet cells, are exposed continuously to stimulation, there is a decreased sensitivity, or adaptation. Sips of milk between bites of brownie might help to prevent the occurrence of adaptation. Exactly how adaptation occurs in the receptors has not yet been explained.

Temperature

Charlie should have won the wager with the person who said he could tolerate a lit cigarette on his hand for 15 seconds. What Charlie did not know was that this man's hand was heavily callused from years of playing handball. When the cigarette was applied, it touched only layers of dead skin that acted as an insulator and prevented pain. After some time, the dead skin probably transferred some of the cigarette's heat to the living cells below the callus, giving at least a sensation of warmth. When the skin is warmed, it causes a temperature increase in the skin's fluid. An increase in temperature affects certain cells in the skin known as **warm receptors**. If the skin is cooled, there is a decrease in the temperature of the skin's fluid. This decrease activates cells in the skin known as **cold receptors**. It is not yet known exactly how these temperature changes activate the receptors. When warm or cold receptors are activated, generator potentials are produced. When the generator potential is great enough to reach the threshold of a neuron, an impulse is formed.

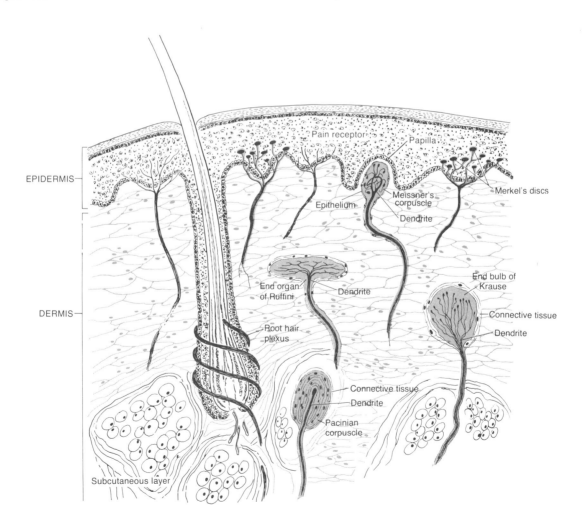

Figure 6–4 Different layers of skin have different kinds of receptors that react to pressure, touch, temperature, and pain.

Smelling, Tasting, and Touching

The Headliner

ARTIFICIAL SWEETENERS: THE FIELD IS WIDE OPEN

No single sugar substitute now on the drawing boards—neither a natural one nor a synthetic—is apt to meet all the demands placed on such a product by government agencies, food processors and everybody who eats.

* * *

Why is it so difficult to come up with something that sweetens? Part of the reason is that scientists do not understand what happens physiologically and on a molecular basis when something sweet touches the tongue and causes a message to be transmitted to the brain saying "sweet."

* * *

"There is no logical way to research for them, no good theory that tells you how to synthesize a new one," says Dr. Robert M. Horowitz of the U.S. Department of Agriculture Fruit and Vegetable Chemistry Laboratory in Pasadena.

Ideally, the way to create a new synthetic would be to understand the underlying biochemical, physiological and neurological principles of sweetness. Then a molecule with the appropriate configuration could be devised. Because there is no model for a "sweet" molecule, most of the synthetic ones have been discovered accidentally by scientists who were looking for something else. Even when such a molecule is discovered, it often must undergo considerable manipulation in the laboratory by researchers to eliminate some undesirable characteristic such as aftertaste or to make it sweeter by changing a few atoms here and there.

A few years ago Dr. Glenn H. Hamor, professor of biomedical chemistry at the USC school of pharmacy, spent a year adding various chemical groups to, or removing them from, the basic molecule for saccharin. The goal was to learn what chemical groups were responsible for the sweet taste. He was not successful.

In the course of these experiments Hamor noted that one of the split saccharin molecules resembled that of a local anesthetic. So he set out to synthesize a new local anesthetic using saccharin as the starting point.

After injecting the new compound in animals, Hamor learned that he had discovered not a new anesthetic but a new drug with the potential for halting epileptic seizures. The antiepileptic drug is now being tested by the National Institutes of Health; it is tasteless.

Another example of serendipity in sweetener research is provided by the work of Dr. Horowitz, the federal Fruit and Vegetable Chemistry Laboratory researchers in Pasadena, and his coworker, Bruno Gentili.

About 15 years ago Horowitz and Gentili became interested in learning what is required chemically to make a bitter compound. They selected as their starting point the chemical in grapefruit peel that makes it taste bitter. It is called disaccharide neohesperidose.

Eventually in their research process they learned that this intensely bitter compound could, by certain chemical processing, be transformed into products that were intensely sweet. One of them, called neohesperidin dihydrochalcone or neo DHC, is about 1,500 times as sweet as sugar and about five times as sweet as saccharin.

Despite the fact the scientists originally had no intention of discovering a new sweetener, this sugar substitute is perhaps as close as any other new product to receiving FDA approval as a sweetener additive.

* * *

SOURCE: Excerpt from a longer article by Harry Nelson, Times Medical Writer, *Los Angeles Times,* May 8, 1977. Copyright © 1977 by Los Angeles Times.

If your skin were touched with an object that was the same temperature as your skin, you would feel neither warmth nor cold. The temperature of the object would be at **physiological zero**, the temperature of your skin. If you were holding a hot cup of water in your hand, the blood vessels near the surface would become engorged with blood in order to cool the skin. If you were holding a cold dish of ice cream, the blood vessels would constrict to keep in the body's heat. Thus, physiological zero, or the temperature of your skin, changes. In order for you to feel something as warm, or cold, the stimulus must be above or below physiological zero. For example, when you hold a dish of ice cream, the dish is below physiological zero, and you feel a sensation of cold.

Adaptation

When you first step into a hot shower, it seems very hot but soon becomes comfortable. Your first jump into a swimming pool makes you feel cold, but soon the water feels comfortable. This seeming change in temperature, from cold to comfortable, occurs because the cold receptors stop being activated when the temperature remains constant. This process is adaptation. The warm and cold receptors in your skin are sensitive to changes in temperature, but they become less sensitive if the temperature remains constant. However, if you were swimming in a very cold pool or taking an extremely hot shower, the receptors would not adapt completely. At extremes of hot or cold, very little adaptation occurs, and for good reason. It could be very dangerous for you to adapt to swimming in icy-cold water.

Receptor to Cortex

If the warm or cold receptors in your skin are activated, you do not know whether you are warm or cold until the impulses reach the cortex. If you hold a cup of hot coffee in your right hand, the warm receptors are activated, causing generator potentials that trigger impulses in connecting neurons. These neurons have long axons that carry the impulses into the spinal cord. Once in the spinal cord, there are several synapses with other neurons, until the information is traveling up the left side of the spinal cord. Temperature information from the right-hand or right side of the body travels up the left side of the spinal cord to terminate in the left side of the brain. If the left side of your spinal cord were damaged, you would lose sensations on the right side of your body.

Temperature information from your right hand travels up the left side of the spinal cord and synapses in the thalamus. If one impulse from one warm receptor arrives in the thalamus, it is unlikely that the thalamus will be activated. There must be many impulses from many receptors before a neuron in the thalamus is activated. If a minute amount of hot water were placed on your thumb, you probably would not feel the drop as hot. If a larger part of your thumb were placed in hot water, more warm receptors would be activated, causing more impulses to activate the neurons in the thalamus. This means that your sense of temperature is not as precise as some of the other senses. For example, your visual sense is more accurate since a smaller number of visual receptors can activate a neuron in the thalamus. It is probably more important for your survival that you be able to see with great accuracy than it is that you know whether a tiny drop of water is hot or cold.

In the Cortex

You can tell whether your thumb is in a cup of hot coffee or your foot is in a cold shower because these pieces of information terminate at different places in your cortex. After leaving the thalamus, information is sent to the primary projection area of the cortex, the somatosensory area. Different areas of the somatosensory cortex receive information from different parts of the body, as illustrated in Figure 6–5. As you can see, information from the trunk is projected to the top of the somatosensory cortex, while information from the tongue is projected to the bottom. If the thumb area of the somatosensory cortex were electrically stimulated, you might feel warm or cold sensations even though the receptors in your thumb were not activated. If the somatosensory cortex were surgically removed, you could no longer tell exactly which part of your body was feeling hot or cold. However, you would have general feelings of warmth or cold. This tells us that information from the temperature receptors travels to areas of the cortex other than the somatosensory area. The sense of temperature differs from most other senses in that you do not have a severe loss of the sensation when the primary projection area is destroyed. We will see that the same is true for pain.

If your brain is functioning normally, you should know that your thumb is hot as soon as information from the temperature receptors reaches the somatosensory cortex. However, this is really a hypothetical question, since the somatosensory area is probably never activated by itself. Almost immediately, impulses are sent from the somatosensory cortex to association cortex. If having your thumb in hot water reminds you of the last time you were burned, it is because the association areas have been activated.

Pain

If a cigarette were accidentally touched to your hand, or your finger were slammed in a door, you would first feel a sharp, quick pain followed by a slow, burning pain. In the skin as well as in various joints, muscles, and **viscera** (internal organs), there are receptors for pain called **free nerve endings**. The free nerve endings look like minute pieces of string with frayed endings. It is thought that there

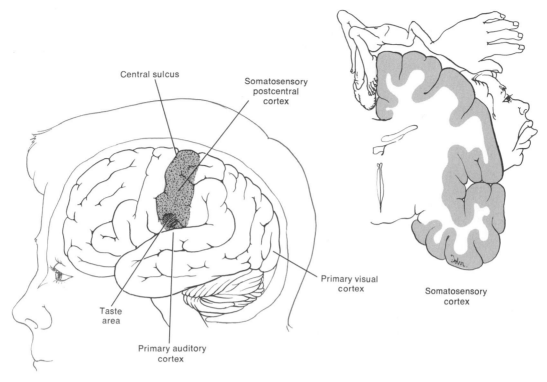

Figure 6–5 The side view of the brain in the skull shows the cortical areas for touch, temperature (somatosensory), and taste in the parietal lobe; vision in the occipital lobe; and audition in the temporal lobe. The figure on the right represents the amount of somatosensory cortex devoted to different areas of the body. The more sensitive the area, the larger the amount of cortex. For example, the fingers are very sensitive so they have more cortical area and are shown larger here than the toes, which have less cortical area and are shown smaller.

are two different pain systems: one for quick pain and one for slow pain. The sharp, quick pain results from activation of free nerve endings that produce generator potentials, which trigger impulses. This information travels on very fast conducting fibers, called **A fibers**. When you slam your finger, impulses reach your brain in a fraction of a second, causing the quick, sharp pain. The dull, slow pain results when other free nerve endings are activated and the information travels on slower conducting fibers, called **C fibers**. The A fibers are axons with large diameters, and because of this they can conduct impulses very quickly. In contrast, the C fibers have small diameters and slower conduction rates.

You may have felt pain after being bruised, cut, pushed, hit, or mauled. Pain occurs when you touch a surface having a temperature above 45°C (113° F) or below 10°C (50° F), when oxygen is stopped to some part of the body, and when the dentist touches an exposed nerve in your tooth. There are several different kinds of headache pain. Constant tensing of muscles in the forehead often leads to tension headaches. Accumulation of fluids in the sinuses results in increased pressure and sinus headaches. And it is thought that the dilation of blood vessels surrounding the brain exposes the receptors in the vessels to certain chemicals that cause the pain of migraine headaches.

In some cases, you may not notice pain immediately.

You may not notice a bad scratch if it occurs while your team is scoring a touchdown. The pain from a tension headache may come and go, depending on how absorbed you are in your work. In a more extreme case, the pain from a flesh wound may go unnoticed while a soldier is fighting for his life. These are examples of how you can ignore pain when your attention is focused on something more dramatic or engrossing. In these cases it is likely that pain receptors are being activated and information is being sent to the brain. The failure to notice pain does not depend on events at the receptor, but on events in the brain. Although the neural information about pain reaches the brain, it may go unnoticed because of excitement, distraction, or learned techniques, such as self-hypnosis or yoga, that prevent your paying attention to pain. People differ widely in their ability to shift their attention and not feel pain.

Thumb to Brain

If you accidentally hammered your left thumb, you would activate receptors for fast and slow pain. Both types of receptors (slow-conducting, type C, and fast-conducting, type A) have long axons that enter the spinal cord. In the spinal cord there would be several synapses until the impulses traveled up the spinal cord. Most of the information from pain receptors in your right thumb and from the right side of your body travel up the left side of the spinal cord and terminate in the left side of your brain. However, some information from pain receptors travels up the same side of the spinal cord. Thus, some information from pain receptors in your left thumb would terminate in the left side of your brain.

In the Brain

When impulses from pain receptors reach your brain, they are processed somewhat differently than the other senses. Some impulses go to the thalamus, others to the reticular formation and hypothalamus. Although all the senses send impulses into the reticular formation, the sense of pain sends proportionately more than the other senses. After leaving the thalamus, some pain impulses go to the somatosensory cortex in the parietal lobe. However, the primary projection area for pain is not entirely localized in the somatosensory area, since damage to this area will not entirely eliminate pain. Other areas of the cortex also receive and process information from pain receptors, among them the frontal lobe. We know this because severing the connections to the frontal lobe is one of the few ways that pain of terminal diseases can be treated. Following this surgery, patients report they still have the sensation of pain but no longer find it as aversive.

Localization of Pain

For the senses of temperature and touch, each part of your body sends its information to a distinct part of the somatosensory cortex. This is not true for the sense of pain. You may wonder, then, how you localize the pain as coming from your left thumb. When you strike your thumb, both pain and touch receptors are activated, and information for the touch receptors is sent to a distinct area of the somatosensory cortex. You feel the pain because pain receptors send their information to the brain, and you know the pain is in your left thumb because the touch receptors send their information to a specific area of the brain. Your brain combines this information so that you feel the pain as localized in your thumb.

Very often you must rely on the sense of touch to tell where your cut, scratch, or bruise is located. You can more easily localize pain on your skin, where there are many touch receptors, than in your viscera, where there are fewer touch receptors. During heart attacks, people report feeling pain in their left arm or shoulder when the pain is actually coming from the heart muscle. This is called **referred pain**, because pain coming from one place inside your body or viscera is referred, or is felt as coming from skin or muscle in another part of the body. One reason for feeling referred pain is that your heart and viscera do not send their infor-

mation to separate areas on your somatosensory cortex. Localization of sensations from areas such as toes or fingers is much easier, since they do have separate areas in the somatosensory cortex.

Another reason that you localize the pain from your heart in your left arm is that neurons coming from the heart enter the spinal cord at the same place as neurons coming from the arm. Once in the spinal cord, some of the neurons coming from your heart may synapse with neurons coming from your arm. Possibly some neurons carry combined information from the touch receptors in the arm and the pain receptors in the heart. Information from these neurons would ultimately terminate in the area of the somatosensory cortex involved in arm sensations. Thus, pain from the heart muscle would be "felt" in your arm because some impulses from pain receptors in the heart terminate in the arm area of the somatosensory cortex. Just as you see with your cortex rather than your eyes, you feel pain with your cortex rather than your heart.

Gate Control Theory

If you hit your thumb with a hammer, your first response might be to rub the painful area. Rubbing the area gives some feeling of relief, probably as a result of events that take place in the spinal cord. When neurons carrying information from pain receptors reach the spinal cord, they form synapses with other neurons in the cord. When you rub the injured area, you activate many touch receptors whose neurons also form synapses with other neurons in the same area of the spinal cord. Information from the touch receptors is thought to inhibit or interfere with the synapses that carry information from pain receptors. This idea has been called the **gate control theory** of pain (6–2). When the touch receptors are activated, the gate for pain information is closed and you feel less pain. When the touch receptors are not activated, the gate is open and more impulses reach the cortex, causing you to feel pain.

Touch

Charlie certainly should have won the bet about recognizing colors with the finger tips, since it is most unlikely that anyone can do this. There have been reports of individuals who claimed to recognize colors using only their fingertips (6–4), but one individual who made the claim had actually learned to peek around the blindfold. This is probably how Charlie lost the bet.

Although your fingers cannot see colors, they can feel differences in texture between a glossy magazine page and a dull newspaper page, they can vary their pressure so that you do not break an egg or crush a paper cup, and they can make hundreds of other fine adjustments.

Receptors

If your skin is stroked lightly, receptors near the surface of the skin and others at the base of the hair follicles are activated. If you shake hands, receptors deeper in the skin are activated by this greater pressure. The receptors that provide information about different kinds of touching and pressure are called **tactile receptors**. These receptors come in various sizes and shapes: some are free nerve endings that look like frayed strings, some look like strings with tiny disks at the end, and others look like strings with their ends wrapped in layers like onions. The latter are called **Pacinian corpuscles** (pa-SIN-ee-in) and are large enough to be visible to the naked eye. They are located deep in the skin, where they respond to deep pressure. Figure 6–4 shows a small section of skin with its various tactile receptors.

As you climb the stairs, this seemingly simple movement is made possible by a series of very fine muscular adjustments. In order for your muscles to adjust the foot so that it can be raised and placed on the next step, your brain must know the continuous position of your foot. Information about the position of your foot as well as your other limbs is made available by receptors in the joints. The receptors in the joints that provide information about where your limbs are in space are called **kinesthetic receptors** (kin-es-THET-ic). A blind person can walk and climb stairs and reach for a light switch because the kinesthetic receptors supply information about where the limbs are in space. One kinesthetic receptor is the Pacinian corpuscle. When you move your arm, pressure is applied to the Pacinian corpuscles located in the arm's joints. The pressure on the Pacinian corpuscle causes a generator potential, and the more the pressure the larger the potential. When the potential is sufficient to reach the neuron's threshold, an impulse is triggered. The other tactile and kinesthetic receptors function in a way similar to the Pacinian corpuscle. Pressure activates the receptors to produce generator potentials that trigger impulses, which travel into the spinal cord on long axons.

Adaptation

If a bowling ball were placed in your lap, you would feel the weight as long as the ball were there. The receptors for deep pressure, the Pacinian corpuscles, continue to be activated by the weight of the ball and show little adaptation. In contrast, if a feather were placed on your skin, after a time you would stop feeling it. In fact, without looking, you would think nothing was there, because the receptors sensitive to light pressure adapt very quickly. When the pressure of the feather on the skin is constant, the receptors stop responding. If the feather were moved across the skin, different receptors would continually be activated so that adaptation would not occur. Thus, the receptors for light pressure adapt unless the stimulus is moving, while those for deep pressure show very little adaptation.

If there were only light pressure receptors in your fingers, you would have difficulty holding a pencil or a coffee cup. Since light pressure receptors adapt quickly, you would probably lose sensation and drop the pencil or coffee cup. Fortunately, you can hold a pencil or coffee cup indefinitely because there are other tactile receptors in your fingers that continue to respond to steady, light pressure. These nonadapting receptors tell you that the fingers are touching a pencil or some other object, such as a coffee cup.

Another reason you can hold a cup of coffee is that the kinesthetic receptors in the finger joints show almost no adaptation. You can keep your fingers curled around a cup because of these kinesthetic receptors and you can keep the right amount of pressure on the cup because of the tactile receptors in the skin.

Kinds of Receptors

Throughout the layers of the skin, as well as in the muscles and joints, are receptors that have different adaptation times. Here are examples of four main types.

1 *Tactile receptors–light pressure:* respond to light touch and adapt very quickly. Many are located in the fingers and are involved in identifying textures (smooth or rough).

2 *Tactile receptors–light pressure:* respond to light pressure and show almost no adaptation. They are located mostly in the fingertips.

3 *Tactile receptors–deep pressure:* respond to deep or heavy pressure with little or no adaptation. They are located deeper in the skin. One type of deep pressure receptor is Pacinian corpuscle.

4 *Kinesthetic receptors:* respond to movement and position of the limbs. They are located in the joints and show almost no adaptation. These are the receptors that allowed you to keep your fingers curled around the coffee cup. (Pacinian corpuscles also serve this function but are not the only type of kinesthetic receptor.)

Skin to Brain

You know there is a cat brushing your left leg because the cat exerts pressure on the skin that activates the tactile receptors, that produce generator potentials, that trigger nerve impulses. The impulses are sent into the spinal cord on long axons. Some of the information crosses over as it enters the spinal cord. Other information crosses over to the opposite side when it arrives just below the brain in the midbrain. By the time the information from your left leg or left body reaches the thalamus, almost all of the impulses have crossed over to the right side of the thalamus, specifically the **ventrobasal nucleus**. It is unlikely that you would have a sensation of being touched when impulses reach the thalamus. From the ventrobasal nuclei of the thalamus, information is projected to the primary projection area, the somatosensory cortex, shown in Figure 6–5. Notice that the area lies just behind the central sulcus in the parietal lobe.

Somatosensory Cortex

The reason you can tell that the cat is brushing against your left leg as opposed to your right arm is that information (tactile, pressure, and kinesthetic) from the various parts of the body terminates in discrete areas of the somatosensory cortex. There are different areas in the somatosensory cortex for the leg, hand, tongue, and other body parts. Your fingertips and lips have large areas on the somatosensory cortex while your legs and back have smaller areas. The more sensitive an area of the body, such as the fingertips and lips, the larger its area on the somatosensory cortex. The less sensitive an area of your body, such as your back, the smaller its area on the cortex. When a receptor in a sensitive area is activated, the impulses from that one receptor are probably sufficient to activate neurons in the thalamus and cortex. However, when receptors are activated in a less sensitive area, there is a great deal more convergence, and many receptors must be activated before their impulses will activate neurons in the thalamus and cortex. So your fingers are more sensitive than your back for two reasons. First, the skin on your fingertips has many more receptors than the skin on your back. Second, there is a larger area devoted to the fingertips in the somatosensory area of the cortex. This means that there are literally more cortical neurons devoted to your fingertips.

If the somatosensory area in your right hemisphere were removed or destroyed, you would be unable to tell if the left side of your body were touched, you would be unable to distinguish between different shapes or textures, and you would have great difficulty locating your limbs in space with your eyes closed. If only a part of the right somatosensory area were damaged, you would lose sensations only in that part of the body represented on the damaged area. That is why a gunshot wound in the middle of the somatosensory cortex could, for example, destroy sensations from the lower face and lips and leave sensations from other body areas intact. If an area of your somatosensory cortex were electrically stimulated, you would feel tingling in the corresponding part of the body. For instance, you would feel tingling in your thumb from stimulation of the thumb area of the somatosensory cortex even though the receptors in your thumb were not activated.

If your right arm were removed because of an accident, you might still continue to feel itching, pressure, or pain "in your right arm." Although your arm was not actually there, you might have feelings in it because neurons in your cortex were activated. Feeling sensations from a limb that has been removed is called the **phantom limb phenomenon**.

Touch Recognition

Although you might have some sensations of touch as soon as impulses reach your somatosensory cortex, this area alone cannot tell you if you are touching a rabbit or a baseball. In order for you to recognize a rabbit by touch, impulses have to reach the association areas of the cortex. The association areas add meaning to the stimulus (soft, pleasant, cuddly) and allow you to name the object (rabbit) and add other kinds of associations (Easter rabbit). With only your somesthetic area, you might know that you are touching something. With your association areas, you can recognize that object as a rabbit that is pleasant to hold.

Senses Are Similar
Receptors

Although your eye has a shape quite different from your nose, which has a shape quite different from your tongue or skin, each of these structures contains receptors that have the same function. The variously shaped receptors react to an energy change with an electrical change, or generator potential. Receptors in the eye, ear, nose, and skin do not respectively see, hear, smell, and feel. Instead, these receptors convert energy, whether it is light waves, sound waves, chemicals, or pressure, into generator potentials. If the generator potential is large enough to reach the neuron's threshold, an impulse is triggered. Receptors are the initiators of impulses.

Only when impulses reach various areas in the brain do you experience seeing or hearing or touching. And it is possible to "see" or "hear" or "touch" without activating the receptors. A blow to the back of the head, affecting the occipital lobe of the brain, may result in the experience of "seeing stars." You would "see stars" because neurons in the visual cortex that are usually excited by input from rods and cones have been activated instead by a blow to the head.

Adaptation

If a cone in the retina were exposed to a continuous beam of light, it would soon cease responding with a generator potential. When a receptor is exposed to a constant stimulus, the receptor stops responding, and this is known as adaptation. Adaptation is common to all receptors, but less so for pain and certain tactile and kinesthetic receptors.

Primary Projection Area

Hypothetically, you might first have experiences of seeing or hearing or touching when nerve impulses reach their primary projection areas in the cortex. If the primary projection area were electrically stimulated, you would have sensations of light, sound, or tingling, depending on which area were stimulated. If the primary projection area were destroyed, you would suffer loss or decrease of sensation in whichever sense area was affected. If your association areas were destroyed, so that you had to depend completely on your primary projection areas, you might sense something when impulses reached the primary projection area. However, this something would be a very simple sensation. For you to recognize or feel or sense complex stimuli, impulses must reach the association areas. In the normally functioning brain, association areas are usually activated after primary projection areas.

Association Areas

Once impulses reach association areas, a flash of light becomes a flower, a tone becomes a song, and an odor becomes a mouth-watering hamburger. The association areas add meaning to the hundreds of stimuli you sense throughout the day. Because we each have different learning experiences and feelings, the kind of meaning added to a stimulus is different for each person. An absolutely sure wager for Charlie is to bet that he does not see or hear or feel the same things that you do.

Comment

A famous line of poetry says that a "Rose is a rose is a rose." From what you have learned about sensory function, adaptation, and association areas, you know that a rose is never just a rose. It is never the same for any two persons. If you hear someone say, "Beauty is in the eye of the beholder," you will know that the idea is almost right. Beauty is not in the eye, tongue, or nose of the beholder, it is in the brain. Each of your senses sends an incredible amount of information to your brain. As you process this information, you are constantly adding meaning, so that your world is like no other's.

SELF-TEST 6

1 When you peel an onion, it releases molecules into the air. An onion is a _____ substance.

volatile

2 You can smell an onion because its airborne molecules reach a membrane in the upper nose called the _____ membrane, which is covered with _____ , under which are the _____ .

olfactory / mucus receptors or olfactory cells

3 When the molecules or chemicals from the onion dissolve in the mucus, they activate the receptors to produce _____ .

generator potentials

4 If the generator potentials are large enough, they reach the neuron's _____ and trigger an _____ .

threshold impulse

5 Unlike the other senses, olfaction does not synapse in the _____ . Instead, olfactory nerves synapse in the _____ and then terminate in cortex areas at the base of the brain called the _____ .

thalamus olfactory bulb olfactory tubercle or prepyriform cortex

6 The stereochemical theory states that different odors are coded by certain sized and shaped _____ "keys" fitting into like shaped and sized _____ "locks."

chemical receptor

7 When a receptor is exposed to a constant stimulus and the receptor stops producing generator potentials, this is called _____ . When neurons of the brain stop responding to receptors, this is called _____ .

adaptation habituation

8 The interaction between the two senses of gustation and olfaction is most apparent when you have a cold. Foods taste bland because you do not have the sense of _____ .

smell or olfaction

9 Like smell, taste is called a _____ sense because the stimulus for it is _____ .

chemical / chemical

10 The receptors for taste are located in the mouth and mostly on the tongue. When a chemical from a food dissolves on the tongue, it activates the _____ , which produce _____ , which trigger _____ .

taste cells or receptors generator potentials impulses

11 Taste receptors on certain areas of the tongue respond more to one taste than to another. Receptors on the tip respond most to _____ tastes. Those on the front edges respond most to _____ tastes. Those on the back edges respond most to _____ tastes. Those on the back in the middle respond most to _____ tastes.

sweet / salty sour bitter

12 If you burnt the tip of your tongue, the receptors for _____ tastes would be destroyed. After a few days your taste sensitivity would return because _____ are continuously being replaced.

sweet receptors or taste cells

13 After leaving the thalamus, taste information is projected to the primary projection area located in the _____ cortex in the _____ lobe.

somatosensory / parietal

14 When impulses reach the _____ area, you might have a sensation of sweetness, but you will not know that the sweet taste is a peach until impulses reach the _____ areas in the cortex.

somatosensory association

15 You know you are sitting in a hot bath because certain cells in your skin called _____ are activated by heat.

warm receptors

16 Hot water increases the temperature of skin fluid, which activates the warm receptors, which produce _____ .

generator potentials

17 When you pick up an ice cube, you know it feels cold because the decrease in skin temperature activates the _____ .

cold receptors

18 The temperature of your skin is called _____ . If something feels warm, it is _____ skin temperature, and if something feels cold, it is _____ skin temperature.

physiological zero / above below

19 When you first get into a bath, it may seem very hot and then become comfortable. This decrease in sensitivity to hot water is called _____ .

adaptation

20 The warm and cold receptors are sensitive to _____ in temperature and are less sensitive if the temperature remains _____ .

changes
the same or constant

21 If you put your left toe into hot water, impulses from the left toe enter the spinal cord and travel toward the brain up the _____ side of the spinal cord.

right

22 For one neuron in the thalamus to be excited, it must receive impulses from _____ temperature information receptors in the skin.

many

23 After leaving the thalamus, temperature information goes to the primary projection area located in the _____ cortex, which is right behind the _____ sulcus.

somatosensory / central

24 You know that your thumb is hot or your leg is cold because different areas of the body are represented in distinct areas of the _____ cortex.

somatosensory

25 The receptors for pain are thought to be _____ , which look like pieces of string with frayed endings.

free nerve endings

26 Information for sharp pain is carried in axons that have a _____ diameter and conduct impulses at _____ speed.

large
high

27 Information for dull pain is carried in axons that have a _____ diameter and conduct impulses at _____ speed.

small
slow

28 Most, but not all, information from pain receptors in your left toe enters the spinal cord and travels toward the brain up the _____ side of the spinal cord; some information travels up the _____ side of the spinal cord.

right
left

29 Before reaching the cortex, information from pain receptors synapses in the _____ and in other brain areas, such as the _____ and _____ .

thalamus / hypothalamus reticular formation

30 After leaving the thalamus, pain information proceeds to the _____ in the parietal lobe, as well as to other parts of the cortex.

somatosensory area

31 Because there is no one _____ for pain, there is no one part of the cortex that can be removed to eliminate pain completely.

primary projection area

32 You are able to locate the exact part of the body that has been injured by using information from your sense of _____ , which, unlike pain, does have a _____ area for each part of the body on the _____ .

touch / distinct or discrete somatosensory cortex

33 You may feel pain on your body surface although the pain is actually originating from another place inside the body. This is called _____ pain.

referred

34 During times of excitement or distraction, you may be injured and not feel the pain because you have shifted your _____ to some other event.

attention

35 If your skin were touched lightly, the touch would activate _____ receptors near the surface. If your hand were squeezed, the squeeze would activate _____ receptors deeper in the skin.

tactile
tactile

36 You would be able to serve a tennis ball with your eyes closed because receptors in the joints, called _____ receptors, provide information as to where your limbs are in space.

kinesthetic

37 When pressure is applied to the Pacinian corpuscle, either from movement of a joint or from heavy pressure, it causes the Pacinian corpuscle to produce _____ that can trigger _____ .

generator potentials impulses

38 If someone sat in your lap, you would feel the presence a long time, since deep _____ receptors do not show _____ .

pressure
adaptation

39 Other receptors that show little adaptation are the _____ receptors and certain light _____ receptors.

kinesthetic / pressure

40 Information from tactile or kinesthetic receptors on the left side of the body synapses in the right _____ of the thalamus and goes to the _____ side of the brain.

ventrobasal nucleus / right

41 After leaving the ventrobasal nucleus of the thalamus, information from tactile and kinesthetic receptors terminates in the _____ , located in the _____ lobe.

somatosensory cortex parietal

42 An area that is very sensitive to tactile stimulation, such as the lips, has a _____ area on the somatosensory cortex. An area that is less sensitive to tactile stimulation, such as the back, has a _____ area.

large

small

43 You might have a sensation of smoothness when information from the tactile receptors reaches the _____ . You know that the object is a snake when the information reaches the _____ areas.

somatosensory area /
association

44 In spite of their varying shapes and sizes, all receptors have the same function, which is to transform some energy change into a _____ .

generator potential

45 If the generator potential is large enough to reach the neuron's _____ , it will trigger an _____ .

threshold
impulse

46 When a continuous stimulus is applied to some receptors, they stop producing generator potentials, and this is called _____ .

adaptation

47 You do not feel any sensations until information from the receptors reaches their particular _____ areas.

primary projection

48 The areas in the cortex that provide meaning and interpret what you sense are called _____ areas.

association

REFERENCES

6-1 Amoore, J. E. The current status of the steric theory of odor. *Annals of the New York Academy of Science* 1964, 116: 457–476.

6-2 Melzack, R. and Wall, P. D. Pain mechanisms: a new theory. *Science* 1965, 150: 971–979.

6-3 Moncrieff, R. W. The characterization of odors. *Journal of Physiology* 1954, 125: 453–465.

6-4 Youtz, R. P. Can fingers "see" color? *Psychology Today* February 1968.

Sexual Behavior 7

How Your Head Knows about Your Sex

Boy or Girl?

Greg and his parents thought about it for months, and they decided he should remain a boy. Greg had a girlfriend and sometimes became aroused when he was with her. He had sisters, and it was clear his interests and thoughts were different from theirs. Greg was happy being a boy. He did not want anything to change.

Following his last medical examination at age 13, the doctors had told Greg he was different from other boys. According to his genes, he was a female. His ovaries had begun to secrete female hormones that had caused his breasts to develop noticeably. Although his sexual organs appeared to be those of a male, his penis, which was very tiny, was actually an enlarged clitoris. At his birth, Greg's parents had been told he was a male, and so they had raised him as a boy. His parents, sisters, and friends all thought of him as male. But now he was beginning to develop the physical characteristics of a female. If nothing were done, Greg would continue to develop the physical sexual characteristics of a female. The problem was that he was genetically and anatomically a female but had been raised as a male.

So the doctors had counseled Greg's parents and his parents had talked it over with Greg. He told the doctors that he considered himself a male and wished to remain a male. He told them that he wanted his breasts removed and that he wanted to be injected with male sex hormones. Finally, he wanted the doctors to explain how all this had happened.

Greg's story comes from the case history of a teenager who had to decide whether to keep or to change his sex. There have been a number of cases in which doctors and parents assigned the label "boy" or "girl" to a baby only

to discover later that the label did not match the child's genetic makeup (7–19). Sometimes, because of hormonal malfunction, a baby's sex organs are neither clearly male nor clearly female. These infants may be labeled as being of one sex while genetically they are the other. Such cases indicate that the way you think of yourself sexually does not follow automatically from your genetic makeup.

Sex and Chromosomes

Greg was conceived like any other infant. Of the 10 to 100 million sperm that one ejaculation deposits into the vagina, only one of these reaches, penetrates, and fertilizes an egg. The fertilized egg or ovum is called a **zygote** (ZEYE-goat). Although smaller than a pinhead, the zygote contains all the information necessary for that miniature cell to develop into an adult human.

The kind of sex chromosomes you received when the egg was fertilized determined the sex organs you would later develop. The female's egg contains only one kind of sex chromosome, called **X**. The male's sperm may contain either a sex chromosome called **X** or a sex chromosome called **Y**. If the egg is fertilized by a sperm with a Y chromosome, the result is a genetic male with the XY combination. It is the Y of the XY combination that contains the instructions for the development of male sex organs, penis and testes. If the egg is fertilized by a sperm with an X chromosome, the result is a genetic female, XX, and the zygote contains instructions for the development of female sex organs: vagina, clitoris, and ovaries. At conception, Greg was a genetic female with XX chromosomes that contained instructions for the development of female sex organs. But at birth his sex organs had resembled those of a

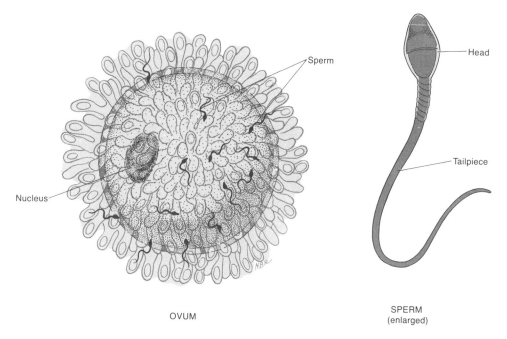

Labels on figure: Sperm, Nucleus (pointing to OVUM), Head, Tailpiece (pointing to SPERM)

OVUM

SPERM
(enlarged)

Figure 7-1 When an ovum is penetrated and fertilized by a sperm, which is many times smaller, the result is a single cell that contains all the information for the development of a human being.

male because of an hormonal malfunction during his mother's pregnancy. Although his clitoris resembled a tiny penis, he had no testes and had the ovaries of a normal female. The sex chromosomes contain instructions for the development of sex organs. The development of sex organs is influenced by hormones and is only the first in a series of steps leading to whether you think of yourself as a man or woman.

Abnormal Chromosomes

The normal condition is to have an XX or XY combination of sex chromosomes. Other patterns do occur, such as X, XXY, or XYY, and these patterns may be accompanied by physiological and psychological changes. For example, if a child has only one X chromosome, she is female. At 15 years of age, this child will be short for her age, have no breast development, no widening of the hips, and no pubic hair, and she will be sterile. She may or may not have a deficit in general intelligence. The condition is called **Turner's syndrome,** and its most notable characteristic is the lack of sexual development at puberty.

If a child is born with an XXY pattern, he is a male but his testes will not develop. As an adult he will be sterile. About half of the males with this condition are also mentally retarded. The condition produced by the XXY pattern is called **Klinefelter's syndrome**.

A chromosomal pattern that has produced much debate is the XYY pattern. This pattern tends to result in a male who is tall, has lower than average intelligence, and periodically may engage in antisocial behavior. The XYY

pattern has been found to be 15 times more common in criminals than in normal adult males. At the same time, there are males with the XYY pattern who are not necessarily tall, who have superior intelligence, and who have never been violent. At present we can only say that the XYY pattern, coupled with a certain environment, may predispose an individual to be aggressive (7–8). In any case, the overwhelming amount of aggression is committed by men with normal XY combinations and only a tiny fraction by men with XYY patterns. In all these examples, however, an abnormal number of sex chromosomes—one too many or one too few—may result in very noticeable physical features (lack of breast development, extreme tallness) and psychological traits (mental retardation, aggressive acts).

Gonads

Following fertilization of the egg, the zygote divides over and over and over, slowly beginning the process of developing into a human body. At this stage of development, the new being is called an **embryo**. After the eighth week, the embryo is termed a **fetus**, and it is during this time that the testes or ovaries begin to develop. These are the glands that produce reproductive cells later in life, and together they are called **gonads**. Male gonads, or testes, are external (outside the body). Female gonads, or ovaries, are internal (inside the body). Greg developed ovaries because he had sex chromosomes, XX, that carried instructions for the development of female gonads. If Greg had had XY chromosomes, he would have developed male gonads. It is the

Sexual Behavior

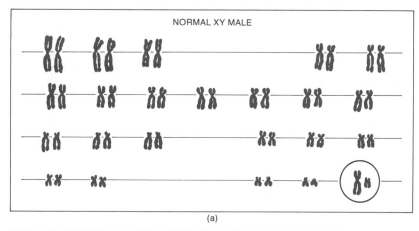

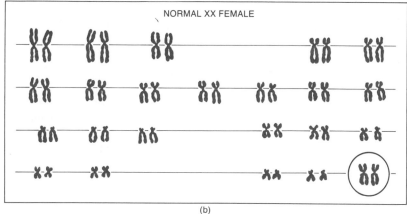

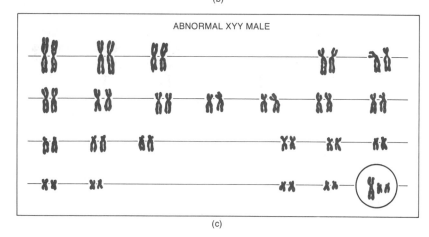

Figure 7–2 There are 23 sets of chromosomes and the last set, the sex chromosomes, contains genetic information for sexual development. (a) The last set is an XY pattern, which usually results in male sexual development. (b) The last set is an XX pattern, which usually results in female sexual development. (c) The last set is an XYY pattern, which usually results in male sexual development. The effect of the extra Y chromosome was thought to be related to other physical and behavioral developments, but so far this relationship has not been proved.

Y chromosome of the XY combination that carries the instructions for the development of testes.

Penis or Vagina?

Regardless of whether it is genetically male or female, the embryo in its early weeks has the capacity to develop either a penis or a vagina and clitoris, called **external genitalia**

(gen-ah-TAIL-ee-ah). Which genitalia develop depends upon certain hormonal conditions. An embryo with female chromosomes, XX, has the capacity to develop the genitalia of either a male or a female. The hormones make the difference. The same is true for an embryo with male chromosomes, XY.

Normally, the formation of male genitalia follows the formation of male gonads. After testes have developed in the male fetus, they begin secreting male hormones or **androgens** (AN-dro-gens), the primary one being **testosterone** (tess-TOSS-ter-own). The presence of testosterone causes the fetus to develop a penis. If testosterone is not present, the fetus will develop a clitoris and vagina. In order for the fetus to develop male genitalia, testosterone or an androgenlike hormone must be present. In order for a fetus to develop female genitalia, no hormones need be present —not even female hormones. If the male hormone testosterone is present, the fetus will develop a penis, regardless of whether it is genetically male or female. When androgens are present in the developing genetically female fetus, the female genitalia become masculinized. The clitoris becomes enlarged to resemble a tiny penis, and the vaginal opening is reduced in size or disappears altogether.

In Greg's case, there was a problem with one of his glands, the adrenal cortex. Instead of secreting its usual hormones, the adrenal cortex secreted a hormone that acted like an androgen. Because there was a male hormone present, the developing external genitalia were masculinized. That is how Greg could be a genetic female, XX, but have external genitalia that looked more like a male's.

Sexual Identity

When Greg was born, the doctor said, "It's a boy." Following this simple pronouncement, a series of forces were set into play so that Greg was raised as, treated as, and thought of as a boy. These forces included the behavior and attitudes of parents, relatives, friends, and strangers, and they shaped Greg to think of himself as a male. A term for all these forces and learning experiences is **socialization**. The way you think and feel about yourself sexually is called your **gender identity**. Usually your gender identity matches your sex chromosomes and organs. But not always. For example, a man may have male sex chromosomes and male sex organs but think of himself as a woman. He would be genetically and anatomically a male but would have a female gender identity. Greg's male gender identity could not have been caused by his chromosomes, since these were female. His gender identity, as well as yours, has been primarily determined by socialization.

Sex and Hormones

Hypothalamus

A brain structure located at the middle base of the brain, the hypothalamus, functions somewhat differently in males and females. In females, the hypothalamus causes the first menstrual period to occur and thereafter causes different hormones to be secreted in a sequence leading to ovulation. To control menstruation, the hypothalamus acts on the anterior pituitary. The anterior pituitary then acts on the ova-

ries, causing them to secrete **estrogen** (ESS-tro-gen) and **progesterone** (pro-GES-ter-own), the primary female hormones. These female hormones are secreted in a cyclic sequence. In the male, the hypothalamus causes a steady, noncyclic secretion of sex hormones.

Apparently, in both male and female embryos, the hypothalamus is originally programmed for cyclic release of hormones. This cyclic ability persists unless testosterone is added during a critical period of fetal development. If testosterone is present in the fetus—produced by the fetal testes—testosterone acts on the hypothalamus and abolishes its capacity to cause cyclic hormonal secretions. So the presence of testosterone in the fetus not only influences development of male genitalia, it also acts on brain tissue, the hypothalamus, to influence future secretion of sex hormones.

Puberty

Although the hypothalamus is programmed during fetal development for either producing the cyclic female or noncyclic male pattern of hormonal secretion, the hypothalamus waits for approximately 12 years before putting one of these patterns into action. Around the age of 12, something triggers the hypothalamus to initiate the secretion of hormones and begin the sexual changes seen during puberty. In a girl, the ovaries experience a tremendous increase in hormone production. The result is breast development, pubic hair, and widening of the hips, all called **secondary sex characteristics**. For a boy, the secondary sex characteristics appear as pubic and facial hair and lowering of the voice. The male secondary characteristics result from an enormous increase in the testes' production of male hormones.

Up to the age of puberty, both males and females have very low levels of both male and female hormones, secreted by the adrenal cortex. These low levels of male and female hormones are normally not sufficient to cause the occurrence of secondary sex characteristics.

The dramatic physical changes that take place during puberty begin with the hypothalamus. Some cue from the body causes the hypothalamus to begin secreting its own hormones, which are called **releasing factors** or **RF's**. These two releasing factors then act on the anterior pituitary and cause it to release two hormones, **follicle stimulating hormone** *(FSH)* and **leutenizing hormone** (LH). The hypothalamic releasing factor for FSH is abbreviated FSH-RF. The hypothalamic releasing factor for LH is LH-RF. FSH-RF and LH-RF cause their respective hormones to be released into the blood stream.

In the female, follicle stimulating hormone, or FSH, travels through the blood stream to the follicles in the ovaries. There it promotes development of the egg and secretion of the female hormone estrogen. When the estrogen in the blood reaches a certain level, it causes the anterior pi-

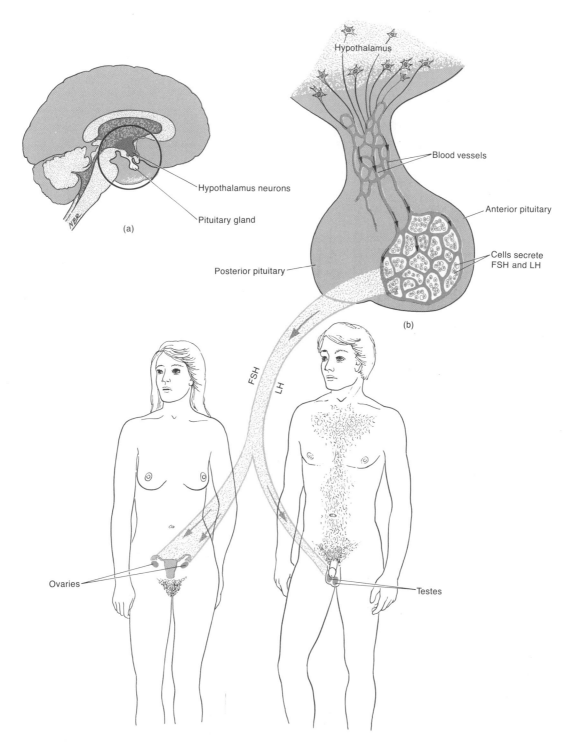

Figure 7–3 Development of secondary sexual characteristics. (a) Middle view of brain shows location of hypothalamus, which controls the pituitary gland immediately below. (b) An enlargement of the pituitary showing the anterior pituitary, which secretes FSH and LH, which in turn act on the gonads (ovaries and testes).

tuitary to secrete LH, which acts to release the egg from the follicle. A high level of estrogen in the blood also acts back on the pituitary to turn off secretion of FSH. After the egg has been released, LH aids in helping the follicle to

secrete progesterone, the other major female hormone. A high level of progesterone in the blood acts back on the pituitary to turn off secretion of LH. Each of these feedback systems works through the hypothalamus and its releasing

Sex and Hormones

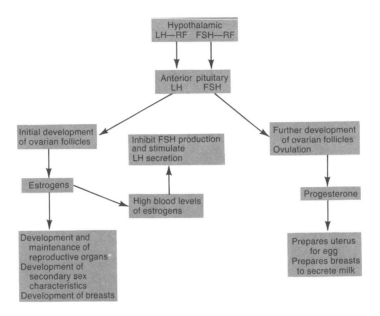

Figure 7–4 Control of female sexual hormones.

factors. If the egg is not fertilized, it is sloughed off through menstruation and the cycle begins again.

In the male, the hypothalamus secretes the same releasing factors as in the female: FSH-RF and LH-RF. These two releasing factors cause the anterior pituitary to release FSH and LH, the same hormones secreted in the female. The difference is that these hormones in the male are secreted steadily rather than cyclically, and they act on different target organs. In the male, FSH acts on the testes to aid in maturation of sperm, and LH acts on other cells in the testes to cause secretion of testosterone, the primary male sex hormone.

Thus, for both males and females at puberty, the hypothalamus acts on the anterior pituitary, which in turn triggers the gonads to flood the body with sex hormones.

Aggression

In the fetal stage, the presence of testosterone causes the hypothalamus of the male to function differently from that of the female. Does the presence of testosterone affect the brain in other ways and cause males to engage in behaviors that are different from those of females? For example, one of the differences found between boys and girls is that boys are generally more aggressive and engage in more fights, rough and tumble play, and sporting activities (7–14). Since boys are exposed to testosterone as fetuses, it is tempting to ask whether the more aggressive behavior of boys can be attributed to the presence of testosterone rather than to socialization. To answer this question, it would be necessary to give testosterone to a developing female fetus. This has been done in monkeys, and there are some examples where it has occurred by accident in humans.

During pregnancy, a female monkey was injected with testosterone. When the baby monkey was born, it was a genetic female but had a well-formed penis. It had no testes. The question was whether the presence of testosterone in the developing fetus had had some effect on the brain and therefore would result in male behavior patterns. In general, male juvenile monkeys show more rough and tumble play than females, use more threatening facial expressions in play, and engage in more sexual play. If testosterone is involved in creating these behaviors, the genetic female monkey whose mother was given testosterone during pregnancy would show a more aggressive pattern of play. That is exactly what happened. This suggests that tes-

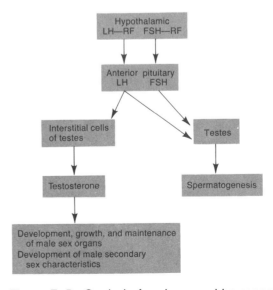

Figure 7–5 Control of male sexual hormones.

tosterone has two effects in monkeys: (1) it masculinizes fetal female sex organs, an effect also seen in humans, and (2) it acts on the brain in some manner to bring about specific patterns of behavior, such as rough and tumble play, playful threats, and sexual play (7–6, 7–20). It is not known whether the second result is also seen in humans.

Specific Effects

In the 1950s a hormone was administered to pregnant mothers to prevent miscarriages. At the time it was not known that this hormone had testosterone-like effects. The hormone, called **progestin** (pro-GES-tin), caused the genitalia of genetic females to be masculinized. However, the infants were born with normal ovaries, which would become functional at puberty. Later these infants had operations to correct the masculinization. The case of the human mothers taking this testosterone-like hormone during pregnancy was very similar to that of the pregnant female monkey injected with testosterone. The monkey's child, a genetic female exposed to testosterone in the uterus, showed malelike behaviors when it was growing up. Would the human infants, genetic females exposed to testosterone-like hormone, develop so-called male behavioral patterns? The answer is that they were no more aggressive, nor did they engage in more fights than were observed in normal, unexposed girls. The exposed girls did show more interest in and engage in more sporting activities as compared with normal girls (7–3, 7–4). Some investigators suggest that the increased interest in sports parallels the increased rough and tumble play in

the monkey exposed to testosterone during pregnancy. In addition, they suggest that the increased interest in sports was probably caused by the testosterone-like hormone affecting the brain and its neural circuitry (7–19). This is the same as saying that the brains of the female fetuses were changed by exposure to the testosterone-like hormone, and the result was a predisposition to be interested in and engage in sports. There is a problem with this interpretation. Did the exposure to the masculinizing hormone somehow influence this interest in sports? Or did the parents, who were warned about problems during pregnancy, encourage their daughters to engage in healthy sporting activities? It would be difficult to say to what extent the interest in sports came from the hormones and to what extent it came from the parent's influence.

Suppose male fetuses were exposed to female hormones. Later on, would these boys show less assertiveness and less athletic ability because of exposure to female hormones? There have been cases in which male fetuses were exposed to double the normal amount of female hormones. Mothers who had diabetes were given female hormones, estrogen and progesterone, to help them cope with the problem of being diabetic and pregnant. Twenty of the male children of these diabetic mothers were studied when they were 16 years old and compared to normal, unexposed males. The experimenters wanted to know if behavior commonly attributed to males, aggressiveness and athletic ability, would be different in these exposed males. They report that the exposed males were less aggressive and had less athletic ability than other males with normal fetal development

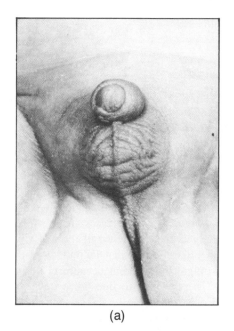
(a)

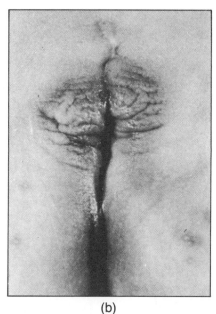
(b)

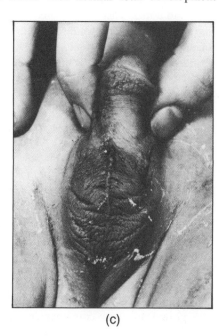
(c)

Figure 7–6 Hormonal malfunction. (a) Infants with female chromosomes, XX, are sometimes born with a micropenis because of a hormonal problem. (b) In some cases, the micropenis is surgically removed and changes are made to resemble female genitalia. (c) In other cases, the micropenis remains and surgical changes are made to resemble male genitalia. (From J. Money and A. A. Ehrhardt, *Man and Woman, Boy and Girl*, Baltimore: The Johns Hopkins University Press, 1972.)

(7–25). However, there is a problem in interpreting these results. The mothers of these exposed males were diabetic and as a result may have been overprotective of their children, discouraging aggressive or sporting activities.

There is a serious problem, then, in trying to determine the specific effects of sex hormones. The effects of socialization, including the parents and all other forces that shape the child's interests, thoughts, and beliefs, are very powerful. The effects of socialization can be so overriding that it is difficult to determine which behavioral patterns (interest in sports) might have a genetic or hormonal cause and which are due to socialization (mother's influence). In the monkey, socialization is also at work, but probably less than at the human level. In monkeys it is not as difficult to determine if hormones or socialization cause certain behavioral patterns, such as rough and tumble play. At the human level, because of the problems of socialization, we cannot say whether the finding that boys are more aggressive than girls can be attributed to the presence of testosterone.

Sexual Interests

If a male were castrated (removal of the testes but not the penis) before puberty, he would have no secretion of testosterone at the time puberty normally occurs. As a result, he would not develop secondary sexual characteristics. There is some evidence that he could have an erection, but he would probably have little sexual interest or motivation (7–19). A female with Turner's syndrome would be analogous to a male castrated before puberty. Since she would have no ovaries, she would have no secretion of estrogen or progesterone. She would not develop secondary sexual characteristics and she would have little interest in sexual behavior (7–2). Neither of these teenagers would develop the sexual interests and motivation seen in teenagers with normal secretion of sex hormones. On the other hand, if sex hormones were administered to these teenagers, they would develop secondary sex characteristics as well as sexual interests. So it appears that the presence of sex hormones at puberty is necessary for the development of sexual interests and behavior. It is possible that the secretion of sex hormones at puberty increases sexual motivation directly, through some action on the brain. It is also possible that secretion of sex hormones increases sexual interests indirectly, through the development of secondary sexual characteristics. That is, once you see your breast development or pubic hair you think of yourself in a sexual way and begin to show an interest in sex. Perhaps sexual interests grow from some combination of these two factors.

Sexual Preferences

Greg was interested in sex and found himself sexually aroused by girls. The occurrence of female hormones in his body at puberty may have contributed to his increased interest in sexual behavior, but these hormones did not determine who he would prefer sexually. The presence of female hormones did not mean he would be aroused by males or prefer males, since, in fact, he preferred females as sexual partners. Likewise, the occurrence of female hormones in a normal female does not determine an interest in a specific sex. Nor does the occurrence of male hormones in a normal male determine which sex he will prefer. Scientists believe that the occurrence of hormones at puberty serves to bring out a sex preference, one that you have already learned through socialization (7–19).

There have been other genetic females like Greg who were raised as males, developed a male gender identity, and preferred females. There have been cases of genetic males who, because of hormonal malfunction, had tiny penises and no testes. Some of these infants were raised as males, assumed the male gender identity, and preferred females. Others were raised as females, assumed the female gender identity, and preferred males (7–19). There also have been cases of genetic males who were exposed to male hormones and developed male genitalia but who, when adults, assumed a female gender identity and sometimes requested a sex change. In similar cases, genetic females have assumed male gender identity. These individuals are called **transsexuals** (7–7). All these examples indicate that neither your genes nor your hormones necessarily determine your preferences for a sexual partner. Sex hormones may be necessary for the development of sexual interests, but they do not seem to determine what the preference will be. Instead, sexual preferences and identities seem to depend to a large extent upon socialization.

Gay Behavior

For decades homosexual, or gay, behavior was considered abnormal or deviant, and there are still laws in some states prohibiting this behavior. In 1972 the American Psychiatric Association voted to remove the label "neurotic or abnormal" from gay behavior. Today, this association and many other professional groups consider gay behavior to be yet another normal expression of sexual behavior. Sexual preferences vary widely among individuals and include no preference, heterosexual, homosexual, and bisexual, or some combination of these. Since the preference of the majority is heterosexual, it was often thought that individuals with other sex preferences might be different because of some hormonal imbalance. There were two questions: do gays have a different level of sex hormones, and is a different level of sex hormones responsible for their being gay?

Most studies on gays have focused on males and have compared hormone levels of active male gays with those of active male heterosexuals. One study found that active male homosexuals have a significantly lower level of testosterone than do male heterosexuals (7–2). Another study

TRANSSEXUAL BIAS CALLED A 'DISGRACE'

More than 3,000 sex change operations have been performed in the United States in the last 10 years, and one of the biggest problems today, says a doctor involved in many of them, is the continuing prejudice toward transsexuals.

"Prejudice towards transsexuals has been a disgrace in this country," said Dr. Roberto C. Granato, who performed the sex change operation on Dr. Renee Richards, whose participation in women's tennis competition has been the center of recent controversy.

Dr. Richards, who once played tennis as Dr. Richard Raskind, advanced Tuesday to the women's quarterfinals of the $60,000 Tennis Week Tournament at South Orange, N.J.

Granato, a urologist and professor at Columbia University's College of Physicians and Surgeons, said more and more doctors were performing the procedure as it became accepted in the medical community.

"I'm glad more doctors are doing it because I've spent a good length of time teaching residents and presenting the technique to such organizations as the American Urological Assn., the American Medical Assn. and the American College of Surgeons," Granato, a 50-year-old Argentinian, said.

Granato has performed more than 200 sex reassignment operations in the last seven years.

"At first I encountered prejudice from the medical community, the nursing community and the lay community," he said. "But little by little, that has broken down. Now those same people want to learn about the procedure. They want to help."

In male-to-female surgery, the male sexual organs are removed. The urethra—the canal that carries urine from the bladder to be expelled—is preserved and trimmed to female size, and the skin of the penis is kept and used later as lining of the new vagina. The female clitoris is created with erectile tissue from the penis.

The vagina is placed in the normal area between the bladder and the rectum. This means the interior wall of the vagina is in direct contact with an erogenous nerve network, permitting orgasm during intercourse. Breasts are increased with silicone.

The patient is in the hospital for eight days, and in four to eight weeks, she can have normal sexual intercourse, Granato said.

The female-to-male operation is more complex and not as rewarding for the patient, Granato said, because it is difficult to obtain erectile tissue for a penis. He said he has only been involved in three female-to-male operations.

"Before I consider operating, the person has to have a complete evaluation from a psychiatrist, counseling, and must have taken female hormones for at least a year and undergone all the beautification and cosmetic processes as a female," he said. "Then I do it, after written advice from a psychiatrist."

SOURCE: *Los Angeles Times,* August 26, 1976. Copyright © 1976 by Los Angeles Times.

Dr. Raskind, the male at the left, underwent a transsexual operation and hormone treatment to become Dr. Renee Richards, the female at the right. (Wide World Photos.)

115

found that active male homosexuals, as well as transsexuals and transvestites, have a level of testosterone significantly lower than heterosexuals (7–22). Although these studies reported lower levels of testosterone, we cannot conclude whether the lower level of testosterone influenced sex preference or whether being gay caused the level of testosterone to be lower. Since homosexuality is not widely accepted and in many states is against the law, gays may be under more emotional stress than heterosexuals. It may be that the emotional stress is causing low levels of testosterone in gays. There is some evidence for this interpretation, for a study of heterosexual men showed that they had reduced levels of testosterone while participating in a training program they considered very stressful (7–13).

The answer to the first question is yes: males with a gay preference have a lower level of testosterone than those with a heterosexual preference. But so do men who are transsexuals or transvestites, and so do heterosexual men undergoing stressful training. At present there is no answer to the second question, whether lower levels of testosterone cause gay behavior. From the above study on lower testosterone levels in stressed heterosexuals, it appears more likely that stress is causing the lower levels of testosterone in gays.

Sexual Motivation

As an adult, if you were suddenly drained of all your sex hormones, would you still have sexual motivation? The answer to this question would be clear if you were a rat, rabbit, mouse, or guinea pig. If testes or ovaries are removed from one of these adult animals, with a resulting loss of hormones, sexual behavior and motivation cease in a few days or weeks. If an adult dog or cat is deprived of sexual hormones, and the animal has had prior sex experience, the dog or cat may continue to have sexual behavior for as long as a year. If adult monkeys are deprived of hormones, there is a decrease in the amount of sexual behavior, but they still engage in sexual responses (7–11). Thus, in animals with more evolved brains, hormones have less control over sexual behavior. In all of these animals, injections of sex hormones will return their sexual behavior to previous levels.

For humans the answer to the question is more complicated. There are cases in which sexual hormones are removed from adult humans. For example, if a female has her ovaries removed (ovariectomy), her primary source of estrogen and progesterone is eliminated. She still has a small amount of female hormones normally secreted by the adrenal cortex. Following an ovariectomy and without hormone replacement, women often report no decrease in sexual behavior. Some report an increase, saying they no longer fear pregnancy, and only a few report a decrease. If hormones were primarily responsible for sexual behavior and motivation in humans, you would expect all of these

women to show some decrease, which they do not. A woman who reports a decrease in sexual behavior may be responding to psychological factors: she is convinced that she will have less sexual motivation, she thinks her sexual behavior will be impaired, or she thinks that in some way she is less a woman. In humans psychological factors can cause a decrease in sexual motivation and behavior. When there are changes in human sexual behavior, it is often impossible to distinguish between physiological and psychological causes.

Castration

Paul was 47 years old. He had sexually assaulted two young boys, and this was not his first offense. After conviction, the judge told him that he faced imprisonment for an indeterminate period, possibly for life. At the suggestion of his attorney, Paul asked about castration. The judge ruled that castration could be part of his rehabilitation program, possibly leading to probation. In actuality, would castration reduce Paul's sexual motivation and cure his problem of sexually assaulting young children?

For men, castration involves removal of the testes and their replacement with artificial testes for cosmetic purposes. With testes removed, the amount of testosterone in the body decreases to approximately the level before puberty. If a male were castrated before puberty, he would be capable of an erection but there would be no development of secondary sexual characteristics and there would be a lack of sexual motivation (7–19). Once puberty is passed, however, is male motivation maintained by testosterone or by previous sexual experiences stored in the brain? Do adult males with lower levels of testosterone have less sex drive?

In Denmark between 1929 and 1959, approximately 900 adult men were castrated for therapeutic purposes. These men had been convicted of rape, sexual attacks on young persons, incest, or indecent exposure. Only those who believed castration was the best solution to their problems were selected for castration. These men were given extensive psychological evaluations and were counseled about the positive and negative effects of castration. Specifically, they were told that their sex lives were partially dependent upon hormone production from the testes. They were warned that, in spite of the castration, they would have to take care to avoid sexually provocative situations. The direction of their sexual drives would not be changed, although the intensity would be lessened.

Of the 900 men convicted of sexual offenses and castrated, only 10 were arrested again for the same sexual offense. Ninety percent of the men interviewed were competely happy with the effects of castration (7–23). Some of these men were still capable of having an erection and engaging in intercourse. There are at least two interpretations for these results. One is that castration caused the men to commit fewer sexual offenses, that the loss of testosterone lessened their sexual motivation. Another interpretation is that psychological factors decreased their sexual motivation. The men selected for castration were those who expected castration to help and who also wanted to be helped by the operation. In addition, the castration did result in certain physiological changes, such as loss of body hair and softening of the skin. These changes may have strengthened the men's belief that castration would reduce their sexual motivation. For these men, it is most likely that changes in sexual behavior were caused both by physiological factors (loss of testosterone) and psychological factors (belief that sexual motivation would decrease). Some of these men did continue to engage in sexual behavior, so the lack of testosterone did not necessarily cause a complete loss of sexual behavior. It appears that if you were drained of sex hormones as an adult, what happened to your sexual behavior would depend to a large extent on your previous sexual experiences and upon what you now believed would happen to you.

Reversible Castration

Henry was an adult male reportedly arrested for sexually exhibiting himself, as often as 10 times daily. He was injected with a drug called Depo-Provera (technical name: medroxyprogesterone acetate). After his injection with the drug, Henry's sexual exhibitions decreased to zero. Did the drug change his sexual motivation? Depo-Provera has drastic effects on sexual functions: after three injections 10 days apart, the level of testosterone is lowered to that of a castrated person, the penis cannot erect, semen is not produced, and orgasm does not occur (7–18). Henry may have lost the motivation to exhibit himself because he could no longer have an erection, rather than because his desire to exhibit decreased. The inability to have an erection has dramatic psychological consequences, especially for an exhibitionist. Several weeks after the drug injections ceased, sexual functions would return to normal.

Individual Psychology

It is very difficult to determine the extent to which hormones support sexual motivation in the adult human. In many animals, it is easy to determine the role of hormones in sexual behavior, but in humans it would be difficult to remove only the sex hormones WITHOUT also causing the person to think, "Now my sex life will decrease" or "I will lose sexual motivation." The psychological consequences of thinking these thoughts can be dramatic decreases in sexual motivation. There are cases of healthy men and women with normal hormonal levels who cannot reach orgasm, presumably because of psychological problems (7–9). Following castration in the male, there are widely variable differences in the loss of ability to have an

erection and ejaculation. Since the ability to ejaculate is more dependent on hormones, ejaculation disappears first. The loss of ability to have an erection varies from weeks to years and seems to be influenced by the emotional or psychological factors accompanying the idea of castration (7–19). In addition, it is known that both males after castration and females after ovariectomy can and do have sexual desires although their level of sex hormones is nil. Hormones may play a role in the sexual behavior of humans, but it appears that psychological factors are equally or more important.

Sex in the Brain

For therapeutic reasons, a patient had an electrode implanted into the **septal** area of his brain. When a small electrical current was applied to the electrode, the surrounding neurons were activated and the patient had an erection and pleasurable feelings that resulted in an orgasm (7–17). Erection and ejaculation have also been produced in monkeys from stimulation of the septal area and hypothalamus, as well as other areas in the **limbic system** (7–15). The limbic system consists of many interconnected nuclei located in different areas of the brain. Besides sexual behavior, the limbic system is involved in emotions and the formation of memories.

A man was arrested for sexually molesting little boys, and the treatment in his case was very radical. He was subjected to psychosurgery, in which part of his brain was destroyed. Before any patient agrees to surgery, the doctor must explain all of its effects. Then the doctor and patient reach an agreement on whether or not the surgery will be performed, as was done in this case. However, there has been much discussion as to whether psychosurgery was justified as treatment for the man's offense. Animal studies have shown that the hypothalamus is an important area for controlling sexual behavior. Placement of sex hormones into the hypothalamus will cause rats and cats to engage in sexual behavior (7–5). On the basis of the animal data, a neurosurgeon in Germany destroyed a small area in the ventromedial nucleus of the hypothalamus in males convicted of child molesting. Following this surgery, there was either a total or partial elimination of sexual behavior (7–21). Patients with this brain lesion no longer sexually molested young boys or engaged in any kind of sexual behavior. The details of this study are not available, so it is difficult to determine whether the patients lost sexual motivation as well as the ability to have an erection or orgasm. However, this study does suggest that in humans, as in animals, the hypothalamus plays an important part in sexual behavior.

In a young male patient with grand mal epilepsy, both temporal lobes were lesioned in an attempt to eliminate the seizures. That part of the temporal lobes destroyed included the temporal cortex, amygdala, and part of the hippocampus, as well as their connections to and from the rest of the brain. Among other changes following this surgery, the patient began to exhibit himself sexually to nurses and other visitors to the hospital (7–24). From this case, as well as from related reports on epileptic humans, it appears that the temporal lobe area is involved in sexual behavior. This same effect, increased sexual behavior, was produced years earlier in monkeys from lesions of the same areas, the temporal lobes (7–11). Studies on brain stimulation and lesions in animals and humans seem to indicate that the limbic system (septal area, hypothalamus, hippocampus, and amygdala) and temporal cortex are areas most directly involved in sexual behavior.

Sexual Reflexes

Jeff's spinal cord was severed above his waist in an automobile accident. From his waist down, he had no voluntary movements or any sensations. He could still think erotic thoughts and enjoy looking at erotic pictures, but neither thinking nor looking produced an erection because of his severed spinal cord. If his penis were manually stimulated,

Jeff could have an erection and ejaculation, but he would not know he was having an erection or ejaculation unless he were watching. The reason Jeff could have an erection and ejaculation is that both of these responses are reflexes, controlled by the spinal cord. The parasympathetic division of the autonomic nervous system controls erection, and the sympathetic division controls the ejaculation. Similarly, in the female, the swelling of the vaginal lips due to increased blood flow and the lubrication of the vagina are reflex responses, controlled by the autonomic nervous system through the spinal cord. Because these sexual responses are reflexes, you cannot do them at will, but must either see or think of something erotic or have the genital area stimulated to trigger the reflex. Although these reflexes are controlled by the spinal cord, they can be inhibited by the brain. If you are anxious or nervous, you may have difficulty having an erection or vaginal lubrication.

Sexual Response

The couple began to touch and kiss. After only a short time, 3 to 8 seconds, Bob felt his penis become erect. At ap-

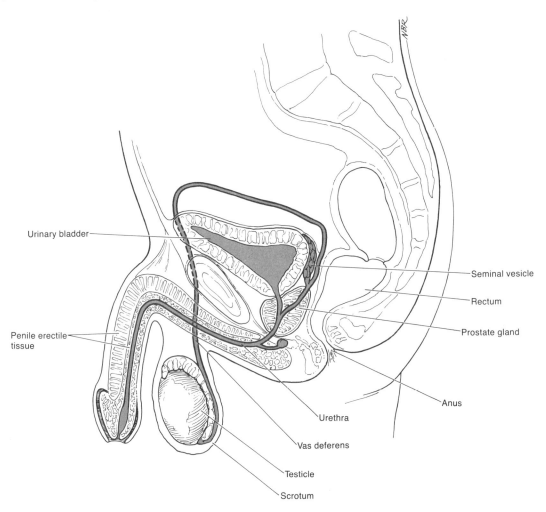

Figure 7–7 Male sexual organs.

Sexual Behavior

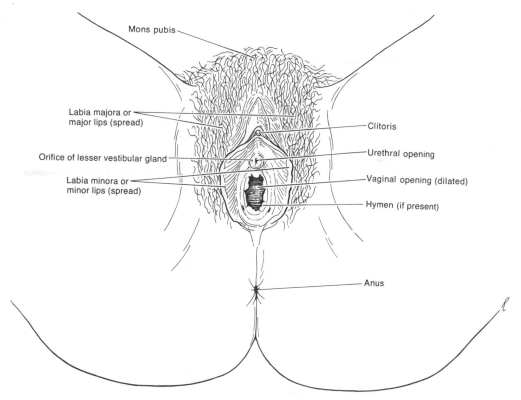

Figure 7-8 Female sexual organs.

proximately the same time, 5 to 15 seconds, Judy noticed some wetness or vaginal lubrication. The reflex responses of penile erection and vaginal lubrication are analogous and can happen very quickly. These responses occur during the first state of sexual response, call **excitement**.

After they had undressed each other and began to fondle, it was unlikely that Bob and Judy noticed what physiological changes were occurring in their bodies. Each was breathing more rapidly, which is called **hyperventilation**. Each one's heart rate was almost double, from a normal 70 beats per minute to between 100 and 160. Although his penis had become erect during the excitement phase, there was a further increase in penile circumference. Bob's testes were drawn upward and because of blood engorgement were approximately 50 percent larger. The entrance and outer third of Judy's vagina had become engorged with blood so that the diameter of the vagina was reduced approximately 50 percent. Her **minor labia,** sometimes called the **sex skin**, changed in color from bright red to burgundy. These responses occur during the **plateau phase** of sexual response and are a continuation of the arousal seen during the excitement phase.

If stimulation is continued, the **orgasmic phase** of sexual response occurs. During this phase, there is hyperventilation, and heart rate may increase to 180 beats per minute. It is now recognized that a woman reaches orgasm through direct or indirect stimulation of the clitoris (7-10). During orgasm Judy experienced contractions of the vagina, of the

muscles in the genital area, and of the muscles surrounding the anus. These contractions are the physiological basis for the experience called **orgasm**. Immediately before Bob's orgasm, there was a contraction of those organs involved in gathering the semen for ejaculation: **prostate** (PROS-tate) and **seminal** (SEM-in-all) **vesicles** (VES-ah-coles). As these contractions occurred, he had the feeling of impending ejaculation and could not stop ejaculation from occurring. During ejaculation, muscular contractions propel the **semen** from the penis. The semen consists of sperm and a fluid from the prostate gland. In the male, the physiological bases for orgasm are the contractions that occur in the muscles during ejaculation. Thus, in both male and female, the experience of orgasm has its physiological basis in the muscle contractions in the genital area. Pleasure from the experience described as orgasm depends upon the physiological sensations coming from your genital area, previous sexual memories and experiences, and your present state of mind. There is one important difference between males and females following orgasm. If stimulation is continued in the female, she may proceed to have a second or third or more orgasms in succession. Women differ in whether they prefer to have a single or multiple orgasm. In contrast, after orgasm the male experiences a brief period during which a second orgasm is not possible.

Following orgasm, Bob and Judy experienced a decrease in heart rate and breathing. Bob noticed a loss of penile erection and a period during which he was incapable of

Sexual Response

another orgasm. Following Judy's orgasm, since stimulation was not continued, there was a decrease in blood accumulation in the genital area and the sex skin lost its color. These responses occured during the **resolution phase** of the sexual response cycle. Our knowledge of these four phases of sexual response cycle—excitement, plateau, orgasm, and resolution—derives from the pioneering work in sexual behavior by William Masters and Virginia Johnson (7–16).

Male Sexual Problems

A somewhat common problem among inexperienced males is **premature ejaculation.** The treatment involves helping the person to recognize physiological cues that ejaculation is about to occur. To do this, his partner manually stimulates his penis until he feels near the point of ejaculation, at which time stimulation is stopped. This procedure is repeated until he learns the cues signaling ejaculation and can tolerate more and more stimulation without having ejaculation. This start-stop technique has proved very effective in treating premature ejaculation.

The opposite of having too little control over the ejaculatory reflex is having too much control, as in **retarded ejaculation**. This problem is usually caused by psychological factors, such as anxiety or tension. Feelings of guilt, anxiety, or nervousness can prevent erotic sensations or thoughts from being processed in the brain and so prevent sexual reflexes from occurring. One treatment for this problem is to have the two people at first engage in sex play without attempting orgasm. Then they have sex play with orgasm but without the male entering the vagina. When the male is comfortable having orgasms near the vagina, the final step is to have an orgasm in the vagina.

Anxiety, worry, or tension can prevent a male from having an erection. This condition is called **secondary impotency**. The treatment involves reducing the fear or anxiety through masturbation or sex play without intercourse. If erection occurs during these activities, then sex play with intercourse is the next step.

Female Sexual Problems

Anxiety, tension, or feelings of guilt can prevent a woman from having sexual feelings. This condition, previously know as frigidity, is now called **secondary general sexual dysfunction**. Treatment for this problem involves engaging in a series of sensuous and erotic exercises in a relaxed atmosphere. These exercises, called **sensate focus**, help the woman focus on, or experience, sensations from the body. The exercises are continued until the woman experiences sexual feelings and can become sexually aroused.

If a woman can reach orgasm through masturbation but not during intercourse, it is called **secondary orgasmic dysfunction**. If she has experienced sexual arousal but never has had an orgasm, her problem is called **primary orgasmic dysfunction**. The reasons for orgasmic dysfunction vary from the male's ignorance of the importance of clitoral stimulation to inhibition of the female's sexual responsiveness because of feelings of guilt or anxiety. Treatment for this problem involves removing inhibitory feelings by helping the woman feel comfortable with having an orgasm by herself and then gradually working toward having an orgasm with her partner. Often her partner may need some instruction in techniques that help a woman reach orgasm (7–9, 7–10).

In most of these sexual problems, the individuals have normal hormonal levels, are physically healthy, and have no apparent physiological cause for these difficulties. These problems illustrate how important psychological factors are in controlling sexual motivation and behavior.

Comment

As far as sexual behavior is concerned, what happens in your head is probably more important than what happens in your genitals.

SELF-TEST 7

1 If you thought of yourself as female, you would be said to have a female _____ identity.

gender

2 Your gender identity and sexual preference usually, but not always, match your _____ makeup and _____ organs.

chromosomal or genetic sex

3 As the case of Greg illustrates, your genetic and physiological makeup does not necessarily determine your _____ identity.

gender

4 During the first seven weeks, the embryo can develop the external _____ of either sex.

genitalia

5 A fetus with XX chromosomes will normally develop female gonads or _____. A fetus with XY chromosomes will develop male gonads or _____, which secrete _____ .

ovaries
testes / androgens or testosterone

6 A fetus that is genetically male will not develop male genitalia unless the gonads of the fetus secrete _____.

testosterone

7 A fetus that is genetically female will normally develop female genitalia without the secretion of female _____.

hormones or estrogen and progesterone

8 If a female were born with one X chromosome she would have _____ syndrome. At puberty she would not develop secondary sexual characteristics.

Turner's

9 Normally, a person who has the chromosomes, hormones, and sex organs of a female will develop a female gender identity. The gender identity of an individual depends upon physiological makeup as well as upon the effects of _____.

socialization

10 The presence of testosterone during fetal development causes some change in the hypothalamus, so that at puberty there is a _____ pattern of hormone secretion.

noncyclic

11 At puberty the hypothalamus begins to secrete two releasing factors: _____ and _____, which trigger the anterior pituitary to secrete _____ and _____.

FSH-RF / LH-RF
FSH / LH

12 Although the _____ secretes LH and FSH in both males and females, the effects are different. In males the hormones act on the _____, and in females they act on the _____.

anterior pituitary
testes / ovaries

13 In females FSH is involved in the development of the _____ and secretion of _____. LH acts to release the egg from the _____ and promotes the secretion of _____.

egg / estrogen
follicle / progesterone

14 In males the maturation of the sperm is aided by _____, while _____ causes the secretion of testosterone.

FSH / LH

15 At puberty, the sudden increase in the male sex hormone, _____, and the female sex hormones, _____ and _____, causes the development of _____ _____ characteristics.

testosterone
estrogen / progesterone
secondary sexual

16 If there were no secretion of _____ at puberty, you would not develop secondary sexual characteristics and you would probably have little interest in _____ behavior.

hormones
sexual

17 It seems that the secretion of male or female hormones at puberty does not determine what your sexual _____ will be but rather brings out the one you have learned through _____.

interest or preference
socialization

18 If a monkey fetus that was genetically female were exposed to testosterone, at birth it would have a _____ genitalia, and while growing up it would show more _____ responses compared with other female monkeys.

masculinized / male or rough and tumble

19 In humans, those genetic females who were exposed to a testosterone-like hormone as fetuses later on showed more interest in _____ activities. This effect may have been due to the presence of _____ during fetal development or to the kind of _____ these girls had.

sporting
hormone or testosterone-like hormone /
socialization

20 In humans, those genetic males who were exposed to estrogen as fetuses later on showed less interest and ability in athletic activities. This effect may have been due to the presence of _____ during fetal development or to the kind of _____ these boys had.

estrogen
mothers or socialization

21 At the human level, it is difficult to determine whether exposure to _____ during fetal development or the learning that occurs during the process of _____ or a combination of the two is responsible for the difference between behavioral patterns of males and females.

hormones
socialization

22 If you were studying a group of men and discovered that they had low levels of testosterone, you could say that these men were probably _____, _____, _____, or _____.

gays / transsexuals / transvestites / stressed heterosexuals

23 If you were to remove the sex hormones from adult rats or rabbits, their sexual behavior would _____. If you were to remove sex hormones from cats and dogs, their sexual behavior would eventually _____, depending upon their previous _____.

stop or cease
cease / experience

24 Following ovariectomy adult human females may report that their sexual behavior has _____, _____, or _____. It seems clear that hormones are not the main determinants of sexual _____ in humans.

increased
decreased / stayed the same / motivation

25 Following castration, adult males may show a decrease in sexual behavior after a number of months, or perhaps after a number of years. This decrease is probably due to the lack of testosterone in combination with _____ factors associated with the surgery.

psychological

26 If males or females do not have sex hormone secretions at puberty, they do not develop _____ and the usual interest in _____ behavior.

secondary sexual characteristics / sexual

27 In humans there may be some minimal level of _____ necessary to maintain sexual behavior. It is difficult to study the effects of hormones on sexual behavior since _____ factors play such an important part in human sexual motivation and behavior.

hormones
psychological

28 If a male were given the drug Depo-Provera, he would not be able to have an _____.

erection or orgasm

29 Erections and orgasms in monkeys or humans have been elicited by electrical stimulation of the _____ area.

septal

30 Sexual behavior has been reduced or eliminated in humans by making a lesion in the _____.

hypothalamus or ventromedial nucleus

31 Increased sexual behavior has been reported in monkeys and humans after removal of the _____.

temporal lobes

32 If a person had his or her spinal cord severed at the waist, he or she could still have an erection or lubrication since these responses are _____ controlled by the _____.

reflexes / spinal cord

33 The first phase of the sexual response cycle is called _____. During this phase, the male response of _____ is analogous to the female response of _____.

34 The second phase of the sexual response cycle is called _____. During this phase, both sexes show _____ and increased _____. In addition, the male has an increase in the size of his _____ and _____. The female has a reduction in the size of the outer third of her _____ and there is a change in the color of her _____.

35 In the female, the physiological basis of the experience called orgasm is in the contractions of the _____ in the genital area. In the male, the basis is in the contractions of the muscles involved in _____.

36 The intensity of the feelings you experience during orgasm depends upon the _____ from the muscles, your previous sexual _____, and your _____ state of mind.

37 The third phase of the sexual response cycle is called _____. Following orgasm, there is a period during which another orgasm is not possible for the _____. In contrast, with continued stimulation, the _____ can experience another or multiple orgasms.

38 In order of occurrence, the four phases of the sexual response cycle are _____, _____, _____, and _____.

39 If a male has a problem with reaching ejaculation too quickly it is called _____. A problem in being able to ejaculate at all is called _____.

40 Anxiety and tension can cause a male to experience difficulties in having an erection, and this is called _____.

41 Feelings of guilt or anxiety can prevent a woman from having sexual feelings, and this is now called _____ dysfunction.

42 If a woman can reach orgasm by masturbating but not by having intercourse, it is called _____ dysfunction.

43 The above sexual problems are not caused by _____ problems but rather by _____ factors.

excitement
erection / lubrication

plateau
hyperventilation / heart rate / penis / testes / vagina / minor labia or sex skin

muscles
ejaculation

sensations or feedback
experiences / present

orgasm
male
female

excitement / plateau
orgasm / resolution

premature ejaculation
retarded ejaculation

secondary impotency

secondary general sexual

secondary orgasmic

physiological /
psychological

REFERENCES

7–1 Beach, F. It's all in your mind. *Psychology Today* July 1969, 3:33.

7–2 Bekker, F. J. Personality development in XO-Turner's syndrome. In J. H. F. van Abeelen (Ed.), *The genetics of behaviour*. New York: American Elsevier, 1974.

7–3 Ehrhardt, A. A., Epstein, R., and Money, J. Fetal androgens and female gender identity in the early treated andrenogenital syndrome. *Johns Hopkins Medical Journal* 1968, 122: 160–167.

7–4 Ehrhardt, A. A. and Money, J. Progestin-induced hermaphroditism: IQ and psychosexual identity in a study of ten girls. *Journal of Sex Research* 1967, 3: 83–100.

7–5 Fisher, A. E. Chemical stimulation of the brain. *Scientific American* June 1964, 210: 60–68.

7–6 Goy, R. W. Experimental control of psychosexuality. In G. W. Harris and R. G. Edwards (Eds.), *A discussion on the determination of sex*. London: Philosophical Transactions of the Royal Society, 1970, 259: 149–162.

7–7 Green, R. *Sexual identity conflict in children and adults*. Baltimore: Penguin, 1974.

7–8 Jarvik, L. F., Klodin, V., and Matsuyama, S. S. Human aggression and the extra Y chromosome: fact or fantasy? *American Psychologist* 1973, 28: 674–682.

7–9 Kaplan, H. S. No-nonsense therapy for six sexual malfunctions. *Psychology Today* October 1974, 8: 77–86.

7–10 Kaplan, H. S. *The new sex therapy*. New York: Brunner Mazel, 1974.

7–11 Klüver, H. and Bucy, P. C. "Psychic blindness" and other symptoms following bilateral temporal lobectomy in rhesus monkeys. *American Journal of Physiology* 1937, 119: 352–353.

7–12 Kolodny, R. C., Masters, W. H., Hendry, J., and Toro, G. Plasma testosterone and semen analysis in male homosexuals. *The New England Journal of Medicine* 1971, 285: 1170–1174.

7–13 Kreuz, L. E., Rose, R. M., and Jennings, J. R. Suppression of plasma testosterone levels and psychological stress. *Archives of General Psychiatry* 1972, 26: 479–482.

7–14 Maccoby, E. E. and Jacklin, C. N. What we know and don't know about sex differences. *Psychology Today* December 1974, 109–112.

7–15 MacLean, P. D. and Ploog, D. W. Cerebral representation of penile erection. *Journal of Neurophysiology* 1962, 25: 29–55.

7–16 Masters, W. and Johnson, V. *Human sexual response*. Boston: Little Brown, 1966.

7–17 Moan, C. E. and Heath, R. C. Septal stimulation for the initiation of heterosexual behavior in a homosexual male. *Journal of Behavior Therapeutics and Experimental Psychiatry* 1972, 3: 23–30.

7–18 Money, J. The therapeutic use of androgen-depleting hormone. In H. L. P. Resnik and M. E. Wolfgang (Eds.), *Sexual behaviors: social, clinical and legal aspects*. Boston: Little Brown, 1972.

7–19 Money, J. and Ehrhardt, A. A. *Man & woman boy & girl*. Baltimore: Johns Hopkins University, 1972.

7–20 Phoenix, C. H., Goy, R. W., and Young, W. C. Sexual behavior: general aspects. In L. Martini and W. G. Ganong (Eds.), *Neuroendocrinology*. Vol. 11. New York: Academic Press, 1967.

7–21 Roeder, F. and Muller, D. The stereotaxic treatment of paedophilic homosexuality. *German Medical Monthly* 1969, 14: 265–271.

7–22 Starka, L., Sipova, I., and Hynie, J. Plasma testosterone in male transsexuals and homosexuals. *The Journal of Sex Research* 1975, 11: 134–138.

7–23 Stürup, G. K. Castration: the total treatment. In H. L. P. Resnik and M. E. Wolfgang (Eds.), *Sexual behaviors: social, clinical and legal aspects*. Boston: Little Brown, 1972.

7–24 Terzian, H. and Ore, G. Syndrome of Klüver and Bucy reproduced in man by bilateral removal of the temporal lobes. *Neurology* 1955, 5: 373–380.

7–25 Yalom, I. D., Green, R., and Risk, N. Prenatal exposure to female hormones. *Archives of General Psychiatry* 1973, 28: 554–561.

Emotions

Loving, Hating, Crying, and Laughing

An Emotional Poem

A famous poem begins:

How do I love thee? Let me count the ways.

What would you think if the ways included:

I love thee with irregular breathing.
I love thee with increased blood pressure.
I love thee with hormone secretions.
I love thee with a smile.

and

I love thee with my septum.

Although it is true that loving includes changes in breathing, blood pressure, hormones, and behaviors like smiling and brain activity, you would think that the experience of love also includes many different feelings, some impossible to describe. The scientist knows that there is more to love than bodily changes, but she cannot take a picture of love or measure it or point to it. She cannot dissect your brain to locate where the feeling of love is coming from. Because of all these "cannots," we know far less about the physiological or neurological bases of emotions than we do about reflexes or the senses. For example, vision has a known stimulus, light waves, and we can easily measure the response of seeing. In learning about vision, we can study animals, because seeing in animals has some of the same properties as seeing in humans. But what is the known stimulus for love, and how do you measure the response of loving, and how do you study loving in animals?

Feelings and Behavior

When the scientist thinks about loving, she has feelings of happiness, excitement, warmth, and satisfaction. These feelings are hers and may be different from yours. You cannot know about her feelings unless she chooses to reveal them. Even then, you cannot be sure that she has accurately understood or communicated her feelings. You can only know what she tells you about the feelings, her **verbal report**. Because these feelings are private and are experienced in her head, they are **subjective**, or personal, as opposed to **objective**, or observable. Part of experiencing love or hate or joy or any emotion is personal, or subjective feelings.

Some people say that romantic love is when you cannot sleep, or when you lose your appetite, or when you want to be with the person most of the time. Part of loving includes **behavior** that can be measured: how many hours of sleep, how much eaten, how much time with the person. These behaviors are observable, and so they are different from the subjective feelings in your head. The scientist can define love or any emotion on the basis of your behaviors (crying, eating, laughing) or on the basis of your verbal report of subjective feelings (happiness, excitement, satisfaction). But would the definition of love based on your behaviors and subjective feelings also apply to others? Probably not.

In order to arrive at a valid definition of love, it would be necessary to ask hundreds of people what they felt and what they did when loving. The same would be true for other emotions. For example, we could ask you what you felt and could observe your behavior while you were being suspended over the edge of a cliff, were receiving a thousand dollars, or were being kissed by your mother. It would be necessary to repeat this procedure using fire fighters, law enforcement officers, business people, doctors, and plumbers, asking what each person felt and observing what each person did. We would probably find that, under the same conditions, people would sometimes feel and behave similarly. For instance, while suspended over the edge of a cliff, most people might report feeling fear and would be observed trying to grab on to something. We probably would also find that, tested under the same conditions, different people often feel and behave differently. Seeing an accident, some people might feel fear, and others, curiosity. They might also show different behaviors, such as giving help or leaving the scene. To complicate matters further, the sex, age, and background of each individual would cause varying feelings and behaviors under the same conditions. It appears that we are caught between using a different definition of love for each person or using the same definition for all, even though it might not apply to everyone. For example, defining love as a feeling of happiness excludes those who are in love but are worried and unhappy about losing the one they love. For the scientist to be able to study brain and body responses involved in an emotion, such as love, that same emotion must occur with some reliability for different people.

The problem is basically the same in using either feelings or behavior to define an emotion. Different people experience different feelings in response to the same stimulus. In a group of people waiting in line, for example, feelings may range from good-natured indifference to extreme anger. Similarly, people show a whole variety of behaviors even when they report the same feelings. For example, most people would say they were happy at winning a contest, but some would laugh, others would cry, and some might show no change in behavior at all. It is not surprising that we lack knowledge of brain and body responses involved in love, as well as in other emotions, because they are so difficult to define. To count the ways that the brain and body love is not going to be easy.

Physiological Responses

If you were a scientist studying physiological response, you might consider the above problems and try a different approach to defining emotions. Perhaps a better way to define an emotion is to measure all of the physiological changes that occur when a person meets her sweetheart, receives a new car, or takes a final exam. During each of these situations, you could measure changes in heart rate, blood pressure, respiration, skin resistance to electricity or skin resistance response (SRR), hormonal secretions, and activity of various brain structures. Then you could check which pattern of physiological changes accompanies which emotional state. If you observed a reliable pattern of changes in heart rate, blood pressure, hormonal secretions, and brain activity under conditions that were considered fearful, and you never observed this pattern under any other conditions, then

you could define fear by a certain pattern of physiological responses. Using this pattern of physiological responses, you would know which emotion the person was feeling without having to ask. By analogy, it's possible to tell without asking if a person is awake or asleep from recordings of EEG waves and muscular activity. Whether you are sleeping can be accurately defined by a pattern of physiological responses. Could love, hate, or other emotions be defined by patterns of physiological responses?

Autonomic Nervous System

While feeling love or fear, you may experience butterflies in your stomach, a dry mouth, cold fingers, deep breathing, tears, or a pounding heart. These physiological responses are controlled automatically by the autonomic nervous system, which you learned about in Chapter 4. When you are feeling calm and relaxed, your heart rate, blood pressure, and breathing are maintained at a normal level by the parasympathetic division of the autonomic nervous system. The parasympathetic division is involved with responses that conserve and restore bodily energy, such as lowering blood pressure or heart rate or stimulating digestion. When you are feeling very fearful or angry or happy, your blood pressure and heart rate increase, the adrenal medulla releases epinephrine and norepinephrine, and blood is diverted from the stomach and skin to the muscles. These physiological responses prepare you for action and are controlled by the other part of the autonomic system, the sympathetic division. So the physiological responses occurring during emotional states are controlled by the two divisions of the autonomic nervous system. It would be a mistake to assume that the parasympathetic system was always active during pleasant emotions and the sympathetic during unpleasant ones. The pleasant feeling accompanying digestion occurs during parasympathetic activity. But the production of tears, blushing, and gastric movements leading to vomiting, which are not always pleasant, are also caused by parasympathetic activity.

Physiological Patterns

Does the autonomic nervous system produce a different pattern of physiological responses for each different emotion? Generally, the answer is no. The pattern of physiological responses occurring during intense anger is very similar to that occurring during extreme elation. When you are feeling joy or grief or fear, a similar pattern of physiological responses may occur. However, there may be a difference between the physiological responses occurring during anger and those occurring during fear. There is some evidence that the level of epinephrine is elevated during states of fear, and the level of both epinephrine and norepinephrine is elevated during states of anger (8–2). Although there may be some difference in responses during

Figure 8–1 In these two girls, grief-stricken over the motorcycle death of a friend, the sympathetic division is activated to help their bodies cope with the stressful news. If stress or excitement becomes too great, the heart may beat so rapidly that it does not pump effectively and too little blood reaches the brain. This is why people may faint when learning of a death or other shocking event. (Wide World Photos.)

fear and anger, it is difficult to tell from physiological responses alone whether you are feeling fear, anger, joy, or happiness. At the present time, it is difficult if not impossible to define an emotion on the basis of a certain pattern of physiological responses. Your head may know whether you are feeling love or hate but apparently your autonomic nervous system does not always recognize the difference.

Injected Emotion

When you feel your heart pounding or your hands trembling or your face blushed, are you feeling love or joy or hate? Suppose you were injected with a substance that caused increased heart rate, flushed face, and tremor in the hands. Would feeling these physiological responses cause you to feel a certain emotion? For example, during fear the amount

of circulating epinephrine increases; therefore, we might expect that if you were injected with epinephrine, you would report feeling fear. In one experiment, human subjects were given injections of epinephrine (adrenalin) but were told it was a vitamin compound. The subjects were not forewarned about the physiological responses they would feel, and there were some very curious results. As the physiological responses began, the researchers placed the subjects in two different environments. Some subjects were placed in a room with a person who was laughing and happy. These injected subjects reported feeling happy. Others were placed in a room with a person who was displaying very angry behavior. These injected subjects reported feeling angry (8–32). All injected subjects felt approximately the same physiological responses, but, depending upon the surroundings, they felt very different

Physiological Responses

127

emotions—happiness or anger. The injection of epinephrine did not produce any specific emotion but rather caused a general feeling of arousal. The specific emotion felt by the aroused person depended upon the way that he perceived, interpreted, and thought about his surroundings. Perceiving, interpreting, and thinking about your environment, collectively called **cognitive functions**, are very important in determining the appropriate emotion. This view is the **cognitive theory** of emotions (8–32).

Source of Feelings

If your spinal cord were severed at the neck, there would be no sensations from your stomach (butterflies) or heart (pounding) or palms (sweaty). Without these responses from your body, would you continue to feel emotions? After accidents that sever the spinal cord at the neck, patients can talk, see, and hear, but they have sensations only from the face and head area. Such persons have been studied to see whether they still have emotional responses, such as fear and anger. These patients do report feeling fear and anger, but they judge these emotions to be less intense than when their spinal cord was intact and they could feel sensations coming from the body (8–15). Apparently you have memories of emotional feelings stored in your brain and can still experience these feelings even though there are no sensations (pounding heart, sweaty palms) from the rest of the body. However, without the sensations of sweaty palms, dry mouth, and pounding heart, the emotion is experienced as less intense. You can fall in love with only your head, but it will feel less intense than falling in love with your head and your body.

Lingering Feelings

A strong emotional feeling, such as the fear at seeing an accident or the joy of seeing a loved one after a long absence, may last a considerable period of time. The emotional feeling may persist because you are remembering the incident over and over and thus are feeling the emotion over and over. Another reason emotional feeling persists is the circulating level of hormones, epinephrine and norepinephrine, secreted by the adrenal medulla during emotional states. The hormone norepinephrine is not easily metabolized and remains circulating in the body, causing physiological arousal. Circulating epinephrine and norepinephrine do not produce a specific emotion, but rather a general feeling of arousal. The circulating norepinephrine and epinephrine maintain the body in a state of arousal that contributes to the intensity and length of the emotional experience. For example, the excitement of a ride on a roller coaster will cause an increase in epinephrine and norepinephrine, the increase will make you feel aroused, and the feeling of arousal may cause you to enjoy the next ride more intensely.

Components of Emotion

It is no surprise that experiencing an emotion is a very complicated affair. When you are feeling jealous, there are three components to this feeling: the subjective, the behavioral, and the physiological. The subjective feeling is the component that occurs in your head and cannot be observed. Since people whose spinal cords have been severed can experience emotions, we know that the head or cognitive contribution to emotion is considerable. The behavioral response, which is observable, may include crying, shouting, hugging, and other actions. The behavioral response (crying) may be the same for different emotions (happiness or grief). Sometimes the behavioral responses of others (laughing) provide cues as to which emotion is appropriate to feel (happy). The physiological component, which may include dry mouth, sweaty palms, rapid heart rate, and increased hormonal secretions, can also be observable. Sometimes the physiological response is seen directly (as in blushing), sometimes it is observed with the use of equipment (as in blood pressure). The pattern of physiological responses may be the same (increased heart rate, blood pressure, and hormonal secretions) for different emotions (fear, love). Although these physiological responses are not essential to feeling an emotion, your perception of them can enhance how much you feel emotions such as love, hate, or joy. If you are feeling afraid, the pounding of your heart may make you feel even more afraid. The subjective, behavioral, and physiological responses that accompany an emotion are organized by structures in the brain. The next question is which structures of the brain are involved in which emotions. Is it true that you love with your septum?

Studying the Brain

If we wanted to know which brain structures were involved when you were feeling love or hate or anger, we might insert electrodes into the brain and record electrical activity or withdraw samples and analyze the neurotransmitters in various brain areas. Brain structures could also be removed and we could see which emotions remained after removal of a particular area. None of these procedures is carried out on the healthy human brain, and with good reason. When wires or tubes are placed into the brain to record activity or analyze chemicals, neurons are destroyed and do not regenerate. The same is true if a brain structure is removed: the neurons do not regrow. Since damage to the brain is not reversible, there would be serious ethical questions about studying a human brain using these methods. As a result, it is very difficult to obtain direct information about how brain structures are involved in emotions in humans.

There are circumstances in which the brain is explored. If a person is wounded, has a tumor, or has a kind of epilepsy that cannot be controlled by medication, it may be necessary for a neurosurgeon to operate on the brain. Before

GIRL IS PSYCHOLOGICAL VICTIM OF SLAYER

No one seeing 17-year-old Monica Silbas help her volleyball team win second place over the weekend would have guessed that for 36 hours last week she had lain, mute and still, on a hospital bed—a reaction to the shooting rampage at California State University, Fullerton, that left seven people dead.

Not that Monica—who lapsed into a torpid state after she witnessed the bloodbath last Monday—is totally out of danger yet. She is still a patient at Mercy Hospital in Santa Ana, but her prognosis is good and she is due to be released soon. She seems to have been helped by the volleyball game at the university which was a calculated risk on the part of her psychiatrist, Dr. Jay Needler of Santa Ana, who gambled that her intense desire to compete would help bring her back to the real world.

"The first word Monica uttered on Wednesday night was 'Coach,'" Needler said. She said it when she saw her coach, Art Jones, on television. Later, he visited her in the hospital and asked her if she wanted to play in Saturday's Upward Bound game. She nodded. "If you want to play, you have to talk," he said. Then Monica finally talked. "When do I get out of the hospital?" she asked.

But none of Monica's torpid behavior was voluntary, Needler said. Not the mutism, the limp body or the total absence of bodily reflexes. Her eyes remained shut for twelve hours, then fluttered open to a fixed stare. Later she giggled at inappropriate times.

"She just couldn't respond," said Needler. "Not to her parents, her brothers and sisters, her priest, or anyone. The shock was too great. She is a normal, bright, active intelligent girl with no previous psy-

chiatric history who has just gone through an enormous emotional cataclysm."

But she wanted to be in the volleyball game, he said, and that wish helped bring her out.

Was hers an uncommon response to witnessing carnage?

In some ways yes, Needler said, but it is not difficult to understand that a sensitive adolescent girl might react this way. Even men in war have had such reactions.

"In World War I, they called it 'shell-shock,' although no shells were involved. In World War II, it was 'battle fatigue.'"

Pressed for a diagnosis, Needler said Monica's condition might be called "post-traumatic hysteria," although he feels such labels are arbitrary and often misleading.

Catatonia, a word previously used by the news media, is too strong a term, Needler said. It refers to a more serious condition of muscular inflexibility.

Monica, an alert lively girl, was able to talk about her own experiences Saturday night at the hospital while she was guest of honor at a brief birthday party—her 17th—thrown by about 30 of her friends from Santa Ana Valley High School. "I was on campus that morning because I am a member of Upward Bound—an accelerated summer college program for high school students from disadvantaged or minority homes. I had just gotten to the Upward Bound office in the library basement when I heard a shot.

"At first, I thought it was a firecracker but someone yelled, 'He's shooting,' and I saw a man with a gun run by. Then I saw a woman lying on the floor riddled with bullets. There were dots of red on her pink dress. When someone shouted, 'Get out of sight . . . get in an office

and lock the door' I did that."

Then she stood against the wall trembling, frozen, and not responding for an hour or more while people tried the door, the phone rang and people called her name. "I just froze—I closed out the world," she said.

When she emerged from the room and saw two bodies covered with sheets on the floor, she sat down and wept. It was the last emotion she was to show for almost two days. By the time she had arrived at the hospital by ambulance, she had, in her own words, "frozen" again.

"Her ability to cry, to show her feelings that way, even briefly, is what helped her recover," Needler said.

But he was with her as much as 14 hours a day at the height of her crisis and she and her family will probably "need supportive help . . . perhaps with a group . . . for some time to come," he said.

Later, the report came through that Monica "was very upset" at the possibility she had talked too much about her experience, in violation of police instructions.

"She is feeling guilty," her mother, Dolores, who works as a food attendant in the Mercy Hospital kitchen, said. "We realize now it will take a while."

* * *

Psychiatrists talked of cases similar to Monica's.

"I remember one at Harvard," said Dr. Charles Wahl, a Beverly Hills psychiatrist:

"A man was turning a corner when he saw a bank robber shoot five people while trying to escape. He became frozen with terror. He didn't know whether to flee or intercede. As a result, he did nothing—just froze there immobile.

"Often this happens to people who have a strong sense of rectitude, who are especially 'good' or try hard to do the right thing," Wahl said. "They are often unusually upset at seeing anything so alien and horrifying as senseless carnage."

surgery, these patients are given a series of tests to measure sensory, muscular, and psychological functioning. After brain surgery, the patients are tested again. With varying degrees of success, it is possible to use these tests to determine something about the function of the brain area removed. Much of our knowledge about the human brain and emotional behavior comes from patients who have undergone corrective surgery. We know much more about how the brain organizes emotional behavior in the rat or cat or monkey, since their brains have been studied extensively. Remarkably similar behavioral changes have been observed in monkeys and humans following destruction of certain brain areas. At the same time, there have also been remarkable differences. Because of these differences, we must use caution in generalizing animal results to humans. We are not completely confident that the findings from animal brains apply to human brains.

Human Temporal Lobe

A young adult had severe epileptic seizures that disrupted his life and could not be controlled by medication. As a last resort, the doctors decided to remove part of his brain. It was thought that removal of the tips of the temporal lobes might eliminate the seizures. For some unknown reason, abnormal electrical activity may begin in the temporal lobe and initiate epileptic seizures. Abnormal electrical activity usually indicates that there are neurons firing when they should not be. In this case, the patient did have abnormal electrical activity, or brain waves, in the region of his temporal lobe. The surgeons removed the tip of the temporal lobe on one side and found that the seizures did not decrease. Next they removed the tip of the temporal lobe on the other side. After the surgery, doctors noted some dramatic changes in the patient's behavior. He became very unemotional and showed no signs of affect when visited by his friends or family. He began to eat many times a day and ask for food frequently. He began to display himself sexually to those who passed by. His conversation deteriorated to the point that he was using one word instead of sentences to ask for things (8–35). His seizures decreased for a time, but six months later they returned. Because of this and other side effects of the surgery, he had to be confined to a mental hospital. In this tragic example, removal of the temporal lobes to treat seizures produced very detrimental side effects. It is not always the case that brain surgery produces debilitating side effects, but it is always a possibility. From this study, it seems that the temporal lobes are involved in sexual behavior, eating habits, manner of speaking, and other emotional behavior, as suggested by loss of **affect**, or emotionality.

Monkey Temporal Lobe

When the doctors removed the temporal lobes in the above patient, they could have had some idea of what behavioral changes might occur. Some 18 years earlier, this same surgical removal of both temporal lobes had been performed on monkeys (8–20). Following surgery, the monkeys behaved much differently. Although usually aggressive, they became tame. They showed less fear of snakes, which they normally avoided. They displayed increased sexuality by mounting inappropriate objects, such as chickens. Their dietary habits changed from vegetarian to meat-eating. They explored all types of objects by placing them in their mouths. This series of behavioral changes following temporal lobe removal has become known as the **Kluver-Bucy** (KLU-ver-boo-see) **syndrome**. The fact that removal of the

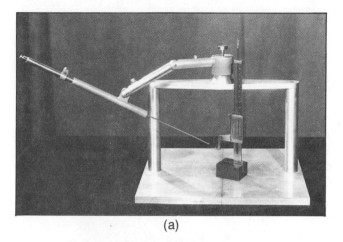

(a)

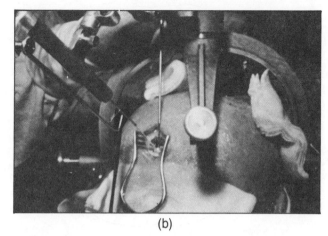

(b)

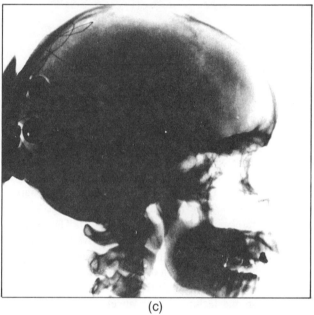

(c)

Figure 8-2 Electrodes placed into the human brain. (a) The electrode is positioned in a special instrument called the stereotactic holder. Using this holder, the surgeon can determine the direction and depth that the electrode should reach in the actual brain. (b) The skull of a patient with the stereotactic holder attached. The electrode is being lowered into the brain according to the measurements taken earlier. There is no pain when the electrode is lowered into the brain because the brain itself has no pain receptors. The electrode can remain in the brain for weeks and is held in place by a special metal plug or cement. (c) An x ray of a human brain after electrodes have been placed into the brain. The electrodes appear as fine lines, and the round disks on the back of the head are the metal plugs holding the electrodes in place. (Photos from V. H. Mark and F. Ervin, *Violence and the Brain*, New York: Harper & Row, 1970.)

temporal lobe's tips in the human patient had effects very similar to those in monkeys tells us two important things: first, that areas in the temporal lobe are probably involved in emotional behavior, and second, that research in monkeys can sometimes help us to understand the structures and function of the human brain.

Limbic System

The last time you were angry or happy or jealous, various structures in your brain were active. Some of the brain structures thought to be involved in emotional behavior are collectively called the **limbic** system. The limbic system evolved millions of years ago in reptiles, which indicates that it is a very old part of the brain. The limbic system includes the amygdala, hippocampus, hypothalamus, and septal areas. It is thought that these areas are involved in your loving, hating, and other emotions.

To learn what a brain structure does, you might implant a fine wire, or electrode, into it and apply current. This current would activate the surrounding neurons. When the neurons in the brain structure were activated, the animal would perform some behavior. You could then assume that the particular brain structure was involved in that behavior. Alternatively, you might lesion, or destroy, part or all of the structure and then observe which behaviors were eliminated. Another approach would be to inject chemicals that would excite or inhibit neurons in the specific brain structure and observe the animal's behavior or lack of it. Finally, you could place electrodes into the structure and, instead of applying electrical current, record the electrical activity of the neurons when the animal was engaged in various behaviors: sleeping, eating, or attacking. All of these techniques—electrical or chemical stimulation, lesions, and electrical recordings—have been used to discover how the brain organizes emotional behavior.

Human Amygdala

During corrective or exploratory surgery in humans, electrodes have been implanted in the amygdala, which is lo-

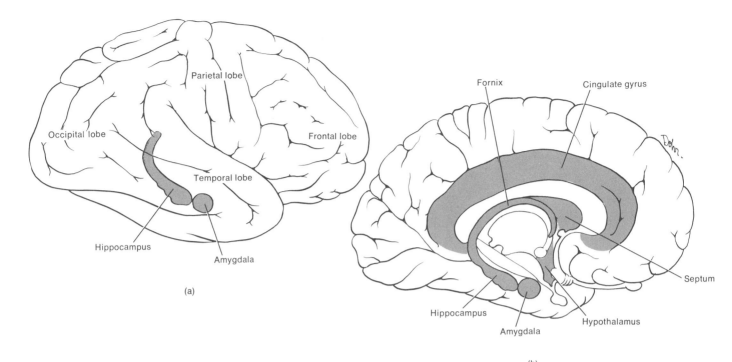

Figure 8-3 Control of emotional behavior involves the limbic system. (a) Side view of the brain showing part of the limbic system, amygdala, and hippocampus, buried deep in the temporal lobe. (b) Middle view of the brain shows location of limbic system structures: amygdala, hippocampus, cingulate gyrus, septum, and hypothalamus.

cated in the tips of the temporal lobes. During electrical stimulation, many patients have reported feeling fear (8–9) while only one patient reported feeling either fear or anger (8–2). Another patient reported the feeling of losing control when one area was stimulated and the feeling of relaxation and calm when another area was stimulated (8–23). When the amygdala has been removed from humans, the general finding has been one of reduced emotionality or affect, apathy, and lack of social interactions (8–26, 8–33, 8–35). These findings suggest that different areas within the amygdala are involved in different emotions that include a general feeling of affect and the specific feelings of fear, anger, and calmness. In addition, stimulation of the amygdala has produced brain waves similar to those seen during epileptic seizures (8–23). It is possible that the amygdala is involved in the initiation of some epileptic seizures. Also, the amygdala has connections with many other brain areas, especially the hypothalamus. So stimulation of the amygdala might produce a feeling like fear through its own activity or through activation of other areas, such as the hypothalamus.

Animal Amygdala

If the amygdala of a cat is electrically stimulated, you see the following responses, depending on which area is activated: (1) attention or alerting, (2) emotional responses of fear or anger, (3) physiological responses of salivation, urination, or defecation, and (4) responses associated with eating, such as sniffing, chewing, and licking. The response

of fear in the cat is consistent with the findings in human patients. However, the response of anger or rage seen in animals is rarely produced in humans (8–9). The other responses indicate that the amygdala is involved in many different behaviors in addition to emotional responses.

If stimulation or activation of the amygdala results in fear or anger, then perhaps removal of the amygdala would result in an animal lacking fear or anger. This is essentially what happens. Following removal of the amygdala, animals show loss of fear, are placid, and are less active (8–6). If the boss or dominant monkey of a group has its amygdala removed, the animal usually loses its position of dominance (8–31). The results from these studies in rats, cats, and monkeys indicate that destruction of the amygdala caused animals to be tamer, less fearful, less aggressive, and less dominant. Many of the effects following amygdala destruction are the same as those noticed by Kluver and Bucy after destruction of the temporal lobes. This similarity indicates that it was the destruction of the amygdala area in the temporal lobes that was responsible for most of the effects called the Kluver-Bucy syndrome. In animals and possibly humans, the amygdala is involved in emotional behaviors that include fear, anger, placidness, or tameness. If your loving involves these behaviors, then your amygdala may be involved.

Human Hippocampus

If all of your hippocampus were removed, you would find it difficult to remember what you did yesterday or the day

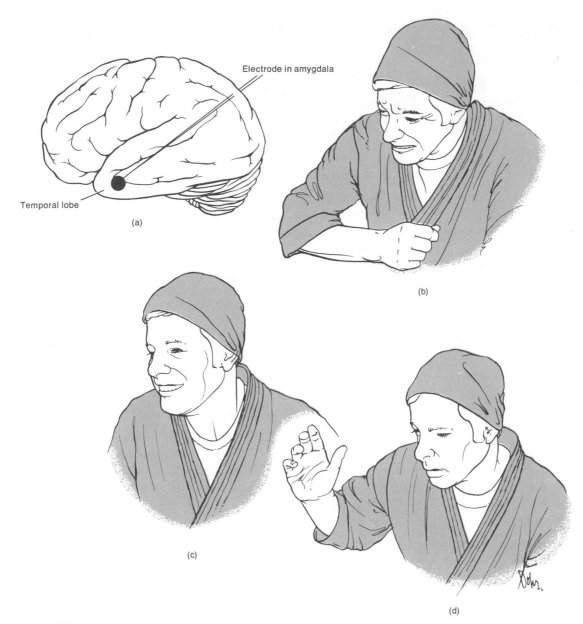

Figure 8-4 Effects of brain stimulation in a human patient. (a) Electrode was implanted into the amygdala. (b) Stimulation at 5 milliamperes causes the patient to appear aroused, angry, and say, "Don't do this to me. I don't want to be mean. I just want to hit something." (c) When stimulation is reduced to 4 milliamperes, the patient breaks into a wide smile and says, "I know it's silly, what I'm doing." (d) Again, stimulation at 5 milliamperes causes patient to feel angry and say, "Don't let me hit you." He raises his arm as if to strike. Afterward, the patient said that while the stimulation was not painful, he did not want it repeated. This is an extremely rare example of stimulation causing anger in a human; there are more examples of stimulation causing fear. (Redrawn from H. E. King, Psychological effects of excitation in the limbic system. In D. E. Sheer (Ed.), *Electrical Stimulation of the Brain*, Austin: University of Texas Press, 1961.)

before, or, for that matter, what you just read. But your memory for events before the operation would be intact (8–34). Located in back of the amygdala in the temporal lobes, the hippocampus is involved in memory, especially memory of recent events. Even though patients with their hippocampus removed have severe memory problems, they do not show any gross emotional changes. The word *gross* is important. It is difficult to test for subtle changes in

emotional behavior, especially when the patient may have had behavioral problems that were partly responsible for the surgery in the first place. If the patient had a tumor or had epileptic seizures that necessitated the removal of the hippocampus, it is difficult to decide whether changes following surgery are due to removal of the tumor or of the hippocampus or are due to lack of epileptic seizures. To say there are no gross emotional changes is to say that the per-

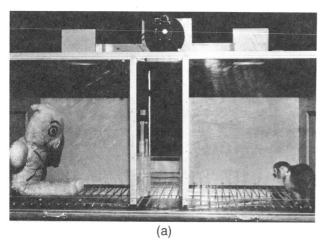 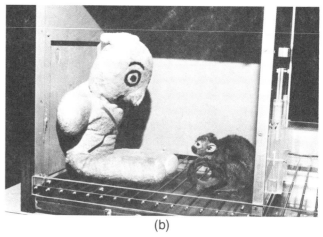

(a)   (b)

Figure 8–5 Amygdala and fear. (a) A normal monkey shows fear of the teddy bear, as indicated by its refusal to enter or approach the bear's compartment. (b) After removal of the temporal lobe tip, including the amygdala, the monkey enters the teddy bear's compartment, sits next to it, and displays none of its former fearfulness. (Photos from R. Plotnik, Changes in social behavior of squirrel monkeys after anterior temporal lobectomy. *Journal of Comparative and Physiological Psychology*, 1968, 32: 369–377.)

son does not exhibit any changes in emotional behavior that are clearly obvious. From studies on humans with their hippocampus removed, we know that this brain structure is involved in recent memory, but we are less certain of its function in emotional behavior.

Animal Hippocampus

If the hippocampus is removed from a rat, its survival ability is severely impeded, since the rat approaches a cat it normally would avoid (8–18). It is hard to know whether removal of the hippocampus makes the rat less fearful or merely causes it to move and explore more than it would normally, so that it enters the cat's area (8–3). When the hippocampus is removed from monkeys, they show less fear of humans and are not frightened by previously avoided stimuli (8–10). The results from monkeys and rats indicate that the hippocampus may be involved in fearful behavior. However, the animals may be less fearful because they move around more, cannot remember that the object is to be feared, or are so distracted that they do not notice the fearful object. Like humans, rats with hippocampal damage also show a problem in remembering recent events. Animals with this lesion will return again and again to a food box in which they have just been shocked (8–16).

The hippocampus has connections with many other brain structures, especially the hypothalamus and the septal area. As is probably true for most brain areas, there is no single function for these structures. Instead, each is involved in many functions that may include emotional, physiological, and behavioral components. Furthermore, when complex behaviors such as fear are evoked, there is certainly more than one brain area involved.

Septal Area

If you were given one electrode to stimulate one area of your brain, you should probably choose the septal area.

When this area is electrically stimulated in humans, they report feelings of pleasure (8–11). Stimulation of this area in animals also seems to result in pleasure, since animals work hard at a task to produce the stimulation (8–27). In addition, stimulation of the septal area in monkeys causes penile erection (8–22), and in some humans, sexual feelings (8–24). The septal area in monkeys and humans is located in the center of the brain. Compared with that of rats and cats, the septal area in monkeys and humans is proportionally much smaller. The septal area has connections with many brain areas, especially the hypothalamus and hippocampus.

If stimulation of the septal area results in pleasure, you might think that its destruction would result in some unpleasant emotion, such as rage or anger. Stimulation of an area sometimes results in one effect while removal of that same area results in the opposite effect. This opposite effect is the ideal result and does not happen consistently enough to be stated as a rule, only as a possibility. In the case of the septal area, stimulation produces pleasure and destruction does produce rage. If the septal area is removed, a rat will become vicious and will attack anything and everything (8–4). From this we infer that the neurons in the septal area, or those passing through it, normally act to suppress or inhibit attack. When they are removed, the attack behavior occurs. The septal area may suppress the hypothalamus or other areas with which it is connected. If an animal with a septal lesion is handled or placed in the company of other rats, the viciousness disappears in a few weeks and the animal appears as before. When this same septal lesion is produced in monkeys, no emotional changes are detected (8–5). This is an example of a similar lesion producing very different responses (rage and nothing) in different animals (rats and monkeys). You can see that it is sometimes dif-

134   **Emotions**

ficult to generalize the findings from animal to animal, much less from animal to humans.

Since all of these brain areas are interconnected, you might wonder what would happen if first one structure were lesioned and then a second. If the septal area is destroyed first, a rat will become vicious. If the amygdala is then destroyed, the rat will become tame (8–19). This finding means that the amygdala must be present for the vicious behavior to occur. It does not mean that the septal area acts directly on the amygdala. It only means that the amygdala is somehow involved in the behavior released by a septal lesion. Since stimulation of the septal area produces pleasurable and sex-related feelings, it is possible that this area is involved in the emotion you know as love.

Hypothalamus

If you could see impulses flowing from the amygdala, septal area, and hippocampus, one of the areas you would see them flowing into is the hypothalamus. The **hypothalamus**, located below the thalamus in the middle base of the brain, is a collective name for a group of 20 different interconnected nuclei. These 20 nuclei are the reason why the hypothalamus has so many different functions.

It is possible to produce increased heart rate and other physiological responses that prepare the body for action by electrically stimulating the back part, or **posterior hypothalamus**. The posterior hypothalamus seems to activate the sympathetic nervous system, which readies the body for action. If the front or anterior part of the hypothalamus is stimulated, the heart rate is slowed and the animal becomes calm. This area, the **anterior hypothalamus**, seems to control the parasympathetic nervous system, which helps the body to conserve energy and maintain an optimum state for proper functioning (8–13). Electrical stimulation of the hypothalamus in humans has produced autonomic responses similar to those reported for cats (8–37). Thus, the hypothalamus is involved in controlling both parts of the autonomic nervous system, the sympathetic and parasympathetic divisions. When you are loving and your heart is beating wildly, your mouth is dry, and your palms are sweaty, it is the posterior hypothalamus controlling the sympathetic nervous system that is producing these results. So you also love with your hypothalamus.

If the hypothalamus is electrically stimulated, a cat will show rage and even attack the experimenter if he or she moves (8–14, 8–36). The same thing happens if the hypothalamus is lesioned. It is not so surprising that stimulation and lesion can produce the same result when you remember that the hypothalamus is actually composed of 20 nuclei. Some of these nuclei may be involved in the excitation of attack and others in the inhibition. In addition, certain areas of the hypothalamus appear to be involved in certain kinds of attack by cats. If stimulated in one area of the hypothalamus, the cat will quietly stalk and kill a rat. If stimulated in another area of the hypothalamus, the cat's killing behavior will be more explosive and vicious (8–7).

This rat-killing behavior is probably not aggression but rather a type of hunting behavior that a cat normally shows. There is probably no behavior in humans that is equivalent to the cat's hunting response, so it is difficult to generalize these results to humans.

When two or more monkeys are placed together, they establish within minutes who is the boss or dominant monkey and who is the submissive one. The dominant monkey has priority over food, drink, and location in the cage. The submissive monkey is kept in its place by the threats and aggression of the dominant monkey. It is very difficult to reverse this dominance pattern since any attempts at reversal are met with attack by the dominant monkey. In one experiment, reversal did take place when the submissive monkey was electrically stimulated in its hypothalamus. During hypothalamic stimulation, the smaller, submissive monkey repeatedly attacked the larger, dominant monkey, and eventually the smaller monkey assumed the rank of boss (8–30). This is not strong evidence that the hypothalamus is involved in aggressive behavior, but it does suggest some possible role. There are very few examples of hypothalamic stimulation in humans. One case is reported in which a slow-growing tumor pressed on the hypothalamus. Pressure on the hypothalamus might stimulate it in a fashion similar to electrical stimulation. In this patient, there were unprovoked outbursts of rage against the examining doctors and nurses (8–29). If you were going to guess what areas of the brain are active when you are enraged, you should probably include the hypothalamus.

The hypothalamus also seems to be involved in very divergent behaviors. Stimulation of some areas of a cat's hypothalamus caused the animal to be calmed or drowsy (8–13). Stimulation of other areas in rats seemed to produce pleasure, since the animals worked hard to press a lever to produce the stimulation (8–27). Evidently the hypothalamus is involved in a range of emotions, from calmness to pleasure to rage to aggression, and it is involved in the autonomic response that conserves the body's energy and prepares it for action.

Frontal Lobe

One area of the brain, the frontal lobe, was lesioned in more than 5,000 human patients as treatment for various mental disorders. Today, a **frontal lobotomy**, as lesioning of the frontal lobes is called, is rarely if ever performed. In these lobotomies, the surgeon did not actually remove the entire frontal lobe. The very tip of the frontal lobe is called the **prefrontal area**, and in back of this are the premotor and motor areas that control voluntary movements. In the frontal lobotomy, the prefrontal area was lesioned and the motor areas were left intact. Very often the brain tissue was not removed, but a cut was made so that it was isolated and became nonfunctional. The use of the prefrontal lobotomy as treatment for mental disorders had its beginnings in a 1935 experiment on chimps. After making a mistake on a learning task, one chimp would throw violent temper tan-

(a)   (b)

Figure 8–6 Brain stimulation causes opposite responses in two different social situations. (a) If the stimulated monkey is dominant, stimulation causes it to attack the monkey crouched on the floor. The platform on top of the stimulated monkey's head connects to the electrodes in its brain; the collar around its neck contains the remotely controlled stimulator. This particular brain stimulation was unpleasant because the monkey, if given the chance, would turn it off by pressing a lever. (b) If the stimulated monkey is submissive, stimulation causes it to make a submissive response (mouth open, teeth exposed) in the presence of a dominant partner that is near the back of the cage. These two examples show how brain stimulation may produce opposite responses depending upon the animal's environment. (Photos from R. Plotnik, D. Mir, and J. M. R. Delgado, Aggression, noxiousness and brain stimulation in unrestrained rhesus monkeys. In B. E. Eleftherion and J. B. Scott (Eds.), *The physiology of aggression and defeat.* New York: Plenum Press, 1971.)

trums, roll on the floor, urinate, and defecate. After its prefrontal lobes were lesioned, this chimp no longer showed temper tantrums. Now when it made mistakes, it remained calm through the testing (8–17). On the basis of these results, neurosurgeons thought that this treatment might relieve symptoms of intense anxiety, obsessional behavior, or rage. Some patients did benefit from this treatment but others did not. Results were not consistent among patients, there were unwanted side effects, and the symptoms often remained. The side effects included the appearance of tactless and inappropriate behavior in social situations (peeing in public), inability to express feeling for other people's problems or one's own, a general dulling of emotions, and the inability to plan ahead. In spite of these changes in social and emotional behavior, prefrontal lobotomy did not usually affect overall general intelligence as measured by a standard IQ test. With all of these disturbing side effects, frontal lobotomies were finally abandoned. From these thousands of cases, we have learned that the frontal lobe is involved in social, emotional, and planning behaviors. We have also learned that the effect of frontal lesions is different for different people, suggesting that the function of the frontal lobes may be slightly different for each of us.

Cortex or Neocortex

The term **cortex** literally means bark or outer layer. The cortex is the outermost part of the brain, and it is the area of your brain that was the last to evolve. The cortex of the frontal parietal, occipital, and temporal lobes is often called **neocortex**, meaning ''new'' cortex. It has many connections with the limbic system, some parts of which (septal area) are considered old cortex or paleocortex. As we use the term cortex, we will be referring to neocortex. It is known that the cortex controls voluntary movements, is responsible for sensing (seeing, hearing, etc.), and interprets and adds meanings to what you sense. Since sensing takes place in the cortex, we can assume that the sequence that results in an emotional feeling frequently begins in the cortex. If you are forced onto the shoulder of the road by a careless driver, the information from your eyes and ears will be projected to your cortex. When this information reaches the cortex, you will recognize, or interpret, the neural activity as being a car swerving into your car, and you will take some action, such as driving onto the shoulder. Your association cortex adds meaning to the sensory information, for example, telling you that the car is dangerously close, that the driver is careless, or that the shoulder is a safe area.

'BRAIN PACEMAKER' SUCCESS REPORTED

Success in treating schizophrenics and other severely mentally ill persons with a brain pacemaker has been reported by a New Orleans psychiatrist-neurologist.

Ten of the 11 patients who have received the tiny device, which corrects electrical disturbances in the brain much like a cardiac pacemaker regulates heart rhythms, are leading close to normal lives after up to 20 years of hospitalization, drugs and shock treatments.

They are no longer receiving medication or other treatment, said Dr. Robert G. Heath, chairman of the department of psychiatry and neurology at Tulane University's school of medicine.

Heath spoke Sunday at the annual meeting of the Society of Biological Psychiatrists here.

The operation has been performed on five schizophrenics, four uncontrollably violent persons and two neurotics. The single failure was a paranoid schizophrenic found to have brain damage in the area in which the pacemaker's electrodes must be implanted.

Heath said that while it is too soon for conclusive results—the first pacemaker was implanted in February of 1976, the last this March —the treatment should be considered for patients who have failed to respond to conventional therapies, particularly those who are developing undesirable side effects from drugs.

* * *

A similar device is being used in several other medical centers to treat epileptics and spastics. However, this is the first reported use for behavioral disorders.

The pacemaker consists of 20 tiny platinum disc electrodes placed on the surface of the cerebellum, the hind part of the brain at the lower back of the head. These are attached to a receiver about the size of a quarter in the left side of the chest, just under the collarbone, by thread-like wires grouped into four silicone-coated bundles running under the skin. None of this is visible from outside.

An antenna, which can be removed for bathing or swimming, is strapped over the receiver. Its battery-powered transmitter is carried in a pocket. Eventually, Heath hopes for a completely implantable unit with a long-lasting power source. At present, the batteries must be changed every week or 10 days and so must be carried outside the body.

The brain is stimulated at five-minute intervals with a pulse that lasts one four-thousandth of a second at three to six volts.

The rationale behind this is that a patient's emotional state can be altered by activating, through electrical stimulation, precise brain pathways. Heath said that many forms of mental illness, whatever the cause, are characterized by electrical disturbances in the brain—for example, misfiring of certain cells.

The areas of the brain that control emotion, however, are deep-seated, and previous attempts to stimulate them have meant digging well into the brain, using electrodes that exited from the scalp and limiting the stimulation to brief periods. The results were inconsistent and short-lived.

Heath said that those deep-seated centers can be reached indirectly by stimulating a precise half-inch area of the cerebellum previously thought to be concerned primarily with motor activity.

Animal and human studies, he said, have shown that stimulation of this easily accessible part of the brain activates cells in the septal region, or "pleasure center," while inhibiting those of the hippocampus and part of the amygdala, the presumed seat of rage, fear and violent feelings.

Patients accepted for the operation had been pronounced incurable by at least two psychiatrists or neurologists. Family consent had to be given as well.

The first patient to undergo the operation was a 19-year-old boy, slightly retarded from birth, who had repeatedly tried to kill himself or relatives. He was confined to a Louisiana state mental hospital. There he was maintained on huge quantities of drugs, kept in physical restraints much of the time and dismissed as hopeless.

* * *

Films of him following the operation but before activation of the pacemaker show a still-sedated, anxious, fearful, uncommunicative and self-destructive boy suffering from the grueling, involuntary movement of tardive dyskinesia.

"From the day the pacemaker was activated the patient's outbursts of violence ceased," Heath said. "His tardive dyskinesia gradually diminished. His behavior has continued to improve. He is now a pleasant and sociable young man. He was enlisted in a vocational rehabilitation course and he is now ready for job placement. Psychological tests, including IQ scores, have shown significant improvement.

"Clinically, the patient has had a complete remission. He copes adequately with the vicissitudes of everyday life. He is receiving no medication. It was necessary for him to visit the state hospital where he had last been a patient, before physicians and nursing staff could believe that it was possible for him to live outside an institution."

The videotapes attest to his progress.

* * *

Nor does the operation erase memory.

As the cortex makes connections with various structures in the limbic system, emotional feelings may be added to this information. For example, you may feel rage at the careless driver, terror of crashing, or relief at finding the safe shoulder.

Possibly some emotional feelings begin at your limbic areas, or at least these areas may contribute to emotional feelings. This idea comes partly from the animal work discussed above, but also from study of human patients. It is from stimulation of limbic areas that humans report emotional feelings. On the other hand, humans very rarely report emotional feelings from stimulation of the cortex (8–9). This is not to say that the cortex is uninvolved in emotional behavior. Rather the cortex and limbic areas probably interact for the production of emotions. Cortical lesions in humans, such as prefrontal lobotomy, do lead to marked changes in emotional behavior. Also, removal of the cortex in cats leads to a great release of emotional behavior, or what has been called **decorticate rage**. Perhaps the cortex is involved in controlling the limbic system during emotional experiences to prevent your emotions from resulting in dangerous behavior, such as attacking the careless driver. So the sequence that results in an emotion often begins with the processing and interpreting of sensory information in the cortex. Emotional feelings may then be added by interactions between cortex and limbic areas. Finally, it is thought that the cortex controls the limbic system so that emotional feelings do not result in dangerous behavior.

Animal Model

In one study conducted with a monkey, the fibers connecting the two brain hemispheres (corpus callosum) were cut so that the right side of the cortex was completely separate from the left side, and neither side knew what the other was doing. In monkeys with normal brains, the right and left sides are constantly transferring information back and forth so that each side knows what the other is doing. With the connecting fibers cut, it was almost as though the monkey had two brains operating independently in the same head. In addition, some of the nerves from the eyes were cut so that the monkey did in fact see one kind of world using its right eye, which now sent information only to the right side; another kind of world using its left eye, which now sent information only to the left side.

In this particular monkey, the amygdala on the right side had been removed. When the right eye was covered, the monkey's left eye saw the world and sent this information to the left side of the brain. The animal was able to see, pick up objects, recognize food, and show other behaviors indicating that its cortex was functioning properly. In addition, when the left eye saw a human, the monkey reacted with anger and rage and could not be approached. With its left brain, in which none of the limbic structures were damaged, the monkey showed normal emotional reactions to humans. Next the left eye was covered, and the right eye saw the world. The right eye sent its information to the right brain. Using its right eye, the monkey could again pick up objects and recognize food, indicating that its cortex was functioning normally. When a human approached, the right eye saw the human and sent this information to the right cortex. Next a dramatic thing happened: the monkey showed no anger or irritability toward the human. Although the cortex had seen the human, it could not interact with the amygdala to form the appropriate emotional behavior. Without the amygdala, there was no anger or aggression (8–6). This is a good example of how the cortex and limbic system interact to form emotions and of how important the limbic system is in the actual feeling of an emotion.

Inherited Temperament?

Suppose your father always smiled at strangers and your mother became very angry whenever someone disagreed with her. Would you have these same emotional patterns? Maybe. If so, would you have **inherited** these emotional patterns from your parents or would you have **learned** them? If you had inherited these emotional patterns, it would mean that somewhere in your brain, possibly the limbic system, you were born with a built-in neural circuit that, when activated, produced smiling at strangers or extreme anger over disagreements. We know that everyone is born with certain prewired neural circuits that result in reflex behaviors: the sucking response, orienting response (turning your head toward a stimulus), and knee-jerk response. You did not have to learn to make the mouth movements involved in sucking. When an appropriate stimulus, such as a nipple, was placed in your mouth, you began to suck. The sucking response is a fairly simple behavior. However, showing an emotional pattern, such as smiling at strangers, is a very complicated behavior. This response involves recognizing strangers, feeling friendly, and, finally, smiling. In humans it is generally thought that specific emotional patterns are not inherited but rather are learned.

There are some who believe that humans inherit a general tendency to be aggressive (8–1, 8–2), although they do not say that we inherit specific emotional patterns. You may wonder how they arrive at the conclusion that aggression is inherited. The evidence for this belief comes in large part from the study of animals, which do seem to have prewired neural circuits. In some fish, birds, or rodents, a certain stimulus triggers a certain kind of aggressive response, and the aggressive response is generally the same for all the animals of a particular species. Some investigators generalize these animal findings to humans and state that humans have also inherited aggression or have an aggressive instinct. Many other scientists consider it a mistake to generalize from the findings that animals have prewired circuits for aggression. In their view, it is a mistake to assume that humans also have prewired circuits for aggression or other emotional behaviors (8–25). In lower animals (rats and cats), it has been possible to locate and stimulate the prewired circuits for aggression. You might think that if these circuits exist in higher animals (monkeys and humans), it should be possible to locate and stimulate them. In fact, brain stimulation in monkeys and humans has rarely produced pure aggression—that is, aggression that is not the result of pain. If there are prewired circuits in the brain, they are certainly difficult to locate (8–28). At the human level, brain research has provided very little evidence of inheritance of prewired circuits for aggression or other emotional behaviors. Your genetic makeup may have contributed to your temperament, but it is most unlikely that your pattern of emotional behavior is prewired in the same way that your reflexes are. If you have a fierce temper, it is probably not inherited from your parents. More likely you have learned your temper from your parents and others.

Comment

The next time you are loving or hating or happy or angry, you will know that you are using your limbic system. You will know that crying may or may not mean you are sad, and blushing may or may not mean you are embarrassed. You will know that your autonomic nervous system does not seem to know the difference between love and hate and jealousy and joy because it tends to act similarly during many different emotions. Finally, you know that it is your head that tells you which emotion you are feeling.

SELF-TEST 8

1 If the scientist cut off your finger and then asked what you were feeling, the scientist would be studying your _____ response during an emotion.

subjective

2 If the scientist cut off your finger and then observed what you did, the scientist would be studying your _____ response during an emotion.

behavioral

3 One problem with defining an emotion on the basis of the behavioral response is that the same behavior may occur when you are experiencing _____ emotions.

different

4 If the scientist measured your heart rate, blood pressure, and hormonal secretions while your finger were cut off, the scientist would be studying the _____ component of an emotion.

physiological

5 One problem with defining an emotion using physiological responses is that the same physiological responses may occur when you are experiencing _____ emotions.

different

6 If your car turned over on the road, the part of your autonomic nervous system that would be active is called the _____ division.

sympathetic

7 As your car was turning over, your sympathetic division would cause an increase in _____ and _____ and cause your adrenal medulla to secrete _____ and _____.

blood pressure
heart rate / epinephrine
norepinephrine

8 When you are home relaxing and listening to soft music, the division of your autonomic nervous system that is active is the _____ division.

parasympathetic

9 If you were injected with epinephrine but told it was a health tonic, any emotional feeling you would experience would depend to a large extent upon the _____.

surroundings or cues or environment

10 Thirty minutes after an airplane crashed into your house, you would still be very emotionally upset. The prolongation of an emotional feeling is partly due to the slow metabolism of the hormone _____, which causes a feeling of _____.

epinephrine or norepinephrine general arousal

11 The next time you smash one of your fingers, you should silently say to yourself, "There are three components to the emotion I am experiencing. My feeling of fear is called the _____ component. My crying is called the _____ component. My heart pounding is called the _____ component."

subjective
behavioral / physiological

12 If your spinal cord were severed at your neck in an accident, you would experience _____ but they would be felt _____.

13 Following the removal of the temporal lobes, monkeys show a series of behavioral changes known as the _____ syndrome.

14 The Kluver-Bucy syndrome results in monkeys that show less _____, explore objects by _____, have changed _____ habits, and show increased _____.

15 Following removal of the temporal lobes in a human patient, he showed less _____, displayed himself _____ to the nurses, began to _____ more and more often, and his conversational fluency _____.

16 When the temporal lobes are removed, two structures buried in these lobes are destroyed. These structures are the _____ and _____.

17 When you are feeling various emotions, a number of brain structures involved are collectively known as the _____ system. This system includes the following structures: _____, _____, and _____.

18 If you wanted to identify which brain areas are involved when a monkey is attacking, you could use one of the following four techniques: _____, _____, _____, and _____.

19 During stimulation of the amygdala in human patients, they have reported a range of emotions that include _____, _____, and _____. (Give three.)

20 If your ordinary house cat had its amygdala stimulated, depending upon the area there could be four different kinds of responses: attention; emotional responses, such as _____; physiological responses, such as _____; and eating responses, such as _____.

21 If you wanted to make a wild animal tame or make a dominant monkey submissive, you would remove the _____.

22 If you were hiring bus drivers and an applicant said he had had his hippocampus removed last year, you would not hire him because he would have difficulty _____.

23 If you asked this same applicant (without hippocampus) where he was born and where he lived five years ago, he _____ tell you.

24 There is some evidence from monkeys and rats that if the hippocampus is removed they will show _____ of normally avoided stimuli, such as humans or cats.

25 One area in the limbic system produces feelings of pleasure or sexual arousal when electrically stimulated. This area is the _____.

26 A rat can be made vicious by removing its _____. This finding cannot be generalized to _____.

27 Impulses from the amygdala, septal area, and hippocampus all flow into the _____, which is located in the middle at the base of the brain.

28 It is possible to cause sympathetic responses by stimulation of the _____ and to cause parasympathetic activity by stimulation of the _____.

29 Stimulation of other areas of the hypothalamus has caused a variety of emotional responses in various animals, including (give three) _____, _____, and _____.

30 Frontal lobotomy, which involves isolating the _____, was used as treatment for various mental disorders but later fell into disuse because the results were _____, the _____ were not always removed, and there were unwanted _____.

31 If you were given a check for a million dollars, the information from your senses would reach your _____, where sensing would take place and meaning would be added. Then the cortex would interact with the structures in the _____, and the emotional feeling would be added.

32 There is evidence that in animals some emotional patterns are _____. That is, they are born with _____ circuits.

33 There is evidence that humans are born with prewired neural circuits for _____, for example, _____. However, there is little evidence that humans are born with or have inherited prewired circuits that result in specific _____ of _____ behavior.

emotions
less intensively

Kluver-Bucy

fear or anger / putting them in their mouths / dietary / sexual behavior

affection or emotion sexually / eat decreased

amygdala / hippocampus

limbic / amygdala hippocampus / septal area

electrical stimulation chemical stimulation lesioning / electrical recording

anger / fear / losing control / feeling calm or relaxed

fear or anger / salivation or urination / licking or chewing

amygdala

with recent memory or remembering his route

could

less fear

septal area

septal area monkeys

hypothalamus

posterior hypothalamus anterior hypothalamus

rage and aggression in cats and monkeys / mouse-killing in cats / pleasure in rats / calmness in cats

prefrontal area inconsistent / symptoms side effects

cortex or neocortex / limbic system

inherited / prewired neural

reflexes / sucking or orienting or knee jerk / patterns / emotional

REFERENCES

8–1 Ardrey, R. *The territorial imperative*. New York: Atheneum, 1966.

8–2 Ax, A. F. The physiological differentiation between anger and fear in humans. *Psychosomatic Medicine* 1953, 15: 433–442.

8–3 Blanchard, R. J. and Blanchard, D. C. Effects of hippocampal lesions on the rat's reaction to a cat. *Journal of Comparative and Physiological Psychology* 1972, 78: 77–82.

8–4 Brady, J. and Nauta, W. Subcortical mechanisms in emotional behavior: affective changes following septal forebrain lesions in the albino rat. *Journal of Comparative and Physiological Psychology* 1953, 46: 339–346.

8–5 Buddington, R. W., King, F. A., and Roberts, L. Emotionality and conditioned avoidance responding in the squirrel monkey following septal injury. *Psychonomic Science* 1967, 8: 195–196.

8–6 Downer, J. L. de C. Changes in visual gnostic functions and emotional behavior following unilateral temporal pole damage in the "split brain" monkey. *Nature* 1961, 191: 50–51.

8–7 Flynn, J. P. The neural basis of aggression in cats. In D. C. Glass (Ed.), *Neurophysiology and emotion*. New York: Rockefeller University Press, 1967.

8–8 Gloor, P. Amygdala. In J. Field (Ed.), *Handbook of physiology*. Vol. 2. *Neurophysiology*. Washington, D.C.: American Physiological Society, 1960.

8–9 Gloor, P. Temporal lobe epilepsy: its possible contribution to the understanding of the functional significance of the amygdala and of its interaction with neocortical-temporal mechanisms. In B. E. Eleftherious (Ed.), *The neurobiology of the amygdala*. New York: Plenum Press, 1972.

8–10 Gol, A., Kellaway, P., Shapiro, H., and Hurst, C. M. Studies of hippocampectomy in the monkey, baboon, and cat. *Neurology* 1963, 13: 1031–1041.

8–11 Heath, R. G. and Mickle, W. A. Evaluation of seven years' experience with depth electrode studies in human patients. In E. R. Ramey and D. S. O'Deherty (Eds.), *Electrical studies on the unanesthetized brain*. New York: Hoeber, 1960.

8–12 Heath, R. G., Monroe, R. R., and Mickle, W. A. Stimulation of the amygdaloid nucleus in a schizophrenic patient. *American Journal of Psychiatry* 1955, 73: 127–129.

8–13 Hess, W. R. *Diencephalon: autonomic and extra pyramidal functions*. New York: Grune & Stratton, 1954.

8–14 Hess, W. and Akart, K. Experimental data on the role of the hypothalamus in mechanisms of emotional behavior. *Archives of Neurology and Psychiatry,* 1955, 3: 143–156.

8–15 Hohman, G. Some effects of spinal cord lesions on experienced emotional feelings. *Psychophysiology* 1966, 3: 143–156.

8–16 Isaacson, R. L. and Wickelgren, W. O. Hippocampal ablation and passive avoidance. *Science* 1962, 138: 1104–1106.

8–17 Jacobsen, C. F. Functions of frontal association areas in primates. *Archives of Neurology and Psychiatry* 1935, 33: 558–569.

8–18 Kim, C., Kim, C. C., Kim, J. K., Kim, M. S., Chang, H. K., Kim, J. Y., and Lee, I. G. Fear response and aggressive behavior of hippocampectomized house rats. *Brain Research* 1971, 29: 237–251.

8–19 King, F. A. Effect of septal and amygdala lesions on emotional behavior and conditioned avoidance responses in the cat. *Journal of Nervous and Mental Disease* 1958, 126: 57–63.

8–20 Kluver, H. and Bucy, P. Preliminary analysis of functions of the temporal lobes in monkeys. *Archives of Neurology and Psychiatry* 1939, 42: 979–1000.

8–21 Lorenz, K. *On aggression*. New York: Harcourt, 1966.

8–22 MacLean, P. D. and Ploog, D. W. Cerebral representation of penile erection. *Journal of Neurophysiology* 1962, 25: 29–55.

8–23 Mark, V. H. and Ervin, F. R. *Violence and the brain*. New York: Harper & Row, 1970.

8–24 Moan, C. E. and Heath, R. C. Septal stimulation for the initiation of heterosexual behavior in a homosexual male. *Journal of Behavior Therapy and Experimental Psychiatry* 1972, 3: 23–30.

8–25 Montagu, M. F. A. (Ed.) *Man and aggression*. 2nd ed. New York: Oxford University Press, 1973.

8–26 Narabayashi, H., Nagao, T., Saito, Y., Yoshida, M., and Nagahata, M. Stereotaxic amygdalotomy for behavior disorders. *Archives of Neurology* 1963, 9: 1–16.

8–27 Olds, J. and Milner, P. Positive reinforcement produced by electrical stimulation of septal area and other regions of rat brain. *Journal of Comparative and Physiological Psychology* 1954, 47: 419–427.

8–28 Plotnik, R. Brain stimulation and aggression: monkeys, apes and humans. In R. L. Holloway (Ed.), *Primate aggression, territoriality and xenophobia*. New York: Academic Press, 1974.

8–29 Reeves, A. G. and Plum, F. Hyperphagia, rage and dementia accompanying a ventromedial hypothalamic neoplasm. *Archives of Neurology* 1969, 20: 616–624.

8–30 Robinson, B. W., Alexander, M., and Bowne, G. Dominance reversal resulting from aggressive responses evoked by brain telestimulation. *Physiology and Behavior* 1969, 4: 749–752.

8–31 Rosvold, H. E., Mirsky, A. F., and Pribram, K. H. Influence of amygdalectomy on social behavior in monkeys. *Journal of Comparative and Physiological Psychology* 1954, 47: 173–178.

8–32 Schachter, S. and Singer, J. E. Cognitive, social and physiological determinants of emotional state. *Psychological Review* 1962, 69: 379–399.

8–33 Scoville, W. B., Dunsmore, R. H., Liberson, W. T., Henry, C. E., and Pepe, A. Observations on medial temporal lobotomy uncotomy in the treatment of psychotic states. *Proceedings of the Association for Research in Nervous and Mental Disease* 1953, 31: 347–358.

8–34 Scoville, W. B. and Milner, B. Loss of recent memory after bilateral hippocampal lesions. *Journal of Neurology, Neurosurgery, and Psychiatry* 1957, 20: 11–21.

8–35 Terzian, H. and Ore, G. Syndrome of Kluver and Bucy reproduced in man by bilateral removal of the temporal lobes. *Neurology* 1955, 5: 373–380.

8–36 Wheatley, M. D. The hypothalamus and affective behavior in cats: a study of the effects of experimental lesions with anatomic correlations. *Archives of Neurology and Psychiatry* 1944, 52: 296–316.

8–37 White, J. C. Autonomic discharge from stimulation of the hypothalamus in man. *Research Publication of the Association for Research in Nervous and Mental Disease* 1940, 20: 854–63.

Hunger, Obesity, and Thirst

Does Your Mouth Have a Mind of Its Own?

Fat People Anonymous

One by one they walked up to the scale with its enormous dial. As they stepped on for the weekly weighing, some took deep breaths, some pulled in their stomachs, and others closed their eyes. Most of them wore extra-large clothes, overflowed the chair when they sat down, and were tired of being stared at. They were obese. They hoped the Fat People Anonymous meeting would help them with their eating problems.

Tom had been on a dozen different diets and had lost and regained hundreds of pounds over the years. Although thin as a child, he had started to eat heavily around adolescence. The more he ate, the more he wanted, until he thought that he was meant to be fat. He weighed 136 kg (300 lb), had high blood pressure, and was worried about his health. On his last diet, he had eaten only protein (meat, fish) and almost no carbohydrates (potatoes, desserts) or fats. In the beginning, he had lost a few pounds, but gradually he had eaten more and more protein and gained more and more weight. The all-protein diet had guaranteed a weight loss. It did not work for him.

After Tom's 136 kg, George seemed small at 102 kg (225 lb). But being only 1.5 m (5 ft), he resembled a cannon ball. He was thoroughly puzzled. He only ate vegetables, fruits, nuts, and cheese and drank raw milk. He could not believe such a healthy, natural diet could result in so much fat.

The last speaker was Diane, and she was very angry. For an entire month, she and her two roommates had kept a record of every meal, potato chip, doughnut, and snack they ate. When they had added up the calories for each day, they had found that she was actually eating less than her roommates on some days and about the same on others. Yet she was gaining weight while her roommates remained slim. She thought her body was working against her best efforts. She wanted to know why.

There was much talk about diets, fasting, starving, and having your mouth wired shut. There was talk about obesity not being a person's fault. If you were a fat baby, perhaps you were predisposed to be fat as an adult. There was talk about surgery. Perhaps the solution was to have part of your intestine or part of your brain removed. And as always there was talk about why slim people remain slim.

Metabolic Rate

Tony, George, and Diane wondered if everything they ate turned to fat. They knew that when they ate a potato, they were consuming approximately 90 calories, a hamburger, 300, and a brownie, 250. The fuel-value, or the capacity of food to produce energy, is based on a measure called a **calorie**. After you eat a hamburger, the 300 calories may be used to produce heat or to fuel your body processes, such as heart rate or digestion itself. Part of the hamburger may be converted to fats, called **lipids**. Lipids are stored in fat reserves called **adipose tissue**. Food calories that are not needed for immediate energy are, indeed, turned into fat and stored.

For a hamburger to become energy, it must undergo a chemical process, or be **metabolized**. The chemical process for turning food into energy is called **metabolism**. Many of the calories contained in foods are actually used up in the processing of foods into energy, that is to say, in the process of metabolism itself. Each person is born with his or her own **metabolic rate**, and the body is not very flexible about changing this rate. A low metabolic rate means that fewer calories are needed and more calories can be turned into fat and stored. Diane was turning more calories into fat than her roommates because she had a lower metabolic rate and possibly engaged in less exercise, which burns calories for fuel.

Unfortunately for people trying to diet, the body does seem to adjust its metabolic rate downward to preserve its fat stores. In other words, if you reduce your calorie intake slightly, your metabolic rate decreases slightly so that the body can operate on fewer calories without using fat stores (9–10). On the other hand, even the slightest excess in caloric intake results in fat storage. During a single year, the average adult male consumes more than a million calories. If only 1 percent of these calories are not expended as energy, they will be stored and the person will gain slightly more than 1 kg (2 lb) by the end of the year (9–27). If you want to maintain a constant body weight, more than 99 percent of your caloric intake must be related to meeting immediate energy needs. If calorie intake exceeds your energy needs by as little as one soda or beer or brownie per day, you will gain almost half a kilogram (1 lb) a month, or approximately 5 kg (10 lb) per year.

Energy Needs

How many calories do you need each day to meet your energy needs and not gain weight? This varies from person to person, depending upon metabolic rate, height, age, degree of physical activity, environment (warm versus cold), amount of stress, and other factors. From your own experiences, you know that some people can eat all they want and not gain weight while others seem unable to lose weight, short of fasting. By monitoring your caloric intake over a period of months and checking whether you are gaining or losing weight, you could probably determine a general range of how many calories you can consume. Eating habits might also affect weight gain or loss. From animal research, it appears that calories consumed in one large meal tend to result in more fat storage and weight gain than the same number of calories consumed in several smaller meals (9–7). Because your body is constantly trying to store supplies and to resist breakdown, most people find that losing or maintaining weight is difficult while gaining weight is easy. If you are gaining weight, it means that you are consuming more calories than can be expended to meet your body's energy needs. The question is why people continue to consume more food than their bodies can use.

Hunger Pangs

When you are extremely hungry, you may experience stomach pains, more commonly called **hunger pangs**. It was once thought that stomach contractions or hunger pangs might be the physical cause of hunger. However, if either rats or humans have their stomachs removed, they show almost normal food intake (9–22, 9–27). Also, humans whose stomachs have been removed or denervated continue to report feelings of hunger. Stomach contractions may contribute to your feelings of hunger, but they are not the critical physical event that causes you to feel hungry.

If your stomach were removed, you would not only get hungry, but after eating you would feel full, or **sated**. Your stomach is not critical for your feeling of fullness, or **satiety** (say-TIE-ah-tee). Only when an extremely large volume of food is eaten does stomach expansion seem to provide cues for your feeling of fullness.

If food were placed directly into your stomach, without going through your mouth, you would still develop feelings of satiety. Humans and rats were equipped with tubes that bypassed their mouths and went directly into their stomachs. Each time the subject pressed a lever, food entered the mouth, there were no sensations from the mouth, or **oropharyngeal** (oh-row-fuh-RAN-gee-al) sensations. Lacking oropharyngeal sensations, humans and rats still consumed normal amounts of food delivered to their stomachs (9–8, 9–23, 9–37). Neither the experience of eating (oropharyngeal sensations) nor the arrival of food in the stomach seems to be the important cue for satiety. What *does* seem to be an important cue is the presence of food in the small intestine, where most nutrient absorption occurs (9–27).

Where Food Goes

Source of Fuel

As you eat a hamburger, you are eating carbohydrates (bun), proteins (lean meat), and fats (animal fat, mayonnaise). All three of these compounds—carbohydrates, proteins, and fats—contain elements—hydrogen, oxygen, and carbon—that can be converted into fuel for the body. The body uses two kinds of fuel: a type of sugar called **glucose** and a kind of fat called **fatty acid**. Glucose is used for energy by all of the cells in the brain and body and is the primary source of fuel for the brain. Except during periods of starvation, when special processes take over, glucose is the only fuel or source of energy for the brain. Fatty acids are metabolized by the cells of the body, but cannot be used by the brain. Much of what occurs in the body during digestion seems to revolve around defending the brain's supply of glucose. It is estimated that the brain consumes as much as 66 percent of the total daily supply of glucose (9–27). Since even brief periods of glucose deprivation can result in permanent brain damage, possibly coma or death, there are many processes that continue the flow of glucose to the brain.

After eating Chinese food, you may feel hungrier much sooner than after eating a dinner of prime rib. Prime rib contains much more fat that Chinese food, and fat provides more than twice as much energy or calories per gram than either carbohydrates (Chinese food) or proteins. Further-

The Headliner

DIETING NO GUARANTEE OF WEIGHT LOSS

Two scientists have proved what many women on a diet already know —that even if you stick religiously to a slimming diet, you don't always lose weight.

What happens is that the slimmers' metabolism, the process by which food is broken down into living tissue, adapts to the diet and it goes on manufacturing "fat" at the old rate, on less food.

This is the explanation put forward in the medical magazine Lancet, based upon tests in which women were put on a diet, under controlled circumstances, and one in three simply could not lose weight.

The volunteers were recruited from 8,000 slimming clubs, according to the nutrition experts who arranged the experiment, Dr. Sally Parsonage and Dr. D.S. Miller.

The women chosen had all attended the clubs for more than six months and had all lost weight for a while when they started their diets, but had later been unable to lose any more.

The 29 volunteers were taken to an isolated country house for three weeks. On arrival, their baggage was searched for illicit food. Throughout their stay, they had no access to food other than the daily diet of 1,500 calories.

They were not allowed outside the grounds unless accompanied by staff members.

After three weeks, the scales showed that nine women had lost no weight at all. Nineteen weighed less —and one luckless lady had actually put on weight.

SOURCE: *Los Angeles Times,* April 13, 1975. Reprinted by permission of Reuters.

---

more, fats are absorbed more slowly from the gastrointestinal tract, and this is why the high-fat prime rib makes you feel fuller longer.

The greater energy value or calorie content of fats means that high-fat diets (butter, cream, fatty meats) lead to greater weight gain than diets with higher proportions of proteins and carbohydrates. Some "high-protein" diets actually contain a high fat content and therefore result in weight gain. Tom's "all-protein" diet contained very little fat, and still he gained weight. This was because he consumed such large quantities of protein that he had far more calories than required for his energy needs. His body converted the excess protein into fat.

Stomach's Function

If your stomach were removed, you could still have sensations of hunger, eat normally, have feelings of satiety, and be able to absorb food (9–21). The primary function of the stomach is to break down food into smaller particles. This process is known as **digestion**. The stomach breaks down, or digests, food by bathing it in **hydrochloric acid** (HCl) and enzymes secreted by cells in the stomach's lining. Hydrochloric acid is extremely powerful, and if a drop were placed on your hand, it would burn or break down the skin. HCl does not destroy or digest the stomach because its walls are coated with protective secretions that are highly alkaline and balance the acidity of HCl. When you think about or smell food or begin to eat, these sensations cause

the parasympathetic division of the autonomic nervous system to stimulate secretion of HCl. The **vagus nerve**, which is part of the parasympathetic system, travels from the brain to the stomach. Impulses in the vagus nerve trigger the secretion of HCl in the stomach. When the stomach is said to be **denervated**, it means that the vagus nerve has been cut and there is less secretion of HCl. The secretion of HCl does not stop entirely because hormones are released when food reaches the stomach, and these hormones also trigger the secretion of HCl. When the concentration of HCl in the stomach becomes very high, there are feedback mechanisms that decrease secretion of HCl.

When people develop ulcers, it means that HCl has actually digested part of the stomach or gastrointestinal tract. Stress and emotional states can increase the secretion of HCl, and too much HCl can cause ulcers. Patients with ulcers are advised to stop drinking coffee or alcohol because these, too, cause increased secretion of HCl. Ulcers are an example of how the brain and body interact. Psychological stressors affect the autonomic nervous system, which triggers the secretion of HCl and causes the stomach to digest itself.

After food is broken down into smaller pieces by the stomach, it moves into the small intestine. During its movement through the 6 m (20 ft) of small intestine, most of the digestion and absorption of food occurs. These processes are regulated by the vagus nerve and by hormones and enzymes found in the small intestine and secreted by the pancreas.

Where Food Goes

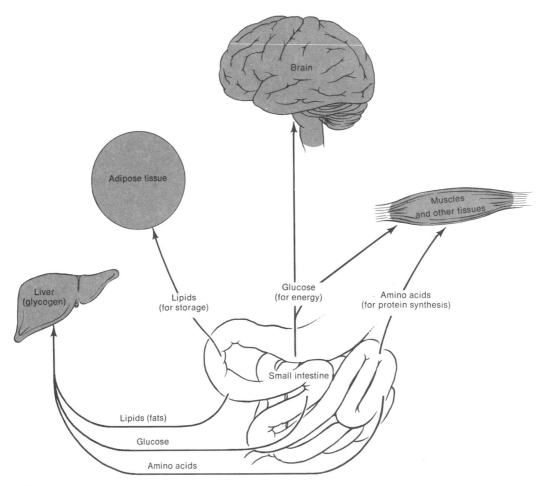

Figure 9–1 After a meal, food passes from the stomach to the small intestine, where the majority of digestion and absorption of foods takes place. The major source of fuel after a meal is glucose, while lipids (fats) and amino acids are stored in the liver and in adipose tissue for later use.

Carbohydrates

Desserts, vegetables, fruit, and alcoholic and soft drinks contain mostly carbohydrates. After leaving the stomach, carbohydrates pass through the small intestine where they are broken down into glucose and absorbed into the blood stream. Most of the glucose is usually used immediately by the tissues of the body. Some of the excess glucose is converted by the liver into **glycogen** (GLI as in eye, GLI-kuh-jen), which is then stored in the liver until needed. Glycogen is a form of carbohydrate that can quickly be turned back to glucose when the body demands immediate energy. When glucose levels become low, the pancreas secretes the hormone **glucagon** (GLUE-ka-gone), which causes the liver to convert glycogen to glucose. Conversion of glycogen is also controlled by the sympathetic division of the autonomic nervous system. In times of stress or emotions, when the body needs extra glucose to provide quick energy, sympathetic nerve fibers act on the liver to cause conversion and release of glucose. The sympathetic division also causes release of epinephrine, which in turn further stimulates conversion and release of glucose.

The glycogen stored in the liver actually represents only a small part of your body's stored energy. Glycogen is also stored in the muscles, where it can be metabolized for energy. However, most of your body's storage (80–90 percent) is in the form of adipose tissue. Much of the excess glucose from a meal is converted into fats or lipids and is stored as adipose tissue. When you eat a candy bar or spoonful of honey for quick energy, you are essentially supplying your body with glucose, which can be metabolized and used very quickly. But any excess glucose from the candy bar or honey will be turned into glycogen and stored in the liver or turned into lipids (fats) and stored in adipose tissue.

Proteins and Fats

Meat, chicken, fish, eggs, and some nuts contain a high percentage of protein. Proteins are broken down in the small intestine into amino acids, which are essentially smaller protein molecules. Amino acids are absorbed into the blood stream. Some of the amino acids circulating in the blood

Hunger, Obesity, and Thirst

stream are taken up by the tissues of the body and used for the synthesis of protein. It is essential that proteins be included in your diet since some of the proteins needed by your body cannot be synthesized from fats or carbohydrates.

If glucose is needed by the body, the liver can convert amino acids into glucose. Excess amino acids are converted into glycogen for storage in the liver or muscles and into lipids for storage in adipose tissue. So if you were on an all protein diet and consumed more calories than your body needed, the excess calories would be turned into lipids and stored in adipose tissue. Consuming excess calories, whether from proteins or carbohydrates, will result in gaining weight from stored adipose tissue.

Butter, cream, oil, and some meats and nuts have a high fat content. Fats are absorbed more slowly from the small intestine than either carbohydrates or proteins. Fats, or lipids, are absorbed into a watery fluid called **lymph** and transported throughout the body to adipose tissues. There, lipids are broken down into two forms, **fatty acids** and **glycerol** (GLISS-uh-ral). Glycerol is a substance that can be readily converted by the liver into glucose. Fatty acids can be used by body tissues for fuel, but cannot be used directly by the brain. In states of starvation, the liver converts fatty acids into substances called ketone bodies, which can be used by the brain (9–10).

Whether you eat only protein, only carbohydrates, or any combination of protein, carbohydrates, and fats, it is clear that all three can be stored as fat. However, if you follow a low-protein diet, you may not get needed amino acids. A low carbohydrate diet may cause constipation. A high-fat diet can cause excessive weight gain. George, the vegetarian, gained weight on his natural diet simply because he consumed more calories than needed for his energy needs. Excess calories, no matter which foods they come from, can be turned into and stored as fat.

Feeling Hunger

Glucose, Insulin, Hormones

After you eat, most of your energy needs are met by glucose, while amino acids and fats are stored for later use (9–10). Depending on the amount and kind of carbohydrates you have eaten, there will be high levels of glucose in your blood for periods ranging up to several hours. The high level of blood glucose causes the hormone **insulin** to be secreted from the pancreas. Insulin causes glucose to diffuse into the cells of the body to be used for energy. If the pancreas does not secrete insulin, as in diabetes mellitus, there is a high level of blood glucose that can neither diffuse into nor be used by the body's cells. Without insulin, the cells starve, even though there are high levels of glucose circulating in the blood. The cells of the brain are not dependent on insulin and can use glucose from the blood.

Several hours after you have eaten, the glucose from the meal has been used by the body for energy. At this point, the body must begin to mobilize the fuels that were stored. When the glucose levels drop, the secretion of insulin decreases, and the pancreas secretes a different hormone, **glucagon**. At the same time, the adrenal medulla secretes epinephrine, and the anterior pituitary secretes growth hormone. These three hormones—glucagon, epinephrine, and growth hormone—help to mobilize fuels for the brain and body. To supply the brain, epinephrine and glucagon cause glucose to be released from the liver. All three hormones inhibit the diffusion of the remaining glucose into the cells of the body so that glucose will be available for use by the brain. All three hormones *stimulate* the breakdown of adipose tissue into fatty acids and glycerol. The fatty acids are then used by body tissues for fuel, and the glycerol is converted by the liver into glucose, which can be used by the brain (9–10).

The way your body obtains its energy immediately after a meal is different as compared with 3 hours later. Imme-

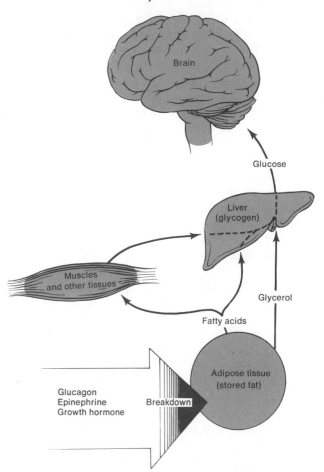

Figure 9–2 Once the glucose from a meal has been used, three hormones – glucagon, epinephrine, and growth hormone – stimulate the breakdown of adipose tissue. The breakdown of adipose tissue produces fatty acids and glycerol, which is converted to glucose for use by the brain.

diately after a meal, your body uses glucose for energy and stores fats and amino acids. Later your body enters a mobilization period during which glucose is reserved for the brain and fatty acids provide needed fuel for the body. How do these different energy situations affect your state of hunger? One possibility is that you begin to feel hungry as soon as you stop using glucose and move into the mobilization period.

Glucostatic Theory

The main source of fuel for the brain is glucose. Could this mean that the level of glucose in the blood affects the brain and results in feelings of hunger or satiation? Individuals with diabetes mellitus have high levels of blood sugar but do not feel full or satiated. In these individuals, the lack of insulin prevents glucose from diffusing into or being used by the cells of the body. Perhaps the critical factor is not merely the level of glucose in the blood, but rather the *utilization* of glucose. This idea led Jean Mayer to formulate the **glucostatic theory** of hunger (9–28). The glucostatic theory states that changes in *cellular glucose utilization* are detected by brain cells that control our feelings of hunger. Some hours after eating, glucose utilization decreases and results in feelings of hunger. After eating, glucose utilization increases and results in feelings of satiety. The one difficulty with this theory is that it is not possible to measure glucose utilization directly. Without a direct measure, it is not possible to relate glucose utilization directly to feelings of hunger or satiety. Some support for the glucostatic theory comes from experiments that measure glucose utilization indirectly (9–27).

How does the brain monitor glucose utilization? Mayer proposed that there are brain cells that act as glucostatic receptors in one nucleus of the hypothalamus known as the **ventromedial nucleus**, or **VMH** (9–28). These cells would be sensitive to glucose utilization and would provide the cues for feelings of satiety. Although there is evidence that the VMH is involved in hunger, there is little to support the idea that the VMH actually contains cells sensitive to glucose utilization (9–27). There is some evidence now that glucose-sensitive cells might be located in peripheral tissue, such as the digestive tract or the liver (9–27, 9–30, 9–33). Cells located in or near the digestive system could monitor changes in glucose utilization almost immediately and relay these changes to the brain through neural pathways. When these changes reached the brain, we would have feelings of hunger or satiety.

Mayer's original version of the glucostatic theory has had to be greatly modified, but there is much evidence to show that glucose utilization plays a part in hunger. For example, insulin injections cause animals to show an immediate decrease in feeding, presumably because the insulin facilitates utilization of available glucose. A short time later, there is a sharp increase in feeding because this utilization has depleted available glucose (9–27). This and many other studies suggest that you may begin to feel hungry when you are no longer using glucose from your most recent meal. But it appears glucose utilization is not the only factor.

Lipostatic Theory

Diane said she ate no more than her roommates, yet she remained obese. From animal studies, there is evidence that the body develops a fixed ratio of body fat to body lean (9–27). Once this ratio of fat to lean is set, the body resists any change in the ratio. The ratio of fat to lean is called the **set-point**. Because of the set-point, Diane does not lose fat or lipid stores when she reduces her food intake moderately. Instead, her body adapts to the lower level of available fuels by reducing metabolism (9–10). When Diane reduces her calories, she may feel fatigued because of reduced fuel but she does not lose weight because her body tries to maintain the established set-point. Only by reducing her calories substantially can she overcome this factor.

The **lipostatic theory** (LIP-oh-static) says that you feel hungry when your fat stores fall below the set-point, and you feel satiated when they rise above the set-point (9–24). The receptor cells for monitoring lipostatic changes have not been located. Experiments on animals indicate that the degree of hunger does not seem to change with the absolute weight level, but rather with the degree of change from the established set-point (9–21, 9–27). If this were true for humans, it might explain why, after severe dieting, it is so difficult for overweight people to maintain a reduced weight level. After severe dieting, there is a change in the ratio of fat to lean, and the individual may be chronically hungry because the fat level is below the established set-point. The body may be trying to return to the former set-point, and so the person may have the feeling of always being hungry.

How much do your parents' genes or your weight as an infant influence the establishment of your set-point and thus your chances of becoming obese? If both your parents were obese, you would be very likely to become obese even if you were adopted by slender parents (9–3). Suppose your parents were slender but you were born a very fat infant. If, out of 100 infants, you were one of the three heaviest, you would be three times more likely to become obese as an adult (9–6). Conversely, if you had been exposed to famine in utero and in early infancy, so that you were a thin infant (of 100 infants, you were one of the 50 lightest), you would be unlikely to become obese as an adult (9–31). This relationship between infant weight and adult weight seems to be independent of parental weight, social class, and education (9–18). The correlation between infant and adult weight has been verified in animal work. Overfeeding and underfeeding rats during the first 3 weeks of life affects their adipose tissue levels in later life (9–12). It appears the body set-point is influenced by both genetic and early environmental factors.

Obesity and Set-Point

If your obesity began in childhood, you would generally possess a higher *number* of fat cells as well as *larger* fat cells. In contrast, those whose obesity began during adult years seem to have only increased size, not increased number of adipose cells (9–20). There is one exception to this rule: if your obesity began in adulthood and is very extreme (170 percent over ideal), you may also have an increase in number of fat cells (9–19). Except in such extreme cases, obesity that begins in adulthood does not involve increased number of adipose cells. When human males became obese as part of an experiment, they showed only an increase in size of adipose cells and not number (9–34). Whether obesity begins early or late may influence how the body develops the set-point and how easy or difficult it will be to lose weight in the future. Whether adipose tissue was developed in childhood or in adulthood may influence the ability of an obese person to lose weight. Generally, you will find it difficult to lose weight if you acquired the adipose tissue as a child. And, if you do lose weight, you may feel depressed and poorly adjusted to your weight loss. On the other hand, if you acquired adipose tissue as an adult, it is easier to lose, and you will feel happier and better adjusted to the prospect of losing weight (9–13). These psychological differences may be related to the physical differences in when the adipose tissue was acquired, and to what the body's set-point is. Animal work showed that once a large number of fat cells had formed, reduced feeding did not reduce the number of cells, only the size of cells

Figure 9–3 On each side of Wonder Woman is a man who weighs over 350 kg (700 lb). A typical breakfast for one of these obese individuals consists of 18 eggs, 2 kg (4 lb) of bacon, a loaf of bread, 2 liters (2 qt) of orange juice, and 16 cups of coffee. The accumulation of adipose tissue seems to affect the body set-point and thus the feelings of being hungry or full. These individuals may feel hungry when their weight drops below 350 kg. (Los Angeles Times Photo.)

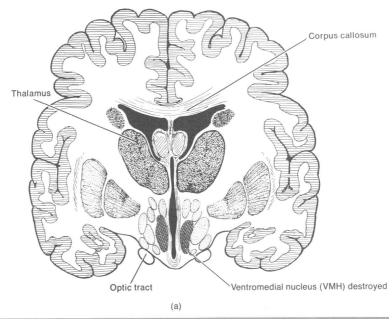

(a)

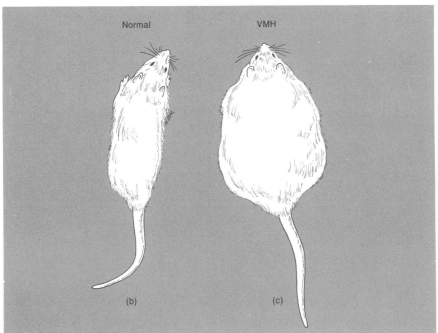

Figure 9-4 Brain and obesity. (a) This brain section shows the location of the ventromedial nucleus of the hypothalamus (VMH), which is involved in the control of eating. If this or surrounding areas are destroyed, the result is an increase in weight. (b) Size of a normal rat whose brain is intact. (c) Size of a rat after destruction of the VMH, showing the doubling in weight.

Hunger, Obesity, and Thirst

(9–18). This does not mean that set-point is permanently fixed. It does mean that some of the problems of the obese—"I cannot lose weight unless I starve," "I feel horrible when I lose weight"—may have a physiological basis. Other problems—eating when not hungry, eating when unhappy—may have a psychological basis.

Liver's Role

Several times larger than the stomach, the liver may very well be the organ that supplies cues for feeling hungry or full (9–10, 9–27, 9–33). From animal research, it seems that cells in the liver respond to the presence or absence of **metabolic fuels** (glucose, lipids, amino acids) and then send nerve impulses to the brain, probably the hypothalamus.

A recent theory of hunger involves the response to metabolic fuels and discards altogether the ideas of glucostatic or lipostatic receptors regulating eating (9–10). This theory, called a **physiological approach**, proposes that the liver

responds to metabolic fuels, regardless of whether they are in the form of glucose, lipids, or amino acids. When metabolic fuels are low, your liver sends impulses to the brain (hypothalamus), which interprets these messages and causes you to feel hungry. When metabolic fuels are high, your liver sends impulses to the brain (hypothalamus) which interprets these messages and causes you to feel sated. According to this theory, an animal overeats and becomes obese after a brain lesion because of a metabolic deficit. Whatever it eats goes immediately to fat stores. Therefore, it is continuously hungry even though it is eating and storing large amounts of food. It would be a mistake to assume that obese humans have a malfunctioning liver. Obese individuals may have metabolic problems, or they may have psychological problems that cause them to ignore metabolic cues.

Hypothalamus

VMH and Satiety

When admitted to the hospital, the woman was rather obese and complained of having to drink and urinate constantly. She was diagnosed as having diabetes insipidus. After 2 months in the hospital, she had gained 24 kg (52 lb). She was eating constantly and consuming approximately 8,000 to 10,000 calories a day. When she died suddenly, her brain was examined. A tumor was found to have destroyed an area in the hypothalamus, the ventromedial nucleus or VMH (9–32). When this same nucleus, the VMH, had been lesioned in rats, it caused them to eat enormous amounts of food (**hyperphagia**) and become obese. Since rats lacking a VMH overate, it was thought that the VMH normally controls the feeling of fullness or satiety. More recent research indicates that the VMH nucleus itself is not a satiety center, but rather part of a system involved in food-intake regulation. In recent times the term **VMH** is applied to both the VMH and an area to its side. The destruction of these two areas results in obesity (9–11).

Except for a very few cases like the one above, it is unlikely that the cause of obesity in humans is damage to the VMH. In addition to causing obesity, a tumor in this area would result in many other symptoms, including diabetes insipidus and disruption of other hormonal functions. A more likely cause of obesity is that the overweight person has learned to ignore signals from the VMH and other brain areas. Stanley Schacter compared the eating behavior of obese humans with that of rats that had the VMH destroyed. He reported many similarities. Rats with destroyed VMH (called "VMH rats") and obese humans both ate larger meals, but they ate less when given undesirable food and more when given desirable food. Both made less effort to obtain food but ate more if it were freely available (9–36). These results led Schacter to conclude that the VMH rats or obese humans were not hungrier but rather were unable to register or respond to bodily cues that signaled fullness

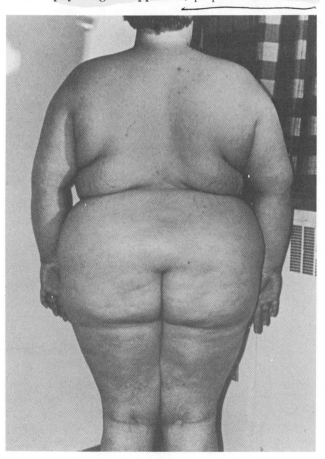

(d)

Figure 9–4 (cont.) Brain and obesity. (d) This patient had a tumor in her hypothalamus near the VMH. It caused her to eat almost constantly and become obese. This is an example of a brain lesion or tumor producing the same results in animal and human. (Photo courtesy of Lester V. Bergman, N.Y.)

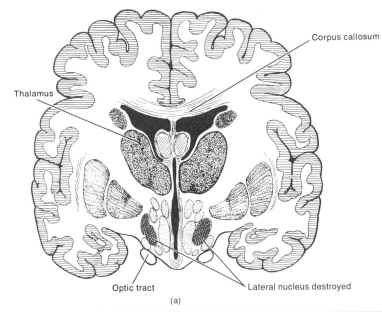

Corpus callosum

Thalamus

Optic tract

Lateral nucleus destroyed

(a)

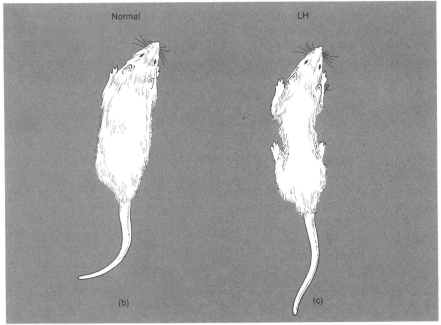

Normal

LH

(b)

(c)

Figure 9–5 Brain and starvation. (a) This brain section shows the location of the lateral hypothalamus, which is involved in the control of eating. If this area is destroyed, the result can be starvation. (b) The size of a normal rat whose brain is intact. (c) The size of a rat after destruction of the lateral hypothalamus. If the rat were not force-fed or fed especially palatable food, such as sweetened meal, it would not eat and would starve to death.

Hunger, Obesity, and Thirst

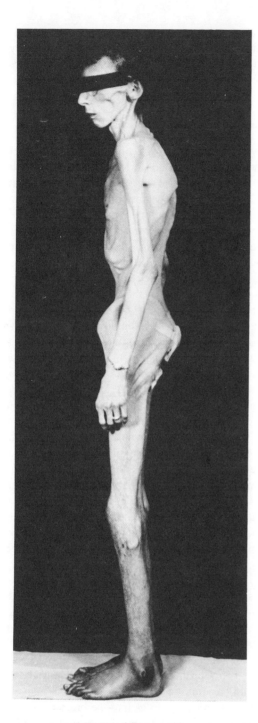

(d)

Figure 9–5 (cont.) Brain and starvation. (d) Two years before this photograph was taken, this woman weighed 60 kg (120 lb). She began to eat less until her weight decreased to 23 kg (47 lb). While the cause was thought to be emotional, the loss of weight would have been similar if she had had a tumor in the lateral hypothalamus. (Photo courtesy of A. J. Bachrach, W. J. Erwin, and J. P. Mohr, The control of eating behavior in an anorexic by operant conditioning techniques. Pages 153–163 in L. P. Ullman and L. Krasner (Eds.), *Case Studies in Behavior Modification*, New York: Holt, Rinehart & Winston, 1965.)

or satiety. We will consider Schacter's view of human obesity later. His view of the VMH rat explains some of the rat's behaviors, but not all. For example, the VMH rat overeats only until it reaches obesity. It then eats just enough to maintain that level of obesity. This suggests that the VMH animal *is* responding to bodily cues, but that the damage to the VMH has caused it to develop a new body set-point. If the animal is starved below this point, it eats vigorously until it returns to the set-point and then eats normally. Obese humans frequently show a similar behavior. After dieting, the obese human may eat excessively and rapidly regain weight to his former level of obesity. Once he is obese, his food intake may be relatively normal. The VMH rat and obese human may be responding to bodily cues that involve a higher set-point.

Lateral Hypothalamus

Mr. A. was 1.8 m (6 ft) tall but weighed only 32 kg (72 lb). Over a period of months, he had lost 27 kg (60 lb), had no appetite, and showed no interest in food. First it was thought that there were psychological reasons for his not eating. But when he developed diabetes insipidus and showed abnormal hormonal secretions, a tumor was suspected and found in his hypothalamus. The tumor had spread into the side or lateral area, called the **lateral hypothalamus**, or **LH** (9–17). In many different animals, it has been shown that if the lateral hypothalamus is damaged, the animal will stop eating and drinking. When an animal or human stops eating, the condition is called **aphagia** (ah-FAY-sha). When an animal or human stops drinking, it is called **adipisia** (ah-DIP-see-ah). If animals with lesions of the lateral hypothalamus or of the entire hypothalamus (lateral and ventromedial hypothalamus) are not force fed, they will rapidly starve to death. If these lesioned animals are force fed and then gradually shifted over to highly desirable foods (chocolate chip cookies), they will recover their eating behavior (9–39). But some problems remain. If these recovered animals are injected with insulin, it causes the available glucose to be used by the peripheral cells and to be rapidly depleted. Normal animals would eat to compensate for this depletion of glucose. Animals with LH lesions do not eat, and they die from the lack of glucose in the blood. Apparently, animals with LH lesions cannot regulate the glucose level in the blood.

These findings, and others using brain stimulation and recording, led some to believe that the lateral hypothalamus might be a "hunger center" in which the cells sensitive to glucose were located (9–27). Since the lateral hypothalamus receives axons from many brain areas, it is no longer thought to be a hunger center, but rather part of a system regulating eating. Like the VMH, the LH seems to be involved in the establishment of the body set-point. Findings from animals suggest that damage to the LH causes a new, lower set-point. If animals are first starved to a lower set-point and then given LH lesions, they show little or no aphagia following the surgery (9–24).

Feeling Hunger

One of the questions asked at the Fat People Anonymous meeting was whether a brain lesion might be the solution to obesity. From research on rats given LH lesions, it would seem that a brain lesion could indeed cause a reduction in appetite and body weight. However, this lesion might also produce a number of side effects, such as diabetes insipidus, abnormal thermal regulation, and hormonal malfunctions. These effects could be expected because the hypothalamus is involved not only in control of eating, but in *temperature, water* and *hormone* regulation. A lesion in the lateral hypothalamus would cause weight loss, but it would also cause many side effects that would interfere with normal bodily functioning.

Specific Hungers

Although you have heard people say they are specifically hungry for pizza or steak or chocolate cake, it is unlikely that there is a physiological cause for these specific hungers. Most likely, these specific hungers or tastes have been learned. If a young child were allowed to select his own foods, would he choose a nutritionally adequate diet? Controversy has raged over this question, and the answer is both yes and no. You have an innate preference for some of the substances you require, such as sodium, which is the Na in NaCl, or salt. Sodium is involved in conduction of nerve impulses and in regulation of body fluids. If a child were fed foods containing too little sodium, he would choose salty foods, such as potato chips, over chocolate ice cream if given the chance (9–27).

If a child were fed foods with very little of the B-vitamin thiamine, she would suffer from nausea and loss of appetite. Eventually, she would develop the symptoms of beri beri, which include neuritis (inflammation of nerves) and edema (accumulation of fluids). Edema causes the swollen bellies seen on starving children. If the child were allowed to select among foods, she would learn to select foods with thiamine since they would relieve her symptoms. In the case of thiamine, you do not have an innate preference. If deprived of thiamine, you can learn to eat foods that contain thiamine and therefore relieve your symptoms. For some substances that your body requires, you have an innate preference (sodium), while for other required substances you may learn to fill the need through trial and error, by choosing certain foods (thiamine) that relieve unpleasant symptoms. This does not mean that a child can learn to select a nutritionally adequate diet. It is only when the substance causes a relief of symptoms, such as nausea, that we learn to select it. Thiamine is one of few substances for which adequate selection has been shown.

There is now some concern over the large amount of sugar consumed by Americans, 22–45 kg (50–100 lb) per person each year. Almost all animals, including humans, have some preference for sweet solutions, and the preference is to some extent inherited (9–29). However, in humans the preference for sweets may be encouraged by eating habits. The emphasis on sweets begins with baby foods, which are sweetened to satisfy the taste preferences of the mother.

Neurotransmitters and Hunger

Nearly everyone at the Fat People Anonymous meeting had tried taking amphetamines to lose weight. At first they had found amphetamines depressed the appetite, but after a few weeks, a tolerance developed so that higher and higher doses were needed to affect appetite. Large doses of amphetamine can have dangerous effects on the cardiovascular system, causing high blood pressure. They can also cause nervousness and sleeplessness. When the dieters stopped taking amphetamines, they resumed their former eating habits and gained back all the weight they had lost.

The reason amphetamine initially suppresses appetite is that it causes an increase in the levels of neurotransmitters in the brain, which are called **catecholamines**. These neurotransmitters include epinephrine, norepinephrine, and dopamine. Neurotransmitters have been studied by injecting them through fine tubes directly into the brain. When norepinephrine was injected directly into the brain near the lateral hypothalamus, it caused rats to eat more (9–14). The result was puzzling. You would expect norepinephrine to cause decreased eating, since amphetamine causes appetite suppression in humans. One solution to this puzzle has been offered: in one area of the hypothalamus, norepinephrine causes increased eating, while in another area of the hypothalamus, epinephrine causes decreased eating (9–25). Amphetamines may have more effect on the epinephrine neurons, which result in appetite suppression or decreased eating. With continued amphetamine usage, the appetite-suppression properties of amphetamines decrease. This is because the body is constantly trying to return to homeostasis—that is, the body counteracts the effects of amphetamine, and returns the amount of neurotransmitters to their former levels. As the body succeeds in counteracting the effects of amphetamine on neurotransmitters involved in hunger, your appetite will return, unless larger and larger, and more harmful, doses are taken.

Instead of injecting drugs into the brain to change levels of neurotransmitters, it is possible to destroy neurons and thus the neurotransmitters stored in their telodendria. There is a system of neurons which contain norepinephrine and travel from the brainstem through the hypothalamus, near the ventromedial nucleus. If this system, called the **ventral noradrenergic bundle,** is destroyed, the result is overeating, or hyperphagia, and obesity (9–1). Another system of neurons contains the neurotransmitter dopamine. This system, called the **nigrostriatal system,** begins in the brain stem and travels through the area of the lateral hypothalamus. If this system is destroyed before it reaches the hypothalamus, the result is animals that do not eat or drink

THE FAT BABY: A BIG, BIG PROBLEM

It may be bothersome to those who still would like to imagine themselves as highly seductive, but the "fat and 40" type of overweight is far less of a problem, from the viewpoint of physical and psychological health, than the obesity that begins in infancy or early childhood.

Since it is likely that the person who is overweight during infancy will end up facing a weight problem as an adult, it would be highly desirable if we could somehow head off infant obesity.

That is not as simple as it sounds because a large number of questions about childhood obesity remain to be answered. When should a baby be considered fat and when simply big? Weight gain alone is not a certain criterion. Some infants who gain weight faster than other infants are also those who may be developmentally advanced. They are longer and larger in all dimensions than are other babies.

We still need to define the truly fat baby who needs immediate preventive management. Some investigators do this by checking weight against length or height and correlating both with standard growth tables for American children. We also need to try to distinguish those overweight babies who will outgrow their baby fat from those who will not. After all, not every fat infant becomes a fat adult.

Factors for Determination

We also must find out why some babies become fat. Heredity, infant and family feeding and eating patterns, the baby's physiology and other factors probably all will prove to be important. There's also a theory that the infant who shows a marked increase in number and size of fat cells is one who will be permanently obese.

Finally, we need to explore methods for treating overweight infants early in life, for once obesity becomes firmly established, it is exceedingly difficult to reverse, as some of us bitterly know.

Infant feeding patterns obviously influence growth. We know for example, that bottle-fed babies usually —though not always—gain weight somewhat more rapidly than do breast-fed infants. This is not always merely fat, however. It can be fat and lean tissue, in varying proportions, depending on the individual baby. Many investigators also believe that the early introduction of solid foods is a factor.

Given the state of our knowledge then, how best do you handle the problem of the fat baby?

First, there is the wait-it-out school of thought. This group argues that reducing diets for babies may slow growth and maturation. Instead of putting the baby on a diet, they suggest waiting until the preschool years to see if it is still necessary then. Meanwhile, moderation should be the path in infant feeding.

Early Weight Control

Then there is the holding-pattern school. Like the wait-it-outers, this second group suggests an approach-with-caution attitude, but extends it through the school years. The preventive measure suggested by this group is to hold weight constant until the child catches up in the growth of lean tissue by paying attention to what the youngster eats and mildly restricting caloric intake. A conscious attempt is also made to increase physical activity.

The now-or-never school believes that obesity must be prevented in the first year or two of life, when the number of fat cells can be influenced. Instead of force-feeding the cells with high-caloric foods, they advocate holding off the use of solid foods, then feeding foods that are low in fat and empty calories.

There are four other approaches. The predestination school believes that genetic endowment is so strong that there is no way to stop the inevitable progress of obesity. As a result, some researchers suggest that the treatment and management of obesity in the mother, either before or during pregnancy, is the way to influence the number of fat cells or fatness of the baby.

Problems in the Family

The it's-all-in-the-mind adherents believe that most childhood obesity is precipitated by deep emotional problems within the family. Only after these problems are solved by long-term therapy, they maintain, is it advisable to begin to modify the child's diet and exercise habits.

The family-centered learning school claims that obesity can be learned from family attitudes toward diet and exercise. The encouragement of eating and the use of foods as rewards are examples of ways infants grow fat.

Finally, there is the all-out physical fitness school, which suggests encouraging exercise as soon as a child is able to walk and teaching by family example the benefits of the physically active life. They suggest vigorous physical activity programs in all the school years, coupled with moderation in eating and caloric intake.

As far as we're concerned, you should raise specific questions with your pediatrician. But in general, we feel that the best course is to delay the introduction of solid foods until the baby is about 4 or 5 months old. Never forcefeed a child or use food as a reward. And see that he or she is encouraged to move about as much as possible even if it takes time that you would prefer to use in another way.

SOURCE: Dr. Jean Mayer and Dr. Johanna Dwyer, *Los Angeles Times*, April 21, 1977. Reprinted by permission of the Chicago Tribune–New York News Syndicate.

and that starve unless they are force fed (9–38). Destruction of the nigrostriatal system produces results very similar to those produced by lesion of the lateral hypothalamus. These studies indicate that different catecholamine systems (epinephrine, norepinephrine, and dopamine) interact to result in feelings of hunger or satiety. Since the catecholamines are so important in hunger regulation, it makes sense that drugs that affect catecholamines (amphetamines) will also affect hunger.

Other Reasons for Eating

Internal and External Cues

For breakfast you had two eggs, toast, and sausages. Lunch was a ham-and-cheese sandwich with a large Coke. There was a candy bar about three o'clock. By the time dinner time arrived, you had consumed well over half of your needed calories, but you were having dinner at your favorite restaurant. You had a giant salad covered with dressing, two pieces of bread with butter, a large steak, and baked potato with butter and sour cream. You had now far exceeded your calorie need for the day, but who can resist cheesecake for dessert? Maybe you did not realize that the cheesecake, along with a good part of the steak and potato, would be stored as fat. Later that evening, you stopped by a friend's house and had two beers and some potato chips. The beer and potato chips would also be stored as fat.

As you can see, some of the eating you do is not related to satisfying calorie needs or physiological deficits. Sometimes you eat in response to learned or external cues: you like to make a huge salad, food smells make you want to eat, you see someone having a baked potato and it looks good, you always have a dessert after a meal, you always munch when you have a beer. It appears that we all eat in response to learned cues. Schacter maintains that compared with normal-weight individuals, obese people are even more dependent upon external cues (9–36). In a series of experiments, he and his associates studied the eating patterns of obese and normal-weight individuals. The subjects were not told the purpose of the experiments, and their eating patterns were observed under the guise of studying taste. The experimenters found that, after eating a roast beef sandwich, normal-weight subjects ate fewer crackers than they ate when their stomachs were empty. In contrast, obese subjects ate the same number of crackers whether or not they had just eaten the sandwiches. The obese subjects ignored the internal cue of having just eaten, of having a full stomach. Normal-weight subjects tended to stop at two sandwiches even if they could have three or more. In contrast, obese subjects ate however many sandwiches they were given, showing that they were more responsive to external cues, the presence of the sandwiches.

In another experiment, researchers either slowed down or speeded up a clock so that it appeared to be closer to dinner time or farther from dinner time than was actually the case. Normal-weight subjects responded to their internal cues and ate the same amount whether the clock was true or whether it appeared to be farther from dinner time. If the clock was speeded up, so that it appeared that dinner time was closer, normal-weight subjects actually ate less because, they reported, they did not want to spoil their dinners (9–35). In contrast, obese subjects ate less when they thought it was earlier (farther from dinner time) and ate more when they thought it was close to dinner time. The obese subjects were eating according to the clock rather than responding to their internal cues. From these experiments, Schacter argues that the problems of obesity result from the fact that the person is not responsive to internal cues and eats mainly in response to external cues.

Others argue that there are other causes of obesity, and that the result of being obese is not a greater dependence upon external cues (9–40). Even though obese persons may eat in response to external cues, they often eat less than normal-weights. They may eat less and still become obese possibly because of differences in activity. When compared with thin females, obese college females ate less but spent only one-third as much time in physical activities. Since calorie needs are closely tied to energy output, a person who exceeds her calorie needs by only 100 calories per day will gain 4.5 kg (10 lb) per year or 45 kg (100 lb) in 10 years. As a result, some researchers feel that it is decreased activity that causes the gradual obesity seen in many middle-aged persons.

Stress

Once an individual becomes fat or obese, he tends to remain that way. An increase in fat causes the body to develop a new weight set-point and to defend the accumulated fat. This is a physiological factor that promotes obesity. There may also be psychological factors. When attitudes toward eating were studied, normal-weight persons reported that they ate primarily in response to hunger. Obese persons, including those who had lost weight and then regained it, reported that they tended to eat in response to loneliness and boredom and in response to many kinds of emotional arousal or stress (9–26). Some people eat to distract themselves from stressful situations. Eating in response to stress seems to be a very common human problem. It is possible that the physiological changes that occur during stress result in feelings of hunger. During stress, the hormones secreted by the sympathetic system cause inhibition of glucose utilization, which may be a cue for hunger. Thus, obesity seems to be related to many different factors, both physiological and psychological.

Losing Weight

You've seen that it is difficult to lose weight because the body has several mechanisms for protecting its stores of fat.

When you reduce your calorie intake, your body makes more efficient use of its available stores. As you start to lose weight, the body tries to maintain its overweight set-point. Nevertheless, it is possible for most of us to lose weight and to establish a new body set-point. If you consistently consume fewer calories than your body needs for energy output, you will lose weight. If you then consume only enough calories to meet your energy needs, you will maintain the new, lower body weight. Programs that have been successful in helping people to lose weight and to maintain the weight loss have focused on developing new eating patterns and becoming conscious of calorie intake. Essentially, these programs make you aware of your eating habits so that you can change them. For example, you may not realize that you gulp down your food and continue to eat long after you feel full, or that you are constantly snacking on candy bars or potato chips. Once you become aware of your over-eating habits, you can develop new eating patterns.

Intestinal Surgery

The woman weighed almost 181 kg (400 lb). She had been on diets and drugs without any success for many years. Her obesity now directly threatened her life. Under conditions such as these, doctors may consider a radical surgical procedure in an attempt to save the person's life. In this surgery, an intestinal bypass is formed so that only a small segment of the small intestine, approximately 50 cm (20 inches), is still in use. The idea is that less food will be digested and absorbed into the body (9–5.)

Early use of this surgical procedure resulted in very high mortality rates, and today the procedure still carries a definite risk of death or serious complications, including liver or kidney malfunction. The effects of removing part of the small intestine include extreme illness (nausea, diarrhea) and extreme weight loss—almost half of the body weight in 1 year. Patients for whom this surgery was successful were found to have greater self-esteem and to be pleased with the surgery, but at the same time, they experienced greater anxiety, depression, and irritability. Some of these problems seem to be psychological consequences of adjusting to being a slimmer person, but some of the problems have a physical basis. Many of the bypass patients develop major physical complications (abdominal distention, kidney stones, thinning of the hair), which in turn lead to discouragement (9–5). These findings indicate that intestinal surgery should be considered only when obesity is so severe as to threaten the person's life.

Why do these patients lose half of their body weight in the first year following surgery? It was thought that by shortening the small intestine fewer nutrients would be absorbed, and the result would be less fat storage. This may explain part of the weight loss. However, one of the primary effects of this surgery is to make the patient sick for weeks or months. Suffering from nausea and diarrhea, patients eat less, and possibly their weight loss is entirely the result of a reduction in eating. Also, after surgery most of the patients developed an aversion to sweet foods (9–4). These studies indicate that the main cause of weight loss following this surgery is the reduced eating that results from illness and changed appetite. Reduced absorption contributes less to the initial weight loss, but may be involved in long-term weight reduction.

Fasting

After fasting for 2 days, you lose 1.5 kg (over 3 lb). The next 2 days you eat very little and gain back more than 1 kg (over 2 lb). How can you lose and gain weight so quickly, when changes in your fat deposits occur at a relatively slow rate? The large weight shifts that accompany fasting result from changes in body water. When you are fasting, you lose body water because you are not consuming salt, which your body needs to retain fluids. As soon as you stop fasting and resume eating, you take in salt, which functions to retain water. How is salt involved in water regulation?

Bodily Fluid

Salt and Water

Your bodily fluids are constantly being circulated and recirculated through your kidneys. On any given day, approximately 166 l (45 gal) of fluid pass through your kidneys. The kidneys filter and send some of the fluid to your bladder for excretion. However, approximately 99 percent of the water that passes through the kidneys undergoes reabsorption from the **tubules**, or collecting ducts of the kidneys. This water is recirculated in the body.

The sodium in salt (sodium chloride) is important in reabsorption. Because there is more sodium present in the surrounding body fluid, there is a tendency for water to flow out of the tubules. This tendency for water to move from an area of lower sodium concentration into an area of higher sodium concentration is called **osmotic pressure**. If sodium were not present in the fluid surrounding the tubules, there would be no osmotic pressure for the water to be reabsorbed. Instead the water would be sent into the bladder and excreted. During fasting, the reduced intake of salt causes a reduction in sodium, which causes a reduced osmotic pressure, so that body water is sent to the bladder and excreted. The presence of sodium is crucial in reabsorbing and maintaining body water.

Sodium Regulation

When you fast, you may also drink less fluids. About two-thirds of the body's fluid is contained inside of cells and is called **intracellular fluid**. The remaining one-third of bodily fluid is found between the cells and in the blood and is called **extracellular fluid**. A reduction in extracellular bodily fluids, as might occur from drinking too little fluids during fasting, is called **hypovolemia** (hi-po-vo-LEEM-ee-ah), meaning reduced volume.

In the kidneys, there are cells that can detect the reduction in body fluids, or hypovolemia. These detectors set off a chain of hormonal events that result in sodium being retained. First the kidneys release the hormone **renin**, which causes formation in the blood of another hormone, **angiotensin**. In turn, angiotensin causes the hormone **aldosterone** to be released from the adrenal medulla. Aldosterone stimulates the reabsorption of sodium from the tubules. The presence of sodium in the fluid surrounding the tubules then causes reabsorption of water and an increase in bodily fluids. Although the body secretes hormones to retain its sodium stores, the reduction of salt intake during fasting cannot be completely compensated, and water loss results.

Blood Pressure

Fasting without sufficient attention to drinking fluids can be dangerous. The sudden loss of bodily fluids caused by reduced salt intake can cause a decrease in blood pressure. For some, a decrease in blood pressure can cause dizziness or fainting. On the other hand, the increased bodily fluids that result from too much salt intake can raise the blood pressure. This is why individuals suffering from high blood pressure, or hypertension, are often placed on so-called salt-free diets. Such diets are never entirely sodium free, but rather sodium-reduced. The reduction in salt intake lowers the level of body water and also blood pressure. Although sodium balance plays an important part in regulating body water, it is not the only mechanism.

Dehydration

During the course of the evening you drank six beers and visited the bathroom frequently. The next morning you felt very thirsty and dehydrated. The reason for frequent urination when you are drinking and feeling dehydration the next morning is that alcohol inhibits secretion of a hormone that functions to retain water. This hormone, **antidiuretic hormone**, or **ADH**, is secreted by the posterior pituitary and acts on the tubules of the kidneys to facilitate the reabsorption of water. If the secretion of ADH is suppressed, as it can be by alcohol or other drugs, you will lose water and become dehydrated.

ADH Regulation
If an area in the hypothalamus were destroyed, you would develop the condition known as diabetes insipidus and would experience excessive water loss, more than 22 liters (6 gal) per day. This area involves two nuclei in the hy-

pothalamus, the **pariventricular** and **supraoptic**, which manufacture ADH. Once manufactured, ADH travels down the axons from the hypothalamic nuclei and is stored in the posterior pituitary. When there is a reduction in bodily fluids, nerve impulses from the hypothalamus stimulate the release of ADH from the posterior pituitary.

When there is a reduction in bodily fluids, there is also a drop in blood pressure. Receptors in the heart monitor blood pressure, and they are called **baro receptors**. These receptors send signals to the hypothalamus when there is a reduced blood pressure, indicating a reduction in bodily fluids. Signals from the baro receptors activate the hypothalamus to trigger the release of ADH from the posterior pituitary, and the presence of ADH facilitates the reabsorption of water in the kidneys.

ADH secretion is also triggered by cellular dehydration. If you eat a high-salt meal or a large amount of sugar, you increase the osmotic pressure in your extracellular fluid. This osmotic pressure draws water out of the cells and causes them to shrink. It is now thought that a tiny nucleus in the hypothalamus contains cells that detect this osmotic condition and stimulate release of ADH (9–15). The ADH then travels to the kidneys and facilitates reabsorption of water. This is another reason why a high-salt diet causes you to retain more water and therefore have a higher body weight and higher blood pressure.

Thirst

Extracellular Thirst

After a bout of diarrhea, you would be very dehydrated and feel thirsty. When you have diarrhea, you lose fluids primarily from the extracellular fluid. This loss of extracellular fluid produces the condition known as **hypovolemia** and causes **hypovolemic thirst**. When you have hypovolemia, you also have lowered blood pressure. This lowered blood pressure activates the baro receptors in the heart and other pressure receptors in the kidney. Nerve fibers carry signals from these receptors to the brain, probably the hypothalamus. If an area of the hypothalamus is destroyed, animals no longer show hypovolemic thirst (9–9). It is also thought that cells in the hypothalamus may respond to the hormone angiotensin, which is activated by hypovolemia, or to changes in the blood pressure in hypothalamic capillaries (9–9). Thus, there are many different signals for hypovolemic thirst. If you have diarrhea or lose a great deal of body water from drinking alcohol, your brain will be signaled in several ways to make you feel thirsty and seek water.

Intracellular Thirst

You finish a very salty meal and feel thirsty. This feeling of thirst does not come from hypovolemia, since the level of bodily fluids has not dropped. Your thirst comes from the increased salt intake, which causes the extracellular fluid to have a higher salt content than the fluid inside the cells, the intracellular fluid. This difference in sodium concentration between the two fluids causes **osmotic pressure** —that is, a pressure for the water in the intracellular fluid to move to the extracellular fluid. In other words, the higher sodium concentration of the extracellular fluid draws water out of the cells. The loss of water from the intracellular fluids results in the cells becoming dehydrated. This causes you to feel thirsty, but in this case, your thirst is called **osmotic** or **intracellular thirst**. It seems that cells located in the hypothalamus and called **osmoreceptors** register osmotic thirst. If these cells are destroyed, animals no longer show osmotic thirst—that is, they no longer drink water in response to salt injections (9–2). The fact that salt causes you to be thirsty and to drink additional water is another reason why high-salt diets cause you to have higher body weight and higher blood pressure.

Comment

From your own experiences, it might appear that the mouth has a mind of its own. You have heard the expression, "My stomach is full but my mouth is hungry." This is another way of saying that you are responding to learned or external cues to eat rather than physiological cues. You may be full but still eat because you see, smell, or imagine food. You may eat even though you have no calorie need or physiological deficit. If you are obese, these learned or external cues may seem even more persuasive, and you have the additional problem of a high body set-point. Just a slight excess each day in calorie intake above energy needs can result in many pounds of fat stored through the years. It is easy to point out the physiological mechanisms leading to obesity, but that does not necessarily change eating habits. Psychological factors may have become more important, and this may be especially true when a person is emotionally upset. The way you eat becomes tied up with the way you think and feel.

SELF-TEST 9

1 A grilled cheese sandwich has the capacity to produce fuel. Fuel value is based on a measure called a _____. For a sandwich to become energy, it must undergo a chemical process called _____.

calorie
metabolism

2 Everyone has his or her own metabolic rate. When you diet, the body adjusts its metabolic rate _____ to save its fat stores. If you eat more than your metabolism requires, the excess calories are turned into _____.

downward
fats or lipids or fat stores

3 Individuals who have had their stomachs removed report feelings of _____ and _____, which indicates that stomach sensations are not the critical _____ for these feelings.

hunger / fullness or satiety / cues

4 When food was delivered directly into the stomach, thus eliminating _____ sensations, humans and rats consumed _____ amounts of food.

oropharyngeal
normal

5 Through the action of the small intestine, a hot dog is turned into two different kinds of fuel for the body: _____ and _____.

glucose / fatty acids

6 As its source of energy or fuel, the brain uses _____ but cannot use _____.

glucose / fatty acids

7 The stomach breaks down or digests a hot dog by bathing it with _____ and with enzymes secreted by cells in its lining.

hydrochloric acid or HCl

8 The secretion of HCl is controlled by the _____ division of the autonomic nervous system as well as by _____ that are released when food reaches the stomach.

parasympathetic
hormones

9 Stress or emotions can affect the secretion of HCl, and if there is too much, the result can be _____.

ulcers

10 If you eat a meal consisting mostly of carbohydrates, they pass into the small intestine where they are broken down into _____. Excess glucose is stored in the liver as _____.

glucose / glycogen

11 The liver can convert glycogen into _____ either from the action of the hormone _____, which is secreted by the pancreas, or from the action of the _____ of the autonomic nervous system.

glucose / glucagon
sympathetic division

12 Glucose that is not used or converted into glycogen is converted into _____ and stored as _____ tissue.

fats or lipids
adipose or fat

13 Eggs, which contain a high percentage of protein, are broken down in the small intestine into _____, which are used for the synthesis of _____. Excess amino acids can either be converted into _____ or _____.

amino acids / protein
glycogen / lipids

14 After you eat a thick slice of homemade bread and butter, the butter will be converted by the small intestine into _____ and _____.

fatty acids / glycerol

15 Immediately after eating, you will have a high level of _____ in your blood. This causes the secretion of the hormone _____ from the pancreas.

glucose
insulin

16 Without the secretion of insulin, glucose cannot be used by the body's cells. This condition is known as _____.

diabetes mellitus

17 Several or more hours after a meal, most of the blood glucose has been used. At this point, the body

has several mechanisms to convert stored fuels into energy: the pancreas secretes _____, the adrenal medulla secretes _____, and the anterior pituitary secretes _____.

glucagon / epinephrine growth hormone

18 One theory of how feelings of hunger originate is based on the utilization of glucose and is called the _____ theory.

glucostatic

19 Problems with this theory include the difficulty in directly measuring _____ and relating it to feelings of _____ or _____.

glucose utilization hunger / satiety

20 Evidence for the glucostatic theory of hunger comes from animal studies. When injected with insulin, animals show a _____, presumably because insulin stimulates utilization of glucose. A short time later, animals _____, presumably because of depletion in glucose.

decrease in eating start eating

21 Another theory that attempts to explain the source of your hunger or satiety says that when your fat stores fall below the _____ you feel hungry. When they rise above the _____, you feel satiated. This is called the _____ theory.

set-point / set-point lipostatic

22 If you were born to obese parents or if you were a fat infant, there is a _____ probability that you would be _____ as an adult than if you had been born a very thin infant.

greater obese

23 If you were obese as a child, you would have a _____ number of and _____ -sized fat cells. Except in extreme cases, if you became obese as an adult, you would have only an increase in _____ of fat cells.

higher / larger

size

24 A human with a tumor in, or a rat with a lesion in, the _____ would eat enormous amounts of food.

ventromedial nucleus of the hypothalamus or VMH

25 There are similarities between rats with VMH lesions and obese humans. After becoming obese, both will eat enough to _____ their obesity. After rats are forced to reduce or obese humans lose weight through dieting, they may eat excessively to reach their former level of obesity, or _____.

maintain

set-point

26 A human with a tumor, or a rat with a lesion, in the _____, will stop eating, which is called _____. In addition, rats with a lesion in this area will not _____, which is called _____.

lateral hypothalamus or LH / aphagia / drink adipisia

27 These two areas, the ventromedial and lateral nuclei of the hypothalamus, are not considered hunger centers but are part of _____ involved in controlling hunger. Both of these areas may be involved in establishing the _____ for the body.

systems set-point

28 When obesity threatens life itself, a radical treatment is intestinal surgery. After surgery, patients show a great reduction in weight because the surgery makes them _____ and they take in fewer _____.

sick calories

29 The physiological approach to the explanation of hunger states that the _____ responds to metabolic fuels and sends impulses to the brain, which interprets these messages and causes you to feel hungry or full.

liver

30 For some foods, there is evidence that we have an innate _____. For others, there is evidence we could learn to choose them to relieve unpleasant _____.

preference symptoms

31 A system of neurons that passes through the hypothalamus and contains the neurotransmitter norepinephrine is called the _____. If this system is destroyed, the result will be an animal that becomes _____.

ventral noradrenergic bundle / obese

32 The system of neurons that contains the neurotransmitter dopamine is called the _____ system. If this system is destroyed, an animal will _____.

nigrostriatal not eat or drink

33 Schacter believes that, compared with normal-weight individuals, obese persons respond more to _____ cues than _____cues.

external or learned physiological or internal

34 There are reports that obese individuals eat in response to loneliness, boredom, and _____.

emotional arousal or stress

35 The presence of sodium in the fluid surrounding the tubules causes an increase in _____ pressure, so that water is _____.

osmotic reabsorbed

36 When there is a reduction in extracellular bodily fluids, the condition is called _____. When this occurs, cells in the kidneys release the hormone _____, which causes the formation in the blood of another hormone, _____. This causes the release of _____ from the adrenal medulla, which stimulates the reabsorption of sodium. Sodium causes the reabsorption of water.

hypovolemia renin angiotensin / aldosterone

37 ADH is manufactured by two areas in the hypothalamus called the _____ and _____ nuclei. ADH is stored in the _____ until it is secreted into the body's blood supply.

pariventricular supraoptic / posterior pituitary

38 If you are thirsty because of a drop in the level of bodily fluids from the extracellular space, as from diarrhea or eating a meal without drinking any fluids, you are experiencing _____ thirst.

hypovolemic

39 If you are thirsty because of a loss of water from the intracellular fluids, you are experiencing _____ thirst.

osmotic or intracellular

REFERENCES

9–1 Ahlskog, J. E. and Hoebel, B. G. Overeating and obesity from damage to a noradrenergic system in the brain. *Science* 1973, 182: 166–168.

9–2 Blass, E. M. and Epstein, A. N. A lateral preoptic osmosensitive zone for thirst. *Journal of Comparative and Physiological Psychology* 1971, 76: 378–394.

9–3 Bray, G. A. The varieties of obesity. In G. A. Bray and J. E. Bethune (Eds.), *Treatment and Management of Obesity*. Hagerstown, MD; Harper & Row, 1974.

9–4 Bray, G. A., Barry, R. E., Benfield, J., Castelnuovo-Tedesco, P., and Rodin, J. Food intake and taste preferences for glucose and sucrose decrease after intestinal bypass surgery. In D. Novin, W. Wyrwicka, and G. Bray (Eds.), *Hunger: basic mechanisms and clinical implications*. New York: Raven Press, 1976.

9–5 Castelnuovo-Tedesco, P. and Schiebel, D. Studies of superobesity. II. Psychiatric appraisal of surgery for superobesity. In D. Novin, W. Wyrwicka, and G. Bray (Eds.), *Hunger: basic mechanisms and clinical implications*. New York: Raven Press, 1976.

9–6 Charney, E., Goodman, H. C., McBride, M., Lyon, B., and Pratt, R. Childhood antecedents of adult obesity. *New England Journal of Medicine* 1976, 295: 6–9.

9–7 Cohn, C. Feeding frequency and body composition. *Annals, New York Academy of Science* 1963, 110: 395–409.

9–8 Epstein, A. N. and Teitelbaum, P. Regulation of food intake in the absence of taste, smell and other oropharyngeal sensations. *Journal of Comparative and Physiological Psychology* 1962, 55: 753–759.

9–9 Fitzsimons, J. T. The physiological basis of thirst. *Kidney International* 1976, 10: 3–11.

9–10 Friedman, M. I. and Stricker, E. M. The physiological psychology of hunger: a physiological perspective. *Psychological Review* 1976, 83: 409–431.

9–11 Gold, R. M. Hypothalamic obesity: the myth of the ventromedial nucleus. *Science* 1973, 112: 488–490.

9–12 Greenwood, M. R. C. and Hirsch, J. Postnatal development of adipocyte cellularity in the normal rat. *Journal of Lipid Research* 1974, 15: 474–483.

9–13 Grinker, J., Hirsch, J., and Levin, B. The affective responses of obese patients to weight reduction: a differentiation based on age at onset of obesity. *Psychosomatic Medicine* 1973, 35: 57–63.

9–14 Grossman, S. P. Eating or drinking elicited by direct adrenergic or cholinergic stimulation of hypothalamic mechanisms. *Science* 1960, 132: 301–302.

9–15 Hatton, G. I. Nucleus Circularis: is it an osmoreceptor in the brain? *Brain Research Bulletin* 1976, 1: 123–131.

9–16 Heatherington, A. W. and Ranson, S. W. Hypothalamic lesions and adiposity in the rat. *Anatomical Record* 1940, 78: 149–154.

9–17 Heron, G. B. and Johnston, D. A. Hypothalamic tumor presenting as anorexia nervosa. *American Journal of Psychiatry* 1976, 133: 580–582.

9–18 Hirsch, J. The adipose-cell hypothesis. *New England Journal of Medicine* 1976, 295: 389–390.

9–19 Hirsch, J. and Batchelor, B. Adipose tissue cellularity in human obesity. *Clinics in Endocrinology and Metabolism* 1976, 5: 299–311.

9–20 Hirsch, J. and Knittle, J. L. Cellularity of obese and nonobese human adipose tissue. *Federation Proceedings* 1970, 29: 1516–1521.

9–21 Hoebel, B. G. and Teitelbaum, P. Weight regulation in normal and hypothalamic hyperphagic rats. *Journal of Comparative and Physiological Psychology* 1966, 61: 189–193.

9–22 Inglefinger, F. J. The late effects of total and subtotal gastrectomy. *New England Journal of Medicine* 1944, 231: 321–327.

9–23 Jordan, H. A. Voluntary intragastric feeding: oral and gastric contributions to food intake and hunger in man. *Journal of Comparative and Physiological Psychology* 1969, 68: 498–506.

9–24 Keesey, R. E. and Powley, T. L. Hypothalamic regulation of body weight. *American Scientist* 1975, 63: 558–565.

9–25 Leibowitz, S. F. Brain catecholaminergic mechanisms for control of hunger. In D. Novin, W. Wyrwicka, and G. Bray (Eds.), *Hunger: basic mechanisms and clinical implications*. New York: Raven Press, 1976.

9–26 Leon, G. R. and Chamberlain, K. Emotional arousal, eating patterns, and body image as differential factors associated with varying success in maintaining a weight loss. *Journal of Comparative and Physiological Psychology* 1973, 40: 474–480.

9–27 Lytle, L. D. Control of eating behavior. In R. J. Wurtman and J. J. Wurtman (Eds.), *Nutrition and the brain*. Vol. II. New York: Raven Press, 1977.

9–28 Mayer, J. General discussion. *Advances, Psychosomatic Medicine* 1972, 7: 322–336.

9–29 Nachman, M. The inheritance of saccharin preference. *Journal of Comparative and Physiological Psychology* 1959, 52: 451–457.

9–30 Novin, D. Visceral mechanisms in the control of food intake. In D. Novin, W. Wyrwicka, and G. Bray (Eds.), *Hunger: basic mechanisms and clinical implications*. New York: Raven Press, 1976.

9–31 Ravelli, G., Stein, A. A., and Susser, M. W. Obesity in young men after famine exposure in utero and early infancy. *New England Journal of Medicine* 1976, 295: 349–353.

9–32 Reeves, A. G. and Plum, F. Hyperphagia, rage, and dementia accompanying a ventromedial hypothalamic neoplasm. *Archives of Neurology* 1969, 20: 616–622.

9–33 Russek, M. A conceptual equation of intake control. In D. Novin, W. Wyrwicka, and G. Bray (Eds.), *Hunger: basic mechanisms and clinical implications*. New York: Raven Press, 1976.

9–34 Salans, L. B., Horton, E. S., and Sim, E. A. H. Experimental obesity in man: cellular character of the adipose tissue. *Journal of Clinical Investigation* 1971, 50: 1005–1011.

9–35 Schacter, S. Eat, Eat. *Psychology Today* April 1971, 45.

9–36 Schacter, S. Some extraordinary facts about obese humans and rats. *American Psychologist* 1971, 26: 129–144.

9–37 Snowdon, C. T. Motivation, regulation, and the control of meal parameters with oral and intragastric feeding. *Journal of Comparative and Physiological Psychology* 1969, 69: 91–100.

9–38 Stricker, E. M. and Zigmond, M. J. Brain catecholamines and the lateral hypothalamic syndrome. In D. Novin, W. Wyrwicka, and G. Bray (Eds.), *Hunger: basic mechanisms and clinical implications*. New York: Raven Press, 1976.

9–39 Teitelbaum, P. and Epstein, A. N. The lateral hypothalamic syndrome: recovery of feeding and drinking after lateral hypothalamic lesions. *Psychological Review* 1962, 69: 74–90.

9–40 Thomas, D. W. and Mayer, J. The search for the secret of fat. *Psychology Today* September 1973, 74.

Sleep and Wakefulness

10

Why You Spend One-Third of Your Life Asleep

A New Record

Randy was a bit skinny for his 17 years, but this did not affect his determination. He wanted to break a record. No one had ever stayed awake for 11 straight days, and Randy wanted to be the first person to do it. In case determination was not enough, he had asked two friends to help keep him awake. At exactly six o'clock in the morning, he awoke and stared at the homemade poster on the wall, "Eleven days or bust." So began an attempt to stay awake longer than any human being had previously been able.

By the end of the first sleepless day, Randy felt he could last 12 or even 15 days. By the second day, he had some trouble focusing his eyes. By the third day, he felt nauseous and could no longer read to stay awake. His friends found it more and more difficult to keep him awake at night. By the fourth day, he sometimes forgot what he was saying, and there were times when he forgot what he was doing. Reporters from the press and TV arrived to cover his attempt at a new sleepless record. By the fifth day, Randy's motivation almost failed. It was lucky that several sleep scientists had come to observe his sleepless behavior. They told of previous studies that reported the fifth sleepless day as the most difficult to conquer. By the sixth day, Randy wanted to sleep as much as a drowning man wants to breathe. One of the scientists told of early studies on sleep deprivation in which puppies that were kept awake for 6 days sometimes died. This thought helped keep Randy awake. By the seventh day, his speech became slurred. His friends and the scientists had to devise all manner of schemes to keep him awake at night.

Randy's father became more and more concerned about his son's health. The father was so nervous that he took

sleeping pills to help him sleep. By the ninth day, Randy showed signs of being irritable and of not being able to finish his sentences. One scientist told of a disk jockey in New York who had stayed awake for almost 9 days. During the last days, the disk jockey had begun to see things that were not there and to suspect people of trying to drug his food. This ninth night, Randy was convinced he was the greatest black football player who had ever lived. By the tenth day, the sleep record seemed unimportant compared to the drudgery and pain of trying to keep his eyes open. If it weren't for the constant hounding of the press and the companionship of the scientists, he probably would have slept then and there. On the eleventh and last night, he stayed awake by playing 100 games on a baseball machine with one of the scientists. Randy beat the scientist every game. The scientist's excuse was that he was tired. Finally, a few minutes past 11 sleepless days, Randy closed his eyes and went to sleep. He had set a new record for going without sleep: 264 hours, or 11 days. He had been on national TV. He had received the personal attention of prominent sleep scientists. They would write about his 11 days without sleep and about what happened on the twelfth day.

The story of Randy is based on the actual case of a seventeen-year-old youth who went without sleep for 264 hours as part of a science project (10–10, 10–18). The scientists were interested in this case because of previous reports of psychotic behavior and hallucinations following prolonged sleep loss. They also wondered if any problems in memory, personality, or behavior would persist when Randy returned to a normal sleep schedule. When the press asked Randy how he had managed to stay awake 11 days, he said that it was simply mind over matter. When the press asked one of the scientists the same question, he replied as follows.

Control of Wakefulness

Sensory Stimulation

What goes on in the brain when you are awake 12, 24, or 264 hours? After several days of staying awake, Randy found that he had to be doing something constantly to stay awake. This suggests that incoming sensory information and constant feedback from his muscles acted on his brain to keep him awake. Suppose most sensory information and muscle activity were prevented. Imagine you are lying on a bed in a barren room. On your eyes are translucent goggles which permit you to see only diffuse light. On your arms are cardboard tubes, and on your hands are heavy gloves, so that you feel little sensation from your limbs. There is no sound in the room. You lie on the bed, and for each day you spend there, you receive 20 dollars. Subjects who actually did this slept more than usual on the first day. But on the second and third days, they slept less. Apparently, the lack of sensory and muscle stimuli can keep you just as awake as if you were engaging in constant activity. What kept the subjects awake was probably not the lack of stimulation itself, but the state of stress caused by the lack. Subjects rarely remained in this condition for more than three days, in spite of what was then a generous salary (10–3, 10–4). Most of them quit because the boredom became overwhelming. This study indicates that sensory and muscle input to the brain may contribute to your staying awake, but that you can also stay awake when this input is reduced. This same point was made dramatically in an experiment using cats. The nerve tracts carrying **somesthesis** (touch, temperature, and pain) and audition were cut. The result was a great reduction in sensory input to the brain. However, without this sensory input, cats continued to show normal patterns of wakefulness and sleep, indicating again that sensory input to the brain is not critical to being awake (10–23).

Brain Function

It is possible to eliminate wakefulness in cats by making lesions in one of two brain areas. One area is the reticular formation in the brain stem. Part of the reticular formation, called the **ascending reticular activating system**, or **ARAS**, sends impulses to the cortex and causes it to be aroused or activated. If an animal is asleep, stimulation of the ARAS will cause the animal to wake up. The other brain area important for wakefulness is the posterior hypothalamus. If this area is destroyed, animals will remain asleep. These two areas, the ARAS and posterior hypothalamus, function to keep the cortex activated. The cortex must be activated in order for you to be awake and conscious.

Biological Rhythms

Most people are normally awake each day for approximately 16 hours and asleep for approximately 8. What would happen to this schedule if there were no time cues, no day and night, no job to get up for? If you lived in a cave, totally removed from all time cues, you would still function on approximately 24-hour cycles. Besides waking and sleeping, other physiological responses occur on a 24-hour cycle. Your body temperature reaches a high point in the middle of the day and a low point very early in the morning, around 4 A.M. Certain chemicals known to be involved in sleep are secreted by animals on a 24-hour cycle (10–31). Biological responses that reach a high or low point every 24 hours are called **circadian rhythms** (sir-KAY-dee-an). Circadian means "about a day." It was because of his circadian rhythm that Randy had the hardest time staying awake at night.

The effects of circadian rhythms are clearly noticed when you fly from one time zone to another. If you flew from the West Coast to the East Coast and arrived late at night, you would still feel wide awake. This is because your

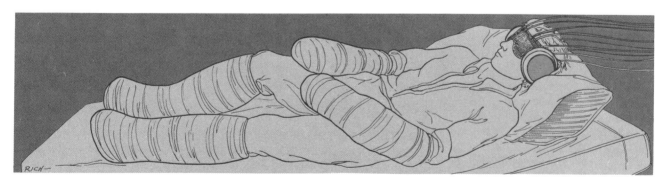

Figure 10–1 A subject can readily tolerate sensory deprivation for one or two days. To isolate the subject from sensory stimuli, he would be placed in a constant-temperature-controlled, sound-proofed room; have cuffs around the hands and feet; and be blindfolded. After this kind of isolation for one or two days, subjects asked to leave the experiment because of the excruciating boredom.

awake rhythm would still be functioning on West Coast time. Inappropriate wakefulness or sleepiness has been called the **jet-lag syndrome**, and it means that the body rhythm time is out of step with clock time. Usually the body rhythm time requires some time to adapt to the new clock time.

Your particular circadian rhythm (sleeping 8 hours and waking 16, or sleeping 7 hours, or whatever) is probably inherited, but as you will see later, it may be possible to modify it somewhat. What exactly controls your biological or circadian rhythm is not known. We do know from the research described earlier that it does not depend upon sensory stimulation. Probably, circadian rhythm is controlled by chemical secretions from the various brain areas involved in wakefulness and in sleep.

Control of Sleep

Just as there is no one answer to why you stay awake, there is no one answer to why you go to sleep. We know that sleep is not simply a matter of fatigue. At times you may go to sleep because of fatigue, but at other times, you may feel too fatigued to sleep. As you have seen, your sleeping follows a circadian rhythm, and, if this rhythm is interrupted, it may be difficult to sleep even though you are very fatigued. Disabled people who are forced to lie in bed all day might be expected to be less fatigued, but they sleep approximately the same amount as active persons.

One possible reason you go to sleep is that the ARAS and posterior hypothalamus, which are involved in wakefulness, are turned off for the night. The specific trigger in the brain that produces sleep is not known but probably is one or several of the chemicals now known to be involved in sleep. In any case, you will see that sleep is far more than a response to fatigue or the mere absence of wakefulness.

Normal Sleep

If you sleep 6 hours and your friend sleeps 8, then 6 is normal for you and 8 is normal for your friend. Each person has a slightly different sleep pattern that is characteristic of and normal for that person. The average length, which is not the same as the normal, is approximately 8 hours. A small percentage of people (less than 8 percent) sleep less than 6½ hours or more than 9½. You might think that short sleepers (6½ hours) are psychologically different from long sleepers (9½ hours). One investigation reported that short sleepers were more efficient, ambitious, and self-confident while long sleepers were more depressed and anxious (10–12), but this finding has not been confirmed. Two other studies have failed to find any personality, academic, or medical differences between short and long sleepers (10–39, 10–40).

From these studies, we can conclude that there are certainly no obvious differences among people based on how long they sleep. Since mental retardates show the same amount of sleep as those with normal or above-average IQ scores, there seems to be little relationship between intelligence and sleep. Finally, there is no sex difference in sleep length, as men sleep approximately the same amount as women. In one sense, the amount of time spent sleeping seems to be the same for everyone—that is, it does not differ with sex or intelligence. In another sense, it is quite different for everyone—that is, individuals may sleep very divergent lengths of time but not differ obviously in other ways.

Measuring Sleep

The sleep scientist watched the endless flow of paper leave the brain wave machine. As she watched, she talked quietly into a microphone. "Randy is going to sleep. He is now fully asleep." Some time later, she noted, "Randy is now probably dreaming. He may be waking up." The scientist was watching Randy's brain waves. Around his head were metal disks the size of dimes. These disks, or electrodes, were attached to his skull with paste. The electrodes were recording the electrical activity from the neurons in the cortex, which lies just under the skull. The cortex contains millions of neurons which, when active, produce electrical changes. The electrical changes recorded on the skull are very tiny, only about a millionth of a volt. In comparison, an ordinary flashlight battery is rated at 1.5 volts. The electrical changes recorded from the skull are fed into and greatly magnified by a device called an **EEG machine**. EEG stands for **electroencephalogram** (e-LECK-tro-in-SEF-ah-low-gram). Brain waves recorded with the EEG machine are logically called EEG's. The scientist watching Randy's brain waves was actually interpreting his EEG pattern.

Interpreting EEG's

If you watched an EEG machine record brain waves on paper, you would see squiggly lines. The lines represent the electrical activity from millions of neurons in the cortex. The squiggles would differ in how close together they came, which is called **frequency**, and in how high they were, which is called **amplitude**. Different combinations of frequency and amplitude indicate different kinds of activity in cortical neurons. If you were awake and alert, your EEG's would have a fast frequency and low amplitude and would be called **beta waves**. Beta waves occur 15–30 times per second and are said to have a frequency of 15–30 Hz (cycles per second). When the cortex is activated or aroused by the ARAS, beta waves are present in the cortex. If you were relaxed and had your eyes closed, the EEG's would

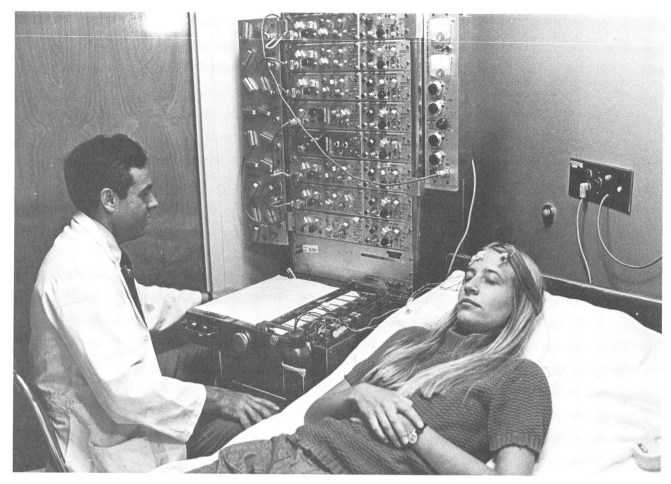

Figure 10–2 While asleep, this person's brain activity is being recorded, amplified, and written out by the machine on the left, called a polygraph. This brain activity is commonly referred to as EEG waves. (Photo courtesy of Sleep Disorders Clinic, Stanford University School of Medicine.)

be slower in frequency (8–12 Hz). These waves are called **alpha waves**. They are slightly higher in amplitude than beta waves, but as you can see in Figure 10–3, they have low amplitudes compared to brain waves observed during sleep. During wakefulness, the EEG's would contain either beta or alpha, low-amplitude waves. Although beta and alpha waves each have a specified frequency range, the frequency varies so that they have a very random appearance on the paper. They resemble writing done while riding on a bumpy road. This random pattern is called **desynchronous**, which is the opposite of a regular, or **synchronous**, pattern, such as one made by a swinging pendulum. Alpha waves are slightly more regular in pattern than beta waves. If you were to fall asleep while hooked up to the EEG machine, your EEG's would become lower in frequency and higher in amplitude. During one period of sleep, **delta waves** would appear. These have a frequency of only 2–4 Hz and are perhaps eight times as large as beta waves. Delta waves occur in a very regular, or synchronous, pattern. From your EEG's and other bodily responses, an experienced sleep scientist would be able to tell fairly accurately whether you were asleep or awake.

Sleep Stages

As you sleep through the night, five different EEG patterns or stages occur in a regular cycle. Formerly, scientists thought that these five EEG stages were associated with five different functions of sleep. They believed that if you missed one of these stages some problem might develop during waking or the next night's sleep. Perhaps you would be less efficient, more irritable, or more fatigued, or have a different sleep pattern the next night.

Suppose you were awakened every time your EEG's showed you to be entering stage 4 sleep. During the night, you would be totally deprived of stage 4 sleep. If stage 4 is essential to sleep or to your functioning properly, then a lack of stage 4 should result in some deficit in behavior. But this does not happen. On the day following no stage 4 sleep, you would show no deficits in personality, mood, or various performance tasks (10–1, 10–14). On the following night, you would show more than the usual amount of time in stage 4 sleep, but that would be the only obvious effect. After years of research on the five stages of sleep, one scientist, Laverne Johnson, concluded that, although

Sleep and Wakefulness

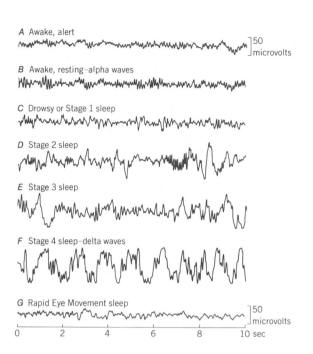

A Awake, alert

B Awake, resting—alpha waves

C Drowsy or Stage 1 sleep

D Stage 2 sleep

E Stage 3 sleep

F Stage 4 sleep—delta waves

G Rapid Eye Movement sleep

50 microvolts

0   2   4   6   8   10 sec

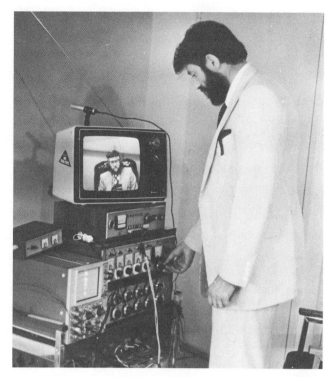

Figure 10–3 A researcher could determine if you were awake or in stage 4 sleep from looking at your EEG record. In the awake or alert state, the EEG waves have a low amplitude, fast frequency, and are desynchronous; in stage 3 and 4 sleep, the EEG's have a higher amplitude, slower frequency, and become more synchronous. (Photo courtesy of Dr. L. Fehmi, Princeton Medical Center, New Jersey. EEG waves courtesy of the publisher from P. Mussen and M. R. Rosenzweig, *Psychology: An Introduction*, Lexington, MA: D. C. Heath, 1973.)

you function poorly after having no sleep, you can function normally after missing some of the stages. Johnson suggests lumping the five sleep stages into two and looking at the functions and cycles of these two sleep states (10–14). That is what we shall do.

Two Sleep States

If you watched Randy's eyes while he was asleep, you would notice that after 90 minutes or so they would be darting back and forth under his eyelids. Throughout the night, there are usually five periods during which his eyes would show these rapid movements. During these darting eye movements, his EEG's would resemble those recorded when he was awake and alert: fast frequency, low amplitude, and desynchronous. His breathing, heart rate, and blood pressure would show increased activity and large fluctuations. Although his brain waves and autonomic responses would look as though he were aroused, the muscles of his limbs and neck would be limp or relaxed, showing little muscle **tonus**. If he were awakened during this period, it is very likely that he would report dreaming. The dream would be detailed and contain several sequences of action. This state of sleep, named after the rapid eye movements, is called **rapid eye movement sleep**, always abbreviated **REM** (pronounced ''rem''). On an average night, you

spend approximately 20 percent of your total sleep time in REM and go in and out of REM an average of five times.

If you spend 20 percent of your sleep time in REM, it means that you spend 80 percent in a state called **NREM** (pronounced ''non-rem''). This is the state you enter when you first fall asleep. There is a gradual change in EEG pattern during NREM sleep toward that of slower frequency and larger amplitude. This is best recognized by the appearance of the slow-frequency and large-amplitude delta waves. Physiological activity declines gradually during NREM sleep, with a slowing of heart rate, respiration, blood pressure, and oxygen consumption and a lowering of body temperature. You do not lose muscle tonus in the limbs or neck during NREM sleep, and there are fewer eye movements than when you are in REM sleep. If you were awakened during NREM sleep, you might report dreaming but the dream would be a fragmentary image, less detailed and sequential than the dreams reported during REM. Throughout the night, you alternate between NREM and REM sleep.

NREM Sleep

Since you spend most of your sleep time in NREM sleep, it must have an important function. It is generally assumed that one function of NREM sleep is to help us recover from

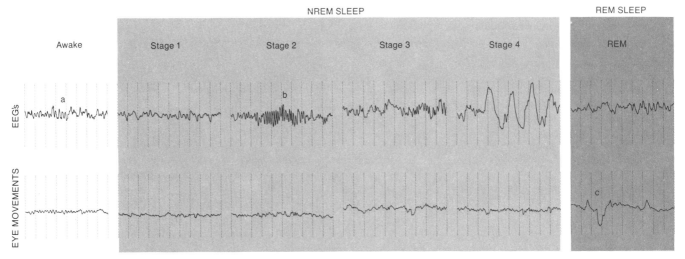

Figure 10-4 Changes in EEG's as a person falls asleep. In an awake but relaxed state with eyes closed, the pattern of EEG's is known as alpha waves and is shown in (a). As the person passes deeper into sleep, short bursts of waves known as sleep spindles occur, as shown in (b). Sleep stages 1, 2, 3, and 4 are known as NREM sleep. During REM sleep, the EEG's have a lower amplitude and faster frequency — very similar to the awake, alert state. Also during REM, eye movements occur, as shown in (c).

the fatigue built up during the day. That is, NREM has a **restorative** function, to recoup our energy and prepare us for the coming day. If NREM is restorative, then someone deprived of NREM should be very fatigued the next day. This idea cannot be tested. It is impossible to deprive someone of all NREM sleep without also eliminating REM sleep. You cannot go into REM sleep without first going into NREM. If there is no NREM, there is no REM. However, subjects have been deprived of approximately 15 percent of their NREM sleep. The portion of NREM sleep during which the large, slow delta waves occur can be eliminated without depriving the person of REM sleep. Delta-wave NREM sleep is usually called **slow-wave sleep** or **stage 4 sleep**. Although lacking slow-wave or stage 4 sleep, subjects showed no specific behavioral deficits (10–1). They did show more than the usual amount of slow-wave sleep the next night, but this rebound effect is difficult to interpret since there are no behavioral changes associated with it. If eliminating the slow-wave part of NREM sleep does not make you more fatigued or less efficient, then either the other stages of NREM take over this function or NREM does not have this function at all. The answer to whether NREM is restorative is probably unanswerable, since total NREM sleep cannot be eliminated without also eliminating REM sleep.

Another function proposed for NREM sleep is that it keeps us inactive when the greatest harm could befall us (10–38). According to this theory, through evolution we have inherited a timing mechanism, sleep, that functions to keep us inactive when our survival is most threatened. It would have been most dangerous for our ancestors to roam at night since many predators have better night vision

than humans. For this reason, humans have evolved with a timing mechanism for being awake in the day and sleeping at night. This timing mechanism has a circadian, or 24-hour day, rhythm. This theory explains why some animals sleep during the day instead of at night. For these animals, most harm would befall them in the daytime, and through evolution they have developed a timing mechanism that is the opposite of humans'. This theory varies from the restorative view of NREM sleep in that it says essentially that we sleep so as not to become injured.

Brain Function

What happens in the brain so that you can go into NREM sleep? The answer seems to involve several chemicals and brain areas and will probably become clearer in the very near future. There is an area in the brainstem called the **raphe nucleus** (rah-FAYE). If most of this area is damaged, a cat will become sleepless, show no NREM sleep, and remain in an almost chronically awake state (10–30). This tells us that the raphe is important for inducing NREM sleep. The raphe has a large concentration of neurons that produce a chemical called **serotonin** (ser-ah-TONE-in). Serotonin is important in controlling NREM sleep. We know this because a cat will show little NREM sleep and remain wakeful if a drug is administered to deplete serotonin (10–25). Evidently the trigger and maintenance of NREM sleep are closely tied to serotonin levels in the brain. According to this idea, you would go into NREM sleep because the raphe nucleus released serotonin, which would act on other brain areas, such as the ARAS, to terminate wakefulness and initiate sleep. The release of serotonin would probably be governed by your circadian sleep rhythm. Evi-

The Headliner

SLEEP FOR THE MEMORY

According to Boston Psychiatrist Chester Pearlman, evidence from both Europe and America is making 1976 ''The Year of REM Sleep.'' Scientists have long known that REM (for the rapid eye movement during periods of dream sleep, which occur three to five times a night in 20-min. segments) serves crucial needs. One of those needs, Pearlman told the Paris conference, has now been clearly identified: REM dreaming is essential to consolidate memories—no dreaming, no long-term memory.

Some ten years ago, French Psychologists Vincent Bloch and Pierre Leconte showed that laboratory rats forgot how to do certain things if deprived of REM sleep after training. In a similar experiment by Pearlman, a rat that had mastered an intricate system of avoiding electric shocks to get food was deprived of REM sleep and then starved to death when tests were repeated.

Among other things, the evidence indicates that the student who stays up all night cramming for an exam is making a mistake. Says Pearlman: ''You introduce a lot of facts that you really can't learn, because staying awake prevents it. The next day you won't be able to remember any of it, and you certainly will not be able to use any of it in the future —it is not part of you.'' A group of researchers at the University of Ottawa showed the same role of sleep in integrating recently learned material into long-term memory: among students enrolled in an intensive language course, those who were learning had an increase in REM sleep; those who were unable to learn had no such increase.

Pearlman and his colleague at the Boston Veterans' Administration Hospital, Psychoanalyst Ramon Greenberg, are among those who argue that REM sleep does more than aid memory: it also helps people cope with daily stress. Paradoxically, it is while sleeping that they assimilate traumatic experiences they have had during the day. In recording the sleep patterns of psychiatric patients, Pearlman and Greenberg found a rise in REM sleep occurred after stressful discussions. In an experiment with nonpatients, the need for REM sleep rose sharply after exposure to distressing movies. The researchers' conclusion: the memory function and coping function of REM sleep are linked. In both cases, the mind must deal with something it has not been prepared to face, and dream sleep makes it possible to consolidate the new material and make it part of oneself. ''We know people generally repress the implications of situations for which they are not prepared,'' says Pearlman. ''The situations usually appear in dreams the next time they sleep and there can be a resolution of the problem.'' Though the functions of sleep are far from being well understood, it is hardly just ''rest.'' The REM period may well be one of the most exciting and active parts of the day.

SOURCE: *Time*, August 23, 1976. Reprinted by permission from TIME, The Weekly Newsmagazine; Copyright Time Inc. 1976.

dence that some mechanism like this exists comes from an experiment with cats. Solutions that were taken from the reticular formation of a sleeping cat caused NREM sleep when injected into the reticular formation of an awake cat. It is not yet known if the solution did in fact contain serotonin (10–7). This study demonstrates that one of the sleep-inducing mechanisms may be a chemical in the brain. The raphe nucleus and serotonin have been most clearly implicated in NREM sleep, but there are probably other chemicals and other brain areas involved in control of NREM sleep, since stimulation of other brain areas will cause cats to sleep.

REM Sleep

As an infant, you spent 50–80 percent of your sleep time in REM. As you matured, there was a gradual decrease in REM until the age of 12 or so, when your adult sleep pattern was established: REM, 20 percent, and NREM, 80 percent.

Since you spend much of your time in REM sleep dreaming, it was once thought that a primary function of REM was to permit dreaming and to fulfill a need for dreaming. The occurrence of dreams, it was thought, caused REM and indicated your need to dream. If this were true, you would expect people deprived of REM and the associated dreaming to show some behavioral changes. This hypothesis can be studied, since it is possible to eliminate REM sleep time completely without eliminating NREM. The researcher watches the EEG's, eye movements, and muscle tonus. Each time the person shows rapid eye movements or fast-frequency, low-amplitude EEG's, or loss of muscle tonus, he is awakened by the researcher. In this way, the subject is never allowed to enter REM sleep. One of the first studies depriving subjects of REM and the kind of dreaming associated with REM reported harmful psychological effects, such as anxiety and irritability (10–6). In addition, subjects spent much more time than normal in REM sleep the next night. Since that study, there have been many others reporting that elimination of REM and the related dreaming does not cause harmful psychological effects (10–14). There were no personality changes in either normal or psychotic subjects. There were few deficits in specific behavioral tasks, such as counting, memory, or verbal learning. Most studies do report that after REM deprivation there is an increase in the amount of REM on the next normal night of sleep. This is called **REM rebound**, and its function is unclear, since there are no behavioral changes associated with it. Consensus now is that the lack of REM and of the type of dreaming that occurs during REM has very little effect on behavior.

During REM the EEG's (fast frequency, low amplitude) and some physiological responses (increased autonomic activity, loss of muscle tonus) are different from those observed during NREM. For this reason, it is thought that REM is a different state and serves a different function than NREM. There have been many hypotheses about the function of REM sleep. No one any longer holds that REM satisfies a need for the sleeper to dream or that dreams cause REM. Instead, the proposed functions of REM range from restoring the brain's chemical balance to evaluating and processing the material from the waking day. It is likely that REM serves several functions, but as yet there is no agreement on what these functions are.

Brain Function

As mentioned before, each person has a pattern of alternating between NREM and REM sleep. Sleep always begins with NREM, and approximately 90 minutes later the first REM period appears. Thereafter, NREM and REM are cyclic, and it is thought that some chemical may trigger REM onset. There is an area in the pons called the **locus coeruleus** (LOW-cus cha-RUL-ee-is) which, if destroyed, eliminates REM sleep in cats. The neurons in the locus coeruleus produce the chemical norepinephrine, which is thought to be involved in controlling REM sleep. When animals are given drugs which interfere with norepinephrine synthesis, the result is a suppression of REM sleep but not of NREM. It is also thought that another chemical, acetylcholine, or ACh, is involved in triggering REM because its injection initiates REM sleep in cats. The alternation between NREM and REM sleep probably involves an interaction between the locus coeruleus, which contains norepinephrine, and the raphe nucleus, which contains serotonin.

REM and Dreams

I dreamt that I had just met a stranger with enormous eyes that looked into my body. The eyes were deep blue and I was sitting in my favorite chair. Each time I tried to move, the stranger's eyes changed color. When I finally walked away, the eyes turned white.

Dreams that occur during REM, like that above, are more detailed and contain more sequences than dreams that occur during NREM. An experienced dream researcher can usually distinguish with great accuracy which dreams occurred during REM (detailed, action sequences) and which dreams occurred during NREM (fragmentary, one scene or image). What do people dream about? We can never know for certain what someone has dreamed, but we can learn a lot about dreams by seeing which dreams are reported most

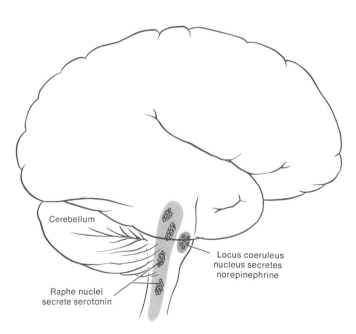

Cerebellum

Locus coeruleus nucleus secretes norepinephrine

Raphe nuclei secrete serotonin

Figure 10–5 Research shows that sleep is controlled by chemicals that are thought to act as transmitters in the brain. It is known that serotonin, secreted by the raphe nucleus in the midbrain, is involved in NREM sleep, while norepinephrine, secreted by the locus coeruleus in the pons, is involved in REM sleep.

Sleep and Wakefulness

frequently. Contrary to what most of us believe, the majority of dreams are not bizarre, unusual, or heavy with emotion. In fact, most dreams have very commonplace settings. They include another person and only occasionally an animal. Most dreams include some activity, such as talking or walking, that is not very strenuous. We dream of misfortune and failure more often than of success and good fortune. We dream about friendly interactions almost as often as aggressive encounters. We dream about sexual interactions very rarely. These data come from analyses of more than 1,000 dreams reported by college students (10–11). College students are not a good representative sample for the entire population. It is possible that persons from different age or cultural groups would have different types of dreams.

It is thought that the length of a dream is about as long as it would take to imagine the same happening while awake. Some of us imagine for seconds, others for minutes, and we probably dream the same way. Although both infants and animals have REM sleep, no one knows if they dream.

What causes dreams? During REM sleep, your EGG's closely resemble those seen when you are awake and alert. When you are awake and can engage in complex mental activities, your EEG waves have a high frequency and low amplitude. This similar appearance during REM sleep probably accounts for your ability to engage in mental activities, or dreaming (10–14). In other words, while it is no longer thought that dreaming causes REM, it is believed that the conditions of the brain during REM make mental activities, such as dreaming, possible.

The meaning of dreams has continued to intrigue and elude us. Current dream research has focused more on what the dream itself means rather than on what may be hidden beneath the obvious. Current research considers dreams to represent a broad range of concerns rather than one concern, such as sexual expression. Recent study has focused less on what symbols mean and more on what the specific images in the dream mean for you as a unique individual. Dream analysis is directed more at studying how a person copes with his or her life rather than treating the dream as a source of information about some deep-seated problem (10–38). Why we dream and what dreams mean make interesting speculation, but it is important to remember that people deprived of REM and accompanying dreams seem to suffer no behavioral problems.

Sleep Deprivation

If deprived of some slow-wave, or NREM, sleep or of all REM sleep, you would show no deficits on personality, mood, or specific behavioral tests. In contrast, if you were deprived of all sleep for 2 days, you would probably become very fatigued, depressed, hostile, and less happy. On specific behavioral tests that require attention, accuracy, or

memory, total sleep deprivation would cause you to do more poorly (10–17). Since total sleep deprivation affects mood and specific behavioral tests, sleep certainly serves some function, be it restorative or protective or both.

The studies on sleep deprivation for periods longer than 2 days report similar findings: increase in depression and lethargy and a decline in the ability to concentrate or to do motor, visual, or perceptual tasks. With prolonged sleeplessness of more than 120 hours, there may be hallucinations, such as seeing a gorilla (10–29). Infrequently, prolonged sleep deprivation may produce psychoticlike behavior, such as suspecting people of drugging your food. Whether psychotic behavior will result from prolonged sleep deprivation probably depends upon the individual personality, since there have been many cases of prolonged sleeplessness without any psychotic episodes. The most dramatic case was that of Randy, who showed no psychotic behavior following 264 hours of sleeplessness.

You might think that the body's physiological responses would begin to deteriorate after 120 or 264 hours of sleeplessness. For example, heart rate, blood pressure, or body temperature might be lower or erratic. In fact, neither 120 nor 264 hours of sleeplessness produced any remarkable changes in heart rate, blood pressure, respiration, or body temperature. Since these responses are controlled by the autonomic nervous system, it appears that this system is somewhat immune to the effects of sleeplessness (10–15). Most studies indicate that you can go sleepless for long periods with little change in physiological responses but much change in mood and behavioral responses.

After sleep deprivation, a REM rebound effect is usually seen in the first night's sleep. In the case of Randy and his 264 sleepless hours, the first night he slept 15 hours and showed REM rebound. When he awoke the next morning, he was essentially normal in mood and behavior, demonstrating the powerful recuperative effects of a night's sleep. His second night's sleep was 8 hours and also showed REM rebound. Followup studies on Randy's behavior as well as studies of other sleepers deprived for 205 hours have revealed no long-term problems in sleep, no emotional upsets, and no personality changes. Although prolonged sleeplessness does cause great stress to the individual, there is no evidence of physiological problems or any long-term effects on behavior.

Sleep Reduction

Many people dream of needing only 4 or 5 hours of sleep a night. There are documented cases of two individuals who slept no more than 3 hours each night, rarely napped, and seemed to lead normal, healthy, productive lives. They had proportionally the same percentage of NREM and REM sleep in their 3 hours of sleep that you have in your 8 hours (10–19). One wonders if the chemical makeup of their brains differed from that of 8-hour sleepers' brains.

We saw in Randy's case that it was not very productive or useful to go totally without sleep. Perhaps it would be possible to reduce one's sleep time gradually to 4 or 5 hours. There have been several attempts by 8-hour sleepers to reduce their sleep time gradually to 4 or 5 hours (10–9, 10–16, 10–26). They did this across many months by going to bed later and always getting up at the same time. There is a cost to this procedure. After reducing sleep time from 8 to 5 hours, subjects began to report that it was extremely difficult to get up in the morning. They were fatigued, had less vigor, had difficulty in concentrating, and felt less happy and friendly. In one study, two subjects asked to end their 4-hour sleep schedule after 3 weeks because of unwanted mood changes and performance deficits. In the other study, subjects did not go below 5 hours because of unwanted mood changes. The most interesting aspect of these studies is what happened after the subjects were allowed to sleep on any schedule they chose. Four months after the studies ended, most of the subjects were sleeping 1 or 2 hours less than when the study began. If you are willing to suffer the discomfort of fatigue and unpleasant mood changes for many weeks, it appears you may be able to cut an hour or two from your sleeping time. You will not be able to decrease your sleep time from 8 to 4 hours, but rather from 8 to 7, or at most 6.

Sleep Problems

Insomnia

Americans spend more than half a billion dollars a year to help them get to sleep. Difficulty in going to sleep, staying asleep, awakening too early, or any combination of these is called **insomnia**. Insomnia can be caused by situational problems, such as a death in the family, financial, marital, or health problems. In these cases, insomnia is transient and usually disappears when the problem is resolved. For example, Randy's father's insomnia disappeared as soon as Randy's experiment was over. In other cases, insomnia is associated with psychological disturbances, such as depression or anxiety, and in these cases it may be more difficult to handle. Under these kinds of circumstances, people sometimes turn to drugs for relief.

The sleep of an insomniac is different from that of a normal sleeper. Insomniacs show more body movements and elevated heart rate and body temperature, indicating that the body is physiologically aroused. If the insomniac seeks relief in drugs, the problem may be relieved initially but usually returns as before. The most common drugs prescribed are **sedatives**, which include **barbiturates** with trade names such as **Seconal (sodium secobarbital)** and **Nembutal (sodium pentobarbital)**. These drugs cause a general depression of neural activity. When an insomniac first begins to take barbiturates, he may go to sleep sooner

than usual, have fewer body movements, and wake up less often during the night. He may be so encouraged by the helpful effects of the barbiturates that he thinks his insomnia is cured. But several problems will arise. He will have to take a significantly larger and larger dosage because the body builds up a tolerance to drugs. A **tolerance** means that it will take a larger and larger dosage to produce the same physical and behavioral effects. Next, the chronic drug user will find that he is beginning to have the same difficulties as before in falling asleep, staying asleep, or both. The result is a return of insomnia, even though he is taking sleeping pills. Finally, there is one more problem. If the chronic user stops taking pills, he will experience very disturbed sleep, with frequent and intense dreams and possibly nightmares. A sudden withdrawal from the long-term use of sleeping pills results in greatly disturbed sleep. Because his sleep is now worse than ever, the chronic user may again return to sleeping pills. Clearly, barbiturates offer no long-term solution to the problem of insomnia and, in one sense, tend to worsen the problem. Sleeping pills also cause a significant reduction in the amount of REM sleep. When drug usage is discontinued, there is a significant increase in REM sleep. The behavioral significance of this REM rebound effect is not known. At present, there are no drugs that treat insomnia without some detrimental side effects (10–21).

"Helping you to get to sleep" is a common advertising theme for many nonprescription drugs, such as **Sominex, Sleep-eze, Nytol,** and **Compoz.** The main ingredient in all of these compounds is a form of **antihistamine (methapyraline).** Antihistamines are taken by people who have hay fever or allergies, and one of their side effects is drowsiness. One study that evaluated the effects of Sominex on insomnia found that, compared with a sugar pill or **placebo,** Sominex had no effect on either going to sleep or staying asleep (10–22). Why do people who take Sominex think it helps them sleep? The answer probably involves the phenomenon known as the sugar pill or **placebo effect.** Very often people experience relief of symptoms (sleeplessness, headaches, pain) when they are given a sugar pill that contains no medicine, a placebo. It appears that if you believe strongly that a pill will help your symptoms then your belief actually produces relief, even if the pill happens to be a placebo. Apparently, Sominex and similar drugs provide relief from symptoms because of the placebo effect (10–5, 10–8).

Narcolepsy

There is a very serious sleep disorder that fortunately is not very common. One person who had this disorder would fall into a deep sleep when stopped for a red traffic light. When the light turned green and other drivers began honking their horns, he would wake and drive away. This condition is called **narcolepsy** and literally involves having a sleep attack. The attack consists of falling into a deep sleep almost without warning. It is sometimes accompanied by loss of muscle tonus so that the person collapses, inability to move when passing from wakefulness into sleep, and hallucinations. It is not known whether narcolepsy has a genetic basis. In some cases, the disorder seems to run in families, which does not necessarily mean it is genetic, and in other cases, there is no family history of the problem. When a sleep attack occurs, there is evidence that this sleep is REM. In a normal adult, there must always be a period of NREM sleep before the person enters REM. In narcoleptics, it appears that REM sleep occurs in the absence of NREM. At present there is no cure for narcolepsy.

Other Problems

As a young child, you may have awakened in the middle of the night completely terrified, unable to remember what had happened. The next morning you did not remember your nighttime waking or your terror. From the ages of 3 to 5, children experience **night terrors**. These occurrences are different from bad dreams or nightmares in that the child cannot recall any specific dream sequence. Night terrors usually occur during NREM sleep and seem to result from being awakened during deep sleep. Night terrors usually disappear as the child grows older.

Starting somewhat later, at approximately the age of 7, a child may experience **nightmares**. Nightmares are awakenings from bad dreams, and the child may recall the frightening events of the dream. It is unlikely that nightmares are associated with any kind of psychopathology. They usually occur during REM sleep and in some cases may persist into adulthood.

Everyone has heard stories of people walking in their sleep. **Sleepwalking** is not a waking dream state, but happens during NREM sleep. It may last from 30 seconds to many minutes, and the person does not report a dream sequence when awakened. Sleepwalking appears to be automatic behavior. It is difficult to awaken the sleepwalker, and if awakened she will be confused as to what she is doing out of bed. If the sleepwalker is not awakened, she will have no memory of walking. Sleepwalking observed in children is usually outgrown.

The most frequent problem in children from 5 to 7 years old is **bed wetting**, or **enuresis** (en-your-EE-sis). Research on this problem has shown that bed wetting does not represent hostile or dependent feelings on the part of the child, as sometimes presumed. Enuresis occurs during NREM sleep. If the bed clothes are not changed, the wetness may be incorporated into a dream during REM, so that the child believes the bed wetting occurred during dreaming. Treatment of this problem involves counseling the parents so they do not make the child feel guilty, as well as treatment of the child. Both drugs and behavior modification have proved successful in treating enuresis.

Sleep as Therapy

In the 1950s, Russian scientists experimented with long periods of sleep as treatment for various emotional problems, such as anxieties, depressions, phobias (fears), and hysteria. Patients were put to sleep with either drugs—usually barbiturates—or a sleep machine. The sleep machine was approximately the size of a typewriter and generated a weak electrical current. Two electrodes were placed on the forehead and two on the back, so that the electrical current passed through the patient's head. When the current was turned on, patients reported a tingling sensation. The daily length of sleep induced by drug or machine varied according to the preference of the investigator, usually from 10 to 13 hours and up to 18. The total length of treatment was 1–3 weeks. Russian scientists reported that the majority of patients experienced an improvement of mental or emotional problems (10–2).

Although these results seemed very promising, sleep as therapy received little study in the United States until rather recently. There is now an interest in something called **electrosleep**, which has been induced by a machine similar to that used by the Russians. Although the process is called **electrosleep** or **cerebral electro-therapy**, none of the studies report whether the patients were actually put to sleep by this machine, which passes an electrical current through the head. Also, the procedure was quite different from that reported by the Russians. The procedure involved giving five sessions of electrosleep, with each session lasting only 30 minutes. The electrical current was increased until the patients reported an uncomfortable feeling, and then the current was reduced until the patients reported feeling nothing. This kind of treatment has been tried on patients with alcoholism with little success (10–36), on patients with anxiety and insomnia with little success (10–24), and on patients with anxiety with some slight success (10–32). From the above studies, there is little evidence that electrosleep is effective. Since there is some question whether the patients were put to sleep, the word *electrosleep* may be misleading. If you see an ad for an electrosleep machine, you would be wise to save your money.

Learning during Sleep

You may have seen ads in the popular press for learn-while-you-sleep programs. The program usually consists of a tape recorder, pillow speaker, and some material (foreign language) that is played while you are asleep. If only it worked! Most research indicates that you cannot learn anything very complex while asleep (10–30, 10–34). If learning occurs, it occurs during the drowsy period between waking and sleeping. If you have studied something just before going to sleep, you essentially are rehearsing it during this drowsy period. Sleep learning is mislabeled, since it actually involves learning when you are awake and drowsy but are not asleep.

Information Processing

Although you cannot learn a foreign language during sleep, your brain can do quite remarkable things during sleep. While asleep, you can hear and wake up to the sound of your name and no one else's (10–27). While asleep, you can hear a weak sound and press a button in order to prevent a fire alarm from going off next to your ear (10–42). While asleep, you can learn a simple discrimination, such as pushing a button in response to one of two tones in order to avoid being awakened by a loud bell and to receive a monetary reward (10–41). All of these studies indicate that you cannot learn complicated material while asleep, but you can and do process information and can learn and perform simple discriminations. While you are asleep, your brain responds to signals that you (your brain) considers important or novel. Your brain responds less to signals it considers unimportant. You may have noticed this phenomenon when you awoke to the sound of your dog barking, baby crying, or window creaking but not to the sound of trucks or buses going by. While asleep, the brain can process important or novel information and can wake up the body if necessary.

States of Consciousness

During wakefulness, NREM, and REM, there are differences in EEG's and/or behaviors. These three conditions are considered to be different states of consciousness. There are other states in which people seem to be neither awake nor asleep, such as when they are hypnotized or meditating.

When hypnotized, does a person have brain waves, physiological responses, or behaviors that are different from those seen when he is awake? The physiological responses (heart rate, respiration, blood pressure) observed during hypnosis are similar to those seen during waking. The brain waves recorded during hypnosis are similar to awake brain waves and are unlike sleep waves. And the behaviors observed under hypnosis (immobility, lack of pain) have been reproduced in suggestible persons when awake (10–33, 10–35). Although there is some controversy over these data (10–13), it appears that hypnosis is another form of wakefulness.

During transcendental meditation, the subject sits in a comfortable position with her eyes closed. She repeats some specific sound over and over in order to help prevent distracting thoughts and, according to the proponents, to free the mind for more creative experiences. Subjects are told to meditate twice a day for 20 minutes. This technique is simple to learn and has achieved great popularity among its many followers. When a person is meditating, are the brain waves and physiological responses different from those observed when she is awake or asleep? First reports claimed that meditators did enter a state with responses different from either wakefulness or sleep (10–37). However, subsequent research has called this finding into question by showing that meditators actually spend much meditation time in a state of sleep, as indicated by their brain waves (10–28). Researchers conclude that the state of transcendental meditation is probably similar to the state of sleep. Whatever state their brain is in, meditators have reported beneficial effects from using this procedure.

Comment

Although we might all like to sleep less, it takes considerable time and some anguish to shorten our sleep by an hour or two. Although we might like to learn while asleep or sleep off our neuroses, there is little evidence that we can do either. Although insomniacs want to sleep better with pills, the beneficial effects of sleeping pills are usually shortlived. Although you spend one-third of your life asleep, not counting time asleep in classes, there is no agreement yet on the function of sleep or what triggers sleep. Perhaps the best thing we can do about sleep is just to lie back and enjoy it.

1   When a cat is deprived of most of its sensory input, it still shows a normal _____ cycle, indicating that sensory input is not essential for _____.

waking or wake–sleep
wakefulness

2   If a lesion were made in either the _____ or _____, it would cause an animal to remain asleep or be in a coma.

ARAS posterior
hyopthalamus

3   The ARAS functions to keep the _____ in an aroused or activated state.

cortex

4   Your wake–sleep cycle revolves around a 24-hour day, and these kinds of cycles are called _____rhythms.

circadian

5   The average length of sleep is approximately 8 hours, although a small percentage of people sleep less than 6½ and more than 9½ hours. The length of sleep is not associated with either _____ or _____.

sex
intelligence

6   The EEG machine records the activity of millions of neurons in the _____. When you are awake and alert, the EEG's have a _____ amplitude, a frequency of _____ Hz, and a _____ pattern and are called _____ waves.

cortex
low / 15–30
desynchronous
beta

7   When you are awake and relaxed with your eyes closed, the EEG's have a _____ amplitude and a frequency of _____ Hz and are called _____ waves.

low
8–12 / alpha

8   Based on EEG's, there are five different patterns that occur during sleep. These five different EEG patterns can be combined into two separate sleep states called _____ and _____.

NREM / REM

9   When you first go to sleep, you go into _____ sleep. During this state, the EEG pattern would change to one of _____ amplitude and _____ frequency with a _____ pattern. There is a decline in _____ activity and no loss of _____ tonus.

NREM
higher / slower
synchronous
physiological / muscle

10 Approximately 90 minutes after entering NREM, you ordinarily go into _____ sleep. During this state, the EEG pattern would resemble EEG's recorded during _____. This sleep state is named after the occurrence of _____, during which people often report _____. Also during this state, there is loss of _____ tonus and an increase in _____ activity.

REM / waking
rapid eye movements /
dreaming
muscle / physiological

11 Several functions have been proposed for NREM sleep. One theory says that NREM sleep is _____, or helps prepare us for the next day's activities. Another theory says that NREM is part of an inherited timing mechanism that functions to keep us inactive when _____.

restorative
most harm would occur

12 If you were deprived of the slow-wave, or _____ wave, component of NREM sleep, there would be no deficit in _____, but there would be a _____ effect in the next normal night's sleep.

delta / personality tests or
behavioral tests / rebound

13 If an area in the brainstem called the _____ is destroyed, an animal will show little NREM sleep and will essentially remain sleepless. Neurons in this area produce the chemical _____, which is thought to be involved in the control of NREM.

raphe nucleus
serotonin

14 There have been several functions proposed for REM sleep. One function no longer given credence is that REM satisfies a need to _____. Current theories of REM function include _____ of what occurred during the waking day or restoring the brain's _____.

dream / evaluation or
processing / chemicals

15 If you were deprived of all REM sleep, there would be little change in your _____ or in specific _____tasks, but there would be a _____ effect in the next normal night's sleep.

personality
behavioral / rebound

16 There is an area in the pons that is involved in REM sleep. This area, called the _____, produces the chemical _____.

locus coeruleus
norepinephrine

17 Although dreams have been reported during both NREM and REM sleep, there is a difference in the kind of dreams. Those reported in REM are more _____ and have more _____ than those reported during NREM.

detailed / sequences

18 When deprived totally of sleep for 2 days or more, your mood changes to one of _____ and you do poorly on tests requiring _____.

depression or being less
happy / attention,
accuracy, or memory

19 Although there is a change in mood and a deficit in performance on behavioral tasks, prolonged sleep deprivation does not seem to cause any change in _____ responses that are controlled by the _____.

physiological / autonomic
nervous system

20 In some studies, sleepers who averaged 8 hours a night gradually reduced their sleep time to 4 or 5 hours. The most significant outcome of these studies was that when subjects were allowed to return to a sleep schedule of their own choosing, they slept _____ than before the study began.

1 to 2 hours less

21 Insomniacs have trouble going to sleep or staying asleep. Once asleep they show more body _____and have a higher activity in _____ responses than normal sleepers.

movements
physiological or heart
rate or temperature

22 The most commonly prescribed drugs for insomnia are _____, which initially bring some relief. However, within weeks the body builds up a _____ to drugs and the _____ returns.

barbiturates
tolerance / insomnia or original sleep problem

23 A very serious but not very common sleep problem is that of having a sleep attack, called _____. During this attack, the person may go immediately into _____ sleep without first going into _____.

narcolepsy / REM
NREM

24 In children, sleep problems that occur during NREM sleep include _____, _____, and _____. Problems that occur during REM sleep include _____.

night terrors / sleepwalking
enuresis / nightmares

25 Although sleep therapy has been used by Russian scientists with claims of high success rates, there is little evidence that the procedure of _____ has beneficial effects on alcoholism, anxiety, or insomnia.

electrosleep

26 While there is little evidence that one can learn _____ material while asleep, there is evidence that while asleep you can learn to perform a simple _____ and that you can and do respond to _____ stimuli.

complex
discrimination
significant or important or novel

27 It is generally accepted that there are at least three states of consciousness: _____, _____, and _____. During these three states, you have different _____ and different _____.

wakefulness / NREM
REM / EEG's / behaviors

REFERENCES

10-1 Agnew, H. W., Jr., Webb, W. B., and Williams, R. L. The effects of stage four sleep deprivation. *Electroencephalography and Clinical Neurophysiology* 1964, 17: 68–70.

10-2 Andreev, B. V. *Sleep therapy in the neuroses.* Translated from Russian by B. Haigh. New York: Consultants Bureau, 1960.

10-3 Bexton, W. H., Heron, W., and Scott, T. H. Effects of decreased variation in the sensory environment. *Canadian Journal of Psychology* 1954, 8: 70–76.

10-4 Brownfield, C. A. *The brain benders.* New York: Exposition Press, 1972.

10-5 Claridge, G. *Drugs and human behavior.* Baltimore: Penguin, 1972.

10-6 Dement, W. The effect of dream deprivation. *Science* 1960, 131: 1705–1707.

10-7 Drucker-Colin, R. R. Crossed perfusion of a sleep inducing brain tissue substance in conscious cats. *Brain Research* 1973, 56: 123–134.

10-8 Evans, F. J. The power of a sugar pill. *Psychology Today* April 1974.

10-9 Friedmann, J., Globus, G., Huntley, A., Mullaney, D., Naitoh, P., and Johnson, L. Performance and mood during and after gradual sleep reduction. *Psychophysiology,* in press.

10-10 Gulevich, G., Dement, W., and Johnson, L. Psychiatric and EEG observations on a case of prolonged (264 hours) wakefulness. *Archives of General Psychiatry* 1966, 15: 29–35.

10-11 Hall, C. S. and Van de Castle, R. L. *The content analysis of dreams.* New York: Appleton-Century-Crofts, 1966.

10-12 Hartmann, E., Baekeland, F., and Zwilling, G. R. Psychological differences between long and short sleepers. *Archives of General Psychiatry* 1972, 26: 463–468.

10-13 Hilgard, E. R. Hypnosis. In M. R. Rosenzweig and L. W. Porter (Eds.), *Annual review of psychology.* vol. 26. Palo Alto, CA: Annual Review, 1975.

10-14 Johnson, L. C. Are stages of sleep related to waking behavior? *American Scientist* 1973, 61: 326–338.

10-15 Johnson, L. C. Physiological and psychological changes following total sleep deprivation. In A. Kales (Ed.), *Sleep physiology and pathology.* Philadelphia: Lippincott, 1968.

10-16 Johnson, L. C. and MacLeod, W. I. Sleep and awake behavior during gradual sleep reduction. *Perceptual and Motor Skills* 1973, 36: 87–97.

10-17 Johnson, L. C. and Naitoh, P. The operational consequences of sleep deprivation and sleep deficit. *Advisory Group for Aerospace Research & Development* 1974, No. 193.

10-18 Johnson, L. C., Slye, E. S., and Dement, W. Electroencephalographic and autonomic activity during and after prolonged sleep deprivation. *Psychosomatic Medicine* 1965, 27: 415–423.

10-19 Jones, H. S. and Oswald, I. Two cases of healthy insomnia. *Electroencephalography and Clinical Neurophysiology* 1968, 24: 378–380.

10-20 Jouvet, M. The states of sleep. *Scientific American* 1967, 216: 62–72.

10-21 Kales, A., Bixler, E. O., and Kales, J. D. Role of the sleep research and treatment facility: diagnosis, treatment, and education. In E. D. Weitzman (Ed.), *Advances in sleep research.* vol. 1. Flushing, NY: Spectrum, 1974.

10-22 Kales, A. and Kales, J. Recent advances in the diagnosis and treatment of sleep disorders. In G. Usdin (Ed.), *Sleep research and clinical practice.* New York: Brunner/Mazel, 1973.

10-23 Lindsley, D. B., Schreiner, L. H., Knowles, W. B., and Magoun, H. W. Behavioral and EEG changes following chronic brainstem lesions in the cat. *Electroencephalography and Clinical Neurophysiology* 1950, 2: 483–498.

10-24 Moore, J. A., Mellor, C. S., Standage, K. F., and Strong, H. A double-blind study of electrosleep for anxiety and insomnia. *Biological Psychiatry* 1975, 10: 59–63.

10-25 Morgane, P. J. and Stern, W. C. Relationship of sleep to neuroanatomical circuits, biochemistry and behavior. *Annals of the New York Academy of Science* 1972, 193: 95–111.

REFERENCES (cont.)

10–26 Mullaney, D. J., Johnson, L. C., Naitoh, P., Friedmann, J. K., and Globus, G. G. Sleep during and after gradual sleep reduction. *Psychophysiology,* in press.

10–27 Oswald, I., Taylor, A. M., and Treisman, M. Discriminative responses to stimulation during human sleep. *Brain* 1960, 83: 440–452.

10–28 Pagano, R. K., Rose, R. M., Stivers, R. M., and Warrenburg, S. Sleep during transcendental meditation. *Science* 1972, 191: 308–309.

10–29 Pasnau, R. O., Naitoh, P., Stier, S., and Kollar, E. J. The psychological effects of 205 hours of sleep deprivation. *Archives of General Psychiatry* 1968, 18: 496–505.

10–30 Rubin, F. *Learning and sleep.* Bristol, England: John Wright and Sons, 1971.

10–31 Rusak, B. and Zucker, I. Biological rhythms and animal behavior. vol. 26. In M. R. Rosenzweig and L. W. Porter (Eds.), *Annual Review of Psychology.* Palo Alto, CA: Annual Reviews, 1975.

10–32 Ryan, J. J. and Souheaver, G. T. Effects of transcerebral electrotherapy (electrosleep) on state anxiety according to suggestibility levels. *Biological Psychiatry* 1976, 11: 233–237.

10–33 Sarbin, T. R. and Coe, W. C. *Hypnosis.* New York: Holt, Rinehart & Winston, 1972.

10–34 Simon, C. W. and Emmons, H. H. Responses to material presented during various levels of sleep. *Journal of Experimental Psychology* 1956, 51: 89–97.

10–35 Simonov, P. V. and Paikin, D. I. The role of emotional stress in the hypnotization of animals and man. In L. Chertok (Ed.), *Psychophysiological mechanisms of hypnosis.* Berlin: Springer-Verlag, 1969.

10–36 Smith, R. B. and O'Neill, L. Electrosleep in the management of alcoholism. *Biological Psychiatry* 1975, 10: 675–680.

10–37 Wallace, R. K. and Benson, H. The physiology of meditation. *Scientific American* 1972, 226: 84–90.

10–38 Webb, W. B. *Sleep the gentle tyrant.* Englewood Cliffs, NJ: Prentice-Hall, 1975.

10–39 Webb, W. B. and Agnew, H., Jr. *Science* 1970, 168: 146.

10–40 Webb, W. B. and Friel, J. Sleep stage and personality characteristics of "natural" long and short sleepers. *Science* 1971, 171: 587–588.

10–41 Weinberg, H. Evidence suggesting the acquisition of a simple discrimination during sleep. *Canadian Journal of Psychology* 1966, 20: 1–11.

10–42 Williams, H. L., Morlock, H. C., Jr., and Morlock, J. V. Instrumental behavior during sleep. *Psychophysiology* 1966, 2: 208–216.

Learning and Memory 11

How Neurons Learn to Remember

The Accident

It was an instant that seemed to last forever. There was a dog in front of her motorcycle, the sound of braking tires, and her screams as she lost control. There was a tree in front of her. Her arm hit with a loud snapping noise. There was an incredible pressure in her head, and then there was nothing.

People were talking in the distance. Their voices grew louder, and she could make out white coats. It was a dream and then it was real. She was lying on her back. There was a pain in her arm and a great pressure in her head. It was an ambulance. The driver asked her what happened. She told of the dog and losing control and hearing her arm snap and cracking into a tree and forgetting to wear her helmet. The driver mumbled something about not wearing her helmet.

She woke the next day in a hospital bed. She did not know where she was or what had happened yesterday or last week. When the doctor visited her in the evening, she did not remember that he had also examined her that morning.

Her mind seemed like a blank. Nothing stayed very long. She could not remember the accident or what had followed or what had happened 2 weeks before. Over the days, memories slowly came back. She gradually pieced together her memories for the weeks before the accident. It was like putting together a jigsaw puzzle. She would have one memory that triggered another and another, until, with time, she could remember the events of the preceding weeks. Then she could remember the summer day and riding her bike in the park. But no matter how hard she tried, she was never able to remember the dog barking or falling off the bike or hitting the tree, even though she had recalled these events in the ambulance. She could not remember the first

few hours in the hospital or the X rays or the arrival of her parents. She was suffering from a loss of memory called "traumatic amnesia." A blow, or trauma, to the head can cause a loss of memory for events preceding, during, and following the accident.

The example of Debby was constructed from actual case histories of individuals who suffered traumatic amnesia (11–37). What happened to her memories, and why do some return?

Remembering

A sharp blow to the head can temporarily wipe out memories of the preceding weeks. Failure to remember events prior to the accident is called **retrograde amnesia**. Retrograde amnesia may cover moments, hours, days, or weeks, depending on how severe the head trauma is. As in Debby's case, recovery from retrograde amnesia is usually complete except for the moments immediately preceding the accident. These events never will be remembered. It seems that the last memories, or those occurring immediately before the trauma, are the first memories to be disrupted and lost. This is called the **last-in/first-out principle** of memory loss (11–36). Hitting the tree was one of Debby's last memories in and one of her first memories out (lost).

For some time after the accident, Debby could not remember the preceding 2 weeks. We know these events remained in her memory since she finally was able to recall them. The trauma of the accident had somehow disrupted the brain mechanisms involved in **recall**, or **retrieval**, of these memories. A blow, or trauma, to the head does two things: it completely eliminates those memories immediately before the blow, and it disrupts retrieval of memories preceding the blow for hours, days, or weeks. Having a memory and being able to retrieve it are very different processes. You can disrupt the retrieval without destroying the memory itself. You may not remember a friend's name and then it suddenly comes to you. When memory of your friend's name does return, it means your initial problem was one of retrieval rather than memory loss. Many techniques for improving memory call for the coding of new memories so that retrieval is made easier. If someone you meet looks like a bear and his name is Bob, you may more easily retrieve his name by thinking of a bear whose name is Bob. When a particular memory does not return, it is possible that the problem is not retrieval but instead is memory loss. **Forgetting** means that the memory is permanently lost. The loss can mean that you absolutely cannot retrieve the memory, that the memory is no longer present in your brain, or that the memory was never formed.

Consolidation

One of the interesting things about Debby's amnesia is that even when she was able to remember events before and after the accident, she was never able to remember those moments immediately preceding the accident. Seeing the dog, feeling her arm break, and hitting the tree were memories that she had had in the ambulance but somehow had lost. The problem might have been retrieval, but it might also have been that these events never became part of her long-term memory. Perhaps a certain time period is required before memories become fixed or converted into long-term memory. In other words, memories may exist first in a temporary state and, with time, become fixed or **consolidated** (11–30). The idea that memories are first temporary and need time to become part of long-term memory is called the **consolidation hypothesis**. This hypothesis says that if neural events underlying memories are disrupted before consolidation can occur, these memories are lost and there is no long-term storage. Possibly the blow to Debby's head disrupted the neural events for memories of the dog, arm, and tree. Since these memories were in a temporary state, the blow prevented them from becoming consolidated into long-term memory.

You look up a new phone number, dial the number, and talk to the person. After the conversation it is unlikely that you will remember the number. The events of dialing and talking, which involve further learning, disrupt the memory of the phone number. When subsequent learning (dialing and talking) acts to disrupt previous learning (telephone number), it is called **retroactive interference**. The consolidation hypothesis explains retroactive interference in this way: subsequent learning (dialing and talking) prevents or interferes with the consolidation of the preceding memory (telephone number), and this latter memory is lost (11–26). Another possibility is that the memory of the telephone number was consolidated but that you cannot re-

trieve it. If you remember the number some time later, it means the memory was consolidated but the problem was actually one of retrieval.

Theory

The scene of the dog running at the bike is registered in the brain through the activity of millions of neurons exciting and inhibiting other neurons. One scientist, D. O. Hebb, proposed that the event "dog running" was actually coded or represented by the activity of a certain combination of neurons. When activated, this combination of neurons would result in the image "dog running." Hebb called this group of neurons a **circuit** because he felt they acted like a closed loop that could reactivate itself. Once this neural circuit was activated, impulses would repeatedly pass over the circuit. The repetition of impulses over the circuit is called **reverberation**. The scene "dog running" is represented or coded in a reverberating circuit that is thought to be the basis for temporary or **short-term memory**. According to this idea of **reverberating circuits**, you can remember a new telephone number for several moments because the event is literally being repeated, or reverberated, in your brain.

If you were to repeat a telephone number over and over to yourself, you would repeatedly activate a reverberating circuit. Hebb proposed that repeated activation of the circuit causes structural changes at the synapses, which make the neurons in the circuit easier to activate. According to this theory, when a telephone number in short-term memory becomes consolidated into long-term memory, it means that structural changes have occurred at the synapses. If the activity of the reverberating circuits responsible for short-term memory were interrupted by a blow to the head, there would be no consolidation and no long-term memory of the telephone number.

Blocking Consolidation

The patient was suffering from severe psychological depression and was unresponsive to therapy or drugs. The psychiatrist recommended electroconvulsive shock treatment. Mental disks were placed on the patient's head, and she was given a muscle relaxant. An electric current was passed through the patient's head. The current was strong enough to excite the neurons in her brain. When the neurons in the motor cortex and other areas of her brain were activated, the result was a convulsion and unconsciousness. The muscle relaxant given to the patient prevented damage to any of her limbs as a result of strong contractions of muscles. When the patient recovered consciousness, she had a retrograde amnesia for the moments preceding the treatment. This observation suggests that ECS had interrupted consolidation in the same way as a blow to the head. Thus, ECS could be used to study the process of consolidation.

A light came on to signal that shock would follow. If the

rat ran to the opposite end of the box, it would avoid the shock. After learning to run to the opposite end of the box to avoid shock, rats were given ECS immediately (within 20 seconds) or at longer intervals (40 seconds to 14 hours). This procedure was repeated for 18 days. Each rat received a daily trial in which it ran to the opposite end of the box to avoid the shock and was then given ECS either immediately after or after longer intervals (11–6). If ECS inter-rupts consolidation, you would assume that rats would not remember the task from day to day and would have to re-learn it each day. When ECS occurred 20 seconds after the trial, the rats showed virtually no learning of the avoidance response (see Figure 11–1). When ECS occurred 1 hour after the training trial, the rats showed improved perfor-mance from day to day, meaning that they were remem-bering and that consolidation was occurring. These results

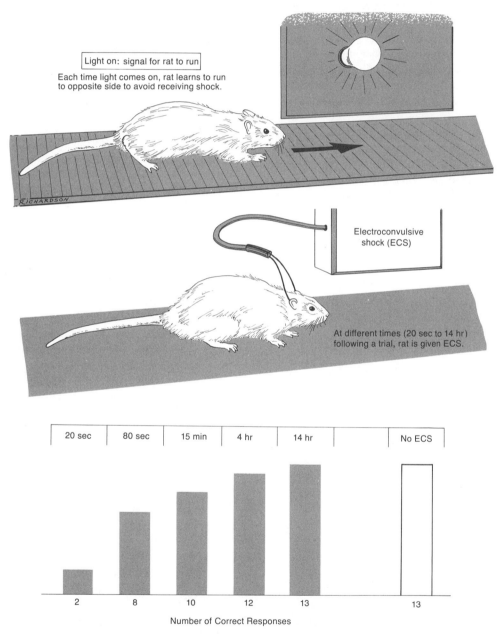

Light on: signal for rat to run

Each time light comes on, rat learns to run to opposite side to avoid receiving shock.

Electroconvulsive shock (ECS)

At different times (20 sec to 14 hr) following a trial, rat is given ECS.

20 sec	80 sec	15 min	4 hr	14 hr		No ECS
2	8	10	12	13		13

Number of Correct Responses

Figure 11–1 What happens to learning when brain activity is disrupted by the administration of electroconvulsive shock? If ECS is given very soon (20 sec) after a trial, a rat makes only two correct responses of running when the light appears. As the ECS is delayed more and more, the rat makes more and more correct responses. If the ECS is given 14 hours after a trial, the rat makes 13 correct responses, which is the same number it makes when receiving no ECS. (Redrawn from C. P. Duncan, The retroactive effect of electroshock on learning, *Journal of Comparative and Physiological Psychology*, 1949, 42: 32–44.)

Remembering

suggest that time is required for memory to become consolidated in the nervous system and that disruption of neural activity can interrupt this process and prevent long-term memory.

Perhaps the rats that received the ECS immediately after running to the opposite end of the box did not make this response the next day because the ECS caused fear. Perhaps they were fearful of that end of the box. Subsequent research showed that one ECS treatment did not seem to cause fear (11–26). This research supports the idea that ECS interfered with remembering the avoidance response (running to the opposite end) by interrupting consolidation rather than by causing fear. Perhaps the rats had consolidated the memory of how to avoid the shock, but they could not retrieve that memory. Although it is possible that ECS disrupted retrieval rather than consolidation, most of the evidence suggests that ECS interfered with consolidation and prevented the memories from ever being stored (11–20).

In other experiments, rats were deprived of oxygen, subjected to seizures, or anesthetized with ether immediately after making some learned response (11–26). These procedures, like ECS, caused loss of memory for the response, or retrograde amnesia. These experiments suggest that a certain time period is necessary for consolidation to occur and that disruption of the nervous activity during this time period prevents consolidation and destroys the memory (11–4).

Aiding Consolidation

Suppose that after reading this chapter on learning you took a drug that stimulated your nervous system. Would the increased neural activity enhance consolidation and improve your ability to remember? In an attempt to answer this question, scientists trained mice to run to the side of a maze that had a black card and to avoid the side with a white card. Some mice received a stimulant drug, pentylenetetrazol, at various times before they made their choice. Others received the drug at various times after choosing. As shown in Figure 11–2, the stimulant drug caused rats to make more correct choices or reduced errors when they were given the drug 5 minutes before or after a training trial. Other stimulant drugs also increased the number of correct choices, if given from 60 minutes before to 60 minutes after training, but not if given after a longer time period (11–26). The researchers suggested that the stimulant drugs had improved memory consolidation by increasing neural excitability during the consolidation period.

The fact that stimulant drugs can improve memory in animals does not mean they can affect humans the same way. Conceivably, in the future, neurochemical treatments could be devised to improve memory in persons with physical brain disorders. However, since the improvement in memory caused by stimulant drugs is very small, it is unlikely that these treatments would enhance memory in the normally functioning brain (11–26). Some children seem to have poor memory because they are very active (hyperactive) and have difficulty paying attention. When children diagnosed as hyperactive are given stimulants, such as amphetamines, some seem to learn better and to have improved memory. In these children, the drug probably helps memory by improving their ability to pay attention and concentrate (see Chapter 13). It is less likely that amphetamines improve the consolidation process. Apparently stimulant drugs can improve memory by increasing ability or motivation to concentrate on a task or by facilitating consolidation after the task is learned. If drugs are given *before* learning, it is impossible to determine whether they are affecting the learning process itself or are affecting attention and memory. In some of the mice studies, the drugs could not have affected attention or motivation during learning because they were administered after learning. In these studies, the drugs were thought to improve consolidation.

Time for Consolidation

After looking up a new telephone number, you repeat it to yourself six times. As you are about to dial it, a horrible automobile accident happens right outside the phone booth. Moments later, when you attempt to dial the number, you find that you cannot remember it. Apparently, seeing the accident disrupted your nervous activity so that consolidation of the phone number did not occur. Or, you did consolidate the number but can no longer retrieve it. In either case, you cannot remember the number. On the other hand, suppose that after repeating the number six times you dial it and reach your party. After the conversation, you get into your car and drive off. Driving down the freeway, you witness a car hit the center divider and turn over. When you arrive at your home, you can still remember the number. In this case, being upset from witnessing an accident did not affect consolidation because seeing the accident occurred some time after you learned the new phone number. How long does it take for consolidation to occur? It seems that memory consolidation does not occur immediately. Memory can be disrupted by ECS or trauma or facilitated by stimulant drugs within 10 to 15 seconds after the event is registered in the nervous system. Most investigators in this field would probably agree that consolidation requires at least that amount of time (11–4). Some researchers have reported that consolidation still may be occurring as long as 15 minutes after some task is learned, but there is no evidence that it continues as long as 60 minutes. These data suggest that you will learn and remember best if you are not distracted or interrupted during the time period when consolidation occurs in your nervous system.

Memory and Engram

Waiting in your car at a stop light, you watch someone wearing an orange jacket ride by on a bicycle. An hour later

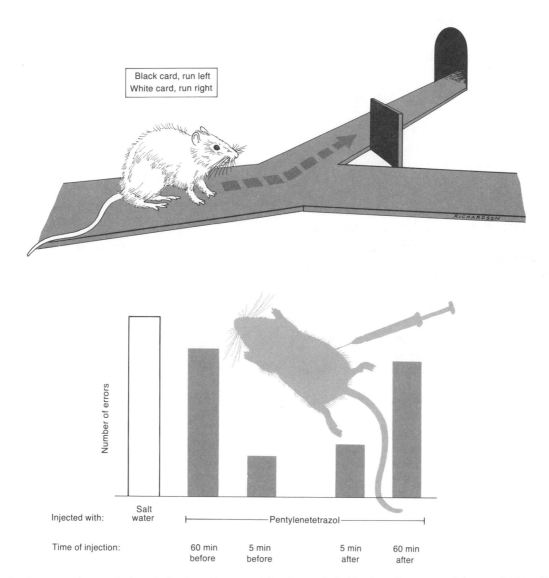

Figure 11–2 A mouse learns to turn left when it sees a black card, right when it sees a white card. Then it receives injections of a stimulating drug, pentylenetetrazol, at various times before or after the trial. If the drug is given 5 minutes before or after a trial, the mouse makes fewer errors — suggesting that the stimulant improves consolidation of long-term memory. If the stimulant is given 60 minutes before or after a trial, there is little effect and the number of errors is somewhat similar to the number made after a control injection of salt water. (Redrawn from J. Krivanek and J. L. McGaugh, Effects of pentylenetetrazol on memory storage in mice, *Psychopharmacologia*, 1968, 12: 303–321.)

you do not remember the person. Suppose you saw someone with an orange jacket and a bare bottom ride by on a bicycle. Not only would you remember the event hours later, you would probably be talking about it. The event ''bare bottom'' was stored in your memory, which means that there has to have been a *physical* change in your brain. The physical representation of a memory is called an **engram**. No one has ever seen an engram for ''bare bottom'' or for any other memory. No one knows exactly what kind of physical change occurs in the brain. But because the brain is made up of physical components like neurons, we know that the formation of memories must involve some

physical change. The term **engram** refers to the physical change in the brain that results in a memory.

Location of Engram

Memories of when you failed an exam, lost a job, or broke up a relationship are engrams that you might like to have removed. Could your family surgeon remove troublesome memories by removing engrams? Scientists have searched for the location of engrams in animals. In experiments, animals learned a task and then parts of their brains were destroyed. The scientists' assumption was that if the engram were stored in certain brain areas, then removing those areas would remove the engram. If the engram were surgically removed, the animal would behave as if it had lost its memory for the task.

After learning to make the correct turns in a maze, rats had various parts of their cortex removed. These experiments were done almost 50 years ago by Karl Lashley (11–20). Much to his surprise, there seemed to be no one area of the cortex that was most important for memory of the maze. Instead, the amount of cortex removed, regardless of its location, was more important. The larger the amount of cortex removed, the more errors the animals made on the maze. Since the amount of cortex removed affected the number of errors, Lashley called this principle **mass action.** Mass action means that memory is affected by the mass or amount of cortex removed: the greater the amount of cortex removed, the greater the loss of memory. Since the location of the lesions did not seem to be important, Lashley proposed that many areas of the cortex can take over the function of many other areas, or that all areas of the cortex are equally important. The idea that location of the lesion was unimportant in disrupting memories and that all areas seemed equally important was called the **principle of equipotentiality.** These two principles, mass action and equipotentiality, are not entirely applicable to the monkey or human brain.

A monkey was trained to press a lever and obtain a banana when shown a picture of a square. It was taught not to press a lever when shown a picture of a circle. After the monkey learned to perform this visual task, a lesion was made in the visual association area of the occipital lobe. Following this lesion, the animal lost its memory that square means banana and no longer could learn this type of task. The same monkey could be trained to press a lever when it felt a rough surface and not to press when it felt a smooth surface. Thus, a lesion in the visual association cortex affects a visual problem but not a tactile one (11–16). These findings show that all the cortex is not equal, and that some of the cortex is associated with visual functions and other parts with tactile functions. Different functions are located in different parts of the cortex. Does this mean that memories or engrams for the square versus the circle problem are located in the visual cortex? By destroying visual association cortex, it is possible that we are destroying the animal's ability to see four lines and perceive these lines as a square. That is, we may be interfering with the animal's ability to perceive visual stimuli. The monkey can see, but it cannot see the difference between a circle and a square. Or, possibly the damage to this area may be destroying engrams that associate square with banana. From these experiments, we know that some functions are localized in the cortex, but we do not know if the function involves perceiving the stimuli (distinguishing between circle and square) or involves the actual engram of events (remembering that square means banana).

During brain surgery in humans, it is often necessary to stimulate the cortex and have the patient conscious so that he can describe the sensations. From the patient's description, the surgeon can determine the function of different areas and be especially careful to avoid parts controlling critical responses, such as speech or voluntary movements. During these operations, stimulation of the cortex in the temporal lobe sometimes produces memories or flashbacks. In a series of reports by Wilder Penfield and associates, there are examples of electrical stimulation causing patients to report memories (11–31, pp. 617, 645):

"I hear my mother and father talking and singing." And after a pause, "Christmas carols."

"Oh, gee, gosh. Robbers coming at me with guns. Oh gosh, there they are, my brother is there. He is aiming an air rifle at me."

"My mother is telling my brother that he has his coat on backwards."

These findings are remarkable in showing that stimulation of certain neurons seems to cause memory experiences. These findings do not tell us whether the engrams for these memories are stored in the neurons of the temporal lobe or elsewhere. Stimulation of neurons in the temporal lobe may excite neurons in other parts of the brain, which in turn cause the memories. In either case, the temporal lobe is involved in the memory process.

If you think back to the example of the bare-bottomed bicyclist, you will discover that you have many memories, and thus engrams, of this event. You saw the bare bottom (visual engram), you heard people talk about it (auditory engram), and you felt embarrassed about bare-bottomed riding (emotional engram). Each of these engrams—visual, auditory, and emotional—may be stored in a different part of your brain. It may be possible to remove the visual engram by removing visual association cortex, but you would still have auditory and emotional engrams. Instead of having one engram located in one part of your cortex, you probably have many engrams associated with the event, and these engrams are located in different areas of your cortex.

Learning and Memory

The epileptic seizures were occurring so frequently that H.M.'s daily life was completely disrupted. In an attempt to control the seizures, surgeons removed part of his temporal lobe, including the hippocampus, from both sides of his brain. After recovering from surgery, H.M. could speak normally, could interact socially with the staff, showed normal emotional responses, and showed a slight improvement on standard intelligence tests. His seizures decreased in both frequency and severity. But now H.M. has one serious problem. Although he can remember events from his early years, he cannot remember what happens from day to day, the name of the doctor that examined him an hour ago, or the headline he read minutes ago. Although he has lived in the same house for 6 years, he cannot remember the address. He cannot find the lawnmower, even though he used it the day before and put it in the garage. He can work on the same jigsaw puzzle repeatedly or read the same magazine again and again without ever remembering that he did the puzzle or read the magazine just yesterday. He cannot remember the names of friends who have visited him repeatedly since the surgery and does not recognize them if he meets them on the street. For the 12 years since his surgery, H.M. has virtually no memory (11–28). For the most part, he has retained the memories of his life experience prior to surgery, but it is as if the record of his life experiences stopped with the surgery. Such a world is difficult to imagine. H.M. describes it (11–36, p. 6):

Every day is alone in itself, whatever enjoyment I've had, and whatever sorrow I've had . . . Right now I'm wondering, have I done or said anything amiss? You see at this moment everything looks clear to me, but what happened just before? That's what worries me. It's like waking from a dream. I just don't remember.

In spite of his day-to-day or long-term memory loss, H.M. is capable of learning new tasks and remembering them for short periods. He was told the number 584 and was asked to remember it for 15 minutes. Fifteen minutes later, he repeated the number showing normal short-term memory. Thirty minutes later, he could remember neither the number nor the scheme he had devised for recalling it. could pay attention and keep the number in short-term memory. Thirty minutes later, he could neither remember the number or the scheme he had devised for recalling it. On one particular task, H.M. was capable of long-term memory. He practiced drawing a star-shaped pattern while looking in a mirror. He showed normal improvement in learning this **perceptual-motor task,** beginning each day at the level he had achieved by the end of the previous day's practice. But even though he improved on this task from day to day, showing long-term memory, he had no memory of having performed the task before (11–29). From the studies on H.M., we can conclude that he has no obvious impairment in short-term memory (remembering 584 for 15 minutes), has long-term memory on perceptual-motor tasks (tracing star), and has memory for events before the surgery. But he cannot consolidate long-term memory for events occurring after his surgery (except for motor skills). Loss of memory following surgery is called **anterograde amnesia.** Since H.M. has no recall of memories following his surgery, this suggests that the area damaged, especially the hippocampus, plays a critical role in memory formation. Since H.M. can pay attention and does have short-term memory, the hippocampus may be less important for these functions.

These same findings, loss of memory for recent, day-to-day events but little loss of memory for earlier events, have also been reported in some chronic alcoholics. Examination of their brains has revealed damage to the hippocampus and related area, the **mammillary bodies** (11–36). (See Chapter 12 for discussion of alcohol and brain damage.) These cases of brain damage in humans seem to implicate the hippocampus in learning and memory. However, there is less evidence from animal research that the hippocampus is involved in learning (11–17). The discrepancy between human and animal research may be explained by the kind of learning on which the animals are tested. Animals are tested on the equivalent of perceptual-motor tasks after hippocampal damage. H.M. showed normal learning and improvement on mirror drawing, a perceptual-motor task, even though he could not remember doing the task. From human data, we would expect little or no loss of learning on perceptual-motor tasks. One researcher, Brenda Milner, suggested that perceptual-motor tasks may be acquired independently of the hippocampus. However, for other learning problems, her work with H.M. and other brain-damaged patients suggests that the hippocampus plays an important role in learning, or in the formation of long-term memory (11–29).

The case of H.M. helps illustrate two questions: Where in the brain does learning occur, and are these areas different from those where memories are stored? Some parts of the brain seem to play a special role in the process of learning and in the formation of engrams. These brain areas may not actually store engrams, but rather play some part in forming them. Once formed, the engrams may be stored in other brain areas. In the case of H.M., it appears that he cannot store new long-term engrams without the hippocampus. Since he still has memories of events before the surgery, these engrams must be stored in places other than the hippocampus. Apparently engrams or memories are stored throughout your brain.

Locating Learning

You learn to recite a poem by heart. Next you are given a lesion in your speech area that makes you unable to speak. When asked to recite the poem, you cannot. The lesion does not interfere with your memory but rather with your ability to recite or perform. When asked to learn a new poem, you can. But since you cannot recite or perform the new poem, it might appear that the lesion has interfered with learning. It is possible to learn something but be unable to *perform* it. The lesion does not prevent you from learning a new poem, rather it prevents you from performing or reciting it. In animals, it is often difficult to determine whether a brain lesion has affected the animal's *ability to learn* a new task (square means banana) or its *ability to perform* the task (lesion causes poor vision). After a lesion, animals might show poor learning, not because learning ability itself has been affected, but because the lesion has changed levels of arousal, motivation, or attention or has impaired sensory or motor ability (11–16). If the animal is poorly motivated,

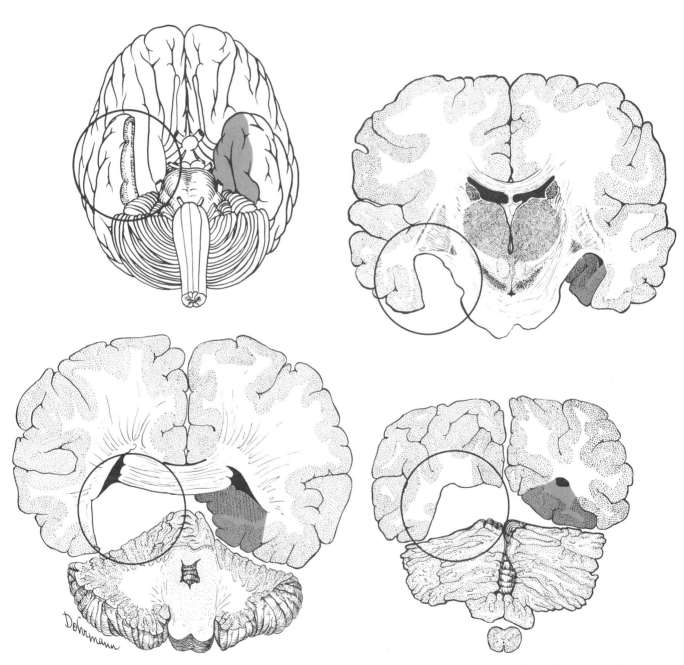

Figure 11-3 In a patient, H. M., the hippocampus was removed from both sides of the brain because of uncontrollable epileptic attacks. These views of the brain show the area of hippocampal removal. After this surgery, H. M. was unable to remember events for more than a few minutes, showing the involvement of the hippocampus in memory. (From B. Milner, The memory defect in bilateral hippocampal lesions, *Psychiatric Research Reports*, 1959, 11: 43–52.)

it may not perform and thus may not learn, even though it has the brain areas to do so. Brain areas involved in motivation and attention are necessary for learning but they may not be involved in the actual formation of the engram.

In literally thousands of experiments, selective lesions were made in animals' brains in an attempt to determine which areas were necessary for learning. If the removal of a particular brain structure could be shown consistently to prevent animals from learning, then researchers could conclude that brain area was essential for learning. The most amazing result from this research was that no one area was found in which lesions could be said to prevent learning without also affecting performance (11–16).

In trying to locate those brain areas essential for learning or for the formation of an engram, we have discovered the following:

1 A lesion that disrupts learning may do so either by affecting the ability to learn or by interfering with performance.

2 The brain may use several different systems to learn a task, so a lesion may affect one system but leave others intact. For example, you might learn to type by touch as well as by looking at the keys. If a lesion destroyed the area involved in learning to type by touch, you might continue to type by sight with little loss in learning.

3 After a lesion, there may be little loss in learning because another area of the brain takes over the function. There is evidence that when one section of the brain is destroyed, axons from surrounding areas send branches, or sprouts, to replace the axons that have been damaged. When remaining axons send out new branches after brain damage, it is called **sprouting** (11–23, 11–32). The occurrence of sprouting may explain why we recover from some types of brain damage.

4 Finally, lesions in one area of the brain may destroy fibers passing through and therefore cause deterioration in other areas of the brain. If an animal were unable to learn a task, it might be the result of damage to one or more brain areas, which makes it difficult to locate the exact area for learning (11–22).

The researcher must consider all these problems before deciding a lesion in a particular part of the brain interferes with the formation of an engram.

Learning Made Visible

Imagine a brain in which electrical activity were visible. When the owner of the brain was learning a new task, it would be possible to observe which areas of the brain were active and thus to discover where learning occurs in the brain. This is essentially what researchers are attempting to do with **electrophysiology**. One type of electrophysiology involves inserting into the brain extremely fine wires called **microelectrodes**, which can record the activity of a few neurons. The activity recorded by the microelectrodes indicates which brain areas are active while the animal is learning a task. One problem with this technique is that it is possible to sample only a very limited number of the millions of neurons in the brain. If there is no activity recorded during learning, it may be because that brain structure is actually not involved or because the microelectrodes are in the wrong areas of the structure. The following experiment, conducted by Richard F. Thompson and associates, is an example of learning made visible. Their study recorded neural activity that represents the earliest events in the formation of an engram (11–41).

These investigators studied rabbits because rabbits have a very simple response that is easy to observe. When a piece of dust or air strikes the rabbit's eye, a membrane flicks over the cornea to protect the eye. This membrane, called the **nictitating membrane (NM)** (NICK-tate-ing), responds automatically to a stimulus, such as dust or a puff of air. Since movement of the membrane occurs automatically after a stimulus, it is a reflexive response. It is thought that neural mechanisms controlling such reflex responses are much simpler than those involved in learning to make a response that square means banana. Since the rabbit's response is a reflex, performance factors such as motivation, attention, or arousal are less important. Researchers hope to discover how learning occurs in the brain by first studying simple reflexive responses, before they go on to study more complex learning.

Normally, the rabbit's nictitating membrane moves only in response to some irritation, such as a piece of dirt or puff of air. If you made a sound, the membrane would not respond. But it is possible to condition the rabbit so that the membrane does move to sound or tone. When this happens, it means that a new association has been made in the rabbit's brain. We will look at the activity of neurons as this new association (tone = movement of membrane) is formed in the brain.

After the rabbits to be conditioned are anesthetized, microelectrodes are surgically placed into the temporal lobe, specifically, in the hippocampus. From the case of H.M., who lost the ability to form long-term memories, we would guess that the hippocampus is involved in the formation of new engrams. The tips of the microelectrodes, invisible to the naked eye, can record the activity of a small number of hippocampal cells while the rabbit's membrane undergoes conditioning to a tone.

The procedure for conditioning the rabbit's membrane is the same as that developed by Pavlov when he conditioned a dog to salivate to a tone. You begin with a reflex response that always occurs as the result of a stimulus. A puff of air always causes the reflex movement of the nictitating membrane. Since the puff of air causes the response with no prior conditioning, the air puff is called the **unconditioned stimulus.** Since the nictitating membrane moves to the puff of air with no prior conditioning, the movement of the membrane is called the **unconditioned response**. Now we add the tone and have the following sequence. The tone comes on first, followed by the air puff (unconditioned stimulus), which causes the nictitating membrane to move (unconditioned response). This sequence is repeated over and over. After many trials, a new association begins to form, so that the tone causes the nictitating membrane to move before the air puff occurs. The membrane movement is now conditioned to the tone. The tone is called a **conditioned stimulus** and the nictitating response to the tone is called the **conditioned response**. The procedure of conditioning a reflexive response (membrane movement) to a stimulus that initially has no effect on the response (tone) is called **classical conditioning**. During classical conditioning, a new association is formed so that the tone becomes capable of eliciting the reflexive response. During the formation of this association (tone = membrane move-

ment), new learning occurs, engrams are formed, and the microelectrodes in the hippocampus record the neural activity.

The neural activity in the hippocampus during conditioning is shown in Figure 11–4. Before training, the hippocampal cells do not respond to the tone alone. Neither do the hippocampal cells respond when only the air puff occurs. But when the tone and air puff are paired, the hippocampal cells begin to respond to the air puff even before the new association is learned. As training continues, the hippocampal cells begin to respond to the tone before the air puff occurs, and this means the membrane is conditioned. In other words, when the tone causes a conditioned response of the membrane, new neural activity appears in the hippocampal cells. So the formation of this new association, membrane movement in response to the tone, is represented by new neural activity in the hippocampus. As

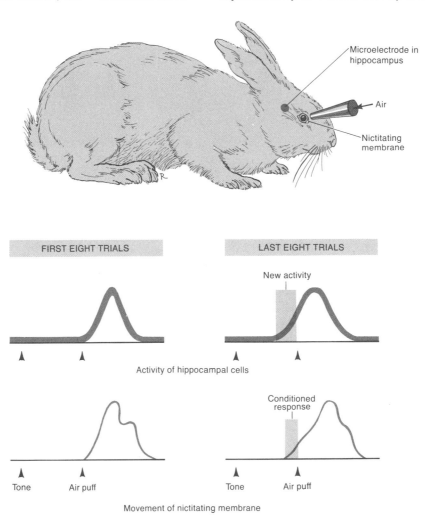

Figure 11–4 The rabbit's nictitating membrane is being conditioned while electrical activity is recorded from its hippocampus. During the first eight trials, there is very little activity of the hippocampal cells before the air puff occurs. During the last eight trials, conditioning occurs, as shown by the movement of the nictitating membrane before the air puff. With this conditioning the hippocampal cells show new activity which also occurs before the air puff. This indicates that the hippocampal cells are involved in the formation of new associations or engrams. (Redrawn from R. F. Thompson, The search for the engram, *American Psychologist*, March, 1976, 209–227.)

Learning and Memory

Thompson suggests, this hippocampal response may be the "earliest event in the formation of the engram."

Perhaps the activity in the hippocampus that we think represents a new association simply represents the movement of the membrane, a motor response. But if the air puff occurs by itself (not paired with the tone), causing the membrane to move, there is no response from cells in the hippocampus. This shows that the hippocampal activity does not represent a motor response of the membrane. If the tone occurs alone, there is no response from the hippocampal cells, indicating that the hippocampal cells are not merely responding to a novel stimulus. Only if the tone is paired with the air puff and a conditioned response occurs (membrane is conditioned to move to the tone), does hippocampal activity appear. Evidently the hippocampal cells are not responding to a novel stimulus or a motor response alone but rather to the rabbit learning the association between the tone and the air puff. From these data, it appears that the hippocampal activity represents the formation of an engram. If these findings are confirmed, it will be an important step in determining where and how engrams are formed in the nervous system.

Engram and Proteins

When you first learned the word **engram**, physical change occurred in your brain. While some researchers ask where that engram is located, others ask what the physical change is. Since the brain is composed of and uses a variety of chemicals in its functioning, many have felt that the formation of an engram must involve some change in chemical composition. Since virtually all brain functions involve the utilization of proteins, it was thought that proteins might be involved in the formation of engrams.

Suppose the learning of a new name involved the formation of new protein. That is, the memory of that name was stored in a new protein molecule. If memories were stored in new protein molecules, it might be possible to enhance memory with treatments that increased protein formation. If memories were stored in particular molecules, it might be possible to remove and reproduce these molecules or even transplant them from one person's brain into another's. If you find it difficult to imagine a complex memory being stored in individual protein molecules, remember how genetic instructions are stored. The complicated instructions for the development of the body are contained in DNA molecules that make up the genes (see Chapter 1). Each cell of the body, including the neuron, has a nucleus. In each nucleus is an acid—deoxyribonucleic acid, or DNA—that contains genetic instructions. Another nucleic acid—ribonucleic acid, or RNA—forms a pattern or template of DNA. RNA is responsible for carrying the genetic instructions from the nucleus to the rest of the cell. Messenger RNA carries the pattern of a DNA molecule into the body of the cell or cytoplasm. Once in the cytoplasm,

the pattern contained in messenger RNA has the instructions for the synthesis of the appropriate protein needed for the development of that cell. The coding of memory or the formation of an engram was thought to occur in a similar way.

Here is how the idea was applied to learning. When you learn a new name, it activates the neuron and triggers the release of a chemical. This chemical causes a previously inactive DNA molecule to begin producing messenger RNA. The messenger RNA carries the DNA pattern into the cytoplasm with instructions for the formation of a new protein which codes the memory. In this way, the new memories would be stored in new protein molecules. Is it true?

Transfer of Memory

If memories were stored in protein molecules, perhaps these molecules and the resulting memories could be transferred from one person to another. Researchers began with a tiny animal, the flatworm, which was trained to avoid shock by contracting when a light came on. After flatworms learned to contract to the light and avoid shock, they were fed to untrained flatworms. Surprisingly, the investigators found that after eating trained flatworms, the untrained flatworms learned the task more quickly (11–24). In subsequent research, James McConnell extracted and transferred RNA from trained to untrained flatworms and concluded that RNA was involved in the transfer of memory (11–25). These experiments created tremendous excitement in the popular press and a general uproar in the scientific community. The question was, what was being transferred? Was it memory or was it something else? Some researchers found that it might not be memory. In other experiments, flatworms received shock but no training to avoid shock. When these shocked flatworms (donors) were fed to others (recipients), the recipients showed improved performance (11–12). This experiment indicates that the memory of avoiding the shock wasn't being transferred, since the donor animals had not been trained to avoid shock. But the story goes on. Contrary to the above study, it was next reported that memory might in fact be transferred, since only donor flatworms that were trained to avoid shock, improved the performance of recipients. In this later study, if the donors received only shock or only light, the recipients did not show any improvement (11–18). Because of the many contradictory results, experiments left unresolved the problem of what was being transferred. Researchers went on to study transfer of memory in rats using extracts of brain RNA or protein. Like the flatworm research, the rat research on memory transfer was conflicting. Results obtained in one laboratory often could not be reproduced in other laboratories or even in the same one (11–18).

More than 10 years have passed since the initial memory transfer experiments. The idea that memory can be transferred or is stored in giant protein molecules has not been abandoned. However, few neuroscientists studying memory today would maintain that this is the only mode or even the major mode of memory storage in the mammalian nervous system (11–19). Although proteins are not generally thought to contain memories, they are certainly thought to play an important role in memory storage. In fact, the role of RNA and proteins in learning has been one of the most intensively researched areas in recent years.

RNA and Protein for Learning

If the formation of RNA does play an important role in learning, then it should be possible to observe increased levels of RNA during learning. How does one observe a biochemical change? One approach has been to inject into the brain a radioactive chemical that binds itself to RNA and makes RNA radioactive. By measuring radioactivity, it is possible to measure changes in the level of RNA. Making RNA radioactive is called **labeling**, and the labeling procedure has been used in one of the most thorough studies of RNA's role in learning (11–10). In this research, the radioactive chemical was injected into the brains of mice shortly before they learned a task. One mouse was then placed into a cage with an electrified floor. The mouse was trained to avoid shock by jumping onto a small ledge when a buzzer sounded. Another mouse, called a **control**, was placed in a similar cage and received the same number of shocks and buzzes but was not trained to avoid the shock. Did the mice trained to avoid the shock have different levels of RNA than the control mice, which recieved no training? The mice that learned to avoid the shock were found to have higher levels of radioactivity labeled RNA in their brain tissue than the control mice. If these results were confirmed by other types of research, they will represent an important step in implicating RNA in learning.

The most well-known experiments on the role of RNA and proteins in learning are those of Hydén and associates (11–14, 11–15). Their results are of special interest because one of the areas in which they found biochemical changes during learning was the hippocampus. They found that a particular protein, S100, increased during learning in certain of the large hippocampal cells. These results take on more significance when added to the finding that hippocampal cells are also active during learning in the rabbit (11–41).

Manipulating RNA and Proteins

If RNA were important for learning, could you improve your memory by taking RNA? There have, in fact, been reports of RNA being administered to aged patients. While the patients were receiving the RNA, they showed improved mental functioning and better memory (11–2). This was an exciting finding, but it cannot be considered evidence that RNA promotes memory storage. There is the

problem of differentiating between RNA's effects on learning and on performance. The RNA may have improved "memory" in the elderly patients through general effects on attention, arousal, or motivation, all of which influence performance.

Is it possible to give someone a pill that would impair memory? If protein synthesis (directed by RNA) is important for learning, a treatment that blocks RNA or protein synthesis should interfere with learning. Few questions have been researched as thoroughly. Thousands of goldfish, mice, and rats have been injected with drugs that inhibit protein synthesis and then tested on learning tasks. The initial results of this type of research were extremely exciting (11–9). If mice were injected with a protein inhibitor and then trained to avoid an area where the floor was electrified, they could remember the task for several minutes to an hour after training. However, they could not remember when tested several hours later. Drugs injected *before* training usually did not impair performance or short-term memory of the task, but did impair *long-term memory*. These findings led to the conclusion that protein synthesis does not play a role in short-term memory, but is involved in the consolidation of long-term memory.

The drugs used to block protein synthesis are very toxic to the animal. Drugs such as puromycin may cause the animal to be sick or to have convulsions. Another drug currently used to inhibit protein synthesis, anisomycin, is thought to be less toxic (11–9, 11–39, 11–40). The drug's toxicity makes it difficult to determine whether the effect on long-term memory is due to interference with protein synthesis or is the result of the animal feeling sick. In spite of these problems, some investigators argue that the bulk of evidence indicates that blocking protein synthesis interferes with long-term memory (11–9).

Changes at the Synapse

While walking through the zoo, you learn the name of a small, fuzzy brown animal called *koala*. You repeat the name over and over to remember it. As you are learning the name *koala*, there are probably changes in your RNA and protein levels in your hippocampal cells and in other brain areas. Many of these changes are probably occurring at the synapse. Learning involves forming new associations, and one of the places in the brain where stimuli are combined or associated is at the synapse. When you see the koala, the sight of the animal activates many neurons in your brain. These millions of neurons communicate with one another at synapses and produce impressions of small, brown, and fuzzy. After you have repeated the name *koala*, a number of times the name alone can cause you to have these impressions. It is generally assumed that when you learn a new association, or form an engram, changes have occurred at the synapse (11–34). Since communication at the synapse involves chemical transmitters, it is frequently assumed that formation of engrams involves changes in the transmitter system.

It is too difficult to study activity at the synapse during something as complex as learning the name *koala*. Instead, researchers are studying what happens at the synapse during a very simple response: if a neuron is stimulated over and over, there is a decrease in activity at the synapse. This decrease in activity, habituation, is studied in simple animals such as the Aplysia, a sea animal, and in the spinal cord of the frog (11–3, 11–8). What happens at these synapses during habituation may be a model for what happens at the synapse during complex learning. It is generally agreed that the decrease in activity (habituation) at the synapse from repeated stimulation is caused by a change in the presynaptic mechanisms, rather than in postsynaptic mechanisms (11–3, 11–8). Also, the habituation does not result because the transmitter is used up or depleted, but because there is less transmitter secreted with repeated stimulation. These changes at the synapse are referred to as **synaptic plasticity**. This type of plasticity may be one of the events that occurs at the synapse during formation of the engram for *koala*.

Stress Hormones and Memory

You can almost always remember the embarrassing moments that have happened to you. Contrast this ease of recall with trying to remember the names of the new people you met last week. One explanation for this difference in recall involves hormones secreted during stress. There is evidence that hormones secreted during stress may facilitate memory storage (11–7). As explained in Chapter 3, in times of stress, the anterior pituitary secretes ACTH, or adrenocorticotrophic hormone. When the anterior pituitary is removed, rats learn poorly. Injections of ACTH serve to restore their learning ability (11–5, 11–7). Further, this influence on learning seems to be a direct effect of ACTH itself, rather than of the hormones that ACTH caused to be released from the adrenal gland. We can conclude this because ACTH continues to affect learning even if the adrenal gland is removed. Parts of the ACTH molecule, called **ACTH fractions**, have also been shown to affect protein synthesis in the brain. When an ACTH fraction was infused into normal men, it caused improved visual memory. This improved memory seemed to result from improved attention (11–38). Research with ACTH and learning suggests that ACTH may facilitate the physical changes (plasticity) necessary for learning (11–7), it may facilitate retrieval of memory (11–33), or it may improve attention (11–38). You may have remembered that embarrassing event because ACTH facilitated plasticity in your brain or because it caused you to pay more attention.

Environment-Altered Brain

Although the child was 12, she seemed no more developed than a 5-year-old. She had not been allowed to play with other children, to go to school, to watch television, or to engage in the hundreds of activities children usually do. For her 12 years, she had been kept in a closet. In addition to stunting her socially, intellectually, and psychologically, this extreme deprivation possibly could have affected her brain. Animal research seems to indicate that isolation can result in less than normal brain development.

Shortly after weaning, when they were approximately 21 days old, some rats were isolated in individual cages. Other rats were grouped together in a large cage that contained many toys for sniffing, climbing, biting, and general interacting. These latter rats were said to be in an **enriched** environment. After 30 days, the brains of the isolated rats were compared with those of the enriched rats. The different environments had caused different brain development. Compared with the isolated rats, the enriched rats had a heavier cortex, especially the occipital cortex. They had a greater amount of metabolic activity, as indicated by an increased ratio of RNA to DNA. They had a greater amount of biochemical activity as indicated by an increase in the enzyme acetylcholinesterase (ah-SEE-til-ko-lin-ESS-ter-aze), which is involved in destroying the neurotransmitter acetylcholine. Their brains showed more branching of dendrites, which are involved in receiving information from other neurons. And the enriched rats had evidence of new synaptic formations (11–1, 11–11, 11–35).

One of the most exciting findings in this research is that some of the changes can also be produced in adult animals placed in an enriched environment. What caused these changes? The increased cortical weight and biochemical and enzymatic activity were not caused by handling the rats, nor by stressing them by tumbling, nor by depriving them of visual stimulation by blinding (11–1). None of these manipulations caused the same brain changes as those produced from being raised in an enriched environment. The important factor seemed to be the animals' experience with the environment. The investigators would not claim that these brain changes resulted from experience or learning, but that is certainly the most interesting possibility. One author suggested that perhaps hormonal or nutritional influences resulting from being in an enriched environment caused the changes (11–11).

Since enriched rats have heavier cortexes and increased biochemical and enzymatic activity, are they more intelligent? Are they faster learners? Compared with isolated rats, enriched rats generally make fewer errors when learning the correct path through a maze (11–11). On other tasks, enriched rats have not consistently been shown to be faster learners. However, one of the difficulties in determining whether enriched rats are more intelligent is finding tasks that are sensitive enough to measure an improvement in learning.

So far, brain changes resulting from isolated or enriched environments have not been demonstrated in humans. If, in the future, the results are shown to be the same for humans, it would mean that an enriched environment could cause beneficial brain changes. An enhanced environment, with greater opportunity for experience and learning, may actually cause brain changes that improve learning capacity.

Comment

When H.M. hears a joke the first time, it is new and very funny. When he hears it the second time, it is still new and funny. When you hear a joke the second time, it is never as funny. You have a neural record or engram of the joke, while H.M. does not. Unlike H.M., you will have some degree of memory for the joke unless something happened to interrupt your neural processes immediately after you heard it. A blow to the head could destroy the memory of a joke by interfering with consolidation.

If we had recorded the activity of cells in your hippocampus while you learned a joke, we might have found the earliest signs of the engram. If we had recorded the RNA levels in your brain during this same period, we might have found that they were different. Although we know that physical changes underlie memory, at present it seems unlikely that you would be able to swallow a pill that contained the chemical memories for a new joke.

SELF-TEST 11

1 When you cannot remember events that occurred before some trauma to your nervous system, you are suffering from _____ amnesia. — *retrograde*

2 The memory loss for a long period (days) preceding an accident is usually a problem of _____ rather than actual _____ of the memory. — *retrieval* / *loss*

3 If the memory loss is permanent, we would say that _____ has occurred. If the memory loss is not permanent and the memory returns, the problem was one of _____. — *forgetting* / *retrieval*

4 Events occurring immediately before a blow to the head may never be placed in _____ memory because the process known as _____ did not occur. — *long-term* / *consolidation*

5 According to the consolidation hypothesis, it requires _____ for memories to become fixed in _____ storage. — *time* / *long-term*

6 After you learn what an engram is, a car drives through your room. You may not remember what an engram is because of the disruption. When previous learning is disrupted by a new event, it is called _____. — *retroactive interference*

7 According to Hebb's theory, you remember a new phone number for a few minutes because the event is being _____ in your nervous system. During short-term memory, impulses continue to circulate through _____ circuits. — *replayed or repeated* / *reverberating*

8 In Hebb's view, this short-term activity is necessary for the _____ of long-term memory. As the impulses continue to reverberate through the circuit, they cause structural or physical changes at the _____. — *consolidation* / *synapses*

9 When rats were given electroconvulsive shock (ECD) after learning a task, the closer to training the ECS occurred, the more _____ was the retrograde amnesia. — *severe or complete*

10 If memory consolidation requires continued neural activity, then drugs that _____ neural activity should improve learning. — *stimulate*

11 There is general agreement that consolidation requires at least _____. There is some evidence that it may still be in progress at _____. But there is little evidence that it is still in progress after _____. — *10–15 seconds* / *15 minutes* / *60 minutes*

12 The physical representation of memory in your brain is known as the _____. — *engram*

13 Lashley's principle of mass action holds that the _____ of cortex removed is critical for memory. His principle of equipotentiality holds that the _____ of the lesion is less important in the rat's brain, or that all areas of the rat's cortex are _____ important. — *amount* / *location* / *equally*

14 After a monkey learns to discriminate between a high tone and a low tone, the auditory association area is removed. Following removal, the monkey can no longer discriminate between tones. This may be because the lesion interfered with _____ or with _____. — *performance or auditory functioning or learning*

15 In human patients, electrical stimulation of the _____ caused the occurrence of memories. This does not necessarily mean that memories are _____ in this area, but it does suggest that the temporal lobe plays a special role in _____. — *temporal lobe* / *stored or located* / *memory*

16 After surgery, H.M. lost his ability for _____ memory. He could remember phrases or numbers briefly, indicating that his _____ was not impaired. — *long-term / short-term* / *memory or attention*

17 From studies on H.M. and chronic alcoholics, it appears that an area important for long-term memory is the _____. — *hippocampus*

18 If the hippocampus is lesioned in animals, they will still be able to learn and remember _____ tasks. This finding in animals is similar to the performance of H.M. on _____ tasks.

perceptual-motor
perceptual-motor

19 An animal learns a task and then has part of its brain lesioned. After the lesion, the animal does poorly on the task. This deficit may be due to the lesion interfering with _____ or _____.

learning / performance

20 If an animal does not show any deficit in performance after a lesion, it may be because the lesion destroyed one _____ but left another intact. Another area of the brain may take over the damaged area's _____ through a process called _____.

system
function / sprouting

21 One way to locate which areas of the brain are active during learning is to record the electrical activity of neurons in different areas. This approach is known as _____.

electrophysiology

22 During classical conditioning of the rabbit's _____ membrane, microelectrodes were placed in the _____.

nictitating
hippocampus

23 In this study, the puff of air was the _____ stimulus and a tone was the _____ stimulus. After a number of trials pairing tone with air puff, the tone was capable of eliciting the _____ response.

unconditioned
conditioned / nictitating
or conditioned

24 When the nictitating response became conditioned to the tone, increased activity was observed in _____ cells. This activity was not observed when only the _____ or only the _____ was presented. This shows that the hippocampal cells were active during the _____ between the tone and the nictitating response.

hippocampal / puff / tone
association

25 It is possible that when you learn something, this learning involves chemical changes in the neuron. Possibly this chemical change occurs in the following way. When you learn something, it triggers chemicals in a neuron to activate a previously inactive strand of _____, which produces _____, which directs the formation of a new _____, which codes the new _____.

DNA or deoxyribonucleic
acid / ribonucleic acid
or messenger RNA
protein / memory

26 When trained flatworms were fed to untrained flatworms, the untrained ones learned the task more quickly. These experiments showed that something was being transferred, but there is no good evidence for transfer of _____.

memory

27 Mice were injected with a radioactive chemical that binds itself to RNA, so that RNA can be measured. Mice that learned to make a response to avoid shock showed _____ levels of brain _____ than mice that received tone and shocks but did not _____ the task.

higher
RNA / learn

28 The experiments of Hydén and associates have shown that during learning there is an increase in a particular _____ that occurs in certain cells of the _____.

protein / hippocampus

29 When a drug that inhibits protein synthesis is injected before training, it usually does not impair _____ but does interfere with _____. One of the problems with using these drugs is that they often make the animal _____.

short-term memory
long-term memory or
consolidation / sick

30 If some neurons are stimulated repeatedly, there is a decrease in activity at the synapse. This is called _____. This decrease in activity seems to involve a change in the _____ neuron and a decrease in the amount of _____ released.

habituation / presynaptic
transmitter

31 When you are stressed, the anterior pituitary secretes _____. If the pituitary is removed, rats show _____ learning unless they are injected with _____.

ACTH or
adrenocorticotrophic
hormone / poorer /
ACTH

32 Some investigators think that this hormone plays a special role in the _____ necessary for learning. Others think the hormone affects primarily _____.

conditions or plasticity
retrieval or attention

33 When rats are raised in an _____ environment, their brains show heavier _____. Their brains also show increased _____ and _____. (Give two.)

enriched / cortex /
metabolic activity or
biochemical activity or
branching dendrites or
synaptic connections

34 These changes could not be attributed to _____ or _____. (Give two.) The important feature seems to be the rats' _____ with the environment; thus, the brain changes might have resulted from _____.

handling or stress or
visual stimulation
experience / learning

REFERENCES

11–1 Bennett, E. L. Cerebral effects of differential experience and training. In M. R. Rosenzweig and E. L. Bennett (Eds.), *Neural mechanisms of learning and memory*. Cambridge, Mass: MIT Press, 1976.

11–2 Cameron, D. E. and Solyom, L. Effects of ribonucleic acid on memory. *Geriatrics* 1961, 16: 74–81.

11–3 Castellucci, V. F. and Kandel, E. R. A quantal analysis of the synaptic depression underlying habituation of the gill-withdrawal reflex in *Aplysia*. *Proceedings of the National Academy of Sciences (USA)* 1974, 71: 5004–5008.

11–4 Chorover, S. An experimental critique of ''consolidation studies'' and an alternative ''model-systems'' approach to the biophysiology of memory. In M. R. Rosenzweig and E. L. Bennett (Eds.), *Neural mechanisms of learning and memory*. Cambridge, Mass: MIT Press, 1976.

11–5 DeWied, D. Pituitary-adrenal system hormones and behavior. In F. O. Schmitt and F. G. Worden (Eds.), *The neurosciences: third study program*. Cambridge, Mass: MIT Press, 1974.

11–6 Duncan, C. P. The retroactive effect of electroshock on learning. *Journal of Comparative and Physiological Psychology* 1949, 42: 32–44.

11–7 Dunn, A. J. Biochemical correlates of training experiences: a discussion of the evidence. In M. R. Rosenzweig and E. L. Bennett (Eds.), *Neural mechanisms of learning and memory*. Cambridge, Mass: MIT Press, 1976.

11–8 Farel, P. B. and Thompson, R. F. Habituation of a monosynaptic response in frog spinal cord: evidence for a presynaptic mechanism. *Journal of Neurophysiology* 1976, 39: 661–666.

11–9 Flood, J. F. and Jarvik, M. E. Drug influences on learning and memory. In M. R. Rosenzweig and E. L. Bennett (Eds.), *Neural mechanisms of learning and memory*. Cambridge, Mass: MIT Press, 1976.

11–10 Glassman, E. and Wilson, J. E. The incorporation of uridine into brain RNA during short experiences. *Brain Research* 1970, 21: 157–168.

11–11 Greenough, W. T. Enduring brain effects of differential experience and training. In M. R. Rosenzweig and E. L. Bennett (Eds.), *Neural mechanisms of learning and memory*. Cambridge, Mass: MIT Press, 1976.

11–12 Hartry, A. L., Keith-Lee, P., and Morton, W. D. Planaria: memory transfer through cannibalism re-examined. *Science* 1964, 146: 274–275.

11–13 Hebb, D. O. *The organization of behavior*. New York: Wiley, 1949.

11–14 Hydén, H. and Lange, P. Protein synthesis in the hippocampal pyramidal cells in rats during a behavioral test. *Science* 1968, 159: 1370–1373.

11–15 Hydén, H. and Lange, P. S100 protein: correlations with behavior. *Proceedings of the National Academy of Sciences (USA)* 1970, 67: 1959–1966.

11–16 Isaacson, R. L. Experimental brain lesions and memory. In M. R. Rosenzweig and E. L. Bennett (Eds.), *Neural mechanisms of learning and memory*. Cambridge, Mass: MIT Press, 1976.

11–17 Isaacson, R. L. Hippocampal destruction in man and other animals. *Neurophychologia* 1972, 10: 47–64.

11–18 Jacobson, A. L. and Schlecter, J. M. Chemical transfer of training: three years later. In K. H. Pribram and D. E. Broadbent (Eds.), *Biology of memory*. New York: Academic Press, 1970.

11–19 Kety, S. S. Biological concomitants of affective states and their possible role in memory processes. In M. R. Rosenzweig and E. L. Bennett (Eds.), *Neural mechanisms of learning and memory*. Cambridge, Mass: MIT Press, 1976.

11–20 Lashley, K. S. *Brain mechanisms and intelligence*. Chicago: University of Chicago Press, 1929.

11–21 Luttges, M. W. and McGaugh, J. L. Permanence of retrograde amnesia produced by electroconvulsive shock. In J. L. McGaugh and M. J. Herz (Eds.), *Memory Consolidation*. San Francisco: Albion Publishing Co., 1972.

11–22 Lynch, G. Some difficulties associated with the use of lesion techniques in the study of memory. In M. R. Rosenzweig and E. L. Bennett (Eds.), *Neural mechanisms of learning and memory*. Cambridge, Mass: MIT Press, 1976.

11–23 Lynch, G., Gall, C., Rose, G., and Cotman, C. Changes in the distribution of the dentate gyrus associational system following unilateral or bilateral entorhinal lesions in the adult rat. *Brain Research* 1976, 110: 57–71.

11–24 McConnell, J. V., Jacobson, R., and Humphries, B. M. The effects of ingestion of conditioned planaria on the response level of naive planaria. *Worm Runner's Digest* 1961, 3: 41–45.

11–25 McConnell, J. V., Schigehisa, T., and Salive, H. Attempts to transfer approach and avoidance responses by RNA injections in rats. In K. H. Pribram and D. E. Broadbent (Eds.), *Biology of memory*. New York: Academic Press, 1970.

11–26 McGaugh, J. L. Neurobiology and the future of education. *School Review* 1976, 85: 166–175.

11–27 McGaugh, J. L. and Herz, M. J. *Memory consolidation*. San Francisco: Albion Publishing Co., 1972.

11–28 Milner, B. Amnesia following operation on the temporal lobes. In C. W. M. Witty and O. L. Zangwill (Eds.), *Amnesia*. New York: Appleton-Century Crofts, 1966.

11–29 Milner, B. Memory and the medial temporal regions of the brain. In K. H. Pribram and D. E. Broadbent (Eds.), *Biology of memory*. New York: Academic Press, 1970.

11–30 Müller, G. E. and Pilzecker, A. Experimentelle Beitrage zur Lehre vom Gedachtniss, *Z. Psychol.*, 1, 326–330. Cited by J. L. McGaugh and M. J. Herz, *Memory consolidation*, San Francisco: Albion Publishing Co., 1972.

11–31 Penfield, W. and Perot, P. H. The brain's record of auditory and visual experience—a final summary and discussion. *Brain* 1963, 86: 595–696.

REFERENCES *(cont.)*

11–32   Raisman, G. The reaction of synaptogenesis in the central and peripheral nervous systems of the adult rat. In M. R. Rosenzweig and E. L. Bennett (Eds.), *Neural mechanisms of learning and memory*. Cambridge, Mass: MIT Press, 1976.

11–33   Rigter, H. and Van Riezen, H. Anti-amnesic effect of ACTH–[4-10:] its independence of the nature of the amnesic agent and the behavioral test. *Physiology and Behavior* 1975, 14: 563–566.

11–34   Rosenzweig, M. R. and Bennett, E. L. (Eds.), *Neural mechanisms of learning and memory*. Cambridge, Mass: MIT Press, 1976.

11–35   Rosenzweig, M. R., Bennett, E. L., and Diamond, M. C. Brain changes in response to experience. *Scientific American* 1972, 226: 22–29.

11–36   Rozin, P. The psychobiological approach to human memory. In M. R. Rosenzweig and E. L. Bennett (Eds.), *Neural mechanisms of learning and memory*. Cambridge, Mass: MIT Press, 1976.

11–37   Russell, W. R. and Nathan, P. W. Traumatic amnesia, *Brain* 1946, 69: 280–300.

11–38   Sandman, C. A., George, J. M., Nolan, J. D., Van Riezen, H., and Kastin, A. J. Enhancement of attention in man with ACTH/MSH 4-10. *Physiology and Behavior* 1975, 15: 427–431.

11–39   Squire, L. R. and Davis, H. P. Cerebral protein synthesis inhibition and discrimination training: effects of extent and duration of inhibition. *Behavioral Biology* 1975, 13: 49–57.

11–40   Squire, L. R., St. John, S., and Davis, H. Inhibitors of protein synthesis and memory: dissociation of amnesic effects and effects on adrenal steroidogenesis. *Brain Research* 1976, 112: 200–206.

11–41   Thompson, R. F. The search for the engram. *American Psychologist* 1976, 31: 209–227.

Human Brain and Higher Functions

12

One Brain Is Actually Two

Split Brain

She watched as Carl left the hospital. For the first time in 10 years, he was free of seizures. He seemed so relaxed, so normal that it puzzled her. The surgeons had literally split Carl's brain in two. She wondered which brain listened when she talked to him, which brain laughed when she told him a joke, and which brain took credit for beating her at checkers. Through the weeks, he carried on as usual: he dressed himself, went for walks, answered the phone, and read a novel. Their friends did not notice anything different about him. She was much relieved.

One morning, she entered the bedroom as he was dressing. Standing quietly in the doorway, she watched a strange spectacle. One of Carl's hands was pulling his pants up while his other hand was pulling them down. After several ups and downs, one hand finally succeeded in pulling the pants up. She wondered if he were joking or if his two separate brains were have a disagreement.

She forgot about this incident until one afternoon when they were in the kitchen. They were disagreeing about what to have for lunch. Suddenly, Carl grabbed her shoulder with his left hand and began to shake her violently. She was afraid and knew he was not joking. As his left hand continued to shake her, she saw that his right was trying to stop his left hand. The shaking stopped as the right hand gained control over the left. A few minutes later, they were conversing normally, as if nothing had happened.

Most days passed without incident. In fact, Carl was usually as normal as anyone. One afternoon they were playing horseshoes in the backyard and Carl was losing. When he finished his last throw, he walked over to the side of the house and picked up an ax that happened to be lying

there. She ran into the house and waited. After a while, he came into the house and asked for a sandwich. She wondered which brain had picked up the ax and what it was going to do with it. Perhaps he was only going to return it to the garage. She could not help thinking that sometimes Carl's right brain did not know what his left brain was doing.

This description of Carl is based on an actual case report. Carl and other patients who had this surgery were seeking treatment for uncontrollable epileptic seizures (12–12). In their cases, drugs were not effective, and a drastic surgical treatment was attempted: the brain was split in two.

Operation

Carl's seizures began with abnormal neural activity in one hemisphere of the brain. This electrical activity would spread on nerve tracts into the adjacent hemisphere, excite more neurons, and result in an epileptic seizure. His doctor thought that if the spread of abnormal electrical activity between hemispheres could be stopped, the seizures might be prevented. This was the idea behind treating seizures by splitting the brain in two.

After the surgeon removed the top of Carl's skull, she gently pried apart the two hemispheres of his brain. The two hemispheres are separated by the longitudinal fissure. Looking down into the longitudinal fissure, the surgeon saw a large white band of fibers that connect the right and left hemispheres, the corpus callosum. The surgeon cut the corpus callosum as well as several other smaller tracts connecting the hemispheres. The result was a brain split into two separate hemispheres: the right hemisphere was isolated

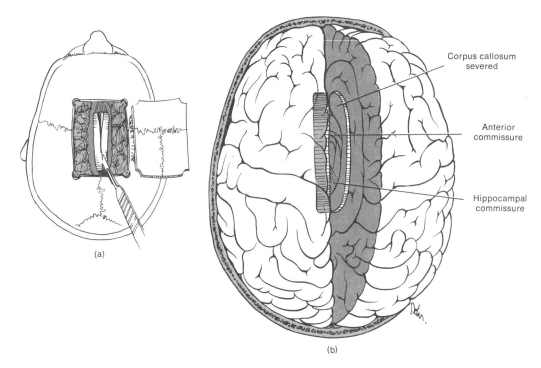

Figure 12-1 The corpus callosum connects the two hemispheres. (a) A section of the skull has been removed and the two hemispheres have been separated to show the location of the corpus callosum. (b) Part of the brain has been removed to show the corpus callosum.

Corpus callosum
severed

Anterior
commissure

Hippocampal
commissure

(a)

(b)

from the left. Normally the right hemisphere communicates with the left hemisphere and vice versa by more than 200 million interconnecting fibers. With many of these connecting fibers cut, the two hemispheres cannot communicate, each hemisphere can function independently, and the result can be the right hand pulling down your pants while the left is pulling them up. With the hemispheres isolated from each other, it is possible to test each one and discover its function. What can Carl's right hemisphere do that his left cannot? What is it like to live in a head that has two separate brains?

Split-Brain Behavior

Six months after Carl's split-brain operation, the average person could not tell from Carl's behavior that his brain had been divided in two. Two years after surgery, a split-brain person can pass a routine medical exam without being detected. Following this operation, there is usually no noticeable change in speech, intelligence, personality, or temperament (12–31). Only infrequently are the two divided hemispheres seen in conflict, as when one hand contradicts the other. In fact, it was first thought that splitting the corpus callosum had little effect on behavior. Only after special psychological tests were devised, did it become clear that the right hemisphere did not know what the left hemisphere was doing and vice versa. It became clear that each hemisphere was specialized in certain functions.

Speaking

Only Carl's left hemisphere could speak. His right hemisphere was mute. This is true for most people, since their speech areas are usually located in their left hemispheres. It is estimated that 70 percent of the general population are right-handers, and of these, the vast majority (95 percent) have the speech area located in the left hemisphere. The remaining 30 percent of the population are either left-handers or ambidextrous. Of these, the majority also have the speech area located in the left hemisphere. Some, however, have the speech area located in the right hemisphere, and a few others have speech areas in both hemispheres (12–36). So almost all right-handers and the majority of left-handers have the speech area located in the left hemisphere. This means that if you were right-handed and a stroke damaged your left hemisphere, you would probably have difficulty speaking. If you were right-handed and a stroke damaged your right hemisphere, you probably would have few, if any, speaking problems.

One of the reasons that Carl seemed normal after the split-brain operation was that his left hemisphere continued to speak and carry on conversations as usual. How do we know that his left hemisphere but not his right can speak? By projecting an image to only one side of the visual area, or field, it is possible to project that image to only one hemisphere. A picture of a rabbit could be projected to Carl's left hemisphere. If asked to name what he saw, he would say, "I saw a rabbit." If a picture of a spoon were projected to his right hemisphere, Carl may answer, ''I saw nothing'' or ''I saw an orange.'' Since Carl's left hemisphere would not see the spoon, his left hemisphere would respond correctly that it saw nothing. But could the right hemisphere actually see the spoon? In addition to being mute, perhaps it cannot recognize objects. Carl is blindfolded and given a box of objects. He is told to reach into the box and pick out the object he saw. He reaches into the box with his left hand because the right hemisphere controls the left hand. Reaching into the box with his left hand, he feels each object and picks out a spoon. The right hemisphere cannot speak, but it can recognize and identify objects by touching or by pointing.

Although the major connections between the hemispheres have been cut, the right hemisphere still receives information and controls the left side of the body and the left hemisphere receives information and controls the right side of the body. This is so because the motor and sensory nerves cross over in the brain stem, and these connections have not been cut. Since the hemispheres are separated, it is possible for each hand to search simultaneously for a

different object that has been shown to its controlling hemisphere. If the right hemisphere sees a key and the left sees a ball, the left hand (right hemisphere) will sort through the objects and pick out a key, while at the same time, the right hand (left hemisphere) will sort through the same objects and select a ball. While searching for these objects, neither hemisphere knew what the other was looking for. When separated, the two hemispheres function independently, and only the left can tell you verbally what is on its mind.

Reading

Carl was seated before the projector that would flash words into the left hemisphere. Whether the words were *steak*, *carrot*, or *bike* (nouns), *sizzling*, *yellow*, or *fast* (adjectives), or *eat*, *grow*, or *ride* (verbs), the left hemisphere had no difficulty in reading or verbally identifying the words.

When words were projected to his right hemisphere, Carl could read *dog*, *cat*, or *carrot* and could point out (using his left hand) this object on a card containing several ob-

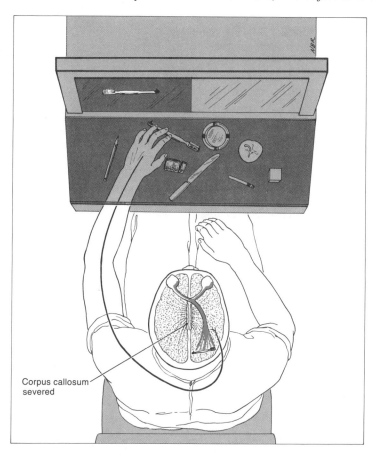

Corpus callosum severed

Figure 12–2 The corpus callosum has been cut in this patient. As he stares straight ahead, a toothbrush is projected briefly on the screen at the far left. This means that the visual information of the toothbrush will be sent to the right hemisphere only. If the subject is asked what he has seen, he may say "nothing" or guess "an apple" because the left hemisphere has not seen the object and in this patient only the left hemisphere can speak. But if the subject is asked to identify the object by touch, he can use his left hand (controlled by the right hemisphere) to correctly pick out the toothbrush from among various objects that are under the counter.

Split-Brain Behavior

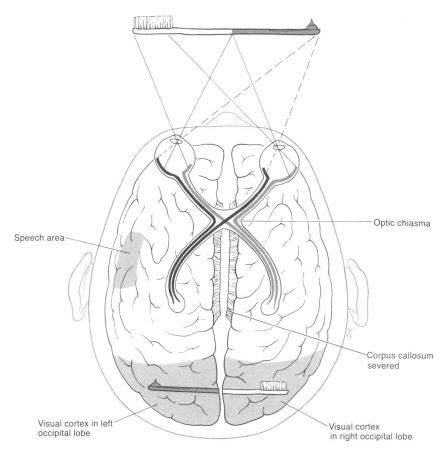

Figure 12-3 In this person the corpus callosum has been cut and the speech area is located in the left hemisphere. If he looks straight ahead at the toothbrush, half of it will be projected to his right hemisphere and half to his left hemisphere. If he were asked what he was looking at, he would reply a handle since that is all the left hemisphere sees. This is a schematic drawing of what happens in the brain.

jects. The right hemisphere could read some adjectives, but not all. Also, if the right hemisphere were shown the word *smile*, and Carl was asked to do what the word indicated, he could not. Carl's right hemisphere had difficulty reading verbs. When the verbs *chew* or *knock* were shown to the left hemisphere, Carl could do the appropriate behaviors, but when these words were shown to the right hemisphere, he could not. The right hemisphere can read nouns, some adjectives, and few if any verbs. The ability to read is more localized in the left hemisphere than in the right.

Writing

Using the special visual-field procedure, a picture of a kangaroo is shown to Carl's left hemisphere. After being told to write the name of the object, he writes kangaroo with his right hand. He has no difficulty in writing the names of objects shown to his left hemisphere or in saying what he saw.

Using the same procedure, a picture of an owl is shown to Carl's right hemisphere. When he is told to write the

name of the object, we find that he cannot write anything with his left hand—he cannot write *owl*. The right hemisphere is mute and usually cannot write.

Spelling

Even though the right hemisphere seems to have difficulty writing, it is able to spell simple words. Using his left hand (right hemisphere), Carl can feel large letters and then spell simple words such as *cup*, *love*, and *not*. In one of the spelling tests given Carl, something very interesting happened. Carl was told to spell the word *dog* using his left hand (right hemisphere). Although the right hemisphere was working on the problem, the left hemisphere had overheard the instructions. During the spelling test, the left hemisphere kept up a running conversation. Knowing that the right hemisphere was trying to spell *dog*, the left hemisphere kept trying to guess what the letters were. Carl's left hand would hold the letter *d* and he would say (his left hemisphere would say) that he was holding an *o*. In spite of what his left hemisphere was saying, which was often wrong, the

Human Brain and Higher Functions

right hemisphere went about the task of correctly spelling the word *dog*. This is remarkable. It means that the right hemisphere not only has its own ability to think and to spell but it can do so in spite of the left hemisphere's distracting comments, wild guesses, and general interference. Although the right hemisphere does have this limited capacity for spelling, it is still the left hemisphere that wins the spelling bees.

Emotional Behavior

Do both hemispheres have a sense of humor? A female patient with a split brain was watching a series of images being projected to her right hemisphere. Placed among the routine set of slides was one of a nude woman. When she saw this slide, the patient broke into a smile. When asked what was funny, she said (her left hemisphere said) she did not know. That is because the left hemisphere had not seen the slide. When the same slide was shown to her left hemisphere, she laughed and said that it was funny to see this slide placed among the others (12–12). From this example, it is apparent that both hemispheres have the capacity to experience emotions. Is there any difference in the kind of emotions controlled by the right or left hemispheres?

When asked to pick out the funniest cartoon in a selection, patients with brain damage to either their right or left hemispheres (not split-brains) were less able to do so than normals. However, the behavior of patients with damage to the right hemisphere was even more unusual. They tended to have one or two reactions: either they laughed at

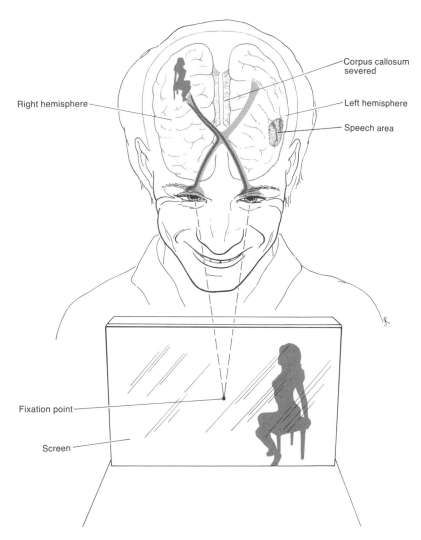

Figure 12–4 A patient with his corpus callosum severed was watching a series of pictures of common objects. He stared straight ahead and the pictures were presented briefly on his far left so that this visual information went only to the right hemisphere. Suddenly, among the pictures, a slide of a nude woman was presented. When he saw this, he smiled, indicating that the right hemisphere could experience emotions. When asked to explain why he was smiling, he could not explain because only the left hemisphere could speak and it had not seen the nude.

nearly every cartoon, whether or not they understood it, or, more often, they showed little emotional reaction, even when they understood the meaning of the cartoon. These and other studies have led some investigators to conclude that the right hemisphere is more important for emotional behavior (12–8, 12–11). However, it is very difficult to interpret what it means when brain-damaged people respond inappropriately to cartoons. Their reactions could be related to perceptual impairments, in that they can see the cartoons but cannot associate or perceive any humor in the cartoons. Or their reactions could be related to impairments in having appropriate feelings, and they may perceive many situations as funny when they are not.

Hemisphere Functions

From studies on individuals with split brains and on others with brain damage, it is possible to gain some idea of which kind of behaviors are predominantly controlled by each hemisphere. The left hemisphere controls the ability to speak and write and is superior at reading, spelling, language skills, and mathematical calculations. It can experience emotions, think, and reason. Behaviors for which left hemisphere performance is poor include recognizing melodies, drawing figures, or assembling blocks into a specific pattern. These latter skills require spatial organization, and the left hemisphere is inferior in this capacity.

The right hemisphere can read, spell, and use language skills with approximately the same ability as a 5- to 7-year-old child (12–22). It can do simple mathematical calculations, can experience emotions, and can think and reason. The right hemisphere cannot speak a sound unless the person happens to be one of the small percentage of people who have the speech area located in the right hemisphere. Compared with the left hemisphere, the right hemisphere is superior at drawing figures and maps or assembling blocks into a specific pattern. These latter tasks involve spatial organization, at which the right hemisphere is superior. It is also superior at recognizing melodies. The right hemisphere seems to be involved in the way you think of your body, or how you form your body image, since damage to the right hemisphere may result in people denying the existence of the left side of their body or improperly dressing the left side (12–10, 12–16).

Each hemisphere is specialized for certain functions. At one time, it was thought that the left hemisphere was the dominant hemisphere because of its speech and language abilities. That is no longer considered to be true, since each hemisphere excels at some behaviors and not at others. If you were a poet, you would certainly need your left hemisphere to write poetry. On the other hand, if you were a musician, you would need your right hemisphere to play melodies. It is not known why certain functions reside in one hemisphere and not in the other. One explanation for the evolution of hemispheric differences is that having separate and complementary functions prevents unnecessary duplications and makes the brain more efficient (12–16).

How the Brain Compensates
Cross-Cuing

The youngest patient to undergo a split-brain operation was 13 years old. During the first couple of years following the operation, he could not verbally identify the objects or words shown to his right hemisphere. Seven years later, he could verbally identify from one to three numbers or letters shown to his right hemisphere. It is possible that his right hemisphere developed some ability to speak, but it is more likely that the right hemisphere relearned how to communicate with the left hemisphere. Consider the following example. Using the special visual-field procedure, a red or green light is flashed to Carl's right hemisphere. He is asked to guess the color, and, since the left hemisphere did not see the color but does the talking, the guesses are as often right as wrong. But if Carl is permitted to correct himself, he can usually get the color right. Here is the sequence that probably happens. The right hemisphere sees the color red. Asked to guess the color, the left hemisphere may say "red." When the right hemisphere hears this response, it knows it is correct and does not try to interfere. On the other hand, if the left hemisphere says "green," the right hemisphere hears the response and knows that it is incorrect. The right hemisphere might then frown or shake the head, which cues the left hemisphere that it has guessed the wrong color. The left hemisphere can then correct its guess to "red." As this example shows, the right hemisphere can communicate with the left hemisphere through a series of nonverbal cues (frown, smile, head shake, blush). This communication is called **cross-cuing**. During the 7 years following his surgery, the patient described above presumably became so good at cross-cuing that he could verbally identify letters shown to his right hemisphere (12–13).

Assuming New Functions

There have been cases of individuals born without a corpus callosum but with several of the lesser connections between the hemispheres. If the hemispheres have been isolated from each other from birth, how does the brain compensate for this lack of communication? When those born without corpus callosums were tested, the findings were startling. These people could write with both hands, draw pictures with both hands, make designs from blocks with both hands, and speak with both hemispheres (12–6, 12–31). Since they could use both hands to write and draw, it means that both hemispheres had developed a function that normally develops in only one hemisphere. The same can be said for speech. The fact that they could speak with both hemispheres suggests that both hemispheres are initially capable of developing speech, and that specialization develops only if the corpus callosum is intact (12–27). These examples indicate that the brain is not a fixed group of neurons, capable of serving one function. Rather, the brain is flexible and can compensate for damage (no corpus callosum) by assuming another function (language in the right hemisphere) or by learning to communicate in nonverbal ways (cross-cuing).

Sprouting

After damage to the brain, a person may find it difficult to speak or write or walk. Some months later, he may have recovered some of these abilities. What happens in the brain to permit these behaviors to return after the damage? The occurrence of a stroke often causes widespread damage, destroying some neurons outright and causing others to be temporarily out of order. Neurons that are temporarily affected may return to normal functioning, and their return may be accompanied by some return in behavior (decreased paralysis, some ability to speak). Recovery of function after damage may also occur as the other parts of the brain learn to take on new functions. When nerve cells or parts of nerve cells in the brain are destroyed, they never return. However, from animal work, there is evidence that undamaged neurons send out new extensions to compensate for the loss (12–19). This increase in neural connections, or sprouting, may be one way the brain compensates for damage and loss of function. Because the brain can compensate for damage in several ways, it is very difficult to predict how many or which functions will return following brain damage. It is known that the brain of a younger person is better able to compensate for damage than the brain of an older person.

Consciousness

Each hemisphere can react to its environment with complex responses, can think, reason, and communicate its awareness. If you remember the spelling test, the right hemisphere proceeded systematically with its own goals (spelling the word) even though the left hemisphere kept up a running conversation and tried to help but really was interfering. The occurrence of separate goals in the two hemispheres was also observed in a split-brain patient when the left hemisphere (right hand) worked on a block-arranging task at which the right hemisphere was better. The right hemisphere (left hand) kept trying to help the left hemisphere (right hand). Finally, the patient's left hemisphere (right hand) grabbed the left hand and had the person sit on it so that it could work on the task without further interference. Evidence from split-brain monkeys also shows that each hemisphere can have its own separate goals. Split-brain monkeys were capable of working simultaneously at two different tasks (12–12). These experiments suggest that each hemisphere has its own state of consciousness and its own goals.

Some individuals never achieve **consciousness**, by which we usually mean self-awareness. They can sleep and wake, react to loud sounds and gross visual stimuli by movement of eyes and facial muscles, can smile, cry, and make crude sounds. They never become conscious in the sense of responding to other people or their environment with anything more than reflexive responses. These individuals are born without any cerebral cortex. Their brains are normally developed up to the level of the thalamus, but beyond that there is nothing—no cortex, and thus no sense of consciousness (12–3, 12–34). Interactions between the cortex, reticular formation, and related brain areas are necessary for the awareness of yourself that is consciousness.

Following severe damage to the cortex, a person may remain alive because the life-sustaining reflexes (breathing, blood pressure, heart rate) are located in the brain stem. In fact, medical technology can maintain unconscious individuals for long periods of time even when brain damage is so severe that they have lost many life-sustaining reflexes. If these patients have no EEG waves, it indicates that the cerebral cortex is severely damaged, and it is extremely unlikely that consciousness will return. That is why many states have now passed laws which define death according to brain function rather than heart function. The ability to be conscious and interact with your environment involves the cerebral cortex. If there are no EEG waves, the cortex is dead and there can be no consciousness.

Anesthetizing a Hemisphere

It is possible to cause a temporary and reversible split-brain situation. It is possible to anesthetize one complete hemisphere—that is, make it unconscious—while the other hemisphere is conscious and functioning. A barbiturate, sodium amylobarbital, can be injected into the blood supply of one side of the brain. The brain receives its blood supply from two arteries: the right carotid supplies the right hemisphere, and the left carotid supplies the left hemisphere. If a barbiturate is injected into the left carotid, the left hemisphere will temporarily be anesthetized or unconscious and will cease to function. The anesthetic effects may last several minutes. If a right-handed person is speaking, and a barbiturate is injected into the left carotid, the person will probably cease talking. This happens because the left hemisphere is anesthetized and no longer is able to function. After a few minutes, the anesthesia wears off and the left hemisphere again resumes its normal functions, including speaking. This procedure is named the Wada Test after the investigator who first used it (12–33).

If a person requires surgery to her temporal lobe, the Wada Test is sometimes administered to determine the location of the speech and language areas. If the surgeon is operating on the right temporal lobe, he wants to know if his patient is one of the few people with speech and language areas located in the right hemisphere. If they are located there, he will try to spare as much of these areas as possible.

Using the Wada Test, a patient was studied to determine if the two hemispheres in a normal brain have separate thoughts and memories. The patient was seated in a chair, and a barbiturate was injected into his left carotid to anesthetize his left hemisphere. A spoon was then placed into his left hand, which is controlled by his right hemisphere. After the left hemisphere recovered from the anesthesia, the person was asked to name the object that had been placed into his left hand. The patient said (his left hemisphere said), "Nothing." Next the patient was asked to use his left hand (right hemisphere) and point to the correct object on a card containing pictures of many objects. The left hand correctly pointed to a spoon. The memory of the spoon is stored only in the right hemisphere, and even though the corpus callosum is intact, the left hemisphere cannot gain access to that memory (12–13). This case shows that the hemispheres in the normal brain may in fact have separate ideas, memories, and thoughts. It is conceivable that even in normal individuals the hemispheres do, at times, function independently.

Consciousness and Control

She was a tiny woman and her face reflected her 64 years. For the last 20 years, she had had a brain disorder, Parkinson's disease. The disease caused a number of strange symptoms: she would literally freeze in her steps for 1 to 60 minutes, she would have episodes of having to run forwards and backwards with the tiniest steps, she always had a blank facial expression although she experienced a wide range of emotions, and her neck was severely bent so that her head almost touched her chest. This disorder can be caused by damage to the basal ganglia, which are involved in starting and stopping movements. The woman kept a diary of what it was like to be conscious of what she wanted to do but to be unable to do it, to be aware of thinking one thing and to have her body do the opposite.

She had just washed her hands and was about to walk to supper, when she suddenly found that she could not lift her feet from the ground, and that the more she fought to do so, the more they "attached" themselves to the ground. Miss D. was alarmed, annoyed, and amused at this novel experience: "It's like they had a will of their own. I was glued there, you know. I felt like a fly caught on a strip of flypaper." And later that evening she added, musingly: "I have often read about people being rooted to the spot, but I never knew what it meant—not until today." (12–25, p. 72)

This is an example of a person being conscious and interacting with her environment but having another part of her brain take control of her body, rendering her helpless to move. In addition, at other times there would be episodes in which this refined, gray-haired woman would gnaw and chew her food with a growling noise.

"I am a quiet person," she expostulated on one occasion. "I could be a distinguished maiden-aunt. And now look at me. I bite and chew like a ravenous animal, and there's nothing I can do about it." (12–25, p. 73)

It is strange to hear someone say that they are chewing food like a ravenous animal and there is nothing they can do about it. It is as if she had a type of split brain, but in this case it is not the two hemispheres that seem to be in conflict, but the cortex and other subcortical areas. One part of her brain tells her to eat like a refined person while another part of her brain not only does not listen but causes her to eat and growl like a dog. This is a dramatic example of being conscious of some behavior but being unable to control it. From your own experiences, you know there are numerous times when you are conscious at some level of wanting to do one thing (do not eat, do not smoke, go and study) and yet you do another (eat, smoke, and not study). Apparently, there are many levels of consciousness that result in different goals and purposes simultaneously. We know that the right and left hemispheres have their own separate functions, thoughts, and memories, and that other areas of the brain seem to have their own powerful impulses. You can see how this might lead to thinking one thing and doing another. What you think and what you do depend on the interaction between thoughts, ideas, and memories from many areas of your brain.

Localization of Language

Carl can neither speak nor write nor read very well with his right hemisphere. Why do most right-handers and the majority of left-handers have the speech and language areas located in the left hemisphere? The area for language is usually located in the left temporal lobe. When this area in the left temporal lobe was measured, it was found to be larger than the corresponding area in the right temporal lobe (12–15, 12–38). This could mean that an individual is born with a larger area in the left temporal lobe and that this and other anatomical differences partly determine the development of language in the left hemisphere. Support for this idea has come from the finding that, even in infants, the area in the left hemisphere where language usually develops is significantly larger than the corresponding area in the right hemisphere (12–36). These researchers suggest that the infant is born with a preprogrammed capacity to process speech sounds in the left hemisphere, and that handedness (learning to use one hand) does not determine the localization of the language area.

Although in an adult the capacity for language is confined to the left hemisphere, this is not the case for a child. Up to the age of 5 to 7, the potential for language and speech is not yet restricted to either hemisphere and may be present in both. Not until the age of 7 to 10 do language and speech become localized in one or the other hemisphere (12–2).

Evidently the localization of language in one hemisphere, usually the left, is developmental and does not finalize until the age of 7 to 10. Early brain damage to the left hemisphere can cause the language area to be localized in the right hemisphere or, less often, in both hemispheres (12–28). Handedness may play some role in localization but it is not primary, since many left-handers have the language area located in the left hemisphere. From these findings, it seems that there is a genetic predisposition for language to be localized in one hemisphere, usually the left, but that both hemispheres are capable of language until the localization is finalized through development.

Brain Damage

Strokes

At about eleven o'clock I experienced another coughing spell, and this one would not stop. My wife became frightened and, wishing to believe that I was teasing her, turned off the TV. Despite my coughing I made a move toward the TV, only to find myself on the floor. Though I did not realize it at the time, the right side of my body had become paralyzed. Bette (his wife) thought for a moment that I was malingering; however, as she explained to me much later, she knew something had happened when I tried to smile at her and only the left side of my face lit up. (12–23, p. 3)*

This person had suffered a stroke. Because his body was paralyzed on the right side, we know that the left side of the brain was involved. An artery in his left hemisphere had become clogged, and this caused a decrease in blood supply to the neurons, which in turn caused damage and disruption of function (paralysis). Strokes are also caused by arteries bursting as a result of high blood pressure. If a stroke is severe, meaning it causes widespread neural damage, the person may die or lose so many functions that he is like a vegetable. Strokes are the third leading cause of death in the United States. If the stroke is less severe, there may be only a small deficit, such as numbness in part of a limb. By studying patients who have had strokes and have suffered brain damage, investigators have obtained some idea of how the brain is organized and carries out complex responses such as speaking, reading, writing, and perceiving.

Difficulty in Speaking

I asked Mr. Ford about his work before he entered the hospital.

"I'm a sig . . . no . . . man . . . uh, well . . . again." These

words were emitted slowly and with great effort. The sounds were not clearly articulated; each syllable was uttered harshly, explosively, in a throaty voice.

"Let me help you," I interjected. "You were a signal . . ."

"A sig-nal man . . . right," Ford completed my phrase triumphantly.

"Were you in the Coast Guard?"

"No, er, yes, yes . . . ship . . . Massachu . . . chusetts . . . Coastguard . . . years." He raised his hands twice, indicating the number "nineteen."

"What happened to make you lose your speech?"

"Head, fall, Jesus Christ, me no good, str, str, . . . oh Jesus . . . stroke."

"I see. Could you tell me, Mr. Ford, what you've been doing in the hospital?"

"Yes, sure. Me go, er, uh, P. T. non o'cot, speech . . . two times . . . read . . . wr . . . ripe, er, rike, er, write . . . practice . . . get-ting better." (12–10, pp. 60–61)†

Imagine what it would be like to speak like Mr. Ford. Every word would be difficult to say. You would speak very slowly, laboriously. You could not use conjunctions, such as *if, and,* or *but*. You would have difficulty reading aloud. You could say only the simplest forms of verbs, so instead of saying "goes, went, will go," you would only say "go." You would rarely speak in complete sentences, and you would speak without melody or fluctuations. There is an area on the side of the left frontal lobe, in front of the motor area, called **Broca's area** (BROKE-caw). If there is damage to this area, the result is the above pattern of speech, called **Broca's aphasia** (ah-FAY-zee-ah). In spite of this problem with speaking, Mr. Ford could sing "Home on the Range," he could repeat words that identify familiar objects (book, car, tree), and he could comprehend what was spoken to him. He could understand such questions as "Does a stone float on water?" and could respond correctly with "No." Mr. Ford could understand more than he was able to indicate by speaking. In Broca's aphasia, it is thought that the person has great difficulty in speaking because of damage to the mechanism involved in producing the motor patterns or movements necessary for speech. The impairment is not simply a loss of speech-muscle coordination—remember, Mr. Ford could still sing "Home on the Range." The impairment is specifically in the motor phase of speech, that is, the production or execution of speech. Mr. Ford could make the sound when it was in a song, but not when it was in a sentence. A response such as speaking is composed of many elements: understanding what is to be said, coordinating speech muscles, and actually speaking the words in coherent sentences. A lesion in Broca's area does not disrupt speech comprehension or speech muscles, but it does disrupt the ability to execute words and speak in sentences.

*From *Recovery from Aphasia* by C. S. Moss. Chicago: University of Illinois Press, 1972.

†From *The Shattered Mind* by H. Gardner. New York: Vintage Books, 1976.

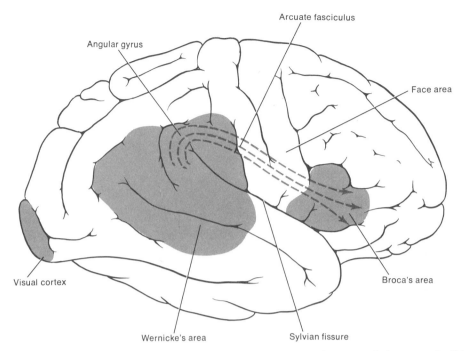

Figure 12–5 The language areas are usually located in the left hemisphere, and damage to this side may result in language problems. Broca's area controls the movement of muscles of the lips, tongue, and vocal cords involved in the production of sounds. If this area were damaged, your speech would be slow and difficult, but your understanding would be intact. Wernicke's area is involved in comprehension. If it were damaged, you could make normal speech sounds (Broca's area), but comprehension would be impaired. Broca's area is connected by a nerve bundle, the arcuate fasciculus, to Wernicke's area. (From "Language and the Brain" by Norman Geschwind. Copyright © 1972 by Scientific American, Inc. All rights reserved.)

Difficulty in Comprehension

''What brings you to the hospital?'' I asked the 72-year-old retired butcher four weeks after his admission to the hospital.

''Boy, I'm sweating. I'm awful nervous, you know, once in a while I get caught up, I mention the tarripoi, a month ago, quite a little, I've done a lot well, I impose a lot, while, on the other hand, you know what I mean, I have to run around, look it over, trebbin and all that sort of stuff.'' (12–10, p. 68)*

No, the above patient is not kidding or engaging in double talk. A stroke caused damage to an area in his left temporal lobe, called **Wernicke's area** (VER-nick-ee). This patient sounds fluent, but if you examine what he actually says, you will find almost no content. This pattern of speaking fluently but with little content is called **Wernicke's aphasia**. A person with Wernicke's aphasia may also have difficulty in naming objects. For *ankle* he may say, ''ankley, no mankle, no knakle.'' For *comb* he may say, ''close, saw it, cit it, cut, the comb.'' But he does know what a comb is because he combs his hair with a comb and not with a spoon. He is unable to find the right word for an object although he knows what the object is and how it is used. The patient's writing is very similar to the way he speaks. The above patient wrote:

*From *The Shattered Mind* by H. Gardner. New York: Vintage Books, 1976.

Philip Gorgan (his name). This is a very good beautifyl day is a good day, when the wether has been for a very long time in this part of the companing. Then we want on a ride and over to for it culd be first time . . . (12–10, p. 71)*

Like his speech, his writing has very little content and seems to ramble on without any purpose. He can read a command, such as ''Pick up the pencil.'' But he cannot carry out the command because he does not understand what he read. He is usually not aware of his own problems in speaking but, to some degree, can distinguish between correct language and double talk spoken to him. In severe cases of Wernicke's aphasia, the patient may have a total lack of comprehension: he does not know that he is speaking nonsense and does not understand any spoken or written words. In less severe cases, he may be able to follow a simple conversation, but comprehension is always disturbed (12–1).

Wernicke's aphasia is an example of how damage to the brain can rather selectively interfere with the ability to comprehend spoken or written words, leaving intact the ability to make the sounds of letters and words. Wernicke's aphasia affects comprehension but not the execution of sounds and words, while Broca's aphasia affects the execution of sounds and words but not comprehension (12–14). These examples illustrate how parts of the brain work together to produce fluent and understandable speech.

Human Brain and Higher Functions

Difficulty in Naming

"What specifically did you do, Mr. MacArthur?"

"Oh, specifically, why sure. Well, I could come in every morning about eight o'clock, check in, you know they have those big new time clocks, and then I'd make the rounds checking on all the fellows, like at the electric lathes, and all that. Is that what you mean?" (12–10, p. 76)*

This patient's reply to the question sounds normal, but on closer inspection lacks a detailed description of what he does. The patient was asked to name objects around the room, the first being a clock.

"Of course, I know that. It's the thing you see for counting, for telling the time, you know, one of those, it's a . . .

"But doesn't it have a specific name?"

"Why, of course, it does. I just can't think of it. Let me look in my notebook." (12–10, p.76)*

It is difficult to imagine that a person could sound normal in speaking, could understand what was said to him, and be able to read but be unable to name a simple object, such as a chair. This problem usually arises from damage to the area where the parietal and temporal lobes come together, the **angular gyrus**, and less often from damage to the frontal areas or other diffuse damage. This inability to name objects is called **anomia** (ah-KNOW-me-ah). You can begin to see how many different elements and brain areas are involved in saying the rather simple sentence, "That is a clock on the wall." To make this response, you must be able to make the sounds for the letters and words (Broca's area), you must be able to comprehend the question, "What is that object?", you must be able to arrange the words of your answer into a meaningful sentence (Wernicke's area), and you must be able to select the correct word to identify the object (angular gyrus).

Difficulty in Reading and Writing

Mr. C. was able to express himself without difficulty, to recognize and name instantaneously obscure technical and scientific instruments, to understand everything said to him, to recall the most minute details of past events. Even more astonishing, he could still write without difficulty, both expressing his thoughts spontaneously and transcribing what was dictated to him; yet he was unable to decipher his own handwriting. . . . In short, all his language functions, including writing, were preserved with the exception of the decoding (reading and recognizing) of words and letters presented to his eyes. (12–10, p. 116)*

Mr. C. could not read letters or words, and this inability is called **alexia** (ah-LEX-ee-ah). Sometime later Mr. C. suffered a second stroke that left him unable to write letters

or words, and this disorder is called **agraphia** (ah-GRAPH-ee-ah). By studying the brains of patients with alexia and agraphia, it is possible to discover something about how these functions are organized and how it is possible for you to read and write (12–4, 12–9). The brain of Mr. C. had several areas of damage that resulted in alexia. His left visual cortex in the occipital lobe was destroyed and so could not send information to the language areas in the left temporal lobe. Also, there was damage to part of his corpus callosum, which prevented information from his right visual cortex from crossing over to the language area in the left temporal lobe. Since his right visual cortex was intact, he could see lines and objects in his left field of vision. However, since the patterns formed by letters and words could not reach the language area, these patterns could not be identified as letters, and thus he could not read. The speech area in the left frontal lobe (Broca's area) and the language area in the left temporal lobe (Wernicke's area) were intact, so he could make sounds, form words, and comprehend what he heard or spoke. The second stroke damaged an area in his left temporal-parietal lobe, which left him unable to write. This area, the angular gyrus, appears to be involved in the visual processing of language. Damage to the angular gyrus of the left hemisphere usually causes agraphia. The case of Mr. C. is a good illustration of how you can see something when impulses arrive at the visual cortex (lines and patterns) but cannot identify these lines and patterns as letters or words until nerve impulses reach the language area in the association cortex.

Difficulty in Recognition

A sixty-year-old man, almost blind in his right eye from an old injury, woke from a sleep unable to find his clothes, though they lay ready for him close by. As soon as his wife put the garments in his hands, he recognized them, dressed himself correctly and went out. In the streets, he found he could not recognize people, not even his own daughter. He could see things but not tell what they were. (12–5, p. 289)†

Which area of this man's brain do you think was damaged? Since he could see objects, it seems that information was reaching the visual cortex in the occipital lobes and that this area was intact. Since he could not recognize objects by sight, it seems that there was damage to association areas, most probably in the **occipito-parietal** lobes. This association area, where the occipital and parietal lobes join, is involved in the identification and recognition of visual stimuli. Since he was able to identify his clothes by touch, it appears that the association area for touch was intact and that it is separate from that for vision. When you can see an object but not recognize it, the disorder is called **agnosia** (ag-KNOW-zee-ah). There are many kinds of agnosias: in

*From *The Shattered Mind* by H. Gardner. New York: Vintage Books, 1976.

†From *The Parietal Lobes* by M. Critchley. London: Edward Arnold (Publishers) Ltd., 1966.

some cases, individuals can recognize objects but not faces, some individuals cannot recognize colors, and others cannot recognize parts of their body (12–2). These examples of agnosia illustrate how the recognition of an object, face, or color depends first upon receiving patterns in your visual cortex (occipital lobe) and then forwarding these patterns to the association areas in the occipito-parietal lobe, where recognition takes place. For complex stimuli, recognition always involves several steps and different areas of the brain.

Localization

As you have seen, patients can lose the ability to speak, read, write, comprehend, or recognize images when dif-

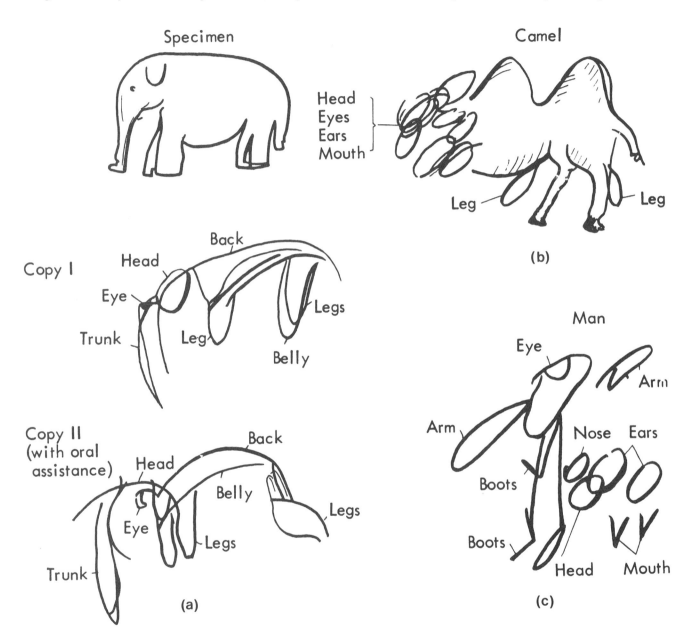

Figure 12–6 Drawings by a patient with damage to the visual area in both hemispheres. (a) The patient was shown a sketch of an elephant and asked to draw it. Copy I and Copy II show the attempts to draw the elephant. Damage to the visual area prevented the patient from completing this simple visual task. (b) The patient was given an incomplete sketch of a camel and asked to draw in the front half. (c) The patient was asked to draw a picture of a man from memory. Both (b) and (c) show great distortions in the visual abilities of this patient following damage to the occipital region. (Figure 40 from *Higher Cortical Functions in Man* by Aleksandr Romanovich Luria, translated from the Russian by Basil Haigh, © 1966 by Consultants Bureau Enterprises, Inc., and Basic Books, Inc., Publishers, New York.)

Human Brain and Higher Functions

ferent areas of the brain are damaged. Many of the areas involved in writing, reading, comprehending, or using language are located in the brain's association areas. It is no surprise then that the greater part of the human cortex is association cortex. Some functions, such as speaking (making sounds), are located in a discrete area of the cortex (Broca's area). Damage in the one area leaves a person mute but leaves other functions, such as comprehension, intact. Other functions, such as recognition of objects or faces, are probably not located in one discrete area, since a difficulty such as agnosia may arise from several different lesions. Thus, for simple functions, such as seeing, hearing, or speaking, there are discrete areas localized in specific brain areas (visual cortex, auditory cortex, Broca's area). For complex functions, such as recognition or comprehension, there are no discrete centers, but rather a combination of areas.

When an area of the brain is damaged, connections to and from other areas are also destroyed. As these connections disintegrate, destruction reaches other brain areas far distant from the originally damaged area (12–18). For example, when we say that the occipito-parietal area is involved in recognition, we mean that there is damage here as well as to its connections and other areas. The combination of lesions results in loss of recognition. The various problems of agnosia, aphasia, alexia, and agraphia help illustrate which general brain areas are involved in a function but do not indicate that a certain function (recognizing) is entirely localized in the area.

Brain Recovery

Early Damage

There have been cases in which an entire hemisphere has been damaged at birth or during the first year of life. Five to ten years later, this early damage sometimes has resulted in uncontrollable seizures. A drastic treatment for this condition is the removal of the damaged hemisphere, which results in the successful elimination of seizures in approximately 70 percent of the cases (12–35). What happens to language, reading, and writing if the left hemisphere is damaged at birth? A remarkable reorganization of brain functions occurs in children with early brain damage. If the left hemisphere is damaged and later removed, the child is able to speak, write, and use language. The early damage to the left hemisphere somehow results in development of speech and language functions in the right hemisphere (12–16, 12–20, 12–35). However, if the right hemisphere must develop the functions of speech and language in addition to its normal functions, there may be a deficit in one of its usual functions, such as spatial organization (12–17, 12–21). Apparently one hemisphere cannot completely assume the functions of both hemispheres. Some functions are completely lost with removal of one hemisphere, even

when the removal occurs very early. If your left hemisphere were removed, the right side of your body would be paralyzed. You would have no sensations from the right side, and there would be a loss of vision in your right visual field. These sensory and motor functions are not assumed by the remaining hemisphere.

Studies of early brain damage show that a hemisphere has the flexibility, or **plasticity**, to develop some functions (language, reading, writing)—but not all (motor and sensory)—normally found in the other hemisphere. In addition, if a hemisphere must assume an additional function, it does so at the cost of a deficit in one of its normal functions.

The brain's flexibility to assume functions lost through damage is dramatically shown in the following case. When he was 5½, the child's left hemisphere was removed to treat uncontrollable seizures. Twenty-one years later, he was given a series of psychological tests to determine which functions his remaining right hemisphere had assumed. As was expected, he was paralyzed on his right side, had no sensations from his right side, and was blind in his right visual area. The right hemisphere does not assume the sensory and motor functions found in the left hemisphere. On the other hand, he was able to speak, read, write, use language, and comprehend so well with his right hemisphere that his score on the standard IQ test was 116 (a score of 100 is considered average). Other tests for language and nonlanguage functions were also in the normal range. He had a job as an industrial traffic controller and was completing his senior year in college with a dual major in sociology and business administration (12–30). The ability of this individual to do well on language tests, maintain a job, and pursue two majors in college demonstrates the extent to which the right hemisphere can function if the left is removed or damaged.

Late Damage

As you grow older, does the brain lose some of its ability to compensate? We have seen that either hemisphere can develop language functions until the child reaches the age of 5 to 7. After the age of 10, brain damage to the left hemisphere usually results in serious speech and language problems, since the right hemisphere lacks the flexibility to completely assume these functions. Damage to the left hemisphere before the age of 10 may result in complete aphasia (no speech) or Broca's aphasia (speech is slow and labored), but the ability to speak usually returns, and the prospects for recovery are very good. This indicates that the right hemisphere has the flexibility to assume language functions. When damage occurs to the left hemisphere after the age of 10, there may be serious language and speech deficits, depending on the severity of the damage. The result may be complete aphasia, or Broca's or Wernicke's aphasia. The prospects for recovery are much poorer than if the damage occurred early, and there will never be complete recovery. With age, the brain loses some of its flexibility to compensate for damage. There can still be recovery in adults, possibily through sprouting or increased activity of undamaged areas, but the degree of recovery is generally less than is seen after early brain damage.

In only three reported cases has removal of the left hemisphere in a right-handed adult been followed by a return of language abilities (12–29). In these cases, the right hemisphere did, for unknown reasons, develop language abilities. In most cases, the right hemisphere of an adult does not assume the language abilities of the left.

Blows to the Head

Since a sport such as boxing involves constant blows to the head, participation might be expected to produce eventual brain damage. More than 200 individuals who had boxed for at least 3 years (and some for 10) were examined for symptoms of brain damage. One in six were found to have signs of brain damage, including problems of coordination (**ataxias**), rigidity in their joints, tremors, and difficulties in speaking (**dysarthria**). The longer their boxing careers, the greater the signs of brain damage. It was thought that these symptoms were caused by damage to the cerebellum and another part of the extrapyramidal motor system, the basal ganglia (12–24).

Blows to the head sustained in other sports have also been shown to cause signs of brain dysfunction. In football players, for example, blows to the head have been reported to cause temporary amnesia (12–37). After repeated falls from horses, jockeys have developed seizures and auditory and visual hallucinations, and on autopsy they have been found to have severe brain damage in many parts of their brains

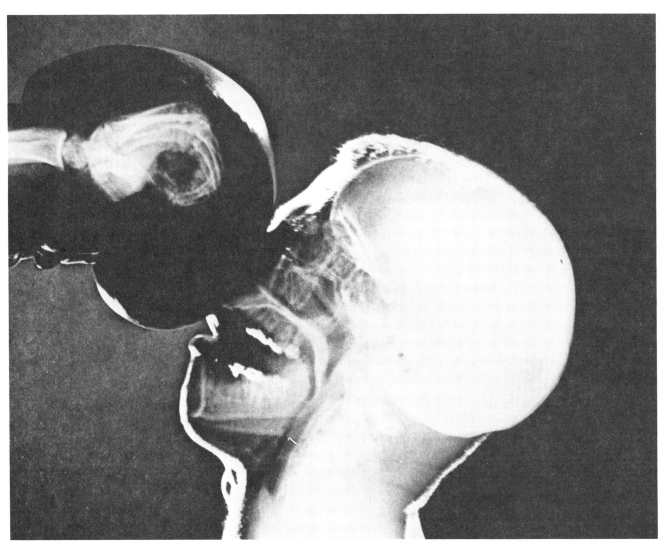

Figure 12–7 Blows to the head. X ray of what happens when the head is struck. The brain is somewhat loosely placed in the skull, so that a blow to the head causes the brain to bang into the skull. Repeated blows to the head may cause hemorrhaging and other damage to the brain. (Photo courtesy of Howard Sochurek.)

Human Brain and Higher Functions

CAULIFLOWER BRAINS

*"He took too many beatings . . .
that just made him sort of simple."
—The Battler,* Ernest Hemingway

With his shuffling gait, slurred speech and foggy memory, the punchdrunk boxer is a stock character in movies and fiction, and a mainstay of many a stand-up comic's nightclub routines. But there is nothing funny about the condition some doctors call "dementia pugilistica." Doctors have known for years that a hard blow to the head can slam the jelly-like brain against the rigid skull and cause permanent damage. Now a trio of British researchers has documented just how serious—and how widespread among boxers—this damage is likely to be. In a study published last month in the journal *Psychological Medicine,* they report that the pounding suffered by boxers can destroy vital brain tissue, producing not only physical symptoms but psychiatric problems as well.

Conducted by Drs. J.A.N. Corsellis and C.J. Bruton with the assistance of a psychiatric social worker named Dorothy Freeman-Browne, the study is not the first attempt to understand why boxers become punchy. But it is the most extensive. Most previous efforts have concentrated on only one or two fighters. The British report is based on posthumous examination of 15 brains collected during the past 16 years, and careful study of the fighters' lives as well.

Varied Lot

The boxers, who fought between 1900 and 1940, were a varied lot.

Three were amateurs; the other twelve were professionals. Their names were not revealed, but two were one-time world champions, while six more held national or regional titles. They also boxed a good deal more than fighters do today; over half had fought in more than 300 contests.

But the fighters, who died between the ages of 57 and 91, had more in common than their professions. Interviews with relatives and friends, plus reviews of boxing journals and other publications, revealed that all were bothered by physical and mental symptoms after they left the ring. Most developed speech difficulties and a Parkinson's-like syndrome with drooling and tremors. Some also became uncoordinated in their movements and unsteady on their feet. In most cases, their minds were muddled. Some developed into alcoholics; some acted as if they were drunk even though they never touched liquor. A few became uncontrollably violent.

The reason for these and other disorders became apparent upon autopsy. All the boxers had suffered serious brain damage. Researchers who examined the boxers' brains found greater degeneration and loss of nerve cells than in those of non-fighters who died at similar ages. They also found an injury that seems peculiar to pugilists. Three-fourths of the former fighters had fenestrations, or "windows," in the septum, a membranous partition between the two halves of the brain; this can result in hemorrhages.

Among non-boxers, only 3% suffered such injuries.

The findings have already provoked an angry outcry from boxing's backers. The sport, they claim, is far safer today than it was a generation or more ago when Bruton and Corsellis' subjects were in the ring. Moreover, defenders of boxing maintain, soccer and rugby players also run the risk of head injuries. While acknowledging that these arguments are partly accurate, Corsellis is unimpressed. As a result of his work, he would support a move to bar boxing.

For the brain damage is not simply the result of an accumulation of blows—like a boxer's cauliflower ears for example—but the result of one or more damaging blows that may occur by chance. "A single punch, or even many punches to the head," says Dr. Corsellis, "need not visibly alter the structure of the brain." But there is still "the danger that, at an unpredictable moment and for an unknown reason, one or more blows will leave their mark." Present boxing conditions reduce the number of professional fights a boxer is likely to endure. Just by being in the ring, however, he exposes his head to punishment more frequently than other sportsmen. And once brain tissue is destroyed, "it is gone for good."

SOURCE: *Time*, October 1, 1973. Reprinted by permission from TIME, The Weekly Newsmagazine; Copyright Time Inc. 1973.

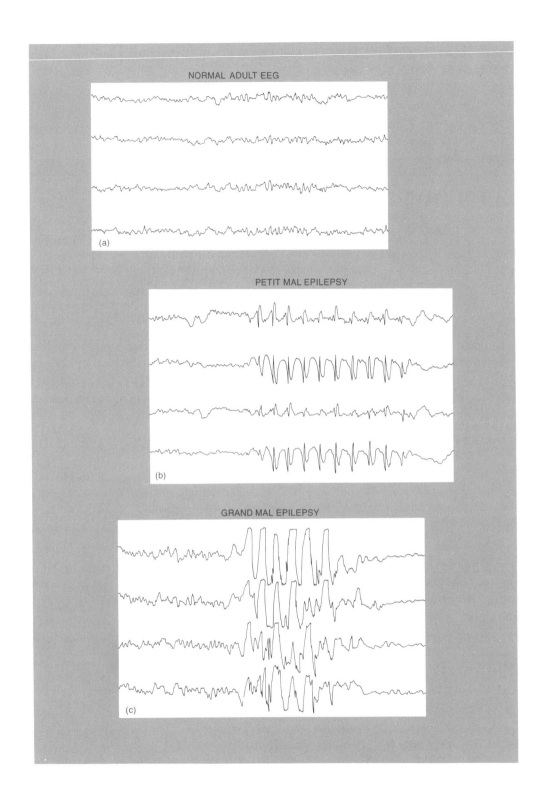

Figure 12–8 Electrical brain activity recorded from the scalp is commonly called EEG waves. (a) Example of a normal EEG pattern. (b) Example of abnormal brain activity occurring during a petit mal epileptic seizure. During this seizure, a person would have a lapse in attention and the eyes might roll up. (c) Example of the high-amplitude EEG pattern occurring during grand mal epileptic seizures. During this seizure, the person loses consciousness, falls down, and shows spastic movements of the limbs.

Human Brain and Higher Functions

(12–7). In general, blows to the head can result in brain damage from which there is never complete recovery.

Epilepsy

It was about eleven o'clock when I put down my pen feeling suddenly tired and saying to myself that I could do no more that night, so I would make a cup of tea and go to bed. I made the tea, looked up at the clock—a strange chance—and saw that it was ten minutes past eleven. The next moment I was still looking up at the clock and the hands stood at five and twenty minutes past midnight. I had fallen through Time, Continuity, and Being. (12–26, p. 7)*

When this person recovered consciousness, she realized she had just had an epileptic attack. There are many types of epileptic attacks. In a **grand mal seizure**, the person loses consciousness and falls to the ground with rigid limb extension and, sometimes, urination. The attack may occur without warning. Grand mal seizures are more common in adolescents and adults than in children. Another kind of attack may last for only a few seconds and may go unnoticed by an observer. In this kind of attack, an individual will suddenly stop what she is doing and stare ahead. Her eyes may roll upwards, and she will be unresponsive, neither speaking nor understanding if spoken to. Sometimes there may be noticeable jerks of the arms and legs. Afterward, the individual will continue whatever she was doing and may not even be aware of having had the seizure. This type is called a **petit mal seizure** (PET-tea-maul) and may occur as frequently as 10–20 times a day. Petit mal and grand mal seizures are two of the more common types of epileptic attacks.

If the seizures begin during the first year of life, there is a possibility that the cause is some abnormality of the brain or injury during birth. Seizures that occur later in life but during the first 20 years, when most seizures begin, may have no easily identifiable cause. When seizures occur after the age of 20, there is a greater chance that some cause such as scar tissue, can be found in the brain. Epileptic attacks can be triggered by emotional disturbances, lack of sleep, flashing lights, and other stressors.

The seizure occurs when neurons in the brain become hyperactive. This abnormal neural activity produces electrical changes that can be recorded with an EEG machine. The abnormal electrical activity may spread to other areas of the brain and result in grand mal or petit mal seizures. There are many causes for the abnormal electrical activity and neural hyperactivity: head injuries, brain infections, scar tissue, deficiency in oxygen because of heart disease, or build up of toxins in the blood because of kidney disease. In some cases of epilepsy, physicians are unable to determine the cause for the abnormal neural activity. In about

*From *About Epilepsy* by D. Scott. New York: International Universities Press, 1973. Reprinted by permission.

one-third of the cases, damage to the temporal lobe is the cause of epilepsy. The temporal lobe's position in the skull makes it especially susceptible to damage from blows and falls (12–32).

Treatment of Epilepsy

The major medication for seizures is a group of drugs called **anticonvulsants**. For grand mal seizures, a commonly used drug is *phenytonin* (common name: Dilantin). Exactly how phenytonin acts is not known, but the drug appears to prevent the spread of abnormal electrical activity in the brain rather than to block the initial occurrence. Phenytonin is one of the anticonvulsant drugs that do not actually cure epilepsy but rather control the occurrence of seizures. Anticonvulsants must be taken regularly, usually for a year or two. After this time, the patient may be withdrawn from drugs, and in some cases the seizures do not return. One problem with anticonvulsants is the occurrence of side effects, such as skin problems, receding gums, and growth of body hair. In certain kinds of epilepsy, surgery is one means of treatment. However, there are very few cases in which surgery can be used effectively. For surgery to be effective, the abnormal electrical activity must be focused. That is, the seizure must begin in one discrete area of the brain. In these cases, the surgeon attempts to remove the area in which the abnormal activity begins. Following surgical treatment, approximately half of the patients are completely cured of seizures, approximately one-third have a reduction, and the remaining patients have little change (12–26). In the case of Carl, the epileptic seizures could not be controlled by drugs and the electrical activity was too widespread to be removed by discrete surgery. Instead, the corpus callosum was cut in order to prevent the abnormal electrical activity from spreading from one hemisphere to the other. This treatment, cutting the corpus callosum, does not always reduce the seizures and is therefore rarely done today.

Epilepsy is an example of how neural activity, which occurs constantly in the brain, may suddenly become hyperactive and have profound effects on behavior. Because all of our behaviors depend upon neural activity, you can see how increased neural activity could result in anything from loss of consciousness to gross body movements.

Comment

It is surprising to realize that you may actually have thoughts, memories, emotions, ideas, and goals in your right hemisphere that are separate from and even different from those in your left hemisphere. Is it any wonder then that you sometimes think one thing and do another, or say one thing and feel another? Complex responses such as reading, writing, naming, comprehending, and speaking can be disrupted by damage to various areas of the brain.

From studying individuals with brain damage, we know that before letters become words, lines become faces, or sounds become sentences, many different areas of the brain must process information. When there is damage to the brain of a young child, the remaining brain areas have the flexibility to assume many, but certainly not all, of the functions lost in the damage. When there is damage to the brain of an adult, the remaining parts have less flexibility to assume new functions and to compensate for the lost behaviors. It is the constant neural activity in and between hundreds of brain areas that is the basis for your consciousness, your behaviors, and you.

SELF-TEST 12

1   The right hemisphere can be isolated from the left by cutting a thick band of fibers called the _____ as well as some smaller connections.

corpus callosum

2   A person with a split brain usually has little or no change in the following behaviors: _____ and _____. (Give two.)

speech, intelligence, personality, or temperament

3   If a right-handed person with a split brain were speaking to you, he would be speaking with his _____ hemisphere.

left

4   If a left-handed person with a split brain were speaking to you, he would probably be using his _____ hemisphere. Chances are much smaller that he would be using his _____ hemisphere.

left / right

5   If the left hemisphere were shown a picture of a monkey, it could identify the object by _____ and _____. (Give two ways.)

speaking, writing, or pointing

6   If the right hemisphere were shown a picture of a snake, it could not identify it by _____, but it could identify it by _____.

speaking
pointing or touching

7   The left hemisphere has no difficulty in reading words. The right hemisphere _____ nouns and adjectives but not verbs.

can read

8   Although both hemispheres can experience emotions, it seemed persons with right hemisphere damage showed _____ responses to cartoons.

less appropriate

9   Compared to the right, the left hemisphere is better at producing the following behavior: _____, _____, and _____. (Give three.)

speaking, writing, reading, spelling, or mathematical calculations

10   The left hemisphere is inferior at tasks such as _____ figures, which require _____ organization.

drawing / spatial

11   The right hemisphere is involved in the way you think of your body, or your _____. It is superior at tasks that involve _____, and also at tasks that involve recognizing _____.

body image
spatial organization
melodies or faces

12   Following a split-brain operation or brain damage, the brain may compensate for loss of function by _____ and _____. (Give two.)

cross-cuing, assuming a new function, or sprouting

13   If you were born without a corpus callosum, it is likely that when tested later your right hemisphere would be able to _____ and _____, and your left hemisphere would be able to _____ using the right hand.

speak / write
draw figures

14   In order for you to achieve and maintain consciousness, two brain structures must be intact: _____ and _____.

cerebral cortex or cortex
reticular formation

15   The area in the left temporal lobe that is involved in language was found to be _____ than the corresponding area in the right temporal lobe.

larger

16   If a stroke caused a person to speak in a very slow, deliberate manner and made reading aloud and speaking in complete sentences difficult, we would say the area of the brain damaged was _____. The brain disorder would be called _____.

Broca's area / Broca's aphasia

17   Although a person with Broca's aphasia has difficulty in speaking, she does not have any difficulty in _____ what she hears or reads.

comprehending

18   If a stroke caused a person to speak fluently but with little content, we would say the brain area damaged was _____. The brain disorder would be called _____.

Wernicke's area
Wernicke's aphasia

19   A person with Wernicke's aphasia has no difficulty in speaking but has great difficulty in _____ what he reads or says and in _____.

comprehending
writing

20   If your job were naming the animals in the zoo, you would lose this ability if the _____ were damaged. This problem would be called _____.

angular gyrus
anomia

21   In order for you to read, information from your visual cortex must reach the _____ area in your _____ lobe where the patterns are identified as letters and words. If the information does not reach this area, the result is a problem called _____.

language
left temporal
alexia

22. In addition to being involved in naming objects, the angular gyrus is important for _____ *visual* processing of language. If this area were destroyed, the person would have agraphia, which means the inability to _____. *write*

23. Individuals who cannot recognize objects or faces or colors usually have damage in the _____ *occipito-parietal* lobe, and this results in a problem called _____. *agnosia*

24. Damage to a certain area of the brain may result in the inability to recognize faces. This function is not necessarily localized in that area, since damage to one area also results in the destruction of _____ to and from the area. *connections*

25. If there is early damage to the left hemisphere, during the first 5-10 years, the right hemisphere can assume the functions of speech and language. But in so doing, it may develop a deficit in some function, such as _____, that is normally found in the right hemisphere. *spatial organization*

26. There are some functions that the right hemisphere does not assume if the left hemisphere is damaged. The functions include various _____ and _____ processes. *motor / sensory*

27. If damage to the brain occurs in adulthood, the lost functions may not be assumed by the undamaged hemisphere, because with age, the brain loses some of its _____ to assume new functions. *flexibility or plasticity*

28. Damage to the brain that occurs in some sports may cause motor behavior problems, such as (give two) _____ and _____, as well as psychological problems, such as _____. *ataxia, rigidity, or tremors / amnesia or hallucinations*

29. If a person has a seizure characterized by loss of consciousness, falling to the ground, and extension of the limbs, it is called a _____ seizure. *grand mal*

30. If a person has an attack that results in a momentary loss of consciousness, cessation of activities, and unresponsiveness, and afterward he does not realize it has happened, the attack would be called a _____ seizure. *petit mal*

31. The seizure, whether it is grand or petit mal, is due to neurons becoming _____ and spreading electrical activity to other areas of the brain. *hyperactive*

32. There are many reasons why some neurons become hyperactive. These include _____ and _____. (Give two.) *head injuries, brain infections, scar tissue, deficiency in oxygen, or kidney failure*

33. Grand mal seizures are often treated with drugs called _____, which do not cure epilepsy but seem to work by _____ the spread of seizures. *anticonvulsants* *preventing*

REFERENCES

12–1 Brown, J. W. *Aphasia, apraxia, and agnosia*. Springfield, Ill: Charles C. Thomas, 1972.

12–2 Brown, J. W. and Hecaen, H. Lateralization and language representation. *Neurology* 1976, 26: 183–189.

12–3 Cairns, H. Disturbances of consciousness in lesions of the mid-brain and diencephalon. *Brain* 1952, 75: 109–113.

12–4 Cohen, D. N., Salanga, V. D., Hully, W., Steinberg, M. C., and Hardy, R. W. Alexia without agraphia. *Neurology* 1976, 26: 455–459.

12–5 Critchley, M. *The parietal lobes*. London: Edward Arnold (Publishers) Ltd., 1966.

12–6 Ettlinger, G., Blakemore, C. B., Milner, A. D., and Wilson, J. Agenesis of the corpus callosum: a behavioural investigation. *Brain* 1972, 95: 327-346.

12–7 Foster, J. B., Leiguarda, R., and Tilley, P. J. B. Brain damage in national hunt jockeys. *Lancet* May 8, 1976, 981–983.

12–8 Gainotti, G. Emotional behavior and hemispheric side of the lesion. *Cortex* 1972, 8: 41–55.

12–9 Gardner, H. The forgotten lesson of Monsieur C. *Psychology Today* August 1973.

12–10 Gardner, H. *The shattered mind*. New York: Vintage Books, 1976.

12–11 Gardner, H., Ling, P. K., Flamm, L., and Silverman, J. Comprehension and appreciation of humorous material following brain damage. *Brain* 1975, 98: 399–412.

12–12 Gazzaniga, M. S. *The bisected brain*. New York: Appleton–Century–Crofts, 1970.

12–13 Gazzaniga, M. S. The Biology of memory. In M. R. Rosenzweig and E. L. Bennett (Eds.), *Neural mechanisms of learning and memory*. Cambridge, Mass: MIT Press, 1976.

12–14 Geschwind, N. Language and brain. *Scientific American* 1972, 226: 76–83.

12–15 Geschwind, N. and Levitsky, W. Human brain: left-right assymetries in temporal speech region. *Science* 1968, 161: 186–187.

12–16 Joynt, R. J. and Goldstein, M. N. Minor cerebral hemisphere. In W. J. Friedlander (Ed.), *Advances in neurology*. Vol. 7. New York: Raven Press, 1975.

12–17 Kohn, B. and Dennis, M. Selective impairments on visuo-spatial abilities in infantile hemiplegics after right cerebral hemidocortication. *Neuropsychologia* 1974, 12: 505–512.

12–18 Lynch, G. Some difficulties associated with the use of lesion techniques in the study of memory. In M. R. Rosenzweig and E. L. Bennett (Eds.), *Neural mechanisms of learning and memory*. Cambridge, Mass: MIT Press, 1976.

12–19 Lynch, G., Gall, C., Rose, G., and Cotman, C. Changes in the distribution of the dentate gyrus associational system following unilateral or bilateral entorhinal lesions in the adult rat. *Brain Research* 1976, 110: 57–71.

12–20 McFie, J. The effects of hemispherectomy on intellectual functioning in cases of infantile hemiplegia. *Journal of Neurology, Neurosurgery and Psychiatry* 1961, 24: 247–249.

12–21 Milner, B. Psychological aspects of focal epilepsy and its neurosurgical management. In D. P. Purpura, J. K. Penry, and R. D. Walter (Eds.), *Advances in Neurology*. Vol. 8. New York: Raven Press, 1975.

12–22 Moscovitch, M. On interpreting data regarding the linguistic competence and performance of the right hemisphere: a reply to Selnes. *Brain and Language* 1976, 3: 590–599.

12–23 Moss, C. S. *Recovery with aphasia*. Chicago: University of Illinois Press, 1972.

12–24 Roberts, A. H. *Brain damage in boxers*. London: Pitman Medical and Scientific Publishing, 1969.

12–25 Sacks, O. *Awakenings*. New York: Vintage, 1976.

12–26 Scott, D. *About epilepsy*. New York: International Universities Press, 1973.

12–27 Selnes, O. A. The corpus callosum: some anatomical and functional considerations with special reference to language. *Brain and Language* 1974, 1: 111–139.

12–28 Selnes, O. A. A note on ''On the representation of language in the right hemisphere of right-handed people.'' *Brain and Language* 1976, 3: 583–589.

12–29 Smith, A. Speech and other functions after left (dominant) hemispherectomy. *Journal of Neurology, Neurosurgery and Psychiatry* 1966, 29: 467–471.

12–30 Smith, A. and Sugar, O. Development of above normal language and intelligence 21 years after left hemispherectomy. *Neurology* 1975, 25: 813–818.

12–31 Sperry, R. W. Lateral specialization in the surgically separated hemispheres. In F. S. Schmitt and F. G. Worden (Eds.), *The neurosciences*. Cambridge, Mass: MIT Press, 1974.

12–32 Sutherland, J. M., Tait, H., and Eadie, M. J. *The epilepsies*. London: Churchill Livingstone, 1974.

12–33 Wada, J. and Rasmussen, T. Intracarotid injection of sodium amytal for the lateralization of cerebral speech dominance: experimental and clinical observations. *Journal of Neurosurgery* 1960, 17: 226–282.

12–34 Williams, M. *Brain damage and the mind*. Baltimore: Penguin, 1973.

12–35 Wilson, P. J. E. Cerebral hemispherectomy for infantile hemiplegia. *Brain* 1970, 93: 147–180.

12–36 Witelson, S. F. and Pallie, W. Left hemisphere specialization for language in the newborn. *Brain* 1973, 96: 641–646.

12–37 Yarnell, P. R. and Lynch, S. The 'ding': amnestic states in football trauma. *Neurology* 1973, 23: 196–197.

12–38 Yeni-Komshian, G. H. and Benson, D. A. Anatomical study of cerebral asymmetry in the temporal lobe of humans, chimpanzees, and rhesus monkeys. *Science* 1976, 192: 387–389.

Behavior Disorders and Drugs 13

Can Pills Change Your Mind?

A Brain Exploded

I am here. I am Mark Vonnegut and all that entails. That's Simon there and Sy there and André there and Sankara there. We all went to Swarthmore. We are in Vancouver, British Columbia, Canada. I can remember lots of things. I can think about things. I can understand what people are saying and they can understand what I am saying.

It never lasts very long. It's lasting less and less. I keep going away. It keeps getting harder and harder to come back. I stop being Mark Vonnegut. Simon stops being Simon and so on. I stop being able to remember things, think about things, or understand what people say. It stops being Vancouver, British Columbia, Canada. I get swept away. I keep making it back, but it's getting tougher and tougher. (13–67, pp. 145–146)*

This person is struggling to maintain his sanity, to control his thoughts, to understand the world around him. This person is literally going crazy.

Time had gotten very strange. Things whizzed and whirled all about me with great speed and confusion. Then everything would stop. There was no more movement, everything was being frozen, solid, life was being drained out of everything. I'd feel a scream building up deep down inside me when suddenly everything would spring to life and begin rushing around again, violently and pointlessly. The scream would come but there'd be no sound. It was all drowned out in the frantic rush of wings beating all around my head. I'd come to myself from time to time and realize that I was walking, half stumbling through the woods. I'd wonder where the hell I was going, what was I doing? I'd take handfuls of snow and press them to my face, trying desperately to get some sort of hold on myself. (13–67, pp. 108–109)*

*From The Eden Express *by Mark Vonnegut. © 1975 by Praeger Publishers, Inc. Reprinted by permission of Praeger Publishers, Inc., a Division of Holt, Rinehart and Winston.*

Day in and day out, his world was changing into one of confusion. Less and less was Mark in control of his thoughts, wishes, and behaviors. During this time, he was not alone. There were voices.

By this time the voices had gotten very clear. At first I'd strain to hear or understand them. They were soft and working with some pretty tricky codes. Snap-crack-pops, the sound of the wind with blinking lights and horns for punctuation. I broke the code and somehow was able to internalize it to the point where it was just like hearing words. In the beginning it seemed mostly nonsense, but as things went along they made more and more sense. Once you hear voices, you realize they've always been there. It's just a matter of being tuned to them. (13–67, pp. 136–137)*

He eventually lost contact with reality, he did not know who he was, he could not understand what was said to him, he knew the voices were real. After attempting suicide, Mark was committed to a hospital for treatment. He was diagnosed as being psychotic, **schizophrenic**. *After a period of various kinds of treatments, he again became rational and wrote a book about his experience (13–67).*

*For many schizophrenics, the world is very similar to that described above. It is a world of confused thinking, delusions, hearing voices, not understanding what is happening, and in some cases the belief that people are out to get you (**paranoia**). In the United States, approximately 1 percent of the population is clearly schizophrenic and another 4 percent have some of the symptoms (13–59). What happens in the brain to cause such bizarre behaviors? Since all of our behaviors, normal or bizarre, ultimately depend on chemical interactions in the brain, we will first see what these chemicals do.*

219

Chemicals and Neurotransmitters

After he was admitted to the hospital, Mark was given a drug called **chlorpromazine** (common name: **Thorazine**). Chlorpromazine (chlor-PRO-ma-zine) affects the chemicals in the brain that are involved in the neuron's function. When an impulse reaches the end of a neuron's axon, it causes the chemicals stored in the end feet or telodendria to be released. These chemicals, neurotransmitters, cross the synapse and act to excite or inhibit the adjacent or post-synaptic neuron. (See Chapter 2 for more complete discussion.) Neurotransmitters are secreted only from a neuron's telodendria and usually act on the dendrites or cell bodies of the postsynaptic neurons. You can read this sentence, think, speak, hear voices, have hallucinations, or ride a bike because of the action of different neurotransmitters in various areas of the brain. When you take a drug, it can act on the presynaptic neuron to affect the secretion of neuro-

transmitters. The drug can act at the synaptic cleft to affect the destruction of transmitters after they are secreted. Or the drug can act on the postsynaptic dendrites or cell bodies and block the neurotransmitter from acting on them. A drug may produce any one or several of these three actions, in any number of brain areas.

In Mark's case, chlorpromazine alleviated his confused thinking so that he gradually became aware of where he was and what had happened to him. This drug affects several neurotransmitters in the brain, especially dopamine and norepinephrine. Apparently chlorpromazine prevents these two transmitters from acting on the postsynaptic neurons, and this is related to the decrease in schizophrenic symptoms (13–60). Dopamine and norepinephrine, along with epinephrine, form a group of transmitters called the **catecholamines** (cat-uh-COLE-ah-means). Another group of neurotransmitters, called **indoleamines** (in-DOLE-ah-means), includes serotonin, which is thought to be involved

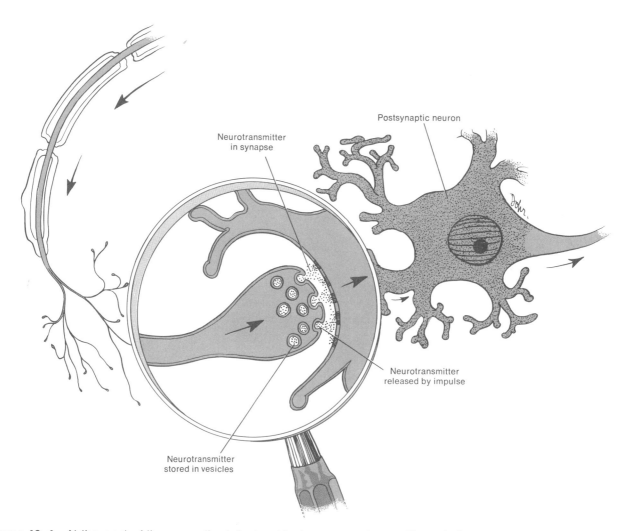

Figure 13–1 At the end of the axon, the telodendria have neurotransmitter substances stored in small packets or vesicles. When an impulse reaches the telodendria, it causes the vesicles to release the neurotransmitter into the synaptic space. The neurotransmitter crosses the synapse and acts on the postsynaptic neuron's membrane, either exciting or inhibiting it.

Behavior Disorders and Drugs

in other psychological problems. Many of the drugs used to treat psychological problems will somehow manipulate these three neurotransmitters.

Deactivation of Neurotransmitters

As you are constantly behaving, there is a constant secretion of neurotransmitters in the brain. If these transmitters were allowed to build up at the synapse, the result might be abnormal behaviors. So there must be a way to destroy or deactivate neurotransmitters. After catecholamines are secreted into the synapse, they act on the postsynaptic neuron's dendrites and cell bodies. Following this action, most of the catecholamines are taken back into the telodendria from which they were secreted. This process of being taken back into the telodendria is called **reuptake**. Catecholamines that are not taken back into the telodendria are destroyed by enzymes. Of the two methods for deactivating or removing the catecholamines from the synapse, the major mechanism is reuptake and the minor one is destruction by enzymes (**monoamine oxidase,** or **MAO**) (13–3). For other transmitters, the major mechanism for deactivation may be destruction by enzymes. For example, the neurotransmitter acetylcholine is primarily destroyed by the enzyme acetylcholinesterase and is not subject to reuptake. Some drugs work primarily by affecting reuptake, while others affect the enzymes. For example, amphetamines interfere with the reuptake of the catecholamines dopamine and norepinephrine. The result is an increase in dopamine and norepinephrine levels at the synapse, which in turn causes behavioral changes such as euphoria, sleeplessness, increased energy, and loss of appetite. When levels of neurotransmitters are changed, there can be dramatic changes in behaviors. The search for the physical bases and treatment of psychological problems, such as schizophrenia, mania, depression, and anxiety, involves determining which neurotransmitters are acting in which areas of the brain.

Physical Basis of Schizophrenia
Genetic Predisposition

Why don't scientists simply measure the neurotransmitters in patients with schizophrenia and determine what is different in their brains? It is not always possible to determine the level of a neurotransmitter from a blood sample. This is because not all chemicals freely pass from the blood supply of the brain to that of the body, and vice versa. Also, there may be enzymes in the liver or other organs that destroy neurotransmitters before they can be measured. Additionally, it is not feasible to place instruments into the normal brain to measure chemicals—this would be a very serious operation and would damage brain cells. Furthermore, there is another difficulty in studying the neurotransmitters and schizophrenia. The development of schizophrenic symptoms may occur quickly or take years, and there may be one or two or a variety of different symptoms. Instead of a single problem called **schizophrenia**, there are four or five different types of schizophrenia. Each type may

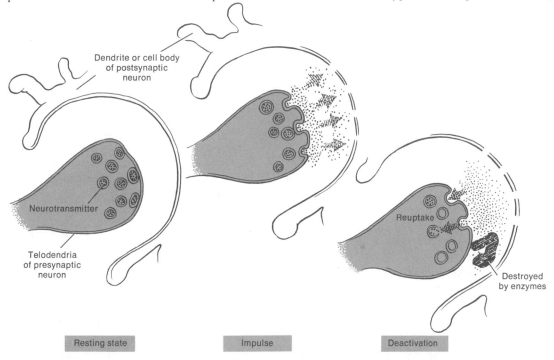

Figure 13–2 In the resting state, the neurotransmitter is stored in vesicles in the presynaptic neuron's telodendria. When an impulse arrives at the telodendria, the vesicles release the neurotransmitter into the synaptic space. After the neurotransmitter has acted on the postsynaptic neuron, it is either taken back into the presynaptic neuron, which is called reuptake, or the neurotransmitter may be destroyed by enzymes in the synaptic space.

have a different cause and may involve different neurotransmitters acting in different brain areas. Nevertheless, in the face of these difficulties, the search for the chemical bases of schizophrenia has seen some progress.

Shortly after birth, a number of children were adopted and raised by foster parents. Later in life, some of these children developed schizophrenia. These children have the genes from one set of parents (biological) and the learning experiences from another set (foster). Because there are two sets of parents, you can ask whether the genes from the biological parents contributed to the later development of schizophrenia, or whether schizophrenia was caused primarily by learning experiences with the foster parents. To answer this question, you can study both sets of parents to determine which set had the higher incidence of serious psychological problems. If the biological parents had a higher incidence of problems than the foster parents, it would be evidence that a genetic predisposition, rather than learning experience, was involved in the development of schizophrenia. If the foster parents had a higher incidence of psychological problems than the biological parents, it would be evidence that learning experience, rather than genes, was one of the major factors. Reseachers found that the biological parents had a higher incidence of psychological problems than the foster parents who had raised the children (13–35). This suggests that one factor in the development of certain kinds of schizophrenia is a **genetic predisposition**. Studies on identical twins (same genetic makeup) who became schizophrenic support this idea. If one identical twin develops schizophrenia, even if raised apart from the other, there is a high probability that the other twin will also. The probability of this happening in fraternal twins (dissimilar genetic makeup) is much lower (13–29). These studies indicate that in addition to environmental factors, there seems to be some kind of genetic predisposition for later development of schizophrenia.

Genes and Enzymes

How might the genes be involved in the development of such a complex behavior as schizophrenia? If the genes carried instructions for the synthesis of too little or too much enzyme, the result might be too little or too much neurotransmitter. Changes in the level of neurotransmitters can cause behaviors such as delusions, hallucinations, and confused thinking. If there is genetic control over enzymes, then enzyme levels should be more similar for identical twins than for fraternal twins. To study this possibility, enzyme levels were measured for the enzyme monamine oxidase, or MAO, which is involved in the destruction of catecholamines. It was found that the levels of MAO were more similar in identical twins than in fraternal twins. This indicates that there are genetic differences in the control of enzyme levels (13–48, 13–76).

If different enzyme levels were involved in causing schizophrenia, you would expect different levels in schizophrenics than in controls. In five of seven studies, there were reports of lower levels of MAO in patients with a lengthy history of schizophrenia and of lower levels in patients suffering from manic-depressive problems (13–9, 13–16). These studies indicate that enzyme levels may be involved in the development of serious psychological problems (13–76).

Another question was whether individuals who were not schizophrenic, but who had low levels of MAO, would have a higher incidence of psychological problems. Perhaps a low MAO level indicates a predisposition to develop serious psychological problems. College students were selected who had either a very low or very high level of MAO and were compared for incidence of psychological problems. Those with a low level of MAO had a much higher incidence of psychological problems than those with a high level. And, those with a low level came from families who had a higher incidence of suicide or suicide attempts. A reduced level of MAO, which affects neurotransmitters, can be related to the occurrence of psychological problems and may be predictive of a possible predisposition to future problems (13–9). MAO levels in college students were computed by analyzing samples of blood from the body. Since not all chemicals freely pass from the blood supply of the body to that of the brain, lower MAO levels in the body do not necessarily mean lower levels in the brain. Thus, in the above study, we do not know if MAO levels were actually lower in the brain.

In some cases, the brains of patients diagnosed as having a long history of schizophrenia were examined after death for abnormal levels of enzymes or neurotransmitters. It was found that the brains from schizophrenics had lower levels of the enzyme **dopamine-B-hydroxylase,** which is important in the synthesis of a catecholamine, norepinephrine. In this study, there was no difference in levels of MAO in the brains of schizophrenics as compared to controls. These researchers believe that one cause of schizophrenia is a disintegration of some brain pathways that utilize norepinephrine (13–74). Changes in levels of another transmitter, dopamine, have also been hypothesized. In spite of findings of lower enzyme levels, there is yet no direct evidence that these conditions cause the schizophrenia symptoms. It is possible that they are one of the causes or that they may be the predisposition for schizophrenia or other problems to develop (13–60).

In addition to their other functions, enzymes can change neurotransmitters into chemicals that can cause hallucinations. Drugs such as **LSD (lysergic acid diethylamide)** or **mescaline** cause hallucinations by adding a structure called the **methyl group** to a transmitter such as serotonin. The addition of a methyl group, which is called **transmethylation,** occurs normally in the brain, and this is how some neurotransmitters are synthesized. It has been suggested that in schizophrenia there is an error in the transmethylation process, and the result is a brain that produces its own hallucinogens, which in turn may cause schizophrenic symptoms (13–60). Support for this idea comes from a study in which schizophrenic patients were given drugs that increased transmethylation—the patients' symptoms became worse (13–2).

Enzymes are involved in thousands of chemical reactions that affect brain activity. Without enzymes, many chemical reactions and their related brain activities would simply cease. Similarly, when the enzymes are changed, brain activity is changed. There are numerous ways that enzymes can be involved in causing psychological problems. Transmethylation is one possibility.

Why is it that some people do and some people do not develop schizophrenia? One explanation may be found in the genes—whether or not you have a genetic predisposition for abnormal enzyme or neurotransmitter levels. But not all individuals with abnormal enzyme levels develop schizophrenia. Whether or not you become schizophrenic must be related to the kind of personality (behavior patterns) you develop and how you respond to pressures in your environment. If you had some genetic predisposition and also had an unusual personality or an unusual response to pressure, the interaction of these factors might result in schizophrenia. Another cause might be that the brain itself, either because of genetics or faulty metabolism, uses transmethylation to change normal neurotransmitters into chemicals capable of producing schizophrenic symptoms. Since everyone's brain appears capable of synthesizing hallucinogens through transmethylation, the actual occurrence may be triggered by the individual's responses to environmental stress. Not only must we search the brain for causes of schizophrenia, but also the person's environment (13–42).

Treatment of Schizophrenia

The single drug most responsible for reducing the number of patients in mental hospitals is **chlorpromazine.** Introduced in the 1950s, chlorpromazine was one of the first drugs effective in the treatment of schizophrenia. Chlorpromazine is from a family of drugs called **phenothiazines** (fee-no-THIGH-ah-zine). The phenothiazines, as well as new drugs, have been used with varying degrees of success in treating schizophrenia (13–14). Sometimes they alleviate the symptoms, such as thought confusion, but there is a certain cost to the patient.

The cost is the occurrence of side effects. While on chlorpromazine, patients tend to be in a lethargic or doped state. After 1 or 2 years on phenothiazines, the patient may develop slow, rhythmical movements of the mouth and lip smacking, as well as unusual movements of the limbs or other parts of the body. These symptoms, called **tardive**

dyskinesia (TAR-diff dis-caw-KNEE-zee-ah), may occur in as many as 50 percent of those patients on phenothiazines for an extended time (13–13). The symptoms do not go away when the drug is withdrawn, which suggests that the drug causes some long-term brain changes. Tardive dyskinesia is a serious side effect and has caused concern that usage of phenothiazines should be limited. There have been attempts to treat tardive dyskinesia with other drugs, but these new drugs may have their own side effects (13–21). Other side effects of phenothiazines may include problems in male sexual response. In one sample of 57 men, 60 percent reported problems with ejaculation (13–36). Although the phenothiazines as well as other drugs can alleviate schizophrenic symptoms, they may at the same time cause other undesirable side effects.

In treating schizophrenia with drugs, doctors and researchers are also concerned over the length of time that the patient must be maintained on the drug. After treatment and discharge from the hospital, many patients remain on phenothiazines for years. In spite of being maintained on drugs, a substantial number of patients experience the return of symptoms, and many must be rehospitalized—from 20 to 70 percent (13–51). In one study, patients were followed for 2 years after discharge from the hospital. After their release, some were maintained on chlorpromazine and were compared with others given inactive pills, or placebos. Of those given chlorpromazine, 48 percent developed their original symptoms or were rehospitalized. Of those given placebos, 80 percent relapsed to their original problems (13–31). This study shows that being maintained on chlorpromazine is more effective than being on a placebo. It also shows that while some patients on chlorpromazine remain free of their symptoms, almost half relapse. Some patients must remain on drug therapy for years, while others receive drug treatment and then go off drugs with no relapse. Finally, there is a small percentage of schizophrenics that is not responsive to any drug treatment. The phenothiazines and other drugs may not cure schizophrenia, but rather function to keep the symptoms under control so that the individual can learn to readjust to his or her world. Since your response to various stressors in your environment affects the level of neurotransmitters in your brain, the removal of these stressors is also a part of curing schizophrenia.

Affective Disorders

One patient entered the hospital talking incessantly and boisterously, chiefly about his plan for peace in the Middle East; he had already made several phone calls about it to the State Department in Washington, Whitehall in London, and to the Presidential Palace in Cairo. His wife reported that he had slept only 3 or 4 hours a night for the past month and that he spent most of the small hours puttering around and singing cheerfully in his basement workshop. Occasionally she found him outdoors clipping the hedge or weeding the flower beds in the wan light of dawn. (13–20, p. 240)*

This patient has excessive energy, sleeps little, and has no idea that there is anything unusual about his boundless behavior. Together, these symptoms are called **mania,** and they interfere with normal functioning in your daily life, job, or family. After 2 weeks of drug treatment, the man described above was less talkative, could speak reasonably about his unusual behavior before coming to the hospital, and could engage in therapy sessions. The drug he received was once used as a substitute for salt but was discontinued because of harmful side effects. The drug is **lithium.** Although very little is known about its action on the brain, lithium may reduce levels of norepinephrine. In the treatment of mania, lithium is more effective than chlorpromazine, and this difference suggests that particular neurotransmitters may be involved in particular psychological problems (13–20). In spite of its success, lithium does not help approximately 20 percent of manics. This indicates that there are different types of mania and different causes, which may involve different neurotransmitters.

Everyone has been depressed at some time in his life. But if you were so depressed that you could not function and thought about suicide, you would be diagnosed as having serious or psychotic **depression.** At one end of affective behavior is the excessive energy of mania, and at the other end is the terrible depth of depression. Patients having severe depression are approximately ten times more common than those with mania. Some scientists have attempted to explain the occurrence of depression and mania on the basis of changes in levels of neurotransmitters (13–57). Possibly during depression there is a lowered level of the catecholamine norepinephrine, while during mania there is an excess. This idea is called the **catecholamine theory of affective disorders**. Support for this theory is seen in the fact that drugs such as amphetamine or **imipramine** (im-IP-rah-mean), which increase levels of norepinephrine, cause an elevation in mood. Drugs such as **reserpine** (RES-er-peen), which decrease levels of norepinephrine, cause depression. The drug imipramine, which increases levels of norepinephrine, is in fact effective in treating depression. In the long-term treatment of depression, one study found that after 1 year, 60 percent of the women who had been discharged and maintained on drugs experienced the reoccurrence of mild symptoms (13–70). These results indicate that, like the phenothiazines used in treating schizophrenia, antidepressive drugs do not cure the problem but rather relieve the symptoms, so that the patient can readjust to the world. As with schizophrenics, there is a small percentage of patients with serious depression that does not respond to

*From *Lithium in the Treatment of Mood Disorders* by A. A. Gattozzi. Rockville, MD: National Institute of Mental Health, 1974. Reprinted by permission.

drug therapy. The catecholamine theory of mania and depression is a starting point for understanding how changes in levels of neurotransmitters could relate to these serious psychological problems.

Tranquilizers

After Barbara had given birth prematurely, her doctor prescribed Librium—ten mg four times a day—to soothe her anxiety about the baby's health. But after a few months she complained that the medication no longer seemed effective. On the basis of the drug manufacturer's claims that Librium was safe, harmless, and non-addicting, her doctor promptly upped the dosage to twenty-five mg four or five times a day.

About a year later, hospitalization for surgery abruptly interrupted her Librium regimen. Two days after her operation, Barbara started to hallucinate, hearing French horns and orchestral sounds, and five days later went into convulsions. She was going through withdrawal from the drug that is supposed to be nonaddicting. (13–46, p. 14)

Literally millions of people take tranquilizers for relief of anxiety, stress, or mild depression. In the United States in 1973 there were 80 million prescriptions written for two tranquilizers, **Librium** and **Valium,** which are common names for two derivatives of the chemical **benzodiazepine** (ben-zoh-die-AS-ah-peen). In 1976 Valium was the most frequently prescribed drug in the United States, surpassing birth control pills and painkillers. The two tranquilizers are frequently prescribed as muscle relaxants. If you took one of these benzodiazepines, you would feel calmness and diminished anxiety. Although these drugs are in wide usage for treatment of anxiety, mild depression, stress, and insomnia, little is known about their action on the brain. It is thought that the benzodiazepines may decrease anxiety by making more serotonin available in the brain (13–75). It is known that the benzodiazepines are not effective in treating schizophrenia.

When you first begin taking benzodiazepines, you may feel more relaxed and less anxious. But, as in the case of Barbara, if you continue to take them on a regular basis, you will discover that a larger and larger dosage is needed to achieve the same physiological or psychological effect. This adaptation to the drug's effect, or tolerance, results in the need to increase the drug's dosage. As Barbara continued to take a high dosage of the drug, her body became **physically dependent** on the drug—this is called **addiction**. Because she was physically dependent or addicted to Librium, withdrawal of the drug caused her to experience insomnia, agitation, loss of appetite, and convulsions. If you are addicted to a drug, stopping the drug causes **withdrawal symptoms**. These symptoms occur because the body has undergone certain changes in order to compensate for the drug's actions. In other words, the body tries to return to its normal chemical state, or maintain homeostasis, despite the presence of the drug. When the drug is suddenly

Figure 13–3 A series of paintings that reflect the artist's perceptual experiences as changed by schizophrenia. Although the subject is always the same, a cat, you can see the schizophrenia-caused distortion, especially in the final picture (bottom right), which shows no similarity to a cat. The artist, Louis Wain, developed schizophrenia in his later years. (© Guttmann Maclay Collection, Institute of Psychiatry, London. Wide World Photos.)

Tranquilizers

DRUG TO SLOW HEART RATE ALSO SEEMS TO HELP BEHAVIOR DISORDERS

A chance observation by an Israeli doctor seven years ago has led medical researchers down a new path in the quest to find a better treatment for schizophrenia.

The story began in 1969 when a 26-year-old woman was admitted to Beilinson Medical Center in Tel Aviv suffering from a peculiar genetic disease called porphyria.

Two of the chief symptoms of acute porphyria are a very rapid heart rate with high blood pressure and mental disturbances.

Dr. Abraham Atsmon and his colleagues gave the woman the generally accepted dosage of a drug called propranolol, now widely used to slow heart rate, but it had no effect. Gradually, the dosage was increased until—when the dosage had reached a level far higher than usually given—the woman's heart rate returned to near normal.

Not only did the heart rate come down, but all the other symptoms, including the mental disturbances, disappeared also, Atsmon recalled last week during talks to physicians here.

The doctors in Israel thought the acute attack of porphyria had passed, so they stopped the drug, Atsmon said.

But within six hours all of the symptoms returned. The drug treatment was resumed and the symptoms again disappeared.

Fascinated by the disappearance of the mental symptoms at those very high doses, Atsmon and his colleagues at Tel Aviv University next tried propranolol on a second patient—also suspected of having porphyria—who was having hallucinations and was in an excited mental state.

The result was the same as in the first case. When the drug was given, the mental symptoms disappeared. When it was stopped, the symptoms returned, Atsmon told doctors during talks at the City of Hope Medical Center and USC school of medicine.

The observations on the two cases subsequently prompted psychiatrists in Israel and in England to begin a study using propranolol as a treatment for psychosis.

To date, 26 patients have been treated at the Beilinson Medical Center in Israel and 55 at Friern Hospital in London.

The British and Israeli psychiatrists, who also were here to discuss their studies, said they were "encouraged enough to keep on with the work," but emphasized that it is still in an early stage.

Nevertheless, Dr. Eugene Roberts, chairman of neurosciences at the City of Hope, said the propranolol studies "give hope for a breakthrough in schizophrenia" for the first time since the introduction of tranquillizing drugs.

"Schizophrenia research is littered with false dawns," cautioned Dr. Neil J. Yorkston, a psychiatrist from Maudsley and Friern hospitals who has conducted the British studies.

One of the undesirable features of the major antipsychotic drugs is their tendency to cause difficulty in arm and leg movement and to produce a "zombie" effect.

But Yorkston said he is encouraged by the lack, so far, of long-term toxic effects of propranolol. Patients who have been ill up to 20 years, despite treatment and antipsychotic drugs, have responded to propranolol treatment, he said. A

few recovered rapidly, but the general rule for those in whom the drug had a good effect, was a slow improvement, he said.

Twenty-eight of the 55 schizophrenics treated by Yorkston have shown improvement, he said. Eleven of the 28 received the standard drug treatment as well as propranolol, but 17 did it on propranolol alone, the psychiatrist reported.

"We conclude that propranolol can cause remission of symptoms when used by itself. We believe it is effective," Yorkston said.

But he pointed out that the kind of study that most researchers agree is essential has not yet been completed. This is the so-called double blind study, in which neither the patient nor the staff knows which patients are receiving the active drug and which are receiving an ineffective sugar pill.

Yorkston said the double blind study now is under way in England and should produce results in about one year.

The studies already made by Yorkston and Dr. Saniha A. Zaki in England and Dr. Ailana Blum in Israel point to schizophrenics who are active, restless and aggressive as being the ones most apt to respond favorably to the drug.

Although the researchers do not know why propranolol works in some mental cases, they believe it slows heart rate by blocking nerve centers that release norepinephrine, a chemical that transmits nerve impulses.

It is suspected, however, that propranolol somehow reduces excessive chemical activity in the brain, thereby restoring it to a more normal level.

SOURCE: Harry Nelson, Times Medical Writer, *Los Angeles Times*, December 27, 1976. Copyright © 1976 by Los Angeles Times.

withdrawn, the body continues to compensate even though the drug is no longer present. As a result, the body overcompensates, and the result is withdrawal symptoms. Different drugs have different withdrawal symptoms. With continued usage of drugs, tolerance almost always develops, while physical dependency or addiction may not always occur. It is thought that tolerance and addiction occur in the brain, probably at the level of the neuron, but the exact mechanism is unknown.

Although tranquilizers may provide initial relief from anxiety or related symptoms, there is less evidence that they are effective over time. In fact, one researcher concluded that anxious patients seem to improve with any kind of attention—whether they are prescribed a drug or placebo—and that it is often difficult to determine whether the drug is any more effective than a placebo in treating anxiety (13–33). Finally, many patients with symptoms of anxiety may recover within 2 weeks with no treatment. From the enormous number of prescriptions written for tranquilizers, it is evident that people seek quick relief from their anxiety or depression. They may come to believe that they cannot function without their daily Valium or Librium, even though it actually may be no more effective in curing anxiety than a placebo. If you believe that a pill is very effective in treating your anxiety, and that you cannot function without it, you are **psychologically dependent** on the pill. In some cases, psychological dependency on a drug can so motivate a person to continue taking the drug that the behavior resembles physical dependence (13–66).

Stimulants

Amphetamines

The patient has just been admitted to the hospital emergency room, so violent that it took three strong men to bring him in. . . . Yesterday John felt that others were looking at him in a peculiar way. He had walked the streets all night and spent his morning looking for gold in the gravel paths of the city park. This afternoon he heard voices talking about him. Hostile, secretive persons were looking at him; he was sure they were planning to kill him. (13–58, p. 42)*

John was diagnosed as having paranoid schizophrenia, until the doctors discovered that he had been taking a drug. For the past 3 months, he had been injecting himself with **methamphetamine** (met-ah-am-FET-ah-mean) (common name: **Methedrine**). There are many examples of heavy amphetamine users like John becoming paranoid and confused (13–58). This finding was also confirmed in the laboratory when four men were given 10 mg of amphetamine every hour of the day and night. Within a period of only

*From ''The True Speed Trip: Schizophrenia'' by S. H. Snyder. Reprinted from Psychology Today Magazine. Copyright © 1972 Ziff-Davis Publishing Company.

2 to 5 days, each of the four exhibited signs of severe or psychotic paranoia called **amphetamine psychosis**. When the drug was stopped, the paranoid symptoms and confused thinking went away in 3 days (13–25). Amphetamine is one of the few drugs that can cause symptoms very similar to those observed in paranoid schizophrenics. As in the treatment of schizophrenia, phenothiazines are effective in treating amphetamine psychosis. The similarities between paranoid schizophrenia and amphetamine psychosis make the latter a possible model for understanding the hows and whys of schizophrenia (13–59).

The amount of amphetamine in the usual pill is approximately 5–10 mg. This amount can cause sleeplessness, loss of appetite, hyperactivity, mild euphoria, and reduction in feelings of fatigue. With each succeeding pill, tolerance develops and these effects decrease. Beginning with 1 or 2 pills a day, the user may eventually reach 100 a day because of tolerance. At this point, the user may turn to taking amphetamine by injection, and continued usage may result in confused thinking, irritability, fear, repititious behavior, hallucinations, delusions, or symptoms similar to paranoid schizophrenia. The user is now addicted to amphetamine, and if the drug is stopped, there will be withdrawal symptoms of great depression with feelings of incredible fatigue. If the heavy user remains off amphetamine for 1 to 6 months, the paranoid symptoms and confused thinking will usually disappear (13–17).

In the brain, amphetamine blocks the reuptake of norepinephrine and possibly dopamine, causing more of these neurotransmitters to remain in the synapse. The increased levels of norepinephrine and dopamine are thought to cause the euphoria, sleeplessness, repetitive behavior, and other effects. In chemical structure, amphetamine is very similar to the catecholamine norepinephrine. Besides affecting transmitter levels in the brain, amphetamine causes a significant increase in blood pressure, blood sugar, breathing, and dilation of the pupils. These physiological responses are similar to those produced by norepinephrine when it is released from the adrenal medulla in times of stress. Since the chemical structures of amphetamine and norepinephrine are similar, you would expect both chemicals to produce similar physiological responses, which, in fact, they do.

There has been much concern over the use of amphetamines to relieve boredom, improve performance, and help in weight reduction. In the case of weight reduction, amphetamines are not effective in the long term because tolerance develops to its appetite-suppressing properties. Also, people on the drug do not learn to change their eating habits. When drug usage stops, they return to the old habit of overeating (13–32). Because amphetamines cause euphoria and feelings of great power, they can relieve boredom and improve performance in sports. But with amphetamine usage, there is the danger of tolerance and having to take ever-increasing dosages, of becoming physically and psychologically dependent upon it, and of possible damage to

Figure 13–4 Examples of the distortions in perception caused by the continued heavy usage of amphetamines. The drawings show feelings of being watched, strangled, and followed, which reflect the paranoia developing from heavy, long-term amphetamine usage. (Reproduced from *Psychology Today* magazine. Copyright © 1972 Ziff-Davis Publishing Company.)

Behavior Disorders and Drugs

health because of increased blood pressure. There is now pressure to limit the prescription of amphetamines to treatment of sleeping sickness or narcolepsy (see Chapter 10) or to treatment of children diagnosed as hyperactive or hyperkinetic (discussed later in this chapter).

Caffeine

If you were not a heavy coffee drinker, 2 cups would cause you to experience some mood elevation and difficulty in going to sleep. It would also cause your brain, especially your cortex, to be aroused. An aroused cortex has EEG waves of low amplitude and fast frequency. One cup of coffee contains between 100 and 200 mg of caffeine, a (12 oz) bottle of cola contains 35–55 mg, and a chocolate bar may have up to 25 mg of caffeine per 30 g (1 oz). Because it arouses the brain, caffeine is classified as a stimulant, although it is far less potent than amphetamine. As a stimulant, caffeine may increase performance on tasks requiring quick reaction times (13–18). The way in which caffeine will affect your performance on nonmotor tasks, such as tests of verbal ability, may depend upon your personality. Under stress of time pressure, caffeine increased the scores of individuals classified as extroverts and decreased the scores of individuals classified as introverts (13–53). This means that drinking coffee before taking an exam may help you perform if you are someone who would be classified as an extrovert and may hinder you if you are someone who would be classified as an introvert.

In low to moderate amounts, caffeine does not usually result in tolerance or addiction. With extremely large doses, from 15 to 18 cups a day, tolerance and addiction can develop along with side effects of lack of appetite, insomnia, irritability, and flushing. After caffeine or any stimulant is metabolized by the body, there usually follows a period when the person feels tired and possibly depressed. This means that if you drank coffee all during the day, you might feel very tired and experience mild depression in the evening. Although you may not develop a physical dependency (addiction) to caffeine, you may become psychologically dependent. You have often heard the remark about needing a cup of coffee in order to get started in the morning or to keep going in the afternoon or to think straight.

Nicotine

Just as some cannot think straight without a cup of coffee, others cannot do so without a cigarette. You may wonder why Americans smoked 620 billion cigarettes in 1976 from packages clearly labeled ''Warning: The Surgeon General Has Determined That Cigarette Smoking Is Dangerous to Your Health.'' Of the many reasons why people continue to smoke, one of them is to satisfy their addiction to **nicotine**. If you are a smoker, you have developed a physical dependency or addiction to nicotine. If you switch to brands with lower levels of nicotine, you may find yourself smoking more cigarettes to obtain the amount of nicotine to which your body has become accustomed. If you stop smoking, you may experience withdrawal symptoms that include headaches, sweating, insomnia, nervousness, and drowsiness. Like caffeine, nicotine is one of the most widely used stimulants. It affects the brain and causes EEG waves indicating arousal. It also stimulates the body by causing increases in blood pressure, heart rate, and release of epinephrine.

If you compare your first smoking experience with your present one, you will see that you have developed a tolerance to nicotine. Your first smoking experience produced sweating, nausea, and even vomiting, but with the continued usage these symptoms have long since disappeared. Evidence is strong that the continued usage of nicotine may result in serious health problems, such as lung cancer and emphysema. Many users do not consider nicotine and caffeine drugs or stimulants since they have become such an integral part of personal and social interactions.

Cocaine

For centuries, workers in the mines of Peru have chewed coca leaves to obtain stamina and to deaden the misery of poverty and hard work. The leaves of the coca plant contain **cocaine,** a powerful stimulant. Either inhaled or injected, cocaine can cause euphoria, feeling of great power, loss of appetite, great indifference to pain, and reduction in fatigue (13–12). The euphoria and other effects from cocaine are very similar to those produced by injections of amphetamine. One difference is that the effects of cocaine are briefer (minutes) than those of amphetamine (hours). Like amphetamine, cocaine has an effect on sexual responses, in that it delays ejaculation and orgasm. Claims that amphetamine and cocaine are aphrodisiacs arise from their ability to prolong the occurrence of orgasm and to intensify the awareness of sensory feelings.

In addition to its use as a stimulant, cocaine is an extremely powerful local anesthetic. When applied to the skin, it blocks nerve conduction that eliminates feelings of pain. Except for its usage as a local anesthetic, cocaine has no other medical applications. Its action in the brain is very similar to that of amphetamine. Cocaine prevents the reuptake of norepinephrine which builds up in the synapse and continues to affect postsynaptic neurons, causing the euphoria and other effects. Once the effects of cocaine have worn off, there are mild withdrawal symptoms, including fatigue, weariness, and depression. The user may wish to alleviate these feelings by taking another dose of cocaine. Cocaine use results in little or no tolerance and no physical dependency or addiction. In this sense, cocaine differs from heroin, to which one may become physically addicted. There have been examples of individuals who developed a strong psychological dependency on cocaine. The most famous of these was Sigmund Freud.

THE CHEMISTRY OF SMOKING

"Don't ask me why I smoke," says the grim-looking man in the Winston cigarette ad. Columbia Psychologist Stanley Schachter, 54, agrees that it is better not to ask. The Winston man—or any other heavy smoker—would probably say he smokes for pleasure, or because it calms his nerves, gives him something to do with his hands or solves his Freudian oral problems. "Almost any smoker can convince you and himself that he smokes for psychological reasons or that smoking does something positive for him—it's all very unlikely," says Schachter, a virtual chain smoker himself. "We smoke because we're phsically addicted to nicotine. Period."

Schachter reached his conclusion after conducting a series of experiments over the past four years. Like other researchers, Schachter and his team (Brett Silverstein, Lynn Kozlowski and Deborah Perlick) found that heavy smokers, given only low-nicotine cigarettes to smoke, tried to compensate; to inhale their normal quota of nicotine, they smoked more cigarettes and puffed more frequently. Even so, some were not able to make up the difference and showed withdrawal symptoms: increased eating, irritability and poorer concentration.

The researchers then went further by testing volunteers to see whether smoking eases stress. On the assumption that the more anxious a person is, the less pain he will tolerate, groups of smokers and non-smokers were asked to endure as much electric shock as they could bear. Smokers proved to be sissies when deprived of cigarettes or given only low-nicotine brands. Those supplied with armloads of high-nicotine brands to smoke accepted a higher number of shocks—but no more than the control group of nonsmokers. Schachter's conclusion: "Smoking doesn't reduce anxiety or calm the nerves. Not smoking increases anxiety by throwing the smoker into withdrawal."

Mindless Machine

Then why do most smokers smoke so heavily when under stress? Schachter's answer: because stress depletes body nicotine, and the smoker has to puff more to keep at his usual nicotine level. The key is the acidity of urine. One result of anxiety and stress is a high acid content in the urine. Highly acidic urine flushes away much more body nicotine than normal urine does. Schachter discovered that smokers who were administered mild acids (vitamin C and Acidulin) in heavy doses smoked more over a period of days than comparable smokers who took bicarbonates to make their urine more alkaline. His tests also show that bicarbonates reduce smoking under stress. One experiment indicates that partygoing increases the acidity of the urine for smokers and nonsmokers alike. "It follows," Schachter says puckishly, "that the concerned smoker should take the Alka-Seltzer before—not after—the party."

Schachter says his findings, which will be published in next month's *Journal of Experimental Psychology,* show that "the smoker's mind is in the bladder. You just don't need the mind to explain smoking. When plasma nicotine is below the smoker's usual level, he smokes; when it is at his level, he doesn't." Schachter agrees with other researchers who have recommended development of a new high-nicotine, low-tar, low-gas cigarette. Current low-tar, low-nicotine brands, he says, may be lethal. "You wind up spending more, smoking more and getting far more dangerous combustion products for the same nicotine payoff as stronger cigarettes. Worse, it's probably a good guess that the low-tar brands are hooking millions of teen-agers. When I was young, that first Camel or Lucky made so many kids sick that they stayed off cigarettes for good. Now so many brands are so weak that the kids don't get sick enough to stop right away. They just get hooked."

Schachter's own "biochemical mechanism" currently requires 2½ packs a day, and he sees little hope of cutting down. "It's possible to control and restrict smoking, but the price appears to be a chronic state of withdrawal." He admits that like millions of other smokers, "I'm not willing to face that withdrawal."

SOURCE: *Time,* February 21, 1977. Reprinted by permission from TIME, The Weekly Newsmagazine; Copyright Time Inc. 1977.

Amphetamines and Hyperactivity

The child was in constant motion, as if he were driven from place to place. He had great difficulty attending to any one thing very long, and the result was poor performance in school. Often he behaved impulsively or acted like a bully in his play and social interactions with other children. This combination of symptoms occurs more frequently in boys than in girls and is often noticed first in the classroom situation. A child with these symptoms is said to have hyperactivity, or **hyperkinesis,** or **minimal brain dysfunction** (MBD). MBD occurs in 5–10 percent of the school population. It has become a very serious problem, both because it is difficult to diagnose and because it raises the issue of whether drugs should be given to young children (13–11).

Although the syndrome is called **minimal brain dysfunction,** there are no definitive signs of brain damage, nor can diagnosis be made on the basis of EEG wave analysis (13–26). There may be related signs, such as noticeable clumsiness, as seen in difficulties in tying shoelaces, buttoning buttons, and throwing and catching a ball. Some believe that MBD may not be caused by actual brain damage but rather by problems arising from genetic factors or maldevelopment in the womb (13–72). To complicate the situation further, MBD symptoms have also been attributed to poor oxygenation of the brain arising from a heart problem, to low blood sugar, to low levels of calcium, and to artificial colors and preservatives in food (13–1, 13–68). Many different factors—genetic, fetal, dietetic, physiological, neurological, and psychological—may give rise to the behavioral symptoms known as MBD.

Children may have these symptoms in varying degrees, from being a nuisance in the classroom, to doing poorly in school, to never sitting in a chair for more than a minute. There is no one sure sign, and diagnosis of MBD may be unwarranted. If drug treatment is recommended, the child will be given either amphetamine or a chemical very similar in structure, **methylphenidate** (common name: **Ritalin**). Since both of these drugs are stimulants, it is difficult to explain how they function to decrease hyperactivity. Possibly the syndrome is mislabeled. Instead of being hyperactive, the children may have an attention problem, and the drug helps them concentrate or be attentive. Although many children show dramatic improvements when given these drugs, there are a number of children diagnosed as MBD (15–25 percent) who are not helped by drugs. Perhaps these children are misdiagnosed as having MBD or do not share the same causes as children who are helped by the drugs.

In the child, as in the adult, the side effects of taking amphetamine or methylphenidate may include insomnia, nausea, and loss of appetite. Most of these side effects diminish over a week's time, as a tolerance to the drug develops. The beneficial effects include reduction in activity and increased ability to hold and maintain attention. Chil-

dren who have been on drugs for long periods—up to 5 years—do have a reduction in hyperactivity, but they may continue to show problems in academic and interpersonal relationships (13–5, 13–45, 13–54). Amphetamine and methylphenidate seem to deal mainly with the symptoms of activity and attention and may be less effective in treating academic and personal problems. These drugs do not cure MBD, but rather reduce some of the symptoms. No one knows the long-term effects of maintaining children, whose brains are still developing, on stimulant drugs. However, it does appear that when children are taken off the drugs in adolescence, many of the behavior problems reemerge.

Opiates: Morphine, Heroin

The resinous material of the opium poppy contains **morphine,** a powerful pain killer, or **analgesic.** Drugs that have analgesic effects similar to that of morphine are called **opiates** or **narcotics.** Of the opiates, **heroin** is the one you hear about most often. It is a synthetic, or manufactured, derivative of morphine. Before 1914 opium was as available as aspirin is today and was used in the treatment of pain and diarrhea. After 1914 the Harrison Narcotic Act placed opiates under strict controls.

Compared to morphine, heroin is more powerful, because it more easily passes from the blood supply of the body to that of the brain. The first injection of morphine or heroin may be unpleasant. Subsequent injections usually produce a pleasant state of euphoria consisting of feelings of well-being and peacefulness. With continued usage of heroin, tolerance develops and the dosage must be increased to achieve the same effects. In one individual, heroin dosage over a 19-day period increased from 18 to 180 mg. With continued usage, a physical dependency or addiction develops so that the body needs the drug's presence to function normally. If the drug is stopped, there are withdrawal symptoms that may include intense craving for the drug, sweating, fever, chills, violent retching, insomnia, and almost unbearable body aches. The severity of these withdrawal symptoms depends upon how long and how much heroin was being used.

Although morphine and its synthetic derivative, heroin, are powerful analgesics, it is not known how they act on the brain. Persons who have taken the drugs report that under the influence of the drugs they still feel pain but are no longer bothered or concerned by it. This means that the sensations of pain remain but that morphine alters the awareness or perception of pain.

It may come as a surprise to learn that morphinelike substances occur naturally in your brain. These substances, called **endorphins** (end-OR-fin), have analgesic actions similar to morphine (13–22). Endorphins may be involved in the physical process that produces opiate addiction (13–22, 13–69), may function as neurotransmitters (13–19), or may be involved in the causation of mental problems

Some treatment programs are based on total drug abstinence, such as synanon, and they have been effective for a small percentage of heroin addicts. Another method has been to maintain the addict on a controlled dose of heroin, as is done in England, or to maintain the addict on a substitute opiate, **methadone,** as is done in America. Maintaining the addict on either drug prevents the occurrence of withdrawal symptoms and allows many addicts to pursue relatively normal lives (13–7). Methadone is a synthetic narcotic that has the analgesic properties of morphine but is dissimilar in chemical structure. Because it can be administered orally, methadone is easier to take than heroin, and its effects are longer lasting. When taken orally, methadone does not produce the euphoria of heroin. However, it does produce euphoria if it is injected.

Another method of treating heroin addicts is to administer drugs that counteract the euphoric effects of heroin. Since they eliminate, or antagonize, the euphoric effects of heroin, these drugs are called **narcotic antagonists**. Much discussion has been centered on whether treatment of addicts with other drugs (methadone, narcotic antagonists) will ever prove to be effective in the long run if users are not also reeducated (13–28). The difficulty in treating heroin addicts involves discovering how the opiates affect the brain and also how to reeducate these people and make their lives meaningful without drugs.

Alcohol

After one or two drinks, you have experiences of mild euphoria, relaxation, and loss of inhibitions. These effects often lead people to think that alcohol is a stimulant. The opposite is true. With continued drinking, alcohol will cause a general depression of neurons in the brain, especially in the cortex and reticular formation. The function of the reticular formation is to keep the cortex aroused and to maintain an alert state. The depressant effects of alcohol on the brain and reticular formation are very similar to those of anesthesia and barbituates in producing sleep and unconsciousness.

If you were to drink 4 oz of whiskey or eight bottles of beer, you would probably be legally drunk (0.10 percent blood alcohol). If you were to quickly gulp a pint of 100-proof whiskey, you would go into a coma because of the depressant effects of alcohol on the brain and reticular formation. If you were to quickly gulp 2 pt, you would probably die. In one 3-day period, five students having a party drank 16 gal of wine, 6 qt of tequilla, 4 qt of gin, 4 qt of bourbon, 2 qt of Cynar liqueur, and one bottle of 190-proof Everclear. Of the five, one died, and his blood alcohol was found to be more than 40 times that of someone considered legally drunk. Another was in a critical condition but survived. The other three had massive toxic reactions, commonly called **hangovers**. Their symptoms included nausea,

Figure 13–5 A woman under the influence of heroin. Heroin, made from morphine, produces a "rush" when injected. The continued usage of heroin results in addiction, and a person will experience withdrawal symptoms when deprived of the drug. (Archie Lieberman, from Black Star.)

by upsetting the chemical homeostasis in the brain (13–4, 13–34). The discovery of endorphins in the early 1970s was the first indication of the presence of morphinelike substances in the brain. Endorphins may be of tremendous importance in explaining how pain awareness is changed, how addiction develops, how addiction might be cured, and how psychological problems develop (13–43).

Treatment of Heroin Addiction

At one time, it was thought that simply withdrawing from heroin, "going cold turkey," would cure the addiction and the drug craving. This kind of treatment has proved unsuccessful: approximately 90 percent of those who go through the withdrawal program return to using heroin within 6 months (13–52).

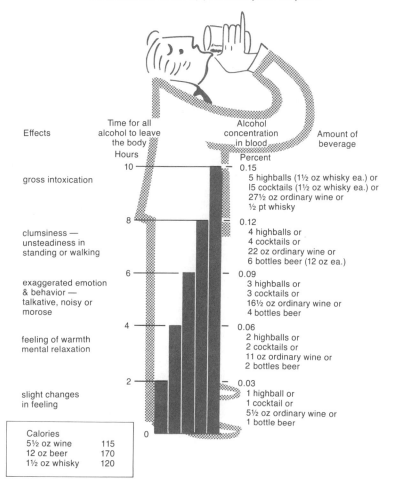

ALCOHOL LEVELS IN THE BLOOD
After drinks taken on an empty stomach by a 150-lb person

| Effects | Time for all alcohol to leave the body Hours | Alcohol concentration in blood Percent | Amount of beverage |

gross intoxication

0.15
5 highballs (1½ oz whisky ea.) or
15 cocktails (1½ oz whisky ea.) or
27½ oz ordinary wine or
½ pt whisky

clumsiness —
unsteadiness in
standing or walking

0.12
4 highballs or
4 cocktails or
22 oz ordinary wine or
6 bottles beer (12 oz ea.)

exaggerated emotion
& behavior —
talkative, noisy or
morose

0.09
3 highballs or
3 cocktails or
16½ oz ordinary wine or
4 bottles beer

feeling of warmth
mental relaxation

0.06
2 highballs or
2 cocktails or
11 oz ordinary wine or
2 bottles beer

slight changes
in feeling

0.03
1 highball or
1 cocktail or
5½ oz ordinary wine or
1 bottle beer

Calories	
5½ oz wine	115
12 oz beer	170
1½ oz whisky	120

Figure 13–6 The effects of alcohol taken on an empty stomach by a person weighing 75 k (150 lb). As alcohol concentration rises in the blood, more and more behavioral deficits are seen. You are legally drunk if the blood alcohol level reaches 0.10 percent. (Reprinted by permission from TIME, The Weekly Newsmagazine; Copyright Time Inc. 1974.)

fatigue, the feeling of dehydration, and a throbbing head-ache. This example clearly illustrates the depressant effects of alcohol on the brain.

Since alcohol depresses the activity of the cortex, it is no surprise that thinking, planning, and processing information may be severely disrupted by moderate to heavy amounts of alcohol (five cocktails or 27 oz of wine). If you have ever had a conversation with someone who was drunk, you know firsthand how alcohol can disrupt most thinking processes. It is well known that alcohol affects motor co-ordination and reaction time, and this is why approximately 50 percent of fatal automobile accidents in the United States involve intoxicated drivers. Moderate to heavy amounts of alcohol can decrease the ability to become sexually aroused and to maintain an erection (13–55). After heavy drinking,

individuals may display more aggressive behaviors, es-pecially if they have a history for this type of behavior (13–6, 13–63). Finally, there is the danger that if barbi-turates are combined with alcohol, the combined depressant effects of these two drugs can result in death.

If you drank two martinis a day, every day, there would be little effect on behavior beyond the initial euphoria or feeling of relaxation. Physiological effects would be few, and you would be unlikely to develop a tolerance to alcohol. On the other hand, if you drank four to six martinis every day, it is likely that you would develop a tolerance. You might increase your drinking, become physically dependent upon it, and, if you stopped drinking, would have severe withdrawal symptoms. These symptoms might include a period of being very agitated, confused, and excitable, with

SCIENTISTS FIND NEW PAIN KILLER

A natural opiate produced by the pituitary gland is a far stronger pain killer than morphine and someday may be useful in treating addiction, researchers say.

Choh Hao Li, director of the Hormone Research Laboratory at the University of California here, said that the first tests on live animals have shown the natural opiate—"beta endorphin"—to be at least 20 to 40 times more effective than morphine when injected directly into the brain and three to four times more effective when injected intravenously.

Li said continuing research on the substance is revealing other opiate properties, such as its ability to relieve morphine withdrawal symptoms.

UC researchers say the test results have far reaching implications not only for pain relief but also for a deeper understanding of narcotics addiction and mental disorders.

One researcher, who declined to be identified, said, "It's a giant step ahead in understanding pain killing. But finding applications will be a long process."

Two experimenters, Horace H. Loh of UC-San Francisco and Eddie Wei of the UC-Berkeley School of Public Health, reported recently that the substance, like morphine, can be addictive. However, they noted that it may be less addictive in practice because it is effective at considerably lower dosages.

Researchers now are working to develop variations of beta-endor-

phin which will be less likely to create dependency.

Yet they concede there are many unanswered questions about why the body produces the substance, why it is addictive and whether the substance is maintained at a constant level or rises under stress.

In 1956, Li first isolated the human growth hormone. In 1975, while researching a substance in camel pituitary glands, he discovered a new peptide, beta endorphin, which he later isolated in human pituitary glands and has since learned to synthesize.

The pituitary, a small gland attached to the base of the brain, has secretions that control the other endocrine glands and influence growth, metabolism and maturation.

SOURCE: *San Diego Union Tribune,* September 23, 1976.

---

insomnia and possibly hallucinations. To decrease or prevent the occurrence of these symptoms, the individual may resume drinking and continue her dependence on alcohol.

Alcoholics

The prolonged and heavy usage of alcohol can result in severe physical and psychological dependency, commonly known as **alcoholism**. It is estimated that in the United States, there are 6–10 million alcoholics. A number of approaches have been tried in the attempt to cure alcoholism (13–50). Alcoholics Anonymous, one of the more successful programs, is based on the idea that an alcoholic must abstain from alcohol totally and permanently. Some programs get the alcoholic to associate aversive events with drinking. In these programs, you might be given a drug, antabuse, which will make you sick if you take a drink, or you might be shocked each time you drink. The difficulty with these treatments is that once the person leaves the program, the drug or shock is gone, and the person tends to return to former drinking habits. The most controversial program involves teaching alcoholics to learn to control

their drinking—that is, to drink socially and in moderation. While some researchers have called this last approach promising for some alcoholics (13–39), others have said there is not enough evidence that alcoholics can abandon abstinence in favor of controlled drinking (13–49). The latter researchers caution against widespread acceptance of a controlled drinking treatment program for alcoholics until the long-term effects have been established.

Alcohol and Brain Damage

The man appeared badly undernourished for his 54 years. Medical examination showed that many of his movements were poorly coordinated (ataxia), that he could not, when asked, move his eyes to the right or left, and that he could not remember incidents that had occurred to him months or years before his illness. The inability to recall memories that occurred before the onset of the illness is called **retrograde amnesia**. When asked to listen to a simple story and then repeat it 10 minutes later, he could not. The inability to learn or form new memories is called **anterograde amnesia**. Although he did have evidence of amnesia, he could often remember events that had happened to him as a child or young man, which showed that some memories were preserved. Sometimes he was **confused** and would think the doctor was his brother or the patient in the next bed was his mother. When asked what he had done the week before, he often made up responses, such as, ''I was flying a plane and the weather was very bad until I landed and rented a car at the airport.'' The patient had never left the hospital. Making up answers to questions is called **confabulation**. All of these symptoms, called the **Korsakoff syndrome,** were the result of heavy and prolonged consumption of alcohol.

The brains from patients with Korsakoff syndrome were studied to determine which areas were destroyed. There was damage in the cerebellum, which would explain the ataxia. Damage was found in the thalamus, especially the mammilary bodies, and less often in the hippocampus. Damage to the mammilary bodies, hippocampus, and other brain areas probably results in the memory losses. It is thought that the major damage to the brain is not caused by the alcohol itself, but rather by the vitamin B deficiency that alcohol produces. Vitamin B is soluble in water, and large amounts are lost because of the excessive urination caused by alcohol. In addition, the heavy drinker tends to skip meals and does not replenish his supply of vitamin B. When patients with Korsakoff syndrome were given vitamin B, especially thiamine, their physical symptoms (ataxia and lack of voluntary eye movements) were the first to clear up. For the other symptoms—amnesia, confusion, and confabulation—administration of thiamine results in very slow improvement, and in 80 percent of the cases, recovery is not complete (13–65). It appears that administration of thiamine early in the course of the illness may prevent Korsakoff syndrome from occurring, but once sufficient damage has occurred, there is little or no recovery. Alcoholics who do not develop Korsakoff syndrome may develop problems in abstract reasoning and thinking (13–23). Korsakoff syndrome and related deficits in abstract reasoning are examples of how the neurons in the brain can be affected by a metabolic problem—in this case, probably lack of vitamin B.

Hallucinogens

I lost all count of time. I noticed with dismay that my environment was undergoing progressive changes. My visual field wavered and everything appeared deformed as in a faulty mirror. Space and time became more and more disorganized and I was overcome by a fear that I was going out of my mind. The worst part of it being that I was clearly aware of my condition. My power of observation was unimpaired. . . . Occasionally, I felt as if I were out of my body. I thought I had died. My ego seemed suspended somewhere in space, from where I saw my dead body lying on the sofa. . . . It was particularly striking how acoustic perceptions such as noise of water gushing from a tap or the spoken word, were trans-

formed into optical illusions. I then fell asleep and awakened the next morning somewhat tired but otherwise feeling perfectly well. (13–38, p. 90)*

This is the first LSD (lysergic acid diethylamide) experience, recorded by the scientist who discovered it by accident. LSD is so powerful that several doses of the drug could be placed on the head of a pin, and 30 gm (1 oz) would be sufficient to supply 300,000 human adult doses. Drugs that can produce hallucinations, such as LSD, are called **hallucinogens** or **psychedelics**. After taking a moderate dose of LSD, you may pass through several stages. At the beginning, there may be physical symptoms, such as sweating, nausea, headache, and chills. Next you may look at a rose and think it is the sun, or have the feeling that you are hearing visual sensations or, as in the example, see the sound of gushing water. All of these are examples of distortions in perceptions. There may then be a period in which you feel that you are confronting yourself, or having great feelings of oneness or unity with God or the universe. The kind of LSD trip depends to a great extent upon the setting, the person's frame of mind, how comfortable she feels, and how secure she feels with the people or surroundings. When given in a bland laboratory setting, LSD can produce a very different experience than when taken privately. LSD can also produce terrifying effects. These effects can sometimes be terminated with chlorpromazine, the same drug effective in treating some forms of schizophrenia. Yet, in some individuals, chlorpromazine may actually intensify a bad LSD experience. After taking LSD repeatedly, some persons experience flashbacks weeks or months after taking the drug. The cause of the flashbacks is unknown.

LSD is thought to affect the brain in two different ways. One is by acting on the neurotransmitter serotonin. (Serotonin is also involved in sleep, as discussed in Chapter 10). The other is by increasing the reticular formation's sensitivity to incoming sensory stimuli (13–40). Increased sensitivity of the reticular formation might explain how visual and auditory experiences become so distorted. With continued usage, a person may develop a tolerance to LSD, but there is no evidence that a physical dependency develops. There has been much discussion as to whether LSD causes chromosomal damage or birth defects. Current research indicates that LSD does not cause any more chromosomal damage than other drugs, such as caffeine or aspirin, and that it probably does not cause birth defects (13–15, 13–41).

At one time, LSD was used in the treatment of serious psychological problems and alcoholism, and in treatment of terminally ill patients, to help them adjust to chronic pain

*Reproduced by permission of the Minister of Supply and Services Canada from the Interim Report of the Commission of Inquiry into the Non-Medical Use of Drugs, G. Le Dain, Chairman, Ottawa, Canada, 1970.

Figure 13-7 Hallucinogenic drugs, such as LSD, cause alterations in perception so that ordinary things become extraordinary. (Robert Foothorap / Jeroboam, Inc.)

and impending death. It is rarely used today because the superiority of LSD to other treatment has never been established (13–7, 13–71).

Other drugs that can produce hallucinations include **psilocybin,** which is found in mushrooms, and **mescaline,** which come from a spineless cactus called **peyote.** It is thought that both LSD and psilocybin affect the neurotransmitter serotonin, while mescaline acts on norepinephrine. As is becoming clear, most of the drugs that have been discussed seem to act on serotonin, norepinephrine, or dopamine.

Marihuana

In 1976 a Berkeley professor of medical physics told a county medical society that marihuana can cause a person to become withdrawn and confused and could destroy a person in a few years. This statement is contrary to most recent findings, which indicate that, in moderate doses, marihuana is a relatively harmless drug. The idea that smoking marihuana destroys all motivation and causes con-

fusion is called the **amotivational syndrome.** Since this idea was presented, studies on college students have found no motivational differences between users and nonusers (13–30). In fact, even those who had smoked 7–25 cigarettes a day for 10–25 years showed no evidence of a difference in motivation levels or ability to think straight (13–56).

Serious health hazards that have been attributed to smoking marihuana are chromosomal damage, suppression of ability to fight off infections (immunological response), interference with the sexual reproduction system, and brain damage. We will look at the current findings in each of these areas.

If marihuana caused chromosomal breakage, there is a possibility that the damaged chromosomes would cause birth defects. In the early 1970s, there were several reports of marihuana causing such breakage (13–61). In these studies, the subjects were not asked about previous drug usage or about their concurrent usage of drugs other than marihuana. When other drugs were excluded during usage of marihuana, chromosomal breakage was not observed (13–47). This later study supports the position that chromosomal breakage occurs no more frequently from marihuana usage than from taking caffeine or aspirin.

Several studies found that marihuana usage depressed the ability of the body's white blood cells to fight off disease and infection, which is called the **immune response** (13–27). Later research showed that after subjects smoked three or four times a week over a long period there was no change in the immune response (13–73). Finally, in those individuals who smoked 7 to 25 cigarettes a day for 10–25 years, there was no more incidence of infection (13–56). In this study, the individuals were originally selected on the basis of good health, so those who might have been prone to more infections might not have been included. In any case, it now appears that moderate usage of marihuana—three to five cigarettes per week—does not suppress the immune response.

If you are a male and smoke an average of five joints a day, you might have some decrease in male sex hormones. When males smoked five joints a day, they showed normal levels of the male hormone testosterone for the first 4 weeks. By the fifth week and until the ninth week, when the study was stopped, levels of testosterone dropped by approximately 33 percent but were still within the normal range (13–44). Since these men were kept in a hospital setting, it is not known if their sexual behavior and motivation also decreased. There is little correlation between levels of testosterone and sexual motivation, unless testosterone levels drop to the low levels seen before puberty (see Chapter 6). We do not know what effect being locked up in a hospital for 9 weeks can have on testosterone levels, but we do know that stress can cause a reduction in testosterone (13–37). Levels of testosterone fluctuate normally, and although marihuana was associated with a 33-percent decrease, we do not know how much of this was caused by stress, and whether it affected sexual motivation or sperm production. These results were produced by a large dose of marihuana: five joints every day for 9 weeks. There is little evidence that less intense usage causes any related effects on testosterone levels (13–44).

In the early 1970s, there were reports that usage of marihuana caused brain damage, that there was atrophy or shrinkage of the brain (13–10). The problem with this study was that the subjects had used other drugs, and four of the ten subjects had suffered head injuries. A later study of students who had smoked regularly over at least 3 years showed no difference in brain damage between users and nonusers (13–23). At present, there is little evidence that moderate use of marihuana causes brain damage. Although it is known that the active ingredient in marihuana is **tetrahydrocannabinol,** or **THC,** it is not known how THC affects the neurotransmitters in the brain (13–40).

First-time users of marihuana rarely report any euphoria or feeling of being high. This shows how the surroundings and the person's expectations combine and interact with the drug to produce some experience. If a person is nervous, paranoid, or tense, marihuana may increase these feelings. Regular users report feelings of euphoria, elation, wellbeing, and finally, drowsiness. There is usually a distortion in sense of time, in that events seem to take longer. With large doses, there may be distortions in perception and even visual or auditory hallucinations. Compared with LSD, marihuana is a mild hallucinogenic. There have been no reports of fatal reactions to smoking marihuana, but there have been cases of individuals becoming disorganized, confused, and having hallucinations, so that hospitalization was necessary. This latter experience has usually been the result of massive doses. With extremely high doses, the equivalent of 50–100 cigarettes a day, tolerance and physical dependency may develop. However, with moderate usage, there is no evidence of either tolerance or physical dependency. Most of the current literature suggests that marihuana is a relatively harmless drug in moderate usage

(13–8, 13–64, 13–77). At the same time, as with any drug, there may be side effects (lung cancer) or long-term harmful effects that are as yet unknown.

Comment

The decision of what drugs, if any, you wish to take is influenced by what you know about the drug, social pressures, whether or not a doctor prescribes it, how much you believe you need it, and, finally, the risk to your health. Some believe that all drugs should be freely available and that the government's program of legislating drugs as illegal simply encourages people to seek the thrill of finding and taking drugs (13–62). On the other hand, many want to end the drug problem by obtaining more enforcement and better laws. However, in some cases, it was decided that law enforcement was not the solution. Six states have changed their laws on marihuana so that its uage is a misdemeanor or is handled like a parking ticket. This change in law was partly due to the evidence showing that marihuana is not a dangerous drug, but it was also due to the fact that so many people were using marihuana that law enforcement either was not possible or was too costly. It should also be noted that the most-prescribed drugs, Valium and Librium, are taken by middle-class Americans who may not question this practice because their doctors recommend it. The public is more concerned with hard-drug users, such as heroin addicts. But this too may change, as discussion has begun in the United States about giving controlled doses of heroin to reduce the black market and the crime associated with obtaining it illegally.

Previously, when you heard the term "drugs," you probably thought of marihuana, cocaine, or heroin. Now you know this term applies equally to caffeine, nicotine, Valium, and other compounds. Strictly speaking, we are all, to some extent, drug users. Yes, drugs can change your mind, but often at some cost to you.

1   All of your behaviors depend upon the secretion of _____ from the neuron's _____.

    neurotransmitters / end feet or telodendria

2   If you took a drug, it could affect the _____ of neurotransmitters, it could cause their _____, or it could prevent neurotransmitters from reaching the postsynaptic _____ and _____.

    secretion destruction / dendrites cell bodies

3   Together, the neurotransmitters dopamine, norepinephrine, and epinephrine are called _____.

    catecholamines

4   The neurotransmitter serotonin is from a group called the _____.

    indoleamines

5   After catecholamines are secreted into the synapse, the major mechanism for their deactivation is _____, and the minor mechanism is destruction by _____.

    reuptake / enzymes

6   From studies on adopted children and on identical twins, there is evidence that one factor involved in schizophrenia is a _____.

    genetic predisposition

7   Enzyme levels were studied in identical twins to determine possible genetic factors, and it was found that their levels of _____ were more similar than in fraternal twins.

    monamine oxidase or MAO

8   In patients with a long history of schizophrenia or in manic depressives, the majority of studies found a lower level of the enzyme _____.

    monamine oxidase or MAO

9   When the brains of schizophrenic patients were examined, they were found to have a lower level of the enzyme _____, which is important in the synthesis of the neurotransmitter _____.

    dopamine-B-hydroxylase norepinephrine

10 It is possible for neurotransmitters in your brain to be turned into chemicals that can cause hallucinations, through a process called _____.

    transmethylation

11 One of the drugs effective in treating schizophrenia is _____, from a family of chemicals called _____.

    chlorpromazine phenothiazines

12 One of the side effects produced by phenothiazines involves movements of the mouth and limbs and is called _____.

    tardive dyskinesia

13 The treatment of schizophrenia with phenothiazines or other drugs may, in some cases, eliminate the symptoms. However, the percentage of patients in whom the symptoms return varies from _____.

    20 to 70 percent

14 In the treatment of mania, a drug found to be effective was _____, although approximately _____ percent of the patients were not helped by it.

    lithium 20

15 In the treatment of depression the drug _____ was successful. It worked in the brain by increasing levels of _____.

    imipramine norepinephrine

16 The theory that attempts to explain mania and depression is called the _____ theory of affective disorders. It hypothesizes that during mania levels of _____ are _____ and that during depression these levels are _____.

    catecholamine norepinephrine / high low

17 The most frequently prescribed tranquilizers are from a family of chemicals called _____. These drugs are frequently prescribed for _____.

    benzodiazepines muscle relaxation

18 As you continue to take a drug, your body adapts to its effects and you need a larger and larger dose to produce the same effect. This is called developing a _____. With continued drug usage, the body may grow to need the drug in order to function, and this is called _____.

    tolerance / physical dependency or addiction

19 Although you may not develop a physical dependency on a drug, you may feel that you must have a drug to function, and this is called _____.

    psychological dependency

20 One of the few drugs that can cause symptoms similar to paranoid schizophrenia when used heavily is _____.

    amphetamine

21 Amphetamine psychosis is thought to be caused by blockage of the reuptake of _____ and possibly _____.

    norepineprine dopamine

22 The medical uses of amphetamine include treatment of _____ and _____. It is not effective in programs of weight reduction because _____ develops to the appetite-suppressing properties of the drug.

    narcolepsy / MBD or hyperactivity / tolerance

23 A mild stimulant found in coffee is _____, which causes your cortex to be _____ and may improve your performance on tasks requiring quick _____.

    caffeine / aroused or alerted / reaction times

24 Continued smoking of cigarettes can result in _____ to nicotine, which is classified as a _____ because it causes EEG waves indicating _____.

    addiction / stimulant arousal

25 Cocaine produces stimulant and euphoric effects similar to the drug _____. It is also a powerful local _____, and in the brain it prevents the reuptake of _____.

    amphetamine / anesthetic norepinephrine

26 The symptoms that are called MBD include _____, _____, and _____.

    hyperactivity / difficulty in attending / impulsive behavior

27 MBD may arise from genetic factors, fetal maldevelopment, or physiological problems. Drugs used in the treatment of MBD include _____ and _____.

28 These two drugs work primarily on the symptoms of _____ and _____, and in the long-term treatment do not seem to _____ MBD.

29 Morphine and its synthetic derivative _____ are used medically as powerful _____. The continued use of these opiates results in the development of _____ and _____.

30 There are morphinelike substances in your brain and these are called _____. It is thought that these chemicals may be involved in (give two) _____, _____, and thus causing _____.

31 Although alcohol may relieve inhibitions at the beginning, continued drinking causes depression of the _____ and _____.

32 With moderate to heavy drinking, there are problems in your ability to _____ and in motor _____. Continued heavy drinking results in _____ and _____ to alcohol.

33 Programs for the treatment of the alcoholic include _____ and associating _____ with drinking. The most controversial program teaches _____ drinking.

34 Some alcoholics develop a syndrome called _____, which includes both _____ and _____ amnesia, periods of _____, and possibly _____.

35 It is thought that Korsakoff syndrome is caused by a lack of _____, which causes damage to the brain, especially the _____ and _____.

36 LSD causes hallucinations and intensification of sensory stimuli by acting on the neurotransmitter _____ and by increasing the sensitivity of the _____.

37 Recent studies on the effect of marihuana have shown that it does not seem to cause _____ or _____. (Give two.)

38 There is evidence that after 4 weeks of heavy usage of marihuana, there is a reduction in the levels of _____, which is not always correlated with _____.

amphetamine
methylphenidate

hyperactivity / attention problems / cure

heroin / analgesics
tolerance / addiction

endorphins
producing addiction, functioning as neurotransmitters, or upsetting chemical homeostasis / mental problems

cortex / reticular formation

think or reason
coordination / tolerance
addiction

abstinence / aversive events / controlled

Korsakoff syndrome
retrograde / anterograde
confusion / confabulation

vitamin B or thiamine
mammilary bodies
cerebellum or hippocampus

serotonin / reticular formation

chromosomal damage, suppression of immune response, or brain damage

testosterone / sexual motivation

REFERENCES

13–1 Akerley, M. S. The relationship between problem behavior and food allergies: one family's story. *Journal of Autism and Childhood Schizophrenia* 1976, 6: 75–91.

13–2 Autun, F. T., Bennet, G. B., Cooper, A. J., Daly, R. J., Smythies, J. R., and Zealley, J. The effects of L-methionine (without MAOI) in schizophrenia. *Journal of Psychiatric Research* 1971, 8: 63–71.

13–3 Axelrod, J. Neurotransmitters. *Scientific American* 1974, 230: 59–71.

13–4 Bloom, F., Segal, D., Ling, N., and Guillemin, R. Endorphins: profound behavioral effects in rats suggest new etiological factors in mental illness. *Science* 1976, 194: 630–632.

13–5 Borland, B. L. and Heckman, H. K. Hyperactive boys and their brothers. *Archives of General Psychiatry* 1976, 33: 669–675.

13–6 Boyatzis, R. E. The predisposition toward alcohol-related interpersonal aggression in men. *Journal of Studies on Alcohol* 1975, 36: 1196–1207.

13–7 Brecher, E. M. *Licit and illicit drugs*. Boston: Little Brown, 1972.

13–8 Brecher, E. M. Marijuana: the health questions. *Consumer Reports* March 1975.

13–9 Buchsbaum, M. S., Coursey, R. D., and Murphy, D. L. The biochemical high-risk paradigm: behavioral and familial correlates of low platelet monoamine oxidase activity. *Science* 1976, 194: 339–341.

13–10 Campbell, A. M. G., Evans, M., Thomson, J. L. G., and Williams, M. J. Cerebral atrophy in young cannabis smokers. *Lancet* December 1971, 1219–1225.

13–11 Cantwell, D. P. (Ed.), *The hyperactive child*. New York: Halsted Press, 1975.

13–12 Cohen, S. Cocaine. *Journal of the American Medical Association* 1975, 231: 74–75.

13–13 Crane, G. E. Clinical psychopharmacology in its 20th year. *Science* 1973, 181: 124–181.

13–14 Davis, J. M. Recent developments in the drug treatment of schizophrenia. *American Journal of Psychiatry* 1976, 133: 208–214.

13–15 Dishotsky, N. I., Loughman, W. D., Mogar, R. E., and Lipscomb, W. D. LSD and genetic damage. *Science* 1971, 172: 431–440.

13–16 Domino, E. F. and Khanna, S. S. Decreased blood platelet MAO activity in unmedicated chronic schizophrenic patients. *American Journal of Psychiatry* 1976, 133: 323–326.

13–17 Ellinwood, E. H. and Cohen, S. Amphetamine abuse. *Science* 1971, 171: 420–421.

13–18 Franks, H. M., Hagedorn, H., Hensley, V. R., Hensley, W. J. and Starmer, G. A. The effect of caffeine on human performance alone and in combination with ethanol. *Psychopharmacologia* 1975, 45: 177–181.

13–19 Fredrickson, R. C. A. and Norris, F. H. Enkephalin-induced depression of single neurons in brain areas with opiate receptors—antagonism by Naloxone. *Science* 1976, 194: 440–442.

13–20 Gattozzi, A. A. *Lithium in the treatment of mood disorders*. Rockville, MD: National Institute of Mental Health, 1974.

13–21 Goldman, D. Treatment of phenothiazine-induced dyskinesia. *Psychopharmacology* 1976, 47: 271–272.

13–22 Goldstein, A. Opioid peptides (endorphins) in pituitary and brain. *Science* 1976, 193: 1081–1086.

13–23 Grant, I. and Mohns, L. Chronic cerebral effects of alcohol and drug abuse. *The International Journal of the Addictions* 1975, 10: 883–920.

13–24 Grant, I., Rochford, J., Fleming, T., and Stunkard, A. J. Neuropsychological assessment of the effects of moderate marihuana use. *Journal of Nervous and Mental Disease*, 1973, 156: 278–280.

13–25 Griffith, J. D., Cavanaugh, J., Held, N. N., and Oates, J. A. Dextroamphetamine: evaluation of psychotomimetic properties in man. *Archives of General Psychiatry* 1972, 26: 97–100.

13–26 Grinspoon, L. and Singer, S. B. Amphetamines in the treatment of hyperkinetic children. *Harvard Educational Review* 1973, 43: 515–555.

13–27 Gupta, S., Greico, M. H., and Cushman, P. Impairment of rosette-forming T lympocytes in chronic marihuana smokers. *New England Journal of Medicine* 1974, 291: 874–877.

13–28 Hammond, A. L. Narcotic antagonists: new methods to treat heroin addiction. *Science* 1971, 173: 503–506.

13–29 Heston, L. L. The genetics of schizophrenic and schizoid disease. *Science* 1970, 167: 249–256.

13–30 Hochman, J. S. and Brill, N. O. Chronic marijuana use and psychosocial adaptation. *American Journal of Psychiatry* 1973, 130: 132–139.

13–31 Hogarty, G. E., Goldberg, S. C., Schooler, N. R., and Ulrich, R. F. Drug and sociotherapy in the aftercase of schizophrenic patients. *Archives of General Psychiatry* 1974, 31: 603–608.

13–32 Holden, C. Amphetamines: tighter controls on the horizon. *Science* 1976, 194: 1027–1028.

13–33 Hollister, L. E. *Clinical use of psychotherapeutic drugs*. Springfield, IL: Charles C. Thomas, 1973.

13–34 Jacquet, Y. F. and Marks, N. The C-fragment of B-Lipotropin: an endogenous neuroleptic or antipsychotogen? *Science* 1976, 194: 632–634.

13–35 Kety, S. S., Rosenthal, D., Wender, P. H., and Schulsinger, K. F. The types of prevalence of mental illness in the biological and adoptive families of adopted schizophrenics. In D. Rosenthal and S. S. Kety (Eds.), *The transmission of schizophrenia*. New York: Pergamon Press, 1968.

13–36 Kotin, J., Wilbert, D. E., Verburg, D., and Soldinger, S. M. Thioridazine and sexual dysfunction. *American Journal of Psychiatry* 1976, 133: 82–85.

13–37 Kreuz, L. D., Rose, R. M., and Jennings, R. J. Suppression of plasma testosterone levels and psychological stress. *Archives of General Psychiatry* 1972, 26: 479–482.

13–38 Le Dain, G. *The non-medical use of drugs*. Baltimore: Penguin Books, 1970.

13–39 Lloyd, R. W. and Salzberg, H. C. Controlled social drinking: an alternative to abstinence as a treatment goal for some alcohol abusers. *Psychological Bulletin* 1975, 82: 815–842.

REFERENCES *(cont.)*

13–40 Logan, W. J. Neurological aspects of hallucinogenic drugs. In W. J. Friendland (Ed.), *Advances in neurology*. Vol. 13. New York: Raven Press, 1975.

13–41 Long, S. Y. Does LSD induce chromosomal damage and malformations? A review of the literature. *Teratology* 1972, 6: 75–90.

13–42 Mandell, A. J., Segal, D. S., Kuczenski, R. T., and Knapp, S. The search for the schizococcus. *Psychology Today* October 1972.

13–43 Mark, J. L. Neurobiology: researchers high on endogenous opiates. *Science* 1976, 193: 1227–1229.

13–44 Maugh, T. H., II. Marihuana: new support for immune and reproductive hazards. *Science* 1975, 190: 865–867.

13–45 Minde, K., Lewin, D., Weiss, G., Laviguer, H., Douglas, F., and Sykes, E. The hyperactive child in elementary school: a 5-year controlled follow-up. *Exceptional Children* November 1971, 215–221.

13–46 Murray, L. The growing scandal about Valium and Librium. *Playgirl* January 1976.

13–47 Nichols, W. W., Miller, R. C., Heneen, W., Bradt, C., Hollister, L., and Kantor, S. Cytogenetic studies on human subjects receiving marihuana and Δ-9 tetrahydrocannabinol. *Mutation Research* 1974, 26: 413–417.

13–48 Nies, A., Robinson, D. S., Lamborn, K. R., and Lampert, R. P. Genetic control of platelet and plasma monoamine oxidase activity. *Archives of General Psychiatry* 1973, 28: 834–838.

13–49 Pendery, M. and Maltzman, I. The question of controlled social drinking as a treatment goal for alcohol abusers: a reply to Lloyd and Salzberg. *Psychological Bulletin,* in press.

13–50 Pomerleau, O., Pertschuk, M., and Stinnett, J. A critical examination of some current assumptions in the treatment of alcoholism. *Journal of Studies on Alcohol* 1976, 37: 849–867.

13–51 Prien, R. F., Levine, J., and Switalski, R. W. Discontinuation of chemotherapy for chronic schizophrenics. *Hospital and Community Psychiatry* 1971, 22: 4–7.

13–52 Regush, N. M. *The drug addiction business*. New York: Dial Press, 1971.

13–53 Revelle, W., Amaral, P., and Turriff, S. Introversion/extroversion, time stress, and caffeine: effect on verbal performance. *Science* 1976, 192: 149–150.

13–54 Riddle, D. K. and Rapoport, J. L. A 2-year follow-up of 72 hyperactive boys. *The Journal of Nervous and Mental Disease* 1976, 162: 126–134.

13–55 Rubin, H. B. and Henson, D. E. Effects of alcohol on male sexual responding. *Psychopharmacology* 1976, 47: 123–134.

13–56 Rubin, V. and Comitas, L. *Ganja in Jamaica*. Garden City, NY: Anchor Press, 1976.

13–57 Schildkraut, J. and Freyhan, F. A. Neuropharmacological studies of mood disorder. In J. Zubin (Ed.), *Disorders of mood*. New York: Grune & Stratton, 1972.

13–58 Snyder, S. H. The true speed trip: schizophrenia. *Psychology Today* January 1972.

13–59 Snyder, S. H. *Madness and the brain*. New York: McGraw-Hill, 1975.

13–60 Snyder, S. H., Benerjee, S. P., Yamamura, H. I., and Greenberg, D. Drugs, neurotransmitters, and schizophrenia. *Science* 1974, 184: 1243–1253.

13–61 Stenchever, M. A., Kunysz, T. J., and Allen, M. A. Chromosome breakage in users of marihuana. *American Journal of Obstetrics and Gynecology* 1974, 118: 106–113.

13–62 Szasz, T. *Ceremonial chemistry*. Garden City, NY: Anchor Press, 1975.

13–63 Taylor, S. P. and Gammon, C. B. Effects of type and dose of alcohol on human physical aggression. *Journal of Personality and Social Psychology* 1975, 32: 169–175.

13–64 Tinklenberg, J. R. (Ed.), *Marijuana and health hazards*. New York: Academic Press, 1975.

13–65 Victor, M., Adams, R. D., and Collins, G. H. *The Wernicke-Korsakoff syndrome*. Philadelphia: F. A. Davis, 1971.

13–66 Vinar, O. Dependence on a placebo: a case report. *British Journal of Psychiatry* 1969, 115: 1189–1190.

13–67 Vonnegut, M. *The eden express*. New York: Bantam, 1976.

13–68 Walker, S., III. Drugging the American child: we're too cavalier about hyperactivity. *Psychology Today* December 1974.

13–69 Wei, E. and Loh, H. Physical dependence on opiate-like peptides. *Science* 1976, 193: 1262–1263.

13–70 Weissman, M. M., Kasl, S. V., and Klerman, G. L. Follow-up of depressed women after maintenance treatment. *American Journal of Psychiatry* 1976, 133: 757–760.

13–71 Wells, B. *Psychedelic drugs*. Baltimore: Penguin, 1973.

13–72 Wender, P. H. The case of MBD. *Hastings Center Studies* 1974, 2: 94–102.

13–73 White, S. C., Brin, S. C., and Janicki, B. W. Mitogen-induced blastogenic responses of lymphocytes from marihuana smokers. *Science* 1975, 188: 71–72.

13–74 Wise, C. D., Baden, M. M., and Stein, L. Postmortem measurement of enzymes in human brain: evidence of a central noradrenergic deficit in schizophrenia. *Journal of Psychiatric Research* 1974, 11: 185–198.

13–75 Wise, C. D., Berger, D. B., and Stein, L. Benzodiazepines: anxiety-reducing activity by reduction of serotonin turnover in the brain. *Science* 1972, 177: 180–183.

13–76 Wyatt, R. J., Murphy, D. L., Belmaker, R., Cohen, S., Donnelly, C. H., and Pollin, W. Reduced monoamine oxidase activity in platelets: a possible genetic marker for vulnerability to schizophrenia. *Science* 1973, 179: 916–918.

13–77 Zinberg, N. E. The war over marijuana. *Psychology Today* December 1976.

Selected Readings

Starved Brains

Roger Lewin

We know the picture well: the bloated bellies, stick-thin arms, and sad listless eyes that mark severe malnutrition. Countries sapped by chronic food shortages or thrown into despair by sudden devastating famines and war have burned those images into our conscience. But less dramatic, and therefore more insidious, are the effects of long-term undernutrition, which more than 300 million children already suffer.

Although these children may escape the worst rigors of starvation, there is now mounting and inescapable evidence that their intellectual development suffers damage from which there is no chance of complete recovery.

The beautifully complex architecture of the human brain follows an innate blueprint, but factors in the environment of the growing infant partly influence its final form, and therefore its final performance. One major factor during the early stages of brain development, we now realize, is an adequate supply of food. Without the necessary flow of nutrients the brain simply cannot create the structures—the cells, the wiring, and the complex circuits—that fuse to form the functioning human mind.

Researchers in Europe, Africa and South America are also learning of a delicate but crucial interplay between adequate diet and environmental stimulation in the first two years of life. During this critical period the brain's potential has to be reached, or it is too late. There is no second chance. An infant deprived of

nutrition or stimulation will never develop to full mental capacity. The implications of this situation are frightening: cycles of poor nutrition and environmental poverty enhance each other, leading to personal suffering and chronic social malaise. Today 70 percent of the world's population seriously risks permanent brain damage.

The critical period of development of the human brain results from its peculiar pattern of growth. At birth an infant's brain has already reached 25 percent of its adult weight, and by six months it is half way to the final target. In comparison, total body weight at birth is a mere five percent of its adult maximum, and reaches the 50 percent mark only at age 10.

Until recently we had no clear picture of the stages and timing of human brain growth. Now, John Dobbing and Jean Sands of the University of Manchester, England, have examined the composition of almost 150 human brains ranging in age from 10 weeks of gestation to seven years. What they found helps us understand the effects of malnutrition in children.

Progress of the Brain

Basically, the brain grows in two stages. First, between weeks 10 and 18 of pregnancy, the adult number of nerve cells develops. Second, beginning about week 20, the brain's packing cells (the oligodendroglia) begin to appear, followed by the production of the insulating material (myelin) that coats the long fibers along which the nerve cells send their messages. This second stage continues for at least two years after birth; myelination progresses at a lower rate until the age of four years. The second stage, known as the brain growth spurt, represents the most vulnerable period of brain development. It is the critical period when inadequate nutrition and lack of stimulation inflict the most lasting damage.

Before Dobbing and Sands laid out clearly the timing of the human brain's growth spurt, we assumed that most of the brain's important development took place prenatally and was more or less complete by birth. But their demonstration that about five sixths of the growth spurt comes *after* birth forced an awareness of the hazards of prolonged malnutrition in the early years of life.

There are several ways of exploring what happens to an infant nurtured in an impoverished womb and born into a world where he or she is deprived of food. One can study what physically happens to the brain or one can examine the physical and behavioral consequences of malnutrition in animals. Or one may observe children born under deprived circumstances and determine the effect of environmental factors in improving or worsening their condition.

One thing that is more or less safe from nutritional insult in the growing human brain is the number of nerve cells it contains. Because this number is established very early in pregnancy, at a time when outside nutritional factors fail to impinge on the developing fetus, the brain's basic nerve-cell complement escapes unscathed. There is, however, a major exception. The cerebellum, a wrinkled structure at the back of the brain that coordinates movement of the arms and legs, is vulnerable to nutritional deprivation because its nerve-cell generation and growth spurt are delayed. A starving brain risks delayed creation of the oligodendroglia and the later myelination of the nerve fibers.

Post-mortem examinations of human beings can't answer questions about these early developmental phases, so we have to rely on animal experiments. This approach is justified, because although the *timing* of the growth spurt in human and other animal brains differs, the *stages* are identical. Dobbing and his colleagues find that rats with malnutrition have significantly smaller brains than healthy rats, with the cell deficit concentrated in the oligodendroglia. Starved rats also show reduced myelination, and some enigmatic enzyme imbalances too. The cerebellum, compared with the rest of the brain, suffers more; it weighs less and doesn't have the adult complement of nerve cells, due to its delayed growth spurt. The particular vulnerability of the cerebellum is important because damage to this structure goes a long way toward explaining the reported clumsiness and reduced manual skills of malnourished children.

Malnourished Neurons

One thing that brain researchers readily admit is that they have measured what is easiest to measure. The feature of brain development that is probably most difficult to quantify, but is almost certainly the most important, is the lacework of connections between the nerve cells (neurons). Reliable reports show that the major part of the nerve fibers, the axons, shrink in diameter in malnourished animals. But the really crucial area of interneuron communication centers on the end of the axon, where it branches into literally thousands of tiny fingers that make contact with the neighboring neurons. B. G. Cragg from Monash University, Australia, has had a crack at this problem, and what he finds is most disturbing.

Cragg did some microscopic investigations of the cerebral cortex in rats malnourished early in life. In what must have been a crashingly tedious experiment, he counted the number of minute nerve endings (the synapses) in the cortex of undernourished animals. He found a 40 percent reduction, compared to normal rats. Cragg suspects too that some of the synapses may have been unable to function because of molecular breaks. The creation of the interneural network is one of the brain's major construction projects during the first two years of life, so Cragg's result is crucial and needs to be confirmed. If the undernourished cerebral cortex really lacks almost half of its interconnections (or even a 10th), the consequences for brain function are frightening. The planet may be raising a generation of clumsy, feeble-minded millions.

A crucial point about all these experiments is that moderate degrees of malnutrition—of the sort that 300 million children experience daily—can produce these physical side effects and deficiencies. More important, we cannot repair these physical deficiencies by normal feeding once the brain growth spurt has passed.

The typical undernourished child is shorter and lighter than his counterpart in affluent countries. He is about 70 percent of his correct weight, and the brain weight and head diameter are marginally smaller as well. The next step we've taken is to find out what this means for intellectual and social activity.

In the attempt to find the consequences of chronic undernutrition, most research groups have used the longitudinal study, observing the progress of a group of children over a period of years. For example, Joaquín Cravioto and Elsa DeLicardie studied a group of infants born in 1966 in a small rural village in southwest Mexico. They have been observing the children ever since. The village has a "normal" background of undernutrition, but the researchers concentrated on 22 children who at times had had almost no food and thus had been severely malnourished.

Food and Language

Cravioto and DeLicardie studied nutrition and mental development against the background of social and economic factors. Their outstanding discovery was the effect of malnutrition on language development and verbal-concept formation. As a group, the severely malnourished children began to lag behind in language at about six months. At the age of one year the matched control group had language development equivalent to 334 days, compared with 289 days for the hunger group. By three years the gap was 947 days to 657.

Because verbal concepts are a basic area of human intelligence, the researchers gave children tests to measure their understanding of 23 pairs of opposites (such as big-little, long-short, in-out). At 31 months of age the control group of normals understood an average of 5.46 concepts, compared with 3.92 for the malnourished children; by 46 weeks their scores were 16.92 and 12.16, and at 58 weeks the controls knew 20 of the concepts, three ahead of the malnourished group. Even after 40 months the children who had suffered malnutrition in infancy were behind the control children in language development and concept formation. Although the worst physical symptoms of their malnutrition were gone, and although they did make up some of the lost ground, they didn't catch up with their healthier playmates. The trend line suggests they never will.

Because the poverty that produces severe malnutrition also produces deprived environments, Cravioto and DeLicardie compared the home lives of the children. They used the Caldwell Inventory of Home Stimulation to measure factors such as frequency and stability of adult contacts, the number of voices the child hears, availability of toys and games, whether the child's needs are met, and how many restrictions there are on the child's activity. The researchers found that the malnourished infants came from homes that were significantly impoverished in activity that brings the human mind alive.

Although this poor environment of the malnourished children contributes to their slowed intellectual development, Cravioto claims that it is not the sole explanation. This conclusion is supported by Stephen Richardson and his colleagues, who studied a community of children in Jamaica, and found that malnutrition is as damaging as an impoverished social life. Richardson measured the physical and intellectual status of a group of boys, aged seven to 11 years, who had during the first two years of their lives suffered severe malnutrition. These children were smaller in stature, lighter in weight, and had smaller heads than normal children. Behaviorally, they were disadvantaged too:

they did less well in formal tests of reading, writing and arithmetic; teachers found their school performance to be poorer, with more special problems in classwork.

• • • •

Further, the previously malnourished children were less popular among their schoolmates. When Richardson asked all the children to pick the three peers in their class with whom they most preferred to spend their time, they named the malnourished children much less frequently. This is a tricky result to untangle, but the cause may have some parallels with the observation that malnourished animals are socially disturbed and more irritable. Perhaps the children were too.

Poor Nutrition Vs. Poor Environment

The researchers also measured the children's home environments, and this time found that not all of the malnourished children came from impoverished homes. So they were able to compare four groups: malnourished children from rich environments, malnourished children from deprived environments, healthy children from rich environments, and healthy children from deprived environments.

The results showed clearly how a home that is poor in stimulation and opportunity for a child will impair his or her intellectual development, regardless of the extent of the malnutrition. Among healthy children, those from stimulating environments averaged 71.4 on an intelligence test, while those from deprived environments averaged 60.5. Malnourished children from enriched homes scored 62.7. But the combination of malnutrition *and* a poor environment produced the deadliest deficit in learning of all, averages of only 52.9.

One report that seemed to counter the evidence for the prolonged effects of malnutrition comes from the Columbia University School of Public Health and Administrative Medicine, which detailed the intellectual performance of 19-year-old Dutch youths entering the army. These men had either been born or were young infants during the famine the Nazis imposed on their country during World War II. These young men showed normal intelligence, which suggested that malnutrition has no lasting effect on mental development. The crucial fallacy in such a conclusion is that the Dutch famine was very short, only six months, and before and immediately after the famine there was no severe food shortage. Any brain growth deficit inflicted by this brief famine would therefore be made up for by enhanced development within the two and one quarter year brain growth period. The Dutch infants, who went hungry for a brief period but otherwise were well-nourished in infancy and childhood, are thus not comparable to the Mexican and Jamaican children, who live in a state of chronic malnutrition.

Curing Deprived Children

Now researchers are beginning to ask what can be done to help children who do not get adequate food and environmental enrichment. Leonardo Sinisterra and his colleagues in Cali, Colombia, are giving malnourished children food and supplemental schooling from the age of three and a half on. Compared with their fellows, the children in his program have a marvelously rich environment indeed. They build with wooden blocks and even make large-scale structures with poles and planks; they paint pictures of their environment, make up stories, and even act out adult situations; and they get an expanded view of the world by going on trips into the country, all of which are outside the experience of most of the poor children of Cali. These children are now five years old, and have made remarkable strides toward catching up with the intellectual ability of more affluent children, both in verbal reasoning and general intelligence.

Sinisterra gave a second group of formerly malnourished children one part of the treatment but not the other: they got good food, but no extra schooling. So far, it looks as though they are doing no better than malnourished children who have had no supplementary program. The reason seems to be that the children did not get the additional food until they were three and a half, well after the critical brain growth period had passed.

One aspect of intellectual performance remains resistant to repair in malnourished children, regardless of whether or not they get additional food and special schooling—short-term memory. So far no program has been able to help deprived children gain a normal ability to remember what they just learned.

Another compensation study is underway in a poor agricultural village in Mexico, Tezonteopan. Few families in Tezonteopan show signs of severe and clinical malnutrition, but almost all are chronically underfed, barely managing to survive. Passive children and tired mothers barely communicate, rarely play. Adolfo Chavez is studying the long-term effects of supplementary food on both parents and children. He began his food supplements with pregnant women and continued them throughout the brain growth spurt, i.e., until the children were over two years old.

For a start, the supplemented mothers produced babies that were roughly eight percent heavier than normal in the village, and this weight advantage continued and expanded. But behavioral differences appeared rapidly too. The test children showed superior language development within the first year, and in simple physical activity they far outshone their underfed fellows. On a measure of movement, they were three times as active by age one year, and four times as active by age two.

Further, the well-fed children spent less time in their cots, walked at a younger age, were more vigorous in play, and were more likely to take the lead in play, and were generally much more independent. And because of their greater activity and exploratory behavior, their parents and siblings took a greater interest in them, which in turn was strengthened by the infants' tendency to smile more. The whole family dynamics gained a higher level.

Some Tezonteopan fathers even took an active part in child care, something they almost never do. They were enthused by having a vigorous, alert child. Several were so impressed with their "special" children that they declared to Chavez, "This child will not be a farmer like me."

Chavez's work reveals the tragedy and the promise. Millions of people today accept deep, grinding hunger and poverty as normal and inevitable, and pay the price with lowered intellect and activity. We know that if the brain is not well fed during its critical period of growth, it will never develop to the full and rich potential that is our heritage. We also know that massive doses of good diet, fun and games, teaching and stimulation can help to overcome the intelligence gap that malnutrition leaves in its wake.

Ultimately, the efforts to untangle the effects of malnutrition and a poor environment may make little difference in the real world, where the two exist in a vicious circle. Poverty inflicts a double insult—its victims condemned to a dearth of food and a sterile environment. The combination is at work daily, eroding the mental capacity of 300 million children.

Genetic Engineers
Now That They've Gone Too Far, Can They Stop?

Caryl Rivers

Human control of human life has always been a vision with a dark underbelly of nightmare. The classic image is Mary Shelley's "Frankenstein"—alive, but grotesque and misshapen. In Aldous Huxley's *Brave New World*, babies pop like olives out of bottles to confront a society in which human beings are manufactured, chemically adapted and conditioned to the functions they are expected to perform. There are grave taboos associated with the wellsprings of life. It is a territory, like that of the ancient Indian burial grounds, into which one does not trespass without arousing the ire of the gods.

Some may think it excessive to begin the consideration of such a serious scientific topic as The New Biology, with nightmares. But sometimes the prophets and the poets who probe the shadows see more clearly than the scientists. Some nightmares turn solid. Hiroshima ten seconds after zero made all those medieval murals depicting the terrors of hell seem pale by comparison. The human capacity to destroy can outrun even the human imagination.

There are, of course, other human capacities—to create and to cure. They are the compass points for those who want to chart a full ahead course for genetic technology.

Most of us remember encountering Gregor Mendel and his peas in high school biology, and learning that the tiny microscopic specks inside our cells were called genes and were the carriers of heredity. Alone, or in combination, those particles would determine the color of our eyes and the range of our abilities in math. The process was inevitable. We inherited our genes from our parents and we were stuck with what we got.

But the past three decades have seen an explosion of knowledge in the biological sciences. "Genetic engineering" is in its infancy, but the infant shows signs of maturing at an alarming rate.

The cells inside our bodies house as much activity as a steel mill going full blast, and are densely populated.

The genes are composed of hundreds of subunits linked together in a spiral shape. Hundreds of genes linked together form the long, threadlike strands of genetic material called DNA (deoxyribonucleic acid) that is the main substance of the chromosomes. DNA is the basic genetic material, the "governor," so to speak, of the mechanisms of cell reproduction.

In the early 1950s two young scientists, Francis Crick and James Watson, working in Cambridge, England, developed a model of the DNA molecule. It was found that DNA transmits its messages in a four "letter" code, each letter being a specific chemical compound. The messages are carried by RNA, another chemical compound. The achievement won the Nobel prize for Crick and Watson, and the science of molecular biology took off like an express train.[*]

The New Biology raises the most immediate and perhaps the most far-reaching questions in the field of human reproduction. There are two types of cells in the human body: body cells, which contain a full set of chromosomes, and sex cells (sperm or egg), which each contain only half the required number. It takes a merger of sperm with egg for human reproduction to begin. The merger occurs inside a woman's body, but what if it were to happen outside, in a test tube? Would the cells continue to grow and divide? In 1959 an Italian scientist, Dr. Daniele Petrucci, announced he had achieved test-tube fertilization. His work was condemned by the Pope, and the scientist destroyed the results. The Papal frown did not dissuade all scientists, however, and the most advanced work with what is called *in vitro* vertilization is now going on in England.

In vitro means, literally, "in glass," and a husband-and-wife team in the physiology department of Cambridge University have devised a way to obtain healthy human eggs for their experiments. Dr. R. G. Edwards and Dr. Ruth Fowler work with volunteer subjects,

---

*A recent book, Anne Sayre's *Rosalind Franklin and DNA* (Norton), argues that Franklin, a scientist who worked with Watson and Crick, has not been given due credit for solving the riddle of DNA. Sayre says that without the work done by Franklin—the refined use of X-ray crystallography to gather data on DNA—the achievement of Watson and Crick would not have been possible. (Franklin died of cancer in 1950 at age 87.)

usually women who are unable to conceive because of blocked Fallopian tubes. (Sperm must travel up the tubes to merge with an egg before conception can occur naturally.) The women are given fertility drugs, which cause the production of a number of eggs. These are removed from their uteruses by minor abdominal surgery. Edwards and Fowler bring the eggs together with sperm in culture dishes, and they have been able to produce human embryos in very rudimentary stages.

Both doctors see their work as being in the best traditions of medical science, since its aim is to enable women with blocked or damaged tubes to conceive. An egg is removed from a woman, fertilized with her husband's sperm, then reimplanted in her uterus. So far, the embryos have not attached themselves to the lining of the uterus so that pregnancies would result.

But embryo transplants have been done in animals, cattle in particular, with success. In fact, in the 1960s sheep embryos were implanted into the uterus of a rabbit—flown from England to South Africa in their temporary "incubator"—and then removed from the rabbit and implanted into other female sheep, who later gave birth to ewes.

No one knows what effect the handling of human embryos would have on their development. Would the result be a high proportion of damaged babies? Paul Ramsey, the Yale theologian who has written extensively on the ethics of genetic control, says that *in vitro* fertilization is unethical experimentation subject to absolute moral prohibition. Another objection to work with human embryos is that too little research so far has been done with primates, the animals closest to humans in complexity.

Some scientists, while arguing for caution, feel that the fear of gross abnormalities may be overstated. Mouse embryos have developed to normal birth even after extreme manipulation. They question whether *in vitro* fertilization is any riskier than what is going on right now. For example, physicians give women fertility drugs that often result in multiple births despite the dangers to the embryos of prematurity, stunted growth, and respiratory disorders. Often, one or more of the fetuses does not survive.

Edwards and Fowler feel that an additional benefit of their work is that they will be able to bypass sex-linked diseases. This might work in the case of hemophilia where male children are afflicted and female children are not. Edwards and Fowler say, "Placing female embryos in the mother would avoid the birth of affected males, though half of the female children would be carriers of the gene."

In vitro fertilization also raises a welter of legal and social questions. If a damaged child resulted from an embryo transplant, could the parents sue the doctor for malpractice? Could the child sue the parents? That sounds bizarre, but there is a legal theory called "wrongful life," which holds parents responsible for willful damage done to a child before its birth. The doctrine is not established and perhaps never will be, but there have been cases argued, including one involving a blind child born to a syphilitic mother.

Does a childless woman have a *right* to have children? Is infertility a sickness, to be "cured" by any process, no matter how risky?

Perhaps even more disturbing questions for society are raised by bolder applications of embryo-transplant technology. If a cow embryo can be transplanted from one womb to another, why not a human embryo? A woman with a heart condition who could not undergo the rigors of childbirth could still be the mother of her own natural child. A "test tube" embryo could be implanted into the uterus of another woman, who, out of friendship or for payment, would carry and deliver the child.

It is possible that this technology would mean still another way that women's bodies would be used—as temporary havens for other people's children. One could imagine a flourishing "rent-a-uterus" business. One British doctor has even suggested a "reasonable" price for such a service—2,000 pounds (or about $4,000). It wouldn't be the first time that poor women found that their bodies are their one salable commodity.

How far should we go in manipulating embryos? There has been speculation that in the future we may be able to change the sex, the hair color—even the intelligence of embryos. The most outageous fantasy is that of "designing" people—a legless astronaut for a life in space or a human being with gills to live in the oceans.

It is not the fantasies that are disturbing. Asexual reproduction, or cloning, may be possible in the next 10 years, or sooner. Have we, as a society, thought much about where we will draw a line?

James Watson, whose work 20 years ago helped create The New Biology, has been outspoken in calling for serious concern: "If we do not think about (the matter) now, the possibility of a . . . free choice will one day suddenly be gone."

Dr. Sissela Bok, who has written extensively on medical ethics, and who now lectures at Harvard and at Simmons College, shares that concern. "In some ways," she says, "our society is so brittle that it cannot take much more strain in regard to questions of living, dying, and being born." We must be very conservative in our attitudes toward the new technology, she believes. It is not right for one doctor to forge ahead.

But there is at least one who is going to try. One unnamed American scientist told science writer Albert Rosenfeld, "If I can carry a baby all the way through to birth *in vitro*, I certainly plan to do it—although obviously, I'm not going to succeed on the first attempt—or even the twentieth."

Whether or not we tamper with it, the very fact that we are coming to know more and more about the machinery of heredity will bring us to difficult—sometimes agonizing—choices. Already much can be learned about an embryo through an increasingly common procedure known as amniocentesis. (In amniocentesis, a hypodermic needle, inserted through the mother's abdomen into the amniotic sac, is used to withdraw amniotic fluid which contains fetal cells.) Examination of the cells can reveal some 60 genetic disorders. The woman who finds that the embryo she is carrying has a serious genetic defect can choose to abort. Amniocentesis can also detect the sex of the fetus from the chromosomal structure of the cells.

Despite the fact that amniocentesis is no longer an exotic procedure and is an essential diagnostic tool, some women who seek it find resistance from physicians similar to the opposition that they find doctors have toward abortion. In a survey of 25 couples, Dr. John Fletcher of the Interfaith Metropolitan Theological Education, Inc., in Washington, D.C., found that five of the couples had encountered opposition from doctors. One 40-year-old mother of three was told that her mental health needed attention because she sought amniocentesis. Another woman, a carrier of the gene for a rare and usually fatal disease, Lesch-Nyhan syndrome, said that one doctor "as much as called me a murderer when I said I wanted the test."

As fetal detection becomes more sophisticated, choices will get tougher. One case, presented in a scientific journal as a question of "bio-ethics" is a good example. A woman in her forties with three children sought amniocentesis to test for Down's syndrome (mongolism). The test showed the fetus was a male, with no evidence of Down's syndrome. But the fetus did have an extra "Y" (male) chromosome, an abnormality whose effect is not known. There has been some evidence presented that "extra Y" males are prone to aggression and antisocial behavior, but that evidence has been vigorously disputed. Was the woman's physician obliged to give her the full report, or just to tell her there was no sign of Down's syndrome?

The fact that amniocentesis can detect the sex of the fetus presents another moral quandary. A Utah doctor wrote an outraged letter to the *Journal of the American Medical Association* in 1972, citing what he called a "possible abuse of prenatal chromosome evaluation of the fetus." A 38-year-old patient, mother of one boy and two girls, asked for amniocentesis to rule out Down's syndrome. The embryo was diagnosed as a normal female. The woman decided to abort, since she and her husband wanted another son, not a daughter.

Is it morally right for parents who want a child to abort a normal fetus simply because it is the "wrong" sex? This raises questions even for strong supporters of the idea that a woman should have control over her own body. Is abortion a proper method of sex selection? Studies of preferences for sons or daughters done in the United States have consistently favored male children so one suspects that the majority of the aborted fetuses would be female.

Selective abortion is not the only method of choosing the sex of a child. It is probable that in the next few years the technology will be available to preselect the sex of a child before conception. (If a sperm bearing an X chromosome fertilizes an egg, the child will be a female; if a Y chromosome, a male.) There have been numerous articles and books about possible methods of sex selection based on the fact that male sperm swim faster than female sperm. But such methods are usually based on the timing of intercourse and are rather hit-and-miss, since it's hard for a woman to tell precisely when ovulation occurs. More effective techniques will probably be available in the near future based on the differences in sperm. Male and female sperm differ not only in speed but in weight (female sperm are heavier). This makes it possible to separate them.

Reports in the British journal *Nature* in 1973 said that strong antibodies directed against substances in male sperm of mice reduced the likelihood of their fertilizing an egg. The male sperm were in effect "hobbled," leaving the race to the X-bearing sperm. It is also possible to collect Y-bearing sperm in a condition that would allow them to be used in artificial insemination, ensuring a male child. A sperm separating technique which results in a high percentage of male offspring is being used in some American fertility clinics. One clinic is also accepting applications from couples who want male children. One argument for the use of such techniques is that if parents could choose the sex of their children, it would tend to lower population levels.

But what effect would sex selection have on the ratio of males to females in society? At first, a rash of boy babies could be expected. Some demographers believe the balance would right itself. Marc Lappe, Associate for the Biological Sciences at the Hastings Center (an institute set up to examine the ethical and social questions proposed by science and technology) suspects the opposite. By artificially selecting one sperm type over another, "we may be selecting for sperm that would produce offspring whose own gametes (be they sperm or egg) would again have a predilection for the same sex." We might not be selecting just a male child, but a dynasty of male children. He feels that, given the sexual inequality in society, we are not ready to assume the responsibility of sex selection.

Still another thorny question may arise from our increasing knowledge about genetic makeup. Today, people who seek genetic testing do so voluntarily. At what point will society step in and say we *must* be tested?

Mass genetic screening may be on the horizon. In some states, testing of newborns for PKU (phenylketonuria)—a genetic disorder that causes retardation and can be treated by special diet early in life—is mandatory. In some areas, testing for sickle-cell disease, a disorder that mainly affects blacks—is mandatory for schoolchildren or for persons about to marry. The National Research Council of the National Academy of Sciences has called mass screening a progressive health concept. But there is confusion about *victims* of sickle-cell disease and carriers of the *trait*. The latter are not sick, but have sometimes been refused insurance, or fired from jobs because of the confusion. The various states have a confusing welter of laws regarding testing for PKU, sickle-cell, and other genetic disorders.

According to Tabitha Powledge, research associate for genetics at the Hastings Center, the increasing knowledge society will have about each of us may cause our options to become narrower and narrower. She uses as an example the research on certain chemical substances in the human body called antigens. Some antigens seem to be statistically associated with the presence of certain diseases. If, at some future time, we could screen for those antigens to identify people with a predisposition toward a certain disease, we might, for example, be ruled out of a job because of a disease we don't have but might get, or we could be denied insurance, or rejected by potential spouses.

A bitter battle over screening for another genetic disorder—the "extra Y" chromosome—erupted in Boston in 1974. Since 1968, all the baby boys born at the Boston Hospital for Women had been screened for chromosomal abnormalities, including the extra Y. Psychiatrist Stanley Walzer of Harvard Medical School followed the development of 40 of these boys. A citizens' health-advocacy group called Science for the People (which included some of Dr. Walzer's peers at Harvard and the Massachusetts Institute of Technology) attacked the study. They charged that the children would be unfairly stigmatized by being labeled as "extra Y" males.

In the past few years there have been widespread reports in the press about the extra Y chromosome as the "criminal" chromosome. Dr. Walzer said publicly that the "criminal-chromosome" theory was nonsense, but that there were indications that some extra-Y males may have behavioral problems and learning disabilities.

It was an example of a head-on clash between two well-intentioned groups. Dr. Walzer and his colleagues doing the study believed that the information would be helpful to the children and the parents. As a parent,

I would certainly want to know if my child had any abnormality that could lead to problems. I hope I would have the wisdom to deal with the information wisely. On the other hand, as Science for the People argued, children who are expected to be "problems" usually live up to those expectations. What would happen when a boy got into normal kid's mischief in school if his medical records showed an extra Y? Would a teacher or principal mark this as the beginning of a pattern of "antisocial" behavior? The study was finally halted after a heated public debate. In the next few years we will see more of these battles over genetic screening.

It is not only in the area of human reproduction that The New Biology raises controversial issues. The invasion of the cellular mechanism has been relentless in the past five years. For example, in 1970 Dr. H. Gobind Khorana headed a team at the University of Wisconsin that achieved the first synthesis of a gene in a test tube. The methods for chemical synthesis had been established—theoretically now any gene could be made in the test tube. In 1975 a team of biochemists at Harvard artificially reproduced a mammalian gene—a much more complex structure than the one produced five years previously.

Scientists have not only duplicated genes, but they have changed cell construction. In 1971 a team of scientists at Oxford University corrected a defect in a cell. They worked with mouse cells that were not able to produce a necessary enzyme. The deficient mouse cell was injected with some healthy pieces of chick chromosome using an inactivated mouse virus as a carrier. The same enzyme deficiency in humans produces the rare and fatal Lesch-Nyhan syndrome. The new genetic material enabled the mouse cells to produce the enzyme, and the new genes not only remained part of the permanent cell machinery, but were duplicated as new, healthy cells grew and divided. The journal *Nature* said the achievement meant that it was now possible in principle to remove defective cells from a human patient, to introduce new genes, and to return the cured cells to the patient.

However, the genetic mechanisms of the human body are very complex and the day of genetic medicine—the curing of genetic disease by the transfer of material into cells—is probably a long way off. Which is not to say that science hasn't taken the first tentative steps in that direction. The first known attempt at gene therapy came in 1970, and it caused an international controversy which is still going on. Two sisters, then seven years and two years, were brought into a hospital in Cologne, Germany; they were suffering from a rare, hereditary enzyme deficiency which caused high levels in their blood and spinal fluid of a substance called arginine. The girls suffered from palsy, epileptic seizures, and retardation.

An American virologist, Dr. Stanfield Rogers at Oak

Ridge National Laboratory, worked with German doctors to attempt gene therapy. They injected the girls with a virus, which had caused a lower concentration of arginine in the blood of laboratory workers exposed to that virus than to a control group who was not. Could the virus eliminate the lethal substance in the children's blood? Possibly, but there was also a known risk. The virus, when tested on rabbits, produced cancerous skin lesions.

The therapy was tried, and in 1975 Dr. Rogers announced that it had failed, possibly because the virus used was not full-strength. It had deteriorated in storage. He said they would try again, although this time there was no possibility that the girls could be helped. Their symptoms were then irreversible. But could the knowledge gained help others in the future? Or would the second injection of the cancer-causing virus possibly doom them to even more suffering? Scientists on both sides of the Atlantic were bitterly divided over the case. The questions in this debate will be raised again and again as society grapples with the risks and benefits of genetic medicine.

Possibly the most significant development in genetic research has been the success of "gene transfer" techniques. For the first time scientists can take a gene out of its environment and get a closer look at its machinery—why it shuts off and on, how it transmits messages. By understanding the behavior of a gene, scientists may be able to probe the causes of the uncontrolled cell growth of cancer. Scientists have been able to use enzymes like a surgeon's knife, to lift pieces of DNA out of complex cells and put them into laboratory bacteria, where they can multiply. The "transferred" genes are usually housed in bacteria known as *E. coli*, a common inhabitant of the human colon. The new techniques enable researchers to combine genetic material in a way never before possible, to concoct a "genetic stew." A Swedish team, for example, has crossed genes of different species to produce live hybrid cells. The team combined human cells with those of rats, mice, and even insects.

What if a bit of this stew were to escape from the lab, in a tiny piece of the *E. coli*. The bacteria might travel to its natural habitat in the human gut, depositing there pieces of genetic material unknown to nature.

Since one of the substances used for gene transfer—a genetic material called a plasmid—can confer resistance to antibiotics, the specter has arisen of mass infections for which there is no known cure. Could gene-transer procedure create the "Doomsday Bug"? The incidence of laboratory-acquired infections—5,000 cases in the past 30 years—suggests it could.

In 1974 a group of American scientists were so alarmed by the possible hazards of gene transfers that they called for an international moratorium. At the "Asilomar" conference held in Pacific Grove, California, in 1975, an international group of scientists met and hammered out safety guidelines for work with hybrid cells. It was probably the first time in the history of science that scientists gathered together to discipline themselves before—not after—the dangers have materialized.

However, in the face of such potential hazards, are voluntary safeguards enough? And are these being discussed in the right places by the right people? The places where decisions about research are made—congressional and corporate offices, government agencies, university science departments—are conspicuous for the absence of certain people. Women and minorities are not often included in high-level decisions. In our society, the mechanisms for bringing disenfranchised groups into decision-making are few. In some scientific quarters, there is suspicion of the public process. It 1971 during a Senate hearing on a bill to set up a commission to look at issues in the biological sciences. Senator Walter Mondale (D.-Mont.) expressed surprise at the resistance to what he called a "measly little study commission." He said, "I sense an almost psychopathic objection to the public process, a fear that if the public gets involved, it's going to be antiscience."

In fact, it was the emotionally charged issue of research on aborted fetuses that prompted Congressional action. Senator Edward Kennedy (D.-Mass.) introduced a bill that led to the National Commission for the Protection of Human Subjects, which had a majority of nonscientists as members. The commission is an advisory body to the Department of Health, Education, and Welfare. Its first job was to draw up a set of guidelines for fetal research, which it did in 1975. The commission is now looking into the question of research involving prisoners and minorities, but it will be phased out of existence after its final report, sometime in 1977.

The Pandora's box of genetic technology may be opened and its inhabitants long gone before the public process catches up. The revolution in molecular biology will affect the destinies of women in a profound way, but few women will be asked to be involved in policy decisions that will chart its direction. Do we want proxy mothers or clones or handy methods for choosing the sex of our children or mass genetic screening? Do we as a species have the wisdom to direct our own evolution by tinkering with our genes? Dr. Leon Kass of the Kennedy Institute Center for Bioethics at Georgetown University says, "We triumph over nature's unpredictabilities only to subject ourselves to the still greater unpredictability of our capricious will and our fickle opinions. Thus, engineering the engineer as well as the engine, we race our train we know not where."

And if women remain mute, we will simply go along on the ride.

Cloning: A Generation Made to Order

Human reproduction begins with the merger of the sex cells, sperm and egg. Since each contains only half a set of chromosomes, the joining of sperm with the egg is the first step in the creation of a new and unique individual, with traits inherited from both parents. But this is not the only possible way for life to begin.

The other type of cells in the human body already has a full set of chromosomes. All the genetic information necessary for an organism to reproduce itself is contained in the nucleus of every cell in that organism. If body cells could be made to divide, the result would be asexual reproduction—the production of offspring with only one parent. Such a process is already being used with other species—it is called cloning. It has been tried successfully with plants, fruit flies—and more significantly, with frogs.

In 1968, J. B. Gurdon at Oxford University produced a clonal frog. He took an unfertilized egg cell from an African clawed frog and destroyed its nucleus by ultraviolet radiation. He replaced it with the nucleus of an intestinal cell of another frog of the same species. The egg, suddenly finding itself with a full set of chromosomes, began to reproduce. It was "tricked" into starting the reproductive process. The result was a tadpole that was a genetic twin of the frog that donated the cell. The "mother" frog contributed nothing to the genetic identity of the tadpole, since her potential to pass on her traits was destroyed when the nucleus of her egg was obliterated.

How would it work with human beings? Roughly the same way. A healthy egg could be removed from a woman's body, in the same way that Edwards and Fowler obtain eggs for their work. But instead of fertilizing the egg with sperm, scientists could destroy the nucleus of the human egg and replace it with a cell taken from the arm or anywhere of a donor we'll call John X. The egg would be reimplanted in the uterus of a woman. Although its identity would be wiped out with the destruction of its nucleus, it could nonetheless start to divide, because it had received the proper signal—the presence of a full set of chromosomes. The baby that would be the result of that process would have only one parent—John X. It would, in fact, be a carbon copy of John X—his twin, a generation removed. (Or her twin, if the cell donor were female.)

In March of this year scientists announced major progress on the hunt for the substance that "switches on" the reproductive mechanisms of the cell. Gurdon's first experiments with the frog proved that such a mechanism exists and that all cells—not just sex cells—could be made to reproduce. Now, work done by Gurdon at Cambridge and by Ann Janice Brothers at the University of Indiana is moving science closer to discovering the identity of the "master switch."

Gurdon inserted the nuclei of human cancer cells into immature frogs' eggs, and the human cell nuclei responded in dramatic fashion, swelling in size to as much as a hundredfold.

Brothers, working with amphibians, axolotls, has observed that a molecule identified as the O+ factor appears to be the substance that signals the reproductive process to carry on. Eggs produced by axolotls that did not contain the O+ factor did not develop past very rudimentary stages until they were injected with O+ substance. Brothers and her colleagues at Indiana report that O+ appears to be a large protein molecule that is somewhat acidic. The scientists are working to isolate and define that molecule. The identification of the "master switch" would be a giant step toward understanding cancer and would bring the day of human cloning closer.

The consequences of human cloning are almost impossible to imagine. Widespread human cloning would alter human society beyond recognition. The family would no longer exist, sexuality would have no connection with reproduction. The idea of parenthood would be completely changed. The diversity of human beings provided by sexual reproduction would vanish. One could imagine entire communities of people who looked exactly the same, whose range of potential was identical. Some scientists have suggested that "clones and clonishness" could replace our present patterns of nation and race.

The misuses of cloning are not hard to predict. Would an aging dictator try to insure the continuance of his regime by an heir apparent who was his genetic double? Would women and men project their egos into the future by producing their own "carbon copies"? Would society choose to clone our most valued citizens? Artists? Generals? Members of elite groups? The capacity of our species to change and adapt may be rooted in the diversity of the gene pool. By tampering with that process we could be limiting our own ability to survive.

There are some who believe that current work in test-tube fertilization to extract eggs is a first step in the direction of cloning. There have been some estimates that human cloning will be a reality within the decade. Who will say where we draw the line?

Why Brain Nerves Can't Repair Themselves

Unlike many parts of the body, including peripheral nerves, nerves in the brain and spinal cord are unable to repair themselves if damaged. A team of Swedish neurologists suggests one explanation of this phenomenon in the May 22 *Nature*. Niels-Aage Svengaard heads the team at the Univesity of Lund.

The tiny blood vessels that usually protect central nervous system neurons from harmful substances in the bloodstream— the so-called blood-brain barrier— do not replenish themselves among damaged central nerves, the group found. So even if central nerves manage to resprout new axons, these axons will probably not survive because they will be attacked by immune fighters or other harmful substances in the bloodstream.

The team also suggests that a defect in the blood-brain barrier might be a major factor in multiple sclerosis and other neurological disorders that comprise long-term degeneration of nerves.

The tiny blood vessels in the central nervous system are unique with respect to their barrier mechanisms, preventing, to a varying degree, many types of substances from passing into the brain and spinal cord from the blood. So Svendgaard and his co-workers postulated that damage to, or defects in, the barrier might underlie nerves' inability to repair themselves if damaged.

In testing this hypothesis they found that if peripheral nervous tissue were transplanted into the brains of experimental animals, nerves in the brain would form functional connections with the implanted tissue. At first the nerve connections functioned well, but then they showed signs of damage, resulting in a progressive deterioration of the entire nerve network. In contrast, such degeneration was not noted in the brain neurons outside of the implanted tissue area.

So Svendgaard and his team determined whether the inability of the central nerves to survive in the implanted tissue was due to a failure of the blood-brain barrier to develop in the implanted tissue. They transplanted nerves from the iris of the eye into the brains of rats. Some of the rats were injected with nerve transmitter chemicals known as catecholamines, which act as an index of whether or not the barrier is present, because they cannot get through the blood-brain barrier.

The iris transplants in the brain, the investigators found, were rapidly supplied with nerves from the brain. In fact, within three weeks the nerve density of the irises was close to normal. But the investigators found that no tiny blood vessels invaded the iris transplants. And the catecholamines, in those animals which were injected with the substance, managed to get into the iris transplants and totally destroy the brain nerves that had reinnervated them. So it looked as if brain nerves could innervate the implanted tissue, but a blood-brain barrier failed to develop in the implanted tissue to protect against harmful chemicals.

Then the investigators did a reverse experiment. They transplanted central nervous system tissue to peripheral nervous tissue in the eye. Here again, implanted nervous tissue was innervated by nerves from the host tissue. But in this situation, a blood-brain barrier did develop in the implanted tissue.

The two experiments show that whether or not the blood-brain barrier develops in regenerating nerves depends on the kind of host tissue that is present. In other words, central nervous system nerves in the brain were unable to provide a blood-brain barrier for the implanted iris (peripheral nervous) tissue. Peripheral nerves in the eye did provide a barrier for the implanted central nervous system tissue.

Central nerves cannot naturally regenerate themselves, the investigators conclude, because they cannot make a new blood-brain barrier for their regenerated parts. And if a blood-brain barrier is not present, antibodies, lymphocytes or other substances in the blood could well invade the new nervous tissue and destroy it.

This latter contention, in fact, is supported by other investigators' evidence that if lymphocytes get into the brain and spinal cord of experimental animals, they produce multiple sclerosis-like damage.

Extracerebral Elements of the Mind
When and How the Mind Is Formed

J. M. R. Delgado

In Plato's works, Socrates is presented as a kind of intellectual midwife who extracted knowledge already existent in the person he questioned. According to the doctrine of recollection, learning is only the remembering of knowledge possessed in a former life. In *Phaedo*, the second argument for the survival of the soul is that knowledge is recollection, and therefore the soul must have existed before birth.

Aristotle rejected the theory of inborn ideas and proposed the metaphorical *tabula rasa*, which was subsequently accepted in the seventeenth and eighteenth centuries by empirical physiologists, including Locke and Helvétius. The newborn mind was considered a blank tablet on which experience would write messages, and the dissimilarities between individuals were attributed solely to differences in education.

The Aristotelian principle, "Nihil est in intellectu quod no prius suent in sensu" (St. Thomas, *De Veritatis*, II, 3), repeated among others by Leonardo da Vinci ("Ogni nostra cognizioni principia dai sentimenti"), expressed the idea still prevalent in present times that "nothing is in the intellect which was not first in the senses." Some authors, including Epicurus and the sensualists, stressed the importance of sensory inputs to its limit, proposing that the intellect is only *what* is in our senses.

Between the extremes of considering the mind either sophisticated or naive at birth, contemporary opinion holds that both genetic and experiential components are essential, although their functions and relative importance remain controversial. According to several child psychiatrists, heredity and experience are equipotent (156, 225). Piaget (178) has emphasized that while the human brain is an almost entirely hereditary regulatory organ, it has practically "no hereditary programming of these regulations, quite unlike the case of so many instincts in birds or fishes. . . ." Intelligence combines two cognitive systems: experience and endogenous regulations. The last system is a source of intellectual operations; by prolonging the feedbacks and correcting the mistakes,

it transforms them into instruments of precognition.

The genetic determination of mental functions has been supported by Rainer (181), who believes that the fertilized ovum contains "the primordia of what we later call mind," and that "the newborn infant is already as much of an individual 'mentally' as he is physiognomically." According to the evolutionary theories of William James (119), "the new forms of being that make their appearance are really nothing more than results of the redistribution of the original and unchanging materials . . . the evolution of the brains, if understood, would be simply the account of how the atoms came to be so caught and jammed. In this story no new *natures* [James's emphasis], no factors not present at the beginning are introduced at any later stage."

In agreement with these ideas, Sherrington (206) writes: "Mind as attaching to any unicellular life would seem to me unrecognizable to observation; but I would not feel that permits me to affirm it is not there. Indeed, I would think that since mind appears in the developing soma, that amounts to showing that it is potential in the ovum (and sperm) from which the soma sprang. The appearance of recognizable mind in the soma would then be not a creation *de novo* but a development of mind from unrecognizable into recognizable."

The importance of the prenatal period as a determinant of future behavior crystallized in the concept of "ontogenetic zero" (88) has been accepted by most child psychologists (30). At the moment of fertilization, the life of a unique individual is initiated (at birth a child is already nine months old); and some experts have suggested that its beginning should be traced back through evolution of the parental reproductive cells or even through previous generations.

These theories have the merit of stressing the role of genetics in the formation of the mind, but they give the false impression that genetic factors alone are able to create a mind, or that in some mysterious way, a minute, undeveloped mind already exists in the cells. At the core of this discussion is the meaning of "potentiality," which is a convenient concept provided that we understand its imitations. If we say "a block of marble is potentially a piece of sculpture," we mean that marble is an element which can be shaped into a symbolic pattern by using chisels and hammers with appropriate skills. We may say that all shapes and artistic creations potentially exist in the marble, but the reality is that in the absence of a sculptor, the piece of stone lacks, per se, the essential elements to become a work of art. It would be incorrect to think that tools or skills are hidden within the block of marble, or that if we waited long enough, a statue would emerge spontaneously from the block. This type of incorrect reasoning has been called the "error of potentiality" (137). It has infiltrated the field of embryology and has influenced analyses of the origin and evolution of mental functions by assuming, at a certain stage of development, the existence of properties which are present only at a later stage and which depend on a series of essential conditions neither present in nor determined by the stage under consideration.

If we say that the mind is in the sperm, we can also say that each man has one million children, that a newborn baby will be the inventor of spaceships, or that a worm may evolve into a monkey. These statements may be potentially valid, but their fulfillment is contingent upon a constellation of factors which are not present in the original material. In spite of his genes and his potentials, a man cannot create a single child without the collaboration of a woman; and a baby will not invent rockets unless he is exposed to a highly sophisticated level of physics. We believe that worms have evolved into more complex forms of life, and that potentially they may produce dinosaurs, supermen, or inhabitants of the moon, but before we allow our imagination to wander among the limitless possibilities of nature, it is preferable to identify the factors responsible for the observed reality among an infinite number of theoretical potentials.

According to early theories of preformism, the germinal cell—the ovum—held a miniature organism with microscopic eyes, arms, legs, and other parts of the body which eventually would grow. The ovaries of Eve had potentially the bodies—and minds—of all mankind. As soon as scientific embryology began, it was evident that the germinal cell did not contain a compressed homunculus, but only a plan which required the interaction of other elements in order to develop into a human being.

A relatively small group of organization centers (the genes), with the collaboration of molecules supplied from the outside (the mother), produce another series of organizers (enzymes, hormones, and other active substances) which will arrange patterns of molecules for the construction of cells, tissues, and organs and will also produce a new series of organizers to direct the interaction of these new elements. The organizers are not completely stereotyped in performance but are influenced by their medium. A particular gene may have different phenotypic effects in different environments, and "genes control the 'reaction norm' of the organism to environmental conditions" (31). Blood vessels, muscles, and the various organs are differentiated; neurons appear, their interconnections are established, and the brain evolves. Chromosomes have neither heart nor brain—only a set of architectonic plans which under suitable conditions will evolve into a complete organism. These plans are unfulfilled for millions of sexual cells and for countless embryos that are casualties in spontaneous abortions. The possibilities of evolution are far from accomplished realities.

If we accept these ideas, we may also state that the fecundated germinal cell does not talk, understand, or think, and that the resulting embryo has no mental functions before the medullary plate rolls up to form the neural tube. When can we detect the first signs of a functioning mind? How are they correlated with the anatomical development of the central nervous system? The study of these questions may be simplified if we first examine the initial signs of a functioning brain as revealed by behavioral expression in lower animals. Before the development of muscles, motor neurons are already growing out to establish neural contacts with them. The order of growth is a "progressive individualism within a totally integrated matrix, and not a progressive integration of primarily individuated units" (34). Motions, therefore, are basically a part of a total pattern, and their relative individualization is only a secondary acquisition. Some efferent motor pathways appear before any afferent fiber enters the cerebrum. Initially, the cerebral association system develops toward the motor system and the peripheral sensory fibers grow toward the receptor field. Significant conclusions from these facts are that "the individual acts on its environment before it reacts to its environment" (35), that efferent nerves must be stimulated by products of the organism's metabolism, and that "behavior in response to such stimulation is spontaneous in the sense that it is the expression of the intrinsic dynamics of the organism as a whole" (37). Total behavior is not made up of reflexes; rather, "the mechanism of the total pattern is an essential component of the performance of the part, i.e., the reflex," and behavior therefore "cannot be fully expressed in terms of S-R (Stimulus-Response)" (37). It is significant that in man vestibular connections develop before vestibular sense organs, because this reveals that "the cerebral growth determines the attitude of the individual to its environment before that individual is able to receive any sensory impression of its environment. Hence, the initiative is within the organism" (36).

Some of these findings have been confirmed in the toadfish and the cunner (228). On the first day that the cunner larva swim around freely, they do not respond to external stimuli. Thus under natural conditions, this species moves about without an effective exteroceptive mechanism, evidently propelled by a "mechanism of motility activated from within." The afferent sensory system grows gradually until it finally "captures" the primitive motor system. The conclusion is that behavior has two components: "endogenous activity, the fundamental motility conditioned by the inner physiological adjustments of the organism; and exogenous activity, the oriented activity by which endogenous activity is so modified as to render response to external stimuli possible" (70).

This information emphasizes the importance of genetic determination and indicates that some mechanisms for behavioral performance are organized in the absence of environmental inputs. It is generally accepted that development of the nervous system is basic for the onset and elaboration of mammalian behavior, but it is not clear whether any factor can be singled out as decisive. Without synaptic conduction, impulses obviously cannot be transmitted: thus the functional maturity of synapsis must be essential (104, 144, 205, 241). Objections have been raised about the acceptance of synaptic permeability as the main reason or onset of behavior (140), and other factors may be equally important. Activity of peripheral nerve fibers is considered essential for the differentiation and specificity of behavioral performance (72, 78), and the anatomical development of neurofibrillae may be specifically related to the onset of behavior (136). These and other studies have provided important information, but its interpretation has often been biased by methodological distortions.

It is a common error in behavioral embryology, and in science generally, to try to simplify the observed phenomena and to reduce causality to a single factor, excluding all other variables. This is the *fallacy of the single cause* (121), or failure to understand that a biological phenomena is always the product of a complex situation, not of a single determinant. With this pitfall in mind, we must face the task of identifying the several elements essential for the development of any given phenomenon, and both conduction and synaptic mechanisms are certainly basic for the onset of behavior.

Myelin is a substance with insulating properties covering the nerves, and its appearance in neuronal sheaths has often been associated with the onset and differentiation of behavior by neuro-anatomists. A correlation perhaps exists for some specific behavior patterns in the cat and the opposum (138, 226), but most authors today agree that the myelogenetic law cannot be generalized. In the newborn rat, myelination does not take place for several days although the fetus starts moving many days before birth, and some

discrete reflexes and inhibitory activity in higher centers can be observed in a rat fetus nineteen days after conception (5). Myelination, therefore, cannot be interpreted as necessary for the conduction of impulses or for functional insulation.

Differences in anatomical and behavioral evolution certainly exist between mammals and lower life forms. In the guinea pig, for example, limbs are well formed in the embryo before appearance of the first behavioral response, while in the salamander motor behavior is initiated before morphological differentiation of the limbs. Evidently embryologic studies of man cannot be as extensive and as well controlled as those of amphibia, but valuable information on this subject already exists (30). Inside the uterus, the human embryo has a comfortable and sheltered life without facing responsibilities or making choices. Cells multiply automatically and organs take shape while the growing fetus floats weightless in the silent night of amniotic fluid. Food and oxygen are provided and wastes are removed continuously and effortlessly by the maternal placenta. As the fetus grows, many organs perform something like a dress rehearsal before their functions are really required. This is usually referred to as the principle of anticipatory morphological maturation. The heart starts to beat when there is no blood to pump; the gastrointestinal tract shows peristaltic movements and begins to secrete juices in the absence of food; the eyelids open and close in the eternal darkness of the uterus; the arms and legs move, giving the mother the indescribable joy of feeling a new life inside herself; even breathing movements appear several weeks before birth when there is no air to breathe (1).

Some extensive information about human fetal behavior has been obtained by indirect methods in pregnant women, while other findings were obtained directly from fetuses surgically removed for medical reasons (112, 155, 176). The first movement observed in a four-millimeter-long, three-week-old fetus is the heart beat, which has intrinsic determinants because it starts before the organ has received any nervous connections. The neural elements needed for a reflex act can be demonstrated in the spinal cord at the second month of embryonic life, and at that time, cutaneous stimulation may induce motor responses. A fourteen-week fetus shows most of the responses which can be observed in the neonate with the exception of vocalization, the tonic grasping reflex, and respiration. With fetal growth, spontaneous motility increases inside the mother's womb and it is well known that responses from the fetus may be elicited by tapping the mother's abdominal wall.

Sensory perception of the fetus has been investigated in detail by several scientists (27, 30, 240). Cutaneous reception is well developed long before birth, and mechanical or thermal stimulation of the skin elicits appropriate motor activity related to the stimulated area. The existence of pain perception is doubtful. Proprioceptors of the muscles (the spindles) develop at the fourth month of fetal life and the labyrinth is evident even earlier. Both organs are active during fetal life; they are capable of postural adjustments and may be partially responsible for fetal motility in the uterus.

The possibility of fetal perception of gastrointestinal movements, hunger, thirst, suffocation, and other types of organic experience has been debated, and it is generally accepted that internal stimuli may activate skeletal musculature. Distinction of sweet from other tastes and of unpleasant odors such as asafetida has been demonstrated in premature babies, showing that these receptor mechanisms are already developed. It is doubtful, however, that with the nose and mouth immersed in amniotic fluid, the fetus could have gustatory or olfactory experiences before birth.

The auditory apparatus is well developed at birth, but the general consensus (180) is that the infant is deaf until the liquid of the fetal middle ear is drained through the Eustachian tube by breathing, crying, and perhaps yawning. Loud noises, however, might be perceived, and some cases of presumed fetal hearing have been reported (79).

The optic apparatus is sufficiently developed in the newborn infant to permit perception of light and darkness, but the optic nerve is not yet fully developed, and its evolution continues after birth and is probably influenced by sensory perception (180). It is highly improbable that the fetus has any visual experience during its uterine life.

In summary, it is unlikely that before the moment of birth the baby has had any significant visual, auditory, olfactory, or gustatory experience, and it is probable that it has received only a very limited amount of tactile, organic, and proprioceptive information. The newborn has an elaborated system of reflexes; and coughing, sneezing, sucking, swallowing, grasping, and other actions may be evoked by the appropriate sensory stimulation. In an experimental study of seventeen behavioral responses, their intercorrelations proved to be zero, indicating that "there is no mental integration in the newborn child" (82). This integration usually takes place during the first postnatal month.

Whether or not the fetus was capable of conscious experience was a classical philosophical and psychological problem debated at length with a flourish of words and speculations but with little factual support (39, 86, 135, 147, 175). It is difficult to understand the basis of this controversy since there is no evidence that the fetus has visual, auditory, olfactory, or gustatory

stimulation. The possibility of fetal awareness is therefore reduced to a limited input of organic sensations of proprioception and touch in the absence of the main sensory faculties. Whether or not these phenomena can by themselves create consciousness is mainly a question of definition and arbitrary agreement, but it may be stated that they cannot produce manifestations comparable to those of consciousness in children or adults, which are mainly based on visual and auditory perception and experience. The mystery is perhaps insoluble due to the impossibility of establishing verbal communication with the newborn.

Anticipatory morphological maturation is present in various mechanisms which remain quiescent in the fetus, ready to perform with physiological efficiency as soon as they are needed. Their necessary links are established before birth and are triggered by appropriate stimulation. These functions, which include oral suction, respiration, kidney secretion, and gastrointestinal activity, are able to act several weeks before an expected delivery, in case the baby is born prematurely.

No comparable provisions exist for mental functions. The newborn brain is not capable of speech, symbolic understanding, or of directing skillful motility. It has no ideas, words, or concepts, no tools for communication, no significant sensory experience, no culture. The newborn baby never smiles. He is unable to comprehend the loving phrases of his mother or to be aware of the environment. We must conclude that there are no detectable signs of mental activity at birth and *that human beings are born without minds.* This statement may seem startling, but it should not be rejected by saying, "Well, you don't see mental functions during the first few days, but everything is ready for action; wait a few weeks, or perhaps a few months; it is just a slight lack of maturity, but the baby's mind is there." Potentiality should not be confused with reality. A project is not an accomplished fact, especially when essential elements are lacking in the original design. Naturally a baby lacks experience, but by recognizing this fact, we are accepting the essentiality of extracerebral elements which originate in the outside world and are independent of both the organism and its genetic endowment. As Cantril and Livingston (29) have said, organisms are in a constant "transaction," in a "process of becoming," constantly changing into something different from what they were before. Early in life, an infant is attracted to sources of comfort and repelled by sources of distress. These experiences lead to the "intelligent" recognition of objects and persons associated with positive or negative reinforcement, and they will determine selective patterns of behavioral response. "It is at this point, we think, that 'mind' is born" (29).

The concept of the mindless newborn brain is a

useful hypothesis because it clarifies our search for the origin of the mind. If this origin depended on genetic endowment, then mental functions should appear in the absence of other external elements (as respiratory functions do). If genetic determination alone is not sufficient, then we must investigate the source and characteristics of the extracerebral elements responsible for the appearance of the mind as the baby matures.

Evolution and the Brain

Stephen Jay Gould

Nature discloses the secrets of her past with the greatest reluctance. We paleontologists weave our tales from fossil fragments poorly preserved in incomplete sequences of sedimentary rocks. Most fossil mammals are known only from teeth—the hardiest substance in our bodies—and a few scattered bones. A famous paleontologist once remarked that most of mammalian history involved only the mating of teeth to produce slightly modified descendant teeth.

We rejoice at the rare preservation of soft parts— mammoths frozen in ice or insect wings preserved as carbonized films on beds of shale. Yet most of our information about the soft anatomy of fossils comes, not from these rare accidents, but from evidence commonly preserved in bone—the insertion scars of muscles or the holes through which nerves pass. Fortunately, the brain has also left its imprint upon the bones that enclose it. When a vertebrate dies, its brain quickly decays, but the resultant hole in the skull may be filled by sediment that hardens to produce a natural cast. This cast can preserve nothing of the brain's internal structure, but its size and external surface may faithfully copy the original.

Unfortunately, we cannot simply measure the volume of a fossil cast to obtain a reliable measure of an animal's intelligence; paleontology is never that easy. We must consider two problems.

First, what does brain size mean? Does it correlate at all with intelligence? There is no evidence for any relationship between intelligence and the normal range of variability for brain size *within* a species (fully functional human brains range from less than 1,000 to more than 2,000 cubic centimeters in volume). The variation of individuals within a species, however, is not the same phenomenon as variation in average values for different species. We must assume that, for example, average differences in brain size between humans and tuna fish bear some relationship to a meaningful concept of intelligence. Besides, what else can paleontologists do? We must work with what we have, and brain size is most of what we have.

Secondly, the primary determinant of brain size is not mental capacity, but body size. A large brain may reflect nothing more than the needs of the large body that housed it. Moreover, . . . the relationship of brain size to body size is not a simple one. As animals get larger, brains increase in size at a slower rate. The brains of small animals are relatively large; that is, the ratio of their brain weight to body weight is higher. We must find some way to remove the influence of body size. This is done by plotting an equation for the "normal" relationship between brain weight and body weight.

Suppose we are studying mammals. We compile a list of average brain and body weights for adults of as many different species as we can. These species form the points of our graph; the equation that fits these points indicates that brain weight increases about two-thirds as fast as body weight. We can then compare the brain weight of any given species with the brain weight for an "average" mammal of that body weight. This comparison removes the influence of body size. A chimpanzee, for example, has an average brain weight of 395 grams. An average mammal of the same body weight should have a brain weight of 152 grams according to our equation. A chimp's brain is, therefore, 2.6 times as heavy as it "should" be (395/152). We may refer to this ratio of actual to expected brain size as an "encephalization quotient"; values greater than 1 signify larger than average brains; values less than 1 mark smaller than average brains.

But this method imposes another difficulty on paleontologists. We must now estimate body weight as well as brain weight. Complete skeletons are very rare and estimates are often made from a few major bones alone. To pile difficulty upon difficulty, only birds and mammals have brains that completely fill their cranial cavities. In these groups, a cranial cast faithfully reproduces the size and form of the brain. But in fishes, amphibians, and reptiles, the brain occupies only part of the cavity, so the fossilized cast is larger than the actual brain. We must estimate what part of the cast the brain would have occupied in life. And yet, despite this plethora of difficulties, assumptions, and estimates, we have been able to establish, and even to verify, a coherent and intriguing story about the evolution of brain size in vertebrates.

California psychologist Harry J. Jerison has reccently marshaled all the evidence—much of it collected during his own labors of more than a decade—in a book entitled *The Evolution of the Brain and Intelligence* (New York, Academic Press, 1973).

Jerison's major theme is an attack upon the vulgar notion that vertebrate classes can be arranged in a ladder of perfection leading from fish to mammal through the intermediary levels of amphibian, reptile, and bird. Jerison prefers a functional view that relates the amount of brain to specific requirements of modes of life, not to any preordained or intrinsic tendency for increase during the course of evolution. The potential "brain-body space" of modern vertebrates is filled in only two areas: one occupied by the warm-blooded vertebrates (birds and mammals), the other by their cold-blooded relatives (fish, amphibians, and modern reptiles). (Sharks provide the only exception to this general rule. Their brains are much too big—quite a surprise for these supposedly "primitive" fishes, but more on this later.) Warm-blooded vertebrates, to be sure, have larger brains than their cold-blooded relatives of the same body size, but there is no steady progress toward higher states, only a correlation between brain size and basic physiology. In fact, Jerison believes that mammals evolved their large brains to meet specific functional demands during their original existence as small creatures competing on the periphery of a world dominated by dinosaurs. He argues that the first mammals were nocturnal and that they needed larger brains to translate the perceptions of hearing and smell into spatial patterns that animals active in daylight could detect by vision alone.

Jerison provides his tidbits within this framework. I hate to confute a comfortable item of received dogma, but I must report that dinosaurs did not have small brains—they had brains of just the right size for reptiles of their immense dimensions. We should never have expected more from *Brontosaurus* because large animals have relatively small brains, and reptiles of any weight have smaller brains than mammals.

The gap between modern cold- and warm-blooded vertebrates is neatly filled by intermediate fossil forms. *Archaeopteryx*, the first bird, is known from fewer than half a dozen specimens, but one of them has a well-preserved brain cast. This intermediate form with bird feathers and reptilian teeth had a brain that plots right in the middle of the unfilled area between modern reptiles and birds. The primitive mammals that evolved so rapidly after dinosaurs became extinct had brains intermediate in size between reptiles and modern mammals of corresponding body weights.

We can even begin to understand the mechanism of this evolutionary increase in brain size by tracing one of the feedback loops that inspired it. Jerison computed the encephalization quotients for carnivores and their putative prey among ungulate herbivores for four separate groups: "archaic" mammals of the early Tertiary (the Tertiary is the conventional "age of mammals" and represents the last 70 million years of earth history); advanced mammals of the early Tertiary; middle to late Tertiary mammals; and modern mammals. Remember than an encephalization quotient of 1.0 denotes the expected brain size of an average modern mammal.

	Herbivores	*Carnivores*
Early Tertiary (archaic)	0.18	0.44
Early Tertiary (advanced)	0.38	0.61
Middle to late Tertiary	0.63	0.76
Modern	0.95	1.10

Both herbivores and carnivores displayed continual increase in brain size during their evolution, but at each stage, the carnivores were always ahead. Animals that make a living by catching rapidly moving prey seem to need bigger brains than plant eaters. And, as the herbivores increased their brain size (presumably under the intensive selective pressure of their carnivorous predators), the carnivores also evolved larger brains to maintain the differential.

South America provides a natural experiment to test this claim. Until the Isthmus of Panama rose just a couple of million years ago, South America was an isolated island continent. Advanced carnivores never reached this island, and predatory roles were filled by marsupial carnivores with low encephalization quotients. Here, the herbivores display no increase in brain size through time. Their average encephalization quotient remained below 0.5 throughout the Tertiary, and they were quickly eliminated when advanced carnivores crossed the isthmus from North America. Again, brain size is a functional adaptation to the ways animals make a living, not a quantity with an inherent tendency to increase. When we document an increase, we can relate it to specific requirements of ecological roles. Thus, we should not be surprised because sharks have such large brains; they are, after all, the top carnivores of the sea, and brain size reflects mode of life, not time of evolutionary origin. Likewise, carnivorous dinosaurs like *Allosaurus* and *Tyrannosaurus* had larger brains than herbivores like *Brontosaurus*.

But what about our preoccupation with ourselves; does anything about the over-all history of vertebrates indicate why one peculiar species should be so brainy? Here's a closing item for thought. The most ancient brain cast of a mammal in our order of primates belongs to a 55-million-year-old creature named *Tetonius homunculus*. Jerison has calculated its encephalization quotient at 0.68. This is, to be sure, only two-thirds the size of just an average living mammal of the same body weight, but it is by far the largest brain of its time (making the usual correction for body weight), and it is more than three times as large as an average mammal of its period. Primates have been ahead right from the start; our large brain is only an exaggeration of a pattern set at the beginning of the age of mammals. But why did such a large brain evolve in a group of small, primitive, tree-dwelling mammals, more similar to rats and shrews than to mammals conventionally judged as more advanced? And with this provocative query, I end, for we simply do not know the answer to one of the most important questions we can ask.

The Human Brain

E. A. Shneour

The human brain is the culmination of almost 3 billion years of evolutionary history. It reflects the highest degree of biological development achieved by any living thing. The most complex structure in creation, it is the site of man's supremacy in the animal kingdom. It is the organ that allows him to dominate his environment and control his destiny.

The earliest known living cells appeared in the primitive oceans of the planet earth more than 2.7 billion years ago, and their remains have been found in Precambrian rocks of what is now Africa.[1] These cells, probably similar to today's blue-green algae, were completely passive organisms, unable to respond to changes in the environment. Their survival and reproduction depended upon the maintenance of a favorable supply of energy from sunlight and food from the oceans. These tropical waters then still contained an accumulation of foodstuffs left over from an earlier period, during which the first organic matter was formed on the primitive earth,[2] described by the English biologist J. B. S. Haldane as "a hot thin soup."

Under these mild conditions the cells floating in the waters proliferated, and competition for food and light began in earnest. These independent cells did not have a nervous system, let alone a brain. But some of them acquired, by random mutation, the ability to identify food and light and, most importantly, to respond to these stimuli by swimming into the areas of their greatest abundance. This evolutionary change gave the cells that had acquired it an enormous competitive advantage over cells not so endowed. The eventual result of this struggle for survival was the disappearance of the more primitive cells as they were swamped by a greatly increased number and diversity of the more advanced ones.

Thus response to the environment was a vital aspect of evolution, of which the eventual development of the human brain is the ultimate expression. Evolution by natural selection is one of the greatest conceptions of modern man, ranking with Einstein's special theory of relativity. It is certainly the most important concept in biology, and one in which the brain plays a major role. Like all brilliant insights, Darwin's theory of evolution by natural selection is based on simple propositions: (1) progeny outnumber their parents; (2) in spite of this high fecundity the total population remains relatively stable because of limitation of space and available resources; and (3) the abundant progeny are endowed with a much greater diversity of traits than are their parents. Charles Darwin's deduction from these simple premises was that there was in nature a continuous struggle for existence, and that only those best fitted to their environment would survive and reproduce their kind, while those with unfavorable attributes would be eliminated.

[1] A. Holmes, "The Oldest Dated Minerals of the Rhodesian Shield," *Nature* 173 (1954), p. 612.

[2] S. L. Miller and H. C. Urey, "Organic Compound Synthesis on the Primitive Earth," *Science* 130 (1959), p. 245.

A remarkable and well-documented example of natural selection occurred in the mid-1800s, during England's industrial expansion.[3] Most of the moths in the countryside were light-colored, but scientific observers of the time noted that the light-colored moths were gradually being replaced by dark ones until as many as 90 per cent of them in the industrial areas were dark. This puzzling phenomenon was eventually explained as follows: While the country remained rural, the light-colored moths matched well the color of the tree trunks, while the dark moths stood out and easily fell prey to hungry birds. As the soot from coal-burning factories gradually darkened the trees, the situation was reversed, i.e., the light-colored moths now stood out and were early and frequent victims of bird predators, while the dark moths now were able to blend with their surroundings and thus survive and reproduce their kind in increasing numbers over their light counterparts.

Evolution did not proceed gradually and inexorably in one, preordained direction. Chance played a dominant role, and diversity insured that at least some cells possessed traits that would be advantageous in the existing environment. The environment itself, of course, changed also. Some advantages in one circumstance could prove disastrous in another.

By trial and error, by modifications that appeared and then disappeared when they proved to be evolutionary dead ends, and by random, lucky, and timely appearance of attributes that were favorably matched by environmental changes, did evolution go forward. The development of a nervous system proved to be perhaps the most radical improvement that a group of cells could achieve for its collective survival and prosperity. This occurred early in the geological history of the planet.

Single cells evolved to form clusters of cells able to interact with each other and to specialize. Some members of the clusters became proficient at gathering food, others at digesting it, while still others connected themselves into a net capable of identifying and transmitting information about the environment throughout the colony. This was the beginning of the development of a true nervous system—a primitive nerve net, to be sure, but effective enough to recognize both opportunity and danger.

We still find on the shores of seas and oceans descendants of these early animals. They belong to the phylum known as the coelenterates, which includes the hydra, the jellyfish, and the sea anemone.

The nerve net was only the first step up the evolutionary ladder in the developing nervous system. It provided the organism with the simplest possible mechanism for gathering information about basic environmental variables. But the response of such an organism to a stimulus was very slow and uncoordinated (as anyone who has ever touched a sea anemone and watched it close on his finger can testify), because there was no central direction of the functions of the neural net. The acquisition of a neural center, called *cephalization*, was the process by which a brain eventually emerged.

An interesting modern example of this developmental stage of the nervous system is found in the flatworm planaria. It has a head, with a very primitive brain and simple light-sensitive spots that could be called eyes. Because the planaria has eyes and other sense organs and because information about the outside world can be conveyed by these sense organs to the brain, this little flatworm can respond more quickly to what goes on around it, can move about more rapidly, and can do much more as a living organism than can the jellyfish. But the flatworm brain is very limited; it cannot coordinate movement. In fact, one can surgically remove the planaria's brain, and the flatworm will still be able to move around as if nothing had happened, except for the loss of sensory response to the environment.

Coordination of movement by the brain is such a complex function that apparently the brain could not achieve it at this point in evolution without help from the peripheral nerve net. This became possible with segmentation of the organism into separate parts able to handle local problems without reference to the brain. Only when it was necessary to take concerted action could the brain override local intersegmental reflexes and coordinate a mass response by the whole organism. Such is the case, for instance, with the earthworm. And anyone who has ever observed an earthworm, or sacrificed part of one to a fishing hook, will recognize that earthworm segments seem to have a life of their own, in addition to an integral one possessed by the whole animal controlled by its brain.

This segmentation is found in a much more elaborate form in man. The human nerve net consists of nerve fibers that issue from the spinal cord, between the vertebrae, and radiate to specific areas of the human body. Thus man can in effect be sliced into some thirty-three segments, most of which can handle simple reflex actions (such as jerking a hand away from a hot stove without direction and immediate action of the brain) but which are connected with and coordinated by the brain.

The geology of the earth began with the formation of the earth's crust about 4.6 billion years ago. The first 4 billion years have left very little in the way of a fossil record. This long and dimly perceived era is known as the Precambrian. Beginning with the Paleozoic era, which started about 600 million years ago, abundant

[3] H. B. D. Kettlewell, "The phenomenon of Industrial Melanism in Lepidoptera," *Annual Reviews of Entomology* 6 (1962), pp. 245-62.

fossil records exist, and most of the stages of evolution described up to this point took place during the early part of the Paleozoic era.

About 500 million years ago there appeared a group of animals whose likes had never been seen before on the earth. Although these animals were quite different from their ancestors, they nevertheless retained such successful features as cephalization and segmentation of their nervous systems. The most significant feature they possessed, however, at least during a part of their life, was a stiff rod below the spinal cord, which ran from top to bottom along the back, the *notochord.* A few of these animals, of which the contemporary primitive fish amphioxus is a leading example, retained the notochord throughout life. But most of the others gradually substituted for the notochord a series of vertebrae. The vertebrates are unique in that they possess an internal skeleton, articulated at the spine and protecting the central nervous system, surmounted by the brain, which is in turn protected by the skull. A rigid structure confers the mechanical advantages of rapid motion and greatly increased animal size, as well as the less obvious advantage of safety. The skull provided a secure housing for the brain and its associated major sense organs of vision, sound, and smell. Protected from the environment, these organs were able to develop more rapidly and with much greater sophistication than those of other living organisms. The notochord, therefore, proved to be a quantum jump in evolution. It made possible high mental capabilities, including intelligence.

The predominant subphylum of the vertebrates includes the fishes, reptiles, birds, and mammals, of which man is the most highly advanced example. Because of their brain and central nervous system, the vertebrates are immeasurably more efficient and responsive to the environment than any other living thing. They literally took over the earth in succession: first the fishes, then the reptiles, the mammals, and finally modern man.

The Paleozoic era lasted until 225 million years ago and ushered in the Mesozoic era, which lasted for more than 150 million years. The Mesozoic was the age during which the great reptiles, the dinosaurs, the largest animals in geological history, roamed the earth. An example was the 65-foot-long *Brontosaurus.* This great reptile was controlled by an amazingly minuscule, one-pound brain surmounting its 35-ton bulk. . . .

Almost unnoticed, there appeared during that time an increasing number of small, warm-blooded, furtive, and inconspicuous mouse-like animals. The dinosaurs from their august fleshy pedestals did not seem to care; they all but ignored these swift-moving, relatively intelligent creatures that arose from the reptiles themselves and started the long line of mammals (Latin, *mammae:* breasts). Their brain was orders of magnitude more advanced than that of the dinosaurs. One of the main reasons for this advantage was that the most successful among them were placental; that is, they carried their young within the mother's body, protected from the environment during a long and laborious growing period, which allowed for extensive development, and they were fed from milk-secreting mammary glands after birth during the remainder of this process. Thus their brain could reach potentials beyond anything that had ever been possible before.

About 75 million years ago, after the longest reign of any group of animals on earth, the dinosaurs disappeared, with a suddenness that has still not been satisfactorily explained. But it seems likely that their inadequate brain must have played a significant, if not a major, role in their swift decline. . . .

Thus, with increasing variety and sophistication of functions, the brains of the vertebrate animals reflected these changes by striking increases in both proportion and size.

The disappearance of the dinosaurs coincided with significant climatic changes and with the beginning of the modern era, the Cenozoic. As the dinosaurs left a competitive void, the population of mammals literally exploded both in numbers and in kind.

The climate of the earth during the early years of the Cenozoic era was warm, humid, and milder than it is today. Palm trees were growing on the site of what is now London, and in the United States these trees could be found as far north as the Canadian border. It was the golden age of mammalian diversification into the many orders that are the immediate ancestors of the vertebrate animals of today. One of these orders, the primates (Latin, *primus:* first) had acquired, through evolution, two extraordinary advantages, which laid the basis for the eventual dominance of man and his technology. These were the opposable thumb, which made it possible for these animals to grasp objects, and stereoscopic vision. The eyes of other animals are found on opposite sides of the head, and their vision covers separate fields of view.

The achievement of stereoscopic vision required that the eyes migrate to the front of a flattened face, so that the sight of one eye would overlap that of the other. Stereoscopic vision allowed the accurage judgment of object size and distance. Coupled with hands skilled at grasping, these sensational attributes allowed rapid and safe movement from branch to branch, avoiding ground-based predators. This endowment permitted the primates to pick fruits and to catch swift-moving insects for food. The coordination of sight with manipulation also gave them the ability to make and use tools and weapons and to engage in hunting. A dramatic and sustained increase in brain size, complexity, and competence took place simultaneously with the development of these skills and gave effect to these evolutionary manipulative and visual advantages.

In one of the best analyses to date of brain evolution, Dr. Philip Tobias of Columbia University graphically demonstrated that increasing brain size is the most striking sustained trend shown in the hominid (family of man and his ancestors) fossil record. A larger brain, the most evident hallmark of that evolution, must have conferred a clear advantage, and down through the ages this attribute must have afforded greater opportunities for survival than did a smaller brain.[4]

These advantages were to have very great survival value, because soon afterward the primates were subjected to drastic changes in climate. These changes were heralded by one of the most geologically disturbed periods of the earth's history, involving violent volcanic activity and extensive mountain-building, which changed the face of continents. The vast lava beds of the Columbia Plateau in the northwest United States, the Alps, the Caucasus, and the Coast Range of California are testimony to these gigantic upheavals, some of which continue to this day.

Concurrent with these events, the climate grew progressively colder, signaling the coming of the first of several ice ages, about 2 million years ago. Surprisingly, however, these great periods of widespread glaciation do not appear to have caused the extinction of many animals or plants, but did result in a rapid redistribution of living things over the surface of the planet. Some large mammals, such as the mammoth, the mastodon, the ground sloth, and the magnificent saber-toothed tiger, did become extinct, but it seems more likely that their disappearance was the result of hunting by early man.[5] Evidently, as soon as he appeared on earth, ancestral man's ability to play havoc with his environment was already manifest. Most important, however, is the fact that the ice age saw an extraordinarily rapid advance in the evolution of the hominid primates. . . .

As the earth's climate cooled, the early hominid *Ramapithecus*, the oldest fossil man known (whose remains amount to only pieces of a jaw), roamed the remaining tropical areas now known as India and Africa. *Ramapithecus* gave way to *Australopithecus*, whose remains have been found in widely scattered parts of the world, suggesting a very wide distribution. *Australopithecus* was a biped of small stature, with a brain only one third the size of that of modern man. *Australopithecus* was followed by a number of increasingly larger and more man-like primates with many

confusing names and descriptions; actually, the main sequence is simple and relatively well established.[6]

The several hominids recognized by anthropologists overlapped each other, so they were often found to be contemporary for a period of time. *Australopithecus* was the ancestor of *Homo erectus*, and like him was a ground dweller and a fashioner and user of progressively more sophisticated stone tools. *Homo erectus* probably lived between two hundred thousand and seven hundred thousand years ago. His descendants belong to the genus *Homo sapiens*, of which "Neanderthal man," clearly a member of the family of modern man, is the best-known early example.

It has often been stated that since early members of the hominid family had the appearance of apes, Darwin's theory of evolution meant that man must be descended from monkeys. This is not true. While at first glance it might have been difficult to tell *Australopithecus* from a contemporary ape, since both could walk on two feet in an upright position and had opposable thumbs and stereoscopic vision, they nevertheless differed in one striking and fundamental respect: *Australopithecus* and his descendants had overwhelmingly larger brains and overridingly higher intelligence than the apes that were contemporary with them[7]. . . . The hominids kept pace with these developments and stayed continuously ahead of the apes. . . .

The most recent genus of man, *Homo sapiens* (Latin, *homo:* man; *sapiens:* wise), is only a few thousand years old, having appeared during the last glacial age. His kind is found in great variety all over the world, with differences in skin color, stature, and temperament. But this great diversity arose from the same ancestral stock and shares many more common features than differences. Among these shared features is the anatomy of the brain itself. The average adult brain weighs approximately 1,400 grams (3 pounds) and represents about 2 per cent of the total body weight. Its growth is a remarkable phenomenon. . . .

It is clear . . . that while the rate of growth is greatest before birth, the major increase in the size of the human brain occurs soon after birth. The brain nearly triples in size during the first year of life, a growth rate that is not shared by any other animals and that is a direct result of man's placental origin. An infant with a full-sized brain could not be delivered through the female pelvic canal, and yet without a fully developed brain man could probably not have survived as a species. The evolutionary solution to this problem was to delay a major part of brain development until the period immediately following birth. This solution, however, created a new

[4] P. V. Tobias, *The Brain in Hominid Evolution* (New York: Columbia University Press, 1971), p. 114.

[5] A. L. McAlester, *The History of Life* (Englewood Cliffs, N.J.: Prentice-Hall, Inc., 1968), p. 127.

[6] Ibid., p. 139.

[7] H. J. Jerison, *Evolution of the Brain and Intelligence* (New York: Academic Press, 1973).

problem. Rapid postnatal growth of the brain requires a sustained supply of appropriate nutrients in adequate quantity, without which normal brain development would be jeopardized. No other organism shares this vulnerability with man to the same degree.

But while postnatal growth of the brain is a spectacular event, the prenatal period is even more remarkable. One of the earliest recognizable primordial tissues in the human embryo is the neural plate, the first evidence of cephalization.[8] This is an amazingly early start for brain development, and it may help to explain the brain's extended vulnerability to unfavorable influences, including malnutrition. During the nine months of gestation, the developing brain recapitulates much of the past evolutionary history of the species, all the way from the single cell that emerged some 3 billion years ago, through the various stages of intermediate evolution, to man. This process is as precisely programmed as the bulding of a complex architectural edifice, with a tyranny of time that cannot be overcome. Each specific part of the structure is scheduled to be completed at a given time and place, and in its proper position in the sequence. The raw materials needed must be available in full and exactly specified measure, and the energy resources must be in readiness to fashion the job. Any failure of logistics is fatal to the brain substructure involved; it will never be properly completed, and the resources will be employed elsewhere and differently, adapting the resulting defect in the least damaging way possible. While a great deal of redundancy, which can mitigate and even overcome a potential defect, is built into the process of growth, a chronic deficiency of resources such as may be caused by malnutrition cannot always be reversed, and a defective substructure will result.

The structures and functions of the brain still defy detailed analysis and complete understanding. Since man first became conscious of his existence, philosophy has been concerned with the nature of the thought processes as well as with the nature of man himself. It has been known since antiquity that the brain was a unique organ that most likely was the repository of man's divinity and that the frontal lobes behind man's characteristically high forehead were the site of his intellectual superiority. It is that part of the cranial cavity which has expanded the most in hominid evolution. . . .

Few surgeons or medical investigators dared enter the mysterious confines of the brain, and most of it remained forbidden territory until relatively recent times. This taboo was lifted in the nineteenth century, on the bloody battlefields of Western Europe were field surgeons were forced to conclude with amazement that men could sometimes survive even with part of the brain shot away.

There is also the story of an American railroad foreman, Phineas Gage, who was immortalized by a strange accident. In September 1848 he was preparing a blasting charge in a rock with a heavy tamping iron when the charge exploded, propelling the 1¼-inch-thick iron rod backward with terrific force. The rod bored completely through Gage's skull from front to rear, and continued beyond for some distance. Gage did not even lose consciousness at the time of the accident. In fact, he was able to walk unassisted and carry on a normal conversation with the physician who attended his wound. Phineas Gage lived for twelve more years and became a legend in medical literature. The remarkable aftereffects of his experience are on the record.[9] Though there is evidence for some reduction in Gage's mental faculties and particularly for a degradation of his personality, he was able to live a relatively normal life. At autopsy it was found that his brain had suffered severe damage not only in the left frontal lobe, the site of entry of the iron, but also in the right frontal lobe, mainly because of the infection that followed the accident.

These examples underscore the resiliency, redundancy, and near invulnerability of the mature brain, protected as it is by a rigid bony structure and bathed in a hydraulic medium called the cerebrospinal fluid.

The brain of primates, including man, consists of two lobes, or hemispheres, on each side of the cranium, separated by a deep longitudinal fissure. Though the brain appears as a gel-like, gray-to-pink mass, it is in fact very highly differentiated into many smaller parts, each of which performs specific functions. But, as we have seen in the case of Phineas Gage, at least some of these functions can be transferred to other parts of the brain when normal performance is affected by either damage or destruction.

These many parts divide into two broad segments, the paleocortex (the "old" or primitive brain) and the neocortex (the "new" brain). The proportion of each varies as the evolutionary ladder is climbed. Man's brain is 85 per cent neocortex and only 15 per cent paleocortex. It is in this 15 per cent of the "old" brain that most of the prior history of brain evolution is found. Many of the old functions, such as swimming coordination in the fish and flying coordination in the bird, are still there, buried in the paleocortex. The paleocortex is the control site of the elemental requirements for life: respiration; visceral, spinal, and postural reflexes, movement coordination; regulation and transmission of impulses; hunger, thirst, and sex drives.

But it is the spectacular size of the neocortex that

[8] A. L. McAlester, op. cit., p. 96.

[9] Both Phineas Gage's pierced skull and the heavy tamping iron are on display at Harvard University.

eventually gave man his unique standing on the planet. It is that part of the brain which comprises the frontal lobes and contains the elements of his transcendental advantages in the animal kingdom; it is the site of consciousness, intelligence, and memory.

The mature human brain contains about 11 billion nerve cells (neurons), whose functions are directly related to the acquisition, transfer, processing, analysis, and utilization of information. There are also billions of supporting cells, called neuroglia, which serve primarily to maintain the integrity of the nerve-cell network and to manufacture an essential fatty structure, myelin.

To generate a human brain of 11 billion neurons requires the production and differentiation of about twenty thousand neurons *per minute* throughout the entire period of prenatal life.[10] These neurons are joined together in a vast entanglement of fibers and filaments that the writer George Gray has called "the great ravelled knot."[11] It is in these woven cellular circuits that the machinery of the brain discharges its unique functions. The brain-neuron complement can be described as a properly interconnected slab 12,000 cells long by 12,000 cells wide by 70 cells thick.[12]

One of the most important properties of the human brain during development is its plasticity, or ability to change and be molded under the influence of the external environment. It is able to receive and use stimuli from the outside during its exceptionally long developmental period. These stimuli can actually cause both structural and functional changes, which will then affect the way the brain will respond to these same stimuli in the future.[13] This is one of the ways in which learning takes place.

While neuroglia may be replaced by new cells during the lifetime of the individual, the neurons are not replaced. Humans are born with their full complement of neurons. After birth the brain continues to grow and mature by an increase of neuroglia and by addition of the myelin they produce. The neurons migrate to their final location before the maturity of the organism, and with these changes the die is cast. Each and every neuron is as old as the individual; the neurons that die are never replaced. Thus prenatal malnutrition can seriously affect a person's entire life by severely inhibiting the number of neurons produced before birth....

The brain has an extraordinarily high sustained demand for oxygen and nutrients. This is because the brain is never at rest and maintains the same level of utilization of resources whether one is asleep or engaged in highly intellectual activity. Although the weight of the adult human brain is but 2 per cent of the total body weight, it consumes 20 per cent of the total oxygen (the figure is 50 per cent for the infant) and 20 per cent of the total nutrients of the body. It uses more than 500 calories out of a 2,500-calorie diet, mostly in the form of glucose. To provide this disproportionate amount of body resources, a rich blood supply is carried through the brain; about 800 ml. (1½ pints) of blood flow through the brain every minute. But, paradoxically, the brain has practically no margin of metabolic safety and no reserves. A five-second interruption of blood flow brings unconsciousness, and irreversible damage or death follows a few minutes' deprivation. There exists no good explanation for this puzzling condition. One would logically suppose that this master organ should be able to handle such an emergency. A reasonable answer would seem to be that the extraordinary demands made by the many functions of the human brain are already straining the limits of the relatively small skull cavity. There is neither space nor resource left for anything else, even lifesaving reserves. It is not surprising, therefore, that the complete development of the human brain is essential for the many specialized activities it must continuously carry out. Any impairment of structural or functional integrity will inevitably be accompanied by a substandard level of performance.

Despite this vulnerability to sustained pre- and early postnatal malnutrition, and to oxygen deficiency, the human brain is superbly equipped to resist metabolic assaults from the environment, once it reaches maturity. It has repeatedly been shown that even starvation will cause no permanent damage, and the transitory impairment of functions can be completely reversed once adequate nutrition is re-established.

Thus the biological potential of the human species is derived primarily from the extraordinary competence of the human brain; but this capacity can be approached only when the long, vulnerable, and critical period of development can be allowed to proceed without significant interference.

[10] C. R. Noback, *The Human Nervous System* (New York: McGraw-Hill Book Co., 1967), p. 65.

[11] G. Gray, "The Great Ravelled Knot," *Scientific American*, October 1948.

[12] S. Deutsch, *Models of the Nervous System* (New York: John Wiley & Sons, 1967), p. 258.

[13] R. J. Harrison and W. Montagna, *Man* (New York: Appleton-Century-Crofts, 1969), p. 95.

Systemic Hypertension and the Relaxation Response

Herbert Benson

The relaxation response is defined as a set of integrated physiologic changes that may be elicited when a subject assumes a relaxed position, often with closed eyes, within a quiet environment, engages in a repetitive mental action and passively ignores distracting thoughts. The physiologic changes that result include decreases in oxygen consumption, heart rate, respiratory rate and arterial blood lactate, and slight increases in skeletal-muscle blood flow and in the intensity of slow alpha waves on the electroencephalogram.[1-4] These changes occur concomitantly and are different from those observed during quiet sitting or sleep.[4,5] They are consistent with generalized decreased sympathetic-nervous-system activity, although in one study, direct measurement of plasma norepinephrine during elicitation of the relaxation response did not reveal a statistically significant decrease.[6]

Walter R. Hess described physiologic changes in the cat that were very similar to those of the relaxation response in man.[7] Hess produced these changes by electrical stimulation of the hypothalamus. He believed that the response functioned as a protective mechanism against overstress and that it counteracted the emergency reaction, or fight-or-flight response, previously described by Walter B. Cannon.[8]

The fight-or-flight response has been defined as an integrated hypothalamic response that consists of increases in catecholamine production, blood pressure, heart rate and respiratory rate, and a marked increase in skeletal-muscle blood flow.[8,9] Epidemiologic and experimental studies indicate that environmental conditions that repeatedly bring forth the fight-or-flight response may lead to sustained elevations in blood pressure in monkeys and in man.[10,11] If environmental factors that produce the emergency reaction are important in the pathogenesis of hypertension, then behavioral interventions that are thought to counteract this reaction, such as elicitation of the relaxation response, are of interest for the prevention and treatment of this disease.

Technics That Elicit the Relaxation Response

Technics have existed for centuries, usually within a religious context, that are capable of evoking the relaxation response.[1,2] These technics are found in virtually every culture, and their underlying principles are not unique to any specific religion or way of life. Four elements appear to be integral to these various practices: a repetitive mental device, a passive attitude, decreased muscle tonus and a quiet environment.

The first element consists of a constant mental stimulus—for example, a word, sound or phrase repeated silently or audibly. To be effective, the repetitive stimulus must free the subject from logical, externally oriented thought. The second element, a passive attitude, is perhaps the most important. If distracting thoughts occur during the repetition, the subject should disregard them and redirect attention to the repetition. The subject should not worry about how well he is performing the technic but should adopt a "let-it-happen" attitude. The third element, decreased muscle tonus, requires a comfortable posture that involves minimal muscular work. The fourth element consists of a quiet setting with few environmental stimuli. A quiet room is often used, as is a place of worship. In many technics, the subject is instructed to close his eyes.

One example in which these four elements are found is "The Prayer of the Heart" or "The Prayer of Jesus," a repetitive early Christian prayer,[1,2] which was described by Gregory of Sinai in the 14th century at Mount Athos in Greece:

Sit down alone and in silence. Lower your head, shut your eyes, breathe out gently, and imagine yourself looking into your own heart. Carry your mind, i.e., your thoughts, from your head to your heart. As you breathe out, say "Lord Jesus Christ, have mercy on me," say it moving your lips gently, or simply say it in your mind. Try to put all other thoughts aside. Be calm, be patient and repeat the process very frequently.

From the Department of Medicine and the Thorndike Laboratory, Harvard Medical School and Beth Israel Hospital, Boston, MA 02215.

Supported in part by grants (HL10539, RR-01032 from the General Clinical Research Centers Program of the Division of Research Resources and MH 25101) from the U.S. Public Health Service.

These Seminars are supported in part by a grant to the Beth Israel Hospital from the Schering-Plough Corporation.

Reprinted, by permission, from *The New England Journal of Medicine* 1977, 296:1152-1156.

Similar practices were used in Judaism in the first century B.C. and are found in an early form of Jewish mysticism, Merkabolism.[1,2] In this meditative practice, the subject sat with his head between his knees, whispered hymns or songs and repeated the name of a magic seal.

In the East, meditational technics capable of evoking the relaxation response were developed much earlier and became a major element in religion and everyday life. The Indian scriptures, the Upanishads, of the sixth century B.C. describe attainment of a unified state with the Brahman (the Deity) by means of restraint of breath, withdrawal of senses, meditation, concentration, contemplation and absorption.[1,2] Eastern technics that are currently popular are various forms of yoga, including transcendental meditation.

Secular technics may also elicit the relaxation response. These methods include autogenic training,[12] hypnosis[13,14] and sentic cycles.[15] On the basis of the four elements that are common to these technics and that elicit the relaxation response, a simple, noncultic method has been developed in our laboratory.[5] The instructions for this technic are:

Sit quietly in a comfortable position. Close your eyes. Deeply relax all your muscles, beginning at your feet and progressing up to your face. Keep them deeply relaxed.

Breathe through your nose. Become aware of your breathing. As you breathe out, say the word "one" silently to yourself. Continue for 2 minutes. You may open your eyes to check the time, but do not use an alarm. When you have finished, sit quietly for several minutes, at first with closed eyes and later with opened eyes.

Do not worry about whether you are successful in achieving a deep level of relaxation. Maintain a passive attitude and permit relaxation to occur at its own pace. Expect distracting thoughts. When these distracting thoughts occur, ignore them and continue repeating "one."

Practice the technic once or twice daily, but not within two hours after a meal, since the digestive processes seem to interfere with elicitation of anticipated changes.

This simple method leads to the same hypometabolic changes observed during the practice of other meditational technics. In one study, 17 normal subjects learned this relaxation technic simply by reading an instruction sheet and practiced it for no more than an hour before they were studied.[5] The experiment consisted of five consecutive 12-minute periods, during which oxygen consumption, carbon dioxide elimination and respiratory rate were measured. The first, third and fifth periods served as control periods, during which the subjects sat quietly and read material of neutral emotional content. The second and fourth periods consisted of either another control condition, during which subjects were instructed simply to sit quietly in a comfortable position and to close their eyes, or the experimental condition, during which

the subjects practiced the relaxation technic. The order of presentation of the control and experimental procedures was randomly assigned. There were no statistically significant differences between the values of the three control (reading) periods for oxygen consumption, carbon dioxide elimination and respiratory rate. Sitting quietly with eyes closed failed to produce significant changes from these control values. During the period when the technic was practiced, however, there were significant decreases in oxygen consumption (13 per cent), carbon dioxide elimination (12 per cent) and respiratory rate (four breaths per minute), as compared to the control periods of reading or sitting with eyes closed (P<0.01 by Dunnett's multiple-comparison procedure). The respiratory quotient remained the same during all periods.

Relaxation Response in Patients with Hypertension

Prospective studies have established that regular elicitation of the relaxation response lowers blood pressure in both unmedicated and medicated patients with hypertension.[16-22] In an investigation by our laboratory,[16,17] 86 subjects with hypertension, who were attending introductory lectures on transcendental meditation, agreed to delay their instruction, to participate in the study. The blood pressures in these volunteers were measured every five minutes during a period of 15 to 20 minutes, until both systolic and diastolic pressures were within 5 mm of mercury of the preceding measurement. In the subjects who were accepted, either systolic blood pressure exceeded 140 mm of mercury or diastolic pressure exceeded 90 mm or both measurements exceeded these levels on the last blood-pressure recording. Weekly base-line measurements of blood pressure were made for approximately six weeks before the subjects were taught to elicit the relaxation response by means of transcendental meditation; the subjects served as their own controls. There was virtually no change in blood pressure during the six-week control period. After the subjects had meditated twice a day for two weeks or more, their blood pressures were measured in an identical manner approximately every two weeks for five to six months. Measurements were taken at random times of the day but never during or immediately after meditation.

On each day of measurement during the control and experimental periods, the subjects completed a questionnaire that assessed the amount and type of medication that they were taking, their dietary habits and their frequency of meditation. The subjects were instructed to take the medications prescribed by their physicians. During the study, however, 50 of the original 86 volunteers altered their own antihypertensive-medication regimens or their diets and were thus excluded from analysis. Of the remaining 36 patients, 22 received no antihypertensive medications during the study, and 14 remained on unaltered medication schedules.

During the control period, systolic blood pressures averaged 146.5 mm of mercury, and diastolic pressures averaged 94.6 mm in the 22 unmedicated subjects. During the experimental period, in which the subjects regularly elicited the relaxation response, these pressures decreased significantly; average systolic pressure was 139.5 mm of mercury (P<0.001 by paired t-test), and diastolic was 90.8 mm (P<0.002). In the 14 subjects whose drug regimens were not changed, control systolic blood pressure averaged 145.6 mm of mercury, and diastolic pressure 91.9 mm. During the experimental period, the mean systolic pressure decreased to 135.0 mm of mercury (P<0.01), and diastolic to 87.0 mm (P<0.05). In both medicated and unmedicated subjects who chose to stop the regular practice of meditation, both systolic and diastolic blood pressures returned to their initial high levels within four weeks after termination of the practice.[18]

Other researchers have also reported decreased blood pressure in patients who regularly elicited the relaxation response. Datey et al. investigated medicated and unmedicated subjects with hypertension, who brought forth the relaxation response by means of a yogic technic, "Shavasan."[19] Statistically significant decreases in systolic and diastolic blood pressure were noted, and the drug requirement was reduced in many patients. In two well controlled longitudinal investigations, Patel obtained greater reductions in blood pressure with a combination of a yogic technic and a biofeedback technic in 20 medicated patients with hypertension.[20,21] Average systolic blood pressure in her subjects was reduced by 20.4 mm of mercury, and mean diastolic pressure by 14.2 mm (P<0.001). In the control group, matched for blood pressure as well as age and sex, no statistically significant changes were observed.

Stone and De Leo have further substantiated the usefulness of the relaxation response in the treatment of hypertension.[22] In their subjects, urinary sodium excretion exeeded 124 meq per liter throughout the experiment. Mean arterial blood pressure did not change in the control group, but in the group who elicited the relaxation response for six months by means of a Buddhist meditation exercise, systolic blood pressure with the subject upright was decreased by 15 mm of mercury, and diastolic pressure by 10 mm (P<0.05). These patients also exhibited significant decreases in plasma activity of dopamine-beta-hydroxylase (P<0.05), in both the supine and upright positions, and a reduction in furosemide-stimulated renin activity in the upright position.

In contrast, another study showed no change in plasma renin activity in 20 patients with hypertension, who elicited the relaxation response by transcendental meditation.[23] The patients in this study served as their own controls. No statistically significant decreases in systolic or diastolic blood pressure were observed after six months of meditation. However, systolic blood pressure decreased significantly, approximately 10 mm of mercury, during the first three months of meditation (P<0.05). In addition, virtually all blood pressure levels were reduced from the control readings obtained before the study. Heart rate was also decreased throughout the investigation. This decrease, approximately eight beats per minute, was statistically significant at the first, second and fourth months. Furthermore, the majority of patients reported a greater sense of physical and mental well-being as a result of meditation. The authors concluded that meditation could be of adjunctive value in the long-term management of hypertension.

In a recently completed, controlled, prospective study by investigators at the Harvard School of Public Health and our laboratory, the relaxation response elicited during "relaxation-response breaks" significantly lowered blood pressure in a normotensive working population (P<0.05 for systolic blood pressure and <0.01 for diastolic pressure by two-tailed t-test).[24] These decreases occurred during periods of the work day when the subjects were not practicing the noncultic technic formulated in our laboratory.

The results of these various investigations demonstrate that regular elicitation of the relaxation response lowers blood pressure in both untreated and pharmacologically treated hypertensive patients and in normotensive subjects. The relaxation response probably reduces blood pressure by centrally altering sympathetic-nervous-system activity, an action similar to that of many antihypertensive drugs. It is unlikely that regular elicitation of this response alone provides sufficient therapy for severe or moderate hypertension. However, it should act synergistically with antihypertensive drugs to lower blood pressure and thus involve less pharmacologic intervention and fewer drug side effects. In mild, borderline and labile hypertension, regular elicitation of the relaxation response may be of great value since it could supplant the use of drugs. In normotensive persons, this behavioral intervention may be a prophylactic measure against hypertension. Moreover, since the rate of development of atherosclerosis is directly related to the level of blood pressure,[25] it may be desirable to lower blood pressure, even within the ranges now considered normal.

Side Effects of the Relaxation Response

The side effects of regularly eliciting the relaxation response appear to be minimal and are essentially those of praying twice daily. Excessive elicitation of this response, for many hours a day, month after month, may induce symptoms that range in severity from insomnia to psychotic manifestations, often with hallucinatory behavior (Benson H: unpublished data). These side effects are difficult to evaluate, but they may be related to sensory deprivation. No adverse side effects have been observed, however, in subjects who have regularly elicited the response twice daily for 10 to 20 minutes over a period of five to six years. Indeed, many patients have reported pleasurable feelings during and after elicitation of the relaxation response. Several have described feelings of warmth in the extremities or feelings of mild sexual arousal; most have reported a general sense of rest and well-being. In several of my patients who were taking either propranolol or insulin, the dosage had to be decreased because of marked bradycardia or hypoglycemia.

Behavioral Factors in Hypertension

The hypothesis that behavioral factors are important in the pathogenesis of hypertension is strengthened by the finding that the behavioral intervention of eliciting the relaxation response significantly reduces blood pressure in subjects with or without hypertension. The role of behavioral factors in the development of this disease should be taken into account in an assessment of the risk-benefit ratio of currently extensive hypertension detection and treatment programs. If behavioral factors can lead to transient, or even permanent, elevations in blood pressure,[11] could not these widespread and intensive educational efforts be counterproductive? By describing hypertension with phrases such as "the silent killer," these programs create an exaggerated sense of its serious implications. This emphasis may influence the initial and subsequent blood-pressure measurements, so that hypertension may seem to be present. This problem does not arise in other health programs— for example, those directed at detection and treatment of carcinoma or glaucoma, in which the diagnoses are not so influenced. In detection of hypertension, however, recognition of behavioral factors should dictate a standardization of initial blood-pressure measurements, which should be performed in environmental settings conducive to obtaining an accurate blood pressure with the subject resting. Standardization could decrease the likelihood of an inaccurate initial diagnosis of hypertension and prevent the subsequent vicious circle of anxiety, further hypertension and pharmacologic therapy; thus, the possibility of iatrogenic hypertension would be minimized.

Conclusions

The relaxation response appears to be a valuable adjunct to pharmacologic therapy for hypertension, and it may also be useful as a preventive measure. This response can be elicited by noncultic technics or by other methods, which some patients may prefer. A religious patient, for example, may select meditative prayer as the most appropriate method for bringing forth the relaxation response. The freedom to choose a technic that conforms to a patient's personal beliefs should enhance compliance. Elicitation of the relaxation response is a simple and natural phenomenon; it does not require complex equipment for monitoring of physiologic events or involve the expense and side effects of drugs.

Discussion

A PHYSICIAN: How often did your subjects meditate?

DR. BENSON: Twice a day for 20 minutes, but one of our current studies suggests that once a day may be enough to reduce blood pressure.

A PHYSICIAN: Does repeated elicitation of the relaxation response affect the ability to produce a fight-or-flight response as a reaction to danger?

DR. BENSON: We have not studied that possibility, but patients report that they are better able to mobilize when they need to, and that, because they regularly elicit the relaxation response, they are generally less anxious.

DR. JOHN W. ROWE: Is the response the same in patients with different types of hypertension?

DR. BENSON: It seemed at first that the response would be most helpful in essential hypertension, but the technic has proved useful in secondary forms as well. In one of my patients with chronic glomerulonephritis, systolic blood pressure has decreased from approximately 180 to 120, and diastolic from approximately 120 to 80 mm of mercury. Her blood pressure has remained at these low values for two years, and her medications have been reduced to almost homeopathic levels.

I am indebted to Ms. Jamie B. Kotch, Ms. Karen D. Crassweller and Mrs. Nancy E. MacKinnon for assistance.

REFERENCES

1 Benson H, Beary JF, Carol MP: The relaxation response. Psychiatry 37:37-46, 1974
2 Benson H: The Relaxation Response. New York, William Morrow, 1975
3 Wallace RK, Benson H: The physiology of meditation. Sci Am 226(2):84-90, 1972
4 Wallace RK, Benson H, Wilson AF: A wakeful hypometabolic physiologic state. Am J Physiol 221:795-799, 1971
5 Beary JF, Benson H: A simple psychophysiologic technique which elicits the hypometabolic changes of the relaxation response. Psychosom Med 36:115-120, 1974
6 Michaels RR, Huber MJ, McCann DS: Evaluation of transcendental meditation as a method of reducing stress. Science 192:1242-1244, 1976
7 The Functional Organization of the Diencephalon. Edited by JR Hughes. New York, Grune and Stratton, 1957
8 Cannon WB: The emergency function of the adrenal medulla in pain and the major emotions. Am J Physiol 33:356-372, 1914
9 Abrahams VC, Hilton SM, Zbrozyna AW: Active muscle vasodilatation produced by stimulation of the brain stem: its significance in the defense reaction. J Physiol (Lond) 154:491-513, 1960
10 Benson H, Herd JA, Morse WH, et al: Behaviorally induced hypertension in the squirrel monkey. Circ Res 26 & 27:Suppl 1:I-21-I-26, 1970
11 Gutmann MC, Benson H: Interaction of environmental factors and systemic arterial blood pressure: a review. Medicine (Baltimore) 50:543-553, 1971
12 Autogenic Therapy. Vol 1, Autogenic Methods. Edited by JH Schultz, W Luthe. New York, Grune and Stratton, 1969
13 Barber TX: Physiological effects of "hypnosis." Psychol Bull 58:390-419, 1961
14 Gorton BE: The physiology of hypnosis: a review of the literature. Psychiatr Q 23:317-343, 457-485, 1949
15 Biomedical Engineering Systems. Edited by M Clynes, J Milsum. New York, McGraw-Hill, 1970
16 Benson H, Rosner BA, Marzetta BR, et al: Decreased blood pressure in borderline hypertensive subjects who practiced meditation. J Chronic Dis 27:163-169, 1974
17 Idem: Decreased blood pressure in pharmacologically treated hypertensive patients who regularly elicited the relaxation response. Lancet 1:289-291, 1974
18 Benson H, Marzetta BR, Rosner BA: Decreased blood pressure associated with the regular elicitation of the relaxation response: a study of hypertensive subjects. Contemporary Problems in Cardiology. Vol 1, Stress and the Heart. Edited by RS Eliot. Mt Kisco, New York, Futura, 1974, pp. 293-309
19 Datey KK, Deshmukh SN, Dalvi CP, et al: "Shavasan": a yogic exercise in the management of hypertension. Angiology 20:325-333, 1969
20 Patel CH: Yoga and bio-feedback in the management of hypertension. Lancet 2:1053-1055, 1973
21 Idem: 12-Month follow-up of yoga and bio-feedback in the management of hypertension. Lancet 1:62-64, 1975
22 Stone RA, De Leo J: Psychotherapeutic control of hypertension. N Engl J Med 294:80-84, 1976
23 Pollack AA, Case DB, Weber MA, et al: Limitations of transcendental meditation in the treatment of essential hypertension. Lancet 1:71-73, 1977
24 Peters RK, Benson H, Peters JM: Daily relaxation response breaks in a working population: 2. Blood pressure. Am J Public Health (in press)
25 Freis ED: Hypertension and atherosclerosis. Am J Med 46:735-740, 1969

Effects of Learning on Visceral Functions — Biofeedback

Neal E. Miller and Barry R. Dworkin

The brain has a major role in regulation of respiration, heart rate, blood pressure and release of hormones such as ACTH, and in the complex control of temperature and electrolyte balance. The lower centers of the brain, which regulate many of these vital visceral functions, were once thought to be largely autonomous, but recent research emphasizes many anatomic and functional connections between the higher and lower centers of the brain. Furthermore, the visceral organs are represented at the brain's highest level, the cerebral cortex. This presentation reviews recent findings on psychologic and learned effects on the visceral processes and some therapeutic approaches based on these findings.

From the Rockefeller University, 1230 York Ave., New York, NY 10021, where reprint requests should be addressed to Dr. Miller.

Supported in part by a research grant (MH 26920) from the U.S. Public Health Service.

Reprinted, by permission, from *The New England Journal of Medicine* 1977, 296: 1274-1278.

Effects of Psychologic Stress

Epidemiologic and quantitative studies of patients exposed to different degrees of stress because of drastic events (for example, loss of a spouse) have shown that psychologic stresses, such as fear, frustration or lack of social support, increase the probability of a wide range of medically adverse consequences. In addition to such well known psychosomatic conditions as peptic ulcers and hypertension, these disorders include coronary heart disease, stroke, diabetes, cancer, tuberculosis, influenza and pneumonia.[1] Animal experiments, under more rigorously controlled conditions, have supported the clinical impressions. This presentation is primarily concerned with the effect on stress of one of the higher psychologic functions of the brain—i.e., learning.

Effects of Learning on Fear-Induced Psychosomatic Symptoms

In some experiments, animals that had learned a response that enabled them to avoid electric shocks were found to have increased susceptibility to experimental infections and to implants of malignant tumors.[2] But a few investigators reported opposite effects. The discrepancy may depend on differences in the experimental protocols or on biologic differences (e.g., the intensity and duration of the stress, the effect of corticosterone on the implanted tumor tissue, a subtle interplay between psychologic and immunologic factors or various combinations of these influences that remain to be elucidated).

In the studies involving electric shocks, the psychologic effects were not clearly isolated from the possible physical effects of the painful stimuli. This difficulty was avoided in an experiment in which the hearts of animals were stimulated via a chronically implanted electrode. The animals were tested in a room in which they had received painful electric shocks to the feet on previous days. Testing the animals in the room that they had learned to fear greatly lowered the threshold for evoking a repetitive and life-threatening ventricular arrhythmia. This study isolated the role of learned fear because no shocks were given on testing days.

In related studies, rats exposed to unpredictable electric shocks were compared with rats that received exactly the same electric shocks but had learned to discriminate between dangerous and safe signals. The unwarned group showed more fear in the experimental situation and had five times as many stomach lesions as the control group. Furthermore, when pairs of rats were given identical electric shocks those that were able to learn a simple coping response (which involved turning off the shock) showed fewer behavioral symptoms of fear and also fewer stomach lesions than their experimental partners. These experiments illustrate that learning has an important role in induction or reduction of fear, and that fear, in turn, can have pathologic effects on the heart and the stomach.[1]

Classically Conditioned Visceral Changes

In the studies described above, fear was learned through classical conditioning: the fear that the painful electric shocks elicited as an unconditioned (innate) response was conditioned to the previously neutral cues in the experimental situation, and these cues then elicited the fear. Similarly, electric shocks can be used to condition a variety of visceral responses to previously neutral cues. Some of the responses that can be conditioned in this way are dilatation of the pupils, vasoconstriction, decreases in the electrical resistance of the skin, contractions of the spleen, increases in blood pressure, antidiuresis and changes in heart rate. Presumably, these responses are all part of an extensive pattern of fight-or-flight behavior.[3]

Some of the foregoing visceral responses can also be conditioned when the unconditioned response is elicited by stimuli other than pain.[3] Thus, either a burst of exercise or an intravenous injection of nitroglycerin can be used to condition tachycardia. An infusion of pituitary extract can induce antidiuresis, and a water load diuresis.

In hungry animals, food can condition salivation and secretion of various digestive juices. Intestinal contractions and temperature changes can also be conditioned. Paired with the injection of morphine, a stimulus can acquire the ability to elicit the hyperthermia and changes in the electrocardiogram induced by the drug. Because conditioned responses are usually studied only one at a time, more information is needed about the variety of patterns and the degree of specificity that are possible.

Some Paradoxical Learned Effects

Habituation to the analgesic effect of small doses of morphine appears to be learned; the analgesic effect can be elicited by the perspicuous cues associated with administration of morphine, and it disappears when these cues are radically changed—effects that do not occur with a purely physiologic process. Furthermore, this habituation has been found to be associated with a conditioned hyperalgesia that is opposite to the unconditioned effect of this drug.[4] A number of other presumably conditioned responses are paradoxically opposite to the unconditioned responses used to reinforce them. A moderate injection of insulin produces hypoglycemia, but if the injection is repeatedly preceded by a neutral stimulus, the result is conditioned hyperglycemia. Often, a painful electric shock causes unconditioned tachycardia but a conditioned bradycardia. These paradoxical, opposite responses cannot be explained by the classical theory that conditioning involves the transfer of a response from the unconditioned to the conditioned stimulus.

Instrumental Learning

One possible explanation for these paradoxically opposite conditioned responses is that they are produced by instrumental learning and reinforced by counteracting the disturbance (e.g., tachycardia or hypoglycemia) elicited by the unconditioned stimulus. To give another example of instrumental learning, when a novice golfer is learning to sink a 300-cm putt, there is, unfortunately, no unconditioned stimulus that innately elicits the desired response—a perfect putt every time. He has to learn by trial and error. Whenever he comes nearer to or, better yet, sinks the putt, this success serves as a reward to reinforce (or to increase the probability of recurrence of) the responses that produced the successful outcome. The reward does not elicit the correct response, but it strengthens it. Because learned responses are instrumental in achieving a goal, such learning is called instrumental learning, trial-and-error learning or operant conditioning. Food for a hungry animal, water for a thirsty one, sex and escape from pain all function as rewards. Many, but not all, rewards clearly serve the function of restoring homeostasis. The same reward may reinforce any of a number of desired responses—for example, food can be used to train a hungry dog to stand up, to sit down or to roll over. Similarly, a given response may be reinforced by any of a number of rewards. Thus, a much wider range of possibilities is involved in instrumental learning than in classical conditioning.

Effects of Instrumental Learning on Visceral Responses

The traditional view has been that visceral responses can be modified only by classical conditioning but not by instrumental learning. This assumption no longer appears to be true.[1] If thirsty dogs are rewarded with water for increasing their rate of salivation, they can be trained to achieve more than double that rate; if they are rewarded by water whenever they decrease their salivation, they can be trained to decrease it to one seventh of the original rate. Water itself has no unconditioned effect. The training procedure in this experiment was to record the time between drops of saliva and to reward the dog whenever there was a small spontaneous fluctuation in the desired direction. As the dog learned, the criterion for reward was made progressively more difficult. In other studies, both rats and monkeys were trained to increase or decrease their heart rate or their blood pressure to avoid electric shock. In one of the most striking experiments, avoidance of electric shock, combined with a reward for food, was used to train baboons to increase their blood pressure approximately 30 mm Hg and to maintain this increase for as long as 12 hours.

Similarly, human subjects have been taught definite, although in some cases limited, control over heart rate, blood pressure, galvanic skin response, vasomotor responses and dysrhythmias. Most investigators have found large individual differences in the ability of human subjects to learn control of a visceral response; the basis for these differences is unclear. Also unknown is whether subjects who are unusually good at controlling one response will be good at controlling others.

Possibilities for Producing Visceral Changes

Whenever a visceral change appears to be produced, either by classical conditioning or by instrumental training, there are a number of different possibilities:

In the first place, a learned skeletal response may have a direct mechanical effect on the transducer used to measure the visceral change. This apparent response is a pure artifact; care is required to avoid it.

Secondly, a learned skeletal response may also have a purely mechanical effect on the visceral process. For example, in Yoga exercises that seem to stop the heart for brief periods, an exaggerated Valsalva maneuver builds up enough pressure in the thoracic cavity to cut off venous return. Although this maneuver eliminates both heart sounds produced by the action of blood on the valves and the pulse, the electrocardiogram shows that the heart is beating rapidly.

Thirdly, a learned skeletal response may affect the receptive field of an innate visceral reflex. For example, urination can be elicited if the abdominal muscles are used to increase pressure on the partially filled bladder; sufficient pressure stimulates the stretch-reflex receptors and causes a reflex emptying. However, such skeletal maneuvers are not essential for the control of urination. When the skeletal muscles in human subjects are completely paralyzed by curare or succinylcholine, the subjects have to be maintained by artificial respiration, but they can initiate or terminate urination on command. Certain hysterical patients hyperventilate—an action that reduces partial pressure of carbon dioxide in the blood and stimulates the receptors for reflexes that produce tachycardia. Some patients can arrest an attack of paroxysmal tachycardia by taking a sudden deep breath and thereby stimulating the vagal reflexes. Although these learned effects are medically important, they do not indicate learning by the autonomic nervous system.

Fourthly, skeletal and visceral responses may be inextricably linked together as parts of a centrally integrated pattern that can be elicited by learning. When my colleagues and I asked patients paralyzed by poliomyelitis to grip a pneumograph cuff with the hand of a paralyzed arm, both blood pressure and heart rate increased; yet recordings of the pressure in the cuff and of the electromyograph from the muscles showed no skeletal responses to stimulate the receptive field of a visceral reflex, either directly or through metabolic products of muscular contractions. In a study of dogs that reacted to a conditioned stimulus for electric shock by a flight-or-fight pattern of skeletal responses, heart rate also increased, and there was a strong antidiuretic response of the kidneys; the dogs that did not show this pattern of skeletal responses did not exhibit these conditioned visceral responses. To demonstrate that this kind of a pattern is central, the peripheral links described in the first three possibilities discussed above must be ruled out, as they were in the patients paralyzed by poliomyelitis. The findings in these patients showed that the central connections of the autonomic nervous system could be modified by learning.

Fifthly, a specific learned visceral response may be elicited directly, without any necessary skeletal links. Many skeletal responses that occur as part of a centrally integrated pattern are not inextricably linked together. With sufficient practice, such responses may become highly specific, as in wagging one finger, or they may be modified into entirely new patterns, as in playing a Beethoven sonata. That visceral responses can also be learned specifically was suggested in our studies of patients with poliomyelitis, most of whom learned to change their blood pressure without changing their heart rate. The alteration in blood pressure alone could not have occurred as part of a central pattern that involved commands to the paralyzed

muscles because these commands altered heart rate as well as blood pressure. Nonparalyzed human subjects can also be taught to change their blood pressure without changing their heart rate, to change their heart rate without changing their blood pressure, or to change both in the same direction or both in opposite directions. Such changes are often relatively small. In a number of other studies training of human subjects to change their galvanic skin responses has not affected other autonomically mediated responses, such as heart rate or finger blood volume.

In investigation of the specificity of visceral responses, it is especially important to rule out the possible peripheral effects of skeletal responses that may be highly specific. Although experiments in our laboratory and in others with rats paralyzed by curare provided evidence for specificity, neither we nor they have been able to replicate these experiments, and the question of specificity remains unsettled.[1]

Therapeutic Applications

The clinical application of research on visceral learning is often called biofeedback. To describe biofeedback, I should like to return to the example of the novice golfer, who is learning to sink a putt. If both the golfer and coach are bindfolded, they will not know whether any putt succeeds or fails. Such knowledge of results, or feedback, serves as a reward or a punishment and is necessary if the golfer is to learn. Most patients are strikingly poor at correctly perceiving their visceral responses, such as blood pressure, and some are even poor at perceiving tension in certain skeletal muscles. With the use of modern instruments, however, feedback that relates to certain biologic functions, or biofeedback, can be supplied. The availability of biofeedback, like removal of the blindfold from the golfer and his coach, should be useful for any response that can be learned, but whose learning is impeded by inadequate perception of that response. In addition to supplementing inadequate perception, biofeedback can help the patient learn to improve the perception of certain visceral events, much as expert instruction can help medical students learn to improve their perception and interpretation of heart sounds. Such improved perception of responses seems to improve control over them; if it can be achieved, it also frees the patient from the need to rely on the biofeedback instruments. An attractive feature of biofeedback is that it helps the patient to learn to do something for himself.

But biofeedback is still only an experimental technic. Before it can be meaningfully applied to clinical disorders, elaborate controls are required. For example, a number of things complicate the evaluation of any new type of therapy. One of these is a natural tendency for the body to heal itself. Another is the spontaneous fluctuations in many chronic diseases, along with the probability that patients will seek treatment when they are feeling worse than usual and will be discharged when they are feeling better than usual. Finally, there is the powerful placebo effect. On the other hand, preliminary results with certain applications are encouraging enough to merit further evaluation.

Cardiac Arrhythmias

One of the early applications of biofeedback was in the treatment of premature ventricular contractions.[5] Electrocardiographs and programming equipment were used to control an array of lights that informed the patient when his interbeat interval increased, decreased or remained relatively constant. To convince them that they could control their hearts, patients were first trained to increase their heart rates a few beats per minute and then to decrease them by the same amount. They were then asked to maintain their heart rates within a narrow range and were taught to identify a premature ventricular beat. Interestingly enough, some of the patients initially thought that these beats, which they could feel, were normal, and that their hearts were stopping when they could not feel the premature beats. With feedback, most of the patients learned to turn the premature beats on and off at a request, a type of specific voluntary control that did not seem likely to be a placebo effect. As learning progressed, the feedback was gradually phased out. Most of the patients learned to control their premature beats outside the laboratory. In two patients, followed up after one and five years, these lower levels were verified by continuous 10-hour, portable electrocardiographic tape recordings, taken while the patients performed normal daily activities. Unfortunately, no records were made before treatment. Computer scoring of portable electrocardiographic tape recordings provides the technical capability to evaluate such treatments, by comparing objective scores on the heart's performance during routine activity before and after training. Promising, but highly preliminary, results have been obtained in several other cardiac dysrhythmias.

Blood Pressure

One special class of patients, those with severed spinal cords, show an unusual ability to learn to produce large, prompt, voluntary increases in systolic blood pressure, ranging from 10 to 65 mm Hg.[6] Most of these patients have hypotension, and, in the restricted subsample with severe postural hypotension, the learned ability to increase blood pressure has definite therapeutic value. These patients quickly learn to identify the stimuli produced by rapid, large increases in pressure and then to practice by themselves. With practice, the higher pressure is maintained with progressively less conscious effort. The specific voluntary control argues against any plaebo effect, and the learned increases are apparently not produced by changes in breathing or by commands to paralyzed or intact muscles. These patients show abnormally large, spontaneous fluctuations in blood pressure; perhaps the homeostatic controls that limit the magnitude of spontaneous and learned changes are weakened by the spinal-cord lesion. A drug that weakens homeostatic controls would be useful for research and perhaps even for therapy.

A number of behavioral approaches have been used to treat hypertension. In one, instruments provide patients with moment-to-moment measurements of blood pressure that are indirectly recorded. In another method, simpler equipment provides feedback on the electrical resistance of the skin, and patients are trained to increase this resistance—a change that presumably involves a decrease in sympathetic activity. Other procedures attempt to produce relaxation by Jacobson's method of progressive relaxation,[7] by autogenic training, by the relaxation-response version of transcendental meditation or by the relaxation of specific muscles with the help of feedback from electromyographic recordings. Hypnosis and training in Yoga have also been used. All these procedures are reported to produce moderate and approximately similar decreases in diastolic blood pressure, averaging about 10 mm Hg, with a considerable range of individual differences.[8] The similarity of these results suggests that the same mechanism, perhaps a general relief from stress, is involved.

Gastrointestinal Symptoms

A few stubborn cases of ruminative vomiting have been treated with an electromyograph that detects the first signs of regurgitation and administers a mildly punishing electric shock. In a few patients with emotional diarrhea, feedback of bowel sounds has been provided by an electronic stethoscope that was placed on the abdomen and connected to a high-fidelity amplifier and loud speaker. The patients were praised for changing the sounds in the requested direction; as they gained control the symptoms subsided. Over 20 resistant cases of fecal incontinence have been successfully treated with one balloon that produces rectal distention and two others that provide the patient with information on the contractions of the internal and external sphincters. The external sphincter, of course, is somatically innervated.

Headaches and Bruxism

In a number of studies, sensitive electronic thermometers have been used to train patients with migraine headaches to warm their hands; the patients then reported fewer headaches. Other investigations have indicated that patients subject to tension headaches can obtain relief by learning to relax their frontalis muscles. In these and other applications of relaxation training, electromyographic recording from the muscle produces a signal, such as successive clicks that become slower as the muscle relaxes.

Recent reports indicate that the electromyograph can also be used to teach patients with bruxism to relax their jaws and stop grinding their teeth. Interestingly enough, some of these patients must be taught to correct a wrong perception; they report a feeling of tension in their jaw muscles, which they think they can relieve by clenching their teeth.

Neuromuscular Rehabilitation

Increasing use is being made of electromyographic feedback in neuromuscular rehabilitation.[9] Some of the disorders to which it has been applied are peripheral nerve-muscle damage, spasmodic torticollis, stroke hemiplegia and cerebral palsy. In many of these cases, the more perspicuous feedback has helped to motivate both the patient and the therapist.

It is apparent that many patients have untapped potentialities for learning. Therefore, to control for the effects of extra attention, studies comparing feedback technics with more conventional ones should be conducted.

It should be emphasized again that none of the foregoing applications of biofeedback have been thoroughly evaluated and that many of them are used in conditions, such as headaches, that are subject to large placebo effects.

Goals Achieved by Certain Symptoms

That visceral responses can be modified by learning suggests that some psychosomatic symptoms may be learned because they are instrumental in achieving some rewarding goal (i.e., secondary gain). Interruption of the symptom motivates some patients to learn a more acceptable means of achieving the goal; but those who cannot do so may resist therapy or acquire a new symptom. In this situation, the therapist must teach the patient another way to achieve the goal. On the other hand, if the symptom results from a misperception of internal cues or has an organic basis that can be counteracted by learning, there may be no strong secondary gain with which to deal. Perhaps its absence explains why some of the most successful applications of biofeedback appear to involve symptoms with organic origins.

REFERENCES

1 Miller NE: Applications of learning and biofeedback to psychiatry and medicine, Comprehensive Textbook of Psychiatry. Second edition. Edited by AM Freedmann, HI Kaplan, BJ Sadock. Baltimore, Williams & Wilkins, 1975, pp. 349-365

2 Stein M, Schiavi RC, Camerino M: Influence of brain and behavior on the immune system: the effect of hypothalamic lesions on immune processes is described. Science 191:435-440, 1976

3 The Cerebral Cortex and the Internal Organs. Edited by WH Gantt. New York, Chemical Publishing Company, 1957

4 Siegel S: Evidence from rats that morphine tolerance is a learned response. J Comp Physiol Psychol 89:498-506, 1975

5 Engel BT, Bleecker ER: Application of operant conditioning techniques to the control of the cardiac arrhythmias, Cardiovascular Psychophysiology. Edited by PA Obrist, AH Black, J Brener, et al. Chicago, Aldine, 1974, pp 456-476

6 Miller NE: Fact and fancy about biofeedback and its clinical implications, Catalogue of Selected Documents in Psychology, Vol 6, No. 1329. Washington, DC, American Psychological Association, 1976

7 Jacobson E: Progressive Relaxation. Second edition. Chicago, University of Chicago Press, 1938

9 Shapiro AP, Schwartz GE, Ferguson DCE, et al: Behavioral methods in the treatment of hypertension. 1. Review of their clinical status. Ann Intern Med (in press)

9 Inglis J, Campbell D, Donald MW: Electromyographic biofeedback and neuromuscular rehabilitation. Can J Behav Sci 8:299-323, 1976

Observing the Brain Through a Cat's Eyes

Roger Lewin

What does a baby see when it gazes out on the world around itself? Does it pretty much see what its parents see? Or does each baby see a "mud-luscious, puddle-wonderful" world quite different from the one its parents—and for that matter, all other babies—are looking at?

Scientists and philosophers have argued this question of vision since Aristotle's day. But now researchers experimenting on cats have made revolutionary discoveries about the way we see—discoveries that apply not only to cats but also to the people who feed them.

The main revelation is that the ability to "see straight" does not develop in children automatically, that is, quite apart from any outside influences. Instead, the researchers have found, our visual machinery is strongly shaped by our early experiences—experiences that drastically affect the way we see the world in later life and that may even determine how gifted we will be musically and linguistically. It may be that areas of great potential in child development are being wasted simply because we don't teach the right things at the right time, the time when children's brains are most receptive.

The pioneers of the vision research on cats are two Harvard biologists, David Hubel and Torsten Wiesel. When they began their study, in the early Sixties, they expected to find that a cat's early environment has some small shaping influence on the way its vision develops. But like all the other biologists now interested in the work, Hubel and Wiesel have been absolutely amazed by the remarkable flexibility and plasticity displayed by the cat's visual system as it slowly develops. It now appears possible to persuade nerve cells in the cat's brain to do jobs for which they were never designed. Even if the rest of the brain is capable of only a fraction of the plasticity evident in the workings of the visual cortex, there is still a great deal of scope for external influences affecting the way the brain develops.

In the beginning Hubel and Wiesel looked at the activity of nerve cells in the so-called primary area of the visual cortex. These cells turned out to be

Saturday Review/World, October 5, 1974. Copyright ©1974 *Saturday Review/World*.

"feature detectors"—that is, they respond to specific shapes seen by the eye. Generally, there are two types of feature detectors: the ones that are found in many animal species and others that are specific to a particular species. These latter usually enable the animal to flourish in its behavioral environment. For instance, the frog has visual cells that are almost lightheartedly called "bug detectors"; these react when an object the size of a fly enters the animal's field of vision. One can argue that these specific feature detectors are programmed genetically, but it is also tempting to think that they may be at least partly shaped by early environmental influence.

The feature detectors, which Hubel and Wiesel located by means of minute electrodes pushed into the adult cat's brain, turned out to be orientation-selective; that is, they respond to—or, in scientific terms, are "specific to"—any line or edge moving across the animal's visual field along a particular orientation or angle. Any one cell is specific to a particular orientation, but all angles through the entire range of 360 degrees are "covered" by the population of nerve cells in this area of the brain. The Harvard team also discovered that most of the cells here are binocular, or wired up to both eyes.

In contrast to the adult cat, the visually naive kitten has practically no mature feature detectors. The cells are certainly present in the brain, but they have not yet been recruited to their job. The binocular connections in the kitten are just like the adult's. In one of Hubel and Wiesel's early experiments to try to discover the forces (genetic or environmental) that convert an infant eye to an adult one, they kept a growing kitten in total darkness and then examined its brain. They discovered that the binocular wiring had remained intact, but that the feature detectors had suffered terribly, remaining very immature. Here was a strong indication of environmental input determining brain development.

Next Hubel and Wiesel tried covering just one of an animal's eyes to see what that does to the brain. This time the feature detectors worked fine, but the binocular connections were thrown awry; they had all gone to the one seeing eye. Hubel and Wiesel found that the visual brain was plastic only during a "sensitive period" of the animal's life: from three weeks to three months. Again, this fits in with the notion that early experience is important in brain development.

The obvious implications of this work for an understanding of human development soon drew other research teams in to probe the problems, and the results have been astounding. For instance, Colin Blakemore and his colleagues in Cambridge, England, have found that in a visually experienced kitten they can induce the switch from inbuilt binocularity to monocularity after just *six* hours' vision through one eye. The change isn't made immediately; a period of consolidation is required following the programming exposure. Blakemore likens this response to learning and memory: in learning, an experience is slotted into a temporary store (short-term memory), and then a more permanent record is made (long-term memory).

The binocular/monocular switch is even more remarkable because it can be repeated again and again. If first one eye is covered, and then the other, and so on, the brain connections with the eyes will switch each time to the seeing eye, but once again this elaborate neural dance is possible only during the sensitive period.

The most remarkable results come from the plasticity of the feature detectors. Following up the early Harvard experiments, Colin Blakemore and Graham Cooper at Cambridge and Nico Spinelli and Helmut Hirsch at Stanford hit on the same idea: to put visually naive kittens into artificial environments to see if the feature detectors can be manipulated. It turns out that they can.

For instance, the Cambridge kittens were reared in visual environments consisting only of vertical stripes *or* horizontal stripes, not both. When the animals emerged from their striped worlds into the real visual world, they behaved in a most extraordinary way. "Horizontal" cats were perfectly capable of jumping onto a chair to settle down for a sleep; but when walking on the floor, they kept bumping into the chair legs, just as if the legs were invisible. In contrast, "vertical" animals had no difficulty in negotiating the chair-leg hazards, but they never tried to jump onto a chair; it was as if the seat were not there.

When the Blakemore team looked inside the kittens' heads, the animals' curious behavior was explained at once. The vertical cats had no horizontal feature detectors; so they literally could not see anything that was composed of horizontal lines, like the seat of a chair. And the horizontal animals had only horizontal detectors, which made it impossible for them to see the vertical chair legs. These animals really were blind to things in their environment that were perfectly visible to you and me and to any self-respecting cat,

all because of their unusual early experience.

This curious saga gets more curious still. Very recently Blakemore and his team, and California researchers Jack Pettigrew and Horace Barlow, managed to pervert all of the orientation detectors in cats; the researchers made the detectors respond to spots, not lines—something that the cells were never "designed" to do. The trick was simply to bring up the animals in a spotty environment rather than a stripy one. Electrodes probed into the animals' brains revealed that it was spots displayed in the visual field that excited the cells in the visual cortex, not lines as in normal animals. Because the animals have to create a picture of their external world by synthesizing the responses of these nerve cells, it is anyone's guess what the unfortunate felines actually "saw" when they emerged—probably a fuzzy, hazy picture, somewhat like a fog.

Blakemore and Don Mitchell, a colleague from Dalhousie University, Canada, decided to measure the speed at which the character of the feature detectors is specified. The researchers were more than astounded at the result, for they discovered that, with as little as one hour's visual experience, the way an animal's feature detectors function can be pretty well changed. The analogy with learning again enters one's mind.

Most people now agree that the cat's "visual-sensitive" period falls within the three-week-to-three-month span that Hubel and Wiesel noticed, with the most sensitive time occurring at about five weeks. This makes good developmental sense, because it is at this time that the animal's eyes have just about swung round to their correct positions in the sockets and the fluid within the eyes has become clear. But what about humans? Is there the same plasticity? If so, is there a sensitive period? If so, when is it?

Inevitably, the evidence for humans has to be rather more indirect than it has been for cats, but the indications are that there is not much difference between us and our feline cousins. For instance, infants with uncorrected squint or severe astigmatism finish up with permanent defects; spectacles cannot help them because it is the brain that appears to be at fault, not the eyes. In contrast, astigmatism that develops in adulthood can be corrected optically. This indicates that, like the brain of the cat, the immature human brain *is* plastic, while the adult brain is not. Blakemore says that the human visual-sensitive period probably spans the years from two to four. Visual defects really should be corrected before then.

Possibly the most intriguing discovery in this whole tale has come just recently from Canadian researchers Robert Annis and Barrie Frost. They examined the visual abilities of city-dwellers and compared them with those of Cree Indians living in tepees on the east coast of James Bay. In the past, researchers had found that "normal" people have better visual acuity (can see most sharply) in the horizontal and vertical axes. But what Annis and Frost found throws into question this concept of normality. They discovered that the Cree Indians have no particular axis of high visual acuity and are not especially attuned to horizontal and vertical lines. These people had, of course, been brought up in the country and away from the city, which is dominated by rectangular shapes. It may well be that the normal horizontal and vertical visual-acuity preferences are imposed on us simply because we live in a rectangular world. If houses were spherical instead of boxlike, things might be different. Despite the Cree Indians' lack of particular acuity in vertical and horizontal axes, they'd be able to get around New York City just as well as the rest of us. The crucial point is that human vision does appear to display the same kind of plasticity found in the experimental cats. And what is true of vision probably applies to our other senses as well.

Pediatricians have long recognized that infants should not be closeted in drab, visually unstimulating nurseries; the work with cats now gives that intuitive realization some scientific backing. But can we go further than this? Will a child become a musical genius if he is bombarded with Beethoven, Bach, and Berlioz from the day he is born? Will talking to a child in a spectrum of languages enhance his linguistic talent? And will one be the parent of a great mathematician if one teaches his infant the elements of logic at a tender age? The answer to all of these is, probably, "up to a point."

Almost certainly, the learning capacity of the human brain has not been exploited to the full by current educational approaches. The essential point is the possible existence of sensitive periods, not just for visual development, but for music, language, logic, and artistic talents. For instance, everyone acquires the elements of his language between the age of two and four. So why wait another six years before teaching a child a second and third language? The brain is clearly attuned to language acquisition in the early years, and there is a lot of evidence about the ease with which youngsters pick up a foreign language to which they are exposed. It would probably be a mistake to try to teach children two languages at once when they are only two years old, because there would be retroactive interference between the languages. But a child of four could start on a new language.

Musical talent very often runs in families. It may be "in the genes," of course, but there is undoubtedly a large environmental element, too. Children exposed to a lot of music when young are almost always more musically talented than average; how much this development is due to encouragement and opportunity is difficult to tell. But evidence that the musical brain becomes keyed in to its early experiences comes from the observation that people who develop perfect pitch while exposed to a slightly out-of-tune instrument always match their pitch to the instrument's. Although playing Beethoven to one's infant will probably not cause an environmentally generated reincarnation of the grand master, it may well produce a more-than-usually musically talented child.

Probably the most important skill that children learn is *how* to learn. The mark of intelligence is the facility for solving problems. Too often we give children answers to remember rather than problems to solve. This is a mistake. Unless children develop the art of problem-solving—whether by analytical logic or by non-sequential intuition—their brains will remain underexploited. Everyone knows that infants go through a period of being intensely curious. This curiosity is probably a behavioral expression of the brain's most sensitive period for acquiring knowledge and learning techniques.

Researchers will now turn their minds to discovering more about specific sensitive periods in the development of the brain, whether it be for language acquisition, enhancing musical talent, or simply learning how to learn. Unless these periods are exploited to the full at the right time, their potential may be lost forever.

Eye Diseases

What Can Be Done About Them?

Phyllis Lehmann

In a world so dependent on the printed word, electronic images, and complex tools, it is not surprising that visual impairment ranks just after heart disease and arthritis among chronic diseases that most severely interfere with a normal life.

The National Eye Institute estimates that nearly four million new cases of eye disease occur each year in the U.S., requiring more than 31 million visits to the doctor.

Some diseases—such as the highly infectious trachoma, which still causes widespread blindness in many parts of the world—have been virtually wiped out in this country. But as life expectancy increases, those associated with aging—cataracts, glaucoma, degeneration of the retina—have become leading causes of blindness.

Fortunately, there are heartening developments in research on the causes, prevention and treatment of eye diseases. As Dr. W. Morton Grant, the David Glendenning Cogan professor of Ophthalmology at Harvard Medical School, points out in *The Horizons of Health* (Harvard University Press), extensive study of the living eye dates back only about 50 years. Yet, thanks to such developments as X-rays, ultrasound and radioisotopes, it is now possible for scientists to investigate what is going on in the diseased eye. Instruments are available for measuring the pressure inside the eye and even inside the blood vessels of the eye. Improved surgical techniques have simplified cataract operations and are restoring vision in once hopeless cases of retinal disorders. Scientists are on the threshold of discovering the biochemical causes of such disorders as glaucoma and those associated with diabetes.

Diseases of the Retina and Choroid

Diseases of the retina, the light-sensitive tissue at the back of the eye, and the choroid, an underlying layer rich in blood vessels that help nourish the retina, are responsible for more cases of blindness in this country than any other eye disorders.

For a number of the disorders there is no known

cure or means of prevention. But through medical and surgical improvements, doctors can preserve or restore vision for many victims. Retinal and choroid diseases include:

Diabetic Retinopathy

Before the advent of insulin in 1921, few diabetics lived long enough to develop eye complications. Today diabetic retinopathy threatens the vision of more than 300,000 people each year and is responsible for about 10 per cent of all new cases of blindness. Among those aged 45 to 74, it accounts for 20 per cent of all loss of sight and is the leading cause of all newly reported blindness between the ages of 24 to 64.

In some way that is still a mystery to scientists, diabetes causes the blood vessel system in the retina to go awry. In the severe form of the disease, abnormal blood vessels grow on the surface of the retina and often protrude into the center of the eye, where they may hemorrhage into the vitreous—the clear gel that fills the eye and keeps it from collapsing like a deflated balloon. When the blood-filled vitreous prevents light from reaching the retina, vision is impaired.

Two exciting new techniques, photocoagulation and vitrectomy, are helping to lower the rate of blindness from diabetic retinopathy. An NEI study of more than 1,720 patients at 16 medical centers nationwide has shown that photocoagulation (the use of a laser or xenon arc beam to destroy abnormal blood vessels and diseased retinal tissue) can reduce the risk of blindness from this disease by more than 60 per cent.

Macular Degeneration

The macula, a tiny area in the center of the retina that gives us sharp color vision and the ability to read and see fine detail, is especially prone to deterioration. Macular degeneration caused by aging is the leading cause of newly reported blindness over age 64. Many other victims, still able to walk around unaided, have trouble reading signs and recognizing faces.

Scientists suspect that macular degeneration is caused by a breakdown in the supply of blood to the retina, but the disease remains largely a mystery. Once a person goes blind, vision often cannot be restored. Such new techniques as fluorescein angiography, in which a fluorescent dye is injected into the blood stream and its passage through the retinal vessels photographed, make it easier for specialists to pinpoint the type and location of macular disorders.

Uveitis

This term refers to a whole family of diseases that cause inflammation of the uveal tract—the choroid, iris, and ciliary body (the tissue that secretes the aqueous fluid that flows through the front part of the eye and which controls the focusing of the lens). Symptoms range from pain, redness, and hypersensitivity to light in acute cases, to slightly veiled vision or floating spots—probably caused by inflamed cells in the vitreous—in chronic cases. Uveitis can be detected in a routine eye examination. Untreated, it can lead to other eye diseases, such as glaucoma.

For the most part, causes of uveitis remain unknown. Some research indicates that prostaglandins, a group of substances commonly released by the body after cell injury, appear within the eye in certain types of uveitis, and may contribute to the inflammation. Scientists now are testing drugs that counteract the prostaglandins. Currently, cortisone is the most popular and effective treatment for uveitis.

Retinitis Pigmentosa

There is no known treatment to prevent a person who carries the gene for retinitis pigmentosa from gradually losing night vision and side vision. The first symptom generally is loss of night vision, which shows up in childhood or adolescence. Fortunately, not all victims go blind. Many even retain their reading vision, although it may be severely limited to a small central field.

Retinitis pigmentosa gets its name from unusual deposits of black pigment scattered through the retina and especially around the edges. Considerable progress is being made in understanding the possible causes of the disease. It is now believed to result from changes in the pigmented layer of the retina which plays an important role in the normal growth and renewal of the light-sensitive retinal cells.

Detached Retina

This is one retinal disorder that lends itself readily to surgical repair if detected early enough. When a tear or hole develops in the retina, fluid from the vitreous can seep between the inner and outer layers of the retina and cause them to separate. If they separate completely, blindness results.

A common symptom is the feeling that a curtain has been drawn across the eyes. Seeing sootlike spots or flashes of light can indicate tears in the retina or a problem in the vitreous that may lead to retinal detachment. Before actual detachment occurs, tears or holes in the retina can sometimes be sealed by beams of intense light (photocoagulation) or by extreme cold (cryosurgery).

If a detached retina is diagnosed early, the separated layers can be reattached in 85 per cent of cases and vision often restored.

Often, vitreous lost through the detached layers of the retina is replaced during surgery by a salt solution, which helps keep the layers in place and maintains the shape of the eye. Under investigation for holding badly detached retinal layers in place is a gas, sulfur hexafluoride, which has the unusual property of swelling when it is injected into the eye.

Glaucoma

More than one million Americans, the majority of them over 35, suffer from glaucoma. Though treatable if diagnosed early, the disease remains a leading cause of blindness.

In the normal eye, a fluid known as aqueous humor, secreted into the eye to nourish the cornea and lens, can pass out into the bloodstream through a system of tiny drainage channels. In glaucoma, this filtration area becomes blocked. The aqueous humor builds up, causing increased pressure that eventually damages the optic nerve.

Glaucoma is most common among people with a family history of the disease. It can be detected by a simple procedure known as tonometry, which measures pressure within the eye. This test should be performed regularly every year, especially after age 30, and if there is a family history of the disease.

An attack of acute glaucoma can cause blurred vision, an illusion of colored halos around lights, enlarged pupils, and pain. Because the pain can produce severe nausea and vomiting, acute glaucoma is frequently misdiagnosed in hospital emergency rooms as an abdominal condition. Anyone who suffers this combination of symptoms should seek immediate medical attention.

There are two common types of chronic glaucoma: open-angle, in which the space, or angle, between the iris and the drainage channels is open but the drains themselves are obstructed, and acute angle-closure, in which the angle is unusually narrow and may become suddenly blocked if the iris should be pushed forward. Often there are no obvious symptoms of the more common open-angle type, and the disease can advance to a severe state before the victim is even aware of it. Once the optic nerve has been damaged, however, reversal of the damage is impossible.

The angle-closure type can give some advance warning in the form of pain, blurred vision, or a halo effect. One method of treating it is to remove a piece of the iris.

If detected early by examination, open-angle glaucoma can usually be successfully controlled, but not cured, with drugs. The most common, pilocarpine, is now available in the form of a wafer that is inserted under the eyelid about once a week. For young people and those with mild cases of glaucoma, this is more convenient than applying drops several times a day.

Because pilocarpine constricts the pupil, allowing less light into the eye, the patient experiences dimmed vision, especially when inside a building or during evening hours. Timolol, a new drug still under investigation, shows promise for lowering pressure within the eye without producing this unpleasant side effect.

Several exciting lines of research may lead eventually to prevention of glaucoma. Scientists have noted, for example, that long-term use of cortisone and related drugs to treat eye inflammations causes increased eye pressure in some people, particularly those who have a family history of glaucoma. This discovery opens up the possibility of a blood test to identify very early those most likely to develop the disease.

Dr. Grant reports that a great deal of attention is now centering on the optic nerve and how it is damaged by glaucoma. Some people are able to withstand eye pressure without any harm to the optic nerve while others go blind from just a slight increase in pressure. The ultimate goal of research in this area, Dr. Grant says, is to find some way of treating weak optic nerves to make them better able to withstand pressure. Most present treatment is aimed at reducing the pressure.

Cataract

Contrary to popular belief, a cataract is *not* a film or membrane that grows over the eye. It is a cloudiness or opacity in the lens—the normally clear portion of the eye between the iris and the vitreous that helps focus images on the retina. When the lens is clouded, light has trouble getting through to the retina, and vision is impaired.

Typically, a person who develops cataract in one eye will develop it in the other. Common symptoms of the disease are hazy vision, double vision in one eye, and a dazzling sensation while driving at night, because the clouded lens scatters light from the headlights of approaching cars.

No one knows for certain what causes cataract. The most common form, known as senile cataract, is associated with normal aging of the eye and afflicts more than two million Americans over age 65. Recent studies at Columbia University and the Massachusetts Institute of Technology indicate that clumping of protein within the lens reduces transparency. Researchers suspect that high concentrations of calcium may be responsible for the protein clumps. If their theory proves accurate, it may be possible to develop drugs that would inhibit the clumping process and delay the formation of cataracts.

Another form of cataract is sugar cataract, which occurs in diabetics. Sugars in the lens are metabolized to sugar alcohols; these accumulate in the lens and cause it to swell and cloud. Scientists have recently developed an experimental drug that slows down the formation of sugar alcohols in animals. The next step is a drug that works safely and effectively in humans. The sugar cataract is rare in humans; most likely, the process may help accelerate the formation of senile cataracts in diabetics. More important is the fact that the same basic process which causes sugar cataracts to form may cause early damage to blood vessels in diabetic retinopathy and in other vascular complications of the disease. Thus an inhibitory drug may be more useful in preventing these complications than for the sugar cataracts themselves.

For now, surgery is the only treatment for cataract. The most common operation is complete removal of the clouded lens. Modern refinements in cataract surgery include introducing an enzyme to weaken the ligaments that hold the lens in place and using an extremely cold probe which freezes to the lens so that it can be lifted easily from the eye.

A recently developed method of removing cataracts is phacoemulsification, in which the surgeon pulverizes the lens with high-frequency sound waves and draws out the fragments through a hollow needle.

To replace the natural lens, cataract patients may be fitted with thick lenses that magnify 20 to 35 per cent. The glasses produce distortion and limit side vision. Contact lenses are an alternative and give better sight, but many elderly patients do not have the dexterity to handle them. The intraocular lens, a tiny plastic device inserted into the eye during surgery, enables a person to see almost normally, but this technique is suited only to a minority of patients.

Corneal Disease

Because it is exposed, the outer portion of the eye is susceptible to all sorts of bacterial, fungus, and viral infections and to allergic reactions. Of all these, diseases that afflict the cornea are the most serious. Because it is packed with nerves, so it can detect if something is on the surface of the eye, corneal disorders are also the most painful of all eye problems. If the cornea becomes clouded or scarred from untreated disease or injury—or despite treatment—the patient can go blind or suffer impaired vision.

The most serious and most common corneal diseases are viral infections which, unlike bacterial infections, often resist drug treatment. The most prevalent is caused by the herpes simplex virus, the one responsible for cold sores. Because the virus lodges in the nerves at the back of the eye, infection often recurs.

A major breakthrough in combating herpes simplex came in the 1960s with discovery of idoxuridine (IDU), the first drug used successfully to treat a human virus infection. A new drug, vidarabine, which is just as effective as IDU but without some of the unpleasant side effects, has just been put on the market. Although these drugs alleviate the symptoms of herpes simplex infections, no drug has yet been found that will actually kill the persistent virus.

Some of the discomfort of corneal disease can be alleviated by the new, fluid-filled soft contact lenses, which are now widely used as "bandages" to prevent the eyelid from rubbing against a tender cornea.

For those who do go blind from corneal disease, transplants offer a second chance for normal eyesight. They are the most successful of all human transplants because the absence of blood vessels in the cornea reduces the danger of tissue rejection.

A recent major advance in cornea transplants was the development by University of Florida scientists of a new tissue culture solution in which fresh corneas can be kept for up to a week with no special handling. Previously, many cornea transplants had to be done on almost an emergency basis, because fresh corneas begin to deteriorate after 48 hours, even under refrigeration.

Sensory-Motor Disorders

Probably less is known about this category of diseases—which involve the nerves or muscles of the eye or interfere with the transmission of visual information to the brain—than about any other eye disorders. The NEI estimates that 31,500 people in this country are blind because of atrophy, or wasting away, of the optic nerve. The most common types of sensory-motor disorders include strabismus and amblyopia, two conditions which occur in early childhood and should be corrected as soon as possible.

Will There Ever Be an Eye Transplant?

Looking far into the future, one question in eye research is whether doctors will ever be able to transplant a working eye from one human being to another or implant an artificial eye that will work like a natural one. For the time being such feats belong to science fiction. Next to the brain, the eye is the most complex organ in the human body and, in fact, could be considered an extension of the brain. The optic nerve alone has 150 million fibers to carry messages to the brain. But in an age when tiny beams of light can repair damage deep within the eye and when parts of the eye can be replaced by pieces of plastic or a salt solution, nothing can be considered permanently impossible.

Shutting the Gate on Pain
Ronald Melzack

The age-old practice of using pain to kill pain has never been readily accepted by the medical profession. The various methods seem not only unscientific, but downright barbaric. However, the use of acupuncture to induce analgesia (insensitivity to pain), first in Chinese and later in Western hospitals, is changing medical opinion about this folk practice. Moreover, research on the chemical basis of acupuncture is producing surprising insights into the nature of pain itself.

When the first reports and films of acupuncture being used during surgery reached the West in 1971, they seemed to support what doctors in China claimed.

Reprinted by permission from *Science Year. The World Book Science Annual.* Copyright © World Book-Childcraft International, Inc. *Editors' note:* Figures have been omitted.

They could perform painless surgery after inserting long, fine needles into specific points in the skin. Most Western doctors were skeptical at first. They attributed the analgesia to hypnosis, or even propaganda and fakery. Then, firsthand observations by visiting Western doctors began to show that the analgesia, for many people, is a genuine experience.

For example, Dr. E. Grey Dimond of Kansas City, Mo., observed an operation in Canton in 1971 in which the patient had part of his stomach removed under acupuncture analgesia. Four acupuncture needles were attached to a direct-current (DC) battery that sent electrical pulses through them. The man reported that all he felt was a pulling sensation in his internal organs. In 1972, British physician Peter E. Brown witnessed a lung removal in Shanghai. This time, only one acupuncture needle was used. It was rotated manually by the anesthetist, and the patient said that he was able to feel only an occasional pulling sensation.

The first writings on acupuncture were compiled about 500 B.C., though scholars think they originated as traditional treatment passed on by word of mouth as long ago as 2700 B.C. By A.D. 400, a complex system of medicine had developed around the writings that included elaborate charts tracing the circulation of the blood and guidelines to treat virtually every kind of pain or major disease. It is interesting to note that the charts were in use long before the English physician William Harvey published his research on blood circulation in 1628.

The traditional Chinese explanation of acupuncture is that the body contains two universal forces, the spirits (Yin) and the blood (Yang), which circulate through a series of 12 invisible channels called meridians. When Yin and Yang fall out of harmony, pain and disease occur. By inserting needles at one or more of 365 specific points designated on the meridians, the acupuncturist somehow brings the Yin and Yang into harmony again.

While the use of acupuncture during surgery is highly dramatic, the most common use is to relieve headache, backache, and other forms of pain. In fact, acupuncture is related to other forms of intense surface stimulation generally described as "counterirritation" in Western medical texts. Among the oldest techniques used to control pain are applying mustard plasters, ice packs, or hot-water bottles to various parts of the body. The Druses who live in Syria and Lebanon put hot nails on a patient's arms and legs to control pain, believing that this drives out pain-producing spirits. The ancient Greeks and Romans applied hot cups to a person's back to ease leg and back pains. Cupping is still used in Italy, Greece, Eastern Europe, China, and Africa. A small, heated jar or cup is placed on the back with the open end down. As the air in the cup cools, a partial vacuum develops that sucks the skin into the cup, breaking blood vessels and creating a black-and-blue area. Although this is moderately painful, it seems to relieve far more severe pains in other parts of the body for long periods of time.

Other counterirritations include pushing threads through the skin and moving them back and forth, applying substances that blister the skin, and cutting the skin. In many parts of Africa, prolonged, severe headaches are sometimes treated effectively by tribal doctors who make large cuts into the scalp and briefly scrape the skull. This process is known as trepanation.

Interestingly enough, acupuncture has been "rediscovered" by Western doctors many times since it was described in a book by the Dutch physician Willem Ten Rhyne in 1683. However, the technique was discarded each time because so many flamboyant claims were made for its curative powers. Unfortunately, its usefulness against pain also was lost each time. This will happen again, I fear, unless we carefully analyze its properties, determine the neurophysiological mechanisms that explain them, and incorporate these into our knowledge and treatment of pain.

Fortunately, the renewed interest in acupuncture this time has sparked widespread research. Perhaps the most exciting research is being carried out on rats and rabbits by Dr. Hsiang-tung Chang and his colleagues at the Shanghai Institute of Physiology. They have recorded electrical activity in several areas of the central nervous system—the spinal cord and the brain—that are known to transmit pain messages when parts of the body are injured. When they inserted acupuncture needles into areas on an animal's body comparable to acupuncture points on a human body, the pain signals stopped. This confirms the belief that acupuncture works on pain through known pathways in the central nervous system.

Scientists in other parts of China have carried out experiments that lead to the same conclusion. They have also used pressure cuffs that prevent the flow of blood and "spirits" along the so-called meridian channels, but do not stop the normal action of nerve impulses. The pressure cuffs also do not affect the pain-killing aspect of acupuncture. Experimenters have also found that acupuncture points for the relief of pain have no effect on pain when an analgesic drug is injected at acupuncture sites before the sites are stimulated. They also discovered that most acupuncture points lie over or near major sensory nerves, the nerves that receive and carry impressions from the outside world to the central nervous system. These observations, together with data from many other experiments being carried out in China lead unequivocally to the conclusion that acupuncture's effects on pain must be due to neurological mechanisms. Reports in early 1974 on studies at Peking Medical College have suggested that chemicals are released in the nervous system by acupuncture. These chemicals can be withdrawn from one animal and injected into another, thereby diminishing its response to pain.

However, three aspects of acupuncture still seem to defy current medical knowledge. These are: (1) control of pain by stimulation, (2) interaction between distant sites in the body, and (3) prolonged time of relief after stimulation stops. All three are so unusual that they cause skepticism among physicians trained in Western medical practice. Yet, interestingly, all three are found in Western medical literature.

The first, control of pain by stimulation, involves fairly intense stimulation of tissues by the acupuncture needles. This stimulation is caused either by twirling the needles or applying an electrical current. If the pain is not blocked, herbs are sometimes placed on the acupuncture sites and burned. This procedure, called moxibustion, stimulates the tissues still more.

In Western medical literature there is considerable evidence to show that brief, mildly painful stimulation can substantially relieve more severe pain, and that the relief lasts much longer than the period of stimulation. For example, vigorously massaging the sensory nerve that serves the lower head and jaw may permanently abolish the excruciating pain of *tic douloureux*, which causes convulsive spasms of the face and mouth. In rare cases, similar kinds of pain may be alleviated or abolished for many days by slowly withdrawing the fluid that surrounds the spinal cord with a hypodermic needle and then reinjecting it very rapidly.

The second aspect of acupuncture is that of stimulation at one site that affects pain at a distant site. For example, in one Chinese hospital the needles were inserted in a patient's forearms during a thyroid operation. For a similar operation in another hospital, the needles were placed in the neck and wrists.

Western doctors have actually known about the interaction between pain and stimulation at distant sites in the human body since 1946. Janet Travell, who later became President John F. Kennedy's personal physician, and Seymour H. Rinzler made some interesting discoveries during research on unusual pain patterns. They mapped more than 40 patterns of pain within which pain can be readily started or stopped by pressing on specific trigger zones. Travell and Rinzler found that many of the trigger zones extended outside the area of pain, and some were a considerable distance away from the areas they affected. Travell also noted that virtually every trigger zone is at or near one of the major acupuncture points shown on acupuncture charts.

Travell and Rinzler found that dry needling—simply moving a needle in and out of the trigger zone without injecting any substance—sometimes relieves pain. They relieved a shoulder pain, for example, by dry needling a trigger point at or near the site of the pain. Intense cold may also bring relief. At first, they assumed the cold produced local analgesia, but they now believe that the intense stimulation itself relieves the pain. Remarkably, this intense stimulation has abolished pain for days, weeks, and in some cases permanently.

The fact that pain can be relieved by stimulation at a point some distance from its source is particularly evident in treating patients with severe phantom-limb pain. Phantom-limb pain is the feeling of burning or shooting pains that seems to come from a leg or an arm after it has been amputated. Doctors in San Francisco found, in 1954, that injecting a saline solution under the skin of an amputee's lower back produces a sharp, localized, burning pain that radiates into his buttocks and thighs, and sometimes into the phantom limb. The pain lasts only about 10 minutes, yet it may partly or completely relieve phantom-limb pain for hours, weeks, or much longer.

The duration of acupuncture stimulation and the analgesia it produces are not related in any simple way. Analgesia tends to develop slowly. Twenty minutes' stimulation is usually needed to produce sufficient analgesia to carry out a surgical operation. Furthermore, acupuncture analgesia may sometimes last for several hours after the stimulation has stopped.

Such prolonged pain relief is particularly puzzling. It suggests that memorylike mechanisms may be involved. In fact, the very existence of phantom-limb pain supports this suggestion. This pain endures long after the injured stump tissues heal. Moreover, the "remembered" pain may include that incurred in the limb before it was severed. In one case, a patient who had a wood sliver jammed under a fingernail shortly before he lost his hand in an accident subsequently reported feeling a painful sliver still under the fingernail of the hand that was no longer there.

There is also experimental evidence of a memorylike mechanism in pain. In 1947, researchers at The Academy of Medical Sciences in Moscow injected turpentine under the skin of a cat's paw. A temporary inflammation caused the cat to flex its paw excessively when it walked. After the inflammation healed, the animal walked normally. The Russian scientists then severed connections between the cat's brain and the rest of its body and found that the animal once again flexed its paw abnormally. This indicated that a memory record of the pain existed for the cat.

Although we do not understand this aspect of pain, we can use certain theories of memory to speculate on how pain memory works. One theory holds that nerve impulses triggered by the original stimulus activate nerve fibers (neurons) in a reverberating circuit. That is, neuron A activates neuron B, which in turn activates A again, and so on. Theoretically, activity may persist for prolonged periods in such a circuit. It is also conceivable that some sort of change occurs at the connecting junctions between neurons so that a permanent or semipermanent trace of the stimulation remains in the nervous system long after the event occurred. Still another theory is that neuron A activates an inhibitory neuron B, which briefly prevents further activity in neuron A. When neuron B returns to its normal state, release of its inhibitory effect causes neuron A to fire spontaneously and recreate the sequence of events. Presumably, such activity in the nervous system could persist indefinitely.

If some pains result from such memorylike mechanisms, it is conceivable that acupuncture needles could act by disrupting these processes and that the effects would last after the needle is withdrawn. Such mechanisms should also be turned off by analgesics and, indeed, some doctors have injected such drugs into trigger points to stop pains in many parts of the body.

According to the traditional view of pain, known as the specificity theory, specific pain receptors in the body tissues send pain signals directly to a pain center in the brain. The process resembles a simple telephone switchboard—a signal is dialed at one end and a bell rings at the other. This theory assumes that the amount of pain is proportional to the intensity of stimulation, and that the location of the stimulus determines the location of the pain.

However, the specificity theory cannot account for the three properties of acupuncture analgesia—control of pain by stimulation, interaction between distant sites in the body, and prolonged relief after stimulation stops. Scientists have therefore been searching for a more comprehensive theory of pain.

One such alternative is the gate-control theory, which physiologist Patrick D. Wall of University College in London and I proposed in 1965. It provides an explanation for the effects of acupuncture stimulation. Although the gate-control theory is still controversial, recent evidence provides increasing support for it. It is now widely taught in Western medical schools, and is even used by many physiologists and physicians in China to explain acupuncture analgesia.

The theory suggests that the transmission of pain signals from the body to the spinal cord and the brain is a dynamic process capable of variation, not a fixed, unchanging one. The variation stems from a series of gatelike mechanisms in the pain-signaling system. If a gate can be closed, full analgesia follows because pain signals from injured tissues cannot reach the brain.

The gates can be opened or closed to varying degrees by nerve impulses in the large- and small-diameter fibers in each sensory nerve running from the body's surface to the spine and the brain. Activity in large fibers tends to close gates and lessen the pain, while small-fiber activity tends to open gates and increase pain. Activity in the fibers that descend from the brain stem reticular formation, which coordinates information from the sense organs and various parts of the brain, can also open or close gates. This part of the nervous system receives impulses from all the sensory systems as well as other brain areas. It normally keeps the gates partly closed, but it can close them entirely or open them wide. Fibers from the cortex of the brain—the center of the memory, attention, anxiety, and interpretative functions—also can either open or close gates.

The gate-control theory suggests that acupuncture stimulation might alter pain signals in several ways. For example, gently stimulating the skin and underlying tissues with an electric current usually activates more large fibers than small fibers. This tends to close gates and block the pain signals that result from an injury. This can explain "local" analgesia when the acupuncture needles are inserted near the site of surgery.

The modulating system in the brain stem, which I call the "central biasing mechanism," shows how analgesia may also be produced by stimulating distant sites. Neurons in the brain stem reticular formation are known to receive impulses from widespread regions of the body. When particular points in the reticular formation are electrically stimulated, analgesia is produced in a large part of the body. Stimulation at specific sites of a rat's brain stem may produce complete analgesia in from one-fourth to one-half of the rat's body.

In addition, the fibers that descend from the cortex can block pain signals. In this way, psychological processes such as expectation, suggestion, and anxiety can affect pain. Anxiety and fear, for example, are known to heighten the perception of pain. A given intensity of shock or heat is far more painful when a person is anxious than when he is not. Dogs raised in isolation and protected from normal injuries are not as anxious about pain as nonisolated dogs. The isolated ones frequently fail to respond normally to such painful stimuli as a pinprick or a flaming match.

Lowering the level of anxiety also decreases the level of pain. Relaxation, distraction, strong suggestion, and faith in the physician and his techniques have all been demonstrated to diminish pain. For example, many of the soldiers who were severely wounded during the fighting at the Anzio Beachhead in Italy during World War II denied feeling pain from their wounds. The emotions activated by their relief at no longer having to endure the anxiety of battle apparently reduced their pain. An unusually small number of them—only one out of three—had enough pain to require morphine, while among civilians with similar wounds, four out of five demand morphine to kill the pain. So, the mere suggestion that acupuncture is effective may play some sort of role in the easing of pain.

Although acupuncture could activate all of these

mechanisms to abolish pain temporarily or permanently, we have yet to prove that this explains how major surgery can be performed with acupuncture analgesia. I believe that the patient's faith in acupuncture, as a result of long cultural experience, and the explicit suggestion that he will feel no pain, greatly eases anxiety from the outset. In addition, the sensory stimulation from the needles activates brain-stem areas that also tend to close the transmission gates and block the pain signals that are produced by an injury.

Support for the gate-control theory has come from electrical stimulating devices, developed in 1971, that have been used to close the pain gates. These small, battery-driven stimulators, about the size of a pack of cigarettes, stimulate nerve endings when their electrodes are placed over the site of the pain. A low-intensity current activates the large nerve fibers, which prevent pain signals from being transmitted from peripheral nerves to cells in the spinal cord. Stimulators are now being used to treat such ailments as back, arthritic, and phantom-limb pains. Most of them produce a tingling sensation that is followed shortly by a sharp decrease in pain. Low-intensity stimulation may be continued for hours at a time, and the relief it brings often outlasts the period of stimulation by several hours.

We have also used electrical stimulators in my laboratory at McGill University in Montreal in a way that closely resembles acupuncture analgesia. The electrodes are placed over trigger zones associated with the particular pain pattern that is to be relieved, or on the acupuncture points that are believed to be related to the painful area. The trigger zones, or acupuncture points, are then stimulated at a high intensity— usually at a mildly painful level. Stimulation for 15 or 20 minutes often relieves pain for several hours, sometimes for several days. The results of these studies so far are extremely promising and point to exciting new methods of pain control.

When I first began to study the effects of pain nearly two decades ago, my laboratory work with animals was done with the dispassionate curiosity of the experimenter. But after visiting the pain clinic operated by William K. Livingston at the University of Oregon Medical School and seeing human beings suffering terribly from many different types of pain, my whole attitude toward my research changed. I have since directed it toward finding the causes of pain and doing something to alleviate it. I hope that my present work on using electrodes at trigger points will provide a method that physicians can use to control pain selectively, particularly for the chronic forms of pain that incapacitate so many people.

Hypnotic Procedures and Surgery

A Critical Analysis with Applications to "Acupuncture Analgesia"[1]

John F. Chaves[2] and Theodore X. Barber

Perhaps the most dramatic phenomenon associated with hypnotism is the reported ability of selected hypnotic subjects to undergo major surgery without experiencing pain (Esdaile, 1850; Kroger, 1957; Mason, 1955; Werbel, 1965). Most investigators appear to agree with Orne (1965) who noted that "from a clinical point of view there is no question that in suitable subjects hypnosis can induce a degree of anesthesia which will completely block the subjective appreciation of pain [p. 288]."

Although the success of "hypnoanesthesia" in surgery is widely taken for granted, it has not been

[1]Some of the material in the present paper was originally presented in popular form in a recent book (Barber, Spanos, & Chaves, 1974). The present paper is thoroughly revised, extended, and supplemented by recent material. The writing of this paper was supported in part by a research grant (GM 22771-01) from the National Institute of General Medical Sciences. We thank Dr. C. Richard

Chapman for making available to us the translations by Mark Harris and Andrew C. N. Chen of the articles that appeared during 1973 in the Chinese Medical Journal. For critical comments on the manuscript we are indebted to S. Aleo, M. W. Ham, R. F. Q. Johnson, and N. P. Spanos.

[2]Reprint requests should be sent to Dr. John F. Chaves who is now at the Department of Applied Behavioral Sciences, School of Dental Medicine, Southern Illinois University, Edwardsville, Illinois 6226.

The American Journal of Clinical Hypnosis 1976: 18: 217-236.

critically evaluated. In the present paper we critically analyze the phenomenon with the aim of enhancing our understanding of hypnotism and the perception and control of pain. The paper is divided into four sections. The first delineates the nature of surgical pain. The second summarizes a number of reports that indicate both the successes and failures of hypnotic procedures in surgery. The third section specifies six factors that appear to play a prominent role in the apparent successes of "hypnoanesthesia." The final section shows that many of the factors involved in "hypnoanesthesia" are also relevant in accounting for the apparent successes of acupuncture in surgery.

Pain and Surgery

The term *pain* refers to a variety of sensations—for example, throbbing, burning, pricking, or sharp sensations—that vary in intensity and that have a unique "unpleasant" quale. However, pain as a sensation is usually closely associated with anxiety, fear, apprehension, worry, and other "emotions" or "reactions to the sensation" (Beecher, 1959). In general terms, if an individual is anxious or fearful when he is exposed to pain-producing stimulation, he tends to report that the pain is more intense. On the other hand, if he is relaxed and not anxious or fearful, he tends to report that the pain is less intense (Barber, 1959; Beecher, 1946, 1959). Furthermore, some procedures that are said to reduce "pain" may actually reduce anxiety, fear, worry, and other emotions that usually accompany the sensation of pain. Patients who have undergone prefrontal lobotomy typically report that they feel the pain (sensation) but that it does not bother them anymore (Barber, 1959). Also, the pain relief that follows the administration of morphine may be due, in part, to the reduction in anxiety and fear. Although the patient who has received an opiate may still experience pain sensations, the reduction in anxiety, fear, and apprehension appears to play a role in his report that pain is reduced (Barber, 1959, 1970; Beecher, 1959; Cattell, 1943; Hill, Kornetsky, Flanary, & Wikler, 1952a, 1952b; Jaffe, 1970; Kornetsky, 1954).

In the following discussion, we shall make a distinction between pain sensation per se, which we shall at times simply refer to as *pain*, and anxiety, fear and other emotions which are usually closely associated with the sensation of pain. Of course, since the "sensation" and "emotions" are difficult to separate, problems arise in making this distinction. However, to understand the effects of hypnotic procedures, it is necessary to make a distinction along these lines (Barber, 1959, 1960; Shor, 1959). The data to be reviewed strongly suggest that the major effect of

hypnotic procedures in surgery is the reduction of fear and anxiety.[3] However, by reducing anxiety, hypnotic procedures at times also appear to change the perception of pain; as Ostenasek (1948) pointed out, "When the fear of pain is abolished, the perception of pain is not intolerable."

Pain (Sensation) in Surgery

Although surgical procedures give rise to anxiety, fear, worry, and other emotions, they usually give rise to fewer and less intense pain (sensations) than is commonly believed. Pain (sensations) is produced when incisions are made into the skin and other external tissues such as the conjunctiva, the mucous membranes of the mouth and nasopharynx, and the stratified mucous membranes of the genitalia, as well as some deeper tissues (such as the deep fascia, the peritoneum, the periosteum, the tendons, and the rectum) (Lewis, 1942). However, most of the remaining tissues and organs of the body give rise to little or no pain *when they are cut*. In summarizing the studies that document these points, Lewis (1942) noted that subcutaneous tissues give rise to little pain when cut and that only slight pain is elicited when muscles are incised. Also, compact bone can be bored without pain, the articular surfaces of joints are insensitive, and the great omentum can be cut without pain. Among the internal organs that produce little or no pain when cut, Lewis included the brain, liver, spleen, kidneys, stomach, jejunum, ileum, colon, lungs, surface of the heart, esophageal wall, uterus, and internal portions of the vagina.

In brief, the skin and other ectodermal tissues and some deeper tissues are sensitive when cut but most tissues and organs of the body give rise to little or no pain when incised by the surgeon's scalpel. Although *cutting* the internal tissues and organs is usually *not* an adequate stimulus to produce pain, *pulling or stretching* the internal organs does give rise to pain.

These data can be placed in broader context if we look carefully at the reports of surgery performed only with local anesthetics.

Major Surgery with Local Anesthetics

At the present time, pain-relieving drugs are used routinely in major surgery. However, prior to the 1840's

[3]Instead of speaking in terms of "reduction of anxiety," we could speak in terms of "production of relaxation." We shall use the concept of "anxiety" instead of the closely related concept of "relaxation" because the latter term at times refers to muscular relaxation and, it appears to us, that it is the "mental relaxation" which is practically equivalent to "lack of anxiety" that is the important effect of hypnotic procedures.

(before the discovery of chloroform, ether, and other general anesthetics), patients underwent surgery without the benefit of chemical pain-killers. The great majority of patients moaned, struggled, or screamed but some "bravely made no signs of suffering at all" (Trent, 1946) and others appeared to experience very little if any pain (*e.g.*, Freemont-Smith, 1950; Tuckey, 1889, pp. 725-726).

Although early reports indicated that only a small proportion of patients could easily tolerate major surgery without any chemical anesthesia, reports which began to appear around 1900 indicated that major surgical procedures could be accomplished with little or no pain if local anesthetics were used to dull the pain of the initial cut through the skin. Lennander (1901, 1902, 1904, 1906a, 1906b) performed a large number of major abdominal operations while using only local anesthetics such as cocaine. After anesthetizing the skin, the remainder of the operation was accomplished with little or no pain even though additional pain-relieving drugs were not used.

Lennander's findings were replicated by Mitchell (1907). Among the surgical procedures performed by Mitchell using only local anesthetics such as cocaine were appendectomies, mastectomies, suprapubic cystostomies, laparotomies, excisions of the glands of the neck and groin, herniorrhaphies, and cholecystostomies. After performing several amputations with local anesthetics, Mitchell (1907) commented as follows:

The skin being thoroughly anesthetized and the incision being made, there is little sensation in the subcutaneous tissues and muscles as long as the blood vessels, large nerve trunks and connective tissues are avoided . . . The same insensibility to pain in bone has been noted in several cases of amputation, in the removal of osteophytes and wiring of fractures. In every instance after thorough cocainization of the periosteum, the actual manipulations of the bone have been unaccompanied by pain. The patients have stated that they could feel and hear the sawing, but it was as if a board were being sawn while resting on some part of the body [p. 200].

The data summarized above indicate that although many tissues and organs give rise to pain (sensations) when they are stretched or pulled, most internal tissues and organs give rise to little or no pain when they are cut by the surgeon's scalpel. Of course, anxiety and fear of being cut play a major role in surgery. At the present time, surgery is usually carried out with general anesthesia primarily because of the anxiety and fear that is aroused and because it is very difficult to carry out an operation when the patient is tense, when his muscles are not relaxed, and when he does not remain perfectly still. Nevertheless, if the patient can tolerate the pain associated with the initial incision through the skin, and if he can remain relaxed

and still, many major surgical procedures can be accomplished with little additional pain.

Successes and Failures of Hypnotic Procedures in Surgery

When "hypnotic procedures" are used in surgery the patient is given repeated suggestions that he is becoming relaxed and is entering a hypnotic state and he is also given suggestions that pain will be reduced or obliterated.[4] Some reports indicate that hypnotic procedures are of little value in surgery whereas others indicate that they can be immensely useful. Let us summarize a number of reports that represent the broad range of effects that have been noted.

If we look back at the early reports of "painless surgery" under mesmerism or hypnotism, we find that, although the procedures reduced anxiety and fear, the extent to which they reduced pain as a sensation may have been exaggerated. For example, in a classic report, Esdaile (1850) stated that he had performed over 300 major operations and numerous minor surgical procedures during a six-year period while he was working in India. His report is frequently cited as demonstrating "painless surgery" utilizing mesmerism or hypnotism. However, a careful reading of Esdaile's cases indicated that, although anxiety, fear, and other emotions were apparently reduced to a marked degree, the surgery may not have been as free of pain sensations as has been supposed.

During Esdaile's stay in India, the government of Bengal appointed a committee to investigate his claims of efficacy of mesmerism in surgery (Braid, 1847). Esdaile selected 10 patients to be observed by the committee. He later excluded 3 of the 10 patients, however, because they could not be mesmerized. In the remaining seven cases, surgery was carried out while the patients were in a "mesmeric trance." In one case, involving the tapping of one side of a double hydrocele, the results were regarded as inconclusive. Although the patient tolerated the procedure without apparent pain, the other side of the hydrocele was tapped while the patient was completely awake and he still reported no pain. Moreover, it was noted that numerous patients had tolerated this procedure while awake without showing signs of pain.

The six remaining cases all involved more extensive

[4]Many other factors are also present when hypnotic procedures are used in surgery. These additional factors, which will be discussed later in this paper, include, for example, the following: the patient is carefully selected; there is a close interpersonal relationship between the patient and the physician; and the patient is exposed to special preparation or "education" prior to surgery and to distractions during the surgery.

surgery, including amputations and removal of scrotal tumors. In each case, the patients testified that they had not felt pain during surgery. However, three of the six patients seemed to be in pain; the committee's report stated that they showed "convulsive movements of the upper limbs, writhing of the body, distortion of the features, giving the face a hideous expression of suppressed agony; the respiration became heaving, with deep sighs. There were, in short, all the signs of intense pain which a dumb person undergoing operation might be expected to exhibit, except resistance to the operator." The remaining three patients did not show the aforementioned signs of pain; however, during the surgery, two of the three showed erratic pulse rates suggesting that some anxiety or pain may have been present. In summary, the committee's report indicated that Esdaile's surgery may not have been as uniformly painless as has been supposed.

The discovery of the anesthetic properties of chloroform, ether, and nitrous oxide during the 1840's led to a rapid decline of interest in mesmerism. Its staunchest advocates, however, remained loyal, pointing out the dangers associated with gaseous anesthetics and noting with satisfaction that not a single operative death could be attributed to mesmerism.

About 50 years later there was a revival of interest in hypnosis, as it was now called. Bramwell (1903) reported that he found he could "sometimes induce anesthesia by suggestion, and from that time occasionally performed surgical operations during hypnosis [p. 161]." However, all of the cases reported by Bramwell involved either dental extractions or other minor surgical procedures.

Moll (1889) took a more critical look at the use of hypnotic procedures in surgery, arguing that "a complete analgesia is extremely rare in hypnosis, although authors, copying from one another, assert that it is common [p. 105]." Moll also gave his own examples, for instance ". . . I once hypnotized a patient in order to open a boil painlessly. I did not succeed in inducing analgesia, but the patient was almost unable to move, so that I could perform the little operation without difficulty [p. 330]."

From around 1955 to the present, interest in the reduction of surgical pain by hypnotic procedures has increased markedly. Numerous clinical reports (*e.g.*, Kroger & DeLee, 1957; Owen-Flood, 1955; Scott, 1973), several books (Coppolino, 1965; Marmer, 1959; Werbel, 1965), and a symposium concerning "hypnoanesthesia" (Lassner, 1964) have been published. In most of the cases that have been reported, it appears that anxiety and fear were attenuated and the patient was able to tolerate the surgery. However, the extent to which pain as a sensation was attenuated is open to question. Let us look at a few examples.

Cooper and Powles (1945) used hypnotic procedures in six cases involving minor surgery (two whitlows, two palmar abscesses, and two axillary abscesses). One case was regarded as unsuccessful because of anxiety and apprehension on the part of the patient. Another case, however, was described in detail since it was regarded as a typical example of the successful use of hypnotic procedures. The patient was an 18-year-old soldier who required incision of two axillary abscesses. He was premedicated with 1½ gr. Nembutal (pentobarbital). Suggestions for relaxation and sleep were continued for 10 minutes together with additional suggestions of anesthesia for the shoulder, axilla, and arm. During the incision "there was considerable grimacing and some movement of the contralateral shoulder." Although it was concluded that the patient showed "satisfactory anesthesia," the "grimacing" and "movement of the shoulder" suggest that some pain sensations may have been present. Moreover, it is not clear in this report to what degree the apparent reduction in fear and anxiety might have been due to the Nembutal.

Anderson (1957) reported that he had performed major surgery, including abdominal explorations, cesarean sections, and exploration of the common duct, with the aid of hypnotic procedures. One case was presented in detail. The patient was a 71-year-old man who underwent abdominal exploration. Since his physical condition was very poor and general anesthesia was contraindicated it was decided to use hypnotic procedures. The patient underwent extensive hypnotic training sessions for two weeks prior to surgery. The training sessions included rehearsal of the operative procedure. During the abdominal exploration, the patient "partially broke his hypnotic trance" necessitating the administration of 5cc. of 2% thiopental (Pentothal). Subsequently, a common duct stone was removed. The report does not give any details about how the patient "partially broke his hypnotic trance" but, presumably, he showed sufficient signs of pain to necessitate the use of Pentothal.

Schwarcz (1965) utilized hypnoanesthesia in two surgical cases. In one case a suprapubic prostatectomy was performed on a 61-year-old man who was described as capable of achieving a "somnambulistic stage." Because of a heart problem, the patient was classified as only a fair operative risk and it was decided that hypnotic procedures should be used. The morning of the surgery, the patient was given a narcotic analgesic (100 mg. Demerol), together with a sedative (100 mg. Nembutal), and 0.4 mg. of atropine. A longitudinal midline incision was made, whereupon the patient showed "a wrinkling of the brow" and a 10 mm. Hg. increase in blood pressure. No further signs of pain were noted during the surgery. The patient reported amnesia for the surgery. It appears to us that in this case the hypnotic procedures reduced anxiety and fear, probably reduced the doses of drugs that were required, and possibly reduced the intensity of pain. However, to draw this conclusion definitively it is necessary to determine (by means of "control" patients) how much anxiety and pain is experienced during this type of surgery and what minimal doses of drugs are required when hypnotic procedures are not used.

Schwarcz's second patient was seen for a transurethral resection of the prostate. The patient had a history of decompensated syphilitic heart disease with an aortic aneurysm. Two previous attempts at surgery under general anesthesia had to be postponed because of drastic reductions in the patient's blood pressure. It was then decided to use hypnoanesthesia. During four training sessions he was found to be a good hypnotic subject. The patient remained quiet during the surgery, but his blood pressure rose from a preoperative level of 140/96 to 170/120. After surgery, he reported that "he had had a pleasant dream and had felt no pain." This successful case indicates that hypnotic procedures can be useful with selected surgical patients. Even though the rise in blood pressure suggests that some anxiety or pain may have been present, the patient was able to tolerate the surgery satisfactorily.

In a more recent first-person account (Reis, 1966), the patient was a nurse-anesthetist who required biopsy of a breast tumor and excision of thyroid nodules. The patient had previously worked with the surgeon and had great confidence in him. Prior to surgery, 75 mg. of meperidine hydrochloride (Demerol) and 0.4 mg. of atropine were administered. The breast incision reportedly felt "as if a fingernail were being drawn over the skin." The neck incision "felt sharper than the two previous incisions but was still not painful." The patient attributed her ability to tolerate the procedure without pain to her confident expectation that she would not feel pain. She also reported that, several years earlier, she had been given a post-hypnotic suggestion that she would be able to use hypnoanesthesia successfully. No indication is given, however, that the patient thought she was in a "hypnotic trance" during the surgery. This case suggests the need to test the hypothesis that patients who approach this type of surgery (biopsy of tumor and excision of nodules) with little anxiety and with expectation that they will not experience pain require less chemical analgesia than those who are highly anxious.

An exceptionally successful use of hypnotic procedures in major surgery has been presented by Mason (1955). The case involved a bilateral mammaplasty performed on a 24-year-old woman who suffered from grossly hypertrophied breasts. Surgery was done in two stages. During the first stage, general anesthesia was used resulting in a stormy post-operative course.

The patient was quite anxious when informed that a second operation would be needed. On this basis, hypnoanesthesia was suggested and the patient was found to be a good hypnotic subject. The patient had two impacted wisdom teeth that needed to be removed, so it was decided to use this opportunity to determine whether she could tolerate the procedure with hypnoanesthesia. The hypnotic procedures were successful; both teeth were removed without noticeable pain. When the dental operation was successfully completed, it was decided to go ahead with the second stage of mammaplasty. The night prior to surgery, the patient was given 130 mg. of sodium amytal but no other medication was administered before, during, or after surgery. Prior to the hypnotic induction, the sensitivity of her entire chest and breast was determined using pinpricks. It was noted that there was a diminution of pain sensitivity over the outer and upper quadrant of her left breast and left nipple. This reduction in pain sensitivity was attributed to the previous surgery. A hypnotic induction procedure was then administered and analgesia was suggested for the chest wall and both breasts. While the incision was being made the patient did not flinch or withdraw, although she reported pain when the surgeon went too far laterally, "apparently beyond the area of suggested anesthesia." The patient was quite talkative during surgery and did not show anxiety or pain. The whole procedure took 70 minutes. When the operation was over, the patient said "Good show!" and asked to sit up. Blood pressure was the same before and after surgery, 140/80, and it was noted that during surgery her pulse rate stabilized at 96.

This is one of the most impressive cases reported in the recent literature since no premedication or analgesics were used. We have only one minor reservation with regard to this case: it is clear that the previous surgery had left some degree of insensitivity in part of the breast area and we do not know what role this played in producing the apparent marked reduction in pain that was observed with hypnoanesthesia. With this tentative proviso, we can conclude that with this patient hypnotic procedures appeared to markedly reduce both anxiety and pain.

In brief, the cases summarized above, taken together with other similar cases that have been reported (Bernstein, 1965; Bonilla, Quigley, & Bowers, 1961; Chaves & Barber, 1974b; Goldie, 1956; Hoffman, 1959; Kelsey & Barron, 1958; Steinberg & Pennell, 1965; Taugher, 1958; Winkelstein & Levinson, 1959), appear to indicate that: (a) Hypnotic procedures are effective with many but not all selected patients in producing relative calmness during surgery with an apparent reduction in anxiety. (b) In most instances, pain-relieving drugs are used together with the hypnotic procedures, although the doses of the drugs are usually less than those typically used in surgery. (c) In a small proportion of cases, pain-relieving drugs were not used during surgery with hypnotic procedures; in some of these cases, the patients seemed to experience pain sensations but in other cases the patients appeared to experience very little if any pain.

The question now before us is: Which of the many factors that accompany the use of "hypnotic procedures" are effective in producing the relative quietude, the reduction in anxiety and fear, and the apparent reduction, in some cases, of pain sensitivity? Although systematic research is needed to provide a definitive answer to this question, the data available at present indicate that the following six factors play an important role in producing the effects that are attributed to "hypnotic procedures": with few exceptions, the patients are (a) carefully selected, (b) given an opportunity to form a close relationship with the physician, (c) given special preoperative preparation or "education," (d) given pain-relieving drugs, (e) exposed to suggestions of anesthesia or analgesia and (f) exposed to distractions during surgery. We shall discuss each of these factors in turn.

Six Factors that Play an Important Role in the Success of "Hypnotic Procedures"

Selection of Patients

There is a consensus among investigators that the successful use of hypnotic procedures in major surgery is only possible with a small proportion of the general population. There is disagreement, however, concerning just how small this proportion might be. Kroger (1957) and Lederman, Fordyce, and Stacy (1958) conjectured that 10% of the population can successfully undergo surgery with hypnoanesthesia. Wallace and Coppolino (1960), on the other hand, carefully surveyed the literature and found that no published studies had appeared which substantiated the 10% figure. Moreover, their own experience suggested that the true figure is probably far lower than 10%. They concluded that "the 10% estimate is an oft-repeated but unsubstantiated quantity and that the true percentage of successful cases is much below that figure [Wallace & Coppolino, 1960, p. 3265]."

Since it is necessary to select patients very carefully for surgery with hypnoanesthesia, it is useful to determine how these patients differ from those who are regarded as unsuitable. At least one important difference is that those who are selected are more responsive to suggestions (more "hypnotizable") than those who are

not. In addition, the selected patients may differ in other important ways from those not selected. For example, they may be less anxious regarding the surgery, may have formed a closer relationship with the surgeon or anesthesiologist, and may have more positive attitudes toward the use of hypnotic procedures in controlling pain. We shall examine these factors in a latter section of the paper. It should be noted, however, that these preexisting differences may play an important role in enabling the selected patients to manifest relative calmness and lack of anxiety during the surgery.

Interpersonal Relationship

As compared to regular surgical patients, patients who are to undergo surgery with hypnoanesthesia often form a very close interpersonal relationship with the physician. The opportunity to form a close relationship is usually provided by "training" sessions in which the hypnotic procedures are practiced (Anderson, 1957; Betcher, 1960; Marmer, 1956; Schwarcz, 1965; Tinterow, 1960). The establishment of a close, supportive relationship between the patient and the physician may have at least two important consequences: (a) it might be expected to minimize the fear and anxiety which accompanies surgery; and (b) it might lead the patient to deny or to minimize the pain sensations that he experiences (Hilgard, 1973; Kaplan, 1960). With regard to the latter possibility, it has been noted:

The physician who has invested time and energy in hypnotizing the patient and suggesting that pain will be relieved, expects and desires that his efforts will be successful, and by his words and manner communicates his desires and expectations to the patient. The patient in turn has often formed a close relationship with the physician-hypnotist and would like to please him or at least not to disappoint him. Furthermore, the patient is aware that if he states that he suffered, he is implying that the physician's time and energy were wasted and his efforts futile [Barber, 1970, pp. 211-212].

Motivation to deny or minimize pain is also present in other clinical situations in which the patient has formed a close relationship with the medical staff. For example, Mandy, Mandy, Farkas, and Scher (1952) indicated that natural-childbirth patients, who report to the physician and his associates that they were pleased with natural childbirth, at times admit to an independent observer that the procedure was more painful than anticipated but that this fact was not reported to the medical staff for fear of disappointing them. Since an important similarity between "hypnoanesthesia" and "natural childbirth" is that both provide the opportunity for a close patient-physician relationship, the motivation to deny or minimize the pain experienced must also be considered in evaluating the use of hypnotic procedures in surgery.

Preoperative Preparation or "Education"

In addition to the close interpersonal relationship that may develop, extended contact between the patient and physician also provides an opportunity for the patient to learn more about the specific surgical procedures and to familiarize himself with the medical setting. This kind of preoperative preparation or "education" may help to reduce the patient's anxiety.

Schultz (1954) provided a description of the kind of preoperative preparation or "education" that is commonly made available to candidates for hypnoanesthesia:

Every patient during the preparatory hypnotic sessions must be led to experience the operation or the labour with all details. For instance, if a thyroidectomy were imminent, the hypnotic preparation was done in the sense that every detail was gone into. For example: "Now your skin is smeared with iodine" (slight touching of the throat with cotton). "Now your skin is stretched" (corresponding straining of the skin of the throat). "Now the knife is going through the skin of your throat" (marking with a pencil the line of incision with a very slight pressure). "Now blood is running down the outside of your throat. You feel the warm fluid; you know 'it is my blood,' and remain absolutely calm, with no pain, no anxiety . . ." [Schultz, 1954, p. 24].

Such preoperative preparation or "education" can clearly minimize any surprise during the actual surgery and may be helpful in reducing anxiety.

The available data indicate that even minimal efforts at preparing the patient for surgery can be quite beneficial. Egbert and his associates (Egbert, Battit, Turndorf, & Beecher, 1963; Egbert, Battit, Welch, & Bartlett, 1964) found that a 5 or 10 minute preoperative visit by an anesthesiologist had a greater calming effect on surgical patients than 2 mg./kg. of pentobarbital sodium which was the routinely employed preoperative medication. Moreover, they found that patients who were given detailed information about their surgery and the kind of post-surgical pain they might expect required smaller doses of narcotics for post-surgical pain than uninformed control patients. In addition, the informed patients were discharged from the hospital sooner than the controls.

Since preoperative familiarization with the medical setting and with the surgical procedures appears to reduce anxiety, and since such familiarization is often provided prior to hypnoanesthesia, it may be that some of the benefits ascribed to the hypnotic procedures may actually be due to the special preparation.

Use of Drugs (Analgesics, Anesthetics, and Sedatives)

The vast majority of patients undergoing surgery with hypnotic procedures also receive narcotic analgesics, local anesthetics, and sedatives alone or in combination. In a previous section of this paper, in which we presented typical cases of hypnoanesthesia, we noted that pain-relieving drugs were usually used together with the hypnotic procedures. In fact, few, if any, present-day investigators seriously suggest that hypnoanesthesia should be used as the sole anesthetic in major surgery. Marmer (1964), for example, stated that "It is only in isolated and rare instances that hypnosis can be used to perform painlessly any surgical procedure [p. 20]." In a similar fashion, Zwicker (1964) emphasized that "hypnosis cannot and should not compete with general anesthesia achieved by chemical means [p. 31]."

The present-day use of pain-relieving drugs in surgery with "hypnoanesthesia" has not received sufficient emphasis. For instance, textbooks on hypnosis commonly discuss cases in which "hypnoanesthesia" was successful in surgery while failing to mention that pain-relieving drugs were also used. In fact, if we look carefully at the kinds of drugs that were used, and we also keep in mind that many tissues and organs of the body fail to give rise to pain when they are incised, much of the mystery of "hypnoanesthesia" disappears. Let us look at two examples.

After describing several cases of minor surgery, Crasilneck, McCranie, and Jenkins (1956) also presented a case of major surgery—a temporal lobectomy—which was performed on a 14-year-old girl suffering from epilepsy. The patient was exposed to a hypnotic induction procedure together with suggestions of analgesia. The authors stated that "the scalp line of incision was injected with a 2% solution of procaine." Later, "it was necessary (twice) to inject the scalp with additional local anesthetic because of the patient's perception of pain. . . ." The patient also complained of pain when the dura mater was being separated from the bone. At another point, "as a blood vessel in the hippocampal region was being coagulated, the patient suddenly awoke from the hypnotic trance." In addition, during the surgery, the patient was given 100 mg. of thiopental sodium intravenously. During most of the surgery, while cutting into brain tissues, the patient appeared comfortable and did not seem to experience pain. Although the hypnotic procedures appeared to be helpful in relaxing the patient and in reducing anxiety and fear, it is questionable whether they produced a marked reduction in pain sensations. It should be noted that (a) the patient reported pain, as would be normally expected, when the dura mater was separated from the bone and when a blood vessel was coagulated, (b) the scalp, which is sensitive to incision, was dulled by the use of procaine (Novocain), and (c) since the brain is generally insensitive to incision, the patient naturally experienced little or no pain sensations when it was cut. In brief, this case, and also other similar cases (Finer, 1966; Schwarcz, 1965; Werbel, 1965) seem amazing only when one incorrectly assumes that insensitive tissues such as the brain are sensitive to cutting and when one fails to note that a local anesthetic was used to dull sensitive areas such as the skin.

Marmer (1956, 1957, 1959) also used hypnotic procedures in a large number of surgical cases, but always in combination with analgesics and sedatives. A typical case presented by Marmer (1956) involved a thoracotomy and resection of the lung. The 25-year-old female patient was exposed to a hypnotic induction procedure the night before surgery and, again, just before surgery. In addition she was given the following medications: 0.10 gm. pentobarbital (Nembutal), 50 gm. diphenhydramine hydrochloride (Benadryl) orally, 100 mg. meperidine hydrochloride (Demerol), 0.40 mg. scopolamine, and 50 mg. thiamylal sodium (Surital) intravenously. In addition, the skin was infiltrated with 25 cc. of 1% procaine hydrochloride. During dissection of the lung, a solution of 0.1% succinylcholine was given and continued until a total of 100 mg. had been administered. The report does not state whether the patient experienced pain sensations during surgery although, in light of the narcotic analgesics, local anesthetics, and sedatives that were administered, it might have been surprising if she had experienced much pain.

In brief, hypnotic procedures are rarely used *alone* in present-day surgery. With very few exceptions, the hypnotic procedures are combined with pain-relieving drugs. Although the hypnotic procedures often seem to be effective in reducing anxiety and fear and in producing relative quietude, the drugs seem to play an important role in reducing pain.

Suggestions of Analgesia or Anesthesia

Patients selected for hypnoanesthesia often have a pre-existing belief in its efficacy and, during the pre-operative phase and during surgery itself, these beliefs are strengthened by direct and indirect suggestions. In addition, specific suggestions for analgesia or anesthesia are administered prior to and during surgery. Clinical and experimental data support the notion that both direct and indirect suggestions that pain will be attenuated are effective in reducing anxiety and/or pain. Moreover, the indications are that suggestions of analgesia are equally effective regardless of whether or not a formal hypnotic induction procedure is employed. Let us review some of the relevant data.

The effectiveness of indirect suggestions in reducing surgical pain has sometimes been observed serendipitously. A rather striking example was reported by Tuckey:

There are few cases of this kind more remarkable than one related by Mr. Woodhouse Braine, the well-known chloroformist. Having to administer ether to an hysterical girl who was about to be operated on for removal of two sebaceous tumors from the scalp he found that the ether bottle was empty, and that the inhaling bag was free from even the odor of any anesthetic. While a fresh supply was being obtained, he thought to familiarize the patient with the process by putting the inhaling bag over her mouth and nose, and telling her to breathe quietly and deeply. After a few inspirations she cried, "Oh, I feel it; I am going off," and a moment after, her eyes turned up, and she became unconscious. As she was found to be perfectly insensible, and the ether had not yet come, Mr. Braine proposed that the surgeon should proceed with the operation. One tumor was removed without in the least disturbing her, and then, in order to test her condition, a bystander said that she was coming to. Upon this she began to show signs of waking, so the bag was once more applied, with the remark, "She'll soon be off again," when she immediately lost sensation and the operation was successfully and painlessly completed [Tuckey, 1889, pp. 725-726].

While working under primitive conditions in a prisoner-of-war hospital during World War II, Sampimon and Woodruff (1946) found that "the mere suggestion of anesthesia" was sufficient to perform minor surgery on soldiers without apparent pain. More recently, Lozanov (1967) showed that suggestions of anesthesia alone (without formal hypnotic induction procedures) were sufficient to perform a herniorrhaphy with little pain. Hardy, Wolff, and Goodell (1952) found that pain thresholds could be elevated 90% over control levels when a placebo was administered with the suggestion that it was a potent analgesic. Similarly, placebos have been shown to be effective in attenuating anxiety and/or pain in many post-surgical patients (Barber, 1959; Beecher, 1955; Dodson & Bennett, 1954; Houde & Wallenstein, 1953; Laszlo & Spencer, 1953).

Similar results were obtained in a series of recent experimental studies in which the subjects were asked to report the intensity of the pain they experienced. These experiments, which were conducted in our laboratory (Barber, 1969; Barber & Cooper, 1972; Barber & Hahn, 1962; Chaves & Barber, 1974; Johnson, 1974; Spanos, Barber, & Lang, 1969; Spanos, Horton, & Chaves, 1975) and in other laboratories (Blitz & Dinerstein, 1968, 1971; Craig & Weiss, 1971; Evans & Paul, 1970; Hilgard, 1967; Hilgard, Cooper, Lenox, Morgan, & Voevodsky, 1966; Kanfer & Goldfoot, 1966; Morgan, Lezard, Prytulak, & Hilgard, 1970;

Notermans, 1966; Zimbardo, Cohen, Weisenberg, Dworkin, & Firestone, 1966), demonstrated that suggestions that pain will be attenuated, as well as other psychological techniques (expectation of pain reduction, social modeling, and distraction), are effective in reducing reported pain.

In four of the experiments mentioned above (Barber, 1969; Barber & Hahn, 1962; Evans & Paul, 1970; Spanos, Barber, & Lang, 1969) suggestions of anesthesia were given to hypnotic subjects and also to control subjects. All four experiments yielded the same results: the suggestions of anesthesia were just as effective when they were given with or without a formal hypnotic induction procedure. Thus, the formal hypnotic induction procedure *per se* does not seem to increase the efficacy of suggestions of anesthesia in reducing reported pain. An important implication of these findings is that the effectiveness of implicit and explicit suggestions of anesthesia in surgery may also not depend on the presence or absence of a formal hypnotic induction.[5]

To summarize, then, patients who are to undergo hypnoanesthesia for surgery believe that the technique is effective and that the pain of surgery will be reduced or eliminated. These beliefs are reinforced by the physician or hypnotist and, in addition, specific suggestions of analgesia or anesthesia are administered prior to and during surgery. The available data indicate that belief in the efficacy of a technique in reducing pain and explicit suggestions of analgesia or anesthesia are both effective in reducing pain. Moreover, experimental studies indicate that suggestions for pain reduction are effective in reducing reported pain when they are given with or without a formal hypnotic induction.

Distraction

When hypnotic procedures are used during an operation, the patient is typically asked to carry out tasks which can distract him from the surgery. He may be asked to focus his attention on his own breathing, on the voice of the hypnotist, or on specific scenes that are suggested by the hypnotist. The patient may also be asked to engage in a distracting task such as singing (August, 1963) or to report the scenes he has been instructed to imagine. For example, Finer

(1966) required a patient who was undergoing surgery with hypnotic procedures to imagine a television with her favorite program and to give an ongoing commentary describing her imaginings. Betcher (1960) and Van Dyke (1965) have also described the use of suggested imagery in hypnoanesthesia. Let us now examine what role these kinds of distractions might play in the reduction of pain.

Studies have shown that a variety of distractions are effective in reducing reported pain in experimental situations (Chaves & Barber, 1974d). Kanfer and Goldfoot (1966) found that reported pain was reduced when the subjects observed interesting slides, when they verbalized the sensations aloud, and when they paced themselves with a clock. Barber and his associates (Barber, 1969; Barber & Cooper, 1972; Barber & Hahn, 1962; Chaves & Barber, 1974a; Spanos, Horton, & Chaves, 1975; Johnson, 1974) have shown that reported pain can be reduced by listening to an interesting tape-recorded story, adding numbers aloud, thinking about pleasant experiences, and imagining that the painful area is numb.

Notermans (1966) found that pain thresholds could be increased from 40 to 50% when subjects were asked to engage in an irrelevant task (inflating a manometer cuff). A variety of external stimuli, including heat, cold, and electrical stimulation, are also effective in reducing both clinical and experimental pain (Gammon & Starr, 1941).

To recapitulate, we have delineated six factors that seem to play a role in reducing anxiety and pain when hypnotic procedures are used in surgery. As we have noted elsewhere (Chaves & Barber, 1973; 1974c; 1974d), almost all of these factors also seem to play a role in the apparent reduction of surgical pain that has been attributed to acupuncture.[6] We will now briefly review the data which pertain to the use of acupuncture in surgery.

Surgery with Acupuncture

Overview

The recent reestablishment of relations between the United States and China has been accompanied by dramatic and widespread interest in some arcane techniques of Chinese medicine, particularly acupuncture. Although acupuncture had been tried in Europe as early as the 17th century and in the United States

---

[5]Suggestions of anesthesia typically instruct the subject to carry out a "cognitive strategy" for the reduction of pain, for example, to imagine that part of the body has been injected with Novocain and is dull, numb, and insensitive. For a discussion of how suggestions of anesthesia alter responsiveness to noxious stimuli by affecting cognitive-imaginative processes see Barber, Spanos, and Chaves (1974), Chaves and Barber (1974a), Spanos and Barber (1974), and Spanos, Horton, & Chaves, (1975).

[6]The one factor discussed in the present work that does not seem especially relevant in surgery with acupuncture is the interpersonal relationship between patient and physician. Available reports of surgery with acupuncture do not seem to indicate that attempts are made to form an especially close patient-physician relationship.

during the very early 19th century (Cassedy, 1974), its impact was negligible. However, contemporary accounts of surgical analgesia with acupuncture seemed to capture the imagination of both the public and the medical profession. The initial claims for acupuncture not only suggested that it was a new and potent technique for controlling pain, but it also implied that Western medicine had overlooked something fundamental about the nature of pain and its control.

Although early attempts to account for the success of acupuncture analgesia had to rely heavily on anecdotal reports (Chaves & Barber, 1973; 1974c; 1974d; Kroger, 1973), detailed reports, as well as several experimental studies have now become available. These more recent reports provide additional support for the notion that the apparent success of acupuncture analgesia can be explained in terms of the same factors that explain the apparent success of surgery with hypnosis (Chaves, 1975). Let us review, briefly, each of the relevant factors and summarize the supporting evidence.

Overestimation of Surgical Pain

Our previous comments regarding the insensitivity of most tissues and organs to incision have obvious relevance to understanding the effectiveness of surgery with acupuncture. As we pointed out, the skin and other ectodermal tissues give rise to pain sensations when they are cut, but most of the remaining tissues and organs of the body are generally insensitive to incision. However, most of the internal tissues and organs give rise to sensations of pain when they are subjected to pressure, pulling, or stretching. Descriptions of surgery performed with acupuncture indicate that Chinese surgeons work delicately and carefully and are especially careful to avoid putting traction on pain-sensitive tissues (Brown, 1972; Capperauld, 1972; Peking Children's Hospital, 1973; Peking Hsuan-wu Hospital, 1973). When traction on these tissues cannot be avoided, acupuncture patients grimace, sweat, and show other signs of experiencing pain (Capperauld, 1972; Peking Hsuan-wu Hospital, 1973).

The skin generally gives rise to pain sensations when it is cut. In surgery with acupuncture, the incision through the skin also typically gives rise to pain when procaine or other local anesthetics are not used to numb the skin (DeBakey, 1973; Eye, Ear, Nose, and Throat Hospital of Shanghai, 1973; Hunan Medical College, 1973; Peking Children's Hospital, 1973; Peking Hsuan-wu Hospital, 1973). A recent experimental study (Mann, 1973) also showed that acupuncture needles, placed at spots considered appropriate

by the traditional Chinese theory, failed to produce analgesia of the skin (as assessed by repeated pinpricks which were sufficiently strong to draw blood).

Selection of Patients

The widespread assumption that acupuncture is routinely employed for surgery in China is false. Acupuncture is used only when it is fully and enthusiastically accepted by the patient (Bonica, 1974; Chaves & Barber, 1973; 1974b; 1974d; DeBakey, 1973; Dimond, 1971; Hus-Shan Hospital of Shanghai, 1973; Wall, 1974). Although there are no statistics currently available to indicate what percentage of patients in China undergo surgery with acupuncture, there are indications that the percentage is quite small (Bonica, 1974; DeBakey, 1973). The chief delegate of the Chinese physicians who visited the United States in 1973 expressed concern "lest the Americans misunderstand [acupuncture] as an established standard technique [for surgery] in China [Anon., 1972]."[7]

Even though the selected patients are originally enthusiastic, some of them become anxious during the surgery. With these anxious patients who find it difficult to cooperate, the failure rate is "as high as 74%" (Peking Hsuan-wu Hospital, 1973). Moreover, if the patients show a "high degree of apprehension and anxiety" during the surgery, they are given general anesthesia (Peking Hsuan-wu Hospital, 1973).

Preoperative Preparation or "Education"

Typically, acupuncture patients are admitted to the hospital several days prior to surgery and are given a detailed explanation of what will be done, how the operation will proceed, what the acupuncturist and surgeon will do, and what effects the needles will have (Bonica, 1974; Dhangshan County People's Hospital, 1973; DeBakey, 1973; Kroger, 1973; Shanghai Acupuncture Anesthesia Coordinating Group, 1973; Tkach, 1972; Wall, 1974). In addition, the patient is frequently asked to talk to other patients who have had the same kind of surgery and is given a set of acupuncture needles which he is encouraged to try on himself. Surgery with acupuncture is not

[7]DeBakey (1973) concluded from this visit to China that "There appears to be more enthusiasm for acupuncture in America—most of it based on ignorance and wishful thinking—than among the skilled physicians with whom I talked in China. They were open in confessing their own uncertainty about it, modest in discussing its effects, cautious in claiming any kind of medical breakthrough. Although they felt that they were onto something important, they frankly admitted that the use of acupuncture, while widespread, is still experimental [p. 138]."

especially useful in emergency situations where preoperative preparation is not possible. In fact, conventional anesthetic techniques are practically always used for emergency surgery (Capperauld, 1972).

Use of Drugs (Analgesics, Anesthetics, and Sedatives)

We pointed out that the vast majority of patients undergoing surgery with hypnotic procedures receive chemical analgesics, anesthetics, and sedatives. The vast majority of patients underoing surgery with acupuncture also receive these same types of medication. The most common medications that are used during surgery with acupuncture include (a) procaine (Novocain) or other local anesthetics which are applied to the area where the skin is to be cut and to internal structures that are sensitive to incision such as the peritoneum, (b) analgesics such as morphine and meperidine, (c) anesthetics such as sodium thiopental, methoxyflurane, and trichloroethylene, and (d) sedatives such as sodium phenobarbital (Changshan County People's Hospital, 1973; DeBakey, 1973; Eye, Ear, Nose, & Throat Hospital of Shanghai, 1973; Hua-Shan Hospital of Shanghai, 1973; Hunan Medical College, 1973; Peking Children's Hospital, 1973; Peking Hsuan-wu Hospital, 1973; Sin-Kaing Medical Hospital, 1973). The clinical reports from China indicate that these medications may be used alone or in combination. The amount of medication employed varies from relatively small amounts (*e.g.*, 50-60 mg. of Demerol, I.V.) to larger doses (*e.g.*, 10 mg. of morphine) depending on the type of surgery and the extent to which the patient shows signs of pain.

Suggestion

We have already pointed out that acupuncture patients are selected, in part, on the basis of their belief and faith in the efficacy of acupuncture. During the preoperative phase, additional implicit and explicit suggestions are administered to strengthen this pre-existing trust (Kroger, 1973; Wall, 1972; 1974). Although the specific suggestions that are provided to acupuncture patients have not been described in detail, Rhee (1972) has noted that "the acupuncturists whom I have watched work, load their therapy with suggestions."

Distraction

Before and during surgery, the acupuncture needles are stimulated continuously, sometimes manually but usually by electricity. The stimulation of the needles, which begins about 20 minutes prior to surgery and then continues during surgery, gives rise to various sensations that are described as sore, swollen, and heavy sensations and also boring, aching, radiating, and painful sensations (Changshan County People's Hospital, 1973; Chen, 1972; Eye, Ear, Nose, and Throat Hospital of Shanghai, 1973; Hua-Shan Hospital of Shanghai, 1973; Man & Chen, 1972; Mann, 1973; Shanghai Acupuncture Anesthesia Coordinating Group, 1973). There appears to be a growing consensus among Chinese investigators that (a) "the key to successful acupuncture anesthesia is dependent upon sufficient stimulation intensity" to produce the aforementioned sensations and (b) it is not especially important where the needles are placed provided that the needling makes the patient feel sore, swollen, and heavy (DeBakey, 1973; General Hospital of the Kwangchow Division of PLA, 1973; Peking Hsuan-wu Hospital, 1973; PLA General Hospital, 1973; Shanghai Acupuncture Anesthesia Coordinating Group, 1973).

The various deep sensations (including painful and even aching sensations) that are produced by stimulation of the acupuncture needles can very effectively distract the patient from the surgical procedures. For instance, in describing his own sensations while undergoing acupuncture for the relief of post-surgical abdominal pain, Reston (1972) noted that the needles "sent ripples of pain racing through my limbs and, at least, had the effect of diverting my attention from the distress in my stomach." As we have noted previously in this paper, many data support the notion that distraction is an effective technique for reducing pain.[8]

Experimental Studies of Acupuncture Analgesia

Within recent years, a number of investigators have attempted to study the reduction of experimentally-produced pain with acupuncture. Although some of these studies have found small reductions in reported pain (Anderson, Jamieson, & Man, 1974; Smith, Chiang, Kitz, & Antoon, 1974), most investigators find

[8]At first glance, the factors we have delineated may seem unsatisfactory in accounting for anecdotal reports in the popular press which suggest that acupuncture may be useful in performing surgery with rabbits, horses, and other mammals. The validity of these reports cannot be evaluated until studies are carried out which, at least, utilize minimal controls. Since there is evidence demonstrating that, under certain conditions of restraint, many mammals, including rabbits and horses, are refractory to stimuli which are thought to be extremely painful (Ratner, 1967), controlled studies are needed to determine whether acupuncture is helpful in operating on mammals.

it extremely difficult to demonstrate an attenuation of pain with acupuncture (Anderson & Holmgren, 1975; Brennan & Velduis, 1973; Clark & Yang, 1974; Day, Kitahata, Kao, Motoyama, & Hardy, 1975; Holmgren, 1975; Li, Ahlberg, Lansdell, Gravitz, Ting, Bak, & Blessing, 1974; Mann, 1973).

Undoubtedly additional data will be forthcoming that will help clarify the frequent failure of acupuncture to control experimental pain. At this point, however, it seems clear that acupuncture does not consistently produce the "profound insensitivity to pain" sometimes alluded to in the literature (Melzack, 1973).

Conclusion

At first glance, surgery performed with hypnotic procedures or with acupuncture seems very dramatic. It is now clear, however, that these techniques are used only with a small proportion of patients who have been carefully selected and that, even then, the pain reductions that are achieved may be much less than is generally believed. The successes of hypnotic procedures and acupuncture appear more dramatic than they really are because we overestimate the pain of many types of surgery; we fail to consider that, with the notable exception of the skin, the great majority of the tissues and organs of the body are insensitive to incision. Moreover, the assumption that pain reduction is due to "hypnotic trance" or to the acupuncture needles *per se* has led to a failure to consider the role played by a number of psychological factors that are effective in reducing anxiety and pain. These factors include the patient's belief in the efficacy of the techniques, the interpersonal relationship between the patient and the physician, special preoperative preparation or "education," implicit and explicit suggestions of analgesia, and distraction.

Much research remains to be done on the separate and combined effects of all of these factors in minimizing anxiety and pain. Up to now, much of the research documenting the effectiveness of these factors has focused on experimentally-induced pain. More systematic research is now needed to evaluate the role these factors can play in alleviating clinical pain. In fact, it appears to us that by explicitly utilizing these factors—for example, utilizing the distinctive suggestions for pain relief that are part of "hypnosis" and the powerful distraction that is produced by applying electricity to acupuncture needles—, we can reduce the dosages of analgesic and anesthetic drugs that are at present required in surgery.

REFERENCES

Anderson, M. N. Hypnosis in anesthesia. *Journal of the Medical Association of Alabama*, 1957, 27, 121-125.

Anderson, D. G., Jamieson, J. L., & Man, S. C. Analgesic effects of acupuncture on the pain of ice water: A double-blind study. *Canadian Journal of Psychology*, 1974, 28, 239-244.

Anderson, S. A. & Holmgren, E. Effects of conditioning electrical stimulation on the perception of pain. Proceedings of the Third World Symposium on Acupuncture and Chinese Medicine, *The American Journal of Chinese Medicine*, 1975, 3, Supplement No. 1, 21.

Anon., China's doctors on tours. *Medical World News*, Dec. 15, 1972, 13, 34-48.

August, R. V. Hypnosis as sole anesthesia for cesarean section. (Film). Kalamazoo, Mich.: Upjohn, 1963.

Barber, T. X. Toward a theory of pain: Relief of chronic pain by prefrontal leucotomy, opiates, placebos, and hypnosis. *Psychological Bulletin*, 1959, 56, 430-460.

Barber, T. X. "Hypnosis," analgesia, and the placebo effect. *Journal of the American Medical Association*, 1960, 172, 680-683.

Barber, T. X. Effects of hypnotic induction, suggestions of anesthesia, and distraction on subjective and physiological responses to pain. Paper presented at annual meeting of Eastern Psychological Association, Philadelphia, April 10, 1969.

Barber, T. X. "Hypnosis" and pain. In T. X. Barber, *LSD, marihuana, yoga and hypnosis*, Chicago: Aldine, 1970. Chap. 5.

Barber, T. X. & Cooper, B. J. Effects of pain of experimentally-induced and spontaneous distraction. *Psychological Reports,* 1972, 31, 647-651.

Barber, T. X. & Hahn, K. W., Jr. Physiological and subjective responses to pain producing stimulation under hypnotically-suggested and waking-imagined "analgesia." *Journal of Abnormal and Social Psychology*, 1962, 65, 411-418.

Barber, T. X., Spanos, N. P., & Chaves, J. F. *'Hypnosis,' imagination and human potentialities.* New York: Pergamon, 1974.

Beecher, H. K. Pain in men wounded in battle. *Annals of Surgery*, 1946, 123, 96-105.

Beecher, H. K. The powerful placebo. *Journal of the American Medical Association*, 1955, 159, 1602-1606.

Beecher, H. K. *Measurement of subjective responses.* New York: Oxford University Press, 1959.

Bernstein, M. R. Significant values of hypnoanesthesia: Three clinical examples. *American Journal of Clinical Hypnosis*, 1965, 7, 259-260.

Betcher, A. M. Hypnosis as an adjunct in anesthesiology. *New York State Journal of Medicine*, 1960, 60, 816-822.

Blitz, B., & Dinnerstein, A. J. Effects of different types of instructions on pain parameters. *Journal of Abnormal Psychology.* 1968, 73, 276-280.

Blitz, B., & Dinnerstein, A. J. Role of attentional focus in pain perception: Manipulation of response to noxious stimulation by instructions. *Journal of Abnormal Psychology*, 1971, 77, 42-45.

Bonica, J. J. Acupuncture anesthesia in the People's Republic of China: Implications for American medicine. *Journal of the American Medical Association*, 1974, 229, 1317-1325.

Bonilla, K. B., Quigley, W. F., & Bowers, W. F. Experience with hypnosis on a surgical service. *Military Medicine*, 1961, 126, 364-366.

Braid, J. Facts and observations as to the relative value of mesmeric and hypnotic coma, and ethereal narcotism, for the mitigation or entire prevention of pain during surgical operations. *Medical Times*, 1847, 15, 381-382.

Bramwell, J. M. *Hypnotism.* New York: Julian Press, 1956. (Original date of publication: 1903).

Brennan, R. W., & Veldhuis, J. Acupuncture anesthesia and dental pain—a controlled study. In H. P. Jenerick (Ed.) *Proceedings of the NIH Acupuncture Research Conference* (DHEW Publication no. NIH 74-165). Washington, D.C.: U.S. Government Printing Office, 1973.

Brown, P. E. Use of acupuncture in major surgery. *Lancet*, 1972, 1, 1328-1330.

Capperauld, I. Acupuncture anesthesia and medicine in China today. *Surgery, Gynecology and Obstetrics*, 1972, 135, 440-445.

Cassedy, J. H. Early uses of acupuncture in the United States, with an addendum (1826) by Franklin Bache, M.D. *Bulletin of the New York Academy of Medicine*, 1974, 50, 892-906.

Cattell, M. The action and use of analgesics. *Research Publications Association for Research in Nervous and Mental Disease*, 1943, 23, 365-372.

Changshan County People's Hospital. Acupuncture anesthesia in splenectomy: Report of 305 cases. *Chinese Medical Journal*, 1973, (2). (Translated by Andrew C. N. Chen)

Chaves, J. F. Acupuncture analgesia for surgery: A six-factor theory reconsidered. Proceedings of the Third World Symposium on Acupuncture and Chinese Medicine, *The American Journal of Chinese Medicine*, 1975, 3, Supplement No. 1, p. 24.

Chaves, J. F., & Barber, T. X. Needles and knives: Behind the mystery of acupuncture and Chinese meridians. *Human Behavior,* Sept., 1973, 2, No. 9, 19-24.

Chaves, J. F., & Barber, T. X. Cognitive strategies, experimenter modeling, and expectation in the attenuation of pain. *Journal of Abnormal Psychology,* 1974, 83, 356-363. (a)

Chaves, J. F., & Barber, T. X. Hypnotism and surgical pain. In T. X. Barber, N. P. Spanos, & J. F. Chaves, *Hypnosis, imagination, and human potentialities.* New York: Pergamon, 1974, Pp. 79-98. (b)

Chaves, J. F., & Barber, T. X. Surgery with acupuncture. In T. X. Barber, N. P. Spanos, & J. F. Chaves, *Hypnosis, imagination, and human potentialities.* New York: Pergamon Press, 1974, Pp. 135-160. (c)

Chaves, J. F., & Barber, T. X. Acupuncture analgesia: A six-factor theory. *Psychoenergetic Systems*, 1974, 1, 11-21. (d)

Chen, J. Y. P. Acupuncture. In J. R. Quinn (Ed.) *Medicine and Public Health in the People's Republic of China.* Washington, D.C.: U.S. Department of Health, Education, and Welfare, National Institutes of Health, 1972. Pp. 65-90.

Clark, W. C., & Yang, J. C. Acupunctural analgesia? Evaluation by signal detection theory. *Science*, 1974, 184, 1096-1098.

Cooper, S. R., & Powles, W. E. The psychosomatic approach in practice. *McGill Medical Journal*, 1945, 14, 415 438.

Coppolino, C. A. *Practice of hypnosis in anesthesiology.* New York: Grune & Stratton, 1965.

Craig, K. D., & Weiss, S. M. Vicarious influences on pain-threshold determinations. *Journal of Personality and Social Psychology,* 1971, 19, 53-59.

Crasilneck, H. B., McCranie, E. J., & Jenkins, M. T. Special indications for hypnosis as a method of anesthesia. *Journal of the American Medical Association*, 1956, 162, 1606-1608.

Day, R. L., Kitahata, L. M., Kao, F. F., Motoyama, E. K., & Hardy, J. D. A psychophysical evaluation of acupuncture anesthesia. Proceedings of the Third World Symposium on Acupuncture and Chinese Medicine. *The American Journal of Chinese Medicine*, 1975, 3, Supplement No. 1, 27-28.

DeBakey, M. E. A critical look at acupuncture. *Reader's Digest*, Sept. 1973, 137-140.

Demond, E. G. Acupuncture anesthesia: Western medicine and Chinese traditional medicine. *Journal of the American Medical Association*, 1971, 218, 1558-1563.

Dodson, H. C., Jr. & Bennett, H. A. Relief of postoperative pain. *American Surgeon*, 1954, 20, 405-409.

Egbert, L. D., Battit, G. E., Turndorf, H., & Beecher, H. K. The value of the preoperative visit by an anesthetist. *Journal of the American Medical Association*, 1963, 185, 553-555.

Egbert, L. D., Battit, G. E., Welch, C. E., & Bartlett, M. K. Reduction of postoperative pain by encouragement and instruction of patients. *New England Journal of Medicine*, 1964, 270, 825-827.

Esdaile, J. *Hypnosis in medicine and surgery.* New York: Julian Press, 1957. (Original date of publication: 1850).

Evans, M. B., & Paul, G. L. Effects of hypnotically suggested analgesia on physiological and subjective responses to cold stress. *Journal of Consulting and Clinical Psychology*, 1970, 35, 362-371.

Eye, Ear, Nose and Throat Hospital of Shanghai. Laryngectomy under acupuncture anesthesia. *Chinese Medical Journal*, 1973, (2). (Translated by Andrew C. N. Chen).

Finer, B. L. Experience with hypnosis in clinical anesthesiology. *Sartryck ur Opuscula Medica*, 1966, 4, 1-11.

Freemont-Smith, F. Discussion of Beecher's paper on perception of pain. Problems of Consciousness, First Conference. New York: Josiah Macy, Jr. Foundation, 1950.

Gammon, G. D., & Starr, I. Studies on the relief of pain by counterirritation. *Journal of Clinical Investigation*, 1941, 20, 13-20.

General Hospital of the Kwangchow Division of PLA. An inquiry into the analgesic principles of acupuncture anesthesia. *American Journal of Chinese Medicine*, 1973, 1, 172-176.

Goldie, L. Hypnosis in the casualty department. *British Medical Journal*, 1956, 2, 1340-1342.

Hardy, J. D., Wolff, H. G., & Goodell, H. *Pain sensations and reactions.* Baltimore: Williams & Wilkins, 1952.

Hilgard, E. R. A quantitative study of pain and its reduction through hypnotic suggestion. *Proceedings of the National Academy of Science*, 1967, 57, 1581-1586.

Hilgard, E. R. A neodissociation interpretation of pain reduction in hypnosis. *Psychological Review,* 1973, 80, 396-411.

Hilgard, E. R., Cooper, L. M. , Lenox, J., Morgan, A. H., & Voevodsky, J. The use of pain-state reports in the study of hypnotic analgesia to the pain of ice water. *Journal of Nervous and Mental Disease*, 1967, 144, 506-513.

Hill, H. E., Kornetsky, C. H., Flanary, H. G., & Wikler, A. Effects of anxiety and morphine on discrimination of intensities of painful stimuli. *Journal of Clinical Investigation*, 1952, 31, 473-480. (a)

Hill, H. E., Kornetsky, C. H., Flanary, H. G., & Wikler, A. Studies on anxiety associated with anticipation of pain. I. Effects of morphine. *Archives of Neurology and Psychiatry.* 1952, 67, 612-619. (b)

Hoffman, E. Hypnosis in general surgery. *American Surgeon*, 1959, 25, 163-169.

Houde, R. W., & Wallenstein, S. L. A method for evaluating analgesics in patients with chronic pain. *Drug Addiction and Narcotics Bulletin*, 1953, Appendix F, 660-682.

Hua-Shan Hospital of Shanghai. Observations on the analgesic effect of employing the Ch'uan Liao point in neurosurgery: Report of 619 cases. *Chinese Medical Journal*, 1973, (2). (Translated by Mark Harris and Andrew C. N. Chen)

Hunan Medical College. Acupuncture anesthesia in cardiac surgery. *Chinese Medical Journal*, 1973, (2). (Translated by Andrew C. N. Chen).

Jaffe, J. H. Narcotic analgesics. In L. S. Goodman and A. Gilman (Eds.) *The pharmacological basis of therapeutics.* (4th Ed.), New York: Macmillan, 1970, Chap. 15.

Johnson, R. F. Q. Suggestions for pain reduction and response to cold-induced pain. *Psychological Record*, 1974, 24, 161-169.

Kanfer, F. H., & Goldfoot, D. A. Self-control and tolerance of noxious stimulation. *Psychological Reports*, 1966, 18, 79-85.

Kaplan, E. A. Hypnosis and pain. *Archives of General Psychiatry*, 1960, 2, 567-568.

Kelsey, D., & Barron, J. N. Maintenance of posture by hypnotic suggestion in a patient undergoing plastic surgery. *British Medical Journal*, 1958, 1, 756-757.

Kornetsky, C. Effects of anxiety and morphine in the anticipation of painful radiant heat stimuli. *Journal of Comparative and Physiological Psychology,* 1954, 47, 130-132.

Kroger, W. S. Introduction and supplemental reports. In J. Esdaile *Hypnosis in medicine and surgery.* New York: Julian Press, 1957.

Kroger, W. S. Acupunctural analgesia: Its explanation by conditioning theory, autogenic training, and hypnosis. *American Journal of Psychiatry*, 1973, 130, 855-860.

Kroger, W. S., & DeLee, S. T. Use of Hypnoanesthesia for cesarean section and hysterectomy. *Journal of the American Medical Association*, 1957, 163, 442-444.

Lassner, J. (Ed.) *Hypnosis in anesthesiology.* Berlin: Springer-Verlag, 1964.

Laszlo, D., & Spencer, H. Medical problems in the management of cancer. *Medical Clinics of North America*, 1953, 37, 869-880.

Lederman, E. I., Fordyce, C. Y., & Stacy, T. E. Hypnosis, an adjunct to anesthesiology. *Maryland Medical Journal*, 1958, 7, 192-194.

Lennander, K. G. Ueber die Sensibilität der Bauchhöhle und über lokale und allgemeine Anästhesie bei Bruch-und Bauchoperationen. *Centralblatt für Chirurgie*, 1901, 8, 209-223.

Lennander, K. G. Beobachtungen über die Sensibilität in der Bauchhöhle. *Mitteilungen aus den Grenzgebieten der Medizin und Chirurgie*, 1902, 10, 38-104.

Lennander, K. G. Weitere Beobachtungen über Sensibilität in Organ und Gewebe und über lokale Anästhesie. *Deutsche Zeitschrift für Chirurgie*, 1904, 73, 297-350.

Lennander, K. G. Ueber Hofrat Nothnagels zweite Hypothese der Darmkolikschmerzen. *Mitteilungen aus den Grenzgebieten der Medizin und Chirurgie*, 1906, 16, 19-23. (a)

Lennander, K. G. Ueber lokale Anästhesie und uber Sensibilität in Organ und Gewebe, weitere Beobachtungen. *Mitteilungen aus den Grenzgebieten der Medizin und Chirurgie*, 1906, 15, 465-494. (b)

Lewis, T. *Pain.* New York: Macmillan, 1942.

Li Choh-luh, Ahlberg, D., Lansdell, H., Gravitz, M. A., Ting, Ching-Yuan, Bak, A., & Blessing, D. *Acupuncture, hypnosis, and pain.* National Institutes of Health (Mimeo), 1974.

Lozanov, G. Anaesthetization through suggestion in a state of wakefulness. *Proceedings of the 7th European Conference on Psychosomatic Research*, Rome, 1967, 399-402.

Man, P. L., & Chen, C. H. Acupuncture "anesthesia"—A theory and clinical study. *Current Therapeutic Research,* 1972, 14, 390-394.

Mandy, A. J., Mandy, T. E., Farkas, R., & Scher, E. Is natural childbirth natural? *Psychosomatic Medicine*, 1952, 14, 431-438.

Mann, F. Paper presented at New York University School of Medicine, Symposium on Acupuncture, 1973.

Marmer, M. J. The role of hypnosis in anesthesiology. *Journal of the American Medical Association*, 1956, 162, 441-443.

Marmer, M. J. Hypnoanalgesia: The use of hypnosis in conjunction with chemical anesthesia. *Anesthesia and Analgesia*, 1957, 36, 27-32.

Marmer, M. J. *Hypnosis in anesthesiology.* Springfield, Ill.: C. C Thomas, 1959.

Marmer, M. J. Discussion. In J. Lassner (Ed.) *Hypnosis in anesthesiology,* Berlin: Springer-Verlag, 1964.

Mason, A. A. Surgery under hypnosis. *Anesthesia*, 1955, 10, 295-299.

Melzack, R. How acupuncture can block pain. *Impact of Science on Society*, 1973, 23, 65-75.

Mitchell, J.F. Local anesthesia in general surgery. *Journal of the American Medical Association*, 1907, 48, 198-201.

Moll, A. *The study of hypnosis.* New York: Julian Press, 1958. (Original date of publication: 1889).

Morgan, A. H., Lezard, F., Prytulak, S., & Hilgard, E. R. Augmenters, reducers, and their reaction to cold pressor pain in waking and suggested hypnotic analgesia. *Journal of Personality and Social Psychology*, 1970, 16, 5-11.

Notermans, S. L. H. Measurement of pain threshold determined by electrical stimulation and its clinical application. Part I. Method and factors possibly influencing the pain threshold. *Neurology*, 1966, 16, 1071-1086.

Orne, M. T. Psychological factors maximizing resistance to stress: With special reference to hypnosis. In S. Z. Klausner (Ed.) *The quest for self-control*, New York: Free Press, 1965.

Ostenasek, F. J. Prefrontal lobotomy for the relief of intractable pain. *Bulletin of the Johns Hopkins Hospital*, 1948, 83, 229-236.

Owen-Flood, A. Hypnotism and the anesthetist. *British Journal of Anaesthesia*, 1955, 27, 398-404.

Peking Children's Hospital. Acupuncture anesthesia in pediatric surgery: Report of 1308 cases. *Chinese Medical Journal*, 1972, (2). (Translated by Andrew C. N. Chen).

Peking Hsuan-wu Hospital. Acupuncture anesthesia in neurosurgery. *Chinese Medical Journal*, 1973, (2). (Translated by Mark Harris and Andrew C. N. Chen).

PLA General Hospital. Some insights concerning the principles of acupuncture anesthesia. *American Journal of Chinese Medicine*, 1973, 1, 167-171.

Ratner, S. C. Comparative aspects of hypnosis. In J. E. Gordon (Ed.) *Handbook of Clinical and Experimental Hypnosis*. New York: Macmillan, 1967, Pp. 550-587.

Reis, M. Subjective reactions of a patient having surgery without chemical anesthesia. *American Journal of Clinical Hypnosis*, 1966, 9, 122-124.

Reston, J. Now, about my operation. In *Acupuncture: What Can It do for You?* New York: Newspaper Enterprise Association, 1972. Pp. 8-11.

Rhee, J. L. Introductory remarks: "Acupuncture: The need for an indepth appraisal." In *Transcript of the Acupuncture Symposium*. Los Altos, Calif.: Academy of Parapsychology and Medicine, 1972. Pp. 8-10.

Sampimon, R. L. H., & Woodruff, M. F. A. Some observations concerning the use of hypnosis as a substitute for anesthesia. *Medical Journal of Australia*, 1946, 1, 393-395.

Schultz, J. H. Some remarks about the technique of hypnosis as an anaesthetic. *British Journal of Medical Hypnotism*, 1954, 5, No. 3, 23-25.

Schwarcz, B. E. Hypnoanalgesia and hypnoanesthesia in urology. *Surgical Clinics of North America*, 1965, 45, 7547-7555.

Scott, D. L. Hypnoanalgesia for major surgery — A psychodynamic process. *American Journal of Clinical Hypnosis*, 1973, 16, 84-91.

Shanghai Acupuncture Anesthesia Coordinating Group. Why surgical operations are possible under acupuncture anesthesia. *American Journal of Chinese Medicine*, 1973, 1, 159-166.

Shor, R. Explorations in hypnosis: A theoretical and experimental study. Unpublished doctoral dissertation, Brandeis University, 1959.

Sin-Kaing Medical Hospital. Summary of 10 cases of breast cancer surgery under acupuncture anesthesia. *Chinese Medical Journal*, 1973, (2). Translated by Andrew C. N. Chen).

Smith, G. M., Chiang, H. T., Kitz, R. J., & Antoon, A. Acupuncture and experimentally induced ischemic pain. In Bonica, J. J. (Ed.) *International symposium on pain*, New York: Raven Press, 1974, Pp. 827-832.

Spanos, N. P., & Barber, T. X. Toward a convergence in hypnosis research. *American Psychologist*, 1974, 29, 500-511.

Spanos, N. P., Barber, T. X., & Lang, G. Effects of hypnotic induction, suggestions of analgesia, and demands for honesty on subjective reports of pain. In H. Condon & R. E. Nisbett (Eds.), *Thought and feeling: Cognitive alteration of feeling states.* Chicago: Aldine, 1974.

Spanos, N. P., Horton, C., & Chaves, J. F. The effects of two cognitive strategies on pain threshold. *Journal of Abnormal Psychology*, 1975, 84, 677-681.

Steinberg, S., & Pennell, E. L., Jr. Hypnoanesthesia — A case report on a 90-year-old patient. *American Journal of Clinical hypnosis*, 1965, 7, 355-356.

Taugher, V. J. Hypno-anesthesia. *Wisconsin Medical Journal*, 1958, 57, 95-96.

Tinterow, M. M. The use of hypnotic anesthesia for major surgical procedures. *American Surgeon*, 1960, 26, 732-737.

Tkach, W. A firsthand report from China: "I have seen acupuncture work," says Nixon's doctor. *Today's Health*, 1972, 50, No. 7, 50-56.

Trent, J. C. Surgical anesthesia, 1846-1946. *Journal of the History of Medicine*, 1946, 1, 505-511.

Tuckey, C. L. Psychotherapeutics; or treatment by hypnotism. *Woods Medical and Surgical Monographs*, 1889, 3, 721-795.

Van Dyke, P. B. Hypnosis in surgery. *Journal of Abdominal Surgery*, 1965, 7, 1-5, 26-29.

Wall, P. An eye on the needle. *New Scientist*, July 20, 1972, 129-131.

Wall, P. Acupuncture revisited. *New Scientist*, October 3, 1974, 30-34.

Wallace, G., & Coppolino, C. A. Hypnosis in anesthesiology. *New York Journal of Medicine*, 1960, 60, 3258-3273.

Werbel, E. W. *One surgeon's experience with hypnosis.* New York: Pageant Press, 1965.

Winkelstein, L. B., & Levinson, J. Fulminating pre-eclampsia with Cesarean section performed under hypnosis. *American Journal of Obstetrics and Gynecology,* 1959, 78, 420-423.

Zimbardo, P. G., Cohen, A. R., Weisenberg, M., Dworkin, L., & Firestone, I. Control of pain motivation by cognitive dissonance. *Science*, 1966, 151, 217-219.

Zwicker, M. Discussion. In J. Lassner (Ed.) *Hypnosis in anesthesiology*. Berlin: Springer-Verlag, 1964.

No-Nonsense Therapy for Six Sexual Malfunctions

Helen Singer Kaplan

Since William H. Masters and Virginia E. Johnson published their research on the physiology of sexual intercourse, and talk about sex has become respectable, a growing number of men and women know they are being cheated. They are seeking help at new sex therapy clinics throughout the nation.

In our clinic at Cornell University Medical School, we see couples who have one or more of the six basic sexual problems:

1 Male impotence: inability to produce or maintain an erection.

2 Premature ejaculation: inability to control orgasm.

3 Retarded ejaculation: inability to trigger orgasm.

4 General female sexual dysfunction: lack of erotic response to sexual stimulation, commonly called frigidity.

5 Female orgasmic dysfunction: difficulty in reaching orgasm.

6 Vaginismus: spasm of the muscles at the entrance of the vagina, preventing penetration.

As sex therapists we deal first and foremost with immediate sexual problems, so that women and men can enjoy sex to its fullest. However, we also attack the conflicts and defenses that are obstacles to sexual functioning. We are, of course, concerned with *why* a man persists in wilting his erection by obsessively monitoring his own behavior, or why he is so worried about performing sexually, or what experiences and fantasies make a woman so insecure that she cannot ask her lover to stimulate her clitoris. But we are primarily interested in teaching individuals to abandon themselves completely to the erotic experience of sexual intercourse.

To do this, we teach patients sexual exercises to remove the immediate anxieties and defenses that create and maintain their anti-erotic environment. We employ psychotherapy when deep anxieties or underlying pathologies impede our progress. I present a detailed discussion of our philosophy and treatment in *The New Sex Therapy*, published by Brunner/Mazel last spring.

Friction and Fantasy

We begin treatment of all sexual dysfunctions with a psychiatric examination of both partners, a detailed history and assessment of their sexual functioning, and an evaluation of the marital relationship. We give the couple a clear picture of what to expect during treatment, and we make a therapeutic contract with them that clearly establishes their responsibility for treatment.

Sex is composed of friction and fantasy; deficiencies in either can produce problems. A pleasurable sexual response depends both on receiving the proper sexual stimulation and responding freely to it. Most couples with sexual problems practice poor, insensitive and ineffectual sexual techniques.

Some inadequate lovemaking results merely from a couple's misinformation or ignorance about sex. Frequently, for instance, neither spouse knows where the clitoris is or recognizes its potential for eliciting erotic pleasure. They have intercourse as soon as the husband has an erection, and he ejaculates without considering whether his partner is ready. Such couples genuinely wonder why the wife does not reach orgasm. Both partners contribute to this sexual ineffectiveness. She will not ask for the kind of stimulation she wants because she is unaware of her own needs; he doesn't know that he's not a very effective lover. So, in silence, they continue their unsatisfactory sexual habits.

In other couples, feelings of guilt or anxiety about erotic needs prevent one or both partners from enjoying sex. They may actively discourage their partners from stimulating them effectively. Careful questioning often reveals that such persons respond to sexual excitement by immediately stopping the activity which produces it. The man who is excited by an actively seductive woman may literally forbid his wife to be aggressive. The woman who is responsive only to slow tender caresses may push her husband away when he tries to kiss her breasts or to caress her buttocks. Patients who avoid effective sexual expression tend to focus on genital stimulation and on orgasm, and are apt to neglect the sensual potential of the rest of their bodies and of nonorgasmic eroticism.

Some persons have as much difficulty giving pleasure as others do in receiving it. These individuals don't provide their partners with enough sexual stimulation because they lack either the knowledge and sensitivity to know what to do, or they are anxious about doing it. Others are consciously or unconsciously hostile towards their mates and don't really want to please them.

Sexual Defenses

Therapists have overlooked immediate sources of anxiety until the advent of the new sex therapy. Traditional approaches to sexual dysfunction looked for subtle and profound anxiety sources, such as oedipal conflicts and marital power struggles. We find there are also more obvious reasons for sexual anxiety, such as fear of sexual failure, fear that the partner expects too much, or fear that the partner will reject sexual advances. These fears create various sexual defenses and introduce conscious control into lovemaking, which in turn prevents persons from abandoning themselves to the experience.

We have found that the three male dysfunctions, impotence, retarded ejaculation, and premature ejaculation, all seem to be associated with some form of sexual conflict, but there are different symptoms for each dysfunction, and each of them responds to different therapeutic strategies and tactics.

1

Premature ejaculation is one of the most common and easily relieved male complaints. Men with this malady are unable to control voluntarily their ejaculatory reflex. Once they become sexually aroused, they reach orgasm very quickly. Some ejaculate after several minutes of foreplay, others just prior to or immediately upon entering their partner's vagina, and others after only a few pelvic thrusts. The essential problem, however, is not how quickly the man ejaculates, but his inability to control the reflex. In contrast to a premature ejaculator, an effective lover continues to engage in sex play while he is in a highly aroused state. He is able to forestall climax until his partner, who is slower to respond, can reach orgasm. At the least, prematurity restricts the couple's sexuality; at worst, it destroys it.

Most men who suffer this distress are unhappy about their condition, and often employ a variety of common-sense techniques to relieve the difficulty. They shift their attention to non-sexual thoughts during intercourse, tense their anal muscles, bite their lips or dig their fingernails into their palms. In this manner they can delay the onset of intense erotic arousal, but once aroused, they still can't control ejaculation. They feel sexually inadequate, and guilty that they have not satisfied their partners.

The term "primary prematurity" refers to a man who has never been able to control orgasm. If he is otherwise healthy, there is little reason to suspect his difficulty arises from a physical cause. On the other hand, a physician should conduct thorough urological and neurological exams on the secondary ejaculator, a man who has developed the problem after a history of good control. Diseases of the posterior urethra or pathology along the nerve pathways serving the orgasmic reflex mechanisms may cause secondary prematurity. Sex therapy should begin only after a physician rules out any physical basis for the condition.

Small Comfort

Different therapeutic schools emphasize various psychological explanations for premature ejaculation. Psychoanalysts say it is the result of a neurosis, marriage counselors believe it comes from hostilities between the partners, common-sense theorists blame it on excessive sensitivity to erotic sensation. Masters and Johnson contend that stressful conditions during a young man's initial sex experiences bring on premature ejaculation, while Wardell Pomeroy, co-author of the Kinsey reports, says that anxiety is the culprit. All these speculations may be theoretically interesting, but they are of little comfort to the patient.

In 1956, James Semans, a urologist, demonstrated a simple manipulative technique to help cure premature ejaculation. Semans realized that the distinguishing feature of premature ejaculation was the rapidity of the orgasmic reflex. Consequently, his treatment goal was to prolong the reflex. To do this, he directed the patient's wife to stimulate her husband's erect penis until he felt he was just about to have orgasm, and signaled her to stop. When he could recapture control, the patient would tell her to resume stimulation until he again felt the sensations that signaled ejaculation. Again she would stop. Over a period of several weeks the couple practiced this stop-start method until the patient could tolerate stimulation without ordering a halt. At this point, his prematurity was permanently cured.

Semans reported on eight men who were premature ejaculators, and in every case the symptom disappeared. Other clinicians have used his method with the same success. I believe the technique works because it focuses a man's attention on the sensations preceding orgasm. Apparently he has previously failed to acquire control because he has not received, or let himself receive, the sensory feedback necessary to bring the reflex under control.

In our treatment program at Cornell we teach the patient to clearly identify his intensely erotic preorgasmic sensations and, initially, to avoid being distracted by his wife's needs. We advise the couple that, provided they adhere to the prescribed therapeutic exercises, we can cure the symptom in most cases.

We use a variation of the Semans "stop-start" method in our treatment. The couple carries out their exercise assignments in their home. After three or four of these noncoital sessions, the patient usually feels he has attained some improvement in orgasmic control. We then suggest that the couple attempt intercourse using the same stop-start method. They first have coitus with the woman in the superior position, then while both lie on their sides, and finally with the man on top. Since this is usually the most stimulating position for the male, he has conquered his problem when he can maintain control in this position.

Husband First

This procedure can be quite unexciting and frustrating for the wife. Therefore, we suggest that the couple work out an agreement previous to treatment where the husband stimulates his wife to orgasm before or after the stop-start treatment. If the wife is unable to have an orgasm, we tell her that our first goal is to cure her husband's prematurity, then we can shift treatment to her.

If either partner resists any part of the treatment procedures, we root out the cause and intervene with appropriate psychotherapy. This might involve marriage counseling, psychoanalysis, or anxiety-reduction techniques. During therapy we continue to reinforce the couple's progress by reminding them that in a relatively short time, most, if not all, premature ejaculators respond to treatment.

2

Whereas the man suffering from prematurity cannot control orgasm, the retarded ejaculator cannot trigger it. Men with a mild form of this disorder can ejaculate by employing fantasy or distracting themselves from their sexual worries, or by additional stimulation. A few others have never experienced orgasm. At one time clinicians thought retarded ejaculation was a relatively rare phenomenon. Now it appears it may be highly prevalent, at least in its mild forms. At Cornell, we are seeing an increasing number of patients with this difficulty.

The Old-Time Religion

In its mildest form, a man's ejaculatory inhibition is confined to specific anxiety-provoking situations, such as when he is with a new partner, or when he feels guilty about the sexual encounter. The patient who seeks help, however, usually is more severely restricted in his sexuality. The man who suffers from primary ejaculatory retardation has had the difficulty since his first attempt at sexual intercourse, has never achieved orgasm during coitus, but may be able to achieve it by masturbation, manipulation or oral stimulation. Secondary retarded ejaculators enjoyed a period of good sexual functioning before the onset of retarded ejaculation; commonly, a specific trauma brought on their difficulty. Like the premature ejaculator, the retarded ejaculator often anticipates failure and frustration, which can eventually impair his ability to sustain an erection.

Few physical illnesses play a role in retarded ejaculation. Clinical evidence suggests that a strict religious upbringing, sexual conflict from an unresolved oedipal complex, strongly suppressed anger, ambivalence toward one's partner, fear of abandonment, or a specific sexual calamity are causes of retarded ejaculation.

Our treatment goal is to overcome the mechanism that inhibits ejaculation and resolve the underlying problems that impede sexual functioning. We use a series of progressive sexual exercises to relieve the patient of his anxieties and fears about the sexual act. We start with the couple performing the sexual practices that can elicit any existing ejaculatory capacity. As the patient is successful in one situation, he moves on to a more threatening or difficult one. Concurrently, the psychotherapy sessions at the clinic foster the patient's insight into any of his irrational fears, traumatic memories or destructive interactions with his partner that inhibit ejaculation.

Masters and Johnson cured 14 out of 17 retarded ejaculators using a similar method. Our preliminary results are similar to theirs. One of our successful cases was Mr. J., who had been in psychoanalysis for some time when he came to our clinic.

No Ejaculation

We traced Mr. J.'s difficulty to the traumatic termination of a sexual relationship. He had left his wife and four children for another woman, who subsequently left him. He became deeply depressed and sought psychoanalytic treatment. Although his depression subsided during analysis, he continued to have ejaculatory problems.

The patient had remarried, and his new wife agreed to cooperate in our sex therapy program. Before entering treatment, they had worked out a way to have frequent and enjoyable sex, except for the limits imposed by his inability to ejaculate during intercourse. They would engage in imaginative sex play and have intercourse until she reached orgasm. Then she would stimulate him manually or orally until he achieved orgasm.

Treatment in this case was brief and effective. First we instructed the couple to participate in sex play without intercourse or orgasm. Then she stimulated him to orgasm with his penis near the mouth of her vagina. Finally, we told the wife to stimulate her husband almost to orgasm, at which point he was to enter the vagina with strong pelvic thrusting. In order to ejaculate during coitus, Mr. J. initially needed to fantasize that his wife was stimulating him orally, but gradually he could ejaculate without distracting himself from lovemaking with fantasy.

At the same time that Mr. and Mrs. J. practiced the sexual desensitization exercises at home, we conducted psychotherapy with them at the clinic. Their relationship had many immature elements in it. He was infantile, jealous and demanding, and haunted by the fear that his wife would leave him. At times, she acted like a stubborn, irresponsible and provocative child. In the therapeutic sessions we discussed the quality of their relationship from this perspective. Two years after we terminated therapy, we were pleased to learn that the patient had retained his ejaculatory competence, felt well, and seemed more assertive and less anxious.

3

A man who suffers from impotence is often almost unbearably anxious, frustrated and humiliated by his inability to produce or maintain an erection. Although he may become aroused in a sexual encounter and want to make love, he can't. He feels his masculinity is on the line. Clinicians and researchers estimate that half the male population has experienced at least transient impotence. Men seek help only when the problem becomes chronic.

Primary impotence is the rarest and most severe form of the disorder; men who suffer from it have never been potent with a woman, although they may be able to attain good erections in other situations. Secondary impotence is less severe, but still debilitating. These patients functioned well for some time prior to their erective difficulties. The prognosis for treating impotence depends on how long the patient has suffered from it and how severe it is. Here again, the prospective candidate should have a thorough physical checkup before he goes into therapy. Stress, fatigue, undiagnosed diabetes, hepatitis, narcotics use, low androgen levels and other physical factors may cause impotence.

Depression and Discord

Although some traditional therapists believe impotence is always a sign of a deep underlying pathology, we believe there are often more obvious and immediate causes. Fear of sexual failure, pressures created by an excessively demanding wife, and guilt or conflict may prevent a man from producing or maintaining an erection. Therefore, we feel our brief, symptom-focused form of treatment is preferable to lengthy, reconstructive insight therapy that essentially ignores the immediate antecedents of impotence. Masters and Johnson report they cured 70 percent of their secondary impotent patients using treatment very similar to ours.

Because depression or marital discord can accompany or cause impotence, we must often relieve these symptoms before we can treat the man's impotence. Therefore, we always combine sexual tasks at home with therapeutic sessions in the clinic. The following case history demonstrates the variability and flexibility of this combined approach.

A 26-year-old Jewish law student applied for treatment. Although he and his 29-year-old West-Indian wife reported they had enjoyed a good sexual relationship during the year and a half they lived together, he began to have erectile difficulty after they were married, and she admitted that even while they lived together, intercourse was often hurried and more infrequent than she wished. Most recently, the patient had been unable to achieve an erection under any circumstances, and had lost all interest in sex. In the course of our initial evaluation and interview, the patient admitted that he had experienced potency problems with girls of his own ethnic background before he met his wife. But he emphasized that he had functioned well with her at first.

The wife had no sexual problems. She had orgasm during coitus, but only if intercourse lasted for 10 minutes or more. She could climax through clitoral stimulation, but was reluctant to allow him to engage in this activity.

Although there were many elements in the patient's psychiatric and family history that could indicate underlying psychological reasons for his impotence, we did not raise those issues in therapy. They had no immediate relevance to our belief that the cause of the patient's impotence was his wife's demands for frequent intercourse of long duration, and his progressive fear of failure.

We saw the couple in our office once a week. We also instructed them to gently caress each other during sexual play at home, but not to engage in coitus. We encouraged the wife to accept clitoral stimulation to orgasm if her sexual tension became excessive. These exercises produced intense excitement in both partners. He experienced a spontaneous erection, and, "against our advice," their passion led them to try coitus. The wife did not reach orgasm, but the patient felt sufficiently encouraged by his success to attempt intercourse again the following night. This time, he lost his erection when he became afraid he would be unable to sustain it long enough to bring his wife to orgasm.

Erotic Abandon

We talked about their experience in the next therapeutic session. When the wife understood the destructive effect of her sexual demands, she admitted for the first time that her husband was not very skilled at clitoral stimulation. Moreover, she said she felt this form of stimulation was "homosexual." We corrected her misconception and encouraged the couple to communicate more freely with each other about their sexual responses.

This couple developed a good sexual partnership, free of the pressures and demands which had caused his impotence. Without making her husband feel deficient the wife achieved postcoital orgasm by clitoral stimulation when she did not climax during intercourse. He learned to abandon himself to his erotic sensations. We terminated treatment after four therapeutic sessions, conducted over a three-week period, and the couple reported no difficulty in sexual functioning a year later.

This case was relatively simple. Others are more difficult. Impotence can be tenacious, and we often have to employ extensive psychotherapy to relieve the anxieties produced by deep-seated pathology or by marital discord.

In contrast to male dysfunctions, the female sexual dysfunctions are not as clearly understood. For example, the term "frigidity" is confusing on two counts. Because it has traditionally referred to all forms of female sexual inhibition, covering both total lack of erotic feeling and the inability to have orgasm, it fails to convey the fact that these are two separate components of the female sexual response. It also implies that women who suffer from inhibitions are cold and hostile to men, which is both inaccurate and pejorative.

Confusion also centers on the relationship between female orgasm and coitus. Some clinicians believe that if a woman cannot achieve orgasm during coitus, she suffers from sexual dysfunction. Others do not attach any particular importance to how a woman reaches a climax. Our clinical experience supports the second viewpoint. A woman who is otherwise orgasmic, but who does not reach orgasm during coitus, is neither frigid nor sick. This pattern seems to be a

normal variant of female sexuality for some women. Our impression is that eight to 10 percent of the female population has never experienced orgasm, and of the 90 percent who have, only about half do so regularly during intercourse.

We also believe no one can yet resolve the debate about whether there are one or two female orgasms. But physiological data do give us an idea of how women experience climax. Apparently, the stimulation of the clitoris or the surrounding area triggers orgasm, but women respond to and perceive the climax primarily in the vagina.

Women are slower than men to become aroused, and their arousal signs are much less obvious than the male's erect penis. Because men cannot easily discern whether or not a woman is ready for intercourse, and because women are culturally conditioned to put their husbands' needs first, couples often proceed to coitus before the woman is sufficiently aroused to reach orgasm during intercourse.

Gentle Sensitivity

A woman's reluctance to express her needs, however, is not always based on cultural paranoia. Women may run a real risk of displeasing their husbands if they become sexually assertive. Such behavior repels some men, who regard women who assume active roles in sex as aggressive, castrating females. Other men feel threatened when their wives express sexual needs. They think their partners are challenging their sexual adequacy. Too often men fail to realize that they can become good lovers if they simply support their partners with gentle, sensitive stimulation instead of perpetual erection.

The inability of some women to become aroused even though they receive adequate stimulation probably indicates some underlying sexual conflict. A restrictive upbringing; a hostile marital relationship; severe psychopathology; conflicts about the female role in lovemaking; fear of men, of losing control, of rejection and abandonment can cause female sexual dysfunctions.

4

General sexual dysfunction, usually referred to as frigidity, is the most severe of the female inhibitions. Women plagued with it derive little, if any, erotic pleasure from sexual stimulation. They are essentially devoid of sexual feelings. Many nonresponsive women consider sex an ordeal. Those who suffer from primary frigidity have never experienced erotic pleasure, and those who have secondary general sexual dysfunctions responded at one time to sexual stimulation, but no longer do so. Typically, these patients were aroused by petting before marriage, but lost the ability to respond when intercourse became the exclusive objective of all sexual encounters.

To help these nonresponsive women, we create a relaxed, sensuous ambience to permit the natural unfolding of sexual responses during lovemaking. To help foster such an environment, we encourage the couple to communicate openly about their sexual feelings and wishes, and we prescribe systematic sensuous and erotic experiences for the couple to perform at home.

Masters and Johnson developed a technique called sensate focus which is an ingenious and invaluable tool in treating general female sexual dysfunction. This exercise consists of having the couple forego sexual intercourse and orgasm while the wife caresses her husband's body, after which he stimulates her in like manner. By telling the wife to act first, we help counteract her guilt about receiving something for herself, and her fear that her husband will reject her. When we free women from the pressure to produce orgasm, they often experience erotic and sensuous sensations for the first time.

When the patient reports that she feels sensuous and erotic during the sensate focus exercises, we expand the caressing to include light, teasing genital play. After the husband caresses his wife's body he gently touches her nipples, clitoral area, and vaginal entrance. The woman guides his actions verbally and nonverbally. If, during these sessions, he becomes too sexually aroused, we tell the patient to bring him to orgasm manually or orally after she has had a chance to experience nonpressured, reassuring genital play.

Premonitory Sensations

Genital stimulation typically produces a definite increase in the patient's sexual responsiveness. When she reaches a high level of erotic feeling during these exercises, the couple moves on to intercourse. On top of her husband, she initiates coitus with slow and exploratory thrusts at first, while she focuses her attention on the physical sensations emanating from her vagina. If her partner's urge to ejaculate becomes too intense during her thrusting, we tell the couple to separate. The husband manually stimulates his wife until his premonitory orgasmic sensations disappear and they can resume intercourse. They repeat this cycle several times until she feels like driving for orgasm. If she does not want to try to reach climax, the couple proceeds with coitus until the husband reaches orgasm.

Frequently these sexual experiences evoke highly emotional responses and resistances in the patient. We use these feelings to help identify the specific obstacles which impede her eroticism. We deal with these obstacles on both an experiential level and in psychotherapy.

There is a good chance that women who suffer from general sexual dysfunction will improve. To a great extent the outcome of treatment seems to depend on the quality of the patient's relationship with her husband. If he does not reject her and she has no deep-seated psychopathology, the great majority of these women learn to enjoy sex and to reach orgasm.

5

Problems in reaching orgasm are probably the most prevalent sexual complaint of women. A woman suffers from primary orgasmic dysfunction if she has never experienced an orgasm, and from secondary orgasmic dysfunction if the disorder developed after a period of being able to reach orgasm. An inorgasmic woman has an absolute problem if she can't achieve orgasm under any circumstances, and a situational one if she can reach a climax only under specific circumstances. Women who suffer solely from orgasmic problems frequently have strong sex drives. They fall in love, enjoy sex play, lubricate copiously, and love the sensation of phallic penetration. They simply get stuck at or near the plateau phase of the sexual response.

Women who can achieve orgasm only by masturbation when they are alone, or those who must use vibrators for half an hour to reach orgasm obviously have a problem. But when a clinician sees a woman who can climax during masturbation, or when her husband stimulates her either manually or orally, but she cannot reach orgasm during coitus, he often faces a dilemma. It is difficult for a therapist to decide whether she is suffering from a pathological inhibition or whether she merely exhibits a normal variation of female sexuality. If the clinician cannot uncover any sexual anxieties, conflicts or fears during his initial interview with the couple, he should probably reassure them that she functions within the normal sexual range, and encourage them to work out lovemaking patterns that satisfy them both. However, if they still want to achieve coital orgasm, we will accept them, and try to increase her sexual responsiveness. Some of these women learn to climax during coitus, and others do not.

At Home, Alone

The first goal of therapy with a woman who has never experienced orgasm is to eliminate as many inhibiting factors as possible from the sexual environment so she can have her first climax. Because it is the rising tide of clitoral sensations which triggers the female climax, and because women are least threatened when they are alone, we first instruct the inorgasmic woman to masturbate at home alone in an environment free from possible interruption. If several attempts at this fail to produce orgasm, we tell her to use an electric vibrator to stimulate her clitoris. Some sexologists feel the vibrator is the only significant advance in sexual technique since the days of Pompeii. Because the patient may become "hooked" on this device, however, we transfer her to manual stimulation as soon as she has had a few orgasms using the vibrator.

When she can stimulate herself to orgasm regularly, we bring her husband into the treatment program. First we instruct them to make love in the usual way, telling her not to make any special effort to achieve orgasm during coitus. After he has ejaculated, and there is no pressure on her to perform quickly, he uses the vibrator or stimulates her manually to orgasm. We tell her to be utterly "selfish," and to focus on her own sensations. After a few of these sessions some women climax during intercourse without the manual stimulation.

One of our patients was a 28-year-old social worker who had never experienced orgasm. Her husband was a 34-year-old physician. They were very much in love, and were frequent and passionate lovers. During the early years of their marriage, Mrs. E. had simulated orgasm because she was afraid her husband would feel hurt and guilty if he knew she could not climax. A year before they sought treatment, she admitted to Dr. E. that she could not reach orgasm, and since then he had tried to bring her to orgasm by clitoral stimulation.

Mrs. E. arrived for the initial interview alone. She explained she had been reluctant to ask her husband to come because of his busy schedule. This was typical of her overprotectiveness of him. We explained that he would have to participate in treatment, and scheduled the first therapy session for two weeks later. In the meantime we instructed her to try to reach orgasm with an electric vibrator.

Missed Signal

At our next meeting, Mrs. E. told us she had easily achieved orgasm with a vibrator in solitude. But she was afraid to ask her husband to use the vibrator to stimulate her clitoris. She thought it would repel him and make him feel inadequate. He reassured her that this was not true, and said he was eager to try to bring her to orgasm.

We also learned that Mrs. E. never abandoned herself completely to her sexual feelings, because, like many other women, she was overly concerned with satisfying and pleasing her husband. This meant that the couple's lovemaking was never governed by her needs. This was not Dr. E.'s fault. Often he aroused her to a high level of sexual tension, but at this point she would think, "That's enough, he must be getting tired." And she would signal him to begin coitus. Not surprisingly, he misinterpreted her signal to mean that she was ready to commence coitus because she too was ready to have an orgasm.

It became clear that the patient's orgasmic inhibition was not associated with severe psychopathology or marital difficulties. It was her great need to please her husband, motivated by her own insecurity.

We treated this couple by enhancing the communication between them, prescribing sexual experiences to sensitize Mrs. E. to her own feelings, and by helping her develop a sense of responsibility for obtaining her husband's adequate stimulation to bring her to orgasm. Both the therapist and her husband reassured her that her sexually assertive behavior would not diminish her husband's sexual enjoyment or jeopardize their relationship.

We encouraged Mrs. E. to develop sexual autonomy during lovemaking, and to assume responsibility for obtaining pleasure, first during foreplay and then during coitus. We instructed her to ask her husband to stimulate her, and tell him where to kiss and caress her. If he ejaculated during intercourse, she was to ask him to stimulate her to orgasm. We also helped her stop monitoring her own progress toward orgasm, which distracted her from her sexual sensations.

Dr. E.'s acceptance of Mrs. E.'s growing sexual maturity and activity helped her progress. After 12 sessions, she easily reached orgasm via clitoral stimulation and was beginning to experience coital orgasm. Both enjoyed sex tremendously, and after therapy Mrs. E. became more assertive and happier in general.

More common than the woman who has never had an orgasm is the patient who is orgastic in low tension situations, but cannot reach a climax under circumstances that make her even slightly anxious. She may be able to climax during solitary masturbation, but not when she is with a partner. We treat these patients by uncovering and resolving the specific conflicts which inhibit the patient.

Bridge Maneuvers

With a woman who cannot have orgasm during intercourse, our goals are to identify and remove any psychic blocks or marital problems that inhibit her during coitus, to have her perform erotic tasks to heighten her sexual arousal, enhance her awareness of and pleasure in her vaginal sensations and to maximize clitoral stimulation. We find that techniques that combine coitus with clitoral stimulation are very helpful. These are called "bridge" maneuvers.

A great majority of women, including those who suffer from absolute primary orgasmic inhibition, are able to achieve orgasm after a relatively brief period of therapy. Indeed, orgasmic inhibition is virtually 100 percent curable if the sole criterion for cure is the ability to reach orgasm. But, as mentioned before, some women never reach orgasm during intercourse, which suggests that the phenomenon is a normal variant of female sexual response.

6

The third, and relatively rare, female sexual dysfunction is vaginismus. Anatomically, a vaginismic woman is normal, but whenever a man tries to penetrate her vagina, the vaginal muscles literally snap the entrance shut so that intercourse is impossible. Physicians often must conduct vaginal examinations on these women under anesthesia. This disorder is due to an involuntary spasm of the muscles surrounding the vaginal entrance. These patients are usually afraid of vaginal penetration and intercourse. They often suffer from general sexual dysfunction or orgasmic inhibition. However, many women who seek treatment for vaginismus are sexually responsive and highly orgastic.

Vaginismus results from a woman's association of pain or fear with vaginal penetration. The precipitating event may be physical pain or psychological stress. A rigid hymen, inflammatory pelvic diseases and tumors, childbirth pathologies, and hemorrhoids may cause it. Strict religious upbringing, a husband's impotence, or the psychological effects of rape also may bring on vaginismus, or it may result from ignorance and misinformation about sex, or guilt caused by deep sexual conflicts.

Tolerating Motion

Our basic strategy for treating vaginismus is simple, provided all physical pain-producing conditions have been corrected. Our first goal is to uncover the basis for the patient's phobic avoidance of vaginal entry.

Then, with progressive sexual exercises, we try to decondition the involuntary spasm of the muscles that guard the entrance to the vagina.

First we have both the patient and her husband examine her genitals in the privacy of their well-lit bedroom. We tell them to find and examine the exact location of the vaginal opening. In the first sexual assignment, we tell the woman to gently insert her own or her husband's finger into her vagina. When her usual discomfort disappears we tell her to move her finger back and forth inside her vagina until she can tolerate the motion without discomfort. We always allow the woman to control the situation to reduce her fears and apprehensions. Next, the husband or wife inserts two fingers in the vagina, and then rotates them gently, stretching the walls of the vagina. When she can tolerate this, the couple proceeds to intercourse. First they lie still with the man's penis inserted in his wife, then the husband begins gentle thrusting at his wife's signal and withdraws if she wishes him to. Finally the couple thrusts to orgasm. Concurrently we conduct therapy sessions with the couple to work on the patient's phobia about vaginal penetration.

We have achieved excellent and permanent results with women who suffer from vaginismus. Masters and Johnson report they achieved a 100 percent cure rate. We find that the length of treatment is more variable than that for the other sexual dysfunctions because of the tenacity of the phobia. But we have been able to resolve the phobic avoidance in 10 psychotherapy sessions. Within three to 14 weeks, we can go on to cure the vaginal spasm with four to eight home exercise sessions.

Sex therapy promises, and experience suggests it delivers, rapid and permanent relief of distressing sexual problems for many. But we have not scientifically substantiated its merits in a controlled study.

There can be no doubt, however, in light of the clinical evidence and the compelling conceptual considerations which underlie this approach, that the new methods merit further trial and development. We need to know which kinds of problems we can best treat with sex therapy, and under what conditions. We must learn precisely what components of these complex methods are actually responsible for the observed changes. At the present stage in its development, however, sex therapy appears to have great value. Indeed, it may close the door on sexual boredom and agony in America.

Biologic Studies [on Sexual Identity Conflict in Children and Adults]

R. Green

Biologically oriented researchers continue their quest for a physiological, anatomical, or hormonal basis of unusual sexual behavior. History's pendulum continues its swing. At the close of the nineteenth century, biologists reigned and Krafft-Ebing's view that male and female sex centers in the brain controlled behavior was typical of its time. Even Freud postulated a biological foundation for the direction of human sexuality. Thus, sensory overendowment in the region of the anus was thought to predispose males to homosexuality. Over the decades, disappointments in not finding biological differences between homosexuals and heterosexuals, coupled with the advent of psychoanalytic and learning theory formulations, resulted in a full swing. Postnatal experiences were the sole determinants of sexual orientation.

A rapprochement may be upon us. Animal research of the 1960s and hormonal assays of the 1970s have ushered in a gradual return to the middle. Animals have been bred that behave contrary to what might be expected by nature of their anatomy, because of changing sex hormone levels before birth. A behaviorally masculine female rhesus monkey results if she is exposed to high levels of male hormone as a fetus. And, a behaviorally feminine male rat or dog results when deprived of male hormone during a comparable period.

In humans, circulating levels of sex hormones have become amenable to ultrasensitive assay. While previous methods involved breakdown products extracted from whole-day urine samples, newer techniques permit exquisite determinations from small samples of blood. Suddenly, differences in clinical subgroups have been reported, and the study of human sexual behavior has entered a new phase of speculation and research.

During these latter years, isolated patient examples and small patient series have occasionally been published correlating a neuroanatomic abnormality or an unusual hormonal status with atypical sexuality. While many of the case reports are more intellectually titillating than scientifically conclusive, they cannot go unnoticed. They demand attention in any integrated attempt to fathom the determinants of masculinity and femininity.

Chapter 3 from *Sexual Identity Conflict in Children and Adults* by Richard Green, M.D. Copyright ' Richard Green, 1974, Basic Books, Inc., Publishers, New York.

Neuroanatomic Abnormalities and Atypical Sexual Behavior

The presence within the same person of both a physically demonstrable brain abnormality and unusual sexual behavior tempts one to draw a causal relation between the two. Unquestionably, space-occupying tumors can cause personality change, as can patterns of abnormal electrical discharge. Furthermore, from animal experimentation it is clear that there are discrete areas within the brain responsible for some aspects of sexual behavior. Thus it is possible that in humans a lesion could, if properly located, have an effect on sexual behavior.

Unfortunately, detailed clinical histories of patients with atypical sexual behavior and brain pathology are usually missing from case reports. Typically it is reported: "The patient showed no evidence of cross-dressing prior to the onset of his cerebral pathology at age thirty-five." Researchers would be on more solid ground if details were known of cross-dressing activities in childhood and the extent of any undue interest in cross-dressing in subsequent years, even if not practiced. Implications differ considerably whether transvestism with concurrent brain pathology occurs in a person with no previously latent impulses to cross-dress, or in someone with a longstanding preoccupation suddenly rendered less capable of suppression. Furthermore, it is also known that adults with no previous history of atypical sexuality may begin showing such behavior relatively late in life without evidence of anatomic brain pathology.

The Temporal Lobe

With increased sophistication in electroencephalographic techniques for measuring brain waves, interest has focused on abnormal rhythms in association with atypical sexuality. Dysrhythmias are of considerable interest because they may represent subtle evidence of brain pathology, possibly present in populations of seemingly healthy persons. Furthermore, the abnormal locus is accessible to experimental manipulation by the use of drugs that may modify electrical discharge and by restricted surgical removal of abnormal cells.

An oft-quoted case report is that of a man sexually aroused by safety pins who also had temporal lobe epilepsy. A "perverse form of erotic gratification, the contemplation of a safety pin, [had] become attached to the onset of the epileptic seizure. . . ." Surgical removal of the left anterior temporal lobe relieved both the epilepsy and the unusual pattern of sexual arousal (Mitchell et al., 1954).

The case report of a thirty-eight-year-old woman with "sexual seizures" in association with destruction of one temporal lobe is of interest both for the vivid detail of the "automatic" sexual behavior and the subsequent amnesia, characteristic of temporal lobe epilepsy. The patient had primary syphilis at sixteen. At thirty-six she complained of a four-year history of a feeling of itching in the pubic area, accompanied by a feeling that a red hot poker was being inserted into her vagina. The patient would then spread her legs apart, beat both hands on her chest, and "verbalize her sexual needs (often in vulgar terms)." She would have no memory for these episodes. Neurological tests revealed bilaterally dilated brain ventricles and changes consistent with tissue loss in the right temporal lobe. This was thought to be due to syphilis. An anticonvulsant drug brought the seizures under some degree of control (Freeman and Nevis, 1969).

Removal of specific brain areas resulting in changes in sexual behavior is a longstanding observation. Over thirty years ago, Kluver and Bucy (1939) described, in the male monkey, a behavior pattern produced by bilateral removal of the temporal lobe areas. Three to six weeks later these monkeys displayed considerable masturbation and mounting of both males and females. In the human, a case has been reported of a nineteen-year-old male who had a similar operative procedure and who two weeks later showed atypical sexual behavior. He reported his attention was attracted by the sexual organs of an anatomic diagram hanging on the wall and displayed to his doctor that he had spontaneous erections, followed by masturbation and orgasm. He also showed, after surgery, heterosexual indifference, in contrast to his previous behavior, and made homosexual invitations (Terzian and Dalle Ore, 1955).

The role of the temporal lobe in persons requesting sex-change surgery has been studied. One report described nearly half of twenty-six subjects who crossdressed and wanted sex change as having abnormal electrical patterns (Walinder, 1965). However, no matched controls were included in that series, and the criteria of abnormality are not known. Furthermore, another study failed to find the same incidence of abnormality (only two of fifteen transsexuals) (Blumer, 1969).

A larger survey looked at the medical records of eighty-six men in an anti-epileptic clinic in Czechoslovakia. A history indicating brain damage (usually from infection or trauma) was found more often among epileptics who manifested a deviation in sexual behavior than among epileptics with nondeviant sexuality. When comparing sexually typical and atypical men with temporal lobe epilepsy, those with atypical sexuality had developed epilepsy earlier in life (Kolarsky et al., 1967). However, before implicating abnormal brain foci in producing both epilepsy and unusual sexuality, it should be noted that only 10 percent of the epileptic men showed such behavior, an incidence which may be no higher than the nonepileptic population.

Sexual arousal to hair in association with a left temporal lobe tumor has also been described. The patient from age four experienced an intense preoccupation with women's long hair. By ten he had intermittently dressed in women's clothes and, in his twenties, would pay prostitutes to allow him to stroke their hair while being masturbated. Psychologic treatment for the hair fetish resulted in loss of symptoms for eighteen months. Subsequently, major seizures ensued during sleep, and the hair fetish returned. Though his electroencephalogram showed a normal electrical pattern, he was found three months later to have a brain tumor. Both the seizures and the hair fetish came under some degree of control with medical treatment (Ball, 1968).

Focal Brain Destruction As Treatment

Neuroanatomical knowledge gained from animal research has been recently applied to treatment of atypical human sexuality. In the rat, and other species, the ventromedial nucleus of the hypothalamic portion of the brain plays a role in regulating sex hormone secretion. Extending the implications of this finding to the human, a team of surgeons treated a forty-year-old male attracted to young boys by destroying the nucleus in one side of his brain. A seven-year postoperative follow-up report indicated a reduction in sexual drive and capacity for erection and an absence of previous sexual orientation. Urinary hormone levels and seminal fluid were described as normal.

A second patient treated more recently by the same team had a sexual attraction to early adolescent males coupled with an aversion to females. He regarded his behavior as an organic disease and "at once agreed to a stereotaxic procedure to remove the 'sex behavior center.'" At short-term follow-up (six months) he reported no homosexual fantasies and no further revulsion to women. A third patient was an elderly male also sexually attracted to young boys who subsequently reported a sex drive diminished in intensity, but not direction (Roeder and Muller, 1969).

The extent to which the results of this procedure are due to interference with the central regulation of male hormone secretion (with its resultant loss of sex drive) or to a direct destructive influence of a hormone sensitive brain area, *or* to the high motivation for change and expectation of help by patients who agree to such a procedure is difficult to assess. Also, the fact that one-sided brain lesions in animals do not appear to affect sexual behavior makes interpretation of this report difficult.

Neuroendocrine Abnormalities and Atypical Sexual Behavior

Recent studies have focused on the interaction between sex hormones and the developing brain in determining later sexuality. Sex hormones may differentiate the central nervous system in a manner analogous to that in the peripheral reproductive system (Grady, Phoenix, and Young, 1965). Thus, while it was previously known that male hormone was required for the genitalia to proceed along male lines, recent findings suggest that male hormone may also be required for the brain to differentiate in a male-type direction.

Of considerable significance for understanding sexual development is that the basic biologic disposition of mammalian embryos is female. No gonads and no sex hormones are required for a fetus to develop in a female direction. For maleness to emerge, androgenic or male hormones must act at critical developmental periods. This was demonstrated initially in the rabbit when a male fetus castrated *in utero* subsequently developed along female lines (Jost, 1947). In the human, the syndromes of Turner (gonadal dysgenesis) and testicular feminization (androgen insensitivity) strikingly illustrate the analogous phenomenon. Children with Turner's syndrome generally have but one sex chromosome (X), develop neither functional ovaries nor testes (and thus do not secrete gonadal hormones), and appear to be female at birth (Money, 1968). Children with testicular feminization are chromosomally male (XY), have testes that secrete normal amounts of testosterone, but their body cells are unable to utilize it (Simmer, Pion, and Dignam, 1965; Rivarola et al., 1967). At birth they appear to be normal females (Money, 1968).

Excessive Male Hormone in the Female

Early evidence that prenatal levels of androgenic hormone may influence postnatal sex-related *behavior* was first demonstrated in the guinea pig and then the nonhuman primate. In the primate, a "tomboy" female rhesus monkey results if the fetus is exposed to large amounts of male hormone from injections given her mother. Normal preadolescent male and female rhesus monkeys behave quite differently, much in the same way as do boys and girls. The male monkey more often participates in rough-and-tumble play, chasing activity, and threatening behavior. Females who have received male hormone *before* birth, however, in addition to being genitally virilized, are considerably more "masculine" in their behavior. Comparable amounts of male hormone given *after* birth, on the other hand, do not appear to have the same masculinizing effect (Young et al., 1964).

These nonhuman primate studies provide speculative appeal for a related phenomenon operating in man. Although it is not possible to conduct parallel experiments with humans, there are some circumstances in which human females have been exposed to unusually high levels of male hormone before birth.

In the adrenogenital syndrome a defect in the production of some adrenal hormones results in excessive production of others that are genitally masculinizing. This overproduction begins before birth and continues postnatally, unless treated. Fifteen preadolescent girls exposed to excessive androgen before birth, but not after, have been studied. The diagnosis of adrenogenital syndrome had been made in infancy so that androgen excess was medically terminated. This natural experiment is somewhat analogous to the monkey procedure mentioned earlier. These girls were compared with fifteen girls in whom there was no evidence of male hormonal excess before birth. These androgen-exposed girls showed much less interest in doll play, more interest in boys' toys, less satisfaction in being girls, and were more likely to be considered tomboys (Ehrhardt, Epstein, and Money, 1968). However, the investigators point out that seven of the fifteen androgenized girls had been thought to be boys at birth but were reassigned as girls before seven months. Since the parents knew of the genital masculinization at birth, "this knowledge may have insidiously influenced their expectancies and reactions regarding the child's behavioral development."

Also studied were a group of twenty-three adult females who were exposed to excessive androgen levels not only prenatally but, because they were not treated during childhood, for at least eight years *after* birth as well. Sexual preferences as adults were assessed. Of the twenty-three, only two had had frequent homosexual contacts, and neither was exclusively homosexual. None were transsexual and desirous of sex-change surgery (Ehrhardt, Evers, and Money, 1968). Thus high androgen exposure before and after birth does not appear to result in homosexuality or transsexualism in the female.

Finally, a group of ten girls, aged three to fourteen was studied which had been exposed to progestins before birth—administered to prevent abortion in the mother. Progestins, although "female" hormones in that they are similar to progesterone, have a masculinizing effect. Nine of the girls showed a strong interest in boys' toys; six an interest in organized team sports, and nine liked to compete with boys in sports. Only two liked frilly dresses and nine were called "tomboy" by their parents and/or themselves. However, in one family a sister who had *not* received progestin was at least as tomboyish as her hormone-exposed sister (Ehrhardt and Money, 1967). Thus, this latter study, as well as that of the girls with the adrenogenital syndrome, is suggestive of a masculinizing effect on behavior as a result of high prenatal doses of androgen.

Deficient Male Hormone in the Male

Testicular Feminization
The testicular feminizing syndrome (androgen insensitivity) is a human parallel to animal laboratory studies in which male fetuses are deprived of male hormone. These persons, unable to utilize androgen, have undescended testes and the male chromosome pattern XY. At birth, they appear to be normal infant females, are designated female, raised as girls, and later show appropriately feminine behavior. At puberty they develop feminine breasts presumably via the chemical breakdown of testosterone (secreted by the testes) to female hormones. The absence of menstruation (there is no uterus), or removal of an inguinal mass found to be a testis, frequently leads to the diagnosis. Such persons are very feminine, are not aware they are chromosomal and gonadal males, and live their lives as sterile women. It is possible that the absence of male-hormonal influence on the fetal nervous system enhances their capacity to adjust so readily to the female role (Money, Ehrhardt, and Masica, 1968).

Transsexualism
A neuroendocrine basis for transsexualism, where the preferred sex role is opposite to anatomic determinants, is a provocative concept. From animal work it is evident that at least in some species there exists a period of behavioral sexual differentiation in response to male hormone exposure, as well as a period of genital differentiation, and that these two critical time periods may be separate (Whalen, Peck, and LoPiccolo, 1966). Thus it is possible to approach in the laboratory a model of transsexualism in which a "female mind exists in a male body" and vice versa. This could result from a male hormone deficiency at a critical de-

velopmental period, resulting in an anatomically normal-appearing male with an unmasculinized or undifferentiated nervous system. However, it is not necessary to postulate a global neural organization in a male or female direction as the effect of an excess or deficiency of androgen. The effect could be on nonspecific variables such as aggressivity and activity. These factors might subtly influence early mother-child and peer-child relations. For example, a passive boy might be treated more delicately by his parents and might find the games and companionship of girls more aggreeable than the rough-and-tumble of more aggressive boyhood. Evidence presented in this text demonstrates the importance of such early experiences in shaping gender identity and gender role activities.

In the great majority of cases of transsexualism there is presently no evidence that such a hormonal imbalance may have existed. However, there are a few patients in whom there is some basis to make this speculation. Recently there has been reported a series of three males desirous of living as women in whom a testicular defect was discovered (Baker and Stoller, 1968).

Case One appeared to be a normal male at birth and was so raised. However, he developed a feminine social orientation, and behaved as a girl from age four. At twenty-eight, after he had requested surgical sex reassignment to live as a female, microscopic examination of the testes revealed an abnormality with a relative excess of "Sertoli" cells. There is uncertainty as to whether such testes produce abnormal amounts of female hormone; however, it is of interest that Sertoli-Cell tumors in dogs *are* feminizing.

Case Two also appeared to be a normal male at birth but insisted during childhood on behaving as a girl. During adolescence his body became feminized with small but feminine breasts with well developed nipples. Facial hair did not appear until his twenties. At thirty, he requested sex reassignment to live as a female. Testicular examination and chromosomal study revealed an intersexed state, XXY, and small, underfunctioning testes.

Case Three, similarly feminine during childhood, was subsequently diagnosed as having a pituitary gland deficiency, one consequence of which was lowered testicular androgens. As an adult he reported feeling like a woman unless his usual low levels of androgen were supplemented by injections. (It was not possible to rule out the effects of suggestion here on enhanced feelings of masculinity.)

These cases of a female identity in a male, all with evidence of deficiently functioning testes, may represent the clinical result of male hormone deficiency at a critical period in central nervous system development. Or, they may represent the combined effect of specific experiential childhood factors superimposed on a receptive brain substrate with the latter influenced by fetal male hormone deficiency. *Or*, they may represent the coincidental existence of two independent phenomena, feminine identification and hypogonadism.

Most recently, another sample of males desirous of sex change has been studied using sophisticated biochemical measures. Both the pattern of sex hormone secretion and the responsivity of certain tissues to male hormone have been measured. Earlier studies of rodents indicated that a male, deprived of androgen at a critical developmental period, released gonad-stimulating substances in a cyclic pattern similar to the normal female, rather than in the steady male pattern (e.g., Harris, 1964). In rats the pattern is determined by androgen action on the hypothalamus. An indirect way of assessing whether there may have been a deficiency of hypothalamic exposure to androgen during the early development of male transsexuals thus presented itself: determining the release pattern of these substances. The hypothesis was not confirmed. The pattern was revealed to be tonic, i.e., normal male.

In a second strategy, scrotal skin of transsexuals and nontranssexuals was exposed to radioactively labeled androgen, and the quantity later present in the tissues was assessed. Here, again, no differences between the two groups were found (Gillespie, 1971). However, since the peripheral reproductive organs of male-to-female transsexuals are typically normal, there is little reason to suspect a deficiency in androgen utilization at such sites. These studies complement the earlier finding that the concentration of male hormones in plasma and female hormones in urine was the same for male transsexuals and nontranssexuals (Migeon et al., 1969). When coupled with the finding noted earlier that females with the andrenogenital syndrome (and thus exposed to high levels of male hormone) do not become female-to-male transsexuals, and yet another finding that female-to-male transsexuals had normal plasma male hormone levels (Jones, 1971), these are important negative reports. They must be considered by those who would ascribe transsexualism to a purely endocrine etiology.

Homosexuality

A revival of interest in a hormonal basis of homosexuality has been spurred by the development of ultrasensitive measures of gonadal hormones. Several provocative studies have been reported. In one, twenty-four-hour urine samples from forty males were analyzed for levels of two breakdown products of the principal male hormone, testosterone. The ratio of urinary etiocholanalone versus androsterone differed for the homosexuals and heterosexuals. Caution must be exercised, however, before concluding that the different ratio is directly related to sexual preferences. Three *hetero*sexuals reported in the same study, who were severely depressed, also had urinary levels like the homosexuals, as did one heterosexual diabetic (Margolese, 1970). Additionally, a more recent study has been unable to confirm this finding (Tourney and Hatfield, 1972). However, a third study (Evans, 1972) did replicate the Margolese finding, thus leaving the issue unsettled.

Loraine and co-workers (1970) compared a small number of hetero- and homosexual females and males. Levels of male hormone were higher and female hormone lower in four homosexual females, while male hormone was lower than normal in two homosexual males.

A most provocative study has compared thirty young adult male homosexuals with fifty male heterosexuals for plasma testosterone levels and additionally has examined the semen of the homosexuals. Those males who were exclusively or almost exclusively homosexual had testosterone levels approximately one half that of the heterosexuals. Additionally, there was a correlation between sperm count and degree of homosexuality, with fewer sperm being associated with a greater degree of homosexual orientation (Kolodny et al., 1971). Again, caution must be exercised pending confirmation on other subjects with rigorous attention paid to possibly confounding variables, such as stress. It could be, for example, that greater stress experienced by homosexuals, because of societal prohibitions, influences the findings. Evidence exists from other studies that stress lowers the secretion rate of testosterone. In the male rodent, for example, exposure to a variety of stressors not only lowers plasma testosterone but also decreases testicular size (Christian, 1955; Bardin and Peterson, 1967). Additionally, in the human male, exposure to military training and actual combat has been shown to significantly lower both urinary excretion rates and plasma levels of testosterone (Rose et al., 1969; Kreuz et al., 1972). More recently, another team of investigators (Tourney and Hatfield, 1972) has been unable to confirm the Kolodny finding.

Estrogen-Progesterone Treatment of Diabetic Women

During the past two decades pregnant diabetics at the Joslin Clinic in Boston have been given high doses of estrogen along with smaller amounts of progesterone. Hormones were administered during pregnancy in an effort to reduce the high fetal mortality rate associated with diabetes. Forty males born of these pregnancies (twenty aged sixteen; twenty aged six) have been compared with same-aged boys of untreated mothers. Both age groups of hormone-treated boys were found to be less aggressive and less athletic (Yalom, Green, and Fisk, 1973). However, the degree to which chronic illness (diabetes) of the hormone-treated mothers (rather than hormones) affected their sons' behavior is uncertain.

Overview

The additional hormonal dimension required to differentiate male characteristics may help explain why, at the clinical level, psychosexual anomalies are commoner in males (e.g., homosexuality, fetishism, transsexualism, pedophilia, sadism, voyeurism, etc.). In a dual system in which one path automatically evolves and the alternate requires specific influences at specific intervals, more errors are probable along the latter path. An additional nonhormonal hurdle for the male infant may be the necessity of psychologically differentiating himself from the first person with whom he is intimate—a female (Greenson, 1967).

While the measurement of gonadal hormones has been greatly simplified by new techniques, understanding their role has been rendered even more complex. Specific hormonal forms appear to act at specific sites and to affect specific functions. One androgen may be critical for masculine differentiation of the genital system and another for defeminizing specific areas of the brain (Goldfoot, Feder, and Goy, 1969; Luttge and Whalen, 1970, 1971). Thus any hormonal differences shown in human subgroups must take into account laboratory findings on the possible sites and modes of action of the compounds under study.

Sex Chromosomes and Sex Behavior

It is a comparatively recent development that chromosomes have become individually visible. Only within the last few years have the consequences of omissions and excesses of chromosomal elements become known. As the incidence of sex chromosome anomalies in the male is about one in five hundred consecutive births, the number of persons so affected is considerable. Controversy exists over the possible interrelation of these chromosomal abnormalities and cross-gender behavior. Several male patients have been described with an extra X chromosome (presumably a step toward genetic femaleness) who are also transvestites or transsexuals (Money and Pollit, 1964; Baker and Stoller, 1968). However, it is difficult to rule out sampling bias as the numbers are small, and such patients are more likely to find their way into the literature. It is also difficult to control for the influence of the somatic manifestations of having an extra X chromosome (a degree of female-type breast development, small genitalia) on a male's self-concept. The issue may be settled by prospective studies in which males identified at birth as having an extra X chromosome undergo longitudinal psychologic study.*

The importance of direct chromosomal observation notwithstanding, that ability may historically come to be but a small beginning. The person with testicular feminization has a normal male chromosomal pattern (44 + XY). Yet, hidden within a normal-appearing chromosome is an invisible genetic defect that renders that male incapable of realizing its masculine potential.

The manner in which gonadal hormones, brain anatomy, and sexual behavior are interrelated defies precise description. If man were solely dependent on relatively simple chemical-cellular interactions, responding as lower animals in a relatively more programmed manner, delineating key mechanisms would be difficult enough. In the human, overlaid with the profound influences of a lifetime of interpersonal experiences and mediated by a more sophisticated central nervous system network, the task of orderly arrangement of all the operant influences approaches the insurmountable. For the present we must content ourselves with descriptions of case reports that alert us to the finding that striking relationships among gonadal hormones, anatomical structures, and sexual behavior may exist. Each new finding merely enlarges the complexity with which the relationship can be viewed. It would be equally hazardous to accept a purely neuroanatomic or neuroendocrine basis of human sexual behavior as it would be to discard all the above findings as irrelevant and inconsequential to man when viewed against psychoanalytic or learning theory formulations.

*S. Walzer, personal communication, 1972.

The Promise and Peril of Psychosurgery

Richard Restak

Psychosurgery is a term used rather broadly these days to describe surgical, electrical, and other alterations of the brain to change human behavior. An important distinguishing feature of any psychosurgical procedure is irreversibility. Once the brain tissue is altered, it can never be the same again. Since the brain is the essence of what we refer to as personality, it follows that psychosurgery irrevocably alters personality. Even at its best, therefore, psychosurgery is the most hazardous form of psychiatric treatment yet devised and currently the most controversial.

Over the past year experts in medicine, behavior, ethics, and law have clashed over the most fundamental question in the field: Who should designate candidates for psychosurgery and for what symptoms? Should a brain operation to reduce aggression, say, be recommended by a neurologist? A psychiatrist? A social worker? This confusion is inherent in our primitive understanding of the way the brain functions. Since we do not know how it performs "normally," we are even more at a loss to predict how it will perform after surgery. Some examples:

- In San Francisco a fifty-five-year-old minister suffering from an incurably painful cancer undergoes "psychosurgery." In three months he returns free of pain to the pulpit after an absence of four years.
- In Jackson, Mississippi, a psychosurgeon operates on a fourteen-year-old boy with explosively violent behavior. After the surgery he is withdrawn and cannot remember his address. After further operations he is described as "deteriorated intellectually."

Last spring the National Institute of Mental Health sponsored a conference on psychosurgery. Appearing by invitation was Dr. O. J. Andy, director of neurosurgery at the University of Mississippi School of Medicine in Jackson. Dr. Andy, perhaps this country's leading proponent of psychosurgery as a solution to the problem of chronic psychiatric disease, explained his position to the conferees:

All abnormal behavior results from structurally abnormal brain tissue. Now, psychiatric techniques are in most instances futile in dealing with these abnormalities. In fact,

Saturday Review World, September 25, 1973. Copyright 1973 Saturday Review, Inc.

adequate therapy can be obtained only by techniques, such as surgery, which deal directly with the structurally abnormal brain tissue.

(When pressed on this point, Dr. Andy is willing to admit that no one has demonstrated abnormalities in the structure of brain tissue in psychiatric disease.)

It is unfortunate that our institutions are constantly filled with patients having behavioral disorders which do not respond to psychiatric and medical therapy and which would respond to surgery but are denied appropriate treatment for a variety of rational and irrational reasons. My own clinical interest has been in the realm of controlling aggressive, uncontrollable, violent, and hyperactive behavior which does not respond to medical or psychiatric therapy. I have developed a clinical description of such behavior: the Hyperresponsive Syndrome. This is erratic, aggressive, hyperactive, and emotional instability which in its full-blown expression terminates in attack. These are the patients who need surgical treatment. In addition, there are others: patients who are a detriment to themselves and to society; custodial patients who require constant attention, supervision, and an inordinate amount of institutional care. It should be used in children and adolescents in order to allow their developing brain to mature with as normal a reaction to its environment as possible.

Dr. Andy went on to explain that many of his subjects have been children aged seven and over; at least one was a child of five. The goal in each case is "to reduce the hyperactivity to levels manageable by parents."

The exact number of operations performed by Andy lies between forty and fifty, but he is not sure exactly how many. Moreover, several children have had more than one operation; in at least one case, five different operations were required in order to bring about "behavioral control."

At one point in Dr. Andy's address, he was interrupted by a question regarding the medical ethics of his psychosurgical procedures. He replied:

The ethics involved in the treatment of behavioral disorders is no different from the ethics involved in the treatment of all medical disorders. The medical problems involving behavior have a more direct impact on society than other medical problems such as coronary or kidney disease. Still, if treatment is desired it is neither the moral nor the legal responsibility of society what type of treatment should be administered. The ethics for the diagnosis and treatment of behavioral illness should remain in the hands of the treating physician.

As of this writing, Dr. Andy has returned to Mississippi to continue his highly individual approach to disturbed behavior or, as he prefers to call it, "structurally abnormal brain tissue." What further operations will be performed will be entirely up to Andy and the other psychosurgeons across the country. At this point there are no binding standards of performance by which psychosurgeons can be judged.

The concept of modifying behavior by surgically cutting parts of the brain is not new. First references to such a procedure can be traced to the Roman observation that insanity might be relieved by a sword wound in the head. But all modern psychosurgical methods date from physiologist James Fulton's observation that cutting a specialized group of nerve fibers from the frontal lobes of the brains of two chimpanzees, Becky and Lucy, led to a taming of the animals. The chimps could remember old tricks, even learn new ones, but accepted test situations and frustrations with a "philosophical calm."

In 1936 Egas Moniz, a Portuguese neurologist, applied a similar technique to uncontrollable psychotics. Thirteen years later Moniz won the Nobel Prize and was commended for "the development of prefrontal leucotomy in the treatment of certain psychoses." The number of lobotomies, as this procedure came to be called, performed by Moniz is unknown. Any exact computation is complicated by Moniz's early retirement from neurologic practice several years before a violent death at the hands of a crazed former patient.

In 1942 Walter Freeman, a neurologist, and James Watts, a neurosurgeon, both at George Washington University Hospital, reported that extreme depression and agitation, even hallucination, could be greatly alleviated by cutting the fibers leading from the frontal lobes of the brain to the neighboring thalamus. The connections between these two structures are normally responsible for a delicate interplay between thought (a frontal lobe function) and emotion (at least partly a thalamic function). After cutting these connections, the doctors reported that exaggerated emotional responses decreased. Although hallucinations might continue, they would be far less terrifying.

The Freeman-Watts treatment spread quickly, and during the 1940s somewhere in the range of 50,000 patients were lobotomized in the United States alone. Freeman, a lobotomy zealot, calculated he had personally performed over 4000 operations, using a gold-plated ice pick, which he carried with him in a velvet-lined case. After the local application of a mild pain killer, Freeman would plunge the ice pick through the thin bone of the upper inner angle of the eye socket, severing the frontal nerve connections to the thalamus. No elaborate preparations or precautions preceded this grisly operation, which often took place in the patient's home or in Freeman's office at St. Elizabeth's Hospital. Freeman's enthusiasm for "ice-pick surgery" knew no bounds; several former associates, who prefer to remain unnamed, can recall long lines of patients waiting for treatment outside Freeman's office.

Unfortunately, these lobotomies, especially as practiced by Freeman, often resulted in a zombielike state known as the *frontal lobe syndrome*. Common symptoms included indifference to other people, convulsive seizures, and intellectual impairment. Patients often became self-centered and utterly dependent on others for the simplest routines of day-to-day living.

During the succeeding thirty years, psychosurgeons developed a less crude method of eliminating undesired emotional responses. This involved tampering with the limbic system, or emotional brain—the target of present-day psychosurgery. The limbic system, though still not totally defined, includes such areas as the hippocampus, the amygdala, the cingulum, and the hypothalamus. In lower animals these structures form the basis for emotional reactions. Tampering with the amygdala, for instance, produces in an animal drowsiness, indifference to surroundings, loss of appetite, and a peculiar symptom known as psychic blindness. The animal may stare for hours at food, not realizing it is meant to be eaten. Studies on the human limbic system have established the existence of emotional centers similar in structure, and presumably in function, to lower animals. Proponents argued that operation on these limbic areas produces less "blunting" of the personality than is caused by lobotomies.

With the discovery of tranquilizers in the early Fifties, interest in surgery on both the frontal lobes and the limbic system declined sharply. A drug called Thorazine was widely used as a kind of chemical lobotomy. It soon became apparent, however, that the use of this "miracle drug" carried its own penalties, particularly drug allergies, serious blood abnormalities, paradoxical reactions resulting in further excitement rather than calm, and a bizarre disorder of muscle tone and movement known as tardive dyskinesia. These failures resulted in a resurgence of interest in psychosurgery.

In the last twenty years at least eight different surgical procedures have been developed in which surgical incisions are made in one or more portions of the limbic system. The two commonest operations used today are cingulotomies and amygdalotomies, which involve deep cuts into these two key areas of the emotional brain. According to limbic-system theory, disturbed emotional patterns (violence, deep depressions, suicidal tendencies, etc.) are partly the results of a form of "short circuitry" between the limbic system and the rest of the brain. Cutting of the amygdala or cingulum is intended to interrupt these faulty "connections" in the hope that new "connections" will develop or that the interruption will abolish the disturbed behavior patterns. In actuality, the correlation between behavior patterns and limbic structures is at best disputable.

Surgical advances in the last fifteen years have led to increasingly precise "targets" within the limbic system. The most innovative development involves stereotactic surgery, a revolutionary treatment for Parkinson's disease in the days before the discovery of the drug L-Dopa. Stereotaxis involves the use of a tiny probe guided externally through a small opening made in the skull. By three-dimensional visualization tiny, accurate cuts can be made in any part of the brain. This procedure markedly reduces the incidence of complications. In many instances ultrasonic beams and radioactive substances have also been used to destroy brain tissue thought to be responsible for emotionally disturbed behavior.

A major advance in the last five years has been the use of small electrodes to stimulate parts of the limbic system. Because the patient is awake, the effects produced by electric stimulation can be described by the patient. If a certain area is found to produce the symptoms for which treatment is sought (rage, depression, etc.), that area can be destroyed. This method has been used for years with good results in the treatment of epilepsy. Its value in treating behavioral disorders, however, has never been established.

Publications regarding psychosurgical operations number many thousands by now. They are, for the most part, contradictory, confusing, and marred by the absence of scientific objectivity. Yet despite the confusion, contradictions, and, occasionally, downright deception, certain accepted facts have emerged. For one thing, tampering with the frontal fibers is almost certain to produce indifference and apathy. Secondly, certain patients have reacted poorly to psychosurgery regardless of the type of operation. Schizophrenics have done worst of all and have been eliminated from the patient pool of even the most enthusiastic of psychosurgeons. So-called psychopaths or sociopaths have not done much better. In fact, the number of patients who stand to gain from psychosurgical procedures turns out to be remarkably small. It includes severe obsessive-compulsives, such as perpetual hand washers, who may excoriate their hands and arms by two or three hundred hand washings a day, and a limited number of severe and unremitting depressives, who, failing to respond to antidepressant medications or even electroconvulsive therapy, gravitate toward inevitable suicide. In addition, psychosurgery may help the terminal cancer patient whose mind is never entirely freed from a totally pain-ridden, drug-addicted existence.

Beyond these few cases, however, lies considerable evidence that the procedure is more often dangerous and even irresponsibly applied. At least one West Coast neurosurgeon, for example, has taken to performing psychosurgery on children as an office procedure. As a result of such abuses, psychosurgery is under challenge as a violation of medical ethics and the individual patient's civil rights.

The most pointed legal objection to psychosurgery revolves on loopholes in the present structure of "informed consent": the extent to which the patient has been informed regarding all possible consequences of psychosurgery. Dr. Harold Edgar, associate professor of law at Columbia University Law Center and author of a forthcoming book on psychosurgery, writes:

As things stand now, the surgeon is covered as long as he explains to the patient and relatives the uncertainties in the methods and gets them to agree to it without guarantee. It is quite possible that some families would be willing to consent to almost anything to get a troublesome relative off their hands. There must be protection against the collusion of such families with overzealous psychosurgeons. The unwilling patient's right must be safeguarded.

The case of obtaining informed consent from prisoners is even more sensitive. Robert C. Neville, of the Institute of Society, Ethics, and the Life Sciences, Hastings-on-Hudson, New York, cites the case of "Thomas the Engineer," who was asked to submit to a behavior-control experiment:

When under the influence of calming electrical stimulation, he consented to a psychosurgical procedure to destroy certain brain cells. When the effects of the stimulus wore off, he refused consent. What is informed rational consent in such a setting?

The question came to a court test in July, and the decision clarified the ambiguous legal position of psychosurgery. A Michigan court ruled that state funds could not be used to finance psychosurgery on mental patients despite the patient's willingness—even enthusiasm—for undergoing the procedure. The patient, convicted eighteen years ago for the rape and subsequent slaying of a nurse, was judged criminally insane and committed to Ionia State Hospital in Detroit. His eligibility for discharge notwithstanding, he requested psychosurgery to eliminate the possibility of losing control and killing again. No coercion was brought to bear; the operation was not a precondition to release.

Still, the voluntary nature of the consent was questioned by Att. Charles Halpern of the Center for Law and Social Policy in February at the Society of the Neurosciences in Washington. "There is simply no way," he said, "to ensure that a person in the hospital for eighteen years, with a likelihood of imprisonment for more time, can ever make a voluntary judgment on whether he should have this operation."

During court hearings Dr. Ayub Ommaya, director of the research section of the National Institute of Neurologic Diseases and Stroke, also questioned the scientific premise of the proposed electrode operation. "The role of psychosurgery," Ommaya testified, "has little, if any, applicability for violent behavior."

A similar, federal-level setback for psychosurgery occurred on June 26. The National Institutes of Health rejected a $1.2 million grant proposal by Dr. Vernon Mark of Harvard and other doctors who have pioneered the use of amygdalotomy to treat violent or irrational behavior. The work of the Boston group, in fact, had provided much of the incentive for the Michigan program. Mark and his colleagues had advocated the idea that much crime and other violence have their roots in medical, rather than social, causes—a concept that had already won them grant money from the Nixon administration.

According to Dr. Edgar, the definition of psychosurgery as an experimental process could resolve some ambiguities. This would require additional safety and quantitative procedures, such as the maintenance of control groups, which are not currently observed. A bill providing guidelines for all human experimentation has been introduced in Congress by Sen. Edward Kennedy.

The issue of behavior modification is perhaps the century's most compelling medical-social issue. Current fads for ESP and biofeedback reflect our enthusiasm for controlling mental processes with techniques similar to those for controlling our physical environment. Psychosurgery, the most extreme and dramatic form of such modification, involves particularly anguishing decisions that must be made now. Unfortunately, the issue is becoming so politicized that reasoning based on facts is seriously hampered. On December 27, 1972, for example, an open session on psychosurgery and behavioral control at the American Association for the Advancement of Science meetings in Washington was disrupted by demonstrators.

In light of such profound disagreements, certain measures seem justified:

1 It is time for a temporary moratorium on all forms of psychosurgery undertaken primarily to modify behavior.

2 We need a clearinghouse of information on the topic of the effects of brain lesions on behavior. As things now stand, the facts are scattered in hundreds of journals. The clearinghouse would enable the evaluation of the data already accumulated from twenty years of various psychosurgical procedures.

3 From here it should be possible to determine national standards of practice concerning (a) when and if psychosurgery is indicated, (b) what procedures offer reasonable hope of result, and (c) most important, what patients are eligible for psychosurgery and under what circumstances.

4 There is an urgent need for measures that will protect the individual patient from having psychosurgical procedures imposed upon him against his will or in a setting in which informed consent or the capacity to choose is impaired.

5 Since the results of psychosurgery have not been established, all psychosurgical procedures should be considered "experimental" and subject to strictly imposed controls. Such operations should be carried out only in a clinical institution able to provide total therapeutic care and follow-up. Non-medical disciplines must have significant influence in the control of psychosurgery.

Some critics have suggested we immediately outlaw psychosurgery altogether. But even this isn't as simple as it seems. What is to be done for tortured compulsives whose senseless rituals defy treatment by any other form? What of the terminal cancer patient whose personality threatens to shatter under the daily strain of unendurable pain? What of the patient who refers himself for a psychosurgical procedure? What are his rights in a possible setting of controlled and reasonably predictable operations? At this point these questions cannot be answered for want of the facts. Only by implementing measures similar to those listed above can we make a good case to abandon—or expand—the use of psychosurgery.

Modulation of Emotion with a Brain Pacemaker

Treatment for Intractable Psychiatric Illness

Robert G. Heath[1]

During the past 16 months, we have applied a new treatment to patients with intractable mental illness, some of whom also had seizures. Involving use of an implantable pacemaker that permits electrical stimulation of specific sites on the surface of the cerebellum, the procedure alters the patient's emotional state by activating precise brain bathways in a particular way. The technique evolved from data collected during therapeutic use of depth electrodes in patients and from extensive data obtained from experimental studies in animals to demarcate the neural basis of behavioral phenomena, particularly of emotion.

Since 1950, electrical stimulation of the brain has been used at Tulane to treat a variety of intractable psychiatric and neurological illnesses (16, 21, 25-27, 29, 31, 34). By implantation of electrodes into multiple preselected brain sites of patients capable of reporting thoughts and feelings, we have also been able to make long term observations of functional brain changes while simultaneously monitoring mental activity. Certain consistent correlations have been observed. Activity of the septal region (20, 33), as defined in the early 1950s, and of the corticomedial amygdala correlates with pleasurable emotion, whereas activity of the hippocampus and dorsolateral amygdala, as well as at periaqueductal sites of the mesencephalic tegmentum, correlates with adversive emotion.

The following specific correlations established in our earlier patient studies are most pertinent to the new therapeutic approach:

1 Psychotic behavior, regardless of the cause, is associated with aberrant electrical activity, in the form of spike and slow waves, in the septal region.

2 Intense emergency emotion (rage, fear, violence, aggression) is associated with high amplitude spindle activity in the hippocampus and associated sites.

3 The clinical epileptic seizure is preceded by seizural-type electroencephalographic (EEG) activity propagated at certain subcortical sites, including the hippocampus and amygdala.

Our original therapeutic rationale was that repeated stimulation of specific brain regions would correct aberrant brain activity and thereby eliminate signs and symptoms of the resultant illness. Attempting to correct brain rhythm permanently by repeated stimulation is essentially the same principle as for the kindling effect (13, 39). It is predicated on the concept of the brain's plasticity, that is, activity of the brain can be modified by repeated electrical stimulation. Prior to recent technical advances, it was necessary for stimulating electrodes to exit from the brain. Further, stimulation could be applied only intermittently for brief periods. Although the intermittent therapeutic stimulation was delivered to some patients over periods as long as 2 years, our techniques failed to produce consistent lasting changes in brain function and associated clinical improvement. Whereas some patients showed long term improvement, many tended to relapse.

Data gathered during therapy of patients, however, provided meaningful direction for anatomical and physiological experiments in animals. Using a variety of methods, we have extended the delineation of the central nervous system network for emotional expression (14-16, 23, 24, 32, 33).[2] We have also shown that brain sites for emotional expression are anatomically connected and functionally related to sensory relay nuclei for all modalities, to sites involved in facial expression and motor coordination, and to sites contain-

[1]Professor and Chairman, Department of Psychiatry and Neurology, Tulane University School of Medicine, 1430 Tulane Avenue, New Orleans, Louisiana 70112.

Neurosurgical procedures were performed by Raeburn C. Llewellyn, M.D., Professor and Chairman, Department of Neurosurgery, Tulane University School of Medicine, and staff.

This research was supported in part by grants-in-aid from the Ittleson Foundation, Inc. and the J. Aron Charitable Foundation, Inc. of New York, N.Y., and the Zemurray Foundation of New Orleans, Louisiana.

The author gratefully acknowledges the techical assistance of Charles J. Fontana, Stanley B. John, and Herbert J. Daigle.

[2]Clark, G. M., Ellison, J. P., and Heath, R. G. Some afferent connections of the septal region of the cat: A study using the horseradish peroxidase retrograde transport method. To be submitted to Exp. Neurol.

ing specific nerve cell chemical transmitters. In animals, moreover, we have demonstrated functional relationships among brain sites during altered emotional states and in association with epilepsy (17, 19, 28).

Of significance is the interrelationship between deep cerebellar nuclei and rostral sites (rostral forebrain sites and temporal lobe deep nuclei), where activity has been shown to correlate with emotion and with seizures. That finding led us to stimulate deep cerebellar nuclei in treatment of psychotic and epileptic patients. As with supratentorial stimulation, however, improvement was not always sustained. Nevertheless, recordings obtained in the patients corroborated our findings in experimental animals: that activity in the deep cerebellar nuclei relates meaningfully to activity of the supratentorial structures (29). Computer analysis has indicated that intense adversive emotion of animals and human subjects is associated with bursts of EEG activity, occurring simultaneously, at certain specific frequencies, in deep cerebellar nuclei, in the hippocampus, and less consistently at other connected sites (29, 45).

Among many recent animal studies we have conducted to clarify further the functional relationships in the pathways for emotional expression is an investigation of effects of cerebellar stimulation on unit recordings in supratentorial sites where activity recorded in human subjects has correlated with emotional expression (30). Stimulation of the cortex of the rostral vermis of the cerebellum activated cells in the fastigial nucleus and, through this, inhibited single unit activity in the directly connected hippocampus, a site where high voltage activity has consistently been recorded concomitant with adversive emotion.... Further, unit activity was facilitated in the septal region, the site where high voltage activity correlates with pleasurable emotion.... The delay time for potentials evoked in both the septal region and hippocampus was 0.5 millisecond longer following stimulation of the cerebellar cortex than with stimulation of the fastigial nucleus (30). The finding suggested that the effects of cerebellar cortex stimulation on hippocampal and septal recordings were indirect, passing through one synapse, possibly in the fastigial nucleus. These effects were induced only when the cerebellar cortex was stimulated at a focal site on the rostral vermis. Stimulation at certain other sites of the cerebellar cortex sometimes induced opposite effects.

These basic anatomical and physiological data formed the foundation of a hypothesis concerning the neurological basis for disorders of behavior and for epileptic seizures. The recent development of an implantable receiver,[3] permitting brain stimulation

[3]Clinical Technology Corporation, 4440 Broadway, Kansas City, Missouri 64111.

(without exiting wires) at selected parameters for an indefinite time, provided a method for testing the hypothesis. We reasoned that the new technique might prevent the relapses that occurred after intermittent stimulation of our early patients.

Hypothesis

We postulate that a stimulus that activates the physiological system for pleasure while inhibiting the system for adversive emotion (which is also involved in the spread of seizural activity) can be effective therapy for behavioral and seizural disorders.

The Psychotic State

The following is not meant to be a complete formulation of the psychotic state; rather, the focus is on the critical physiological alteration of the brain occurring during the psychotic state that forms the rationale for this therapeutic approach.

On the basis of early findings in patients, we consider the psychotic state to be a consequence of a disruption of the physiological mechanism for emotional expression. Particularly involved are brain sites where activity correlates with pleasurable emotion and levels of awareness, as well as sites that are anatomically and functionally related (sensory relay nuclei affecting sensory perception, nuclei for putative transmitter chemicals, and the superior colliculus for expression of the face and eyes).... Spiking in recordings from the septal region correlates with the psychotic state, and high amplitude activity in the hippocampus is characteristic of intense emergency behavior. Conceivably, delivery of a stimulus capable of continuously modulating the physiological circuitry for emotion so as to activate the septal region while concomitantly inhibiting activity of the hippocampus should override the dysrhythmia demonstrated in psychotic patients (including schizophrenics), and abolishing the dysrhythmia should eliminate the symptoms arising from the defects in pleasure and lowered awareness that are responsible for disorders of thought. Other associated signs and symptoms should also disappear, such as sensory perceptive defects (hallucinations, distortions of bodily image) that result from propagation of the septal spiking over directly connected pathways to sensory relay nuclei. Finally, associated outbursts of emergency emotion (rage and violence) should be averted by inhibition of hippocampal activity.

Severe Neurotic Behavior

This brief discussion of neurotic behavior is also limited to those points most critical in the development of our rationale for use of this therapeutic procedure.

We consider inappropriate emergency emotion consequent to faulty learning experiences to be the principal pathognomonic factor in neurotic behavior. Otherwise stated, the interaction between drives based on biological needs and cognition with current perceptive input and past learning experiences results in an inappropriate emergency emotion signal (fear or rage, or both). Signs and symptoms are a reparative attempt to alleviate associated painful feelings. If our hypothesis is valid, symptoms of the neurosis should disappear with modulations of the physiological basis of emotion, so as to inhibit brain sites where activity increases with emergency emotion and simultaneously to enhance activity of brain pleasure sites.

Epileptic Seizures

Seizures spread through the same interconnected brain network as that involved in emotional expression albeit through a different type of activity (17, 18, 28, 38). A superimposed rhythm that modulates pathways for emotional expression should therefore also control seizures. Since seizural electrical activity in the hippocampus and parts of the amygdala has consistently preceded onset of the clinical seizure, a stimulus capable of inhibiting hippocampal activity should be therapeutic.

We have been able to test our hypothesis in patients with these various disorders by stimulating specific sites of the cerebellar cortex, shown in animal experiments to activate the pleasure system (septal region) and to inhibit adversive emotion and seizural spread (hippocampus and lateral amygdala).

Implantation and Stimulation Procedure

With the upper part of the chest, neck, and occipital scalp cleansed and draped, a small incision is made on the left side of the chest just below the clavicle for placement of the receiver. An incision is also made through the skin and muscle for a classical suboccipital craniectomy. The receiver is placed over the left chest. Three or four arrays, each composed of five or seven platinum disc electrodes, each 2.0 mm and separated by 4.0 mm (at center), are pulled under the skin into the suboccipital incision by means of a spe-

cial cannula . . . . The chest incision is sutured. The suboccipital craniectomy is then performed, and the dura opened. After cauterization of small veins between the cerebellar surface and tentorium, the electrodes are implanted subtentorially over the rostral vermal and para vermal regions. They are tacked to the dura to hold them in place.

The external battery-operated stimulator, about the size of a cigarette case, is usually worn by the patient in an inside pocket . . . . It delivers the stimulus through an antenna that is taped to the skin directly over the receiver. The wave form is a capacitive coupled monophasic pulse (0.25 millisecond) at 100 Hz. Voltage setting has varied from 3 to 6 volts.

The Patient Group

Eleven patients, representing various categories of illness, are included in this report. Each patient had previously failed to respond to all other known treatment regimens. In every instance, the patient had been pronounced incurable by at least two physicians (psychiatrists or neurologists, or both). The families, as well as the patients themselves (some patients could not fully comprehend), were informed of the rationale for and the details of the procedure and were advised of the experimental nature of its application. The first patient was operated on in February, 1976, and the 11th patient in March, 1977. The follow-up period therefore ranges from 3 to 16 months. Ten of the 11 patients are now out of the hospital, none requiring medication for behavioral symptoms. (The two epileptics are receiving anticonvulsants.) Some are completely asymptomatic. In others, signs and symptoms have been substantially reduced. The 11th patient (case BP-9) had severe previous damage to the cerebellum, the region to be stimulated, and treatment has proved ineffective.

The cases are dissimilar in many respects: diagnosis, duration of illness, educational, environmental, and economic background, as well as time elapsed after operation and activation of the pacemaker. The 11 patients are grouped into four categories, based on predominant clinical features of their illnesses. The Brief Psychiatric Rating Scale (Overall and Gorham) was completed on each patient by at least two clinicians, and the Nurse's Observaton Scale for Inpatient Evaluation (NOSIE) was used by staff. Because of the heterogeneity of the patients, the variations in clinical states, and the profound changes that occurred, the scales proved impractical. For this reason, a brief abstract has been prepared for each patient. For the five schizophrenic patients, Carpenter's (3) system of 12 symptoms for differential diagnosis was used as one criterion in establishing the diagnosis of schizophrenia. Each of the five patients had seven or more of the differential symptoms, reducing the percentage chance of making a false positive diagnosis of schizophrenia to 1.0 per cent. All patients were tested psychologically (the data will be presented elsewhere). Audio-visual tapes were made of each patient before operation and at intervals after activation of the pacemaker.[4]

Group I: Uncontrollable, Violent-Aggressive Behavior

The first two patients represented medical emergencies, with minimal chances for survival for any significant period. Uncontrollable, explosive violence was the principal characteristic of their illness. Both patients had repeatedly demonstrated homicidal and suicidal tendencies, having narrowly escaped death in their suicidal attempts.

Patient BP-1
This 19-year-old man was selected because he was considered to be the most severely ill patient in our state hospital system at that time. Slightly retarded from birth, he was first hospitalized when he was 13 years old. Following private treatment, he had been hospitalized at Charity Hospital in New Orleans, at the Southeast Louisiana Hospital, and, finally, at the East Louisiana State Hospital, where he was confined on a ward for severely disturbed patients. He slashed his wrists and arms on numerous occasions during episodes of violence, and on one occasion, he had attempted to kill his sister. Despite administration of huge quantities of numerous drugs (lithium, imipramine, thioridazine, chlorpromazine, trihexyphenidyl, diazepam, phenobarbital, and antiparkinsonism medication), he had to be kept in physical restraints much of the time. All attending physicians had declared him to be a hopeless case insofar as ever returning to his home.

The patient's postoperative course was turbulent because of the necessary withdrawal of large quantities of drugs and drug-induced tardive dyskinesia. Before the pacemaker was activated, it was necessary to use large amounts of sedation and to continue to use restraints. He was so disturbing to the entire ward that other patients petitioned to have him removed.

From the day the pacemaker was activated, the patient's outbursts of violence ceased. His tardive dyskinesia gradually diminished, and his behavior has continued to improve. He is now a pleasant and

sociable young man. Psychological tests, including intelligent quotient, have shown significant improvement, and he is able to cope adequately with the vicissitudes of everyday life. Clinically, the patient has had a complete remission and requires no medication. He was enlisted in a vocational rehabilitation course and he is now ready for job placement. He had to visit the state hospital where he had last been a patient for physicians and nursing staff to believe that it was possible for him to live outside of an institution.

Patient BP-2
A 19-year-old woman was continuously suicidal and had failed to respond to a wide variety of medical-psychiatric treatments. Attending physicians at DePaul Hospital in New Orleans, as well as those at other hospitals where she had been a patient, declared her incurable. At age 12, she had left home and soon became a prostitute. She began abusing drugs of all kinds, including D-LSD and psylocibin, and she was fast approaching chronic alcoholism. Three years before coming to us for treatment, she began having epileptic seizures. She was hospitalized for the seizures and for psychotic behavior at various facilities. Diagnoses were epilepsy, psychopathic personality, and schizophrenia. She had married an Air Force Sergeant, but he had decided to divorce her because of her incorrigible infidelity, as well as her illness. Suicidal attempts, beginning about 3 years before operation, consisted of wrist slashing (several times), repeated overdosing with drugs, stabbing herself in the abdomen with a large knife (two occasions), and shooting herself through the abdomen with her husband's service revolver. Her intestines were severed and a colostomy was necessary. The patient was coercive and demanding. Thought content was persecutory. Her predominant affect was intense, destructive rage.

Within a month after activation of the pacemaker, there was striking improvement in her behavior and appearance. She became pleasant, cooperative, and alert. Neuroleptic drugs were no longer required. Complete control of grand mal seizures required anticonvulsant medication (diphenylhydantoin). Since her discharge from the hospital, the patient has been followed at monthly intervals, and she continues to show improvement. She is essentially asymptomatic, and is pleasant with sparkling affect. As a result of losing over 20 pounds, she is much more attractive. She is working at part time jobs and plans to return to school to obtain a high school diploma. Referring physicians are pleased with her improvement.

About 8 months after discharge, the patient decided to stop taking diphenylhydantoin and not to use the pacemaker. Within 2 weeks, she had another seizure, but there was no recrudescence of behavioral symp-

---

[4]Sony cassette tapes were shown during the meeting of the Society of Biological Psychiatry, Toronto, Canada in May, 1977.

toms. She has been symptom-free since resuming diphenylhydantoin and reactivation of the pacemaker. Psychological tests given 7 months after the pacemaker was activated were essentially normal, in contrast to preoperative testing.

Group II: Violence Consequent to Demonstrable Organic Brain Damage

The two patients in this group were also uncontrollably violent but, in contrast to the first group, the violence was the result of gross demonstrable organic brain pathology.

Patient BP-6

Employed as a librarian, this 21-year-old woman had been essentially healthy except for seizures that were well controlled with diphenylhydantoin. During a hold-up in November, 1974, she received a gunshot wound to the head, which destroyed much of the frontal lobes. After debridement, her physical recovery allowed her to return home after 2 months. She was maintained on large doses of phenobarbital and also on diphenylhydantoin for her seizures. Although she was severely disabled, she managed to exist at home. Her affect was euphoric. She was unable to comprehend significantly or to carry on a meaningful conversation, and she had to be assisted in walking because of seriously impaired gait. After several months at home, she stopped eating and taking fluids, and a gastrostomy tube had to be inserted. She then continued her passive, but cooperative existence at home for several more months, until December, 1975, when she began to display bizarre, violent behavior accompanied by unaccountable somatosensory complaints. She was admitted to a local hospital, where she was described as paranoid. She was hostile, almost continuously lashing out to strike anyone within reach. On several occasions, she attempted to kill her father by stabbing him with a knife. Bizarre rituals in walking were prompted by her delusion that there was poison on the floor. She groaned and cried out with pain; when questioned, she indicated that pains were everywhere in her body. Her skin was exquisitely tender to touch. After phenothiazines failed to alleviate symptoms, a course of electroshock temporarily lessened some symptoms. A program of maintenance electroshock plus trifluoperazine was then introduced, and she was able to be at home intermittently until the late fall of 1975, when the regimen ceased to be effective. Her demeanor had become one of continual rage, lashing out, and screaming from somatosensory pain. The pacemaker procedure was suggested in desperation, the rationale (based on experiences with other violent patients and on animal experiments) being that it might help to control her violence.

The pacemaker was implanted on November 10, 1976, and was activated a week later. Improvement has been gradual, but consistent. During the first 2 months after activation, the patient's episodes of rage-violence gradually decreased and the peculiar hyperpathia subsided. Since then, her progress has been encouraging. She is increasingly pleasant, her attention span has improved, and she is doing a little reading. Her memory is beginning to return. She is increasingly eating by mouth and has gained needed pounds, but the gastrostomy tube remains because she takes fluids only sparingly. Anticonvulsant medications have been continued, but she has not required neuroleptic medications since activation of the pacemaker.

Patient BP-10

For 11 years, this 20-year-old man had suffered from intractable epilepsy. Seizures were initially petit mal and grand mal, occurring in volleys of three to eight at 6- to 8-week intervals. About 10 years ago, the patient began having episodes of violence. He engaged in unprovoked fights with classmates, and he knocked his mother down on one occasion. The episodes were often associated with inappropriate laughter and expression of referential ideas. Occasionally, content of thought was overtly persecutory. Several months apart at first, the episodes increased in frequency and severity over the past 5 to 6 years. During the 1½ years before operation, he had episodes of several seizures per day with interictal, gross psychotic behavior characterized by auditory and visual hallucinations persisting for several days. Four such episodes occurred in the year preceding operation.

The patient denied using hallucinatory drugs, and toxic screens were negative. Even though serum diphenylhydantoin levels were often low, the patient's family insisted he took his anticonvulsant medication. Careful investigation during one hospitalization showed inadequate serum diphenylhydantoin levels, despite large oral doses. Ultimately his seizures could not be controlled even with parenteral diphenylhydantoin. Adjuncts to the diphenylhydantoin, including phenobarbital, clonazepam, ethosuximide, and carbamazepine, and various combinations, also failed to control the seizures. Because of the frequency of seizural episodes and large quantities of medications, the patient was virtually in a semistuporous state. Results of neurological and medical examinations have always been essentially negative. Possibly the result of cerebral dysrhythmia, the patient displayed blocking, hesitant and slurring speech, and notable gaps of information. Memory and recall were poor, his affect was flat, and associations were loose. Electroencephalograms were notably abnormal.

The pacemaker was implanted on March 16, 1977. Just as it was to be activated, the patient had a seizure, despite being on anticonvulsant medication, and struck his nurse in the jaw, knocking her unconscious. In his struggle, the chest incision where the receiver was implanted was ripped open. The wound was thoroughly washed with antibiotic and resutured. High doses of antibiotic agents for 10 days prevented infection. The pacemaker was then activated. One seizure occurred 2 days later, but without behavioral complications. During the remaining 12 days of hospitalization, the patient had no more seizures. Since his discharge on April 7, 1977, the family has reported one abortive seizure without behavioral complications. He is described as more alert and displaying more affect than he has shown in many years.

Group III: Undeniable Schizophrenia

Because beneficial results had been obtained in two earlier patients who were psychotic, we elected to test the pacemaker procedure in a group of patients who were undeniably schizophrenic. Neither of the previous patients was undeniably schizophrenic, although that diagnosis had occasionally been applied to both of them. In an effort to determine the limitations of the procedure, we searched our area for intractably ill chronic schizophrenics. Five patients in this category have undergone the procedure, four with distinct improvement. Experience indicates that it takes several months for schizophrenic signs and symptoms to subside significantly, episodes in milder form suggestive of the former psychotic manifestations recurring at progressively longer intervals.

Patient BP-5
Since first being institutionalized 18 years ago, this 36-year-old woman had never had a complete remission of symptoms despite large doses of neuroleptic medications and electroshock therapy. Her illness was characterized by disorders of perception: auditory and olfactory hallucinations, and gross distortions of bodily image, the patient believing that her extremities were continuously changing in shape and size. She was extremely guarded and suspicious. A persecutory delusion, resulting in severe phobic behavior, was that proximity to a man would cause her pregnancy. Although signs and symptoms of her illness had never completely remitted, during occasional periods she could be followed at mental health clinics. On her frequent hospital admissions, the diagnosis was always chronic schizophrenia. Before the pacemaker implantation, she was taking long acting fluphenazine (5 ml every 2 weeks), diphenhydramine (25 mg two times/day), flurazepam (30 mg three times/day), and benztropine mesylate (2 mg three times/day). Medical and neurological findings were normal except for chronic obesity, bronchitis secondary to heavy smoking, and recurrent urinary tract infections. When she was not hospitalized, she lived in impoverished rural surroundings in a one-room shack without running water. She was supported exclusively by welfare payments.

On October 20, 1976, 1 week after operation, the pacemaker was activated. Since then, her psychotic signs and symptoms rapidly diminished, and she has required no neuroleptic medications or sedatives. Within 2 weeks, hallucinations and distortions in bodily image had ceased. Delusions and suspicions also disappeared, and the patient has been able to socialize with acquaintances and relatives whom she had avoided for many years because of her delusions. In mid-January, 1977, she entered a halfway house and began vocational rehabilitation training. She has done satisfactorily and expects to obtain a paying job. She now has no psychotic symptoms. The reintegration in her basic behavior has been interesting to observe. Basic schizophrenic defects in affect and association have notably improved so that she is a more responsive person with whom one can empathize. Still not fully resolved are problems that developed as a consequence of her illness and associated environment. She remains fairly dependent and addicted to her welfare situation, but she is slowly and progressively adapting to a more responsible life in the city.

Patient BP-7
This 21-year-old man, who first became psychotic when he was 17 years old, has not had a complete remission since then despite large doses of neuroleptic medications and electroshock therapy. During the past 4 years, he has been hospitalized in four different hospitals, living at home only when his symptoms could be controlled by massive doses of medication. Most neuroleptic drugs were tried, including 8 ml of fluphenazine intramuscularly every week for 6 months preceding operation, a dosage required by his intense agitation and threats to kill his family. He had auditory hallucinations and bizarre thought content, the foremost idea being a "poo fish" in his stomach as a consequence of anal rape. He believed that his thoughts were controlled by the movements of persons in his environment. His affect was flat and unresponsive. The psychiatrist who treated him for many years was also concerned about his home environment, where his mother was overprotective and seductive.

Since activation of a pacemaker, which was implanted on November 17, 1976, the patient has not received neuroleptic medication. Hallucinations have disappeared and delusional thoughts have gradually diminished, now appearing only rarely. The changes in this patient were slow, clear-cut improvement not occurring for 3 months. Arrangements are nearing completion for him to enroll in a trade college. Despite the significant therapeutic effects, rehabilitation of the patient has been difficult. His mother responds to his adolescent demands, but he is gradually becoming more disciplined in such aspects of behavior as keeping regular hours. Since his illness began in early adolescence, considerable maturation is necessary. For example, he continues to be somewhat impulsive and demanding of his mother and he is only now beginning to make some friends. In every respect, however, he is continuing to improve.

Patient BP-8

This 26-year-old woman, the 11th of 14 children, has had auditory hallucinations since early childhood. The voices have episodically incited her to violent, assaultive behavior. Although her education continued into high school, the patient has never worked. During the past 10 years, she has been hospitalized eight times. She is described as sitting alone or wandering aimlessly around her neighborhood during short periods when she was out of the hospital. Her delusions have included fears of rape. Although unmarried, she is the mother of four children. When she was 22 years old, she struck her oldest child in the face with a bottle in response to a voice telling her to kill her children. They are now being raised by the family of the presumed father. Her family picture is bleak, her parents and all siblings being irresponsible and disinterested. Her thought content was repetitive and dominated by what the voices said to her. Until they were discontinued just before operation, the patient had taken neuroleptic drugs since she was 17 years old. For the past 4 years, she has been refractory to electroshock treatment. She was irresponsible about taking medicine, and her last medication before operation was fluphenazine (3 ml intramuscularly every 2 weeks).

Activation of the patient's pacemaker on November 30, 1976, 1 week after operation, produced some change in the patient, particularly in affect. She became bright and more responsive, and psychomotor retardation largely disappeared. She heard voices notably less frequently. In all spheres of sensory perception, she described increased sensitivity. Although psychotic signs and symptoms persisted, they were less intense, and the patient's mother stated that she was functioning better than she had ever seen her. On December 22, 1976, she was discharged to her home, and steps were taken for her participation in a voca-

tional rehabilitation program. On initial follow-up visits, the patient showed further improvement. When she failed to keep one of her appointments, the family was contacted, and we learned that the antenna of her pacemaker had been broken for a week, but no one had bothered to inform us. The patient had a recrudescence of psychotic symptoms, she was readmitted to the hospital, and over the next 2 weeks, there was again partial improvement. Because of the patient's poor family situation, arrangements were made to place her in the vocational rehabilitation unit of a nearby hospital. We also decided to resume small doses of neuroleptic medication temporarily. Vigorously protesting discontinuation of her welfare payments if she were trained for a job, she willfully broke five antennas and one transmitter for her pacemaker, and made overt threats if she did not get her way. We informed her that if she did not stop breaking the equipment, her transfer to a custodial state hospital might be necessary, and we simultaneously stopped medication. She has since shown steady improvement and has not broken any equipment. Although not in complete remission, she is notably improved clinically.

Patient BP-9

Since 1964, this 34-year-old woman has spent most of her life in a state hospital for the chronically ill. A paranoid schizophrenic, her consistent delusion is that someone is going to kill her or her husband. Violent and assaultive principally toward other persons, she has also mutilated herself. All neuroleptic drugs and courses of electroshock failed to induce improvement. A long trial on lithium, prescribed because of mood swings, also failed to alleviate symptoms. She had been almost continuously restrained on locked wards. For years, she terrorized the hospital staff, often assaulting attendants and inflicting serious injuries. The patient's mother had similarly been confined in the same state hospital, and four of her nine siblings had been hospitalized for schizophrenia. In 1965, she married a fellow patient, also a paranoid schizophrenic. On all medical and neurological examinations, the patient was considered within normal limits. Significant in the past medical history was the vague report that she had two grand mal seizures in 1974. Before operation, the patient was so severely disturbed that attempts to obtain a computerized axial tomographic (C.A.T.) scan were unsuccessful.

When the patient's posterior fossa was opened during the surgical procedure on January 12, 1977, to implant the pacemaker, the cerebellum was seen to be adhered to the tentorium. Extensive and diligent dissection was necessary to separate the superior aspect of the cerebellum from the tentorium, with use of bipolar coagulators. The area of adhesion extended about 2.5 cm on either side of the midline of the superior aspect of the cerebellum, the site over which the electrodes are implanted to stimulate the midline cerebellum. Immediately after operation, the patient's assaultive behavior diminished slightly. Activation of the pacemaker on January 18 brought little notable improvement, the patient soon returning to her preoperative state. She was grossly delusional, hallucinatory, and intermittently assaultive, so that restraints were necessary. Neuroleptic medication, discontinued at the time of operation, had to be resumed 2 weeks after the pacemaker was activated. Even in restraints, however, she was able to destroy the pacemaker equipment. She broke eight antennas and smashed four transmitters. In a desperate attempt to use the pacemaker, we resurrected two strait jackets and tailored them with pockets to hold the transmitter. When the patient shredded both jackets after only 6 days of stimulation, we had to conclude that our efforts were futile. The external transmitter and antenna were removed, and she was transferred back to the state hospital on high doses of neuroleptic medication, her condition essentially unchanged. We attribute our failure to help the patient to damage or to destruction of the cells intended for activation by the stimulation. We have left the receiver and electrodes in place and plan to resume stimulation in 2 or 3 months on the possibility that sufficient cells may recover to permit activation of the brain system involved in her illness.

Patient BP-11

A master's degree physicist, this 41-year-old man had suffered auditory hallucinations, extreme depression or anhedonia, and thought disturbances characterized by religiosity since childhood. For the past 20 years, he has had violent episodes and a compulsion to "make inappropriate remarks." Despite his illness, the patient was Phi Beta Kappa in college. He was first hospitalized 16 years ago, and has been under continuous treatment since then. A patient in numerous institutions, he has received all of the latest neuroleptic drugs, tryptophan treatment, and several courses of electroshock. His ability to work gradually diminished, and he became completely disabled 8 years ago. He has frequent compulsions to choke people, and he has attempted to choke his wife or to stab her with a knife on several occasions. Recently, he has managed to stay out of the hospital by taking large doses of medication. His last drug regimen, discontinued just before operation, was 1000 mg of thioridazine and 6 mg of haloperidol daily. His wife reports that he was unable to do anything at home, not even answer the phone.

The pacemaker was activated on March 21, 1977, 2 days after implantation. Almost immediately, the patient responded to the stimulation. Auditory hallu-cinations and frequency of "violence thoughts" were notably reduced, and his mood shifted from depression to optimism. After 1 week of continuous stimulation, he showed further improvement. When his wife visited him 10 days after activation of the pacemaker, he was bright and alert. They dined at a restaurant and visited relatives, and she reported that he socialized quite well for the first time in many years. Thirteen days after activation of the pacemaker, he was discharged with no medication. During the first 2 weeks at home, he was generally more pleasant and affable with family members and friends, and was more alert. Subsequently, there was considerable fluctuation in signs and symptoms and at times it seemed that he might be relapsing. As he became more involved in activities, however, the old symptoms appeared less frequently and his course continues to be one of slow improvement.

Group IV: Neurotic Behavior

Neither patient in this group underwent the procedure for neurotic behavior, but both had neurotic symptoms that have been modified by the pacemaker procedure. The first patient, who presented a picture of hysteria, had been diagnosed by some clinicians as schizotypal or pseudo-neurotic-schizophrenic. The second patient had intractable, intense agitated depression. She is included here because of her lifelong pattern of severe obsessive-compulsive neurotic behavior that preceded onset of the depression.

Patient BP-3

For 6 years, this 36-year-old woman had suffered from a bizarre form of hystero-epilepsy. "Seizures," seven to 10 daily, were of several distinct types. With one type, the patient fell to the floor and had severe motor movements, only vaguely simulating a grand mal attack. During another type of seizure involving "blackout," confusion lasting several hours was associated with severe headaches, for which she began taking strong medications, including meperidine. A third type of seizure consisted of "blindness," not associated with objective changes, which persisted for hours and sometimes for several days. The combination of symptoms increased in frequency, becoming so decompensating over the 3 years before operation that when she was not hospitalized, she remained virtually confined to her apartment. A wide range of treatments, including neuroleptic and anticonvulsant medications, had been tried without success. Hospitalization for a course of hypnotherapy also failed to alleviate signs and symptoms, even though a number of deep trances were induced.

The patient had a pacemaker implanted on April 22,

1976. Several inadvertent experiences with the operation of the pacemaker served as an effective double blind control for the effects of suggestion. Initially activated at a low frequency (10/second), the brain pacemaker only partially controlled the patient's seizures, reducing them to an average of six to eight/day. Without the patient's knowledge, the frequency was then altered to 100/second, and she became virtually symptom-free, experiencing no further seizures. After an additional week of stimulation under our supervision, the patient returned to her home. All medication had been discontinued. She was feeling "so good" that she began planning vacation trips. About a week later, however, she reported the recurrence of a few seizures. A check of the pacemaker disclosed that the frequency had been inadvertently reduced to 40/second when the patient's husband was changing the batteries. The frequency was restored to 100/second, and the patient remained symptom-free for 3 weeks, after which she again reported several seizures. Examination showed the wire inside the insulation of the antenna was broken, and she had therefore not been receiving any stimulation. A new antenna was provided, and the patient and her husband proceeded on trips to Canada and Hawaii. Subsequently, she developed a few sporadic seizures. When the pacemaker equipment was checked, it was found to be defective. At the same time, the patient was experiencing major problems in her family relationships. It was suspected that someone might be tampering with the apparatus, so arrangements were made for her husband to purchase a monitor to make certain the desirable frequency was maintained. In contrast to the number of seizures the patient had before stimulation (five to eight/day), the incidence is now one every 3 days to a week. It is not clear whether the seizures are due to psychological factors or mechanical difficulties with the apparatus. The patient was the third of this series. At the time of her operation, the receiver was placed under the scalp rather than on the chest. Since her hair has grown, it has become difficult to attach the antenna and to hold it in place over the receiver.

Patient BP-4

This 43-year-old woman had been hospitalized almost continuously for 3 years because of severe, agitated depression. All available medications and several courses of electroshock were ineffectual in reducing symptoms. An anxious, controlled obsessive-compulsive throughout her life, she was unable to experience real pleasure. Both parents had a history of psychiatric illness. Her mother was institutionalized after an unsuccessful lobotomy, and her father, a physician who was addicted to drugs, died of an overdose.

Upon activation of the pacemaker 1 week after its implantation on August 3, 1976, the patient reported good feelings of a kind she had never previously experienced. The adversive, continuous tension and apprehension gradually subsided over several weeks, and she increasingly socialized. Four weeks after activation of the pacemaker, she was able to return to her home.

Agitation and depression, the primary reason for introducing the new treatment, disappeared completely within 5 to 6 weeks. The most significant development since has been the reintegration of her predepressive personality. Her tense, rigid, and controlled, sometimes ritualistic, behavior has gradually subsided. She anticipates coming events with pleasure, in sharp contrast to her lifelong pattern of fearful concern resulting in excessive planning and scheduling. In January, 1977, her husband died unexpectedly of a coronary. She met the crisis very effectively. Family members, friends, and business associates of her husband have expressed amazement over her competence and altered behavior.

Discussion

Although the follow-up period for the 11 cases reported here is not extensive, the continuing beneficial effects of stimulation of specific sites of the cerebellar cortex are encouraging. Previously, all of the patients had been exhaustively treated by a variety of techniques and had failed to have a real remission. In the 10 patients who responded positively to the treatment, improvement has continued throughout the posthospitalization period. None is in the hospital and none requires medication for behavioral symptoms. In the two patients with seizures, psychomotor episodes have been completely controlled, whereas grand mal seizures have been completely controlled in one patient and notably reduced in the other. Anticonvulsant medicaton has been continued in both patients. In the 11th patient, whom we failed to help, damage to the cerebellar cortex possibly nullified the effects of stimulation.

Numerous factors have influenced the postoperative course: diagnosis, home environment, socioeconomic factors, but most important, the duration of the illness and the severity of loss of contact with reality. Alteration in affect has usually been the first observable effect of stimulation. As might be expected in view of this observation, those patients with episodic disorders with lucid interictal periods were the quickest to respond to the treatment. In contrast, the very chronically ill, long term psychotics, who had not had periods of lucid thinking for many years (20 years in one patient), have been slower in remitting. Because symptoms persisted, we were sometimes concerned that the patient was relapsing, some requiring 3 to 6 months of continuous stimulation before results were clearly evident. This course seems reasonable, since the procedure does not affect the patient's bank of memories. Rather, it alters awareness, emotional state, and perception, and only thus gradually modifies behavioral patterns based on background memories. Several patients in the series had never been gainfully employed. Fear of losing government checks impaired their motivation to be trained for paying jobs.

The favorable response in this patient group, representing a wide variety of psychopathology, substantiates our original working hypothesis—namely, the principal effect of the stimulation is modulation of affect and, as a consequence, a gradual disappearance of the symptoms of the disorder. Symptoms of violence and uncontrollable aggression were most promptly eliminated.

All of the chronic psychotic patients in this series had received large doses of neuroleptic medication for prolonged periods and were showing varying degrees of side effects as a consequence. Some had distinct movement disorders, a complication that can become almost as disabling as the original illness. In each case, the side effects were also effectively treated with cerebellar stimulation. Although the external power source is somewhat cumbersome, none of the 10 patients who have responded to the treatment has asked to have it removed. In fact, none would relinquish it.

On the basis of existing data concerning the brain's plasticity, one could speculate that the brain dysrhythmia basic to symptoms might be permanently altered within 3 to 6 months, and the electrodes could be removed. Recent evidence suggests, however, that the basis for cerebral dysrhythmia in psychiatric and neurological disorders is often a generalized metabolic defect. Evidence is accumulating that schizophrenia is a metabolic disorder. Should that be the case, indefinite continuous stimulation would be required to prevent the metabolic abnormality from re-establishing the dysrhythmia.

Chronic cerebellar cortical stimulation was first used by Cooper and associates (6-9) in the treatment of epilepsy and certain motor disabilities, principally on the basis of reports by Snider (4, 5, 47), Moruzzi (40), Walker (50), and others, that stimulation of the cerebellar cortex affected cerebral EEG activity. Riklan and associates (43, 44) have reported tension reduction and alerting, as well as some undesirable behavioral effects, in some of Cooper's spastic and epileptic patients. The patients reported here are the first in whom cerebellar stimulation has been used specifically for treatment of behavioral disorders, the ration-

ale for its use being based on more than 27 years of extensive animal experimentation and clinical studies. Whereas Cooper, in treating epileptics and spastics, has stimulated several sites on the cerebellar cortex, our stimuli are directed toward a precise site on the rostral vermis of the cortex. This site was selected because extensive studies in animals had shown that stimulation of the rostral vermis of the cortex effectively facilitated unit recordings in nuclei involved in the pleasure mechanism and, at the same time, inhibited unit recordings in nuclei involved in adversive emotion (30). Cooper reports using a 10-Hz stimulation in treating epileptic patients. The stimulus parameter we found most effective in the animals, and the one we therefore used in patients, is a 100/second nonpolarizing pulse of 0.250 milliseconds duration at 3 to 6 volts (30). The spacing of our electrodes is derived from careful measurements of spread of stimulation currents on the surface reported by Sances, Larson, and associates (35, 36, 46). With further experience, stimulation site and parameter may be modified.

Most of the literature on cerebellar function deals with effects on motor function. The function of the paleocerebellum, including the site stimulated in our procedure, is described in textbooks as being related to the control of equilibrium, maintenance of muscle tone, and integration of synergistic muscular activity involved in gait (2). The pioneering investigations of Dow and Anderson (10) and of Snider and Stowell (48) suggest that the cerebellum subserves additional functions, including sensory perception, and plays an important role in epilepsy.

Various effects have been described as a result of stimulating the vermis of the cerebellar cortex in animals, including changes in EEGs, in posture and motor activity, and in pain threshold. Those changes have not been observed in the patients reported here. Indeed, immediate, dramatic behavioral effect was rare (occurring in only one of the 11 patients). Cooper (6), in contrast, has reported decrease in muscle tone, apparent within 5 minutes, in response to stimuli at parameters that overlap those we use. The fact that Cooper's patients have had rigidity, whereas ours have not, is a plausible explanation for the different findings.

The reports of EEG changes with cerebellar stimulation are inconsistent. Cooke and Snider (4) described EEG desynchronization, and later Snider and Wetzel (49) described EEG changes in scalp recordings, generally toward slower frequencies, in human subjects with cerebellar stimulation. In contrast, Dow and associates (11) reported no changes in electrocorticograms after cerebellar stimulation, and Cooper has likewise reported no changes. In our patients, even in those epileptics who have shown marked improvement, there have been no significant alterations in EEGs with cerebellar stimulation.

Reports of the role of the cerebellum in emotional behavior, based on animal studies, are scattered and inconsistent. The earliest reports by Pagano (41, 42), appearing in the Italian literature, describe an experiment in which injection of curare into the depths of the cerebellum caused friendly dogs to become rageful and to bite. Moruzzi (40), and later Zanchetti and Zoccolini (51), reported inhibition followed by rebound facilitation of sham rage with cerebellar stimulation in decerebrate cats. Bernston and co-workers (1), on the other hand, in stimulating the basal vermis, superior cerebellar peduncle, and fastigial nucleus, reported that unanesthetized cats displayed grooming behavior and changes in appetite, the cats not only eating food, but objects such as rubber and cord. In a series of experiments beginning with recordings in emotionally disturbed (isolation raised) monkeys from Harlow's laboratory, and several studies in both animals and patients, we have demonstrated with depth recordings and with electrical and chemical stimulation the participation of the cerebellum in emotional behavior (19, 22, 29).

The efferent connections of the Purkinje cells of the rostral vermis are principally to the fastigial nucleus. We recently described monosynaptic connections from the fastigial nucleus to the septal region and hippocampus, regions where activity has been correlated with specific emotions (14). Previously, it was believed that the fastigial projections went no further rostrally than the intralaminar thalamus and that most connections were to the vestibular system.

The procedure described here is noninvasive of the brain, as the electrodes are placed over the surface. Although one report based on a monkey experiment described damage in the vicinity of the electrodes (12), Larson and associates (37), using essentially the same stimulator and parameters as ours, have reported no evidence of cerebellar damage after prolonged stimulation of human subjects and animals.

Because of the relatively short follow-up period, the results reported here are not conclusive. They are sufficiently promising, however, for this treatment to be considered for patients who have failed to respond to adequate trials with conventional therapy, particularly those who are developing undesirable side effects from drugs. Our experience indicates a direct relationship between the time required for remission and the time the patient remained psychotic, especially if he had been isolated from society in institutions.

REFERENCES

1 Bernstein, G. G., Potolicchio, S. J., Jr., and Miller, N. E. Evidence for higher functions of the cerebellum: Eating and grooming elicited by cerebellar stimulation in cats.

Proc. Natl. Acad. Sci. U.S.A., 70: 2497-2499, 1973.

2 Brodal, A. Neurological Anatomy in Relation to Clinical Medicine, 2nd Ed. Oxford University Press, New York, 1969.

3 Carpenter, W. T., Strauss, J. S., and Bartko, J. J. Use of signs and symptoms for the identification of schizophrenic patients. Schizo. Bull., 11: 37-49, 1974.

4 Cooke, P. M., and Snider, R. S. Some cerebellar effects on the electrocorticogram. Electroencephalogr. Clin. Neurophysiol., 5: 563-569, 1953.

5 Cooke, P. M., and Snider, R. S. Some cerebellar influences on electrically induced cerebral seizures. Epilepsia, 4: 19-28, 1955.

6 Cooper, I. S. Effect of chronic stimulation of anterior cerebellum on neurological disease. Lancet, 1: 206, 1973.

7 Cooper, I. S., Amin, I., Riklan, M., Waltz, J. M., and Poon, T. P. Chronic cerebellar stimulation in epilepsy. Arch. Neurol., 33: 559-570, 1976.

8 Cooper, I. S., Crighel, E., and Amin, I. Clinical and physiological effects of stimulation of the paleocerebellum in humans. J. Am. Geriatr. Soc., 21: 40-43, 1973.

9 Cooper, I. S., Riklan, M., Amin, I., Waltz, J. M., and Cullinan, T. Chronic cerebellar stimulation in cerebral palsy. Neurology, 26: 744-753, 1976.

10 Dow, R. S., and Anderson, R. Cerebellar action potentials in response to stimulation of proprioceptors and exteroceptors in rat. J. Neurophysiol., 5: 363-371, 1942.

11 Dow, R. S., Fernandez-Guordiola, A., and Manni, E. The influence of the cerebellum on experimental epilepsy. Electroencephalogr. Clin. Neurophysiol., 14: 383-398, 1962.

12 Gilman, S., Dauth, G. W., Tennyson, V. M., and Kremzner, L. T. Chronic cerebellar stimulation in the monkey. Arch. Neurol., 32: 474-477, 1975.

13 Goddard, G. V., McIntyre, D. C., and Leech, C. K. A permanent change in brain function resulting from daily electrical stimulation. Exp. Neurol., 25: 295-330, 1969.

14 Harper, J. W., and Heath, R. G. Anatomic connections of the fastigial nucleus to the rostral forebrain in the cat. Exp. Neurol., 39: 285-292, 1973.

15 Harper, J. W., and Heath, R. G. Ascending projections of the cerebellar fastigial nuclei: Connections to the ectosylvian gyrus. Exp. Neurol., 42: 241-247, 1974.

16 Heath, R. G. Brain function and behavior. I. Emotion and sensory phenomena in psychotic patients and in experimental animals. J. Nerv. Ment. Dis., 160: 159-175, 1975.

17 Heath, R. G. Brain function in epilepsy: Mid-brain, medullary, and cerebellar interaction with the rostral forebrain. J. Neurol. Neurosurg. Psychiatry, 39: 1037-1051, 1976.

18 Heath, R. G. Common characteristics of epilepsy and schizophrenia: Clinical observation and depth electrode studies. Am. J. Psychiatry, 118: 1013-1026, 1962.

19 Heath, R. G. Correlation of brain function with emotional behavior. Biol. Psychiatry, 11: 463-480, 1976.

20 Heath, R. G. Definition of the septal region. In Heath, R. G., and the Tulane University Department of Psychiatry and Neurology, Eds., Studies in Schizophrenia, pp. 3-5. Harvard University Press, Cambridge, Mass., 1954.

21 Heath, R. G. Electrical self-stimulation of the brain in

man. Am. J. Psychiatry, *120:* 571-577, 1963.

22 Heath, R. G. Electroencephalographic studies in isolation-raised monkeys with behavioral impairment. Dis. Nerv. Syst., *33:* 157-163, 1972.

23 Heath, R. G. Fastigial nucleus connections to the septal region in monkey and cat: A demonstration with evoked potentials of a bilateral pathway. Biol. Psychiatry, *6:* 193-196, 1973.

24 Heath, R. G. Physiologic basis of emotional expression: Evoked potential and mirror focus studies in rhesus monkeys. Biol. Psychiatry, *5:* 15-31, 1972.

25 Heath, R. G. Physiological and biochemical studies in schizophrenia with particular emphasis on mind-brain relationships. Int. Rev. Neurobiol., *1:* 229-331, 1959.

26 Heath, R. G. Pleasure response of human subjects to direct stimulation of the brain: Physiologic and psychodynamic considerations. In Heath, R. G., Ed., *The Role of Pleasure in Behavior*, pp. 219-243. Hoeber Medical Division, Harper & Row, New York, 1964.

27 Heath, R. G. Schizophrenia: Biochemical and physiologic aberrations. Int. J. Neuropsychiatry, *2:* 597-610, 1966.

28 Heath, R. G. Subcortical brain function correlates of psychopathology and epilepsy. In Shagass, C., Gershon, S., and Friedhoff, A. J., Eds., *Psychopathology and Brain Dysfunction*, pp. 51-67. Raven Press, New York, 1977.

29 Heath, R. G., Cox, A. W., and Lustick, L. S. Brain activity during emotional states. Am. J. Psychiatry, *131:* 858-862, 1974.

30 Heath, R. G., Dempsey, C. W., Fontana, C. J., and Myers, W. A. Effects of stimulation of the cerebellum on unit recordings from the septal region and hippocampus of cats and rats. Biol. Psychiatry. In Press.

31 Heath, R. G., and Gallant, D. M. Activity of the human brain during emotional thought. In Heath, R. G., Ed., *The Role of Pleasure in Behavior*, pp. 83-106. Hoeber Medical Division, Harper & Row, New York, 1964.

32 Heath, R. G., and Harper, J. W., Ascending projections of the cerebellar fastigial nucleus to the hippocampus, amygdala, and other temporal lobe sites: Evoked potential and histological studies in monkeys and cats. Exp. Neurol., *45:* 268-287, 1974.

33 Heath, R. G., and Harper, J. W. Descending projections of the rostral septal region: An electrophysiological-histological study in the cat. Exp. Neurol., *50:* 536-560, 1976.

34 Heath, R. G., and the Tulane University Department of Psychiatry and Neurology, Eds., *Studies in Schizophrenia.* Harvard University Press, Cambridge, Mass., 1954.

35 Hemmy, D. C., Larson, S. J., Sances, A., Jr., and Millar, E. A. The effect of cerebellar stimulation on focal seizure activity and spasticity in monkeys. J. Neurosurg., *46:* 648-654, 1977.

36 Larson, S. J., Sances, A., Jr., Cusick, J. F., *et al.* Cerebellar implant studies. IEEE Trans. Biomed. Engineering, *BME-23:* 319-328, 1976.

37 Larson, S. J., Sances, A., Jr., Hemmy, D. C., and Millar, E. A. Physiological and histological effects of cerebellar stimulation. Neurosurgery, *1:* 212-213, 1977.

38 Mickle, W. A., and Heath, R. G. Electrical activity from subcortical, cortical, and scalp electrodes before and during clinical epileptic seizures. Trans. Am. Neurol. Assoc., *82:* 63, 1957.

39 Morrell, F. Goddard's kindling phenomenon: A new model of the "mirror focus." In Sabelli, H. C., Ed., *Chemical Modulation of Brain Function*, pp. 207-223. Raven Press, New York, 1973.

40 Moruzzi, G. *Problems in Cerebellar Physiology.* Charles C Thomas, Springfield, Ill., 1950.

41 Pagano, G. Essai de localisations cérébelleuses. Arch. Ital.Biol., *43:* 139-159, 1905.

42 Pagano, G. Etudes sur la fonction der cervelet. Arch. Ital. Biol., *38:* 299-308, 1902.

43 Riklan, M., Cullinan, T., and Cooper, I. S. Tension reduction and alerting in man following chronic cerebellar stimulation for the relief of spasticity or intractable seizures. J. Nerv. Ment. Dis., *164:* 176-181, 1977.

44 Riklan, M., Kabat, C., and Cooper, I. S. Psychological effects of short term cerebellar stimulation in epilepsy. J. Nerv. Ment. Dis., *162:* 282-290, 1976.

45 Saltzberg, B., and Lustick, L. S. Signal analysis: An overview of electroencephalographic application. In Prescott, J. W., Read, M. S., and Coursin, D. B., Eds., *Brain Function and Malnutrition: Neuropsychological Methods of Assessment*, pp. 121-140. John Wiley & Sons, New York, 1975.

46 Sances, A., Jr., Larson, S. J., Myklebust, J., *et al.* Studies of electrode configuration upon cerebellar implants. Neurosurgery, *1:* 209-212, 1977.

47 Snider, R. S. Functional alterations of cerebral sensory areas by the cerebellum. In Fox, C. A., and Snider, R. S., Eds., *The Cerebellum*, pp. 322-333. Elsevier Publishing Co., Amsterdam, 1967.

48 Snider, R. S., and Stowell, A. Receiving areas of the tactile, auditory, and visual systems in the cerebellum. J. Neurophysiol., *7:* 331-357, 1944.

49 Snider, R. S., and Wetzel, N. Electroencephalographic changes induced by stimulation of the cerebellum of man. Electroencephalogr. Clin. Neurophysiol., *18:* 176-183, 1965.

50 Walker, A. E. An oscillographic study of the cerebro-cerebellar relationships. J. Neurophysiol., *1:* 16-23, 1938.

51 Zanchetti, A., and Zoccolini, A. Autonomic hypothalamic outbursts elicited by cerebellar stimulation. J. Neurophysiol., *17:* 475-483, 1954.

Should You Starve Yourself Thin?

Jean Mayer

Unwanted pounds have a way of creeping up on us. An extra pre-dinner drink here, an occasional splurge on a cream-filled pastry there, and suddenly (or so it seems) we're letting out our belts another notch—or staring in disbelief at our bathroom scales.

The typical reaction to such a predicament is a heartfelt cry: "I've *got* to lose weight!" And then, all too often, people embark on fad diets that promise quick—albeit temporary—results: among them low-protein, high-carbohydrate diets; low-carbohydrate diets; high-protein (and high-fat) diets à la Stillman or Atkins; or diets that concentrate on one special food, like grapefruit. In one short binge of unbalanced undereating, they expect to undo the months of nibbling that produced the "spare tire" in the first place.

But for a growing number of impatient souls, even this plan of action is too slow. Instead, they decide to shed excess weight by cutting out food altogether. After all, what could be faster than fasting?

On a purely mathematical level, this kind of reasoning appears flawless. Calories do count: Every time your energy output exceeds your energy intake by 3,500 calories, you will lose about one pound of body fat. Thus, a no-calorie weight loss regimen would seem to be the dieter's dream because, assuming that an active woman or an inactive man expends about 2,100 calories a day, not eating should mean losing about four pounds a week. Indeed, studies have shown that at the beginning of a total fast weight loss is even more rapid.

If that sounds like an ideal arrangement, remember this: Diet fads come and go, but human physiology remains the same. The body, designed for physical activity, is simply not meant to cope with long periods of complete abstinence from food.

Fasting as a method of weight loss was seriously investigated back in the mid-1960's by a number of researchers, including Dr. G. G. Duncan of Philadelphia. Dr. Duncan (who hospitalized his patients for close supervision) focused not only on the amount of weight lost but also on metabolic changes in the body, as measured by blood levels of a number of key compounds. The subjects fasted from five days to two weeks; adolescents under 18 (who are still growing and need more of many nutrients per pound of body weight than do full-grown adults) were not permitted to fast for more than a week.

The findings? Predictably, the patients did lose more weight than a control group on ordinary, calorie-restricted diets, and almost half of them managed to keep their weight down over a fairly long period. After the first day on the fast, a number of patients also displayed a sense of cheerfulness and well-being, and Duncan fund that hypertensives exhibited a lowering of blood pressure. What's more, the fasting subjects lost their appetites.

Impressive results, yes—but these initial changes do not tell the whole story. Other patients in this and other studies reported some weakness, light-headedness and headaches. Some felt transient nausea. And the encouraging loss of appetite proved to be linked to a rise of ketone bodies in the blood—the same substances that in large amounts cause acidosis and coma in diabetics. In similar programs, fasting patients were found to have a high level of uric acid in their bloodstream, a condition that can lead to kidney or bladder stones. A few even developed ulcerative colitis and mental depression.

Why such profound psychological and physical changes? The answer is simple. Although its proponents may claim that "fasting is not starvation"—and although your mind may be well aware that there is plenty of food in the refrigerator—your body is incapable of making that distinction. After a few days on a prolonged and total fast (one that eliminates the intake of everything but water), the body, oblivious to reason, begins to adapt itself to starvation—and some profound and potentially dangerous adjustments begin to take place.

Ordinarily, carbohydrates (starches and sugars) in the diet—not protein, as many people believe—are the body's preferred sources of energy. These carbohydrates are largely broken down into glucose, a simple sugar. (The brain alone requires 400 to 600 calories a day, and under normal circumstances glucose is its only source of energy.) After the immediate need for glucose is filled, the remaining carbohydrates are metabolized into fat as a reserve against future deprivation. A small amount of glucose, however, is stored in the liver in the form of glycogen—just enough, in fact, to tide us over short, foodless spells (from dinner to breakfast, for instance).

What happens, then, when the usual supply of nutrients is cut off by fasting? Since the body needs calories, not only for fuel for physical activity but also to keep basic metabolic functions humming along—

things like breathing, heartbeat and blood flow, digestion, and cell repair and renewal—a decrease in that nutrient supply forces the basal metabolism to slow down. As a result, physical movements become sluggish and uncoordinated, and the ability to concentrate diminishes.

But the problem with prolonged fasting is that mere calorie conservation is not enough. At the beginning of a fast, when there is no energy coming in from food, the body turns to the reserve of glycogen in the liver. When that is used up, since glucose cannot be synthesized from fat, *the body begins to break down its own muscle and tissue proteins to get glucose.* However, protein (from which we can make glucose, though much less efficiently than from carbohydrates) yields only four calories per gram. In addition, for every gram of protein that is lost, three grams of water are lost, too—and it is this drop in body fluids that accounts for the high weight loss during the first days of fasting. Because body fluids also contain a number of essential minerals, a sizable reduction of sodium and some potassium also occurs.

Only after several days of fasting does the body begin to break down fats—a sort of last ditch effort to conserve lean tissues. The brain, too, slowly adapts to using ketone bodies (one of the by-products of this fat breakdown) as a partial substitute for glucose. But since glucose is still needed, some body protein continues to be utilized. In fact, one study showed that after a one-month fast, subjects lost an average of 14 pounds of lean tissue.

Other effects of pseudo-starvation may be less obvious but no less detrimental. For example, fasting advocates talk of substances being "cleansed out of the blood." What they do not understand is that those substances are actually essential vitamins and minerals, which are always lost with the breakdown and death of cells and which are not replenished since no nutrients are being consumed.

Also, fasting puts a great strain on the liver, which must help convert fat into energy, and on the kidneys, which must excrete some of the substances produced by the breakdown of fat and protein.

Still, fasting is not entirely without value. Under carefully controlled conditions, many reputable specialists have used it as a last-resort "diet" for markedly obese patients, as well as for people who must lose weight rapidly for medical reasons (such as an operation that must be performed by a certain date). In these very rare cases, the fasting is either done in the hospital or under the constant and careful supervision of the physician.

By now it should be quite clear that total fasting over an extended period of time is not a harmless, do-it-yourself procedure. Even in a hospital setting, patients who have an infection, diabetes, liver disease, peptic ulcer, renal ailment, who have had a recent heart attack, or who are pregnant or nursing a baby are excluded from fasting. So unless you are prepared to go to the expense of having a physician monitor you closely, to stop driving a car (I'd just as soon be on a highway facing a drunken driver as a fasting teenager), and to do your physical and mental work less efficiently, find another diet.

For after all, although calories count, the way we pare them away matters more. By accepting the idea of "trickle down" weight loss as complacently as we accept "trickle up" weight gain, it is possible to follow a balanced, even tasty, diet and still lose weight. To wit: A daily deficit of 500 calories—the equivalent of about four and a half pieces of fudge, a small hamburger or a malted milk shake—will result in a weight loss of one pound a week. Maybe that doesn't sound like much, but over the course of a year it adds up to more than 50 pounds!

In the long run, only a permanent change in eating habits or exercise patterns (preferably both) will have a long-lasting effect on your weight and physical fitness. So, fast one day every two to four weeks by all means, as an act of self-discipline, as a gesture of unity with the rest of our troubled world or as a means of spiritual renewal. But don't fast over a long period of time in order to lose weight. To put your body through such unnecessary stress for the sake of a few pounds, except in the direst necessity, is indeed the ultimate absurdity.

Current Concepts in Nutrition
Diet and Weight Loss

**Theodore B. Van Itallie
and Mei-Uih Yang**

Body weight is the most important index of nutritional status that is readily available to the physician; however, the ease and simplicity of the weighing procedure have tended to obscure the complexity of the physiologic processes that underlie weight change. Weight loss reflects a deficit of one or more body substances sufficient to produce a net decrease in body mass. For practical purposes, the constituents that can contribute appreciably to weight loss over the short term are water, fat, protein and glycogen. In much longer-term situations, deficits of minerals (from both bone and soft tissues) also make a small contribution to weight loss.

Nature of Weight Loss

In considering the components that are chiefly involved in weight loss, one must remember that protein and glycogen do not exist in the body in anhydrous form but are incorporated into tissues as part of a complex of hydrated organic materials. Thus, when glycogen or protein deficits occur, they are usually accompanied by an "obligatory" water loss that tends to reflect the characteristic hydration ratio (grams of water per gram of constituent) of the body constituent in question. For glycogen, this ratio is 3-4:1. For protein, it is also 3-4:1 (that for nitrogen being 19-25:1). Such ratios can be only approximate because of biologic variation and the existence of a fairly wide range of hydration coefficients in the literature. It remains debatable whether adipose tissue loses water in association with triglyceride mobilization.

In addition to the water losses that are attributable to tissue losses of protein or glycogen, it is very common to observe water deficits (and retentions) that

From the Department of Medicine and the Institute of Human Nutrition, Columbia University College of Physicians and Surgeons and St. Luke's Hospital Center (address reprint requests to Dr. Van Itallie at St. Luke's Hospital Center, Amsterdam Ave. at 114th St., New York, NY 10025).

Supported in part by a grant from the National Institutes of Health (Obesity Center AM-17624).

Reprinted, by permission, from *The New England Journal of Medicine* 1977, 297:1158-1161.

cannot be explained by the putative hydration coefficients of protein and glycogen. In such cases one must conclude that the additional water is being drawn from the extracellular compartment or that a disproportionate loss of cell water (or some combination of both processes) is taking place.

In the early phases of weight reduction, the composition of the loss is especially apt to vary widely, depending on the nature of the diet and the pre-existing nutritional state of the subject. The constituent that is mainly responsible for this variability is water, which can account for up to 100 per cent of weight loss in certain situations (e.g., diuretic treatment). Later in caloric restriction, water can be retained, even to the point of causing weight gain, while net losses of fat and protein continue. When subjects are placed on a weight-reduction regimen, they tend to lose weight rapidly during the first week or two. Much of this initial loss is water, reflecting the natriuresis and reduction in renal concentrating ability that characteristically accompany early starvation or semistarvation. The mechanism of these sodium and water losses is incompletely understood, but increased glucagon secretion may be partly responsible.[1] Also, sodium excretion would be expected to rise because of the increased anion load placed on the nephron by nutritional ketosis. Finally (as mentioned previously), an obligatory water loss (perhaps 600 to 800 ml) accompanies the depletion of body glycogen that occurs during fasting or carbohydrate privation.

In any attempt to assess the meaning of body-weight loss, it is obviously essential to know the rate at which the loss is taking place. To this end, body weight should be measured accurately every 24 hours. In addition, when the effectiveness of a weight-reduction regimen is being evaluated, it is helpful to have some notion of the quality of the loss. One way of judging quality is to estimate the energy value of the loss per unit of weight (pounds or kilograms). For example, the energy value of a given kilogram of weight loss is largest if most of the loss is from the body's fat depot; in contrast, the higher the proportions of protein and water that are lost, the lower the energy value of the weight loss. At any given level of energy deficit, the quality of weight loss is likely to be highest when its rate is slowest. However, this "test" loses its meaning if less water is being lost from the body than would be anticipated from the nitrogen deficit. If the water content of weight loss is excluded from consideration, a judgment about quality can be based on the relative contribution made by depot fat and body protein to the energy deficit.

In the past, it has been customary to assume that, on the average, 1 lb (0.45 kg) of weight loss corresponds to an energy deficit of about 3500 kcal. This value suggests that 98 per cent of the calories being burned over the corresponding period was derived from depot fat, the remainder coming from body protein. As we shall attempt to demonstrate, this level of energy density is rarely if ever achieved early in weight loss and, indeed, in the absence of a disproportionately low rate of water excretion, is likely to occur only in obese subjects who have been fasted or partly starved for a long time. It is also important to emphasize that no convenient methods are available to the physician that will enable him to estimate the composition of a patient's weight loss. However, there is now enough information from scattered research studies to permit the derivation of certain principles that can help him interpret more critically the claims made for certain highly publicized weight-reduction regimens.

The effects of different diets on rate and composition of weight loss are best considered in terms of nonobese and obese subjects and in relation to short-term and longer-term adherence of such subjects to a given weight-reduction regimen. . . .

Responses of Nonobese Subjects to Caloric Restriction: Rate and Composition of Weight Loss

Short-term studies of the composition of weight loss in nonobese subjects on weight-reduction regimens other than starvation are difficult to find in the literature. Brožek et al.[2] have reported on their attempts to estimate the composition of the weight lost by 13 physically active adult male volunteers maintained for several weeks on a 1000-kcal diet consisting entirely of carbohydrate. The subjects lost weight rapidly (1.8 lb, or 0.80 kg, per day) during the first three days of the regimen . . . but exhibited a marked slowing in rate of loss (to 0.5 lb, or 0.23 kg, per day) by the end of the second week of the diet. The variance in rate of weight change was almost entirely attributable to a higher-than-normal water loss in the early phase of dietary curtailment and to some degree of water retention later.

The effect of prolonged caloric restriction on rate and composition of weight loss in nonobese adult subjects was demonstrated by Keys et al.[3] in their classic study of 32 male volunteers who were subjected to a "famine" regimen that lasted for 24 weeks. The test diet provided 1570 kcal per day (vs. a maintenance diet of 3468 kcal per day) and contained 50 g of protein, 30 g of fat and 275 g of carbohydrate.

The mean composition of the weight lost during the first 11 weeks of semistarvation was approximately 40 per cent fat, 12 per cent protein and 48 per cent water . . . . During the 12th to 23rd weeks, the mean composition of the weight that was lost was estimated to be 54 per cent fat, 9 per cent protein and 37 per cent water. Weight was lost much more slowly during the second half of the semistarvation period (0.1 lb, or about 49 g, per day) than it was during the first half, when the rate of loss was 0.3 lb, or 150 g, per day. This reduction in rate of loss reflects the adaptation of the nonobese subjects to the low-calorie diet; indeed, at the end of the 24-week semistarvation period, their basal metabolic rates had dropped by an average of 31 per cent (per square meter of surface area) whereas their voluntary physical activity level had decreased by 55 per cent. Also, the proportion of the energy deficit derived from body fat showed a substantial increase, from a mean of 88 per cent during the first half of the semistarvation period to a mean of 93 per cent during the second half.

In the light of the rule-of-thumb value of 3500 kcal frequently cited as representing the energy deficit needed to induce 1 lb (0.45 kg) of weight loss, it is noteworthy that the energy value of the average weight lost by the nonobese subjects studied so carefully by Keys et al.[3] was about 1910 kcal per 0.45 kg during the first 11 weeks of semistarvation and about 2460 kcal per 0.45 kg during the last 12 weeks of semistarvation. Thus, under conditions of maximal adaptation to undernutrition, the caloric value of 0.45 kg of weight loss in previously nonobese subjects was far below 3500.

Responses of Obese Subjects to Caloric Restrictions

In a series of obese subjects studied on our metabolic ward, the mean rate of weight loss during the first five days of adherence to a 1200-kcal mixed diet was 1 lb, or 0.45 kg, per day.[4] Thus, like lean subjects, these previously well nourished obese persons lost weight rapidly in the early phase of caloric restriction. . . . 66 per cent of that loss was water, and, indeed, the composition of early weight loss in these obese persons was very similar to that of the nonobese subjects studied by Brozek et al.

The effect of drastically changing the proportions of carbohydrate and fat in a low-calorie (800-kcal) diet was also studied in the same subjects. . . . [T]he rate and composition of weight loss over the last three days of a 10-day period during which they were on a balanced 800-kcal diet containing 90 g of carbohydrate are compared with the rate and composition of the weight loss over the last three days of another 10-day period during which they received a "ketogenic" 800-kcal diet containing 10 g of carbohydrate. The absolute rate of weight loss during the last part of the ketogenic diet period was 0.9 lb, or 0.34 kg, per day whereas that during the comparable segment of the nonketogenic diet period was 0.7 lb, or 0.31 kg, per day. . . . [T]he discrepancy in rate of weight loss between the two regimens was caused almost entirely by the higher rate of water loss while the ketogenic diet was being consumed.

The same group of obese subjects was also studied during a 10-day period of starvation. The absolute rate of weight loss (per day) during starvation was 50 per cent higher than that during the 800-kcal ketogenic diet, the increment being related to the greater energy deficit. However, . . . the composition of the loss during the eighth to 10th days of the total fast, with its high proportion of water, was almost identical to that exhibited during the 800-kcal ketogenic diet period . . . .

No long-term study comparable to that of Keys et al.[3] has been carried out in obese persons; however, there is evidence from experiments of shorter duration that, during prolonged energy restriction, obese subjects also adapt by increasing the proportion of the contribution from their fat stores to the fuel mixture being burned. In a series of seven obese subjects studid by Passmore et al.[5] the mean composition of weight loss during adherence for 45 days to a 400-kcal mixed diet was 78 per cent fat, 5 per cent protein and 17 per cent water, indicating that the contribution of fat to the fuel mixture being burned was 98 per cent. From these numbers, one can calculate that the energy value per mean pound (0.45 kg) of weight loss was 3409 kcal. Thus, after six weeks on a diet very low in calories, these obese subjects were oxidizing a fuel mixture much higher in fat and lower in protein-derived substrate than that being utilized by the nonobese volunteers of Keys et al. during the first 11 weeks of a far less stringent diet. Accordingly, it appears that, during marked energy restriction, obese subjects use their fuel reserves more efficiently than lean persons under similar conditions. In addition, during prolonged semistarvation, obese subjects do not exhibit the substantial decreases in basal metabolic

rate (per square meter of surface area) and in voluntary physical activity shown by nonobese persons under comparable dietary circumstances.

On the basis of observations on 18 obese male adults, Runcie and Hilditch[6] have reported that on the 30th day of a total fast, the mean weight loss was 0.8 lb, or 0.37 kg. At this point, 95 per cent of the expended energy was being derived from body fat. This per cent contribution of fat to the fuel mixture oxidized during starvation would be associated with a weight loss having an energy value of about 3300 kcal per lb (0.45 kg). In contrast to the metabolic behavior of these obese subjects is the response of one nonobese male adult studied by Benedict[7] during a 31-day fast. . . . During the last three days of the fast, this subject lost an average of 0.7 lb, or 0.32 kg, per day. According to Benedict's data, the mean contribution of fat to the energy deficit was 84 per cent; therefore, the energy value of the weight lost by this starved and previously nonobese man (1869 kcal per 1 lb, or 0.45 kg) was much lower than that of the starved group of obese patients studied by Runcie and Hilditch.

Protein-Supplemented Fasting

During the last few years, considerable interest has been generated in the possibility that "protein-supplemented fasting" would have a unique advantage when used to induce weight loss in obese subjects. Unfortunately, published data about its metabolic effects do not provide sufficient information to permit calculation of the composition and energy equivalence of weight lost during adherence to this regimen. Several investigators[8,9] have reported that as soon as a total fast is "modified" by the ingestion of protein alone, nitrogen losses cease, and nitrogen retention can occur. However, in obese adults who have not recently restricted their food intake, protein-supplemented fasting (providing 70 to 85 g of protein per day) will induce nitrogen deficits totalling about 30 g (equivalent to 570 to 750 g of lean tissue) over a three-week period. After this degree of protein depletion has occurred, nitrogen equilibrium may finally be achieved. Thus, the "protein-sparing" effect of protein-supplemented fasting, when it occurs, seems to take place only after there has been some loss of lean body mass. Moreover, it is not yet clear whether this effect can be sustained indefinitely, nor has it been shown that dietary protein alone is more effective in preserving body nitrogen than an isocaloric mixture of protein and carbohydrate.

Conclusions

The rate at which the body loses fat is almost entirely dependent on the size of the proximate energy deficit; at any given level of energy deficit, the rate at which the body loses weight depends on the composition of the loss, particularly its water content. The diuresis that commonly occurs early in caloric restriction can be accentuated and prolonged in subjects who consume a low-calorie ketogenic (low-carbohydrate) diet, or who simply fast. During prolonged partial or total caloric restriction, the body adapts by increasing the relative contribution of its fat stores to the energy deficit and by conserving protein and water. Given the same degree of caloric privation, obese subjects accomplish this adaptation far more successfully than their lean counterparts do. Although some consider a low-calorie diet consisting entirely of protein (protein-supplemented fast) to be uniquely advantageous in preserving body nitrogen, it has yet to be demonstrated convincingly that protein alone is more effective in this regard than an isocaloric mixture of protein and carbohydrate.

REFERENCES

1 Sandek CD, Boulter PR, Arky RA: The natriuretic effect of glucagon and its role in starvation. J Clin Endocrinol Metab 36:761-765, 1973

2 Brozek J, Grande F, Taylor HL, et al: Changes in body weight and body dimensions in men performing work on a low calorie carbohydrate diet. J Appl Physiol 10:412-420, 1957

3 Keys A, Brozek J, Henschel A, et al: The Biology of Human Starvation. Minneapolis, University of Minnesota Press, 1950, pp 284, 371

4 Yang M-U, Van Itallie TB: Composition of weight lost during short-term weight reduction: metabolic responses of obese subjects to starvation and low-calorie ketogenic and nonketogenic diets. J Clin Invest 58:722-730, 1976

5 Passmore R, Strong JA, Ritchie FJ: The chemical composition of the tissue lost by obese patients on a reducing regimen. Br J Nutr 12:113-122, 1958

6 Runcie J, Hilditch TE: Energy provision, tissue utilization, and weight loss in prolonged starvation. Br Med J 2:352-356, 1974

7 Benedict FG: A Study of Prolonged Fasting. Washington, DC, Carnegie Institution. 1915, pp 84, 415

8 Marliss EB, Murray FT, Nakhooda AF: Metabolic response to hypocaloric protein diets. Clin Res 24:681A, 1976

9 Bistrian BR, Winterer J, Blackburn GL, et al: Effect of a protein-sparing diet and brief fast on nitrogen metabolism in mildly obese subjects. J Lab Clin Med 89:1030-1035, 1977

The Search for the Secret of Fat

Donald W. Thomas and Jean Mayer

Fatness is within reach of us all. The automobile, calorie-packed processed foods, and a dizzying variety of labor-saving devices assure us of that. And a great many Americans are fat. Precise data on the incidence of obesity in the U.S. do not exist, but samples of our population, analyzed on the basis of height-weight tables, suggest that at least half of the middle-aged persons in the U.S. are overweight. Perhaps the best indication of the prevalence of obesity in the U.S., and the unhappiness associated with it, is the thriving weight-reduction industry.

Reprinted by permission of *Psychology Today* magazine, September 1973. Copyright © 1973 Ziff-Davis Publishing Company.

There have always been fat people and they have often been targets for ridicule. Shakespeare had Prince Hal describe Jack Falstaff as "that trunk of humours, that bolting-hutch of beastliness, that swollen parcel of dropsies, that huge bombard of sack, that stuff'd cloak-bag of guts, that roasted Manningtree ox with the pudding in his belly." Until recently fatness was attributed to gluttony, lack of will, or neurosis. But the same affluence that has contributed so much to fatness has also permitted us to research obesity in detail. Though much remains to be done, we now know many things about obesity that are not commonly known to the obese, to their critics, or to those who treat fatness with simple, universal remedies.

What We Know

We know that fat people are victims of discrimination. The Robert Half Personnel Agency recently made a survey of business executives to check the relationship between weight and salary. They found that 35 percent of the executives in their sample earning $10,000 to $20,000 were at least 10 pounds overweight, while only 10 percent of the executives in the $25,000 to $50,000 wage bracket were that much overweight. In a second study of our own, we showed that an obese woman has one third the chance of a nonobese one of getting into a prestige college, the college of her choice, or indeed any college at all.

We know that fatness is predictable to some extent. It runs in families. Our group found in a study in Boston that only seven percent of the children of normal weight parents were overweight. Forty percent of the children in families with one obese parent were overweight. Eighty percent of the children in families where both parents were obese were overweight. These differences reflected heredity much more than environment. Obesity in adopted children showed almost no correlation with the weight of parents. A large-scale study in London by R. R. J. Withers confirms our findings.

We know that certain body types are less prone to obesity than others. C. C. Seltzer showed that highly ectomorphic individuals with long, narrow hands and feet do not become fat. Obese individuals have different body builds as a rule—more endomorphic and mesomorphic than the general population.

We know from the research of Jules Hirsch and Jerome Knittle that individuals differ in both the size and number of fat cells they possess. Weight reduction decreases the size but not the number of fat cells. How many fat cells a person has, Hirsch and Knittle suggest, may depend on nutrition in early life, as well as on genetic factors.

We know that there are many different kinds of obesity. In mice alone, there are at least a dozen different varieties: some genetically determined forms, such as "yellow obesity," associated with coat color in mice; New Zealand obesity, associated with a form of diabetes; or Bar Harbor hyperglycemic obesity, associated with another form of diabetes and a number of endocrine, metabolic and behavioral peculiarities in mice. We can make a mouse fat by operating on it, or by injecting it with any of four different chemicals. We can induce obesity in a mouse by manipulating its environment, by keeping it immobile, or by putting it on a high fat diet. These various types of obesity correspond to different balances between food intake and spontaneous physical activity, different patterns and number of meals, different blood glucose, blood cholesterol, and life expectancies.

Two Views of Fatness

Research has thus shown that fatness is a hundred times more complicated than was believed 25 years ago. But it has not answered the crucial question, *Why do people get fat?* How does an imbalance between energy intake and energy output develop in a person?

First, and obviously, we think there are a number of possible answers to this question. Having studied a dozen or so different obesities in the mouse alone, nothing we have seen in man leads us to believe that human obesity is a single syndrome.

But if there are a number of possible causes of obesity, there are at least two fundamental views of why people get fat. They differ in important ways. We look at fatness as being, in *most* cases, an internally controlled, physiological phenomenon. Stanley Schachter and his students look at fatness as an externally controlled phenomenon dependent on environmental stimuli.

Schachter suggests that the obese person is in the thrall of food-related stimuli, perhaps because of defective functioning in the hypothalamus.

We believe, in contrast, that more often a fat person is especially sensitive to food-related stimuli because he has found his normal, internal signals of hunger and satiety untrustworthy. The obese person stops relying on internal signals, and begins relying on sensory information. In our view, sensitivity to food-related stimuli is a *correlate* of obesity, not its cause.

Whoever is right, fatness is fundamentally a problem of *surplus energy*. And surplus energy can only build up three ways:

1 One eats more than a normal amount of food.

2 One eats a normal amount, but doesn't get enough exercise to burn up the energy that he takes in.

3 One has a metabolic disorder. The disorder either speeds up the rate at which his body accumulates fat tissue, or slows down the rate at which his body burns fat tissue, or both.

For the past 30 years, the search for the mechanism which controls energy balance has focused on the hypothalamus. The hypothalamus is a structure deep in the brain which plays an organizing role in many important functions, including eating, drinking and sex. A. W. Hetherington and S. W. J. Ranson first showed that lesions within the ventromedial portion of the hypothalamus of rats cause them to gain weight dramatically. Later studies confirmed their findings in many other animals, including mice, dogs, cats, sheep and monkeys. This weight gain, and the complex set of changes in behavior that follow lesioning, is called the VMH syndrome.

The most striking characteristic of this syndrome is

a dramatic increase in the *rate* of weight gain. The rate usually doubles or triples. The increase usually begins immediately after lesioning and persists for several weeks, until the animal has attained perhaps twice its preoperative weight. In some cases, animals triple their weight, the folds of fat and skin draping to the floor like a skirt, concealing their overburdened legs. After this period of explosive gain, however, the animal's weight stabilizes again. The VMH syndrome has a dynamic, then a static phase.

Studies with VMH rats show that:

• Their overall metabolic efficiency is not sufficiently different from that of normal rats to account for the VMH rats' unusual weight gain. The activity level of the VMH rat is lower than the level of the normal rat. But the fat rat has a greater mass to trundle about, and so does not save enough energy by moving less to explain its rapid gain in weight.

• The daily food intake of a VMH rat doubles or triples immediately following surgery. The intake declines to near normal once the rat has reached its new weight plateau. (Identifying gluttony as the essential source of surplus energy, and thus the primary cause of obesity, John Brobeck and his colleagues termed this disorder "hypothalamic hyperphagia.")

Researchers agree that energy surplus builds up in VMH rats because VMH rats overeat. The question is, why do they overeat? What motivates the VMH rat to consume such extraordinary amounts of food immediately following surgery? It is on this point that obesity researchers often part company.

Schachter suggests that a VMH lesion in a rat places its feeding behavior under the control of environmental stimuli. We think he is wrong. We think the VMH lesion alters the internal regulatory mechanism that governs the rat's feeding behavior, presumably through feelings of hunger and satiety.

Neal Miller, C. J. Bailey and J. A. Stevenson, in a now classic experiment, tried to find out whether a VMH obese rat overeats because it is hungrier than a normal rat, or because it has to eat more before it is satiated. They compared the hunger of obese rats and normal rats by measuring the strength of food-seeking behavior in the two groups according to five criteria: (1) how fast the two groups ran down a runway to get food, (2) how hard each group pulled against a force restraining the rats from food, (3) how much each group ate when a weighted lid had to be lifted to get at the food, (4) how fast the two groups pressed levers to produce food, and (5) how much each group ate when quinine in their food turned it bitter.

The results of these experiments showed that while VMH obese rats eat more than normal rats in a free feeding situation, they are consistently less willing to work for their food. This, suggested Miller and his colleagues, showed that VMH rats overeat not because they are hungrier than normal rats, but because they require more food before they are satisfied.

However, John Falk ran a related experiment in our laboratory, and concluded that Miller's results may have been in part artifacts of his experimental conditions. Falk compared the food-seeking behavior (pressing a lever for food) of a group of rats before and after he placed VMH lesions in their brains. He made all the tests with the animals reduced below their normal preoperative weight. Interestingly, all the rats worked harder to obtain food following the operation, and the rats that worked hardest became the fattest when permitted to feed freely once more. Falk's results indicate that an internal drive (hunger) plays an essential role in the overeating of the VMH rat, at least during the initiation of obesity.

Dynamic and Static

The question of what motivates the VMH rat to consume extraordinary amounts of food after surgery has yet to be answered definitively. We believe, however, that the balance of data suggests that some alteration of an internal mechanism that regulates energy balance prompts the VMH rat to overeat. We doubt that a VMH rat's environment dictates its extraordinary, postoperative consumption of food.

In a study on the role of sensory stimuli in obesity, Philip Teitelbaum pointed out important differences between the dynamic and static phases of the VMH syndrome. Teitelbaum found that VMH obese rats in the dynamic phase of weight gain, like normal rats, maintained their daily food intake even when he laced their food with unpalatable cellulose or quinine. This further supports our view that internal drives play an important role in the early stages of VMH obesity. However, Teitelbaum found that once the VMH rats reached the static phase of the syndrome, they became finicky eaters. This suggests that in later stages of VMH obesity, external cues may become important to food intake.

Rats in both phases of the VMH syndrome, unlike normal rats, did respond to diets made more palatable through the addition of sucrose. They ate markedly more food, and gained markedly more weight.

Fat Feeders

Much is known about the behavior of fat rats and mice. Relatively little is known about the behavior of fat people. Through a series of entertaining and informative experiments, Schachter, Richard Nisbett and their colleagues have marshaled evidence to support their view that fatness in humans is determined by environmental stimuli, not by internal, physiological states [see "Eat, Eat," PT, April 1971].

In one study, Nisbett collected a group of subjects for an unspecified psychological experiment, asking them only not to eat lunch before coming to the laboratory. While they were presumably waiting for the experiment to begin, Nisbett offered them a plate on which were one, two or three roast-beef sandwiches. "There are dozens more in the refrigerator by the way," he told the subjects. "Eat as many as you want." Then he departed. That was the experiment.

Some subjects were fat. Others were normal weight. The question Nisbett wanted to answer was simply, how many sandwiches would each subject eat? The results were interesting and confirmed the hypothesis being tested. The normal subjects ate approximately two sandwiches, regardless of how many sandwiches were on the plate Nisbett gave them. Obese subjects ate more than normal subjects when handed three sandwiches, but less when handed only one. Thus, the obese subjects tended to consume whatever food appeared on their plates, while normal weight subjects typically went to the refrigerator, or left the third sandwich untouched, depending on the experimental situation.

Other human studies by Schachter parallel experiments with fat rats. In one, Schachter gave normal weight and obese human subjects either a good vanilla milk shake or one laced with quinine. Like the obese rats in the studies of Miller and of Teitelbaum, the overweight subjects drank more than the other subjects when the shake was good, but less than the normal subjects when the shake was bad.

In another study, Schachter asked normal and obese subjects to fill out questionnaires. He mentioned in passing that they could help themselves to almonds that were in a bag on the desk. For some subjects in both the normal and fat groups, the nuts in the bags had shells, for others they did not. The presence or absence of shells had no appreciable effect on the nut eating of normal weight subjects. But 19 out of 20 obese subjects ate nuts without shells, while only one bothered with nuts with the shells on. These results, of course, are reminiscent of the results of Miller's study showing the unwillingness of fat rats to work for food.

From these experiments, Schachter has gone on to make a cautious point-by-point comparison of the behavior of his obese human subjects, against the behavior of rats in the static phase of the VMH syndrome. He concludes that his fat human subjects may well be the victims of "functionally quiescent" VMH. He suggests that the psychological consequence of the VMH syndrome is the same for humans and for rats: that is, to place eating, and perhaps other behaviors, under the control of external stimuli acting on their senses.

We disagree with Schachter. Food-related cues in the environment do play a critical role in determining the feeding behavior of humans as well as rats, and these cues cause different reactions in the obese of both species. But altered sensitivity to environmental cues is a *characteristic* of the VMH syndrome, not its cause. Consider these problems with Schachter's interpretation:

- To generalize about the cause of human fatness when we know there are dozens of different kinds of obesity is misleading.
- The static, obese rat that he uses as a model behaves very differently from a rat in the initial stages of obesity, as we have already noted.
- The level of general sensitivity to environmental cues is not a good predictor of VMH obesity. In working with a great many fat rats, we have observed no reliable relationship between irritability and degree of obesity. Some fat rats are docile. Others are vicious. Further, minute differences in the location of lesions within a rat's ventromedial hypothalamus can produce extreme finickiness without obesity, or obesity with very little finickiness.
- If VMH obesity is the result of altered reactions to sensory input, why do VMH rats eventually reduce their daily food intake and stabilize their body weight? Early investigators thought it might be because rats entering the static phase of the VMH syndrome are at last recovering from surgery. But this explanation will not work. When starved down to its preoperative weight, then permitted to feed freely once more, a lesioned rat repeats the dynamic phase of the VMH syndrome. It reduces its daily intake only when it has reached approximately the same weight that marked its previous plateau.

Even more striking, Bartley Hoebel and Teitelbaum showed that rats made super-fat through force feeding, then lesioned, refuse food until their body weight *drops* to the "normal" level of obesity among lesioned rats. Thus, it appears that these rats overeat only until they reach a predetermined level of obesity.

- VMH obese rats overeat even when the sights, tastes and smells normally associated with feeding are eliminated. Dennis McGinty, Alan Epstein and Philip

Teitelbaum designed an experiment in which VMH rats fed themselves by pressing a lever to inject food directly into their stomachs. Without the cues which normally accompany feeding, the VMH animals still overate. However, they did not eat as much as they did when the cues were present. The trio concluded that over-responsiveness to sensory cues associated with feeding is not the cause of VMH obesity, but an important determinant in the rate and duration of overeating.

• We have shown in our own studies that the VMH obese rat does not eat with careless abandon. He controls his intake with great precision. He eats in excess of his energy needs, but by an exact amount each day.

Thus, the cause of obesity is not to be found in the environment. It is located in the internal physiology of these fat rats and, we believe, most fat persons. Food intake is controlled by very sensitive neural and chemical mechanisms. In our laboratory, we have been working for years to understand the system in the brain that regulates the sense of hunger and satiety, which in turn regulates energy intake.

We are finding that in the VMH rat, the regulatory mechanism controlling food intake has apparently been altered. Until the rat achieves its new higher "set point" or "privileged weight," daily intake exceeds daily energy expenditure by a constant amount. We thus classify the VMH syndrome as a regulatory syndrome.

One of our major experimental approaches has been to study meal-taking behavior. We ask: "What causes an animal to start eating? What causes it to stop?" These two events define a meal. Rats, humans, and most other animals do not eat continuously, but consume their daily food in a series of discrete meals. Therefore, when a fat subject's daily food intake goes up, he must be eating more meals, bigger meals, or both. He must be snacking, gorging, or both.

A large number of studies, in our laboratory and elsewhere, confirm that the VMH rat characteristically eats no more often than normal, but takes meals that are two to three times the normal size. Our own work shows that even during the dynamic phase of weight gain, the VMH rat controls its daily food intake. For both normal and VMH obese rats, the bigger the meal, the longer the interval between meals. The difference is that if a normal rat and a VMH rat eat the same amount of food, the VMH rat stays satiated for a shorter time.

We conducted a number of experiments that led us to several conclusions:

• No matter how we upset a VMH rat's feeding pattern—by continuously trickling food into its stomach through a tube, or by pumping water into its stomach during its meals—it quickly adjusted to maintain its usual caloric intake each day and to keep its accumulation of fat at a steady pace.

• It is often suggested that human beings who want to lose weight should eat several small meals rather than one or two large ones. We wanted to find out if increased meal size helps to cause VMH obesity. We arranged our apparatus so that spontaneous meals of normal rats were followed automatically by gastric infusion of food to produce the larger meals eaten by VMH rats. The normal rats responded by increasing the interval between meals by the amount necessary to keep daily food intake and weight level stable. Secondly, we allowed a sample of VMH obese rats to eat as many meals as they wanted, but we limited them to small meals. The VMH obese rats responded by increasing the number of meals daily from the usual dozen or so to more than 40. This kept their daily food intake and weight gain at precisely their previous level. From these experiments, we concluded that increased *meal size is not the cause of* VMH *obesity.*

• In another series of experiments, we induced normal rats to overeat by infusing them intravenously with insulin, or by placing a rat and a feeding apparatus in a refrigerator for several days. Increasing the amount of insulin signals the brain that blood sugar is low, and it is time to eat. Refrigeration causes the rat to use up more energy in maintaining body tempeature. In both situations the normal rats increased their food intake by eating more frequent meals of regular size. This was in marked contrast to the feeding pattern of VMH obese rats after surgery: a regular number of very large meals.

• The only way we have been able to get normal rats to eat exceptionally large meals is by injecting them with a chemical called alloxan. Alloxan damages the pancreas, which reduces the amount of insulin in the blood, and thus the availability of blood sugar to the glucose-sensitive cells of the body. While the mechanism of VMH obesity is quite different (insulin levels are greatly increased during the dynamic phase of obesity) this very obviously illustrates the complexity of the problem.

The Inexorable March of Calories

In both rats and human beings, maintaining a constant body weight requires that the number of calories taken in each day balance exactly the number of calories expended in work, metabolic functions, and in maintaining body temperature. Each intake of energy that exceeds energy expenditure by 3,500 calories produces a pound of fat.

In human beings, disease, injury or psychological trauma sometimes result in dramatic weight gains similar to the VMH syndrome. One striking example of this is the recent report of a woman with a medial hypothalamic tumor whose food intake jumped to 10,000 calories a day.

But most people in the U.S. do not get fat in one dramatic burst, and the VMH syndrome does not explain their obesity. Most people in this country get fat in a slow, inexorable accumulation of calories that marks the creeping obesity common to middle age.

The fact that most human beings maintain a relatively constant weight is perhaps more remarkable than the fact that many tend to become obese. It is not uncommon for the weight of an active young adult to vary less than three pounds over the course of a year, an error of approximately two percent, even though the amount and palatability of food consumed, and the amount of physical work done, may vary widely from day to day.

Consider the consequences if such a person were to consume each day only 100 calories more than he needed (for example, by eating one extra ounce of cheese or neglecting to walk 20 minutes). This represents only about three percent of the daily intake of an adult man. In one year he would accumulate an energy surplus of 36,500 calories (365 x 100), or approximately 10 pounds of fat. In five years he would be 50 pounds overweight. Though clearly obese, he could hardly be accused of gluttony. Psychological explanations of obesity are least satisfactory in explaining differences in energy intake of a very few percentage points.

Inactivity: The Likely Villain

This example may help to explain the frustration and anger experienced by some overweight persons when their claims of moderation are met with knowing smiles. While the obese person by definition overeats, he does not necessarily eat a great deal more than his lean companions, and in some cases may eat less.

We believe inactivity is a major cause of creeping obesity. A study by our group in the early '50s compared the caloric intakes and patterns of activity in 28 overweight high-school girls with 28 normal weight high-school girls. The groups were matched for age, height, and socioeconomic status.

Our group found that the overweight girls ate, on the average, several hundred calories *less* per day than their leaner peers. But the overweight girls spent only one third as much time in physical activity as the normal weight girls. This finding has been confirmed for both boys and girls in a number of more recent studies.

A second series of experiments in our laboratory showed the effects of inactivity on rats. Rats were forced to exercise from one to 10 hours on a treadmill each day for a few weeks. Then their food intake and body weights were compared with rats left undisturbed in their cages for the same length of time. The results:

• The rats who exercised from one to six hours increased their food intake to compensate exactly for the increased energy expenditure.
• The rats who exercised more than six hours became exhausted, ate less, and lost weight.
• The rats we left undisturbed in their cages ate more and gained weight.

These results were later confirmed with human studies both in our laboratory and in field settings. These results show that the physiological mechanism regulating weight control works with remarkable precision over a wide variety of energy expenditure, but fails in the extremes.

Obesity is a very complex problem. No single remedy will meet the needs of every fat person. But for the millions of Americans who are experiencing creeping obesity, our work suggests that some of the convenience of our affluent society must be rejected. Walk, don't ride. Take the stairs, not the elevator. Get a sufficient level of physical exercise to keep the body's hunger-satiety control mechanism functioning properly.

Why Sleeping Pills
Are Keeping You Awake

John Wykert

The late Evelyn Waugh's fifty-first winter was miserable. His house was cold, and he was not well. He was growing deaf, drinking steadily, and felt persecuted. He had always been a bad sleeper, but now was worse than ever, despite his heavy use of sleep medications containing bromides. Waugh began to fear that his mind was giving way.

What happened to him was reported by the *British Medical Journal*: in the second half of January, 1954, Waugh sailed for Ceylon, hoping to continue with his writing on the way. While on board ship he suffered from hallucinations that began with his hearing his name in the air. Soon he was unable to sleep. He found it difficult to write coherently when every sentence he wrote was immediately repeated by a bodiless voice. He broke off his journey and came home. He told his priest that he was the victim of diabolic possession and asked for exorcism. Then he saw his psychiatrist, who understood what was happening to him.

According to the *Journal*, "once he had run out of his medicines aboard ship, the persistence of his hallucinations over some weeks fits best with bromism, which would clear up only very gradually." (Bromism is a chronic bromide intoxication with symptoms ranging from foul breath to violent delirium.) Bromides are still an ingredient in some over-the-counter sleep products, despite the fact that late in 1975, a Food and Drug Administration panel of experts judged this ingredient of nonprescription sleep medications to be unsafe—"the effective dose differs little from the poisonous dose."

The FDA monitors drugs continually. Not since 1969, however, have they "formally re-evaluated" prescription "sleepers," and this despite widespread ignorance concerning their proper use. Like Waugh, doctors and their patients at first fail to see any connection between increasing difficulty with sleep and increasing doses of "sleepers." Yet your sleeping pills may well be keeping you awake or causing other troubles. . . .

The continuing threat of "sleepers" to America's insomniacs was demonstrated recently by a young New York couple. No names, please, for you'd recognize the beautiful twosome, staring with appropriate jet-set ennui out of the pages of *Women's Wear Daily*. For a few years they seemed to be everywhere, living a fashioned-in-dream existence.

It was news when they split up. There were hints of this-would-shock-even-you sex practices. Was society's made-in-heaven marriage undone in bed? Yes, undoubtedly. But not quite the way Suzy's readers might fondly imagine.

Would you believe that sleeplessness, or the inability to *fall* and *stay* asleep, sandbagged their togetherness? And also that one chronic insomniac is all that the firmest partnership can handle? Getting on the drug-therapy treadmill finished this couple off. Their complaints of persistent and severe insomnia despite all the drugs they were taking became an obsession with them. The couple's frantic existence was, finally, an attempt to elude insomnia. Their divorce, civilized and cordial, was their way of admitting defeat.

These two sophisticated New Yorkers were innocents when it came to "sleepers" and sleep—they had developed what is called *drug-dependency insomnia.*

Current understanding of this syndrome is due largely to the efforts of psychiatrist Dr. Anthony Kales, director of the Sleep Research and Treatment Center at Pennsylvania State University's Milton S. Hershey Medical Center. More than two years ago, in 1974, Dr. Kales, together with his psychiatrist wife, Dr. Joyce Kales, and associates at the Medical Center, reported a fascinating observation: ten insomniacs who'd been on sleeping pills for a long time, and continued to use them, slept as poorly or worse than a comparable group of insomniacs who were receiving no medication at all. The test lasted two or three nights. What these ten insomniacs made clear is that sleeping pills themselves are the *disorder masquerading as the cure.*

This should not come as much of a surprise. Five of the ten best-selling hypnotics, or "sleepers," are barbiturates. They are the oldest of the most widely used "sleepers" and their action is well known. They depress heart rates, respiration, nerve action, and blood pressure, relax skeletal muscles, and actually interfere with sleep by suppressing the important REM (rapid-eye-movement) sleep stages. They have considerable side effects, all of them undesirable. Notably, the initial dosage becomes ineffective. This is called "tolerance"—a phenomenon in which ever greater amounts of the drug are required to achieve the desired effect.

A German art historian and his wife, a couple in their seventies, had reached the end of a long, despairing road. Money worries, illness, and inevitable infirmities had brought them to the point of no return. Like young lovers seeking to leap into oblivion, they chose a double suicide.

There was only one hitch to their plans. The professor, who had long suffered from insomnia, had been on various barbiturates for many years. When the aged couple were found he was still alive. To his sorrow, he had failed to take into account that a dose lethal to his wife would merely keep him asleep for 24 hours.

Sleeping-pill junkies share with their hard-drug brethren the terrible triad of drug abuse: tolerance, psychological dependence, and physical dependence. In 1974 California sleep specialist Dr. William C. Dement wrote that "almost every hypnotic compound will cause this syndrome when used chronically. . . . Furthermore, in the absence of proof to the contrary, we have concluded that drug dependency will develop in any medication . . . that shows a rapid development of tolerance to its sleep-inducing effects." Yet in America, where almost half of all prescriptions for "sleepers" are for periods of three months or more, most of the testing of sleep products has involved only the effect of a single night of the drug or, at best, a few nights of sleep—one to three nights. These studies are obviously misleading. They are too brief and give no clue to the effectiveness of the drugs over the long haul. Many of the patients who turn to sleep laboratories and researchers for help with their insomnia problems have been taking sleeping pills for a decade or more.

Anthony and Joyce Kales have undertaken what no other sleep researchers have attempted before: testing the effectiveness of available "sleepers." Most recently, they tested Dalmane and Nembutal for 28 nights each. Previously, they had tested Doriden, Noctec, Placidyl, Quaalude, and Seconal, but only for two weeks. All but Dalmane lost their effectiveness within two weeks, either in inducing or in maintaining sleep. Dalmane alone maintained its effectiveness for a full 28 nights.

These findings are astounding when one contemplates the familiarity of "sleepers" and their number— 74 are listed in the drug bible on every doctor's shelf, the *Physicians' Desk Reference*. Despite the many intriguing research reports from the electronic depths of the all-night-sleep research labs, there still exists an appalling lack of knowledge about these widely used and trusted drugs.

The Kaleses' research clearly calls for new evaluations of all "sleepers" to last for a minimum of 28 days. This and other recommendations were made by Dr. Kales in his capacity as consultant to the United States Food and Drug Administration. His recommendations are now included in the soon-to-be-published FDA Guidelines for Evaluating Hypnotic Drugs. But little else seems to be happening.

The extent of insomnia in this country is not known precisely, but an educated guess is that one out of every seven adult Americans suffers from sleeplessness. Moreover, it is estimated that one out of every six adult Americans uses or has used some form of sleep medication once in a while or on a regular basis. United States citizens shell out about $63,780,000 at their local pharmacies in just one year for "sleepers." About $45 million is spent on drugs that are effective for less than two weeks of steady use. This is a considerable sum for America's insomniacs to be spending on generally ineffective as well as harmful products. The amount may well prove to be only one half of what really is spent, since hospital expenditures have not been included.

Late in 1975, the *New England Journal of Medicine* ran an editorial in which Joyce and Anthony Kales explained why sleep medications are so widely misprescribed today. They wrote:

"The physician is often provided insufficient and misleading information, resulting in a general misuse of these drugs." The Kaleses then pointed out that the misinformation derives from generally inadequate clinical testing and incomplete labeling as well as misleading promotional claims made by drug houses.

"One of the primary problems in the labeling and promotion of hypnotic drugs is that blanket statements are made regarding effectiveness without specifying the duration of effectiveness. By stating that a hypnotic drug is effective, the implication is made that the drug is effective not only for short-term use, but also for intermediate and even long-term use," the husband-wife sleep researchers wrote.

"Since pharmaceutical firms are allowed to make such sweeping implications based on data from only one or two nights of drug administration, the firms are not motivated to begin longer-term studies. As a result, short-term studies serve as the only basis for promoting hypnotic drugs as effective treatment for a condition that is frequently chronic. Since the labeling and the promotional material imply that the drugs are effective with continued use, we can understand how the physician unknowingly contributes to the problem."

Given Dr. Kales's definition of chronic use as three months or more, one wonders about a familiar drug ad which ran for years in many of the physicians' publications: "Noctec and the Rest Is Easy," it stated in a charmingly worded distortion.

Dalmane, whose generic name is flurazepam hydrochloride, has been on the market since 1970, and is the first of the new sleep-lab-tested drugs, one of a class of substances, the benzodiazepines, on which are pinned the hopes for better "sleepers" in the future. It is the nation's best-selling "sleeper." Although it is the only drug to have passed the 28-day test devised by the Kaleses' team, there is no assurance of what will happen after day 29. Dr. Elliot D. Weitzman, a neurologist who heads the Sleep-Wake Disorders Unit at New York's Montefiore Hospital, commented: "For the short run, if we feel a medication is indicated, we prescribe Dalmane. But only for several weeks. We cannot answer the question as to Dalmane's *long-term* effectiveness."

At this time it might be advisable to avoid any long-term, continued reliance on Dalmane, and certainly on all other prescription "sleepers." The general wisdom of this is borne out by anyone who naively has descended into the "Valley of the Dolls" to join the characters in Jacqueline Susann's novel. The ascent is painful, as Gerard Souzay, the internationally known French baritone, has reason to know. "I had a crisis several years ago," he told the New York *Times*. "I was traveling all over the world and I lost sleep. So I began taking sleeping pills, and once you do that you cannot stop. I had a real nervous breakdown because of them and it harmed several years of my career. I went to a clinic to get rid of this habit, and I went through hell." A carefully planned, medically supervised withdrawal program was required.

Those who have gone through a withdrawal program bear witness to its difficulties, and especially the need to endure many restless, miserable nights. Above all, there is the lingering inclination to mistrust the evidence, to think that this sleeplessness is true insomnia, not the kind caused by the habit of popping "sleepers." For the hooked barbiturate taker, withdrawal may take from three to twelve months, as he gradually takes fewer and fewer of those blue or red devils, his yellows or nembies. The greater the amount used, the longer the withdrawal process. There are those who have found it easier to get off heroin than barbiturates. The process is especially difficult toward the end, and then medical supervision is closest.

Hard as it may be to re-educate the chronic barbiturate taker, it may be even harder to bring the nation's physicians around.

Explained a New York psychiatrist, who asked that his name not be used: "Doctors would rather use an old, familiar drug no matter how dangerous and difficult. At least they know what to expect. Of course, they do not explain the potential dangers to their patients, and that brings up an ethical issue that bears going into. Except that no one really will. I use barbiturates, and feel comfortable doing so. And I do warn patients to use them only on occasion and never over long periods of time."

The continuing misprescribing of less than effective "sleepers" may be the fault of physicians who fail to listen to their patients. "Doctors do not get at the real problems posed by a patient's sleeplessness," Dr. Weitzman points out. He feels that "the appropriate and correct diagnosis is the problem. And family physicians as well as internists take too little time and effort to discover the real problem that causes the insomnia. It takes just 40 seconds to write a prescription for sleeping pills. That does not get at the problem. On the contrary, the evidence is conclusive that chronic sleeping-pill use can actually produce insomnia and other disturbances."

"Most practicing physicians are quite familiar with the many disadvantages of barbiturate hypnotics and are increasingly aware that an effective and safer alternative is available," wrote Drs. Jan Koch-Weser and David J. Greenblatt in a widely discussed editorial in the *New England Journal of Medicine.* And here is what these doctors at Boston's Massachusetts General Hospital concluded:

"When the benefits, risks, and cost of flurazepam [Dalmane] and barbiturates are compared, the conclusion is inescapable that patients should no longer be exposed to barbiturate hypnotics. Chronic barbiturate takers can be re-educated, and when necessary flurazepam can be substituted. The barbiturate hypnotics have been rendered obsolete by pharmacologic progress and deserve speedy oblivion."

These brave, strong words appeared in the October 10, 1974, issue of the *Journal.* They have failed to resound in the ears of U.S. physicians. The year after this editorial was published doctors wrote some 19 million prescriptions for five barbiturate-type "sleepers." And the public spent some $16.4 million on these supposedly obsolete medications.

Bad old habits may account for some of these prescriptions, but the price of the drugs themselves is also likely to be a factor. Dalmane costs from 10 cents to 20 cents per capsule, whereas some of the barbiturates are available for about 1 cent per piece. The continued use of barbiturates is based on both low price and the erroneous notion that the barbiturates are valuable when used under medical supervision—as Leonie Beamonte discovered in a famed New York hospital, where she was awakened out of a deep sleep to be given a barbiturate. At first, the angry Ms. Beamonte reports, she was zonked by the medication. Four hours later she was wide awake again, tossing and turning, frantic to get back to sleep.

After that experience, Ms. Beamonte refused all so-called nighttime sleep aids the hospital dispensed. Still, to get her way, it required a determined, blue-black-eyes-blazing struggle with the nursing staff and even with the doctor on the ward. But she won. And she slept "just like a baby" during the rest of her hospital stay.

A famed sleep researcher complains that his efforts to educate the hospital staff where his sleep laboratory is located have been "relatively unsuccessful." He has demonstrated the counter-productive effects of prescribing sleep medications as part of a hospital stay. But the nursing staff cannot be budged. They want their wards quiet at night, and more often than not they think they succeed. Perhaps a more valuable notion would be that inexpensive chemical sleep inducers produce poor-quality sleep as well as other problems.

One might expect to find many places where professionals will consult with us about our plight with "sleepers." Not so. The American Association of Sleep Disorders Clinics is something of a fledgling. But the dozen members of the association . . . will presumably supply the quality care U.S. insomniacs have largely been missing.

If prescription "sleepers" are both ineffective and potentially harmful, so also are the freely available over-the-counter drugs. In larger doses than the manufacturers suggest, they may exert impressive side effects. One unsuspected reaction to scopolamine, an ingredient of Compoz, Sleep-Eze, Sominex, and Sure-Sleep, is a condition that is best described as gagaism. How this side effect overwhelmed several Russian émigrés in Paris was described in Janet Flanner's mordant memoir *Paris Was Yesterday, 1925-1939.*

It seems that Prince Yusupoff's valet "encouraged another valet to put scopolamine in the tea of the latter's masters and their guests, of whom the poor Yusupoff was occasionally one," Ms. Flanner reported. The polite poisoning went on for months and induced "gagaism in the noble family and all their tea-drinking friends. This state of complete stupidity, which none of these aristocrats found strange," had other, more observable, consequences.

"Memory vanished, general conversation lagged, the two children dropped behind in their studies and became unable to add two and two without exciting comment from their proud parents. Casual guests popping in for *le five o'clock* were led back to their limousines in a state of complete imbecility." Scopolamine, like the bromides, was recently judged unsafe by an FDA panel, but warnings about the dangers of all nighttime sleep aids are just so many sculptures of snow.

Amnesia may be the core of the matter for the "Valley of the Dolls" people who locate divinity in drugs. Like some primitive tribes, they do not or cannot see a cause-and-effect relationship between the pills they pop and the troubles that ensue. They are abetted in their lack of awareness by the laggard ennui of their own physicians and the astonishing rapacity of drug manufacturers who in their advertisements skirt the truth about sleeping pills. It is a perfect twentieth-century *La Ronde* of mystification.

The safest way to treat insomnia is to avoid sleeping pills altogether. A little protein, a little exercise, and a little sex are all safer, more effective, and less expensive or hazardous in the long run.

The Content of Dreams

W. C. Dement

"I dreamed I was decapitated. My ribs were picked clean . . . no skin . . . no muscle. My body was cut in half. They didn't know who I was, but I still knew who I was. I wanted to pull myself together, but I couldn't."

This dream was recounted to Patricia Carrington during a recent study of the dreams of schizophrenics. (From "Dreams and Schizophrenia," in *Archives of General Psychiatry, 26:* 343-50, 1972.) She studied sixty women, thirty schizophrenics and a control group of thirty nonschizophrenics, then compared the dreams of each group on parameters theoretically related to schizophrenia. Dr. Carrington found that in general the schizophrenic dreams gave the impression of an acute state of emergency or stress, while the control dreams depicted everyday, practical concerns. Among the specific themes that she reported as more common to the schizophrenic patient were physical aggression and environmental threats against the dreamer. The patients dreamed of choking, of being impaled, of being closed in by slowly crushing walls.

Although this example gives an indication of the rather horrifying extremes that dreams can achieve and suggests that they might have some diagnostic utility, a consideration of the study as a whole will also bring out some of the difficulties involved in answering the question, "What do people dream about?" For example, "My body was cut in half." How do we know that this is really what the dream depicted, or that it was depicted realistically? Maybe the dream experience was much less traumatic or totally different, but was altered in the process of remembering and reporting. We would not be surprised at such a possibility in a schizophrenic patient, but we must keep in mind that, until we can directly enter the mind of another person, the dream world is entirely private and we cannot be absolutely sure of what transpires there.

Reprinted with permission of The Portable Stanford from *Some Must Watch While Some Must Sleep* by William C. Dement. Copyright © 1972, 1974, 1976, 1978 by William C. Dement (New York: W. W. Norton, 1978).

Another problem is how to obtain dream samples. REM period awakenings, while they certainly yield greater recall, also alter the dreams by interrupting them before they are completed. Also, the method is too costly in time and energy to be applied readily to large populations. (It might be worth noting that small portable "dream detecting" machines that could be used at home by the subjects are technically feasible.) When spontaneous recall is the only source of dream information, we must assume that most of the dream material is omitted from the sample because it is forgotten. Spontaneous recall was the method used by Dr. Carrington. In addition to the more general problem of forgetting, it is possible that the differences between the schizophrenic and the normal subjects lay not in the dream content *per se*, but in the kind of dream that was spontaneously remembered by each group. Perhaps only the most somber and anxious dreams were recalled by the patients.

Finally, there is the problem of how the tremendous masses of dream data that are often obtained in either kind of study (REM arousals and spontaneous recalls) are summarized and communicated. This task is roughly analogous to summarizing the encyclopedia. What to tabulate, to emphasize? Does one look only at the manifest dream content? Or should interpretive evaluations of the latent content be attempted?

The most objective method for dealing with dream experiences is content analysis. This method is solely concerned with the manifest content of dreams. No interpretations are made and no inferences are drawn about any possible symbolic meaning of the dreams. By far the most extensive attempt to answer the question of what people dream about is the work of Calvin Hall and his associate, Robert Van de Castle. By asking students to write down any dream they remembered, Hall collected thousands of dreams and then applied the method of content analysis in summarizing them. He was eventually able to report that color appeared in 29 percent of the dreams; strangers appeared in 10 percent, somewhat oftener in dreams of women than of men; and so on. Such analysis is affected by the length of the dream, the detail in which it is described, and the idiosyncrasies and personal proclivities of the dreamer.

Several individuals in addition to Hall have used a scientific method for studying dreams. A true pioneer in this area was Mary Whiton Calkins, a psychology instructor at Wellesley College in the 1890s. Introspection was the vogue then, and the papers published by Miss Calkins and her students, Weed and Hallum, are illustrious examples of that method. Miss Calkins said, "It was very simple to record each night immediately after awakening from a dream every remembered feature of it. For this purpose, paper, pencil, candles, and matches were placed close at hand." In spite of the primitive equipment, she and an associate collected 375 dream descriptions, which Miss Calkins proceeded to examine and elucidate in a manner that could still serve as a model of scientific exposition. She found that the majority of the dreams were fairly prosaic; they involved many episodes, people, places, and things that were taken from the current life of the dreamer.

Dr. Fred Snyder, one of the first to do content analysis of REM awakening dreams, arrived at similar conclusions in his paper "The Phenomenology of Dreaming." Snyder found that the most common color in a dream was green, with red fairly close behind. Yellow or blue turned up ony half as frequently as green. Snyder concluded, "The broadest generalization I can make about our observations of dreaming consciousness is that it is a remarkably faithful replica of waking life."

Turning to the determinants of dream content, we are confronted by one of the most fascinating questions of all: Is there a supernatural element that determines what we dream about? Before I discuss this topic, I should present my own personal biases; essentially I have none. The existence of extrasensory perception, telepathic communication, or any event that transcends the physical laws of the known universe is certainly not proven; on the other hand, it has not been disproven. Certainly folklore is replete with accounts of prophetic, telepathic, or ESP dreams. Perhaps the efforts to investigate these phenomena are analogous to the task confronting physicists trying to discover whether there are faster-than-light particles.

The most extensive studies of the phenomenon of ESP and its relationship to dreaming are being conducted by Dr. Montague Ullman and his colleagues at the Maimonides Community Mental Health Center in Brooklyn. Results have varied from very poor to fairly good, and it should be noted that until recently studies were not tightly controlled for biasing effects. In a typical study, "The procedures were designed to investigate the hypothesis that telepathic transfer of information from an A (or knowledgeable 'sender') to a sleeping S (subject or 'receiver') could be experimentally demonstrated." The sender was given sealed envelopes containing reproductions of famous paintings and instructed to open one of these during the night after the subject was asleep. The subject was awakened during REM periods, and dream reports were obtained. Several independent judges were later asked to determine whether there was any correlation between the selected painting and the dream report. The design and controls for judging were elaborately prepared to prevent the possibility of bias.

The total number of correlations was not statistically significant, but there were several instances of unique correspondence between the painting and the dream. When the painting was Chagall's "The Drinker" (showing a man drinking from a bottle), the subject reported, "I don't know whether it's related to the dream that I had, but right now there's a commercial song that's going through my mind . . . about Ballantine Beer. The words are, 'Why is Ballantine Beer like an opening night, a race that finishes neck and neck?. . .'"

At a Stanford alumni conference several years ago, an alumnus in the audience asked me if we had conducted experiments in telepathic dreams. We had, but before I recount our experience, just for the record, I should mention that some of my colleagues threatened to drum me out of our professional societies after they heard of the undertaking. They asked me why we were getting mixed up with such nonsense. You just can't win! Anyway, back to our experiment. During the winter term of 1970-71 I had over 600 students enrolled in a course on sleep and dreams and I thought it would be fun and possibly informative if we conducted an experiment whereby the whole class would try to "send a thought" to people who were sleeping in the sleep laboratory. We indended to test the premise that since single individuals might be able to transmit their thoughts into other individuals' dreams once in a while, 600 people all sending the same thought or image at the same time might be able to really blast through.

Six students from the class who felt they might have special "psychic" talents volunteered to be "receivers." These students prepared themselves by going to bed progressively more early so that on the day of the experiment they were able to arrive at the sleep laboratory for the hook-up at about 7 p.m. Meanwhile, the class gathered at 9 p.m. at the Lucille Nixon Elementary School on the campus, one and one-half miles from the sleep lab. Our first problem was what to transmit. We finally selected several commonplace, unambiguous objects—a horseshoe, a banana, a key. We made slides of these objects as well as of the experimental subjects. We communicated by telephone with the sleep lab so we would know when our subjects began REM periods. The scenario went something like this: first, the laboratory technicians would inform us that a subject was having a REM period; then we would flash his picture on the screen to further identify him to those students who did not know him well; the class would decide on an object to concentrate on; and the picture of that object would be projected on the screen. None of the test images that the class "transmitted" were manifested in the dreams of the students sleeping in the laboratory.

In retrospect, there were many things wrong with this cumbersome and difficult experiment. In particular, one difficulty we did not anticipate was that we could not produce absolute synchronicity in 600 minds. It is actually quite hard to concentrate on a horseshoe for an entire minute, and the atmosphere of 600 students at a "happening" created additional handicaps. Finally, showing a slide of the specific student to whom the "message" was being sent was an additional distraction.

As so often happens in this kind of study, we did get one very tantalizing though completely non-statistical result. During the third REM period of one subject, Rod Boone, the class was concentrating on the slide of a horseshoe. After "concentrating" on this image for one minute, we asked the lab technicians to wake Rod and see if he "got the message." There was no mention of shoes or horses, but Rod did give the rather unusual report that he had been dreaming of staring at himself in a mirror! Perhaps our class, or at least its female contingent, had actually concentrated more on the slide of Rod's good-looking face than on the less inspiring horseshoe.

Dream Sequences

Another approach which was made possible by the discovery of REM sleep and the use of laboratory EEG techniques is to examine multiple dreams of a particular subject on a single night. If we arouse a subject in every REM period, we are likely to get four to eight fairly detailed dream reports. Will these dreams be similar or totally different? We might expect the dreams to be similar just because they occur on the same night. However, we occasionally obtain nightly samples where the dreams seem startlingly unrelated and altogether improbable. A sequence from one of my own nights in the sleep lab started out with two hippopotamuses in a millpond, then a taffy pull in the Russian embassy with Premier Khrushchev as one of the pullers; next a motorcycle

ride through a wheat field. In the last dream of the night I was at my desk in Riverdale, New York, circa 1959, writing some sort of paper. I have often thought of offering a prize for the most interesting night of dreaming—but such an effort might encourage confabulation.

Is it possible that widely disparate dream episodes are related or linked together by some hidden thought or impulse in the mind of the dreamer? Even on the level of overt dream imagery, the degree and variety of possible relationships are virtually infinite. In the most trivial case, five successive dreams might be said to be related to one another if each one contained the image of a tree or if there were people in each dream. At the other end of the scale, dreams might be related in terms of a complex thematic development or restatement that involves virtually the entire content of each successive dream.

The first study on this topic was done by Dr. Ed Wolpert and me back in 1955-56. By awakening subjects ten to fifteen minutes after the beginning of each successive REM period, we obtained thirty-eight nightly sequences of four to six dreams each distributed among eight adult volunteers. In spite of very careful scrutiny, we did not find the exact duplication of a single dream. Many people say they can wake up from a dream, go back to sleep, and continue the dream. But in our study, no dreams in a sequence were ever perfectly continuous with one taking up just where the preceding one had ended. For the most part, each dream seemed to be a self-contained drama, relatively independent of the preceding or following dreams. Nevertheless, the manifest content of nearly every dream exhibited some obvious relationship to one or more dreams occurring on the same night. In the majority of cases, only contiguous dreams were obviously related.

Some of the relationships seemed quite incidental yet intriguing, as in the following example:

(a) ". . . I went inside and started going up an escalator. I could see my wife up ahead of me four or five steps. The place was just mobbed. Then we were going down a hallway and I couldn't get to her. There were cakes of ice in the center of the hallway and people just milling in and out, everyone carrying suitcases and things. Then we started up this next escalator, and there was a girl standing beside me. She had a real shabby suitcase. . . ."

(b) ". . . He was collecting big hunks of watermelon, and I thought I'd get a job helping him, so I started picking them up, and some of them looked more like pieces of ice than they did like watermelon. . . ."

Although the presence of ice illustrates a seemingly trivial relationship between the two dreams, this image, which seems incongruous in both dream narratives, might imply a deeper and more important relationship on the level of the underlying dream thoughts. Thematic correspondence is more extensive in the following narratives elicited from two contiguous REM periods:

(a) ". . . I went in (a house on a hillside) and I had a feeling that I shouldn't be there or that it was somehow slightly naughty to be in there. Anyway, I was inside and I realized there was a gangster somewhere in the house. There was a third party in the room with us, and we were listening to something going on outside the room. Suddenly we had to escape and we all . . . there were three of us, my wife and I and some man, I can't remember who he was but he seemed to belong . . . and we had to get away, so we jumped out the window. Then we got into the car and I yelled to this guy, for some reason, that I ought to drive. He didn't know how to drive our car, but there was something about him—like he was a movie hero or something—and he was taking over. He jumped behind the wheel, and he went roaring up the hill. Someone shot at us out the window as we ran off. . . ."

(b) "It started out with me telling somebody about a murderer. The murderer was supposed to be in this house. I was telling two detectives a rather lengthy story about this gruesome murder. The idea was to lock them in this house with the murderer so they'd catch him. And my wife, or some woman who was somehow related to me, was supposed to leave. So she went outside and I locked them in. Just as I finished locking them in the house it occurred to me that this was a trick, and the murderer was this woman, and she was having me lock the detectives in the house so she could get me. Just as I went running down the porch stairs this horrible knowledge dawned on me. I ran out into the yard and was kind of looking at the house. It was an old house on a hill. The yard was kind of roundish. Suddenly she jumped out of the bushes and began running at me. She looked horrible. She was going to push me off the cliff—part of the hill was a cliff—or kill me somehow. Just before she got to me she changed into a tiger—a tigress. At that moment I woke up crying out."

In each of these dream narratives, a house on a hill is the locale, and the dreamer leaves the house because of some danger. A gangster appears in the first dream and a murderer in the second. However, there seems to be a reversal of circumstances between the two dreams. In the first the danger is within the house, and a safe exit is made by the dreamer and his companions. But in the second the danger is on the outside, and the dreamer is unable to escape but must awaken in terror.

Another longer sequence revealed a very complicated scheme of relationships through four contiguous dreams. The dreamer seemed to be at the center of a kind of classical tragedy, in which those elements of strength which appear in the first dream are the very forces that vanquish him in the fourth. Although the dreams themselves are too long and detailed to be useful here, a summary of the elements will show the skein of interrelationships.

(a) He dreams about a woman whom he has successfully thwarted, and to whom he says: "Let me see your trump card. Let me just look at you." He looks her in the face.

(b) Another man shoots a woman in the back and the dreamer becomes afraid and runs.

(c) The dreamer is seduced by a woman and made to behave passively. A third woman helps to "instruct" him how to make love. Later, he cuts himself on a razor which he has left on a chair and forgotten. The dream ends in a sequence where he is instructing a young boy about the traditionally masculine activity of hunting.

(d) He is playing cards, seated with two women at a bridge table. When he senses something puzzling, he looks at his cards. His are the wrong kind of cards.

As far we we know, the only available method of gathering this type of dream sequence material is the practice of awakening subjects during the REM period. However, this method has at least two important limitations. First, since one can never be certain in advance exactly how long an individual REM period will last, the awakening must occur fairly shortly after the REM period onset. An unknown amount of material is lost because the dream is prevented from reaching its natural termination. Secondly, the procedure of the awakening undoubtedly disturbs the dream pattern. Not only is the dream abruptly and unnaturally terminated, but a series of events, namely the awakening, the description of the dream, and the handling of the recording apparatus, might induce a spurious relationship of one dream to another. An example of this was vividly demonstrated in a dream sequence that occurred when Charles Fisher and I were studying the effects of REM sleep deprivation.

In this study, we hoped to learn whether dreaming represents an oral drive experience. If so, we could possibly substitute eating for dreaming by waking the subject as soon as a REM period started and by feeding him during each of these awakenings. This theory was not substantiated by our experiment—but one of the dream sequences illustrated how the arousal and the interaction between the subject and the investigator can become incorporated into subsequent dreams.

The first subject we tested told us his favorite food was banana cream pie. Mrs. Fisher baked a delicious, creamy confection and we took it to the lab to begin the experiment. Following the usual procedure in REM deprivation studies, we waited until there were several eye movements, then awakened the subject, who reported a short fragment of a dream about walking down a street in Greenwich Village. He ate his first piece of banana cream pie with great gusto and commented, "What a way to do research!" He went back to sleep, began another REM period about an hour later, recalled another dream fragment when we awoke him, and again ate his pie with relish. After three awakenings, three minute dreams, and three pieces of pie, the fourth arousal elicited the following dream: "I was having a cup of coffee and a cigarette." He ate his fourth piece of banana cream pie with a little less enthusiasm and commented, "I always have coffee and a cigarette at the *end* of meals." Describing the fifth dream fragment, he said, "I was given some spaghetti, but I was scraping it off the plate into a garbage can." He ate his fifth piece of pie with obvious reluctance and left the crust. In the sixth dream fragment he reported, "Dr. Dement, I dreamed I was feeding *you* banana cream pie!"

When Rechtschaffen included NREM awakenings in a study of dream sequences, he discovered a thematic continuity in which the vivid perceptual activity of the REM period appeared as a kind of reflection in the NREM awakening and was then transformed into a dream theme in the next REM period. In other words, the NREM dreaming may have some significance in determining the relationship of successive REM dreams. In Rechtschaffen's study some continuity continued throughout the night in both REM and NREM sleep.

We cannot account for what determines thought processes. In wakefulness it is often nothing more than attending to the environment. We know what we would be thinking about during a football game, for example, but with less stimulation our minds can wander in the most improbable directions following random thoughts. Sometimes we have an experience that persists in our consciousness; we have just heard news of the death of a good friend or close relative. The sadness, the upset, the loss stays with us all day and determines our thoughts. Perhaps a similar process takes place in dreaming and other mental activity during sleep; if some significant event has occurred, we will think about it and dream about it one way or another all night long.

This kind of process is found in the dreams of a subject spending his first night in the sleep laboratory. A naïve subject, seeing the rather impressive equipment and having wires attached to his head, will feel extremely anxious; something is going on that has to do with electricity. In a study I did with Ed Kahn and Howard Roffwarg, we looked at first-night dreams and found that about one-third of them clearly depicted the laboratory situation and the feelings of the subject. This figure dropped to about 10 percent on later nights when the subject was confident that the equipment was not dangerous.

Here is an excerpt from a first-night dream: "I dreamed I was lying here and something went wrong so that any second I was going to be electrocuted. I wanted to tear the wires off, but suddenly realized that my hands were tied. I was very relieved when you woke me up."

If dreams occurring on later nights reflect the laboratory situation, they are usually much less fearful: "[I dreamed] you came in and told me there was a big party going on next door. We decided to call it a night and go to the party. After the electrodes were off, I put on a tuxedo and went over. A whole bunch of people were dancing and I saw this girl standing in the corner. . . .".

Herman Witkin and Helen Lewis studied the effects of presleep stimuli on dreaming by showing movies to their subjects before they went to sleep in the laboratory. One of the movies was a color film depicting childbirth; another showed the circumcision rite of a primitive tribe; and the third was a pleasant travelogue. The experimenters found only veiled references to the first two movies in the dreams. In some instances, they reported that the dreams appeared to be influenced by insignificant details that the subjects did not even remember having seen in the movies. From these results, Witkin and Lewis proposed the tentative conclusion that insignificant events may be more influential in determining dream content than significant events. Of course, it is always difficult to assess the "significance" of certain experiences, particularly across the generation gap. In other words, the childbirth and circumcision movies may have seemed more traumatic to the experimenters than they really were for their younger subjects.

Stimuli: External and Internal

We have shown that, in general, stimuli do not instigate dreams. But if a stimulus happens to coincide with a REM period, can it influence the dream content? Anecdotal literature is replete with examples: someone who dreamed of thunder awakened to hear the clatter of horses' hooves on the pavement; someone who dreamed of a roaring conflagration awakened to find a candle flickering by his bed.

One of the first studies of the relationship between stimuli and dream content which utilized the new technique of REM period awakenings was conducted by Dr. Ed Wolpert and myself in 1958. In this study we inserted three different, relatively non-specific stimuli into REM periods. The first stimulus was a 1,000 cps pure tone sounded for five seconds at a level slightly below the awakening threshold of REM sleep. The second was a flashing 100-watt lamp placed where it would shine directly into the sleeper's face. The final stimulus was a fine spray of cold water ejected from a hypodermic syringe. . . . The stimulus was presented after the characteristic change in the EEG and rapid eye movements had signaled the start of a REM period. If the stimulus did not awaken the subject, he was allowed to sleep for another few minutes before being awakened and asked to report his dream recall.

The dream reports were subsequently examined to determine whether the stimulus had been incorporated into the dream. Incidence of stimulus incorporation varied from 42 percent for the spray of water to 23 percent for the light flashes and 9 percent for the pure tone. It should be noted that the water spray, as common sense would tell us, was most easily recognized in the dream reports. Nonetheless, there appeared to be a kind of hierarchy of incorporation. In addition, although a stimulus was presented fifteen times during periods of NREM sleep, no REM periods were initiated and no dreams were recalled on these occasions.

Since the time of this early study, several investigators, with various objectives in mind, have conducted studies using external stimulation. Ralph Berger used spoken names that were either emotionally significant or neutral to the subjects. The names were presented below the threshold of arousal during REM sleep. Berger reported an incorporation rate of about 54 percent but no differences in incorporation between emotional and neutral stimuli. Furthermore, he concluded that perception of external stimuli occurs during REM sleep but that the origin of the stimuli is perceived as a part of the dream.

Vincenzo Castaldo and Philip Holzman used recordings of the subject's own voice and of other voices as their stimuli. When the subject's own voice was played, the principal figure of the dream was more active, assertive, independent, and helpful. When another's voice was played, the main figure was unequivocally passive.

Hoping to provide a conclusive demonstration of the effects of particular stimuli on dream content, several freshmen in my Sleep and Dreams class of 1970-71 conducted an exhaustive study. (The results of this study were recently published in the *Stanford Quarterly Review*, Winter 1972. Other studies done by this class will appear in this undergraduate publication, and I highly recommend it for further reading.) This study involved elaborate procedures and statistical analysis and independent judges were used to rate the amount of incorporation of each stimulus.

The students chose as their stimuli taped recordings of twelve very familiar and evocative sounds such as a rooster crowing, a steam locomotive, a bugle playing reveille, a dog barking, traffic noise, and a speech by Martin Luther King Jr. The subjects were monitored according to the usual procedures, and the sound tape was played starting at approximately ten seconds after the onset of a REM period.

The students found that the sound influenced dream content in 56 percent of the recorded dreams; the locomotive sound was the most effective and traffic noise the least. A strong incorporation of the steam locomotive is illustrated by the following report:

"I dreamed I was riding in a train. I was driving the engine, and the train was in Branner, and right close to the engine there was this pit. It was about two or three stories long, and it was still open, and the train kind of chugged down into it, and it was real scary. I was dreaming the whole time. When I was going into the pit . . . it was amazing because there were some people at the top of the pit watching me go down."

Another area of interest is the effect of internal stimuli on dreams. There are many anecdotal accounts of explorers who were lost and starving and dreamed of sumptuous meals. But Ansel Keys, in his detailed study of the effects of prolonged starvation during World War II, kept track of the dreams of his starving volunteers and found no particular increase in dreams about food and eating. Ed Wolpert and I attempted to determine the effect of thirst on dreams. Three subjects on five occasions completely restricted their intake of fluids for twenty-four hours or longer before sleeping in the laboratory. On each occasion the subjects reported that they were extremely thirsty when they went to bed, and twice the thirst had reached the point at which the subject had dry ips and was unable to salivate. Fifteen dream narratives were obtained under these conditions, and in no case did the dream content involve an awareness of thirst or descriptions of actual drinking. Five of the dreams, however, contained elements that seemed clearly related to the theme of thirst and drinking:

(a) "I was in bed and was being experimented on. I was supposed to have a malabsorption syndrome."

(b) "I started to heat a great big skillet of milk. I put almost a quart of milk in."

(c) "Just as the bell went off, somebody raised a glass and said something about a toast. I don't think I had a glass."

(d) "While watching TV I saw a commercial. Two kids were asked what they wanted to drink and one kid started yelling, 'Coca-Cola, Orange, Pepsi,' and everything."

(e) "I was watching a TV program, and there was a cartoon on with animals like those in the Hamm's beer advertisement."

I was a subject for this thirst study and recall waking up feeling immediately and painfully thirsty. On one occasion I thought I heard raindrops falling on the window. When I looked outside, I saw the full moon and the stars. I think my desire for water was so great that I momentarily hallucinated the raindrops.

Studies of thirst and hunger seem to answer, at least as a first approximation, the question raised by Freud's wish-fulfillment hypothesis, that the dream represents an attempt to fulfill a wish. In Freud's theoretical framework, the wish was not evident in the manifest content, but was in some way disguised. We can see no reason for disguising the wish in the case of thirst. The psychoanalyst would postulate that this wish is fulfilled in a disguised manner when some seemingly unrelated dream event is in fact a symbolic representation of drinking water. This is very difficult to prove or disprove, because even the analysis of the dream by the method of free association would not provide crucial evidence. If the subject were thirsty, very likely his associations to the dream (or to virtually anything for that matter) would eventually drift toward the subject of water and drinking. The fact that dreams may be interpreted or understood in terms of wish-fulfillment simply is not direct proof that the content occurred for the express purpose of fulfilling the wish.

A salient feature of dreaming is often our total inability to exercise control over the events of the dream. Nonetheless, I have found that many of the students and alumni we have questioned report they are able to control dream content on occasion. The fact that nearly every dream takes unexpected and seemingly random jumps and sudden departures makes these occasional episodes of control all the more interesting.

Drugs can exert an influence on the content of dreams, but this effect seems to be somewhat indirect. We know that the chronic use of barbiturates, monoamine oxidase inhibitors, alcohol, or reserpine (rawoulfia serpentina) can lead to nightmares; but in every case the really frightening nightmares occur following withdrawal of the drug when REM sleep is tremendously intensified.

The intensity of brain stem activity and activation of primitive emotional circuits may be what really determine the sense of dread in dreams. It should be noted that an affective response is not always related to the content of the dream. For example, when approaching a door in a dream one may suddenly experience an incredible dread of opening the door and seeing whatever is on the other side, although the response has nothing to do with the specific visual content. Once the dread is present, it may influence what subsequently appears in the dream. In other words, emotion may sometimes determine what we see, rather than always the other way around.

Many people feel that the tapestry of the dream is woven exclusively from the virtually infinite number of sensory images experienced on the preceding day. However, a study by Roffwarg and his colleagues suggests that elements of the dream are derived from sources other than the previous day's experience. These investigators permitted subjects to experience only the color red while awake. They wore red goggles that filtered all light exept a narrow range of frequencies in the red band of the visible spectrum. When subjects saw only red in the day, the red in their dreams increased; but blue, green, and other colors continued to appear in dreams after a week of experiencing only red during the day. Additional evidence is provided by the dream diary of a young man who was paralyzed in a college football game several years ago. Although some of his dreams include experiences in which he is paralyzed and in his wheelchair, others included experiences in which he is able to walk and play football again, and still others include both physical conditions.

Mental activity at the onset of sleep provides another key to determinations of dream content. H. Silberer described a phenomenon in which at the onset of sleep there seems to be a transformation from conceptual and abstract thinking to a kind of perceptual thinking. One can often observe this by waking a subject immediately after he goes to sleep. One subject said, "I was thinking of my mother-in-law's visit, and all of a sudden I saw a big stack of books starting to fall over." Such images appear to be a symbolic representation of a preceding (presumably wakeful) thought, and this is one of the few instances in which transformations are readily observable.

The onset of sleep appears to be related to REM sleep, particularly in regard to the visual imagery and myoclonic jerks. In newborn infants the onset of sleep is REM sleep, and some vestige of this may stay with us throughout life. In normal adults the first REM period is usually removed from the waking world by sixty minutes or more of NREM sleep, allowing ample time for the random thought process to depart from the wakeful setting and mental content. Rechtschaffen's evidence shows that the later in the night the dream is elicited, the less relationship it bears to the events of the previous day and the contemporary world, and the more relationship it bears to the events of childhood. Later dreams seem to draw more and more upon stored images.

Associations that occur as time passes in sleep may be similar to this intrusion of visual images at the onset of sleep. They are not real perceptions, but visual thoughts or brief fragmentary images raised to a more intense level. Even if these associations were to progress as they do in the waking state, by the time the first REM period arrived they would be so far removed from the thought at the onset of sleep that there would be no way of recognizing the connection unless we could trace every step of the circuitous route of the thought process. Even so, it is unlikely that such a con-nection could be made in the absence of an intense preoccupation acting as a link.

Can we dream of things we have never seen? I would say yes—if they are recombinations, inversions, or re-semblances of things we have seen, or if they are things we could draw or conceive of while awake. It is hard to say whether we could dream of something that we could not even conceive of in the waking state.

ECT and Memory Loss

Larry R. Squire

Memory loss has long been recognized as a prominent side effect of ECT. For a decade or two after the intro-duction of ECT, loss of memory was often believed to contribute to ECT's therapeutic effect (1). Today the view is considerably different. Several investigators have demonstrated that the extent of memory impair-ment is not correlated with clinical improvement (2-4). In addition, although right unilateral ECT (5) results in markedly less memory impairment than conven-tional bilateral ECT (6-9), it is clinically as effective, or nearly as effective, as bilateral ECT (10). Thus the available evidence supports the contention that mem-ory loss is an undesirable side effect of ECT that is not related to therapeutic efficacy.

Like the organic amnesias that result from head trauma (11), Korsakoff psychosis (12), diencephalic tumor (13), and temporal lobe dysfunction (14), the amnesia associated with ECT is both anterograde and retrograde. Several general reviews of ECT's amnesic effects are available (15-17). In this paper I will describe recent studies that further clarify the nature and extent of memory impairment.

The first study compared the anterograde amnesic effects of bilateral ECT with the effects of right unilat-eral ECT. The second described retrograde effects of ECT on remote memory. The third reported findings

Presented at the 129th annual meeting of the American Psychiatric Association, Miami Beach, Fla., May 10-14, 1976.

Dr. Squire is Psychologist, Veterans Administration Hospital, San Diego, Calif. 92161, and Associate Professor of Psychiatry, University of California, San Diego, School of Medicine, La Jolla, Calif.

This research was supported by Alcohol, Drug Abuse, and Men-tal Health Administration grant MH-24600 from the National Insti-tute of Mental Health and by Veterans Administration Clinical In-vestigatorship 8084C.

The author thanks Pamela Slater and Paul Chace for research assistance.

involving the reinstatement procedure. (Results with this procedure in animal studies suggest that learned material not ordinarily affected by electroconvulsive shock may be forgotten if a reminder of the material is presented just before the shock is administered (18-20). These reports raise the possibility that eliciting depressive ideation just before administering ECT could be therapeutically advantageous because ECT might produce amnesia for such ideation.) The final study considered memory capacity in terms of objec-tive and subjective estimates of ability many months after ECT.

Anterograde Amnesia Following Bilateral or Right Unilateral ECT

It has been demonstrated repeatedly that bilateral ECT produces a greater impairment of new learning capacity than right unilateral ECT (6-9). In virtually all of these studies, however, learning ability has been assessed with verbal memory tests that are particularly sensitive to dysfunction of the left cerebral hemi-sphere. It is therefore possible that if memory were assessed with nonverbal tests designed to detect dys-function of the right hemisphere the amnesic effect of right unilateral ECT might be similar to or greater than the amnesic effect of bilateral ECT. In two studies of patients receiving bilateral or unilateral ECT (6, 21), impairment of nonverbal memory asso-ciated with bilateral CT was found to be slightly great-er than the impairment associated with right unilateral ECT. However, in the absence of information about how patients with identified unilateral cerebral lesions perform on these nonverbal memory tests, it is diffi-cult to be sure how specifically sensitive they were to right unilateral dysfunction.

My associates and I have recently assessed verbal and nonverbal memory before and after ECT in patients receiving bilateral or right unilateral treatment. To assess verbal memory, patients were read a short story and then immediately asked to recall as much of it as possible. Delayed recall was tested again 16-19 hours later. Patients with identified dysfunction of the left temporal lobe are known to perform more poorly on this test than patients with similar dysfunction of the frontal, parietal, or right temporal regions (22). To assess nonverbal memory, patients were asked to copy a complex geometric design (23, 24). Without forewarning the same patients were asked to copy the design from memory 16-19 hours later. Patients with right temporal lesions are known to be deficient on this memory task, but patients with left temporal lesions exhibit no impairment (25). Tests were administered 1-2 days before ECT and again with equivalent forms 6-10 hours after the fifth treatment of the series.

. . . [B]efore ECT patients in the bilateral group and the unilateral group were nearly identical in delayed recall of the story and in delayed reproduction of the geometric figure. After ECT, patients in the bilateral group showed greater impairment in both verbal and nonverbal memory than patients in the unilateral group. Delayed recall of the story was significantly impaired in the bilateral group ($p<.01$) but not in the unilateral group ($p>.3$). (Differences between and within groups were assessed with t tests.) The scores of the bilateral and unilateral groups were significantly different ($p<.01$). Delayed reproduction of the geometric figure was significantly impaired by bilateral ECT ($p<.01$), and the difference between the scores of bilateral and unilateral groups was just short of significance ($p<.09$).

It has sometimes been assumed that right unilateral ECT causes as much memory impairment as bilateral ECT in aspects of memory function identified with the right hemisphere. Our present results clearly indicate that bilateral ECT impairs memory to a greater extent than right unilateral ECT, regardless of whether the tests used to assess memory are more sensitive to left or right hemispheric dysfunction.

This finding may mean that after unilateral ECT the unaffected hemisphere can always contribute to some extent to performance. This idea is supported by the observation that bilateral medial temporal surgery affects both verbal and nonverbal memory to a greater extent than unilateral temporal surgery (25).

Retrograde Amnesia for Remote Events

It has been reported that convulsive therapy can cause retrograde amnesia for events that occurred close to the time of treatment (15-17). It is now clear that retrograde amnesia can also extend to events that occurred many years before treatment (8, 26, 27). My associates and I have recently assessed remote memory with objective tests that ask about relatively familiar past events. In one test patients were asked to recognize the names of television programs that were broadcast for a single season from 1957 to 1972 (28). The programs, selected from different time periods, were exposed to national audiences to about the same extent, and memory for these programs was acquired close to the time the programs were on the air. Patients who had had a course of bilateral ECT took one form of this test before ECT and another form 1 hour after the fifth ECT.

ECT caused a temporal gradient of impairment in long-term memory (8, 29). Programs broadcast 1-3 years before ECT were forgotten; programs broadcast 4-17 years before ECT were remembered as well after ECT as they were before. Further work indicated that right unilateral ECT caused no deficit in remote memory as measured by this test. Finally, the memory loss associated with bilateral ECT was largely recovered 1-2 weeks after the completion of treatment.

We have also confirmed the clinical impression that in amnesic patients memory for temporal order is more impaired than other aspects of memory (27). Patients were shown sets of three names of television programs and were asked to choose which program was broadcast most recently. In each set of three the correct program name had been broadcast for one season from 1962 to 1973 and the two incorrect program names had been broadcast from 1957 to 1968. After five bilateral treatments, patients developed a marked impairment in their ability to make temporal judgments about this material. The impairment was temporally graded, extending to events that occurred 4-7 years before treatment but not to events that occurred 8-16 years before treatment. The deficit for temporal order information was more persistent than the deficit for recognition of program names and remained unchanged 1-2 weeks after the completion of treatment. Further work is needed to determine how long this deficit remains.

These results indicate clearly that the amnesia associated with bilateral ECT affects not only recent events but also events that occurred many years before treatment. They also indicate that bilateral ECT produces greater retrograde amnesia than right unilateral ECT. Right unilateral ECT caused no measurable loss of memory for remote events; in contrast, a standard course of bilateral ECT led to an impairment in memory for remote events that persisted for at least 2 weeks.

Reinstatement

Normally, the severity of retrograde amnesia is inversely related to the time interval between learning and amnesic treatment. However, several animal studies have suggested that material not ordinarily affected by convulsive stimulation may be forgotten if a reminder is presented just before treatment (18-20).

To assess the reinstatement phenomenon with human subjects my associates and I conducted a study in which inpatients receiving bilateral ECT learned material 18 hours before ECT or about 10 minutes before ECT (30). Alternatively, patients learned material 18 hours before ECT and then were given a reminder a few minutes before ECT. Retention was tested 6-10 hours after ECT. . . . Patients who learned material 18 hours before ECT consistently showed better retention than patients who learned material only a few minutes before ECT (p<.05 by t test). Patients given a reminder just before ECT of material learned 18 hours before retained this material as well as or better than patients not given a reminder. Thus, recalling material from memory just before ECT did not produce amnesia. If anything, the reminder procedure improved retention.

These results cannot rule out the possibility that amnesia might have occurred if the interval between the reminder and ECT had been shorter than the 3 minutes required for administration of medication. Nevertheless, it is clear that amnesia need not occur even when a reminder is given at a time before ECT when memory for newly learned material is disrupted. This finding is of clinical interest because of the possibility that the reminder procedure might be used advantageously with depressed psychiatric patients to improve the effectiveness of ECT. The results of this study provide no evidence that such a procedure would be effective in a clinical population.

Long-Term Effects of ECT on Memory

My associates and I have conducted a long-term follow-up study of patients who had received bilateral ECT, right unilateral ECT, or hospitalization without ECT 6-9 months previously (31). Memory functions were assessed with five different tests of new learning and a test of remote memory capacity; self-ratings of memory functions were also obtained from all subjects. A group of inpatients who at the time of testing were receiving a course of bilateral ECT was also included.

The three follow-up groups did not differ from each other on any of the memory tests. However, the group tested a few hours after the fifth bilateral ECT was impaired on all of the memory tests. . . . As might be expected, the inpatients had more memory impairment than the other groups. There was no significant difference between the retention scores of the three follow-up groups (p>.3 by analysis of variance).

Although no objective evidence was obtained in this study for persisting memory impairment long after ECT, we found in this relatively small sample (N=31) that subjects who had received bilateral ECT reported frequently that their memory was not as good as it used to be (31). Further study of memory complaints involving a larger sample of subjects who had received bilateral ECT or right unilateral ECT 6-9 months before (N=70) indicated that of the 55 subjects who had received bilateral ECT (mean number of treatments=9.9), 37 (67%) indicated that their memory was not as good as it used to be. By contrast, of 15 subjects who had received right unilateral ECT (mean number of treatments=9.4), 4 (27%) felt that their memory was impaired. (Individuals with memory complaints related only to the period of hospitalization were not scored as having perceived memory impairment.)

Such asymmetry in the distribution of memory complaints of bilateral and right unilateral groups could have occurred by chance less than 1 in 50 times (by chi square test). Most of the subjects with complaints felt that ECT was the cause of their memory problems. Eleven of the 37 subjects who had complaints after bilateral ECT selected from four statements the one they felt best described their circumstances. None felt that they had "severe memory problems that interfere with almost everything I do"; 2 felt that they had "many memory problems that are disturbing and that occur frequently"; 6 felt that they had "minor memory problems that occur frequently"; and 3 indicated that they had "only an occasional minor problem."

Unfortunately, the discrepancy between subjective and objective measures of memory function cannot be conclusively resolved at this time. For example, the possibility cannot be ruled out that failures of recall persist after ECT that are not detected by conventional memory tests. We also cannot rule out the possibility that patients receiving bilateral ECT were different from patients receiving unilateral ECT in some way that favored the development of memory complaints. For example, patients receiving bilateral ECT might have initially been more depressed than patients receiving unilateral ECT, or they might initially have had different expectations about memory impairment. Thus it should not be concluded that bilateral ECT causes persistent memory complaints in any depressed patient. However, it seems quite clear that individuals judged clinically appropriate for bilateral ECT do have memory complaints long after ECT.

One possibility that must be considered is that bilateral ECT itself might lead to a lingering sense of memory impairment. Thus the marked impairment of recent and remote memory initially associated with bilateral ECT might cause some individuals to be more sensitive to subsequent failures in recall, even if they occur at a normal frequency. According to this hypothesis, unilateral ECT, which causes less memory impairment than bilateral ECT, would not be expected to lead to memory complaints. In its strongest form, this explanation of memory complaints supposes that bilateral ECT might lead many individuals (with or without psychiatric illness) to have a persistent illusion of memory impairment. It is too early to accept or reject any of the hypotheses outlined here; further work is needed before it will be possible to choose among them.

Conclusions

The findings reviewed above lead to the following general conclusions about ECT and memory loss: (1) bilateral ECT is associated with greater anterograde amnesia than right unilateral ECT, even when memory is assessed with tests known to be particularly sensitive to dysfunction of the right cerebral hemisphere; (2) bilateral ECT also produces more extensive retrograde amnesia for remote events than right unilateral ECT; (3) the activation just before ECT of previously learned material does not cause amnesia for that material; (4) memory substantially recovers 6-9 months after the completion of bilateral or right unilateral ECT, but persisting memory complaints are common in individuals who receive bilateral treatment.

Many different opinions have been expressed about ECT and about the memory loss that accompanies it. In view of the facts presented here, together with the considerable body of information available about ECT, opinions and clinical impressions no longer seem sufficient in most discussions about memory loss and ECT. The experimental findings reported here summarize what is now known about the risks of ECT to memory functions. All other things being equal, right unilateral ECT is preferable to bilateral ECT because the risks to memory associated with unilateral treatment are smaller than the risks associated with bilateral treatment. These risks should be considered together with the benefits of ECT to provide a basis for clinical judgment.

REFERENCES

1 Brengelmann JC: The Effect of Repeated Electroshock on Learning in Depressives. Berlin, Springer-Verlag, 1959.

2 Fink M: Induced seizures and human behavior, in Psychobiology of Convulsive Therapy. Edited by Fink M, Kety S, McGaugh J, et al. Washington, DC, VH Winston & Sons, 1974, pp 1-17

3 Korin H, Fink M, Kwalwasser S: Relation of changes in memory and learning to improvement in electroshock. Confin Neurol 16:88, 1956

4 Ottosson JO: Memory disturbance after ECT — a major or minor side effect, in Proceedings of the First International Congress of the Academy of Psychosomatic Medicine. Edited by Dunlop E. New York, Excerpta Medica, 1967, pp 161-168

5 Lancaster NP, Steinert RR, Front I: Unilateral electroconvulsive therapy. J Ment Sci 104:221-227, 1958

6 Halliday AM, Davison K, Browne MW, et al: A comparison of the effects on depression and memory of bilateral ECT and unilateral ECT to the dominant and non-dominant hemispheres. Br J Psychiatry 114:997-1012, 1968

7 Fleminger JJ, de Horne DJ, Nair PN, et al: Differential effect of unilateral and bilateral ECT. Am J Psychiatry 127:430-436, 1970

8 Squire LR, Slater PC, Chace PM: Retrograde amnesia: temporal gradient in very long-term memory following electro-convulsive therapy. Science 187:77-79, 1975

9 d'Elia G: Unilateral electroconvulsive therapy, in Psychobiology of Convulsive Therapy. Edited by Fink M, Kety S, McGaugh J, et al. Washington, DC, VH Winston & Sons, 1974, pp 21-34

10 d'Elia G, Raotma H: Is unilateral ECT less effective than bilateral ECT? Br J Psychiatry 126:83-89, 1975

11 Russell WR, Nathan PW: Traumatic amnesia. Brain 69: 280-300, 1946

12 Talland GA: Deranged Memory. New York, Academic Press, 1965

13 William M, Pennybacker J: Memory disturbances in third ventricle tumours. J Neurol Neurosurg Psychiatry 17:115, 1954

14 Milner B: Amnesia following operation on the temporal lobes, in Amnesia. Edited by Whitty CWM, Zangwill OL. New York, Appleton-Century-Crofts, 1966, pp 109-133

15 Harper RG, Wiens AN: Electroconvulsive therapy and memory. J Nerv Ment Dis 161:245-254, 1975

16 Dornbush R: Memory and induced ECT convulsions. Semin Psychiatry 4:47-54, 1972

17 Dornbush RL, Williams M: Memory and ECT, in Psychobiology of Convulsive Therapy. Edited by Fink M, Kety S, McGaugh J, et al. Washington, DC, VH Winston & Sons, 1974, pp 199-207

18 Schneider AM, Sherman W: Amnesia: a function of the temporal relation of footshock to electroconvulsive shock. Science 159:219-221, 1968

19 Misanin JR, Miller RE, Lewis DJ: Retrograde amnesia produced by electroconvulsive shock after reactivation of a consolidated memory trace. Science 160:554-555, 1968

20 Lewis DJ, Bregman NJ, Mahan JJ Jr: Cue-dependent amnesia in the K-maze. J Comp Physiol Psychol 81:243-247, 1972

21 Cohen BD, Noblin CD, Silverman AJ, et al: Functional asymmetry of the human brain. Science 162:475, 1968

22 Milner B: Psychological defects produced by temporal

lobe excision. Res Publ Assoc Res Nerv Ment Dis 36:244-257, 1958

23 Osterrieth P: Le test de copie d'une figure complexe. Arch Psychol (FranRf) 30:206-356, 1944

24 Milner B, Teuber H-L: Alteration of perception and memory in man: reflections on methods, in Analysis of Behavioral Change. Edited by Weiskrantz L. New York, Harper & Row, 1968, pp 268-375

25 Teuber H-L, Milner B, Vaughan HG Jr: Persistent anterograde amnesia after stab wound of the basal brain. Neuropsychologia 6:267-282, 1968

26 Squire LR: A stable impairment in remote memory following electroconvulsive therapy. Neuropsychologia 13:51-58, 1975

27 Squire LR, Chace PM, Slater PC: Retrograde amnesia following electroconvulsive therapy. Nature 260:775-777, 1976

28 Squire LR, Slater PC: Forgetting in very long-term memory as assessed by an improved questionnaire technique. J Exp Psychol 104:50-54, 1975

29 Squire LR: Amnesia and the biology of memory, in Current Developments in Psychopharmacology, vol. 3. Edited by Essman WB, Valzelli L. New York, Spectrum Publications, 1976, pp 1-23

30 Squire LR, Slater PC, Chace PM: Reactivation of recent or remote memory before electroconvulsive therapy does not produce retrograde amnesia. Behavioral Biology 18:335-343, 1976

31 Squire LR, Chace PM: Memory functions six to nine months after electroconvulsive therapy. Arch Gen Psychiatry 32:1557-1564, 1975

Shock Treatment, Brain Damage, and Memory Loss
A Neurological Perspective

John Friedberg

A 32-year-old woman who had received 21 ECT treatments stated 5 years later,

One of the results of the whole thing is that I have no memory of what happened in the year to year and a half prior to my shock treatments. The doctor assured me that it was going to come back and it never has. I don't remember a bloody thing. I couldn't even find my way around the town I lived in for three years. If I walked into a building I didn't even know where I was. I could barely find my way around my own house. I could sew and knit before, but afterward I could no more comprehend a pattern to sew than the man in the moon. (1, p. 22)

By 1928, 10 years before the introduction of electroconvulsive therapy, it was known that accidental death by cardiac arrest could result from as little as

Revised version of a paper presented at the 129th annual meeting of the American Psychiatric Association, Miami Beach, Fla. May 10-14, 1976.

Dr. Friedberg is a third-year resident, Department of Neurology, University of Oregon Medical School, Portland, Ore. Address reprint requests to 1120 N.W. 25th Ave., Portland, Ore. 97210.

The author thanks Mrs. Marilyn Rice for her assistance in assembling references.

70 to 80 milliamperes in the human (2). It was also known in this early period that voltage applied to the head, as in legal electrocution, produced hemorrhage and rupture of cranial contents. Ugo Cerletti (3) demonstrated that electricity in the range of 100 volts and 200 milliamperes is rarely fatal when the current path is confined to the head, but does evoke a grand mal seizure marked by a stereotyped succession of events. A tetanic muscular contraction, the "electric spasm," is followed after a latency of seconds by unconsciousness, a high voltage paroxysmal spike and sharp-wave discharge, and a clonic convulsion. Upon recovery of consciousness the subject is left with a transient acute brain syndrome, a high likelihood of permanent brain damage, and greater retrograde amnesia than is seen in any other form of head injury.

Brain Damage in Experimental Animals

Before examining the premise that ECT damages human brains, a brief discussion of the lesions produced in animals by electrically induced convulsions is worthwhile. The many reports on this subject indicate that petechial hemorrhages scattered throughout both white and gray matter and concentrated in the path of the current are the most consistent finding. If animals are sacrificed after a delay of days or weeks following a convulsive series, hemosiderin pigment in phagocytes remains as evidence of vascular insult. Proliferation of glial cells, neuronal changes, and drop-out are also commonly reported.

In 1938, the year of the first use of ECT on a human being, Lucio Bini, Cerletti's collaborator, reported "widespread and severe" brain damage in dogs with mouth to rectum electrode placement (4). At least seven subsequent animal studies employing conventional cranial electrodes supported his findings (5-11). These culminated in the exhaustive controlled experiment by Hans Hartelius in 1952 (12). This researcher found discernible vascular, glial, and neuronal changes in cats subjected to a maximum of 16 shocks. The animals were not paralyzed but were protected from physical injury during the seizure. Damage was slight but consistent, and the author concluded: "The question of whether or not irreversible damage to the nerve cells may occur in association with ECT must therefore be answered in the affirmative." Furthermore, by examination of unlabeled slides alone Hartelius was able to correctly recognize 8 of 8 slides from shocked animals as well as 8 of 8 controls. Although he considered many of the vascular and glial changes to be reversible, there was no mistaking the brain of a shocked animal for that of a control.

Since that time, ECT in humans has been modified through the use of oxygen and muscle paralysis to reduce the incidence of bone fractures. Although it is believed that these modifications also reduce brain damage, there are no animal studies to support this idea. On the contrary, recent work in England by Meldrum and associates (13, 14) on status epilepticus in primates suggests that the overexcited neuron by itself may be an important factor in seizure damage, especially in the hippocampus.

Human Brain Damage

Let us turn now to the neuropathological findings in humans who died during or shortly after ECT. As in lower animals, bleeding is the most frequent nonspecific tissue response to injury and the one seen most often after electric shock. The first autopsy study in this country revealed brain damage identical to that seen in experimental animals. Alpers and Hughes (15) described the brains of 2 women who had received 62 and 6 shocks, respectively. The first woman's seizures had been suppressed by curare. Both brains showed hemorrhagic lesions around small blood vessels, rarefaction of tissue, and gliosis.

Throughout the 1940s similar reports continued to call attention to brain changes after ECT, including cases in which oxygen and curare had been administered (16). In 1948 Riese (17) added 2 more autopsy studies to the growing list and commented, "In all observations of sudden death after electric shock reported so far, petechial hemorrhages, cellular changes and some glial proliferation stand out prominently, as an almost constant whole."

Pathologists were especially interested in cases that discriminated between the direct effect of electricity and the mechanical and hypoxic effects secondary to convulsive motor activity. In 1953 Larsen reported on a 45-year-old man who had been given 4 electroshocks in the course of 5 days. The ECT did not induce any convulsions. The subject died from pneumonia 36 hours after the fourth electroshock. At autopsy fresh subarachnoid hemorrhage was found in the upper part of the left motor region—"at the site where an electrode had been applied" (18).

In 1957 Impastato summarized 254 electroshock fatalities. Brain damage was the leading cause of death in persons under 40 years of age, and nearly one-fifth of all cerebral deaths were hemorrhagic (19).

Some physicians were alarmed by the evidence of human brain damage. In 1959 Allen reported 18 cases in which he had found signs and symptoms of neurological sequelae following ECT. He concluded, "It is probable that some damage, which may be reversible but is often irreversible, is inseparable from this form of treatment," and called for "more serious consideration" of the entire procedure (20).

In 1963 McKegney and associates (21) reported the case of a 23-year-old man who became comatose 15 minutes after a single shock. The significance of this case was twofold: first, a complete physical and neurological examination was reportedly normal prior to ECT, and second, the ECT technique was contemporary and impeccable. The patient had received .6 mg of atropine, 16 mg of succinylcholine (Anectine), and forced oxygenation pre- and post-shock. ECT parameters were conventional, i.e., 130 volts for .3 seconds. Four days later a brain biopsy showed diffuse degeneration of neurons with hyperplasia of astrocytes. The young man never regained consciousness and at autopsy 2 months later evidence of old hemorrhage was found in the brain. This was the last detailed report in the English-language literature.

The damaging effects of ECT on the brain are thoroughly documented. All told, there have been 21 reports of neuropathology in humans (22-36). It is interesting that, despite the importance of a negative finding, there has not been a single detailed report of a normal human brain after shock.

Electroencephalographic Effects of ECT

Like other insults to the brain, ECT produces EEG abnormalities. Diffuse slowing in the delta and theta range, increased voltage, and dysrhythmic activity are seen in all patients immediately following a series of bilateral ECT and, according to Blaurock and associates (37), may persist more than 6 months in 30% of the cases. Such slowing suggests damage to the thalamus.

Sutherland and associates (38) showed that the side of the brain shocked with unilateral ECT could be predicted by double-blind assessment of EEG tracings.

The seizure thresholds of the hippocampus and other temporal lobe structures are the lowest in the brain; considerable interest has centered recently around "kindling," or seizure induction by subthreshold stimulation of these areas in animals (39). The induction of a permanent epileptic disorder following ECT in humans was first reported in 1942 and other reports followed (40).

Memory Loss

ECT is a common cause of severe retrograde amnesia, i.e., destruction of events prior to an injury. The potency of ECT as an amnestic exceeds that of severe closed head injury with coma. It is surpassed only by prolonged deficiency of thiamine pyrophosphate, bilateral temporal lobectomy, and the accelerated dementias, such as Alzheimer's.

After ECT it takes 5 to 10 minutes just to remember who you are, where you are, and what day it is. In the first weeks after a full course, retrograde and, to a lesser extent, anterograde amnesia are evident to the casual observer. But as time passes compensation occurs. As in other forms of brain injury, the subject is often oblivious to the residual deficit. Unless specific memories essential to daily living are discovered to be unavailable the victim may never know for sure the extent of memory loss. Unless sensitive tests for spontaneous recall of personal preshock data are employed, no one else will know either.

The memory loss following ECT generally follows Ribot's law for all pathological amnesias: the new dies before the old. This, of course, is the opposite of normal forgetting. Squire, however, has shown that the loss may extend to items learned more than 30 years before (41).

The effect of ECT on memory was common knowledge within a few years of its introduction. There were reports of persons who forgot they had children (41, 43), although most amnesias involved humbler matters, such as the woman who forgot how to cook familiar dishes (44) and another who couldn't remember her own clothing and demanded to know who had put the unfamiliar dresses in her closet (45). Some doctors dismissed these sequelae as trivial or transient, although one psychiatrist remarked that psychotherapy was useless in patients undergoing ECT because they couldn't remember "either the analyst or the content of the analytic sessions from one day to the next" (46).

Numerous such case reports finally led to a definitive study of the effects of ECT on memory by Irving Janis in 1950 (47). He found that all 19 subjects in a controlled prospective investigation had significant memory loss 4 weeks after ECT, compared to negligible losses among control subjects. He also noted that these losses may involve events of early childhood dating back 20 to 40 years, with the more recently encoded memories being the most vulnerable. Patient E, for example, a 38-year-old woman, had told Janis in an interview prior to ECT that thyroid medication had caused heart palpitations and panic which led to her admission to the psychiatric hospital. When asked after a course of 10 shocks if she had ever taken thyroid she responded, "I don't think so."

In the late 1940s, when the enthusiasm for ECT seemed to have passed its peak (48), Lancaster and associates (49) advocated the use of unilateral nondominant ECT in treating patients who earn their livelihood with retained knowledge. In this variant the current path and most of the damage is confined to the nonverbal side of the brain, usually the right hemisphere. This exploits the well-known neurological phenomenon of anosognosia, or denial, that is associated with right-hemisphere lesions—victims can't verbalize their difficulties. They complain less. Cohen and associates (50), however, using design-completion tests, proved that shock to the right hemisphere produces its own kind of memory loss—visual and spatial. Inglis found in 1970 (51) that the effects of unilateral ECT were comparable to those of right and left temporal lobectomy, with identical impairment of memory and learning.

Recently there has been a good deal of human experimentation in a futile effort to find electrode placements that eliminate amnesia. As the use of ECT has shifted from state hospitals to private practice, the literature has focused more and more on memory loss. Although some studies have purported to show improvement of learning ability after ECT, not one used sham ECT as a control and few used any controls at all.[1]

[1]Sham ECT, an essential control technique, has been employed in only two studies, which were tests of efficacy, not tests of memory loss. Neither study showed any superiority of ECT over the control treatment (52, 53).

In regard to more general intellectual ability, a study in 1973 (54) showed that the performance on the Bender Gestalt perceptual motor test of 20 institutionalized subjects who had received 50 or more ECT treatments 10 to 15 years before testing was significantly impaired compared to the performance of 20 carefully matched control subjects who had not received ECT. The authors inferred that ECT had caused permanent brain damage.

Mechanism of Action of ECT

The mechanism of action of ECT can now be summarized on the basis of evidence accumulated since its introduction. Penfield and Perot showed in the 1950s that memory traces may be evoked by direct electrical stimulation of the temporal lobe cortex, and nowhere else (55). Scoville and Milner (56) discovered that bilateral hippocampal resection utterly abolished the ability to remember any new material, resulting in a catastrophic inability to learn. From numerous studies of the neuropathology of the amnestic-confabulatory syndrome of Korsakoff it is known that the mammillary bodies, the dorsal median nuclei of the thalamus, and the gray matter surrounding the third ventricle and aqueduct are essential to the general memory process. All of these critical brain structures are just beneath the thin squamous plate of the temporal bone, within seven centimeters of the electrodes, in the direct path and highest density of the current during ECT.

Conclusions

From a neurological point of view ECT is a method of producing amnesia by selectively damaging the temporal lobes and the structures within them. When it was first introduced it was only one of several methods of producing brain damage employed in psychiatry, including insulin coma (1927), camphor and pentylenetetrazol (Metrazol) injections (1933), and prefrontal lobotomy (1935). It is the only such method from that era still used on a large scale. It is highly unlikely that ECT, if critically examined, would be found acceptable by today's standards of safety.

From a neurological point of view ECT produces a form of brain disease, with an estimated incidence of new cases in the range of 100,000 per year (57). Many psychiatrists are unaware that ECT causes brain damage and memory loss because numerous authorities and a leading psychiatric textbook (58) deny these facts. Others, who know of its effects, argue that the interruption of unpleasant states of mind is worth the damage. Some are beginning to give the client a truly informed choice, although most state laws still allow ECT to be imposed if the doctor feels that "good cause" exists.

Assuming free and fully informed consent, it is well to reaffirm the individual's right to pursue happiness through brain damage if he or she so chooses. But we might ask ourselves whether we, as doctors sworn to the Hippocratic Oath, should be offering it.

REFERENCES

1 Friedberg J: Shock Treatment Is Not Good For Your Brain. San Francisco, Glide Publications, 1976

2 Jaffe R: Electropathology: a review of the pathologic changes produced by electric current. Arch Neurol Psychiatry 5:838-864, 1928

3 Cerletti U: Electroshock therapy, in The Great Physiodynamic Therapies in Psychiatry. Edited by Sackler A, Sackler R, Sackler M, et al. New York, Hoeber-Harper, 1956, pp 91-120

4 Bini L: Experimental researches on epileptic attacks induced by the electric current. Am J Psychiatry 94:172-174, 1938

5 Heilbrunn G, Liebert E: Biopsies on the brain following artificially produced convulsions. Arch Neurol Psychiatry 46:548-552, 1941

6 Neubuerger KT, Whitehead RW, Rutledge RK, et al: Pathologic changes in the brains of dogs given repeated electric shocks. Am J Med Sci 204:381-387, 1942

7 Heilbrunn G, Weil A: Pathologic changes in the central nervous system in experimental electric shock. Arch Neurol Psychiatry 47:918, 1942

8 Alpers BJ, Hughes J: Changes in the brain after electrically induced convulsions in cats. Arch Neurol Psychiatry 47:385, 1942

9 Alexander L. Lowenbach H: Experimental studies on electroshock treatment: the intracerebral vascular reaction as an indicator of the path of the current and the threshold of early changes within the brain tissue. J Neuropathol Exp Neurol 3:139, 1944

10 Ferraro A, Roizin L, Helfand M: Morphologic changes in the brain of monkeys following convulsions electrically induced. J Neuropathol Exp Neurol 5:285, 1946

11 Ferraro A, Roizon L: Cerebral morphologic changes in monkeys subjected to a large number of electrically induced convulsions (32-100). Am J Psychiatry 106:278, 1949

12 Hartelius H: Cerebral changes following electrically induced convulsions. Acta Psychiat et Neurol Scand Supplement 77, 1952

13 Meldrum B, Roger V, Brierley J: Systemic factors and epileptic brain damage. Arch Neurol 29:82-87, 1973

14 Meldrum B, Horton R, Brierley J: Epileptic brain damage in adolescent baboons following seizures induced by allylglycine. Brain 97:407-418, 1974

15 Alpers BJ, Hughes J: The brain changes in electrically induced convulsions in the human. J Neuropathol Exp Neurol 1:173, 1942

16 Ebaugh FG, Barnacle CH, Neubuerger KT: Fatalities following electric convulsive therapy: report of two cases, with autopsy. Arch Neurol Psychiatry 49:107, 1943

17 Riese W: Report of two new cases of sudden death after electric shock treatment with histopathological findings in the central nervous system. J Neuropathol Exp Neurol 7:98-100, 1948

18 Larsen EG, Vraa-Jansen G: Ischaemic changes in the brain following electroshock therapy. Acta Psychiat et Neurol Scand 28:75-80, 1953

19 Impastato D: Prevention of fatalities in electroshock therapy. Dis Nerv Syst 18:34-75, 1957

20 Allen I: Cerebral lesions from electric shock treatment. NZ Med J 58:369, 1959

21 McKegney FP, Panzetta AF: An unusual fatal outcome of electro-convulsive therapy. Am J Psychiatry 120:398-400, 1963

22 Ebaugh FG, Barnacle CH, Neubuerger KT: Fatalities following electric convulsive therapy. A report of 2 cases with autopsy findings. Trans Am Neurol Assoc, June 1942, p 36

23 Gralnick A: Fatalities associated with electric shock treatment of psychoses: report of two cases, with autopsy observations in one of them. Arch Neurol Psychiatry 51:397, 1944

24 Jetter WW: Fatal circulatory failure caused by electric shock therapy. Arch Neurol Psychiatry 51:557, 1944

25 Meyer A, Teare D: Cerebral fat embolism after electrical convulsion therapy. Br Med J 2:42, 1945

26 Sprague DW, Taylor RC: The complications of electric shock therapy with a case study. Ohio State Med J 44:51-54, 1948

27 Will OA Jr, Rehfeldt FC: A fatality in electroshock therapy: report of a case and review of certain previously described cases. J Nerv Ment Dis 107:105-126, 1948

28 Martin PA: Convulsive therapies: review of 511 cases at Pontiac State Hospital. J Nerv Ment Dis 109:142-157, 1949

29 Riese W, Fultz GS: Electric shock treatment succeeded by complete flaccid paralysis, hallucinations, and sudden death: case report with anatomical findings in the central nervous system. Am J Psychiatry 106:206-211, 1949

30 Liban E, Halpern L, Rozanski J: Vascular changes in the brain in a fatality following electroshock. J Neuropathol Exp Neurol 10:309-318, 1951

31 Corsellis J, Meyer A: Histological changes in the brain after uncomplicated electro-convulsant treatment. J Ment Sci 100:375-383, 1954

32 Madow L: Brain changes in electroshock therapy. Am J Psychiatry 113:337-347, 1956

33 Faurbye A: Death under electroshock treatment. Acta Psychiat et Neurologica 17:39, 1942

34 Maclay WS: Death due to treatment. Proc Soc Med 46:13-20, 1953

35 Matthew JR, Constan E: Complications following ECT over a three-year period in a state institution. Am J Psychiatry 120:1119-1120, 1964

36 Barker J, Baker A: Deaths associated with electroplexy. J Ment Sci 105:339-348, 1959

37 Blaurock M, Lorimer F, Segal M, et al.: Focal electroencephalographic changes in unilateral electric convulsion therapy. Arch Neurol Psychiatry 64:220-226, 1950

38 Sutherland E, Oliver J, Knight D: EEG, memory and confusion in dominant, non-dominant and bi-temporal ECT. Br J Psychiatry 115:1059-1064, 1969

39 Wada J, Osawa T: Spontaneous recurrent seizure state induced by daily electric amygdaloid stimulation in senegalese baboons (papio papio). Neurology 26:273-286, 1976

40 Parfitt D: Persisting epilepsy following shock therapy. Br Med J 2:514, 1942

41 Squire L: A thirty-year retrograde amnesia following electroconvulsive therapy in depressed patients. Presented at the 3rd annual meeting of the Society for Neuroscience, San Diego, Calif. 1973

42 Tyler B, Lowenbach H: Polydiurnal electric shock treatment in mental disorders. NC Med J 8:577-582, 1947

43 Medlicott R: Convulsive therapy. Results and complications in four hundred cases NZ Med J 47:338, 1948

44 Brody M: Prolonged memory defects following electrotherapy. J Ment Sci 90:777-779, 1944

45 Zubin J: Objective studies of disordered persons, in Methods of Psychology. Edited by Andrews T. New York, John Wiley & Sons, 1948, pp 595-623

46 Stainbrook E: Shock therapy: psychologic theory and research. Psychol Bull 43:21-60, 1956

47 Janis I: Psychologic effects of electric convulsive treatments. Part 1: post-treatment amnesias. J Nerv Ment Dis 3:359-382, 1950

48 Spiegel E (ed): Progress In Neurology and Psychiatry: An Annual Review. New York, Grune & Stratton, 1957

49 Lancaster N, Steinert R, Frost I: Unilateral electro-convulsive therapy. J Ment Sci 104:221-227, 1958

50 Cohen B, Noblin C, Silverman A: Functional asymmetry of the human brain. Science 162:475-477, 1968

51 Inglis J: Shock, surgery and cerebral asymmetry. Br J Psychiatry 117:143-148, 1970

52 Miller D, Clancy J, Cummings E: A comparison between unidirectional current nonconvulsive electrical stimulation given with Reiter's machine, standard alternating current electro-shock (Cerletti method), and pentothal in chronic schizophrenia. Am J Psychiatry 109:617-620, 1953

53 Brill H, Crumpton E, Eiduson S, et al: Relative effectiveness of various components of electroconvulsive therapy. Arch Neurol Psychiatry 81:627-635, 1959

54 Templer D, Ruff C, Armstrong G: Cognitive functioning and degree of psychosis in schizophrenics given many electro-convulsive treatments. Br J Psychiatry 123:441-443, 1973

55 Penfield W, Perot P: The brain's record of auditory and visual experience. Brain 86, Part 4, 1963

56 Scoville W, Milner B: Loss of recent memory after bilateral hippocampal lesions. J Neurol Neurosurg Psychiatry 20:11-21, 1957

57 Friedberg J: Electroshock therapy: let's stop blasting the brain. Psychology Today 9(8):18-23, 1975

58 Kalinowsky LB: The convulsive therapies, in Comprehensive Textbook of Psychiatry, 2nd ed, vol II. Edited by Freedman AM, Kaplan HI, Sadock BJ. Baltimore, Williams & Wilkins Co, 1975, pp 1972-1973

Current Perspectives on ECT
A Discussion

Fred H. Frankel

In my view, Dr. Friedberg has weakened his position by the manner in which he has gathered the evidence to support it. The questions he raises are relevant; they have been asked by many others. However, he has attempted to answer them with data that have been carelessly culled from the literature and frequently reported inaccurately.

Dr. Friedberg's evidence against ECT is arranged in four main sections. He reports on the neuropathological findings in experimental animals subjected to electrically induced convulsions, and in humans who have died during a course of ECT or within weeks or months afterward. He then reports studies and subjective accounts of memory loss and, finally, EEG changes. He concludes that "from a neurological point of view ECT is a method of producing amnesia by selectively damaging the temporal lobes and the structures within them." He states that "ECT produces a form of brain disease" of epidemic proportions and asks why doctors, who are sworn to the Hippocratic Oath, are offering it.

Dr. Friedberg has listed 58 references in his article. I have examined 25 of these and selected those which seemed especially relevant to his argument.

In presenting his evidence for brain damage in animals exposed to electrical currents, Dr. Friedberg states: "In 1938, the year of the first use of ECT on a human being, Lucio Bini, Cerletti's collaborator, reported 'widespread and severe' brain damage in dogs. At least seven subsequent animal studies confirmed his findings." The following quotation is from the Bini reference:

We have so far employed exclusively the method of Viale, which consists of passing the street current (120 volts) for a very short time (1/15 to 1/20 second) through the entire body of the animal with one of two electrodes (carbons from a voltaic arc) in the mouth and the other in the rectum.

With this method we succeeded in producing constantly typical epileptic attacks in dogs. During the passage of the current the animal howls and has a violent tonic spasm with opisthotonus which lasts several seconds after the circuit is opened. Then there appear frequent and violent generalized tonic and clonic convulsions with foaming at the mouth, biting of the tongue, and incontinence of urine and feces. The duration of this second phase varies from 1-2 minutes. There follows a comatose state with complete muscular relaxation, absence of corneal and pupillary reflexes and stertorous breathing. In a short time the animal returns to its normal state, so that after a few minutes new seizures may be induced.

The alterations found by us in the nervous systems of these dogs were widespread and severe. (2, p. 173)

Bini did not state how many seizures were induced, but clearly they were multiple, and the current was applied along the course of the entire body, with one electrode in the mouth and the other in the rectum. I cannot seriously believe that Friedberg considers this to be the customary method of administering ECT, and yet he has quoted Bini's report as if the procedures described were analogous to those used today. Furthermore, there is no mention of the method of sacrificing the animals and no consideration of the fact that anoxia or trauma could have contributed to Bini's findings in the central nervous system.

Dr. Friedberg then claims that seven subsequent animal studies confirmed Bini's findings. In doing so, he has revived the controversy that waxed during the 1940s. I have examined five of these references. Far from confirming the point, two (3, 4) unequivocally disagree with the idea that widespread and severe damage results from electrically induced convulsions in animals, *unless* the current is abnormally prolonged or administered repeatedly or in excess of that used in ECT.

The three other studies I examined are the well-publicized reports by Alpers and Hughes (5), Heilbrunn and Weil (6), and Neuberger and associates (7).

Revised version of a presentation at the 129th annual meting of the American Psychiatric Association, Miami Beach, Fla., May 10-14, 1976.

Dr. Frankel is Head, Adult Psychiatric Unit, Beth Israel Hospital, 330 Brookline Ave., Boston, Mass. 02215. He is also Associate Professor of Psychiatry, Harvard Medical School, Boston, Mass.

American Journal of Psychiatry 1977, 134:1014-1019. Copyright 1977, the American Psychiatric Association. Reprinted by permission.

They all reported damage to the central nervous system. However, a detailed study of their comments revealed less than the well-established evidence that Friedberg claims supports his argument. Alpers and Hughes (5) made no mention of the voltage used. Heilbrunn and Weil (6) reported an electrically produced convulsion in 28 rabbits, 16 of which were paralyzed in the lower limbs, bladder, and rectum after the first few shocks. Nonetheless, they were then still shocked daily for several days before being sacrificed and examined. The size of the electrodes and the current used were equivalent to those employed in ECT and were totally disproportionate to the size of the rabbit's brain. In no way can that study be considered relevant to the current administration of ECT. Neuberger and associates reported that although they found pathological changes in the brains of the animals studied, these changes "were not to be regarded as serious."

Space limitations preclude a detailed examination of the other contradictions and inconsistencies that unfold during an examination of Dr. Friedberg's bibliography, but it is necessary to study a few of them in some detail if we are to place his paper in perspective. He has published widely and has worked hard at trying to influence public opinion. He has revived the controversy of the 1940s and 1950s and maintains that the introduction of anesthesia, oxygenation, and muscle paralysis since that time has in no way diminished the risks of ECT. He appears to base his position on the following two principal assertions: 1) he argues as if the damage caused by a single seizure must be as great as that caused by large numbers of seizures concentrated within a brief period of time, and 2) he states emphatically, "Although it is believed that these modifications [of ECT, namely, the use of anesthesia, oxygenation, and muscle paralysis] also reduce brain damage, there are no animal studies to support this idea."

Dr. Friedberg's next sentence is perhaps the most misleading. "On the contrary, recent work in England by Meldrum and associates [8, 9] on status epilepticus in primates suggests that the overexcited neuron by itself may be an important factor in seizure damage, especially in the hippocampus."

The recent reports by Meldrum and associates deal with the effects of prolonged seizure activity in baboons in an attempt to understand the effects of status epilepticus in humans. In the first study (8), seizures were precipitated in 8 anesthetized adolescent baboons by injections of the convulsant bicuculline. The animals were artificially paralyzed and oxygenated, and the seizure activity was recorded on EEG. Physiological factors were monitored. The activity lasted from 3¼ to 7½ hours in 7 of the 8 ani-

mals. The eighth animal experienced a period of 13 minutes of seizure activity and then, after a second injection of the convulsant almost 3 hours later, experienced an additional hour and 49 minutes of seizure activity. The animals were sacrificed during or shortly after the seizures and the brains examined. There were ischaemic cell changes in the brains of the first 7 animals, but not in the brain of the eighth animal, which had experienced only a little over 2 hours of seizure activity. Meldrum and associates (8) noted that in comparison with their previous work, the presence of peripheral motor paralysis and artificial respiration greatly reduced the severity of the systemic changes and modified the pattern of epileptic brain damage.

How do these comments fit in with Dr. Friedberg's assertion that there are no animal studies to support the idea that modifications of ECT reduce brain damage? In support of his position he reported, out of context, a suggestion by Meldrum and associates that the overexcited neuron by itself may be an important factor in seizure damage. The overexcited neuron alluded to in the original paper refers to the neuron after excessive discharge and seizure activity lasting from 3¼ to 7½ hours, which is scarcely comparable to the neuronal activity associated with a single session of ECT.

In a subsequent study by Meldrum and associates (9), 13 baboons were submitted to similar experiments using the convulsant allylglycine. Five animals developed status epilepticus, and in the other 8 animals, 6-63 seizures occurred in a period of 2-11 hours. Progressive hypoglycemia and hyperpyrexia occurred with the recurrent seizures. The animals were sacrificed at varying stages up to 6 weeks after the experience, and the brains examined. The animals that had had 6-26 seizures over a period of several hours showed *no* pathological sequelae. The animals that had had more than 26 seizures, or status epilepticus, showed varying degrees of ischaemic cell change and neuronal loss with gliosis in the neocortex and lesions in the hippocampus. Meldrum and associates felt that the relative importance of the various physiological changes associated with the repeated seizures could not be definitively established, and they concluded that the effects of hypoglycemia, hyperpyrexia, reduced oxygenation, and impaired cerebral perfusion were probably additive in causing the damage.

Dr. Friedberg's discussion of brain damage found at autopsy on patients who died during or after ECT contains an equally unconvincing body of evidence. It leaves the reader wondering, in many instances, about the true nature of the disease for which ECT had been given, how carefully neurological disease had been excluded prior to administration of ECT, and what role cardiovascular and renal disease had played in causing the pathology found at autopsy. McKegney and Panzetta's report in 1963 (10) of a 23-year-old man who became comatose 15 minutes after his first course of ECT and died 2 months later without having regained consciousness illustrates the point very well. The following material is from the original article:

The patient, a 23-year-old, single, white male . . . was initially seen in the emergency department of a general hospital on Apr. 5, 1962 because of withdrawn and bizarre behavior. He had a long history of "emotional difficulty". . . .
The medical house officer who first saw the patient . . . was unable to perform a complete physical examination since the patient seemed purposively to resist, giggling inappropriately at times, curling himself up and lying with his hands between his thighs. Psychiatric consultation at that time suggested the diagnosis of schizophrenic reaction, catatonic type, and the patient was admitted to the psychiatric unit.
The patient remained essentially unchanged throughout the rest of the evening and the following day, lying in bed with his eyes closed. When called by name he would start and half open his eyes, but then close them quickly and turn his back on the examiner. . . . There were considerable posturing and unusual movements. A complete physical and neurological examination, performed on the second hospital day, was negative in all respects other than the behavior noted above. The axial temperature was 37°C; blood pressure 120/72; pulse 58 per minute and regular; respiration 16-20 per minute and regular.
In order that the patient could be fed and more readily mobilized, he was given his first ECT on the morning of Apr. 7 (atropine .6 mpm., as premedication; anectine 16 mgm. intravenously; 130 volts for 0.3 seconds; forced breathing with oxygen pre and post ECT). (10, pp. 398-399)

It was soon apparent that the patient's post-ECT recovery was not normal. The patient died June 11, 1962, more than two months later, without ever deviating from his progressively deteriorating course. Brain biopsy showed diffuse degeneration of neurons with hyperplasia of astrocytes. At autopsy, old hemorrage was found in the brain.

There are several interesting and challenging details of this case report not recounted fully here. I would nonetheless have hoped that Dr. Friedberg, as a neurologist, would have been sensitive to the neurologically salient points in the case. It is most unlikely that the subtle measurements that are part of a complete neurological examination were possible in a patient as uncooperative as this one; and the EEG and cerebrospinal fluid analysis and culture were carried out *after* the ECT, not before it. The diagnosis of catatonic schizophrenia is poorly supported by the information in the case history, and in my opinion the presence of organic brain disease had not been ruled out before the hasty use of ECT to control the patient's symptoms. In the absence of a clear diagnosis, the use of ECT to control symptoms is ill-advised.

Allusions in Dr. Friedberg's paper to several other articles fail to reflect the balanced view that the articles actually convey when read in the original. Interested readers should examine for themselves some of the studies to which he refers. The literature of that period is rich in reports expressing differing views. Dr. Friedberg either ignores them or, as I have indicated, quotes them erroneously.

His comments regarding memory loss after ECT, and EEG changes, are made with the same bold, sweeping strokes. There are occasional complaints of memory loss after ECT, but the results of unilateral electrode placement would not be regarded as a "futile effort" to remedy the problem. Dr. Friedberg would have us believe that because of damage to the right cerebral hemisphere after unilateral ECT, the improvements reported by patients are attributable to their denial of their illness and their inability to verbalize their difficulties. No one who has ever talked with patients and shared their relief and delight at feeling better and capable of a normal life after ECT can take Dr. Friedberg's assertion seriously, especially when 6-12 months later these patients are still functioning and feeling well.

None of my statements should be construed to mean that there are no unanswered questions regarding ECT. I believe there are many unsolved problems. . . . There is no reason to assume that we can induce large numbers of seizures with impunity because less than 26 seizures in Meldrum and associates' baboons did not seem to be associated with cerebral damage. In addition, it is clear that there are insufficient data at this time from which to understand the occasional complaints of persistent memory disturbance after ECT. The APA Task Force on ECT, on which I serve, was established to weigh the evidence as carefully as possible and to assess realistically the cost/benefit ratio of ECT. There is no simple answer to the questions, and Dr. Friedberg's determination to present one has involved him in a report of the literature that is not only inaccurate and careless, but also somewhat indiscriminate. In addition, his reports of memory impairment have been gathered from people who answered his newspaper advertisement soliciting complaints. He headed the advertisement, "Shock treatment is not good for your brain." He is, therefore, basing his conclusions regarding memory loss on a biased sample; in addition, he could have harmed the very people he claims to be helping by reinforcing the secondary gain provided by their amnesia and their overwhelming yet poorly understood anger.

It seems to me that Dr. Friedberg's personal opinions have been presented as scholarly decisions. He has directed them at stirring up emotions in an area already sorely in need of reasoned discourse and a serious effort to understand why, when ECT has brought relief to so many thousands of patients in the past, in some cases it has resulted in dissatisfaction and angry complaints. I hope that he will consider joining the ranks of those who aim to grapple with the issues by carefully and painstakingly sifting the evidence and concentrating on the facts.

*　　*　　*

REFERENCES

1 Frankel FH: Electroconvulsive therapy in Massachusetts: a task force report. Massachusetts Journal of Mental Health 3:3-29, 1973

2 Bini L: Experimental researches on epileptic attacks induced by the electric current. Am J Psychiatry, May Supplement, 1938, pp 172-174

3 Alexander L, Lowenbach H: Experimental studies on electroshock treatment. J Neuropathol Exp Neurol 1:444-446, 1942

4 Heilbrunn G, Liebert E: Biopsies on the brain following artificially produced convulsions. Arch Neurol Psychiatry 46:548-552, 1941

5 Alpers BJ, Hughes J: Changes in the brain after electrically induced convulsions in cats. Arch Neurol Psychiatry 47:385-398, 1942

6 Heilbrunn G, Weill A: Pathologic changes in the central nervous system in experimental electric shock. Arch Neurol Psychiatry 47:918-927, 1942

7 Neuberger KT, Whitehead RW, Rutledge AK, et al: Pathologic changes in the brains of dogs given repeated electric shocks. Am J Med Sci 204:381-387, 1942

8 Meldrum BS, Vigoroux RA, Brierley JB: Systemic factors and epileptic brain damage. Arch Neurol 29:82-87, 1973

9 Meldrum BS, Horton RW, Brierley JB: Epileptic brain damage in adolescent baboons following seizures induced by allylglycine. Brain 97:407-418, 1974

10 McKegney FP, Panzetta AF: An unusual fatal outcome of electro-convulsive therapy. Am J Psychiatry 120:398-400, 1963

11 Stone AA: Mental Health and Law: A System in Transition. Rockville, Md, National Institute of Mental Health, 1975

12 Grosser GH, Persall DT, Fisher CL, et al: The regulation of electro-convulsive treatment in Massachusetts: a follow-up. Massachusetts Journal of Mental Health 5:12-25, 1975

Cerebral Effects of Differential Experience and Training

Edward L. Bennett

. . . [M]any behavioral, physiological, and biochemical differences have been found between animals raised in isolated or impoverished conditions (IC), standard colony conditions (SC), and enriched conditions (EC). Numerous investigators in this country and abroad have begun to study the effects of such differential environments.

The goal of many workers in this area is to determine if any of these differences are in fact closely associated with learning and memory mechanisms. We believe some brain changes may be quite closely related. It is our strong conviction that explanations of long-term memory will ultimately be cast in terms of anatomical changes. At the gross level, these are reflected in changes in measures of cortical weight and thickness and cell size. However, these relatively gross changes may reflect, in part, higher metabolic activity necessary for sustaining higher levels of cerebral (neuronal) activity and, in part, higher levels of biosynthetic activity required for making more subtle anatomical changes.

. . . These comments will include updated results on synaptic differences produced by environmental complexity as studied by electron micrography, some additional observations on the permanence and persistence of EC effects, some observations on age dependence, and some recent work in our laboratory and in Switzerland on enhancement of EC effects. Then I would like to discuss some experiments in progress that attempt to relate EC-IC effects to neural processes concerned with memory. Along the way I would like to suggest several potential areas of future research using differential environments.

Anatomical Differences Produced by Differential Environments

We started looking for fine structural changes about a decade ago. Holloway (1966) first reported differences in dendritic branching on tissue prepared in our laboratories. We recently reported the higher frequency

In M. R. Rosenzweig and E. L. Bennett (Eds.), *Neural Mechanisms of Learning and Memory* (Cambridge, MA: MIT Press, 1976), Chapter 17. Copyright 1976 by Massachusetts Institute of Technology. *Editors' note:* Tables and a figure have been omitted.

of dendritic spines on basal dendrites of occipital-cortex pyramidal neurons in rats raised in enriched environments when compared to littermates raised in impoverished conditions (Globus et al., 1973). Greenough has summarized some of his elegant studies on dendritic branching as well.

With respect to measurements on individual synapses of occipital cortex, an updating of our results brings them more in line with Greenough's. While we originally reported a 52 percent increase in the length of the post-synaptic opaque region in type-1 synapses or asymmetrical axodentritic junctions from layer 3, and a frequency decrease of one-third (Mollgaard et al., 1971), we have not been able to replicate these findings. Our best present estimates based on thirteen complete sets of triplets are much more in agreement with those of Greenough: about a 5 percent EC-IC difference in length ($p < 0.05$) and an 8 percent decrease in frequency (ns) in layer 4 (Diamond et al., 1975). While it would have been nice to have been able to replicate the much larger differences, I feel that the important observation is that differential environments produce synaptic changes that can be detected by current anatomical methods. These are the types of changes that we feel are most likely to be closely associated with memory processes. Certainly this is an area of research that deserves much more intensive investigation. However, such investigations are restricted now by the laborious nature of the research—it requires a great deal of skill, patience, and many months of dedicated work to carry out refined quantitative work at the anatomical level. Ultimately, sufficient resources must be made available so that much of the quantitation can be automated and computerized. Marian Diamond, in collaboration with Leroy Kerth of the Lawrence Berkeley Laboratory, is now undertaking some feasibility studies of more automated quantitation using scanning equipment originally developed for research in high-energy physics.

The Permanence and Persistence of Brain Effects

Greenough has raised the questions of the permanence and age dependence of brain effects of differential environments, and we have new data that bear on these questions.

While certain effects of complex experience may be transient or change in magnitude with time, I believe the conclusion is valid that differences in several cerebral measures are permanent: weight . . . and thickness of cortex; ratio of cortical to subcortical weight, acetylcholinesterase activity and cholinesterase activity; and RNA/DNA ratio . . . . By "permanent," I mean that these differences are maintained for as long as the animals are differentially housed.

A question related to permanence is that of the persistence of effects of differential housing when animals are removed from enriched conditions and placed in impoverished conditions. If some of the effects of differential environments are related to memory storage, we would expect that some cerebral differences would persist for a long time when animals are rehoused, while others, related to early steps in storage, would cease to differ relatively quickly.

Brown (1971) reported surprisingly large (and variable) differences in AChE and ChE activities produced by her version of an enriched environment. She claimed that these effects vanished within a few days after animals were placed into isolation. Under our conditions of EC, we have not found this to be the case—differences in cortical brain-weight measures and AChE activity fall but are measurable for at least seven weeks when our EC rats are placed into IC, and the fall is slower after 80 days of EC than after 30 days of EC (Bennett et al., 1974). . . .

Age Dependence of the Cerebral Effects of Differential Experience

Greenough has already noted that the postweaning age at which animals are housed in differential environments does not appear to be critical for producing differences in certain cerebral measures, including cortical weight and depth. In fact, the differences in brain weights are remarkably similar in magnitude whatever the starting age of the rats, at least to one year of age. . . .

Only one study of which I am aware has investigated the cerebral effects of differential environments in preweaning rats. This is the study of Malkasian and Diamond (1971), who reported that young rat pups living in a multifamily enriched environment had significantly greater cortical depths and larger neuronal nuclear areas, in both the somatosensory and occipital areas of the cortex, than pups from rats raised under standard colony conditions. These authors concluded that these cortical differences demonstrated more plasticity in the neonate than in the young adult rat brain. To date, I know of no experiment in which the

differential environments have been initiated at preweaning ages and then carried through for 30 days or more into postweaning, and the resulting cerebral effects investigated. This may be a fruitful area for further research.

Enhanced EC Effects

When it is realized that an enriched environment can increase brain measures, it is only natural to ask if EC effects can be even further increased; that is, can a "super" EC condition be devised? We have recently shown that certain stimulant drugs can interact with the enriched conditions to produce enhanced cerebral effects (Bennett, Rosenzweig, and Wu, 1973; Rosenzweig and Bennett, 1972), but perhaps some purely environmental methods can be found.

It would appear from his description of procedures that Greenough uses a somewhat larger complement of toys than we do. Several years ago we became aware of a study by Ferchmin, Eterović, and Caputto (1970), who reported small but significant increases in cerebrum weight (total brain excluding cerebellum, medulla, and pons) after as few as four days of EC. They also reported an initial increase in total brain RNA and RNA/mg after four days of EC. However, after eight days of EC, RNA/mg differed only slightly between groups. We were fortunate enough to have Drs. Ferchmin and Eterović in our laboratory for two years, and in discussion it became quite apparent that their EC conditions were considerably more complex than ours. They rotate animals twice a day among four cages, some of which are considerably larger than ours and offer more opportunity for climbing. We have run a number of experiments comparing the effects of what we shall refer to as FEC (Ferchmin EC) to our regular EC and IC conditions.

I shall discuss the weight results first and come back to results concerning nucleic acids later. The most striking observation to be made is that significant weight effects can be found in occipital cortex and total cortex when four days of differential environments are begun at weaning. . . . Thus certain cerebral effects are shown with much shorter durations of differential environments than we had previously realized. The differences obtained by the Ferchmin EC are very similar to those obtained with the usual EC. A possible advantage of FEC over regular EC is seen only in the weight ratio of cortex to the rest of the brain at four and eight days (1.7 vs. 0.2 percent, and 2.6 vs. 1.7 percent).

Two Swiss investigators, Kuenzle and Knüsel (1974) have also attempted to enhance EC conditions in order to get increased cerebral differences. They housed a group of 70 rats in two large cages provided with varied stimulus objects and connected by tunnels. Each day for 29 days food was placed in one of the cages and water in the other, so that the rats had to shuttle back and forth between the two cages. Gradually the rats were made to solve problems and to climb ropes or jump from one platform to another in order to traverse the tunnels. Brain values of rats from this "superenriched environment" (SE) were compared with those of rats of the same strain kept for 29 days in a copy of our typical EC conditions. In three successive experiments SE rats were found to be significantly greater than ECs in cerebral length, weight of occipital cortex, and ChE/AChE ratio in occipital cortex; small but nonsignificant differences in the same direction were found in the RNA/DVA ratio in occipital cortex.

Another, quite different method by which we have tried to enhance the effects of differential environments is through the use of a "seminatural" environment. Our seminatural-environment rats (SNE) live out of doors in 9-m^2 enclosures with a dirt floor 60 cm or so in depth. These animals are exposed to the rigors of Berkeley weather. Rats put into the seminatural environment at about 40 days of age have adapted well, and virtually all have survived. We now have nine experiments in which we can compare rats raised in a seminatural environment for 30 days to rats raised in regular EC conditions at the Field Station in the Berkeley hills. The seminatural environment does bring about moderate but significant increases in cerebral weight measures over the Field Station EC animals, which in turn are significantly different from IC littermates . . . . A limited number of additional control experiments indicate that Field Station EC animals are not significantly different from EC rats maintained in Tolman Hall. (All comparisons are against the appropriate littermate group run in the same experiment. However, different combinations of groups were run in different experiments; thus the overall difference from seminatural environment to Tolman IC cannot be obtained by adding differences of intermediate groups.) Thus, to date, raising rats in a seminatural environment appears to be a simple and effective way to obtain significantly larger EC effects than we have typically obtained. These results suggest that laboratory EC conditions are good but not optimal.

Factors Producing Cerebral Effects

In order to evaluate whether the effects of differential environments can be related to learning and memory mechanisms, we must have a more complete understanding of the factors that produce cerebral differences.

In a number of studies we have attempted to specify some of the factors in the EC condition that produce differences in cerebral measures. Several years ago we discussed possible alternative explanations of cerebral effects of differential experience (Rosenzweig, Bennett, and Diamond, 1972), and we have recently prepared a more thorough and up-to-date review of this question (Rosenzweig and Bennett, 1976). We have shown that neither the greater handling nor motor activity in EC seems to be crucial. EC-IC effects can be found in animals blinded or raised in the dark, although visual deprivation does produce its own effects; and studies by Riege and Morimoto (1970) have shown that stress is not a component of the EC effect. From results of numerous experiments we have also concluded that it is not essential to maintain the IC rats in a room separate from the EC rats: the ongoing laboratory activities associated with maintaining a large number of EC rats do not modify the cerebral measures of the EC rats. However, both social stimulation and stimulation from inanimate objects do contribute to the EC-IC differences.

Recently, while visiting our lab, Pedro Ferchmin performed an experiment for a quite different purpose which also very clearly ruled out many factors as possible contributors to EC effects. Ferchmin wished to test whether any EC effects would be induced by observation learning; that is, would effects be found in rats that were individually housed in small cages within the EC cage? These animals had the opportunity to observe the EC animals, were exposed to the smells and noises of the EC animals, and even had a limited amount of social contact. After 30 days the observer group showed no significant cerebral differences from the IC group but differed significantly from the EC littermates whose cages they shared in a limited way . . . . On measures of exploratory behavior taken during the last two days of the experiment, IC rats fell significantly below EC, and the observer rats were somewhat below IC. We conclude that actual contact with an enriched environment is necessary for the development of EC effects (Ferchmin, Bennett, and Rosenzweig, 1975).

Enriched Environments As a Tool to Study Neural Mechanisms of Memory

If we wish to relate some of the EC effects to memory mechanisms, it is highly desirable, if not essential, to produce at least some of the EC effects by what I shall term "formal training." In this connection, Greenough has reviewed some of his experiments in which tantalizing, and perhaps even significant, differences have been found in certain dendritic measures.

Over the past several years we also have been attempting to produce cerebral differences by formal training, though our measures have been somewhat less refined than those used by Greenough. In our first experiments we trained rats on a series of bar-pressing tasks over a number of days with food reward. Small and marginally significant chemical differences were obtained in cortical samples.

We are now attempting two somewhat different training procedures in hopes of finding clearer effects. In one, the trained rats run for food reward on self-paced trials in an automatic Hebb-Williams-type maze. These rats can be compared to control rats that are equated for motor activity but only run a straight-alley runway for their food. In the first several experiments small differences in cortical weights were found in the expected direction. However, more recent experiments, conducted under what were intended to be more favorable conditions, have not yielded weight effects.

Our second training procedure we call the "group maze." In this procedure a plastic maze is inserted as a second floor inside the EC cage, and animals must go up and down to get food and water. The intervening partitions can be changed, and maze patterns of increasing complexity can be constructed. This is the complex maze (CM). Another group maze is similar except that a simple route leads through the maze from food to water, and this route is never changed; this is the simple maze (SM). Rats in these two conditions can be compared to rats in the regular EC condition, to rats housed twelve to a large empty cage (group condition — GC), as well as to the IC rats. To date we have completed six experiments with three to five conditions in each experiment. Since all experiments did not have all groups, the presentation of results is complicated, but a few general conclusions can be made . . . . It is clear that the rats raised in regular EC, CM, or SM had very similar cerebral measures, and all differed significantly from ICs. Naturally, we were disappointed that the animals in the complex group maze did not differ from those raised in the simple group maze. We next asked to what extent these differences could be due to the social effects of twelve rats living in a large empty cage, since we already knew that the rats we call "social controls," which live three to a relatively small laboratory cage, typically fall between EC and IC rats. Not unexpectedly, twelve rats living in a large empty cage fall about halfway between IC and EC rats, so social stimulation does play an important role but does not produce the whole effect.

Biochemical Effects of Differential Environments

For a number of years we concentrated on measurements of acetylcholinesterase and cholinesterase as indicators of biochemical (and anatomical) effects of differential environments. I shall not review the voluminous data that we have obtained in this area except to say that we have generally found an increase in total AChE activity in the cortex and an even larger increase in ChE activity (Rosenzweig, Bennett, and Diamond, 1972). This is particularly true after 80 days' exposure to the enriched environment. We have interpreted these results as indicating that an increase in glial function of the rat cortex resulted from the enriched environmens (as compared to the impoverished controls). We then turned to an investigation of RNA and DNA content of the rat cortex in the usual EC-IC paradigm and also in animals raised in the light and in the dark. In both cases we found an increase in the RNA/DNA ratio of the more stimulated rat of the comparison pair (EC or light-raised) (Rosenzweig, Bennett, and Diamond, 1972). Our enthusiasm for pursuing such research was dampened at the time by the fact that the methods available for the analysis of brain nucleic acids in the midsixties were either inaccurate or laborious (or both).

Recently we have developed a new and more reliable method for determining nucleic acid content in brain tissue (Morimoto, Ferchmin, and Bennett, 1974). This method uses cetyl trimethylammonium bromide (CTAB) as the specific precipitant for nucleic acids. In a large number of experiments we have found a highly reproducible and significant increase in the RNA/DNA ratio of the cortex when animals are maintained in EC conditions and compared to their IC littermates. This is particularly true for the occipital and total-cortex measures . . . . Little or no change is found in the subcortex. Most of the increase in ratio is due to a decrease of DNA/mg, and this in turn is related to the increase in cortical weight in EC. With experiments of varied durations there first appears to be a small, transient, but significant, increase in RNA/mg in favor of the EC groups, after which the RNA difference again approaches zero. With a short (4-day) exposure to EC an increase in total brain RNA has been found both by Ferchmin, Eterović, and Caputto (1970) and by ourselves. The increase in total RNA and in RNA/DNA in EC is found for experiments of all durations, from 4 days to 165 days.

The Significance of Environmental Complexity for Studying Neuronal and Biochemical Components of Memory

As discussed by Rose, Hambley, and Haywood, and by Dunn . . . , the results of numerous studies have suggested that an increased incorporation of precursors of RNA and protein into brain may be associated with training. Typically, the effects can only be monitored by highly sensitive radioactive-tracer experiments and represent only a transient and quite small increase in the total macromolecular synthesis. Our recent results have shown that the RNA/DNA ratio in the cortex of a rat maintained in EC is significantly and reproducibly larger than that of its IC littermate. The effect can be found within four days after exposure to EC, as shown by both the experiments of Ferchmin's group and our own experiments. Does this increase represent the integrated effect of many individual learning-memory events, which others have shown to cause an increased incorporation of RNA precursors? We would like to believe that this is the case. If so, we would predict several results: (1) RNA will respond more rapidly to altered experience than other brain measures; (2) the increase in RNA/DNA ratio will not persist for as long as the weight effects when EC rats are removed to an IC environment; and (3) eventually an appropriate paradigm clearly involving only training will increase the RNA/DNA ratio of selected brain areas, and this increase will be detectable by nontracer methods. Data that we have just obtained show that, as predicted, RNA does respond sensitively to experience, and the persistence of RNA/DNA effects is much less than the persistence of weight effects. . . . As discussed above, we are still attempting to devise a series of formal training experiments that will reliably produce many of the cerebral differences Greenough and I have discussed. Ultimately, I believe we shall be successful in finding such differences, some of which will be important in elucidating memory mechanisms.

Summary

Differential environments are thought to be a useful paradigm for the study of memory mechanisms. Some of the cerebral differences, such as cortical weight and the ratio of RNA to DNA, have temporal properties consistent with their involvement in memory storage. For example, cerebral differences can be found within four days, differences can be produced over a variety of starting ages and durations of differential environments, and differences persist for months when animals are removed from EC and placed into IC. Active participation in the EC environment is required, and larger differences can be produced when groups of animals are placed in a seminatural environment. Maze experience has produced cerebral differences in excess of those produced by a group of animals in a large empty cage. As Dr. Greenough has stated, "it would be much more difficult to argue that EC rats do *not* learn more than their IC and SC counterparts than it is to argue that they do." We therefore believe that ultimately a number of biochemical and anatomical changes will be found to result from differential environments. Many of these changes, we suggest, will represent the cumulative effect of a number of memorial events taking place in EC conditions.

ACKNOWLEDGMENTS

The research summarized in this chapter has extended over a number of years, and contributions have been made by a number of individuals. These include Pedro Ferchmin, Marie Hebert, Hiromi Morimoto, Donald Dryden, Arun Prakash, and Jessie Langford. Essential support for our research has been most recently provided by NSF Grant GB-30368, and the U.S. Atomic Energy Commission through the Lawrence Berkeley Laboratory.

REFERENCES

Bennett, E. L., Rosenzweig, M. R., Diamond, M. C., Morimoto, H., and Hebert, M. 1974. Effects of successive environments on brain measures. *Physiology and Behavior* 12: 621-631.

Bennett, E. L., Rosenzweig, M. R., and Wu, S.-Y. 1973. Excitant and depressant drugs modulate effects of environment on brain weight and cholinesterases. *Psychopharmacologia (Berlin)* 33: 309-328.

Brown, C. P. 1971. Cholinergic activity in rats following enriched stimulation and training: Direction and duration of effects. *Journal of Comparative and Physiological Psychology* 75: 408-416.

Diamond, M. C., Lindner, B., Johnson, R., Bennett, E. L., and Rosenzweig, M. R. 1975. Differences in occipital cortical synapses from environmentally enriched, impoverished, and standard colony rats. *Journal of Neuroscience Research* (in press).

Ferchmin, P. A., Bennett, E. L., and Rosenzweig, M. R. 1975. Direct contact with enriched environments is required to alter cerebral weights in rats. *Journal of Comparative and Physiological Psychology* 88: 360-367.

Ferchmin, P. A., Eterović, V. A., and Caputto, R. 1970. Studies of brain weights and RNA content after short periods of exposure to environmental complexity. *Brain Research* 20: 49-57.

Globus, A., Rosenzweig, M. R., Bennett, E. L., and Diamond, M. C. 1973. Effects of differential experience on dendritic spine counts in rat cerebral cortex. *Journal of Comparative and Physiological Psychology* 82: 175-181.

Holloway, R. L. 1966. Dendritic branching: Some preliminary results of training and complexity in rat visual cortex. *Brain Research* 2: 393-396.

Kuenzle, C. C., and Knüsel, A. 1974. Mass training of rats in a superenriched environment. *Physiology and Behavior.*

Malkasian, D. R., and Diamond, M. C. 1971. The effects of environmental manipulation on the morphology of the neonate rat brain. *International Journal of Neuroscience* 2: 161-170.

Møllgard, K., Diamond, M. C., Bennett, E. L., Rosenzweig, M. R., and Lindner, B. 1971. Qualitative synaptic changes with differential experience in rat brain. *International Journal of Neuroscience* 2: 113-128.

Morimoto, H., Ferchmin, P. A., and Bennett, E. L. 1974.

Spectrophotometric analysis of RNA and DNA using cetyltrimethylammonium bromide. *Analytical Biochemistry* 62: 436-448.

Riege, W. H., and Morimoto, H. 1970. Effects of chronic stress and differential environments upon brain weights and biogenic amine levels in rats. *Journal of Comparative and Physiological Psychology* 71: 396-404.

Rosenzweig, M. R., and Bennett, E. L. 1972. Cerebral changes in rats exposed individually to an enriched environment. *Journal of Comparative and Physiological Psychology* 80: 304-313.

Rosenzweig, M. R., and Bennett, E. L. 1976. Enriched environments: Facts, factors, and fantasies. In J. L. McGaugh and L. Petrinovich, eds., *Knowing, Thinking, and Believing.* New York: Plenum Press (in press).

Rosenzweig, M. R., Bennett, E. L., and Diamond, M. C. 1972. Chemical and anatomical plasticity of brain: Replications and extensions. In J. Gaito, ed., *Macromolecules and Behavior,* 2nd ed. New York: Appleton-Century-Crofts.

Amnesia after Bilateral Mesial Temporal-Lobe Excision

Introduction to Case H.M.
W. B. Scoville

I have been invited to give a brief description of H.M., a young man who has become a *cas célèbre* in the psychophysiologic study of memory. This man, now 42 years old, has had intractable epilepsy of both major and minor varieties since the age of 16. He is unmarried, living with his mother, and is of a gentle and passive nature. His early history revealed a minor head injury at the age of 7, which was accompanied by loss of consciousness; *petit mal* seizures began three years later, occurring up to 10 times a day by the age of 13. *Grand mal* seizures began at the age of 16 and initially occurred at weekly intervals. They

were characterized by loss of consciousness and tonic-clonic convulsions, with falling and injury frequent consequences. The incidence and severity of these seizures increased over the ensuing 11 years despite heavy and varied anticonvulsant therapy, so that H.M. was effectively prevented from working or otherwise leading a normal life.

Neurologic and radiologic examinations made at various times during this period were within normal limits, as were routine laboratory tests. Electroencephalography (by Dr. W. T. Liberson), though failing to show any localized epileptogenic area, did indicate diffuse slow activity with a dominant frequency of six to eight per second. During a minor clinical seizure, generalized two-to-three per second spike and wave discharges, with a slight asymmetry in the central

Reprinted with permission from *Neuropsychologia* 1968, 6:211-213, W. B. Scoville, "Amnesia after Bilateral Mesial Temporal-Lobe Excision, Pergamon Press, Ltd.

leads, were recorded. The abnormality was further described as having bilateral centro-temporal predominance, but no sharp focus.

Because of the bilaterality of the continued electrographic disturbances, and because of the incapacitating nature of H.M.'s seizures, a bilateral medial temporal-lobe resection was carried out on August 25, 1953. This procedure had been used previously with severely psychotic patients having similar epileptic seizures, and the results had been favourable with respect to epilepsy (Scoville et al [5]). Bilateral supraorbital one and one-half inch trephine holes provided access to the temporal lobes. Electrocorticography was carried out at the time of the operation, postage-stamp surface electrodes being placed on the lateral, inferior and mesial surfaces of the temporal lobes for a distance of 5 cm from their tips. One depth electrode with 8 segments was also inserted, with the tip resting on the hippocampus. The location of the depth electrode was verified by X-ray, and the tracings obtained presumably reflected activity of the uncus, medial amygdala and anterior portion of Ammon's horn bilaterally. No clearcut evidence of an epileptogenic focus was found, either in this mesial region or more laterally. Nevertheless, for the reasons explained above, a medial temporal lobe resection was made. The removal, carried out through the same trephine holes, extended posteriorly from the midpoint of the medial top of the temporal lobes for a distance of roughly 8 cm. In this fashion, the prepyriform gyrus, uncus, amygdala, hippocampus, and hippocampal gyrus were resected bilaterally. The removal was limited superiorly and laterally by the temporal horns, and extended approximately 3 cm posterior to the medial portion of the petrous ridge. The patient remained awake and talking during the operation, which was done under local anesthesia.

Following this operation, H.M. showed a gratifying reduction in seizure-frequency (which has been maintained), but he appeared to have an almost complete loss of recent memory (Scoville [4]). When examined in 1960, seven years postoperatively, he had had no major seizures for two years, although he was on considerably reduced anticonvulsant medication; before the operation, major convulsive attacks had occurred at least once a week. The *petit mal* attacks, which preoperatively had resulted in an almost continuous state of confusion, had also diminished in frequency, from one every hour to five or six per month.

Apart from the severe memory impairment, clinical observations have shown little change from the preoperative picture. The confusion noted above has cleared completely, and there has been some improvement in intellectual function. He has continued to be pleasant and amiable, but occasionally exhibits a rather quick temper, punctuated by displays of stubbornness. He reads magazines and newspapers but totally forgets the contents after 15 minutes; similarly, he solves difficult crossword puzzles and forgets them thereafter. He is unable to find his way home from a nearby store and is therefore not encouraged to go out of the house unaccompanied. He has had no sexual outlets, nor does he appear to have a need of them.

Realizing the seriousness of the memory deficit, the writer embarked upon exhaustive behavioural study of this patient with Dr. Brenda Milner [6], and later upon related animal studies* with Dr. Robert Correll [3]. H.M. and his mother are faithfully cooperative in the continuing studies and have, in fact, agreed to let others check our observations. Thus, H.M. has been seen by Dr. David Drachman, who included his test results in a recently published report on the hippocampal amnestic syndrome [2]. . . . Of special interest is a slight but definite improvement in memory function, noted recently, more than 14 years after operation. H.M. now has a vague notion of some present-day occurrences, with recognition of the name of our President and of past wars, though he still cannot spontaneously remember them.

This one case, so carefully studied, has demonstrated to many the grave danger of bilateral resection of the medial parts of the temporal lobes when the hippocampus is included in the removal. Even at this late date, however, scientific publications continue to propose removal of the hippocampus bilaterally for relief of behaviour disorders, intractable pain, and other reasons [3]; such proposals no longer seem justifiable in view of the profound anterograde amnesia which results.

REFERENCES

1 Correll, R. E. and Scoville, W. B. Effects of medial temporal lesions on visual discrimination performance. *J. comp. physiol. Psychol.* 60, 175-181, 1965

2 Drachman, D. A. and Arbit, J. Memory and the hippocampal complex. *Arch. Neurol.* 15, 52-61, 1966.

3 Gol, A. and Faibish, G. M. Effects of human hippocampal ablation. *J. Neurosurg.* 26, 390-398, 1967.

4 Scoville, W. B. The limbic lobe in man. *J. Neurosurg.* 11, 64-66, 1954.

5 Scoville, W. B., Dunsmore, R. H., Liberson, W. T., Henry, C. E. and Pepe, A. Observations on medial temporal lobotomy and uncotomy in the treatment of psychotic states. *Res. Publs. Ass. nerv. ment. Dis.* 31, 347-369, 1953.

6 Scoville, W. B. and Milner, Brenda. Loss of recent memory after bilateral hippocampal lesions. *J. Neurol. Neurosurg. Psychiat.* 20, 11-21, 1957.

*This work was supported by U.S. Public Health Service Research Grant MH-02267 from the National Institute of Mental Health.

Left-Brain, Right-Brain

Roger W. Sperry

At the upper levels of the brain is a thick bundle of transverse fibers called the corpus callosum, the largest fiber system in the brain, interconnecting the brain's two large cerebral hemispheres. These hemispheres are now commonly known as left-brain, right-brain because, once the corpus callosum has been cut, the two sides of the brain appear to possess such independent capacities and mental properties that each merits a separate name.

The first series of operations creating the split brain in human beings was performed in the late Thirties and early Forties in order to relieve the seizures of persons afflicted with severe epilepsy—the theory being that the corpus callosum transmitted the brain waves which caused the seizures. The operation has proven effective for selected severe cases in minimizing seizures or in stopping them altogether. But the most remarkable effect of this drastic operation was the seeming *lack* of effect on the patient's behavior and personality.

Extensive follow-up studies failed to disclose any definite neurological or psychological symptoms or deficits left by the surgery. That was generally the case in occasional individuals born without a corpus callosum. As late as the early Fifties, the function of the corpus callosum—estimated to contain over 200 million fiber elements, was still an enigma.

This fact prompted my colleagues and me to undertake a series of laboratory studies on surgical sections of the corpus callosum of cats and monkeys. It soon became evident that the surgically disconnected halves of the brain have their own private sensations, percepts, and learning experiences—all cut off from the awareness of its partner hemisphere. We also learned that each brain half stored its own separate chain of memories, which were inaccessible to the other hemisphere.

The split-brained animal, having learned a task with one hemisphere, would have to relearn it all over again from the beginning when it was obliged to use its other hemisphere. Further, the two hemispheres could be trained concurrently to learn mutually contradictory solutions to a task—with no apparent mental conflict. It was as if each hemisphere had a mind of its own.

This finding still did not tell us much about the left-brain, right-brain differences in people, though,

because it turns out that human beings are the only mammals whose left and right brains are specialized for quite different *functions*. This phenomenon is correlated with the power of speech and the related talents that separate us so distinctly from all other animals.

Our first opportunity to study a human split brain came in 1961, when a callosum-cutting operation was performed by Philip Vogel and Joseph Bogen of the White Memorial Medical Center in Los Angeles. The patient was a 48-year-old war veteran whose brain had been severely damaged by bomb fragments. The injury afflicted him with terrible convulsive seizures, which continued to worsen in spite of all treatment. Upon recovery from the surgery, he was free of the seizures and seemed quite normal in his everyday behavior; in fact, he even showed a much-improved sense of well-being. But his surface normality seemed to overlie some startling changes in his inner mental makeup—a suspicion we were to confirm in studies of additional subjects who had had the same operation.

Some of the new insights that evolved from these studies have occasioned an enormous burgeoning of interest in the left-brain, right-brain phenomenon—among psychologists as well as biologists. In the process new concepts of consciousness and the workings of the human brain have emerged. Because of increasing public demands for relevance in government-funded science, I am often asked to spell out some of the more practical implications of our neuroscientific investigations in terms of medical perspective and changing views of man and the human mind.

But before I talk about left-brain, right-brain, I must go back a step or two. When we first launched our investigation into the functional role of brain connections, one of the first things we learned was how much we had to *un*-learn. At that time neuroscience was thoroughly sold on the notion that brain function was infinitely malleable. Among other things, the functional interchangeability of nerves in neurosurgery was taken for granted. Having its "wires" crossed by the neurosurgeon supposedly created no problem at all for the brain back in the Thirties.

In those days if any damage was done to a nerve that normally transmits the necessary messages to, say, the muscles of the face, that nerve would be replaced surgically by a nearby healthy and more expendable nerve, such as the one used in lifting the shoulder. The initial effect would be that the face muscles would move whenever the patient tried to lift his shoulder. However, the doctrine of the day prescribed that if the patient went home and practiced in front of a mirror, those malleable brain centers would shortly undergo re-education to restore normal facial expression, now mediated through the brain centers and nerves designed for shoulder movement.

At the same time, efforts were being made to restore function to legs paralyzed by spinal-cord lesions. The technique involved using one of the main nerves of the *arm* without disconnecting that nerve from the brain centers. The arm nerve was dissected out, full-length, then tunneled under the skin, and connected to the leg nerves so that it would take over the function of the paralyzed limb. Only an early report of this procedure—*not* the final, disappointing outcome—appeared in the literature for perhaps understandable reasons. Nevertheless, exactly the same operation was later (in the Thirties) reported to be a functional success in experimental tests with rats. The motor, the sensory, and even the reflex functions of a paralyzed hind limb were said to have been restored through the transplanted nerves (working via the brain centers) of the forelimb. Thus even scientists trying to follow the most objective standards, now and then deceive themselves in the direction of their preconceptions.

In those days the nervous system was generally supposed to be possessed of a wholesale behavioral plasticity or, as one authority put it, "a colossal adaptation capacity almost without limit." The followers of Pavlov in Russia and John Watson in this country were speculating that it should be feasible to shape human nature into virtually any desirable mold and thus to create a more ideal society, by means of appropriate early training and conditioning.

This kind of thinking was reinforced by other views current in the Thirties. In particular, the prevalent doctrine concerning nerve growth told us that during embryonic, fetal, and early childhood development, fiber outgrowth and the formation of nerve connections in the brain were essentially diffuse and nonselective. That is, a nerve would connect as readily in one place as it would in another, as in any good standard household wiring system. There seemed to be no way by which the nerve circuits that governed behavior could be grown into the brain directly—that is, *pre*-functionally, through inheritance, without being shaped by experience. It was supposed that the adjustment in brain connections depended *entirely* on function and that it began during the earliest movements of the fetus *in utero*, continuing from then on through trial and error, conditioning, learning, experience, through any means but heredity. Our experimental findings in the Forties, however, effect-

ed a 180-degree about-face in our understanding of these matters. As we now know, nerves are *not* functionally interchangeable. The brain is not all that malleable, and the growth of nerve paths and nerve connections in the brain is anything but diffuse and nonselective. Neural circuits for behavior are definitely grown in, pre-functionally, *under genetic control*—and with great precision in an enormously complex, pre-programmed, biochemically controlled system.

This brief historical review is not just an excuse to recall old times. The point is that while all this has now become a matter of history for those of us in the biomedical sciences, the early views that became so deeply entrenched all through the Twenties, Thirties, and well into the Forties have still not been completely shaken off in other areas. The lingering aftereffect of these doctrines may still be found exerting an unwarranted influence on related disciplines, such as psychiatry, anthropology, and sociology, as well as on society at large. The result is that the majority of us still have a tendency to underrate the genetic and other innate factors in behavior.

What dictates which hemisphere is dominant, whether the individual will be left-handed or right-handed? A recent theory put forth by Jerre Levy of the University of Pennsylvania and Thomas Nagylaki of the University of Wisconsin (both formerly at Cal Tech) proposes that there are two genes governing cerebral dominance and handedness. Each of these two genes has two versions, or "alleles"; thus there are four in all. One gene determines which hemisphere of the developing brain will be language-dominant, and a second gene determines whether the preferred hand will be on the same side as, or opposite, the language hemisphere. Without going into the details, if we count up the possible dominant and recessive characteristics contained in these few genes, we come up with nine different combinations of inherited genotypes, each with distinct properties of cerebral dominance and handedness. Some of the left-handers, for instance, will be more resistant than others to reversal by training, because of their genetic pattern.

Now, both the left and right hemispheres of the brain have been found to have their own specialized forms of intellect. The left is highly verbal and mathematical, performing with analytic, symbolic, computerlike, sequential logic. The right, by contrast, is spatial and mute, performing with a synthetic spatio-perceptual and mechanical kind of information processing that cannot yet be simulated by computers. When one is dealing with neurosurgical patients whose left and right hemispheres have been surgically disconnected, it is most impressive and compelling to watch a subject solve a given problem like two different people in two consistently different ways, using two quite different strategies—depending on whether he is using his left or his right hemisphere.

In other words, the nine combinations of genotypes, representing different balancing and loadings of left and right mental factors, provide just in themselves quite a spectrum for inherent individuality in the structure of human intellect. Left-handers as a group have been shown to be different statistically from right-handers in their mental makeup—that is, in IQs and in other test profiles. Similarly, the profiles of males are different from those of females. And females masculinized *in utero* or those lacking one X chromosome are shown to be different from normal females.

Many kinds of tests have shown that the right hemisphere is particularly talented and superior to the left in visual-spatial abilities. This specialty of the so-called minor hemisphere, according to a recent report in the *American Journal of Human Genetics* by Darrell Bock of the University of Chicago and Donald Kolakowski of the University of Connecticut, is tied to a recessive sex-linked gene; that is, a gene linked to the X chromosome, of which the mother has two and the father has only one. In any case, the specialty is shown to exhibit a cross-correlation pattern of inheritance from parents to offspring in such a clear-cut manner that this aspect of cerebral dominance is seen to be purely genetic and other theories dealing with environment, experience, or child development as being responsible for it are ruled out. Because of the distinctly human differences in left-brain, right-brain and the spectrum of variations that genetic inheritance makes possible in brain physiology—and *therefore* in temperament and talents—each individual brain is truly unique. The degree and kind of inherent individuality each of us carries around in his brain—in its surface features, its internal fiber organization, microstructure, and chemistry—would probably make those differences seen in facial features or in fingerprint patterns look relatively simple and crude by comparison.

A second message that emerges from the findings on hemispheric specialization is that our educational system and modern society generally (with its very heavy emphasis on communication and on early training in the three Rs) discriminates against one whole half of the brain. I refer, of course, to the non-verbal, non-mathematical minor hemisphere, which, we find, has its own perceptual, mechanical, and spatial mode of apprehension and reasoning. In our present school system, the attention given to the minor hemisphere of the brain is minimal compared with the training lavished on the left or major, hemisphere.

A third and final message for social change that we get from the world of the laboratory is a complex one that precludes a simple summary. One of the more important things to come out of our brain research in recent years—from my standpoint, at least—is a greatly changed idea of the conscious mind and its relation to brain mechanism. The new interpretation, or reformulation, involves a direct break with long-established materialistic and behavioristic thinking, which has dominated neuroscience for many decades. Instead of dispensing with consciousness as just an "inner aspect" of the brain process, or as some passive "epiphenomenon" or other impotent by-product, as has been the custom, our present interpretation would make the conscious mind an integral part of the brain process itself and an essential constituent of the action. As a dynamic emergent property of cerebral excitation, subjective experience acquires causal potency and becomes a causal determinant in brain function. Although inseparably tied to the material brain process, it is something distinct and special in its own right, "different from and more than" its component physicochemical elements.

Its directive control influence is seen to reside in the universal power of the whole over its parts, in this case the power of high-order cerebral processes over their constituent neurochemical components. On these new terms, consciousness is put to work, given a use, and a reason for being and for having been evolved in a material world. Not only does the brain's physiology determine the mental effects, as has been generally agreed, but now, in addition, the emergent mental operations are conceived in turn to control the component neurophysiology through their higher organizational properties. The scheme provides a conceptual explanatory model for the interaction of mind with matter in terms that do not violate the principles of scientific explanation or those of modern neuroscience.

After more than 50 years of strict behaviorist avoidance of such terms as "mental imagery" and visual, verbal, auditory "images," in the past five years, these terms have come into wide usage as explanatory constructs in the literature on cognition, perception, and other higher functions.

The revised interpretation brings the conscious mind into the causal sequence in human decision making—and therefore into behavior generally—and thus back into the realm of experimental science from which it has long been excluded. This swing in psychology and neuroscience away from hard-core materialism and reductionism toward a new, more acceptable brand of mentalism tends now to restore to the scientific image of human nature some of the dignity, freedom, and other humanistic attributes of which it had been deprived by the behavioristic approach.

Old metaphysical dualisms and the seemingly irreconcilable paradoxes that formerly prevailed between the realities of inner experience on the one hand and those of experimental brain science on the other have become reconciled today in a single comprehensive and unifying view of mind, brain, and man in nature. Within the brain we pass conceptually in a single continuum from the brain's subnuclear particles on up (through atoms and molecules to cells and nerve-circuit systems without consciousness) to cerebral processes with consciousness.

When subjective values are conceived to have objective consequences in the brain, they no longer need be set off in a realm outside the domain of science. The old proposition that science deals with facts, not with values, and its corollary, that value judgments lie outside the realm of science, no longer apply in the new framework. Instead of separating science from values, the present interpretation (when all the various ramifications and logical implications are followed through) leads to a stand in which science becomes the best source, method, and authority for determining ultimate value and those ultimate ethical axioms and guideline beliefs to live and govern by. By the word *science*, I refer broadly to the knowledge, understanding, insight, and perspectives that come from science. But, more particularly, I am thinking of the principles for establishing validity and reliability and credibility of the scientific way as an approach to truth, insofar as the human brain can comprehend truth.

New Hope for Epileptics
"But We Still Have a Long Way to Go"

Interview with Dr. Richard Masland, Executive Director, Commission for The Control of Epilepsy

Q   Dr. Masland, is medical science making any progress against epilepsy?

A   To some extent, yes. Drugs have helped in the treatment, and there are some encouraging new ones on the horizon. Modern technology has also given us a better understanding of the nature of epilepsy, and that will pay off in the long run.

We have also made some progress in coping with prejudices against epileptics, but we still have a long way to go.

Q   How many Americans have epilepsy?

A   We estimate 2 million people. About 150,000 of these have multiple handicaps such as cerebral palsy and mental retardation—and of those, about 70,000 are in institutions.

Q   Is the proportion of Americans with this problem rising?

A   No. Actually there's some indication from a survey at the Mayo Clinic over a 20-year period that the rate is going down.

The likeliest explanation for this is the improvement in maternal and child care. We know that epilepsy is usually the result of a brain injury. In the past, these commonly occurred during the trauma of childbirth or from childhood's infectious diseases such as meningitis and measles that attack the central nervous system.

On the other hand, there's a growing problem with the effects of automobile accidents—now a very significant cause of epilepsy.

Q   Just what is epilepsy?

A   It's generally characterized by recurrent seizures, but epilepsy is not a single disease. It is often a symptom of a brain-injury scar which becomes an irritant and causes the seizure.

The severity of the disease varies widely. A large majority of victims have had only a few seizures and are leading normal lives as adults. On the other hand, a small number—possibly 5,000 to 10,000—have up to 50 to 100 seizures a day.

Q   What kinds of seizures are there?

A   Most commonly, epilepsy takes the form of a convulsion where the individual becomes rigid and

Reprinted from *U.S. News & World Report*, September 5, 1977.

jerks and falls to the ground. This is the *grand mal* seizure.

Other forms are milder—perhaps brief lapses of consciousness in which the person may remain fixed for 15 to 30 seconds, with perhaps a slight flickering of the eyes. Then, as suddenly as it comes, the lapse disappears and the person will have no recollection of it.

There are also instances where the individual loses partial consciousness but can still be normal in appearance and behavior.

Q Is this something that occurs because of ingrained habit or instinct?

A No. It simply means that while a part of the brain has been activated, the remaining part continues to function in an apparently normal way.

Q What are the first symptoms of epilepsy? When does it strike?

A Seventy-five per cent of the cases have their onset before the age of 18. Usually there is no warning. Suddenly the individual has a convulsion.

There is also a rise in the number of new cases in the older-age group because of arteriosclerosis, which often leads to vascular disease of the brain and small strokes, which can bring on epilepsy.

Q How long a time elapses after a brain injury before epilepsy's onset?

A Usually, up to one to two years—but sometimes it may not develop for many years.

Q Can epilepsy be inherited?

A Susceptibility to it exists in everybody, no matter what one's genetic background. But there is a genetic component that makes some people more sensitive to head injuries than others. We estimate that in possibly 10 per cent of the cases, genetics may be the determining factor. In another 30 per cent, genetic susceptibility may be involved. In the majority of cases, genetics are relatively unimportant.

Q Should people with epilepsy have children?

A It all depends on the nature of the epilepsy that a parent has. If it's entirely the result of illness or an injury, then that person's child is no more likely to have epilepsy than any other youngster. On the other hand, if the parent's epilepsy reflects a genetic susceptibility, it will be inherited to some extent.

In most cases, I see no reason why persons with epilepsy shouldn't marry and have children.

Q Does stress aggravate the seriousness of epilepsy?

A It seems to. I've had college students who were doing very well until they came to the final examination, when they stayed up late at night studying or worrying. After taking the examination, they'd have a big letdown and then a seizure or two.

Q Is epilepsy more common in a stressful civilization such as in the U.S. or Europe?

A Actually it's probably more frequent in less-privileged societies because of the higher chance of injury and disease.

Q Epilepsy is a well-known disease in history, isn't it?

A Yes. Julius Caesar had the symptoms So did many other well-known persons, such as Alexander the Great, novelist Fedor Dostoevski, Alfred Nobel—just to name a few.

Q Is a cure for epilepsy on the horizon?

A Unfortunately, no. Since epilepsy is not a single disease, it's not likely there is a single cure.

Drugs are the most effective treatment now to control seizures. Anticonvulsive drugs can reduce the sensitivity of the nervous system, and thus prevent the onset of seizures. The most commonly used drugs are phenobarbital, phenytoin and primidone and ethosuximide.

These drugs may have side effects, but mostly of the moderate kind. The most disturbing one is the sedative effects of barbiturates.

Q What happens to children who take medication?

A That can be a problem. Children—particularly disturbed children—can become overactive when they are given a sedative, just as they become overexcited when they're tired. This means that phenobarbital makes them overactive, aggressive and difficult to handle in about 20 per cent of the cases of children who take it to control epilepsy.

Q You mentioned some encouraging new drugs—

A Yes, we're very much excited about a most promising drug called sodium valproate. It's different from any of the other anticonvulsive drugs in that it works more effectively with less-marked side effects. The drug was discovered in France about 10 years ago, and since then has been used widely in Europe where it has proven very effective. Unfortunately, it's not yet available in the United States.

Q Why is that?

A Because introducing new drugs into this country is time-consuming and costly. Our food and drug laws set very high standards for safety and effectiveness. If all goes well, we hope to have this drug available in the U.S. very soon.

Q Does medical science now have a better understanding of epilepsy than it did, say, 20 or 30 years ago?

A Yes. Our knowledge has increased greatly with the new CAT [computerized axial tomography] brain scanner. For the first time, it is possible to obtain pictures of the brain's interior, and this has helped us greatly in studying a large number of cases. In most instances, there is some evidence on the scan of brain injury which we had not been able to identify before. All this tends to play down the importance of genetic aspects of epilepsy and give us a much better grasp of the nature of the disease.

Q   What first aid can be given a person having a seizure?

A   Actually, very little needs to be done at the time of a *grand mal* type of seizure. Try to make the person as comfortable as possible, clear the area around him to protect him from banging himself, and put something soft under his head.

After the seizure, you want to make sure that breathing is clear. The most serious danger occurs in falling and injuring the head. In addition, a remarkably high number of people with epilepsy have drowned—not from swimming, but in the bathtub or walking along the street and falling into a puddle. It's much safer for such a person to be swimming in a pool where there's supervision than to be in the bathroom alone.

Q   Is there any way to anticipate a seizure and keep it from occurring?

A   Not usually. Sometimes there is a warning—a peculiar sensation which may last for 30 seconds to a minute as the seizure starts. This is long enough for the person to sit down, but not long enough to take medication or anything like that. A person driving a car could pull over to the side of the road.

Q   Can people with epilepsy get a driver's license?

A   In most States, yes—if he or she has been free of seizures for one to two years.

Q   Are there psychological side effects to epilepsy?

A   Yes. The burden of epilepsy is a very heavy one, partly because of society's reaction. People are frightened by epilepsy. They don't understand it. A person with epilepsy may lose friends and have job problems. Frequently people with epilepsy are arrested as drunks. We are trying to encourage the police and emergency-room staffs to check identification when they find a person in a comatose or confused condition. There's a bracelet or necklace for people with epilepsy to wear, or they can carry a card in their wallet that will identify them as having epilepsy.

Q   Is epilepsy related to intelligence?

A   In a small proportion—about 20 per cent—there is some degree of mental retardation. In addition, if the seizures are difficult to control and the person must take large doses of phenobarbital, the drugs produce a sluggishness.

Q   What problems do children with epilepsy face in school?

A   Very often their problems result from a lack of understanding. For example, a child suddenly loses consciousness for about 30 seconds and is completely unaware of having done so. One girl told me how she suddenly saw her teacher standing next to her, very angry because she hadn't answered a question.

Q   Do people with epilepsy have difficulty in getting jobs?

A   Yes. The Commission for the Control of Epilepsy is recommending that industries develop "sheltered" workshops within their establishments so that handicapped people can become full employes like others.

Q   Aren't some occupations, such as working on high scaffolding, too dangerous for people with epilepsy?

A   There's another way of looking at it. We're dealing with degrees of risk. Life is risky. The man who is a window washer on a tall building can have a heart attack or a fainting spell. Obviously there are things that a person subject to seizures shouldn't take on. With a little thought, however, we'll find that these are very few.

Internal Opioid-Like Compounds

Sidney Cohen

One of the most exciting recent research findings in the field of drug abuse, in fact, in all of neurochemistry, has been the discovery that all vertebrates have built-in, anti-pain compounds in the central nervous system. Furthermore, these compounds act on specific receptor sites at nerve cell synapses, the same binding sites occupied by the drugs we call narcotics.

A lock and key relationship exists between these receptor sites and internal or injected compounds with pain-relieving, euphoriant effects. Slight modifications of the structure of opiates, or of their electrical charges will not permit a "fit" with the receptor molecule, and all narcotic activity will be lost.

Drug Abuse and Alcoholism Newsletter, September 1977, Vol. VI, No. 7. Reprinted by permission of the Vista Hill Foundation.

Similarly, certain minor manipulations of the spacial configuration of a narcotic can change it from a strong narcotic agonist to a narcotic antagonist that will prevent any narcotic from producing its effects. This occurs beause a narcotic antagonist like naloxone (Narcan) can displace or prevent an agonist like morphine from occupying available narcotic receptor sites.

The presence of opiate receptors has been assumed for some time, but the puzzling aspect of the situation has been why they should exist. Now the answer is at hand: endogenous opioids fit the receptor molecule and the narcotic drugs also happen to fit into the same site.

The Enkephalins

At present two types of internal anti-pain compounds have been identified: the enkephalins and the endorphins. The term "endorphin" is becoming the generic name for the whole group. Enkephalins are small peptides consisting of five amino acids. One amino acid chain consists of tyrosine-glycine-glycine-phenylamine-methionine, and it is called methionine enkephalin. Leucine enkephalin is similar with leucine substituted for the methionine. It may seem strange that such divergent molecules as the phenanthrene, morphine, the phenyl-piperidine, Demerol, the diphenylmethane, methadone and the amino acid chain of the enkephalins all fit into the same stereospecific receptor site. When seen spacially, however, there are similarities at one part of all these compounds providing grounds for the assumption that they fit into the opiate receptor at that point.

The enkephalins are distributed in the regions of the brain where opiate receptors are known to be concentrated. These include the substantia gelatinosa, a relay area in the spinal cord for burning, dull pain sensation transmission. From there, the noxious sensations are transmitted along the spinothalamic tract, through the periaqueductal gray matter and up into the thalamus and the limbic system. It is known that morphine is more effective against burning pain than sharp pain. The latter has a separate transmission pathway that is less involved in the enkephalin mechanism of control.

It appears that the enkephalins are neurotransmitters modulating pain perception and the emotional response to it. In addition, they may play a role in emotionality, producing feelings of pleasure just as opiates induce euphoria. It is speculated that individuals with low enkephalin levels might be susceptible to depression.

Nerve cells that are modulated by enkephalins in-

hibit the firing of excitatory neurons thus reducing the sensation of pain or of unpleasant emotional effects. Narcotics perform similar functions. They increase the inhibition of the transmission of noxious stimuli by occupying opiate receptor sites that the enkephalins leave vacant.

When a drug like morphine is given in large doses over a period of weeks, enkephalin formation is reduced or eliminated by feedback mechanisms from the receptor sites that are totally occupied. It may be that the enkephalins are involved in the withdrawal syndrome upon sudden discontinuance of a narcotic. The complete absence of the enkephalins may evoke some symptoms of early abstinence. Repeated injections of enkephalins have produced tolerance and withdrawal effects in mice. The narcotic antagonists precipitate withdrawal in animals made tolerant to the enkephalins.

The well-known antitussive and gastrointestinal slowing effects of the narcotics are also possessed by the enkephalins. Concentrations of opiate receptors can be identified in the solitary nucleus which is involved in the cough reflex and in reducing gastrointestinal secretion and motility.

The Endorphins

Three endorphins have been identified: alpha, beta and gamma. They are long-chain peptides consisting of 16 to 91 amino acids. All of them contain the methionine enkephalin sequence. The pituitary gland is one source of the endorphins. Their action is blocked by the narcotic antagonist, naloxone. The long peptide chain prevents rapid degradation so that they are longer acting and more potent than the enkephalins. The endorphins are as much as 48 times more active than morphine when injected into the cerebral ventricles and are three times more active intravenously despite the fact they cross the blood-brain barrier poorly.

The Role of Narcotic Antagonists

The fact that naloxone immediately reverses the effects of endorphins, enkephalins and all the known narcotics is very suggestive that all of these substances act on a common site of action. The more potent the narcotic, the greater affinity it has for the specific opiate receptor.

It has been found that sodium ions increase narcotic antagonist binding and reduce agonist binding. Since sodium ions are readily available, antagonists are ordinarily capable of displacing agonist molecules that have previously located themselves on the specific receptor. Therefore, antagonists are able to quickly reverse the symptoms and signs of narcotic agonist overdose.

One of the most impressive experiences in emergency medicine is the restoration of breathing and consciousness in a moribund patient who had taken an overdose of some opiate. Narcotic antagonists also have provided the means for the breakthrough in identifying the properties of endogenous opioids.

Stimulation of electrodes implanted in the periaqueductal gray matter of six patients with intractable pain provided complete relief in five and partial analgesia in one. When the electrical stimulation was very frequent, tolerance developed to further stimulation and also to narcotics. Naloxone reversed the pain relief provided by electrical stimulation. It is tempting to assume the stimulation was mediated by an endogenous opioid.

When administered to a person who has not recently taken an opiate, the pure antagonists like naloxone produce no visible effects. Theoretically, they should increase pain sensitivity, and preliminary work indicates that this is a possibility. Since enkephalin levels are reported to be elevated in acute schizophrenics and to return to normal as clinical improvement occurs, naloxone has been tried in a small number of hallucinating schizophrenics. In the initial study improvement seems to have occurred, but a later, controlled study was unable to confirm the finding. Very recently, another blind study showed essentially no change in schizophrenic patients and in those with affective disorders indicating that acute blockade of opiate receptors is not associated with global improvement in psychotic symptomatology.

Acupuncture

A recent investigation into the mechanism of acupuncture analgesia has been performed in anesthetized ats. Pin prick stimuli applied to a limb caused an increased firing in dorsal horn cells as measured by recording electrodes, indicating that painful sensations were being transmitted. A needle was placed in the correct acupuncture point, and electrical stimulation was induced. The increased firing in the dorsal horn cells ceased. No block of the firing occurred when the acupuncture needles were placed in "dummy" positions.

From the time course of the inhibition of the firing it seems likely that enkephalins mediated the acupuncture effect. The inhibition of firing was reversed by naloxone, providing further evidence that some internal opioid acting over the opiate receptor sites

must have been responsible for the acupuncture effect. The work has been replicated in rats, but further testing of the above hypothesis is needed before definite conclusions can be reached.

Discussion

The identification of opiate receptors at specific neuronal synapses and of naturally occurring peptides that have analgesic, and perhaps euphoric properties, has many implications—some of which are not yet clearly discernible. We are at the threshold of applying these important pieces of knowledge. A few of the implications that are perceptible now will be discussed.

1 The long held hope that a non-addictive pain-reliever might be constructed receives new support. Two possibilities arise: the synthesis of an amino acid chain with long-acting narcotic properties that can cross the blood-brain barrier is one conceivable direction. A second is that with the current, simpler modes for testing narcotic effects, a drug with just the right combination of agonist and antagonist properties can be developed that provides narcosis with little or no abusable potential. Larger than average doses would produce a reversal of the narcotic reaction because the antagonist would neutralize the narcotic effect.

2 Is it possible that the enkephalins-endorphins are more than anti-nocioceptive agents? Could they also play a role in mood disorders considering the concentration of opiate receptors in limbic system structures? This area is just beginning to be explored.

3 Now that we know that all vertebrates have a built-in method for dealing with pain and other noxious emotions, our ability to help those in distress will be based on more solid grounds than in the past. Analgesics and pain-relieving methods can be more precisely tested, as exemplified by the study of acupuncture described earlier.

4 The issues of tolerance and withdrawal to narcotics must be reopened and our traditional notions reexamined. It is tempting to believe that the new knowledge will provide assistance in the treatment of opiate addiction.

5 The fact that the presence of specific opiate receptor sites has been proven means that their physiology and biochemistry will be intensively scrutinized. Questions of enkephalin blocking, reuptake, turnover and inhibition of the metabolizing enzymes are being studied. The sensitization and blockade of the receptor site will be closely investigated by the many groups involved in opioid transmitter and receptor site research.

Summary

Instead of summarizing what has been written, it seems worthwhile to mention some of the investigators who provided the initial research in the field of endogenous opioids and their receptors. They and their associates are to be congratulated on their contributions. In alphabetical order they are:

Avram Goldstein, Addiction Research Foundation, Palo Alto, California.
Roger Guillemin, Salk Institute, La Jolla, California.
John Hughes, University of Aberdeen, Scotland.
Cho Hso Li, Eddie T. F. Wei and **Horace H. Low**, University of California, San Francisco, California.
Solomon H. Snyder, Johns Hopkins University, Baltimore, Maryland.

Food Additives and Hyperkinesis
Ester H. Wender

The food-additive-free diet now occupies a definite spot on the American nutritional scene. Very few pediatricians remain who have not been asked by concerned parents about giving their child this special diet. The Feingold Association, a national organization with community-based chapters, bears the name of the physician who first claimed a causal association between certain substances added to foods and hyperkinesis and learning disabilities in children. The speed with which this organization has grown and the vocal activity in its individual chapters indicate the basic appeal of the notion of a simple dietary treatment for a common behavioral disorder. As physicians, we must keep an open mind to Dr Ben Feingold's claim, but we also have an obligation to demand that testable hypotheses be stated and then be subjected to careful scientific study. We are also obliged to keep abreast of those studies in order to function as informed consultants to our patients and our communities.

Several good investigations of the dietary treatment of hyperactivity and learning disabilities have been completed. The purpose of this article is to review the general hypothesis and summarize the available data. Some new questions arise as the result of these studies, and these will also be reviewed.

Dr Feingold's basic claim seems simple. He states that approximately 40% of the children who are hyperactive or learning disabled will improve in behavior when placed on a diet free of artificial food colorings or flavorings and free of foods that contain salicylates.[1] At least three aspects of his hypothesis, however, remain unclear: (1) Is the mechanism of the supposed toxicity an allergic one or, as Dr Feingold claims, is it a toxic reaction to a substance or substances of low molecular weight? (2) How does Dr Feingold define the hyperkinetic syndrome or learning disability and what specific behaviors does he claim are affected by the special diet? (3) Which food substances of the three mentioned above are most likely the toxic agent or agents? Food technologists have looked, for example, at Dr Feingold's list of foods that supposedly contain natural salicylates and find inadequate evidence that many of them contain measurable salicylate. The so-called modified Feingold diet makes no attempt to exclude salicylate-containing foods because of this controversy and because Dr Feingold has recently stated (personal communication) that he now thinks salicylates are not the usual source of difficulty.

As these claims began to receive publicity, two interested groups convened study sections to explore Dr Feingold's claims and to recommend appropriate research designs. The Nutrition Foundation convened a National Advisory Committee on Hyperkinesis and Food Additives in early 1975. This group published a report[2] in June 1975 recommending specific research strategies. In the fall of 1975, a similar review was undertaken by the collaborative effort of several interested federal agencies (including the Food and Drug Administration) and resulted in a published report containing similar recommendations.[3] Both groups stressed the need to control for two important treatment variables— first, the diet specifying the removal of certain food substances, and second, the psychological effects on the child resulting from the alteration of living patterns produced by special shopping trips, special food preparation, and changes in the families' perception of the affected child from being "behaviorally disturbed" to "nutritionally damaged." This second variable is well known in behavioral

American Journal of Diseases of Children 1977, 131:1204-1206.
Copyright 1977, American Medical Association.

research as a "placebo effect," namely, the repeated demonstration of measurable effects by the administration of a placebo that the patient perceives as an active therapeutic agent.[4] In order to control these two factors, the following research strategy was recommended: First, patients were to be placed on the special food-additive-free diet with no attempt to disguise this treatment variable. Then, those children who demonstrated measurable behavioral improvement were to be fed "challenge foods" prepared to contain either no artificial food colorings, or one half of the daily estimated average amount of artificial food colorings present in the average American diet. (In all studies so far, two food bars are given daily.) These two challenge foods were to be indistinguishable from each other and were to be administered in double-blind fashion. If artificial food colorings were the specific toxic agent, behavior should remain improved when the child ate the additive-free challenge food and should deteriorate when he ate the food that contained artificial colorings. Such challenge foods were prepared, and three different groups have studied the Feingold hypothesis employing the recommended research strategy. Initial findings from these three studies were reported at the Nutrition Foundation annual meeting in Palm Springs, Calif, in January 1977. What follows is a summary of these preliminary findings.

One study was conducted by Conners and Goyette[5] at the University of Pittsburgh. Previously, this group conducted the only controlled study on this issue to be published in a journal employing the usual scientific review procedures.[6] That study, however, has been criticized because the attempts made to disguise the diet treatment were believed to be inadequate. In its second study, challenge foods were available and the recommended research strategy was employed. Initially, they identified a group of hyperkinetic school children who demonstrated a 25% improvement in behavior based on a standardized rating scale when placed on the modified Feingold diet. In this open clinical trial where no attempt was made to disguise the treatment variable, 28 of 45 children had a favorable response, which is about the same percentage as that reported in open trials by Feingold and others.[3] Sixteen of these 28 initial responders completed the blind challenge portion of the study. Many of the children who dropped out of this phase of the study did so because they seemed unable, for a variety of reasons, to tolerate the challenge food (a chocolate flavored cookie or bar). Dr Conners thought that some of these children might be allergic to chocolate, but no studies were done to verify this impression. This response was equally common whether the challenge food contained additives or not. Of the 16 children who completed the study, one half initially received food-additive-containing challenge foods and were then switched to the additive-free challenge. The other half were on the opposite schedule. Behavioral change was judged by the completion of standardized questionnaires by both parents and teachers during the challenge periods. No behavior differences were noted between the food-additive and non-food-additive periods. In summary, this study failed to demonstrate any behavioral change specifically due to artificial food colorings as measured by parents and teachers during daily activities. However, in an additional phase of their study, Conners et al[6] measured attention and distractibility by a continuous performance task given one to two hours after the ingestion of the challenge food. Brief decreases in attention were noted in the children receiving the additive-containing food that were not seen when the challenge was additive-free, suggesting a transient pharmacological action of the food colorings. This finding needs replication.

A second series of studies were done by Harley and Matthews[7] at the University of Wisconsin Medical School. In the initial phase of their study, a group of children identified as hyperkinetic were placed on special diets (additive-free or additive-containing foods) in a counter-balanced sequence. All food was supplied to the study families and clever disguises were employed to keep the family ignorant of which diet was being fed. Unlike the controlled studies, they found very few children for whom the additive-free diet was helpful. It is my impression that the control diet was well disguised; and this was not, therefore, an open trial. From this initial study, they selected nine children who demonstrated some positive behavioral change to the additive-free diet and subjected them to the challenge foods in a manner similar to the study by Conners and co-workers. When the challenge food was given, behavioral changes were measured by means of parent and teacher questionnaires, psychological tests, and standard classroom observations. One child of the nine studied demonstrated changes in the expected direction.

A third study was conducted by J. Ivan Williams and his group at the University of Western Ontario and by Douglas N. Cram at the Middlesex, London District Health Unit in Ontario, Canada.[8] Their study employed challenge foods using the recommended study design, but also compared the effect of the additive-free diet with that of stimulant medication. A four-cell crossover design was employed, meaning that each of the 26 children participated in each of the four treatment conditions: additive-free diet plus stimulant medication, additive-free diet plus placebo medication, additive-containing diet plus stimulant medication, and additive-containing diet plus placebo medication. Behavioral changes were measured by standardized checklists completed by both parents and teachers. Both parents and teachers noted a definite behavioral improvement when the children were taking medication. Comparing the two diets, behavioral improvement while on the additive-free diet was noted *only* by the teachers and only in the children who were receiving placebo medication. Similar changes were not seen by the parents. Dr Williams interprets this finding as evidence that food colorings produce a short burst effect similar to that found by Dr Conners when tests were administered just one hour after ingestion of the additive-containing food bar. He reasons that this effect was noted only by the teachers because the food bars were given in the morning and at noon. I question this interpretation on two grounds: First, stimulation medication is known to have a short-term effect and is also usually given in the morning and at noon; but its effects have repeatedly been observed both by parents and teachers under double blind conditions. Second, Dr Feingold claims that there is a global deterioration in behavior after even one diet infraction, and these findings are not consistent with that claim. Nevertheless, since both parents and teachers were unaware of the treatment variable, both Drs Conners' and Williams' findings must be pursued by further study; and final conclusions must await these and other results.

It is of interest that during the study, Williams and his groups asked both the parents and teachers to guess which treatment the children had received during each phase of the study. Seventy percent of both parents and teachers correctly identified the medication treatment, but neither group could tell which diet the child was taking. In other words, the teachers' rating scales discriminated the additive-free diet from the diet with additives, but their global ratings did not. These findings suggest that the behavioral change noted by the teachers on the rating scales, though statistically significant, may be so small in magnitude that global improvement was not perceived, an example of the difference between "significance" meaning improbable and meaning appreciable or important.

In my opinion, the studies completed so far refute the general claim that 40% or more of the children with hyperkinetic behavior disorder demonstrate global improvement in behavior and/or learning when fed a diet free of artificial food colorings. Of the 51 children studied under appropriate conditions (combining the Pittsburgh, Wisconsin, and Ontario studies), only one child showed consistently measurable behavioral change in the expected direction. Hence, the more dramatic improvement noted in

open clinical trials probably represents placebo effect. At the same time, two new findings deserve further study. The changes noted in the continuous performance task by Dr Conners' group need to be replicated as do the teacher observations noted by Williams and co-workers. Other studies are underway employing classroom observations as well as questionnaire findings in measuring outcome. Such techniques will help clarify the meaning of "behavioral change," which is so easily affected by observer bias.

Another question frequently raised, but not yet studied, is the possible nutritional impact of the Feingold diet. The unmodified Feingold diet that supposedly eliminates salicylate-containing foods requires exclusion of the fruits most commonly consumed by children. Oranges, apples, and tomatoes, for example, are eliminated (grapefruit, lemons, and limes are allowed). Unless care is taken, such a diet could result in vitamin C deficiency. Otherwise, the diet appears to be nutritionally sound and even superior since most so-called junk foods are eliminated. If the modified Feingold diet is employed, I see no reason to urge families to discontinue the diet when they note favorable behavioral change. One should be alert, however, to families who employ dietary treatment enthusiastically while trained professionals note a persistence of behavioral or learning problems that need treatment. In this instance, endorsement of a special diet may help the family avoid other treatments (such as psychotherapy or medication). At the same time, if families ask my opinion regarding the efficacy of this diet, I feel obligated to state my pessimistic conclusions while keeping my mind open to new findings if and when they may emerge.

REFERENCES

1 Feingold BF: *Why Your Child Is Hyperactive.* New York, Random House, 1975.

2 The National Advisory Committee on Hyperkinesis and Food Additives: Report to The Nutrition Foundation. New York, The Nutrition Foundation Inc, 1975.

3 Interagency Collaborative Group on Hyperkinesis: First report of the preliminary findings and recommendations, US Department of Health, Education and Welfare, 1975.

4 Shapiro AK: Placebo effects in psychotherapy and psychoanalysis. *J Clin Pharmacol* 10:73-78, 1970.

5 Conners CK, Goyette C: Artificial colors and hyperkinesis. Read before the annual meeting of The Nutrition Foundation Food and Nutrition Liaison Committee, Palm Springs, Calif, January 1977.

6 Conners CK, Goyette CH, Southwick DA, et al: Food additives and hyperkinesis: A controlled double-blind experiment. *Pediatrics* 58:154-166, 1976.

7 Harley JP, Matthews CG: Hyperkinesis and food addi-

tives: A challenge experiment. Read before the annual meeting of The Nutrition Foundation Food and Nutrition Liaison Committee, Palm Springs, Calif, January 1977.

8 Williams JI, Cram DM, et al: Examining the relative effectiveness of dietary and drug management of hyperkinesis. Read before the annual meeting of The Nutrition Foundation Food and Nutrition Liaison Committee, Palm Springs, Calif, January 1977.

Schizophrenia

Ross J. Baldessarini

Schizophrenia, a common type of psychotic mental disorder of unknown cause and of varying severity, presents more or less characteristic disturbances of thinking, mood and behavior. The presence of disordered thinking in the face of a relatively clear sensorium is essential for the diagnosis, which is reached by recognition of specific clinical features, and the past history, course of the illness and family history, but not by physical findings or laboratory tests. Common features include misinterpretation or idiosyncratic distortions of reality, and sometimes frank delusions and hallucinations. Mood in the chronic phase of the illness is usually described as flat, apathetic and joyless, or inappropriate to the situation. Behavior and appearance are often odd or even bizarre. The illness typically follows a chronic course including rather quiescent phases interrupted by exacerbations of profound anxiety, florid psychotic symptoms and disorganized behavior. The risk of becoming schizophrenic at some time in life is about 1 per cent throughout the world. Schizophrenic patients occupy more than a quarter of all hospital beds in the United States, although only about 20 per cent are currently hospitalized.

This illness is characterized clinically by considerable variety, and it represents a cluster of several superficially similar conditions that may or may not belong together. The syndrome was defined in Germany by Emil Kraepelin in the 19th century, when, in attempting to establish a systematic psychiatric nosolo-

From the Department of Psychiatry, Harvard Medical School, and the Mailman Laboratories of Psychiatric Research, McLean Division of the Massachusetts General Hospital (address reprint requests to Dr. Baldessarini at Massachusettts General Hospital, Mill St., Belmont, MA 02178.

Supported in part by a research grant (MH-25515) and a research career-investigator award (MH-74370) from the National Institute of Mental Health and by a grant from the Scottish Rite Benevolent Foundation.

Reprinted, by permission, from *The New England Journal of Medicine* 1977, 297:988-995. *Editors' note:* Figures have been omitted.

gy, he lumped together a number of previously discrete conditions (e.g., hebephrenia and catatonia) under the now obsolete and misleading term "dementia praecox," which emphasizes the common onset of the condition in adolescence, or early adult life, and a chronic and inevitably downhill course of the illness into "dementia." The retention of archaic subtypes of schizophrenia ("catatonic," "hebephrenic," "paranoid," "simple" and so forth) as discrete diagnoses is not helpful and should be abandoned. Although individual cases may have more features of one type than another, most have features of more than one subtype, and currently the majority of cases would be called "undifferentiated" or "paranoid" types. Kraepelin's crucial, and almost certainly valid, decision was to distinguish these illnesses from mood disorders (manic elation or excitement and severe depression). Later, Eugen Bleuler, in Switzerland, gave further definition to the concept, coined the still accepted, but somewhat misleading, term "schizophrenia" (fragmentation of mental functions), emphasized that these were probably a group of related illnesses, and accepted the prevalent view that they were characterized by a more or less chronic or progressive deterioration of the personality starting in adolescence. Bleuler also began an unsuccessful trend of seeking specific, fundamental or pathognomonic signs and symptoms of schizophrenia. In modern American psychiatry, the concept of schizophrenia has been so broadened as sometimes to include cases that might elsewhere be called "severe neuroses," "character disorders," "acute psychoses," "affective psychoses" or "behavior disorders of childhood"; even demonstrably organic or toxic conditions are occasionally misdiagnosed as schizophrenia. There is a danger that the concept will degenerate into a synonym for psychosis or severe mental disorder.

A scientifically and clinically more useful recent trend has been to segregate a "core" syndrome based not only on a consistent pattern of the current psychotic mental status but also on past history, family history, response to treatment and outcome of the illness. One product of this trend is increasing skepticism about the automatic inclusion of acute psychoses with schizophrenia, only some of which eventually become chronic or deteriorating illnesses, and many of which seem to represent affective illnesses as judged by favorable outcome (remission or full restitution between later breakdowns), response to lithium as well as to antipsychotic drugs and family history of manic-depressive illnesses much more than of chronic schizophrenia.[1] Although it is usually assumed that there must be many "schizophrenias," or illnesses with similar clinical features, but different causes, there are at present no clinical or physiologic means of establishing such subcategories rationally, although it is crucial to exclude mental syndromes with psychotic features that have demonstrable organic causes. An important method of attempting to define conditions that may be related to schizophrenia has involved studies of illnesses in the families of patients diagnosed with confidence as having chronic schizophrenia. From this method has evolved the concept of a spectrum of disorders that may segregate in families.[2] The components of this "schizophrenia spectrum" are not yet firmly established; they seem to include milder disorders of the personality characterized by some of the peculiarities of thinking and interpersonal deficiencies of schizophrenia, but generally to exclude acute psychoses and obvious mood disorders (mania or severe depression).

Cause

Simply stated, the cause of schizophrenia is unknown. Research in this area is beset with great fundamental difficulties, including the lack of clear, objective and universally accepted definitions of schizophrenia, the difficulty—perhaps the impossibility— of separating genetic and environmental factors and the persistent, but illogical assumption that descriptive biologic, psychologic or behavioral differences imply something about causes. Investigations into the causes of schizophrenia have used genetic, biologic and psychosocial approaches, the last of which are outside the scope of the present discussion.

Genetic Hypotheses

A summary of the present status of the genetic findings on schizophrenia (Gottesman and Shields[2]) is that the greater the degree of the relatedness of a family member to a schizophrenic person and the more severe and chronic his illness, the greater the risk of schizophrenia. Thus, family studies have found that up to the first degree of kinship, risk is little if at all greater than in the general population, whereas the risks for a full sibling, a fraternal twin or a child of a schizophrenic are similar (about 15 per cent) and several times that of less closely related persons. If both parents are schizophrenic, the risk is greater still (probably about 50 per cent), and exceeded only for an identical twin of a schizophrenic patient, for whom the illness was formerly thought to be almost inevitable. Even recent studies conclude that a monozygote has a threefold to fourfold greater risk of schizophrenia than a dizygotic twin of a known schizophrenic patient, although there is no evidence that the experience of being a twin itself contributes to this increased risk. Another attempt to evaluate genetic contributions has involved study of the frequency of psychopathology among natural and adoptive families of schizophrenic patients adopted and separated from their parents early in life; again, schizophrenia is much more common among the biologic relatives. As yet, the available information does not permit the construction of an unambiguous single-gene hypothesis, or even of polygenic hypotheses.

Although the now compelling body of data supporting a familial or genetic component to the transmission of schizophrenia is commonly taken as evidence of a biologic origin (such as an inherited metabolic defect), abundant room for the further entertainment and testing of developmental and psychosocial hypotheses remains. Moreover, some of the genetic findings (e.g., the average concordance rate of only 50 to 60 per cent even between identical twins) strongly indicate that environmental factors must operate. This situation is not unique to schizophrenia, and has many parallels with the inheritance of risk for diabetes or cardiovascular diseases.

Biologic Hypotheses

There are many documented differences between schizophrenics and other subjects, including physiologic responses to drugs or to a variety of stresses.[3] Unfortunately, they may well reflect their general clinical effects of inactivity and social withdrawal, especially in chronically hospitalized schizophrenic patients, and so far have revealed nothing about cause. Pathologic changes in the brain have been reported from time to time in many poorly conceived and uncontrolled studies. By the 1950's, the conclusion became unavoidable that the pathologic changes described were no more than coincidences—artifacts or misjudgments of normal histologic variation. A more recent development in neuropathology has been the application of chemical technics to the search for abnormalities in human brain tissue. Much attention has been paid to assays of enzyme activities related to the metabolism of neurotransmitters, although so far this approach has not led to the description of appreciable changes (e.g., activity of dopamine-sensitive adenylate cyclase) or to findings that have been based on adequately controlled comparisons or that have been replicated (e.g., decreased activity of dopamine-beta-hydroxylase). The current ferment in the development of immunologic and ligand-binding technics to the study of specific enzymes, transmitter binding sites and other macromolecules in brain tissue shows promise in the evaluation of the post-mortem human brain. Such biochemical approaches have already provided important insights into the loss of neurons containing inhibitory neurotransmitters, including gamma-aminobutyric acid in Huntington's disease.

In recent decades, there has been a search for metabolic abnormalities to explain schizophrenia, encouraged by the discovery of inborn errors of metabolism in mental retardation and several other neuropsychiatric diseases of childhood. So far, virtually all investigations of this kind have been unsuccessful or inconclusive. Several claims have been made that there may be a circulating toxic factor in the blood of schizophrenic patients. Thus, their serum has been claimed to cause rats to behave strangely, to induce irregularities in spiders' web spinning and to drive normal volunteers mad. None of these findings has been corroborated in well controlled and objectively evaluated experiments. There have also been reports of altered blood or urine levels of amino acids, amines or their metabolites, of a circulating copper-containing "psychotogenic" globulin ("taraxein"), unique patterns of immunoglobulins and HLA antigens, circulating anti-brain antibodies or other autoantibodies, a lipoprotein (the "S-protein," an alpha$_2$ globulin) capable of affecting the metabolism of indoleamines, an erythrocyte-lysing actor, altered macroglobulins, elevated activity of serum creatine phosphokinase and a unique fatty acid in the skin (methylhexenoic acid). The findings have generally been based on methodologically unsound observations, remain unconfirmed or are not unique to schizophrenic patients. The many observations that severely disturbed metabolism of endogenous hormones (e.g., in hyperthyroidism, myxedema or Cushing's disease) or the administration of exogenous hormones (particularly steroids) can produce psychotic mental changes have also led to searches for endocrine dysfunction in schizophrenia but, again, without demonstration of consistent or unique changes that cannot be interpreted as nonspecific responses to stress.

The initial enthusiasm for the study of hallucinogens such as mescaline or lysergic acid diethylamide has also waned, because it has become apparent that the interesting toxic effects of these substances have little in common with schizophrenia. The fact that mescaline, dimethyltryptamine and several other methylated aromatic amines are hallucinogenic has led to speculation that altered methylation of biogenic amines might produce an endogenous "psychotogen." Large doses of methionine, an important source of methyl groups, can lead to transient psychotic exacerbations in some schizophrenic patients, although the implications of this possibly toxic effect are not clear, especially since methionine loading probably does not increase methylation of amines. Findings of increased amounts of methylated amines (including dimethoxyphenethylamine and N-methylated indolemines) in various body fluids of schizophrenic patients have not been confirmed consistently or demonstrated by unambiguous methods.

A biochemical alteration that had shown some promise of serving as a correlate of vulnerability to schizophrenia is reduced activity of monoamine oxidase in blood platelets. Decreased activity is not an important feature of mania or other acute psychoses, and it had been hoped that it might be a correlate of chronic schizophrenia. There is excellent evidence that platelet monoamine oxidase activity is strongly genetically determined. It is highly correlated between identical twins, even if one is not currently schizophrenic. Since the reported changes in activity in schizophrenia are small, are unlikely to be physiologically important and seem not to occur in the brain, decreased activity is not likely to lead to a pathophysiologically important excess of brain amines. Moreover, these promising observations, unfortunately, have only been partially confirmed: several recent studies have failed to find reduced monoamine oxidase activity in platelets or in skin fibroblasts of schizophrenic subjects.

Much attention has been called to the toxic, psychotic effects of large doses of stimulant drugs, including the amphetamines, since they and the antipsychotic drugs appear to exert specific and opposite effects on the limbic system and other forebrain centers related to mood, volition and thought. These stimulant intoxications appear uniquely to produce acute psychotic disorders (particularly paranoid thinking) in a relatively clear sensorium, as well as stereotyped and repetitive peculiarities of movement that also occur in some cases of schizophrenia. Small doses of the same catecholamine-potentiating stimulant agents can produce transient exacerbations of psychosis in schizophrenic patients. A currently popular unifying theory is that these effects may be exerted by the activation of dopamine as a neurotransmitter in the striatal and limbic systems.[4] The consistent anti-dopamine effects of virtually all antipsychotic agents now available further support the idea that overactivity of dopamine synaptic neurotransmission in the limbic forebrain may be an important aspect of the pathophysiology of schizophrenia.

Treatment

The essential feature of treatment of schizophrenic patients has become the use of antipsychotic medication in adequate dosage. These drugs have helped to revolutionize the modern management of schizophrenia.[5] The original antipsychotic drugs were the rauwolfia alkaloids and the phenothiazines, of which chlorpromazine (Thorazine) is still one of the most commonly prescribed. There are now several modifications of the original phenothiazines, including the piperazine derivatives, which are higher in milligram potency, such as fluphenazine (Prolixin), trifluoperazine (Stelazine) and perphenazine (Trilafon), as well as newer types of molecules, including the thioxanthenes—e.g., chlorprothixene (Taractan) and thiothixene (Navane)—a butyrophenone, haloperidol (Haldol), an indole, molindone (Moban) and a tricyclic piperazine, loxapine (Loxitane). These compounds are sometimes called "tranquilizers," but this term is a misnomer, for it implies that they merely sedate or reduce anxiety in the way that barbiturates or the benzodiazepines (e.g., Librium or Valium) do. Rather, they appear to have unique antipsychotic properties. Their beneficial effects are not limited to schizophrenia, since these drugs are also effective in managing affective (manic or depressive disorders) and even organic psychoses, and are of value for the various types of paranoid illnesses as well.

At present the antipsychotic drugs are the only generally recognized means of physical treatment of schizophrenic patients with scientifically demonstrated efficacy and relative safety. Most currently available antipsychotic drugs also produce a variety of neurologic ("neuroleptic") effects as well, probably as a reflection of their actions as dopamine antagonists in the basal ganglions. These side effects include Parkinsonism and motor restlessness (akathisia), acute dystonia and late ("tardive"), sometimes persistent, dyskinesias.

From time to time, the chronic and poorly understood nature of schizophrenia has led to unfortunate therapeutic fads and misleading claims, and sometimes to extreme measures taken to assist desperate families of patients with chronic schizophrenia. There have been claims that massive doses of vitamins C and B, and particularly of nicotinic acid, may be of some benefit. There is no compelling scientifically acceptable evidence that such treatments are effective, and their long-term safety is not established.

Other features of the management of schizophrenia include the periodic use of hospital care and the combination of medical treatment with psychologic support and efforts at social and occupational rehabilitation. At times, because of severe psychotic decompensation imminent risk of injury or suicide or severe management problems in the community, it becomes necessary to hospitalize schizophrenic patients and to intensify their medical treatment. Modern psychiatric inpatient management can often be handled very well in a general community hospital. Psychiatric hospitals have changed greatly since the 1950's. Very infrequently are locked doors, physical restraints and the untoward consequences of chronic institutionalism necessary. The contributions of psychoanalytic psychiatry to the understanding of the experience of being schizophrenic or living with a schizophrenic patient have been important, but, as a general rule, prolonged and intensive psychotherapy aimed at accomplishing fundamental changes in the personality has not been demonstrated to be an effective primary mode of treatment for severe schizophrenia. On the other hand, active supportive psychotherapy not only is humane but has much to offer in helping schizophrenic patients and their families to cope with what often represents a lifetime of at least partial and unremediable disability.

An important, but difficult, practical and theoretical question is whether modern chemotherapeutic and rehabilitative interventions have been "curative," or even whether they have brought about demonstrable increases in rates or durations of remissions, or a higher average level of reintegration of mental and social function of schizophrenic patients. Although it is clear that adequate doses of antipsychotic drugs are effective in interrupting acute exacerbations of schizophrenic or other psychotic illnesses and serve to hasten and to maintain at least partial remissions, the more chronically and quietly psychotic a schizophrenic patient becomes, the more difficult it is to demonstrate important benefits of antipsychotic drugs in excess of their side effects. Furthermore, since these agents are not without unpleasant subjective effects and some risk of serious neurologic complications, their continued requirement in an individual case needs to be reviewed frequently. An extreme view is that the rate of remission in chronic schizophrenia is not appreciably increased above that encountered before the introduction of antipsychotic medications in the early 1950's, and that what has been achieved is a shift from acute or florid psychotic symptomatology, and social deterioration inherent in prolonged institutionalization, to a more quiet form of chronic illness and marginal-to-inadequate social adaptation. A problem in evaluating this issue is that many administrative and public-health decisions introduced since the 1950's have also altered the pattern of care of chronic psychiatric patients by emphasizing short-term hospitalization and early return to the home or to an alternative sheltered environment. Even the best studies that have demonstrated high relapse rates in schizophrenia if antipsychotic medications are discontinued within the first two or three years after an initial partial recovery and discharge from the hospital have been based on crude measures of relapse, such as severe exacerbations of illness or the requirement for rehospitalization. Thus, the true impact of medications on the long-term outcome and degree of recovery in chronic schizophrenia remains a topic of debate and requires further research. What is clear at present is that antipsychotic drugs, although enormously helpful, are neither specific nor curative for schizophrenia.

[The section "Theories of Antipsychotic-Drug Action" has been omitted.]

The Dopamine Hypothesis in Schizophrenia

A dominant trend in theoretical biologic psychiatry since the introduction of powerful new antipsychotic, antimanic and antidepressant chemicals in the 1950's has been the assumption that an understanding of the mechanism of action of the drugs would lead to important insights into the pathophysiology of the major psychiatric illnesses of unknown cause. This trend has included the assumption, for example, that if antidepressants increase the availability of norepinephrine or serotonin as central synaptic transmitters, perhaps clinical depression reflects a deficiency of the activity of these neurotransmitters. Similarly, it has been suggested more recently that excessive activity of dopamine as a neurotransmitter, particularly in the mesolimbic or mesocortical projections . . . , may be an important feature of the pathophysiology of schizophrenia. Although this class of hypotheses has had a powerful effect of helping to organize and to focus preclinical and clinical research efforts, their support by direct metabolic testing in patients has generally been disappointing.

Clinical evidence in support of abnormal dopamine activity in schizophrenia remains essentially pharmacologic. The cornerstone of the hypothesis is the consistent antidopamine effect of the known antipsychotic drugs. The possibility remains, however, that antidopamine effects are neither necessary nor sufficient in the treatment of schizophrenia, and that their very consistency may reflect the method of selecting new candidate agents by antidopamine effects. Secondly, it is clear that antipsychotic agents are not antischizophrenic, in two senses: they are ameliorative, but not curative, in chronic schizophrenia; and their antipsychotic effects are even more impressive in some other illnesses, such as mania. It is often pointed out that dopamine agonists, such as amphetamines, other stimulants or L-dopa tend to produce transient worsening of schizophrenic signs and symptoms, not only by increasing the rate of production of all thoughts or behaviors, but also by increasing their qualitative abnormality; however, it has also been reported that the same agents can increase mania in some manic patients, decrease it in others and increase dysphoria and agitation in some severely depressed patients. To complicate matters further, apomorphine, presumably a direct dopamine agonist, has repeatedly been found not to induce exacerbation of schizophrenia or mania, and in the past was even reported to be beneficial, or at least sedating in schizophrenia, and so was recommended for its treatment by Bleuler in 1911.

Authors have commonly dealt with these complicating observations by "hedging" in two ways: by pointing out that the effects of the dopamine agonists are, in fact, quite complicated, and by suggesting that excessive activity of dopamine may be generally important in mediating specific features (especially acute features) of many forms of psychotic illness, and not necessarily specific to schizophrenia. The latter suggestion remains a viable theoretical possibility, although this modified form of the "dopamine hypothesis" of psychosis has not yet been extensively tested directly in patients with affective psychoses (psychotic depression or mania). A possible source of difficulty may be the tendency, in constructing biologic hypotheses of the pathogenesis of severe mental illnesses, to concentrate on the acute and florid features of psychoses (e.g., delusions and hallucinations), which are probably the least specific characteristics of schizophrenia. Another possibility must also be entertained: that it may be faulty logic to assume that the opposite of an important effect of a drug must be an important feature of the cause of the illness treated with that drug. This inference seems especially likely if antipsychotic drugs modify fundamental brain mechanisms mediating the expression of psychic alarm and distress. Another old example of this potential logical pitfall is that a study of the actions of mercurial or thiazide diuretics would not necessarily lead to important insights into the pathophysiology of congestive heart failure.

In more direct clinical tests of the dopamine hypothesis, there have been two strategies for attempting to evaluate the functional status of dopamine-mediated synaptic transmission in the human brain; one is a metabolic, and the other a neuroendocrinologic approach. Although there are no direct methods for evaluating the physiological status of central synapses in man, it has been possible to evaluate dopamine turnover indirectly by measuring static levels of its acidic metabolite, homovanillic acid..., in the lumbar cerebrospinal fluid or, better yet, by monitoring its dynamic changes after the administration of probenecid (to block the escape of the metabolite from the cerebrospinal fluid), or after an acute dose of an antipsychotic drug (to induce a rise in the metabolite levels). This approach has led to findings that, although complex and not entirely consistent, do not support the existence of an important increase in the turnover of dopamine, or of increased sensitivity of its receptors (predicting decreased turnover) in schizophrenic patients. The second, neuroendocrinologic, strategy has also been disappointing thus far. The best studied hormonal responses are resting levels or diurnal changes in plasma levels of prolactin or growth hormone, and there is no evidence that these levels, which are known to be strongly influenced by dopamine at the hypothalamus or pituitary, are altered in schizophrenia. These ingenious strategies may not have provided evidence of increased activity of dopamine owing to their evaluation of anatomic sites that may be irrelevant to the pathophysiology of psychosis: the caudate nucleus in most of the homovanillic acid recovered in the cerebrospinal fluid, and the hypothalamus or pituitary in the hormone measurements.

Very recently, several preliminary but provocative studies have contributed further to the evaluation of endocrine function. Thus, apomorphine, L-dopa or ergot alkaloids have been given to patients to increase the agonism of central dopamine mechanisms, and the dynamic responses of plasma growth hormone (increased) or of prolactin (decreased) were evaluated. In one study, the rise of growth hormone was blunted in some schizophrenic patients although a residual effect of antipsychotic drug treatment could not be ruled out; in another study, schizophrenic patients tended to show a wider variation in growth hormone responses than normal persons, suggesting that various subpopulations of schizophrenic patients may exist, whereas the mean trends for the population as a whole were of no consequence.

Thus, in summary, attempts to evaluate the func-

tional status of dopamine mechanisms in some parts of the central nervous system in patients have not supported the predictions of a dopamine hypothesis of schizophrenia, or of psychosis, although in fairness, this approach to clinical pathophysiology in psychiatric patients has only begun. The evidence that can be mustered for abnormally overactive dopaminergic neurotransmission, perhaps in the limbic system, in schizophrenia or in other forms of psychosis, is largely pharmacologic, inferential and indirect.

Conclusions

At present schizophrenia remains a common and severe mental illness of unknown cause. The treatment of its acute and florid psychotic manifestations was advanced greatly by the introduction of antipsychotic drugs in the 1950's. These drugs and associated changes in the pattern of delivery of psychiatric care have led to increased optimism about the treatability of schizophrenia, and to striking reductions in the reliance on prolonged hospital care of patients with chronic schizophrenia. Attempts to understand the mechanisms of action and of the toxicity of antipsychotic drugs have led to impressive strides in the application of neurobiologic technics to preclinical and clinical biologic psychiatry. These advances have resulted in a coherent theory of the interactions of antipsychotic agents with central dopamine receptors—interactions that help greatly to explain the neurologic and autonomic side effects of these agents—but so far have led to few practical innovations in the design of improved drugs. Efforts to extend these insights to an understanding of the pathophysiology or cause of the psychoses have not yet been successful. The attempts have had important beneficial effects of stimulating and focusing clinical research in biologic psychiatry and of reinforcing the relevance of the mainstream of biomedical research to the theory and practice of modern psychiatry.

REFERENCES

1 Pope H, Lipinski JF: Differential diagnosis of schizophrenia and manic-depressive illness: a reassessment of the specificity of "schizophrenic" symptoms in the light of current research. Arch Gen Psychiatry (in press)

2 Gottesman II, Shields J: A critical review of recent adoption, twin, and family studies of schizophrenia: behavioral genetics perspectives. Schizophrenia Bull 2:360-398, 1976

3 Matthysse S, Lipinski J: Biochemical aspects of schizophrenia. Annu Rev Med 26:551-565, 1975

4 Meltzer HY, Stahl SM: The dopamine hypothesis of

schizophrenia: a review. Schizophrenia Bull 2:19-76, 1976

5 Baldessarini RJ: Chemotherapy in Psychiatry. Cambridge, Harvard University Press, 1977

6 Seeman P, Lee T, Chau-Wong M, et al: Antipsychotic drug doses and neuroleptic/dopamine receptors. Nature 261:717-719, 1976

7 Creese I, Burt DR, Snyder SH: Dopamine receptor binding predicts clinical and pharmacological potencies of antischizophrenic drugs. Science 192:481-483, 1976

8 Meltzer HY, Creese I, Burt DR, et al: Dopamine receptors and average clinical doses. Science 194:545-546, 1976

Glossary

A fibers Axons with large diameters that can therefore conduct impulses quickly; they are responsible for the sensations of sharp pain.

Absolute refractory period The period following the action potential when the neuron cannot be fired or conduct an action potential.

Acetylcholine (ah-seat-tul-KO-lean) The transmitter substance secreted by the preganglionic neurons of the autonomic nervous system. Abbreviated **ACh**.

ACTH Adrenocorticotrophic hormone released by the anterior pituitary glands, acting on the adrenal glands to help the body cope with stress.

ACTH fractions Parts of the ACTH molecule that have been shown to affect protein synthesis in the brain.

ACTH-RF A releasing factor produced in the hypothalamus in response to stress, causing the anterior pituitary to release adrenocorticotrophic hormone.

Action potential The sudden influx of sodium ions into the intracellular fluid, also known as the nerve impulse, is repeated down the length of the axon.

Acuity (ah-CUE-it-tee) The ability to distinguish detail.

Adaptation The decrease in the ability to detect a sensory stimulus after continuous exposure to it.

Addiction Physical dependency on a drug caused by the body's development of tolerance, which requires an increasing dose to produce a given effect. Withdrawal symptoms are experienced when the drug is discontinued.

Adipose tissue Fat reserves where lipids are stored.

Adipsia The condition of not drinking.

Adrenal cortex The outside layer of the adrenal glands where corticoids are secreted to help the body cope with stress.

Adrenal glands Two glands located above the kidneys that secrete corticoids, hormones that help the body cope with stress.

Adrenal medulla The inside layer of the adrenal glands where epinephrine and norepinephrine are secreted.

Adrenalin (ah-DREN-ah-lin) Usually called epinephrine, this hormone, secreted by the adrenal medulla, helps the body to mobilize responses to stress.

Affect Emotionality.

Afferent neuron A nerve fiber carrying impulses toward the central nervous system. Also called a **sensory neuron**.

Agraphia The inability to write letters or words.

Alarm stage The initial response to stress.

Alcoholism Physical and psychological dependency on alcohol.

Aldosterone A hormone secreted in the adrenal medulla active in the regulation of bodily fluids.

Alexia The inability to read letters or words.

All-or-none law States that if the threshold of the axon hillock is reached, there will be a nerve impulse. If the threshold is not reached, there will be no impulse.

Alpha motor neurons Neurons having dendrites, cell bodies, and long axons that carry impulses from the spinal cord to muscle tissue.

Alpha waves Low-frequency brain waves (8–12 Hz), of higher amplitude than beta waves, recorded during periods of relaxation or meditation.

Amphetamine psychosis Psychotic paranoia, confused thinking brought on by overuse of amphetamines.

Amplitude A measurement of the strength of signals or wave formations.

Amygdala (a-MIG-da-la) An olive-shaped structure of the brain located in front of the hippocampus and involved in emotional behavior.

Analgesic A pain killer.

Androgens (AN-dro-gens) Male sex hormones.

Angiotensin A hormone secreted in the blood through the action of renin that causes the adrenal medulla to release aldosterone, active in the regulation of bodily fluids.

Angular gyrus The area where the parietal and temporal lobes come together, responsible for the ability to name or identify objects.

Anomia The inability to name or identify objects.

Anterior hypothalamus The front part of the hypothalamus that stimulates the parasympathetic nervous system.

Anterior pituitary The portion of the pituitary gland that is controlled by hormones called thyroid-releasing factors secreted by the hypothalamus.

Anterograde amnesia Loss of recent memory following surgery, particularly the removal of the hippocampus.

Anticonvulsants Drugs administered to epileptics and believed to control the spread of abnormal electrical activity in the brain.

Antidiuretic hormone Secreted by the posterior pituitary and responsible for the moderation of thirst through the monitoring of water levels in the blood and the regulation of kidney function. Abbreviated **ADH**.

Antihistamine A drug that blocks the release of naturally occurring histamine; used to treat allergies.

Antimotivational syndrome Confusion and loss of motivation formerly thought to result from heavy use of marihuana.

Aphagia The condition of not eating.

Area 17 The visual cortex of the brain, responsible for interpreting visual stimuli.

Ascending reticular activating system An area of the reticular formation that promotes wakefulness. Abbreviated **ARAS**.

Association areas Scattered throughout the four lobes of the cortex, these areas are involved in the functions of thinking, reasoning, association, and recognition of sensory input.

Ataxia Loss or lack of muscle coordination.

Audition The process of hearing.

Auditory nerve The bundle of axons that transmit impulses from the cochlea to the brain.

Autonomic nervous system The part of the nervous system that controls the functions of the body, thought to be involuntary. Abbreviated **ANS**.

Axon The tube extending between the cell body and the telodendria of a neuron, specialized for transmitting nerve impulses.

Axon hillock The area in the axon near the cell body where the threshold is lower than for the rest of the axon.

Barbiturates Drugs prescribed as sedatives that act to cause a general depression of neural activity and so induce sleep.

Baro receptors Receptors in the heart that monitor blood pressure.

Basal ganglia The part of the brain that, together with the midbrain, is involved in the control of muscles for walking, swinging the arms, and starting and stopping movements.

Basilar membrane (BAZ-ah-ler) A membrane that divides the cochlea down the middle and that contains the organ of Corti.

Bed wetting A problem frequent in children 5–7 years old, occurring during NREM sleep. Also called **enuresis**.

Behavior The observable responses or activities of an individual or organism.

Benzodiazepine A chemical from which the prescription drugs Valium and Librium are derived, used for the treatment of depression, anxiety, and mild stress.

Beta waves Fast-frequency, low-amplitude brain waves of 15–30 Hz.

Biofeedback Being made aware of physiological changes in the body and, with practice, being trained to control them.

Bipolar cells Cells that have a single dendrite and a single axon extending from opposite sides of the cell body.

Bitter taste One of the four tastes that are the bases of all other tastes; it is detected by receptors at the back near the middle of the tongue.

Blind spot The point at which the optic nerve leaves the back of the eyeball. Since there are no rods or cones located here, the eye is blind to light striking this area.

Brainstem The portion of the brain consisting of the medulla, pons, and midbrain.

Broca's aphasia (BROKE-caws ah-FAY-zee-ah) Resulting from damage to Broca's area and characterized by difficulty in production or execution of speech.

Broca's area An area on the side of the left frontal lobe in front of the motor area that controls complex motor patterns involved in speech.

Bug detectors Complex ganglion cells in the retina of the frog that respond to objects moving across the field of vision.

C fibers Axons of small diameter and low conduction rate responsible for the sensations of slow, dull pain.

Caffeine A stimulant found in coffee, tea, chocolate, and cola drinks that causes arousal of the cortex.

Calorie The unit of measurement of fuel value or capacity to produce energy in foods.

Cataract The condition of the eye's lens when, through disease or injury, it becomes cloudy.

Catecholamine theory of affective disorders The idea that depression and mania are caused by fluctuations in the level of the neurotransmitter norepinephrine.

Catecholamines (cat-uh-COLE-ah-means) The neurotransmitters dopamine, epinephrine, and norepinephrine that mediate the transfer of neural information at the synapse.

Cell body A round protuberance in the neuron providing nourishment for the entire nerve cell and located between the dendrite and the telodendria. Also called the **soma**.

Cell membrane The outside covering of the neuron where the electrochemical processes resulting in the transmission of neural information take place; a baglike structure enclosing a cell, separating and protecting one cell from another and regulating which substances enter and leave the cell.

Central nervous system Comprised of the neurons and nerve tracts of the brain and the spinal cord.

Central sulcus A fissure running down the side of the brain and forming the rear boundary of the frontal lobe.

Cerebellum (ser-ah-BELL-ahm) A structure in the hindbrain regulating coordination, maintenance of equilibrium, and muscle tonus.

Cerebral electro-therapy Passing a weak electric current through the brain of a subject in order to induce sleep.

Cervical (SIR-vee-cul) Referring to the neck area, as in cervical spinal nerves.

Chemical sense A sense dependent upon the chemical stimulation of receptor cells; taste or smell.

Chlorpromazine (chlor-PRO-ma-zine) A drug administered to schizophrenics that acts to affect chemicals of the brain involved in neuron function.

Chromosomes The gene-containing threadlike bodies, constant in number in every cell for each species, that determine the hereditary characteristics of the species.

Ciliary muscles (SILL-ee-airy) Tiny muscles that control the shape of the eye's lens.

Circadian rhythms (sir-KAY-dee-an) Biological rhythms that reach a high and a low point every 24 hours.

Circuit In the theory of D. O. Hebb, a group of neurons that has been coded to carry an impression or memory.

Classical conditioning The process of conditioning a reflexive response to a stimulus that ordinarily has no effect on that response.

Cocaine A stimulant contained in the leaves of the coca plant causing euphoria, loss of appetite, indifference to pain, and feelings of power.

Cochlea (COKE-lee-ah) A coiled tube, the inner ear, that is responsible for transmitting sound vibrations and helping to maintain body balance.

Cognitive functions Perceiving, interpreting, and thinking about one's experience.

Cognitive theory of emotions The idea that one's own perceptions and interpretation of experiences determines the emotions one feels.

Cold receptors Cells in the skin that are sensitive to decreases in temperature.

Compoz A nonprescription drug containing methapyraline, an antihistamine whose side effects may include drowsiness.

Conditioned response A response that is evoked by a conditioned stimulus after conditioning has taken place.

Conditioned stimulus A stimulus that is paired with an unconditioned stimulus and that subsequently can evoke the response made to the unconditioned stimulus; in Pavlov's experiments, the bell that elicited salivation.

Cones Receptors located in the retina that are specialized to be reactive to light and sensitive to specific colors.

Confabulation Compensation for a loss of memory by making up facts that the person believes did occur.

Consciousness Awareness of the self; responding to the environment and other individuals with more than reflexive behavior.

Consolidated memories Memories that have become part of the long-term memory according to the consolidation hypothesis.

Consolidation hypothesis The theory that memory is first stored in a preliminary and more easily lost form and then consolidated and made part of a more permanent, long-term memory.

Contour sharpening The process by which boundaries of objects are made to stand out through the inhibition of receptor cells near those that are responding to the light waves from the object.

Control An experimental procedure. Ideally an experimental group is compared with a control group that is identical in every way except for the factor being studied.

Convergence The process that occurs when information from many receptors is combined to be carried by a few nerve fibers.

Cornea The curved, transparent outer covering of the eye.

Corpus callosum A bundle of nerve fibers about 1 cm thick connecting the two hemispheres of the brain.

Cortex The convoluted portion of the brain responsible for processing, experiencing, integrating, and responding to external stimuli.

Corticoids Hormones secreted by the adrenal cortex in response to stress.

Cranial nerves Twelve nerves attached at various places along the medulla, pons, and midbrain and carrying sensory and/or motor information.

Craniosacral system The parasympathetic division consisting of the axons that leave the brain stem (cranial area) or the bottom of the spinal cord (sacral area).

Cytoplasm A jellylike substance filling the cellular interior in which enzymes are manufactured.

Dark adaptation The time it takes for the eyes to adjust to dim light, determined by the recombination of opsin and a Vitamin A-like chemical into rhodopsin.

Decorticate rage The release of emotional behavior that occurs after removal of the cortex in cats.

Decrement The process of becoming less. An axon is said to conduct without decrement since there is no loss of amplitude when an action potential is conducted along it. Dendrites and cell bodies are said to conduct with decrement because potential loses strength in these parts of the neuron.

Delta waves Synchronous wave patterns of high amplitude and extremely low frequency (2–4 Hz) occurring during stage 4 sleep.

Delusion A sense impression for which there is no external stimulus; a hallucination.

Dendrite The branched end of a neuron that receives

information from the skin or other neurons.

Denervated stomach One in which the vagus nerve, which controls the secretion of hydrochloric acid, has been cut.

Depolarization The point when the action potential of a nerve cell reaches zero.

Depression The affective disorder characterized by unresponsiveness, despondency, and dejection.

Descending reticular formation The part of the reticular formation responsible for the regulation of muscular tension.

Desynchronous wave patterns Random patterns resembling writing done on a bumpy road.

Diabetes insipidus A condition characterized by abnormal thirst resulting from the undersecretion of antidiuretic hormone.

Diabetes mellitus A condition resulting from lack of insulin; characterized by the loss of water due to the excretion of glucose.

Digestion The process of breaking down food into smaller particles that takes place in the stomach.

Dilation The opening of the pupil to allow the entry of more light.

Dissociation The separation of chemical compounds in solution into ions.

DNA (deoxyribonucleic acid) A complex molecule in the genes that through its double helical form is capable of self-replication, containing in its ladderlike connecting chemical rungs the coded information for cell development.

Dopamine-B-hydroxylase An enzyme found to be deficient in the brains of some schizophrenics and responsible for the synthesis of norepinephrine.

Dorsal root The branched connection site of afferent neurons to the spinal cord.

Double helix The structure of the DNA molecule that allows for self-replication and the transmission of complex genetic information.

Down's syndrome Caused by a misplaced chromosome, the syndrome is marked by abnormal physical features such as slanting eyes, protruding tongue, and abnormal brain development.

Dysarthria Loss of ability to speak.

Ear canal A tunnel approximately 2.5 cm (1 inch) long that is responsible for directing sound into the ear.

Eardrum An elastic membrane located at the end of the ear canal; it vibrates when struck by sound waves. Also known as the **tympanic membrane**.

EEG machine A device for measuring brain waves or electrical activity from the neurons of the cortex.

Electrochemical activity The process occurring at the cell membrane through the action of ions and resulting in the transmission of information through the nervous system.

Electrodermal response The comparative ease with which a current passes through the skin, caused by the presence or absence of sweat; the **EDR**, now called the **skin resistance response**.

Electrodes Wires inserted into the brain or disks placed on the scalp used to measure the electrical activity of neurons or to stimulate them.

Electroencephalogram A recording of brain waves or electrical activity from the neurons in the cortex. Abbreviated **EEG**.

Electrophysiology The exploration of brain function through the use of microelectrodes.

Electrosleep Sleep produced by a device for passing a weak electrical current through the brain of a subject.

Embryo The fertilized egg in the first eight weeks of development.

Encephalization The tendency for a group of neurons to develop at the head end of a nerve network, which allows a greater complexity of movement and function.

Endocrine glands Glands secreting their hormones directly into the bloodstream.

Endoplasmic reticulum Folded membrane sheets located throughout the cytoplasm and studded with ribosomes.

Endorphins (end-OR-fins) Morphinelike substances manufactured in the brain that may be active in the process of opiate addiction as well as functioning as neurotransmitters.

Engram The physical change in the brain that results in a memory.

Enriched environment An environment providing maximal stimulation and opportunity for learning and exploration.

Enuresis (en-your-EE-sis) Bed wetting that occurs during NREM sleep often between the ages of 5 and 7 years.

Enzymes Complex organic compounds that are manufactured in the cytoplasm upon instructions contained in the DNA molecules of the genes. Enzymes control cellular development.

Epinephrine (ap-ah-NEF-ah-rin) One of the hormones secreted by the adrenal medulla in response to stress; it stimulates the heart and constricts the blood vessels.

Estrogen (ESS-tro-gen) One of the primary female hormones secreted by the ovaries.

Evoked potentials Brain waves generated by nerve impulses to the cortex in response to a specific stimulus.

Excitatory postsynaptic potential The event occurring when the resting potential of a neuron becomes more positive and the neuron is more likely to begin an action potential. Abbreviated **EPSP**.

Excitatory transmitters Chemical substances thought to make the cell membrane more permeable to positive ions, including sodium.

Excitement phase The first stage of sexual response characterized by penile erection in males and vaginal lubrication in females.

Exhaustion stage   The final stage of the stress reaction characterized by loss of resistance, glandular collapse, and eventually death.

External genitalia   The penis, vaginal lips, vagina, and clitoris.

Extracellular fluid   The one-third of the body's fluid that is found outside the cells.

Extrapyramidal motor system (extra-per-RAM-id-all) The portion of the brain comprised of the basal ganglia, the midbrain, and the cerebellum.

Fatty acid   One of the two substances used by the body as fuel; a kind of fat.

Feedback system   The inhibition of an enzyme or hormone's production by the end-product of the metabolism of that substance; for example, the inhibition of thyrotropin production that suppresses thyroxin secretion when the level of thyroxin builds up in the blood.

Fetus   The developing young in the human uterus after the first eight weeks of development.

Fissure   The valley or bottom portion of a convolution or wrinkle in the cortex. Also called a **sulcus**.

Follicle-stimulating hormone   In males, the hormone acts on the testes to aid maturation of sperm; in females, it acts on the ovaries where it promotes the development of the egg and the secretion of estrogen. Abbreviated **FSH**.

Forebrain   A portion of the vertebrate brain increasingly developed in higher animals and consisting of the brain hemispheres and interior structures such as the hypothalamus and thalamus.

Forgetting   The loss of information from memory.

Fovea (FOH-vee-ah)   An area in the center of the retina containing only cones, which are not activated by dim light; the area of greatest visual acuity.

Fraternal twins   Formed when two ova are fertilized by sperm cells and resulting in two individuals of different genetic makeups.

Free nerve endings   The receptors for pain that look like minute pieces of string with frayed endings.

Frequency   A measurement (usually in Hz) of the rate of waves, such as brain waves or sound waves.

Frequency code   The fact that a strong stimulus can fire a neuron more frequently than a weak one, resulting in the ability to distinguish between strong and weak stimuli.

Frontal lobe   The portion of the brain that controls voluntary movements; one of the four lobes that comprise the hemispheres of the human brain.

Frontal lobotomy   A lesioning of the frontal lobes performed on human patients for the treatment of various mental disorders.

Galvanic skin response   The comparative ease with which a current passes through the skin, caused by the presence or absence of sweat; the **GSR**, now called **skin resistance response**.

Ganglion   A cluster of neurons located at the top of a nerve network. In lower animals, it functions as the primitive forerunner of a brain. In the human brain and in other higher animals, ganglia control specific portions of the body or bodily functions.

Gate control theory   The idea that activation of the touch receptors at the site of a trauma may help to inhibit the pain receptors for that area; thus we rub wounds, massage muscles that are sore.

Gender identity   The individual's attitude toward her or his own sexuality. This may or may not match the configuration of the individual's genetic and anatomical makeup.

General adaptation syndrome   The three stages of stress—alarm, resistance, and exhaustion—as identified by Hans Selye. Abbreviated **GAS**.

Generator potential   The change in a cell's electrical potential caused by the action of some stimulus on the chemistry of the cell.

Genes   Material composed of DNA molecules contained in the chromosomes and carrying instructions for body and brain development.

Genetic predisposition   The tendency of individuals sharing the same genetic structure to develop the same disorders.

Glucagon (GLUE-ka-gone)   A hormone secreted by the pancreas that triggers the conversion of glycogen into glucose.

Glucocorticoids   Hormones released in time of stress that help raise the level of glucose in the blood.

Glucose   One of the two substances used by the body as fuel; a type of sugar.

Glucostatic theory   Jean Mayer's explanation of hunger as being triggered by decreased glucose utilization some hours after eating.

Glycerol (GLISS-uh-ral)   With fatty acids, one of the two substances formed in the adipose tissue from fats and lipids; a substance converted to glucose in the liver.

Glycogen (GLEYE-kuh-jen)   A form of carbohydrate that can be stored in the liver and converted to glucose as needed.

Golgi complex   A network of fibrils, granules, and membranous structures that wraps hormones and other cellular secretions in a membranous covering for transport out of the cell and into the extracellular fluid or blood for dispersal.

Gonads   The ovaries and testes; the reproductive organs.

Graded potential   The continuously changing resting potential of a dendrite or cell body caused by excitatory and inhibitory transmitters.

Grand mal seizure   A brain disorder characterized by loss of consciousness, rigidity, and urination.

Growth hormone   A hormone released in the anterior pituitary and acting directly on the cells of the body to stimulate growth by making proteins available.

Growth hormone releasing factor A hormone secreted by the hypothalamus during adolescence and causing the secretion of growth hormone by the anterior pituitary. Abbreviated **GH-RF**.

Gustation The sense of taste and the process of tasting.

Gyrus (JI-russ) The ridge or top portion of a convolution or wrinkle in the cortex.

Habituation The process that causes the cells of the central nervous system to stop responding after continued input from receptors.

Hair cells Responsible for changing sound vibrations into nerve impulses, these hair-shaped cells produce generator potentials when they are bent.

Hallucination A sense impression for which there is no external stimulus; a delusion.

Hallucinogens Drugs such as LSD and mescaline that produce hallucinations. Also called **psychedelics**.

Hangover Symptoms of nausea, headache, fatigue, and dehydration experienced following heavy alcohol use.

Heart muscle The muscle tissue that comprises the heart; it is neither smooth nor striated.

Hemispheres Literally, half-sphere. In anatomy, the two symmetrical halves of the brain, each controlling the opposite side of the body and including the frontal, temporal, occipital, and parietal lobes.

Heroin An addictive opiate having analgesic effects similar to morphine.

Hindbrain The portion of the brain consisting of the pons, medulla, cerebellum, and reticular formation controlling coordination, vital functions, and the regulation of sleep.

Hippocampus That part of the brain located below and to the side of the basal ganglia and involved in memory.

Homeostasis The maintenance of the body's internal environment in a state of optimal functioning.

Hunger pangs Pains experienced in the stomach but present even when the stomach has been removed.

Hydrochloric acid The chemical secreted by the stomach and responsible for breaking down foods.

Hyperkinesis Occurring in 5–10 percent of school children and characterized by impulsive behavior and short attention span. Also called **minimal brain dysfunction**.

Hyperphagia The tendency to eat enormous amounts of food.

Hyperpolarization The condition of an axon membrane when the potential across the membrane becomes more negative than in the resting state.

Hyperventilation Rapid breathing.

Hypothalamus (hype-po-THAL-mus) The portion of the forebrain that controls basic drives and the internal body environment.

Hypovolemia A reduction of extracellular bodily fluids such as might occur from drinking too little fluids.

Hypovolemic thirst Thirst occasioned by the loss of extracellular fluid.

Identical twins From a single fertilized egg, two individuals develop that have the same genetic makeup.

Imipramine (im-IP-rah-mean) A drug that causes an increase in the level of norepinephrine and an elevation of mood.

Immune response The ability of the body's white blood cells to fight off in n.

Incus One of the three ossicles of the middle ear; it transmits and amplifies sound waves.

Indoleamine (in-DOLE-ah-mean) One of the neurotransmitter substances including serotonin thought to be involved in certain psychological problems.

Inferior colliculus (ko-LICK-u-lus) The area of the midbrain involved in the reflex of turning toward a noise.

Inherited behavior Behavior mediated by built-in neural circuits of the brain.

Inhibitory postsynaptic potential The event occurring when the resting potential of a neuron becomes more negative, making an action potential less likely to occur. Abbreviated **IPSP**.

Insomnia The inability to stay asleep or fall asleep or awakening too early.

Interneuron A nerve cell whose primary function is to carry impulses between different areas of the nervous system.

Intracellular fluid The two-thirds of the body's fluids that are found inside the cells.

Intracellular thirst Thirst caused by the loss of water from the cells, brought on by salt intake.

Iodopsins (eye-oh-DOP-sins) Three different color-sensitive chemicals contained in the cones of the retina that respond to the primary colors.

Ion A chemical particle carrying either a positive or a negative charge.

IQ score A measure of the ability to perform certain tasks that are thought to relate to intelligence. The average is 100.

Iris The muscular disc that varies the size of the pupil and gives the eye its color.

Jet-lag syndrome Inappropriate wakefulness or sleepiness experienced when passing from one time zone to another.

Kinesthetic receptors (kin-es-THET-ic) Receptors in the joints that provide information on the location of the limbs in space.

Klinefelter's syndrome The condition caused by the XXY chromosomal pattern results in male individuals in which testes are not developed and the individuals are sterile. Some XXY persons are mentally retarded.

Kluver-Bucy syndrome (KLU-ver-boo-see) The behavioral changes following temporal-lobe removal, including loss of affect, aggression, and increased sexuality.

Korsakoff syndrome Confabulation, confusion, poor

coordination, and memory loss occasioned by heavy use of alcohol.

Labeling Making RNA radioactive by injecting radioactive chemicals that bind themselves to the RNA, thus allowing minute measurements of the change of RNA level.

Last-in/first-out principle Results in the loss of the last memories immediately preceding certain traumas.

Lateral fissure The boundary of the temporal lobe in the form of a sulcus running laterally up the brain.

Lateral geniculate nucleus (jen-ICK-you-lit) The area of the thalamus where axons of the optic tract synapse. Each **LGN** cell processes input from a specific field of the retinal area.

Lateral hypothalamus The portion of the brain that controls eating and drinking behavior.

Learned behavior Behavior mediated by experience, or socialization.

Lens The transparent portion of the eye responsible for focusing light on the retina.

Librium A trade name for a widely prescribed derivative of the chemical benzodiazepine, used as a tranquilizer.

Lie detector A device for measuring physiological responses such as respiration, skin changes, and blood pressure; also called a **polygraph**.

Light waves Light in its wave form; one of the two ways physicists conceptualize light, the other being in the form of photons.

Limbic area In lower vertebrates, the portion of the forebrain that governs predatory behavior. In higher animals, it is involved in memory functions and the experience of emotions.

Limbic system Consisting of many interconnected nuclei in different parts of the brain and involved in sexual behavior, memory formation, and emotional behavior.

Lipids A group of fatty compounds that, together with proteins and carbohydrates, make up living cells.

Lipostatic theory (LIP-oh-stat-ik) The theory that one feels hunger when the body's fat stores fall below a setpoint.

Lithium A drug used in the treatment of mania believed to act by reducing levels of norepinephrine.

Locus coeruleus (LOW-cus cha-RUL-ee-is) An area of the pons that produces norepinephrine, which is thought to be involved in controlling REM sleep.

Longitudinal sulcus The fissure that divides the brain into a right and a left hemisphere.

LSD (lysergic acid diethylamide) A drug that can cause hallucinations notably through its action on serotonin.

Lumbar (LUM-bar) Referring to the upper back area, as in lumbar spinal nerves.

Luteinizing hormone In females, the hormone acts to release the egg from the ovarian follicles; in males, **LH** acts on the testes to cause secretion of testosterone.

Lymph A watery fluid in which fats or lipids are stored and transported to the adipose tissue throughout the body.

Malleus One of the three ossicles that comprise the middle ear; it transmits sound waves and amplifies them.

Mammillary bodies An area related to the hippocampus and involved in the formation of memories of recent or day-to-day events. Often damaged by alcoholism.

Mania Excessive energy, sleeplessness, elevated mood, boisterousness.

Mass action principle The idea that memories are lost in proportion to the amount of cortex removed; that memories do not occupy a specific location in the cortex.

Medial geniculate nuclei (jen-ICK-you-lit) The area of the brain to which auditory information is relayed from the thalamus.

Medulla (mah-DULL-ah) A structure in the hindbrain controlling respiration and blood pressure.

Mescaline A drug found in the peyote cactus, capable of causing hallucinations through its ability to transmethylate serotonin.

Metabolic fuels Glucose, lipids, and amino acids—the presence or absence of which may trigger the liver to signal the brain of bodily hunger.

Metabolic rate The rate at which an individual converts food into energy in the body.

Metabolism The process of turning food into energy.

Methadone A substitute opiate used to replace illegal heroin while preventing withdrawal symptoms. It can be taken orally without producing euphoria.

Methamphetamine (met-ah-am-FET-ah-mean) A stimulant that may cause sleeplessness, loss of appetite, euphoria, and reduction of fatigue. Commonly called **Methedrine**.

Methedrine A stimulant that may cause sleeplessness, loss of appetite, euphoria, and reduction of feelings of fatigue.

Methyl group The organic radical CH_3 found in many organic chemicals; when added to a neurotransmitter, it may produce hallucinations.

Methylphenidate Under the trade name Ritalin, this drug is prescribed for children with hyperkinesis.

Microelectrodes Microscopically thin wires that can be inserted into the cell bodies of large spinal motor neurons to measure potentials.

Midbrain One of the three divisions of the vertebrate brain; it controls basic visual and auditory functions. Together with the pons and the medulla, it is called the **brainstem**.

Mineralcorticoids Hormones released in time of stress that help regulate the level of sodium and potassium in the body.

Minimal brain dysfunction Occurring in 5–10 percent

of school children and characterized by impulsive behavior and short attention span. Abbreviated **MBD**. Also called **hyperkinesis**.

Minor labia Called the sex skin; the inner folds of skin bordering the vagina and covered by the labia majora.

Misperception A sense impression that does not correspond with the stimulus that created it; seeing a bird and mistaking it for a plane.

Mitochondria The portion of the cell that provides the energy required for cellular functioning through the breakdown of blood sugar or glucose.

Monoamine oxidase An enzyme that destroys the neurotransmitter catecholamines at the synapse after action has taken place. Abbreviated **MAO**.

Morphine A powerful analgesic derived from the opium poppy.

Motor area The portion of the frontal lobe that controls voluntary movement.

Mucus A viscous substance secreted by mucous cells or membranes.

Multipolar neuron A neuron possessing numerous dendrites and functioning to receive information from other neurons. The shape of most of the neurons of the brain.

Myelin sheath (MY-lin) The fatty wrapping of some nerve cells, thought to help the axon conduct neural impulses at greater speed.

Nanometers (nm) The unit of measurement of light waves, corresponding to a billionth of a meter.

Narcolepsy Falling into a deep sleep without warning.

Narcotic antagonists Drugs that counteract the euphoric effect of heroin; used in the treatment of heroin addiction.

Negative ion A chemical particle that will attract ions having positive charges and repel other negative ions.

Nembutal Trade name for sodium pentobarbital, a barbiturate that is prescribed as a sedative and acts to depress neural activity.

Neocortex The area of the brain comprising the cortex of the frontal, parietal, occipital, and temporal lobes; literally, the new cortex.

Nerve A group of axons carrying information to and from the central nervous system. The term nerve is applied only to groups of axons outside the central nervous system.

Nerve impulses A combination of electrical and chemical changes transmitted through the axon of the neuron.

Nerve network In lower animals, the forerunner of a spinal cord, allowing for organized movements and culminating in a ganglion.

Neural information Nerve impulses.

Neuron A nerve cell consisting of the cell body and nerve fibers, specialized for communication.

Neurotransmitters Chemicals released by the presynaptic neurons that excite or inhibit postsynaptic neurons. Also called **transmitter substances**.

Nicotine A stimulant found in tobacco that increases blood pressure, heart rate, and the release of epinephrine.

Nictitating membrane (NICK-tate-ing) Possessed by owls, rabbits, etc., it is designed to protect the eye by reflexively flicking over the cornea in response to foreign stimuli. Abbreviated **NM**.

Night terror Awakening during sleep with a feeling of terror but no memory of dreams, usually occurring in infancy up to the age of 5 and most often during NREM sleep.

Nightmare Awakening from a bad dream, usually occurring during REM sleep.

Nigrostriatal system A system of neurons containing dopamine running between the brainstem and the lateral hypothalamus, destruction of which causes an animal to cease eating and drinking.

Nodes of Ranvier (ron-vee-AYE) Thin places or interruptions in the myelin sheath that covers most large axons.

Nonspecific response So called because it is initiated in response to different kinds of events.

Noradrenalin (NOR-ah-dren-ah-lin) A hormone secreted by the adrenal medulla that is responsible for mobilizing the body's responses to stress. Usually called **norepinephrine**.

Norepinephrine (nor-ap-ah-NEF-ah-rin) One of the hormones secreted by the adrenal medulla; one of the chemical transmitters active at the synapse.

NREM sleep (non-rem) A period of sleep characterized by declining physiological activity and increasing delta waves.

Nucleus A baglike structure inside the cell body containing the genetic instructions necessary for the manufacture of chemicals that control cellular functioning.

Nytol A nonprescription drug containing the antihistamine methapyraline whose side effects may include drowsiness.

Occipital lobe (awk-SIP-ah-tall) An area of the cortex located at the back of the brain and involved in visual sensation.

Occipito-parietal lobes Contain the association areas of the brain responsible for the ability to identify and recognize visual stimuli.

Off cells Ganglion cells that respond when light is turned off.

Olfaction The process of smelling.

Olfactory bulb The brain structure that relays nerve impulses from the olfactory nerve to the olfactory tubercule and the prepyriform cortex.

Olfactory cells Cells of the olfactory membrane that respond to substances dissolved in the mucus.

Olfactory membrane Tissue in the upper part of the nose containing olfactory cells.

Olfactory nerve Short nerve fibers traveling through the spongy perforated section of the skull and connecting the olfactory membrane and the olfactory bulb.

Olfactory tubercule (TWO-burr-cle)   One of the areas at the base of the brain where the sense of smell is controlled.

On cells   Ganglion cells that respond when light is turned on.

On-off cells   Ganglion cells that respond both at the onset and offset of light impulses.

Operant conditioning   The sequence of making a response to receive a reinforcement.

Opiates   Drugs having analgesic effects similar to morphine; heroin and methadone.

Opponent response   The capacity of a neuron to respond to one color by being excited and to another by being inhibited.

Opsin   One of the byproducts of the effect of light on the rhodopsin contained in the rods of the retina.

Optic chiasma (ky-AZ-muh)   The junction of the two optic nerves leading from the retina of the eye to the brain.

Optic nerve   The bundle of ganglion cells that carries nerve impulses from the retina to the brain.

Organ of Corti   Contains the hearing receptors responsible for changing vibratory energy into nerve impulses.

Orgasm   Spasmodic contractions of the sexual organs and the muscles surrounding the anus, accompanied in males by the ejaculation of semen.

Orgasmic phase   The experience of contractions in the vagina and surrounding muscles of the anus in females and the ejaculation of semen by the male, also accompanied by spasmodic contractions of the sexual organs.

Oropharyngeal sensations (oh-row-fuh-RAN-gee-al)   The experience of eating; the sensations of mouth and throat that accompany eating.

Osmoreceptors   Cells located in the hypothalamus that detect osmotic thirst.

Osmotic pressure   The tendency for water to move from an area of low sodium concentration to an area of high sodium concentration.

Osmotic thirst   Thirst caused by the loss of water from the cells, brought on by salt intake.

Oval window   The connecting point of the stapes in the middle ear and the inner ear; it transmits sound vibrations to the fluid of the cochlea.

Pacinian corpuscles (pa-SIN-ee-in)   Touch receptors shaped like strings with their ends wrapped in layers like an onion, located deep in the skin. Large enough to be visible to the naked eye, they are responsible for the sensation of deep pressure.

Pancreas   An organ responsible for the secretion of insulin, which regulates the ability to use glucose from the blood.

Paranoia   The feeling that people are "out to get you." Delusions of persecution.

Parasympathetic division   The part of the autonomic nervous system that helps the body to return to a relaxed state after the action of the sympathetic division.

Parathyroid glands   Located on each side of the thyroid,

these four tiny glands regulate the amount of calcium in the blood.

Parietal lobe (pear-EYE-ee-tall)   The portion of the brain controlling the experience of touch and temperature.

Pariventricular nuclei   An area of the posterior hypothalamus that manufactures antidiuretic hormone, facilitating reabsorption of water in the kidneys.

Parkinson's disease   Symptoms are a shuffling walk, muscle weakness, facial inexpressiveness, and tremor. Caused by damage to the midbrain and/or the basal ganglia.

Perceptions   The sense impressions of external stimuli experienced through one's needs, moods, and experiences.

Perceptual-motor task   A task requiring sensory feedback and muscular coordination.

Peripheral nervous system   Comprised of the nerves in the limbs and trunk outside the brain and the spinal cord and including the autonomic nervous system.

Petit mal seizures   Characterized by unresponsiveness and noticeable jerking of the arms and legs.

Peyote   A cactus producing mescaline, a hallucinogen.

Phantom-limb phenomenon   The feeling of sensations in a limb that has been removed, caused by the stimulation of an area in the somatosensory cortex that controlled the limb.

Phenothiazines (fee-no-THIGH-ah-zines)   A group of drugs including chlorpromazine used in treating schizophrenia.

Photons   Units of electromagnetic radiation; particles or quanta of light energy.

Physical dependency   Addiction to a drug caused by the body's development of tolerance, which requires an increased dosage for a given effect. Withdrawal symptoms are experienced when the drug is discontinued.

Physical stressors   Stressors such as intense cold or loud noise capable of evoking a stress response.

Physiological approach to hunger   The theory that hunger is caused by the deficit of metabolic fuels (glucose, lipids, and amino acids) in the liver.

Physiological responses   Involuntary responses—such as sweating, increased respiration, and heart rate—controlled by the autonomic nervous system.

Physiological zero   The temperature of the skin. A stimulus whose temperature is physiological zero.

Pinna   The portion of the ear that is visible; its shape is adapted to collecting sound waves.

Pituitary dwarf   A person who possesses normal intelligence and body proportions but who attains a height of only 3–4 feet as a result of undersecretion of growth hormone during adolescence.

Pituitary giant   A person possessing normal intelligence and body proportions who may reach a height of 8 feet. The condition is caused by oversecretion of growth hormone during adolescence.

Pituitary gland   A gland located in a bony cavity at the base of the brain, controlled by the hypothalamus and controlling the other glands of the body.

PKU (phenylketonuria) A genetic disorder that prevents normal brain development and results in mental retardation. It is characterized by the faulty metabolism of phenylalanine.

Place theory The theory that tones of different frequencies activate different areas of the basilar membrane. Since different hair cells are located at each area, our perception of pitch depends on the place activated.

Placebo An inactive substance given in place of a drug; a sugar pill.

Placebo effect The experience of relief from symptoms after administration of a drug or substance of no medicinal value.

Plasticity The flexibility of a brain area to develop the capacities and functions of destroyed areas. Also the capacity of the brain to form an engram.

Plateau phase The second state of sexual response, characterized by increased penile erection, hyperventilation, and increased heart rate in the male and by engorgement of the vaginal entrance, changes in color of the minor labia as well as hyperventilation and increased heart rate in the female.

Polarization The existence of a difference in charge between the inside and the outside of a cell membrane.

Polygraph A device for recording changes in skin response, respiration, and blood pressure. Also called a **lie detector**.

Pons A structure located at the top of the medulla involved in the regulation of sleep and the moderation of voluntary movements.

Positive ion A chemical particle that will attract ions having negative charges and repel other positive ions.

Posterior hypothalamus The back part of the hypothalamus that stimulates the sympathetic nervous system.

Posterior pituitary The portion of the pituitary gland controlled by nerve impulses from the hypothalamus.

Postganglionic axons Axons that leave the sympathetic ganglia and synapse with the organs and muscles of the body.

Postsynaptic neuron The neuron on the receiving side of the synaptic cleft.

Prefrontal area Area of the brain controlling psychological function and mood.

Preganglionic axons Axons originating in the central nervous system and synapsing with the postganglionic neurons of the autonomic nervous system.

Premature ejaculation A male sexual problem caused by ineffective control over the ejaculatory function.

Prepyriform cortex (pre-PEER-ah-form) An area of the temporal lobe responsible for sensations of smell.

Presynaptic neuron The neuron on the transmitting side of the synaptic cleft.

Primary colors The three colors—red, blue, and green—from which our perception of all colors is derived.

Primary orgasmic dysfunction A problem experienced by women who have experienced sexual arousal but have never had orgasm.

Primary projection area An area located in the cortex, responsible for processing specific sensory input.

Principle of equipotentiality The idea that portions of the cortex can take over functions of other parts and the consequence that memories may not occupy a specific location in the cortex.

Progesterone (pro-GES-ter-own) One of the primary female hormones secreted by the ovaries.

Progestin (pro-GES-tin) A testosterone-like hormone given to pregnant women during the 1950s to prevent miscarriages. It was found to affect the neural circuitry of the brain.

Propagation The travel of the action potential down the length of the axon.

Prostate (PROS-tate) One of the organs involved in the gathering of semen for ejaculation.

Psilocybin A hallucination-producing drug found in certain mushrooms.

Psychedelics Drugs such as LSD and mescaline that produce hallucinations. Also called **hallucinogens**.

Psychological dependency The belief that one cannot function without a drug.

Psychological stressors Emotional problems, tension, and other psychological factors capable of evoking a stress response.

Psychosomatic diseases Diseases brought about by prolonged stress, including hypertension, ulcers, migraine, colitis, or allergies.

Pupil A hole in the center of the iris through which light rays enter the eye.

Pyramidal system The system that controls voluntary movements; named for the pyramidal shape of the neurons in the motor area.

Raphe nucleus (rah-FAYE) An area of the brainstem where serotonin, which is important in controlling NREM sleep, is produced.

Rapid eye movement sleep The period of sleep when brain waves resemble those of wakefulness and when the eyes are observed to dart back and forth beneath the eyelids. Abbreviated **REM**.

Recall The retrieval of information from memory.

Receptor The specialized tip of the dendrite that is located in the skin and that translates environmental information into neural information.

Referred pain The experience of pain in another area of the body than the site of trauma; most often felt after damage to organs that do not send their information to specific areas of the somatosensory cortex.

Reflex An involuntary response to a stimulus; for example, a sneeze, a knee jerk, or an eye blink.

Reinforcements Rewards or stimuli that increase the probability of occurrence of a previous response.

Relative refractory period The period following the absolute refractory period when the axon can be fired but the threshold is higher than in the resting state.

Releasing factors Hormones secreted by the hypothalamus that cause the anterior pituitary to release its hormones. Abbreviated **RF**.

REM rebound The tendency to increase REM sleep after having been deprived of it.

Renin A hormone released by the kidneys that aids in water regulation.

Reserpine (RES-er-peen) A drug that causes depression by decreasing the level of norepinephrine.

Resistance stage A reaction to prolonged stress characterized by decreased hormonal output that causes psychosomatic diseases.

Resolution phase The final stage of the sexual response cycle, characterized by loss of erection and incapacity for orgasm in the male and decrease in blood accumulation and loss of color in the sex skin in the female. For both sexes, there is a return to normal breathing and heart rates.

Resting membrane potential The voltage (measured in mV) across the membrane of a neuron in its resting state.

Resting state The state of neurons when they are not conducting nerve impulses.

Retarded ejaculation A male sexual problem often caused by anxiety and tension and characterized by inability to experience orgasm.

Reticular activating system (rah-TICK-you-ler) The part of the reticular formation responsible for arousing the brain and keeping us awake. Abbreviated **RAS**.

Reticular formation A structure lying in the center of the medulla and the pons that arouses the cortex for the processing of sensory information.

Retina The area at the back of the eye on which light waves are focused and which contains the receptors that change light waves into nerve impulses.

Retrieval The recall of information from memory.

Retroactive interference New learning or experience that acts to disrupt a previous learning, according to the consolidation hypothesis.

Retrograde amnesia Often caused by trauma and resulting in the loss of memory of events immediately preceding the trauma.

Reuptake One of the two methods of deactivating catecholamines after action, accomplished by the reabsorption of the neurotransmitters back into the telodendria.

Reverberating circuits Thought to be the basis of short-term memory, the neuron groups capable of repeating or reactivating new information.

Reverberation The process of repetition of new information thought to be the basis of short-term memory.

Rhodopsin (row-DOP-sin) A chemical contained in the rods that is extremely sensitive to light.

Ribosome A cell component contained in the endoplasmic reticulum, responsible for the secretion of hormones.

Ritalin The trade name for methylphenidate, which is prescribed for children with hyperkinesis.

RNA (ribonucleic acid) A chemical that carries instructions from the DNA in the nucleus to the cytoplasm, where enzymes controlling cellular development are formed.

Rods Neurons located on the retina that are specialized to be reactive to light, changing light waves into nerve impulses.

Sacral (SAY-crull) Referring to the lower back area, as in sacral spinal nerves.

Saltatory conduction The progress of a nerve impulse along the axon in jumping fashion between the nodes of Ranvier.

Salty taste One of the four basic tastes that are the bases for all other tastes; it is detected by receptors at the edges near the front of the tongue.

Satiety (say-TIE-ah-tee) The feeling of fullness experienced after eating.

Schizophrenia Mental dysfunction characterized by confused thinking, delusions, and often paranoia.

Seconal Trade name for sodium secobarbital, a barbiturate that is prescribed as a sedative and acts to depress neural activity.

Secondary general sexual dysfunction In females, the inability to experience sexual feelings, formerly called frigidity; caused by guilt, tension, or anxiety.

Secondary impotence A male sexual problem characterized by inability to achieve erection.

Secondary orgasmic dysfunction A problem experienced by females who can reach orgasm by masturbating but not during intercourse.

Secondary sex characteristics In females, the development of breasts, widening of hips, and growth of pubic hair; in males, the appearance of pubic and facial hair and the lowering of the voice. Changes experienced at puberty.

Sedatives Drugs, including barbiturates, prescribed to induce sleep.

Selective perception Discriminating among incoming stimuli on the basis of need, experience, or mental state.

Semen The thick, whitish, sperm-bearing secretion of the male sexual organs.

Seminal vesicles (SEM-in-all VES-ah-coles) The enlarged portion of the seminal duct where sperm are stored prior to ejaculation.

Semipermeable membrane The covering of the neuron that permits some ions to pass through while others cannot.

Sensate focus Sensuous and erotic exercises designed to help women focus on or experience sexual stimulation and bodily sensation.

Sensations Sensory experiences uncolored by past learning or feelings.

Sensory gating The process of selective inhibition thought to take place when attention is directed, by which conflicting or irrelevant stimuli are suppressed.

Sensory neuron A nerve fiber carrying impulses toward the central nervous system. Also called an **afferent neuron**.

Septal area One of the components of the limbic system; involved in sexual and emotional behavior.

Serotonin (ser-ah-TONE-in) A chemical produced in the raphe nucleus of the brainstem that controls NREM sleep.

Set-point The body's ratio of fat to lean.

Sex skin The inner folds of skin bordering the vagina and covered by the labia majora. Also called the **minor labia**.

Short-term memory According to the theory of D. O. Hebb, the reverberating circuit that repeats new information and is subject to retroactive interference.

Skin resistance response The comparative ease with which a current passes through the skin, caused by the presence or absence of sweat. Also called **SRR, EDR** (electrodermal response), or **GSR** (galvanic skin response).

Sleep-eze A nonprescription drug containing the antihistamine methapyraline whose side effects may include drowsiness.

Sleepwalking Occurring during NREM sleep, this walking behavior is not a waking dream state and the sleeper usually has no memory of the event.

Slow-wave sleep Delta-wave NREM sleep; also called **stage 4 sleep**.

Smooth muscles Muscles lining the stomach as well as the intestines and the bladder; usually not under voluntary control.

Socialization The process of character shaping in conformance with the standards of one's society.

Sodium barrier The process by which sodium is prevented from entering the neuron through the membrane.

Sodium-potassium pump The process by which sodium is actively pumped out of the neuron and potassium is actively pumped into it.

Soma A cell body.

Somatosensory area An area of the parietal lobe that controls the experience of touch, temperature, and bodily position.

Somesthesis The senses of touch, temperature, and pain.

Somesthetic cortex An area of the brain active in the experience of touch and temperature.

Sominex A nonprescription drug containing the antihistamine methapyraline whose side effects may include drowsiness.

Sour taste One of the four basic tastes that are the bases for all other tastes; it is detected by receptors on the edges of the tongue near the back.

Spatial summation Summation occurring when two impulses take place at different points on the dendrites of cell bodies, reinforcing each other.

Spinal cord A long, white, smooth, ropelike bundle of neurons running through the spinal column of vertebrates.

Spinal nerves A series of paired nerves connecting the spinal cord with the various muscles and organs of the body.

Sprouting The process of sending out new branches by axons after brain damage.

Stage 4 sleep Characterized by delta waves and lowered physiological response; also called **slow-wave sleep**.

Stapes One of the three ossicles of the middle ear; it is attached to the oval window.

Stereochemical theory The idea that odors are coded by the shape of their chemical keys (molecular structure) fitting appropriate olfactory receptors.

Stress response A series of responses involving the sympathetic division and various hormone secretions that enable the body to deal with stress.

Striated muscle Controlled by neurons in the motor cortex, this tissue makes up the muscles that are under voluntary control.

Subjective feelings Private experiences or feelings experienced in the mind.

Sulcus (SUL-kus) The valley or bottom portion of a convolution or wrinkle in the cortex. Also called a **fissure**.

Summation The process by which two excitatory postsynaptic potentials occurring close in time or at different points in a cell body add together to produce one large EPSP.

Supraoptic nuclei An area of the posterior hypothalamus that manufactures antidiuretic hormone facilitating the reabsorption of water in the kidneys.

Sweat glands Glands located in the skin and responsible for the secretion of fluids.

Sweet taste One of the four basic tastes that are the bases for all other tastes; it is detected by receptors at the tip of the tongue.

Sympathetic division Part of the autonomic nervous system involved in preparing the body for action in response to stress or emotion.

Sympathetic ganglia Groups of cell bodies resembling beads on a string alongside the spinal cord.

Synapse (SIN-aps) The tiny space between neurons where the chemical transmission of nerve impulses takes place.

Synaptic cleft The small space between neurons where chemical changes take place resulting in the transmission of nerve impulses.

Synaptic vesicles (VES-icles) Small spherical packets on the telodendria of presynaptic neurons containing chemicals that excite or inhibit the postsynaptic neurons.

Synchronous wave patterns Regularly recurrent wave patterns, such as delta waves.

Tactile receptors The receptors in the skin that respond to different kinds of touching and pressure.

Tardive dyskinesia A side effect of phenothiazines used in the treatment of schizophrenia; characterized by slow, rhythmic movements of the mouth, lip smacking, and unusual movements of the limbs.

Taste cells Cells contained in the taste buds that respond to chemical input to produce generator potentials.

Telodendria (tel-oh-DEN-dree-ah) Hairlike extensions at the end of a nerve cell axon specialized for transmitting information by secreting chemicals that affect neighboring neurons.

Temporal lobe The portion of the brain that controls speech (left temporal lobe) and hearing (right and left temporal lobe).

Temporal summation The process that occurs when two excitatory postsynaptic potentials take place milliseconds apart to produce a stronger EPSP. Either EPSP by itself might be too weak to exceed the threshold, but together they may fire the neuron.

Testosterone (tess-TOSS-ter-own) The hormone produced by the testes that stimulates the development of male secondary sex characteristics.

Tetany A condition caused by decreased calcium production and characterized by uncontrollable muscle contractions.

Tetrahydrocannabinol The active ingredient in marihuana. Abbreviated **THC**.

Thalamus (THAL-mus) A structure the size of a walnut located above the hypothalamus and responsible for relaying neural information from the sensors to the cortex.

Thoracicolumbar area The area comprising the thoracic (chest) and lumbar (upper back) sections of the spinal cord. The sympathetic division originates here.

Thorazine Trade name for chlorpromazine, a drug prescribed for treatment of schizophrenia; it acts to affect the neurotransmitters at the synapses of brain cells.

Threshold The level of electrochemical charge necessary to cause an axon to become active.

Thyroid glands Located on either side of the neck below the voicebox, these glands secrete thyroxin, which controls metabolism and growth.

Thyroid releasing factor A hormone thought to be released by the hypothalamus and responsible for triggering the production of a thyroid stimulating hormone by the anterior pituitary. Abbreviated **T-RF**.

Thyrotropin A thyroid stimulating hormone released by the anterior pituitary in response to stimulation by hormones from the hypothalamus. Also called **TSH**.

Thyroxin The hormone secreted by the thyroid glands that controls cellular metabolism and therefore bodily growth.

Tolerance The tendency of the body to build immunity to a drug so that larger doses are needed to produce a given effect.

Tonus The tension of muscle tissue.

Transduction The conversion of a physical stimulus into a neural impulse.

Transmethylation The addition of a methyl group (CH_3 radical) to an organic compound such as serotonin by psychoactive chemicals like LSD or mescaline.

Transmitter substances Neurotransmitters.

Transsexuals Genetic females who assume male identity and genetic males who assume female identity. Persons who have undergone sex-change surgery.

Tubule A very small tube or connecting duct.

Turner's syndrome Lack of sexual development at puberty and a deficit in general intelligence; indicated by the presence of one X chromosome.

Tympanic membrane An elastic membrane located at the end of the ear canal that vibrates when struck by sound waves; commonly known as the **eardrum**.

Type A personality An aggressive and competitive person who is susceptible to coronary heart attack because of continued stress responses.

Type B personality A person who experiences no pressing urgency, who avoids prolonged stress reactions, and is consequently less likely to develop coronary heart disease.

Unconditioned response A response that occurs on exposure to a stimulus in the absence of conditioning; a reflex.

Unconditioned stimulus A stimulus that prompts a response without conditioning.

Unipolar neuron A sensory nerve fiber connecting the skin and the spinal cord and having its cell body located near the center of the axon.

Vagus nerve Part of the parasympathetic nervous system; it travels between the brain and the stomach and triggers the secretion of hydrochloric acid.

Valium Trade name for a widely prescribed derivative of the chemical benzodiazepine, used as a tranquilizer.

Ventral noradrenergic bundle A bundle of neurons containing norepinephrine running between the brainstem and the hypothalamus, the destruction of which can lead to hyperphagia and obesity.

Ventral root The branched connection site of motor neurons to the stomach side of the spinal cord.

Ventrobasal nuclei (ven-tro-BASE-all) The area of the thalamus in which sensory information about touch, temperature, and pain is relayed to the cortex.

Ventromedial nucleus According to Jean Mayer's glucostatic theories of hunger, the portion of the hypothalamus sensitive to glucose utilization at the cellular level. Abbreviated **VMH**.

Vertebrae A series of connected bones creating a tubelike structure that surrounds the spinal cord.

Viscera The internal organs.

Visual cortex The area of the brain responsible for interpreting visual stimuli; also called **Area 17**.

Volatility The capacity of a substance to give off molecules that can affect the olfactory cells.

Volley theory The explanation of our ability to hear sounds of higher pitch than the firing capacity of neurons.

Voltage A measurement that describes the potential for ionic movement or electric current.

Warm receptors Cells in the skin sensitive to increases in temperature.

Wernicke's aphasia (VER-nick-ees) A condition resulting in loss of content in speech although fluency may remain; caused by damage to Wernicke's area in the left temporal lobe.

Wernicke's area An area of the left temporal lobe affecting comprehension and speech.

Withdrawal symptoms Experienced when an addictive substance is discontinued. Depending on the substance, symptoms might include insomnia, agitation, loss of appetite, or convulsions.

X chromosome The differential sex chromosome carried by all female and half the male reproductive cells. If the male contributes an X chromosome, the offspring will be female.

Y chromosome The differential sex chromosome carried by half the male reproductive cells. If the male contributes a Y chromosome, the offspring will be male.

Zygote The fertilized egg or ovum that carries all of the information necessary for the development of the individual.

Index

Inherited emotional patterns, 138–139
Inhibitory postsynaptic potential
     (IPSP), 29–30
Inner ear, *84–86*
Insomnia, 172
Insulin, 51, 153
     and hunger, 147–148
Intelligence, 7
     and environment, 191–192
Intelligence Quotient: *See* IQ
Internal cues for eating, 156
Internal Opioid-Like Compounds, 377
Interneuron, 18–19, *20,* 29–30
     stimulation of, 25
Intestinal bypass surgery, 157
Intestinal colitis, 68
Intestinal surgery, 157
Intracellular fluid, 19, 27
     and refractory periods, 25
     and sodium regulation, 22, 157–158
Intracellular thirst, 158–159
Involuntary responses, 56–63
Iodopsins, 78
Ions, 19–26
IPSP (inhibitory postsynaptic
     potential), 29–30
IQ: and psychosurgery, 136
     scores of, 7–9, 10
Iris, 74–*75*

Jellyfish: nervous system of, 2–*3,* 4
Jet-lag syndrome, 164–165
JOHNSON, LAVERNE, 166–167
JOHNSON, VIRGINIA, 120

K⁺ (potassium ions), 19–27
KAMIYA, JOE, 67
KAPLAN, HELEN SINGER, 300
KATZ, BERNARD, 28
KENNY, ELIZABETH, 32
Ketone bodies, 147
Kidneys: and bodily fluids, 157–159
     and hormones, 50
Kinesthetic receptors, 101, 102
Klinefelter's syndrome, 108
Kluver-Bucy syndrome, 130–131, 132
Korsakoff syndrome, 235
KOZLOWSKI, LYNN, 230

Labeling, 190
Labia minor, *119*
Language: and brain development, 6
     and brain function, 204–*206,* 209
LASHLEY, KARL, 184
Last-in/first-out principle, 179

Lateral fissure, 44, *45*
Lateral geniculate, 42, 46
Lateral geniculate nucleus (LGN), 81
Lateral hypothalamus (LH), *152*
     lesions of, 153–156
Learned behavior, 9–10
Learned cues for eating, 156
Learned emotional patterns, 138–139
Learning: and environment, 191–192
     location of, in brain, 185–189, 190
     and memory, 184–185
     and proteins, 189–190
     and sleep, 170, 173–174
     and stress, 191
Left-Brain, Right-Brain, 372
LEHMANN, PHYLLIS, 278
Lens, 74–*75, 76*
Lesbian behavior, 114–116
Lesions: and brain study, 131–138
Leutenizing hormone (LH), 110–112
LEWIN, ROGER, 242, 275
LGN (lateral geniculate nucleus), 81
LH (lateral hypothalamus), *152*
LH (leutenizing hormone), 110–112
Librium, 224
Lie detector, 55–*56*
Light waves, 74, *77*
Limbic area, 5–6
Limbic system, 117, 131–138
LINDSAY, ROBERT D., 11–12
Lipids, 143, *146*
Lipostatic theory, 148–151
Lithium, 224
LIU, E. N., 32
Liver: digestive function of, *146*
     and hunger, 151
     and starvation, 147
Lobotomy: *See* Frontal lobotomy
Locus coeruleus, 170
Long-term memory, 180, 182, 185,
     190
Longitudinal fissure, 197
Longitudinal sulcus, 45, 47
Loudness, 85–86
LSD (lysergic acid diethylamide),
     222–223, 235–*236*
Lumbar nerves, 37–38
Lymph, 147
Lymph glands: and stress, 68
Lysergic acid diethylamide (LSD),
     222–223, 235–*236*

MACHADA-SALA, JESU, 11–12
Male: genetic, 107, *108*–110
     sexual problems in, 120

Male hormones, *112*
     See also Androgens; Testosterone
Male-to-female surgery, 115
Malleus, *83–84*
Mammillary bodies, 185
     and alcohol, 235
Mania, 224
Manic depression, 222
MAO (monoamine oxidase), 221–222
Marihuana, 236–237
MASTERS, WILLIAM, 120
MATINIAN, LEVON, 31
MAYER, JEAN, 148, 330, 335
MBD (minimal brain dysfunction), 231
Medial geniculate, 42
Medial geniculate nucleus, 44, 86
Meditation, *64–65,* 67, 174
Medroxyprogesterone acetate, 117
Medulla, 38, 40, *41,* 42
     development of, 4–*6*
MELZACK, RONALD, 281
Membrane, 19–25, 28–32
Membrane potential, 29–30
Memory: brain centers of, 43
     and brain structures, 5–6
     consolidation of, 180–182
     and engram, 182–184, 189
     and hippocampus, 133–134
     and learning, 184–189
     and sleep, 169, 173–174
     and stress, 191
     transfer of, 189–190
Menstruation, 110–112
Mental retardation, 7
Mescaline, 222–223, 236
Messenger RNA, 8
     See also RNA
Metabolic rate, 143–144
Metabolism, 143–144
     regulation of, 47
Methadone, 232
Methamphetamine, 227–229
Methedrine, 227–229
Methyl group, 222–223
Methylphenidate, 231
Microelectrodes, 27, 32, 81, 87
     See also Electrodes
Midbrain, 40, *41,* 42, 43
     development of, 4–*6*
     and touch, 101
Middle ear, 83–85
Migraine headaches, 64
MILLER, D. S., 145
MILLER, NEAL, 62–63, 67, 269
MILNER, BRENDA, 185, *186*

Credits for Chapter-Opening Photographs

1   David Powers, Jeroboam

2   *Bundle of peripheral nerve fibers pulled apart to show its complexity*. Photograph by Lennart Nilsson © 1977 from *Behold Man* © 1973 by Albert Bonniers Förlag, Stockholm, published by Little, Brown & Company, Boston, 1974.

3   The American Museum of Natural History

4   Karen Preuss, Jeroboam

5   *Section of the retina showing outer receptors (rods) synapsing with other cells*. Deric Bownds and Stan Carlson, University of Wisconsin.

6   *Olfactory receptors in the roof of the nose*. Photograph by Lennart Nilsson © 1977 from *Behold Man* © 1973 by Albert Bonniers Förlag, Stockholm, published by Little, Brown & Company, Boston, 1974.

7   Charles Harbutt, Magnum

8   Leonard Freed, Magnum

9   Burt Glinn, Magnum

10   Mitchell Payne, Jeroboam

11   Bruce Kliewe, Jeroboam

12   Karen Preuss, Jeroboam

13   Ken Heyman